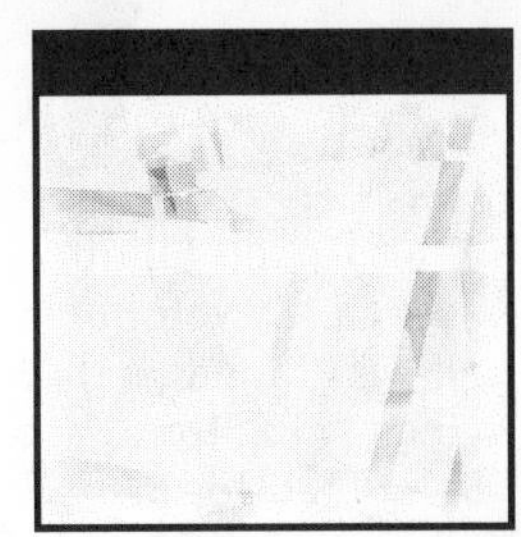

Building J2EE Applications with IBM WebSphere

Dale R. Nilsson
Louis E. Mauget

Wiley Publishing, Inc.

L.C.C. SOUTH CAMPUS LIBRARY

Publisher: Robert Ipsen
Editor: Robert Elliott
Assistant Developmental Editor: Scott Amerman
Editorial Manager: Kathryn A. Malm
Managing Editor: Pamela M. Hanley
Media Development Specialist: Brian Snapp
Text Design & Composition: Wiley Composition Services

This book is printed on acid-free paper. ♾

Copyright © 2003 by Wiley Publishing Inc., Indianapolis, Indiana. All rights reserved.
Published simultaneously in Canada

No part of this publication may be reproduced, stored in a retrieval system, or transmitted in any form or by any means, electronic, mechanical, photocopying, recording, scanning, or otherwise, except as permitted under Section 107 or 108 of the 1976 United States Copyright Act, without either the prior written permission of the Publisher, or authorization through payment of the appropriate per-copy fee to the Copyright Clearance Center, Inc., 222 Rosewood Drive, Danvers, MA 01923, (978) 750-8400, fax (978) 646-8700. Requests to the Publisher for permission should be addressed to the Legal Department, Wiley Publishing, Inc., 10475 Crosspoint Blvd., Indianapolis, IN 46256, (317) 572-3447, fax (317) 572-4447, E-mail: permcoordinator@wiley.com.

Limit of Liability/Disclaimer of Warranty: While the publisher and author have used their best efforts in preparing this book, they make no representations or warranties with respect to the accuracy or completeness of the contents of this book and specifically disclaim any implied warranties of merchantability or fitness for a particular purpose. No warranty may be created or extended by sales representatives or written sales materials. The advice and strategies contained herein may not be suitable for your situation. You should consult with a professional where appropriate. Neither the publisher nor author shall be liable for any loss of profit or any other commercial damages, including but not limited to special, incidental, consequential, or other damages.

For general information on our other products and services please contact our Customer Care Department within the United States at (800) 762-2974, outside the United States at (317) 572-3993 or fax (317) 572-4002.

Trademarks: Wiley, the Wiley Publishing logo and related trade dress are trademarks or registered trademarks of Wiley Publishing, Inc., in the United States and other countries, and may not be used without written permission. All other trademarks are the property of their respective owners. Wiley Publishing, Inc., is not associated with any product or vendor mentioned in this book.

Wiley also publishes its books in a variety of electronic formats. Some content that appears in print may not be available in electronic books.

Library of Congress Cataloging-in-Publication Data:

ISBN: 0-471-28157-3

Printed in the United States of America

10 9 8 7 6 5 4 3 2 1

QA 76.73 .J38 N548 2003

JAN 26 2004

To Karl, Erik, and Nikolaus, my wonderful sons. To my loving wife, Jackie, for holding down the fort when I travel. To my little sister Dawn, who has boundless strength and is always on the go.

—Dale R. Nilsson

To Carey Mauget.

—Louis E. Mauget

Contents

Foreword

The J2EE architecture provides a solid framework for building Java applications. When you write a J2EE component it runs on any platform with a Java Virtual Machine. The J2EE architecture has many different APIs that can be used in combination, enabling a developer to assemble an application that is written only once and runs anywhere. The J2EE components can be shared and reused in different applications. Although the J2EE architecture is an evolving new technology, it is building on a solid base of Open Industry standards. Many development tools, including IBM's WebSphere Studio products, support the J2EE architecture, and a large number of applications and Web solutions are based upon J2EE components.

A J2EE application can take many forms, from a client application that runs on a stand alone PC with a highly robust user interface, to an advanced n-tiered application with a Web interface passing real-time transactions to an enterprise server. You can find numerous examples of the J2EE architecture at http://java.sun.com/j2ee. You can get specific product information on WebSphere at http://www.ibm.com/software/websphere.

The J2EE architecture is managed by Sun Microsystems with the help and support of many active industry partners. The WebSphere product teams at IBM provide world-class tools and runtime services to help make J2EE a reality. WebSphere v5 has made recent, significant enhancements for development and runtime services in support of the J2EE programming model. WebSphere has tools and services that help you develop and run J2EE APIs from applets to web services.

Dale Nilsson and Lou Mauget have done an outstanding job of dissecting the essence of the J2EE architecture and making it a topic that most programmers can easily digest. The many examples in this book show you how to use the J2EE API and harness the productivity and power of WebSphere.

Greg Clark

Director of WebSphere Development and Support

IBM Corporation

Introduction

The use of Java has exploded and it has become the standard for Web development. WebSphere Studio Application Developer (WSAD) was introduced in 2001 as the IBM strategic development environment, replacing VisualAge for Java. WSAD version 5 is J2EE compliant and has tons of tools that help you create many different kinds of applications.

This book helps you learn how to use WSAD with step-by-step instructions, building a variety of sample J2EE applications. This book also has numerous screen captures of the actual WSAD product that give you visual feedback on the progress of your Java applications.

When this book was written, there were hundreds of Java books in publication, many of which focused on a particular Java API such as Servlets, JavaScript, and XML. These books don't show the developer how to combine these different technologies in an application. Another fault of many Java programming books is the pages and pages of API code that only adds to the page count. This book avoids these shortfalls and provides the unique feature of stepping the developer through design decisions while building Java applications.

Overview of This Book

This book is a collection of examples from using WSAD in the real world. The authors worked for IBM for many years in the application development software lab and WebSphere services. They currently work as consultants helping customers develop and deploy J2EE applications.

You will learn how to design, develop, debug, and deploy J2EE applications using WSAD. This book focuses on the good programming architecture and design standards for the J2EE technologies. There is information on how to implement the sample applications and the reasons for the designs. There is Web application deployment and configuration information, but this book is not focused on WebSphere Application Server maintenance.

This book is the result of a truly collaborative effort between the authors. The chapters show the collective knowledge and experience of both the authors and provide the reader with a comprehensive view of the many different ways to harness the power of WSAD. The book has information on migrating from VisualAge for Java and WSAD v4. This is a totally new book with new labs and material using WSAD version 5.

Certification

This book helps prepare you for IBM WebSphere certification, which is part of the JCert Initiative. You will learn how to use the WSAD workbench and its tools by making sample Web applications. Real hands-on experience with WSAD gives you the knowledge to take the WSAD certification test.

You can get more information about the different certification levels and the certification requirements at www.ibm.com/certify and www.jcert.org. There are no certification questions in this book, nor any material focused on the certification test. You can take a sample test at the certification Web site.

How This Book Is Organized

Each chapter in this book starts with a brief description of what is covered and ends with a summary. The book has a number of small applications to illustrate a broad range of J2EE application development topics. This book starts with simpler Java applications, progressing to J2EE Web applications, and finishing with EJBs and Web services. As you progress through the book, the instructions become briefer, and the amount of function in the sample applications increases.

Conventions in This Book

This book contains many instructions for completing the sample Java applications. These instructions are numbered lists and use some conventions to make instructions, tool text, and Java programming information as clear as possible.

The screen captures displayed in the pages of this book are from the Windows version of the WSAD product. In some cases partial screen captures are used that focus on the current topic under discussion. The Linux screens are virtually identical, with only minor system-specific exceptions such as the file dialog and the frame window icons.

Instructions to select menu items are combined in a shortened form. Instead of saying Select File, then select New, then select Project . . . the instructions in the book say Select File > New > Project . . .

WebSphere Studio has many different flavors, including Homepage Builder (WSHB), Site Developer (WSSD), Application Developer (WSAD), and Enterprise Developer (WSED), Device Developer (WSDD). The book is aimed at the broad J2EE market, covering WSSD, WSAD, and WSED. For simplification, when referring to WebSphere Studio the term *WSAD* is used.

The values that you enter in fields in the WSAD tools user interface are shown in bold to differentiate them from instructions. For example, an instruction in the book may read: Enter **John Smith** in the Name entry field.

The instructions to build the samples frequently tell you to press a button on a WSAD tool. Some of these buttons are referred to by their names and others appear with only a graphic image. To make it clearer, there will frequently be a graphic in the margin that gives you a visual cue to the referenced button. For example, you will see the instruction: press the Run button.

A `monospaced font` is used to show code segments. Anything typed in this font should be taken literally and entered exactly as shown. This font is also used for code listings, because it preserves spacing in the code. When entering code or code segments, be aware that many of the lines of code in the book had to be split into two or more lines. This is because of the line width available on the book page is much narrower that what is needed for the code. Every effort has been made to split the lines in a way that will cause no problems, even if you enter them as shown, in multiple lines. However in some cases, for example when we had to split a literal string, you should join the lines in the page into a single line of code.

Terms Used in This Book

A number of terms in this book use Java language statements and Web terms, and these are not necessarily standard English words. For example, the Swing library provides the classes JFrame and FlowLayout. These terms are displayed in a monospaced code font to distinguish them from other text. Later references in this book may use an informal term, for example, frame or flow layout.

The Java language gives you the ability to create many different J2EE components such as applets, applications, servlets, and JavaBeans. All of these components can be part of a Web application, so throughout this book when you create a program that runs in WSAD it is referred to as a Web application.

Throughout this book, we refer to Java classes and objects interchangeably. The correct usage should be *class* for the definition and *object* for an instance of a class. WSAD is a Java development workbench and the use of classes and objects is mandatory.

Who Should Read This Book?

This book is targeted at the reader who is familiar with object-oriented programming and the Java programming language. A general understanding of programming, software development, the use of a Web browser, and Web functions is very helpful. This book is not intended as an introduction to Java programming. There are many sources for learning Java, which include self-study books, interactive CD-ROMs, and formal educational courses.

This book will be a great help for anyone new to WSAD or who wants to get the most out of this comprehensive development workbench. You will learn how to use the WSAD workbench and the development tools, starting from the very basic Java applications and moving to Web applications with EJBs, including their deployment. This book has many examples on proper object-oriented implementations using WSAD construction tools. Even people who are familiar with Java and J2EE will get a lot of valuable information from this book's extensive coverage of the WSAD development tools and the different sample applications.

What's on the Web Site?

The Web site for the book is www.wiley.com/compbooks/nilsson, and it contains a link to the trial edition of WSAD v5. With this version, you can complete all of the sample applications in this book, but it is much better to have a working license for the product. For up-to-date information on the installation of the components on the Web site and other late-breaking news, please read the readme.txt file on the Web site.

Most of the chapters have the source Java code listed for the solution. You can get these files from the Web site to help if you have any problems or to help with entering the code.

The Web site contains the sample code for all the applications in the book. These applications include Java code and other Web resources like HTML files, JSP files, .gif image files, and properties files. If you already have WSAD installed, you still need to load the sample files from the Web site to get some of the projects in the book to work properly.

Summary

WSAD is a very powerful tightly integrated development environment (IDE) with lots of features and functions. Many enterprises have adopted the WebSphere product line for mission-critical Java development. Its feature-rich IDE can be a little intimidating if you are accustomed to editors, compilers, and debuggers that work on files as in the Java Development Toolkit (JDK). This book will help you master the WSAD IDE and help you become confident and productive when writing your own Java solutions. We hope you enjoy the book.

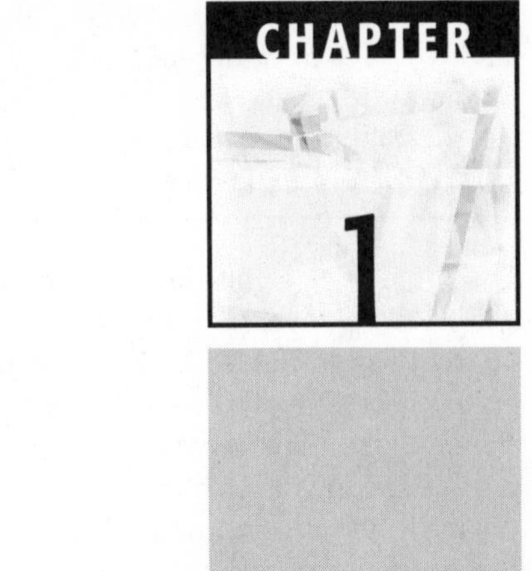

J2EE Overview

What's in Chapter 1?

During the past few years, the J2EE Specification has attained wide acceptance. Now that J2EE has established a good standard for Java development, it is important to have a basic understanding of the J2EE concepts. This book starts with an overview of the J2EE Specification, which forms the basis for the rest of the book.

In this chapter, you will learn about the components that form J2EE. You will feel much more confident about what this software industry term means. You will learn what is included in J2EE and what is not included. This chapter covers the following J2EE concepts:

Architecture— A description of the basic building blocks used for a J2EE application.

J2EE APIs— What Java APIs and version are part of J2EE.

Packaging— A standard consistent way to organize your Java software for run time.

Roles— Formal standard definitions of the different participants in the software development process.

Security— A description of the types of services needed for a J2EE application and how it should work.

All of the J2EE topics give you the background to understand the vocabulary and jargon of Java development.

What Is J2EE?

The Sun J2EE Specification is 174 pages long, and it references other Java specifications and APIs. So, an easy definition for J2EE would be "a big complex Java architecture," but that would not do J2EE any justice. A better description of J2EE is "a set of integrated Java APIs that enable client-server Web applications." If you want to see the complete J2EE Specification, you can get it from the Java Web site at http://java.sun.com/j2ee/download.html.

Java has evolved through many iterations. The initial Java Development Kits (JDKs) had basic classes and were geared largely toward client-server programming. As the initial Java APIs became solid and reliable, many developers created great Java programs and put them into production. The goal of the Java runtime environment is to stay forwardly compatible. Applications that work on a certain version of an API should work on a later version, but the inverse is not true. The Java APIs are not backwardly compatible.

As the Internet revolution exploded, Sun continued to improve Java and its APIs, adding many Web interfaces and redesigning the APIs for better object-oriented design. This situation caused some Java APIs to be incompatible with other APIs. Also, there are stable APIs that were getting bug fixes and new APIs that were changing and not very stable. Java developers and companies that use Java found that they needed guidance on which Java APIs are stable and compatible.

Sun decided to bring order to chaos, so they defined a set of Java APIs and their versions and called these Java 2 Enterprise Edition (J2EE), which is actually JDK v1.2. The J2EE APIs have evolved to the later version, 1.3, and version 1.4. Version 1.4 builds on the previous versions, and it is not a radical change from good Java programming. Future enhancements for J2EE are promised and are covered at the end of this chapter.

Reasons for Using J2EE

The J2EE standard, although it may appear at first to be a little complex, actually makes developing real-world Java applications much easier. We cannot say that it makes Java development easier, because there are a lot of different Java APIs, and the J2EE architecture is designed to separate application code into discrete units that can follow the Model-View-Controller Architecture. The following are some of the many benefits to using J2EE:

Hardware independence— Java's slogan of "write once, run everywhere" means that your J2EE will work on different hardware and software platforms.

Code separation— J2EE is designed so that there can be a clear separation between Business, View, and Controller objects. This separation allows a team of developers to work on different pieces at the same time.

Compatibility— With so many Java APIs available, the J2EE specification lists specific versions of the Java APIs to ensure compatibility.

Scalability— The J2EE architecture enables you to build pluggable components that can deployed on multiple servers.

Tool independence— J2EE is an open architecture with many tool APIs. Many tool providers have tools for various parts of J2EE.

The J2EE specification has helped bring some order to the Java development environment. It unifies the many APIs, and it provides a common base from which tool developers and application developers can work.

J2EE Tiers

The J2EE architecture is designed to address the problems of both application client and Web architectures in one. J2EE is designed to handle multiple tiers. This architecture is sometimes referred to as a three-tiered architecture with client, server, and enterprise components, as shown in Figure 1.1. This is a simplified view of what you see in many complex systems. Quite often there are many middle-tier servers and sometimes multiple back-end enterprise servers.

The application client architecture is sometimes referred to as *fat client* architecture, because it relies on running code on the client machine. This approach is good for high-performance graphical applications, but it assumes that the client PC has enough memory and disk space for adequate performance. WebSphere Studio Application Developer, or WSAD, is an example of an application client application, a program that runs completely on one system with a user interface.

The Web architecture that J2EE supports is commonly referred to as *thin client* architecture. Chapter 11, "JavaServer Pages," and Chapter 19, "Displaying Data," cover the J2EE model one and model two design examples that show you how to use the J2EE APIs to make robust scalable Web applications.

J2EE Architecture

The different tiers utilize different J2EE components. Most of J2EE is focused on components that run on the J2EE server and communications with the server. Figure 1.2 shows the three J2EE tiers: the Client tier, the J2EE Server tier, and the Enterprise tier. Each tier has specific J2EE APIs that enable the development of open scalable Web applications. The next section covers the different required and optional J2EE APIs.

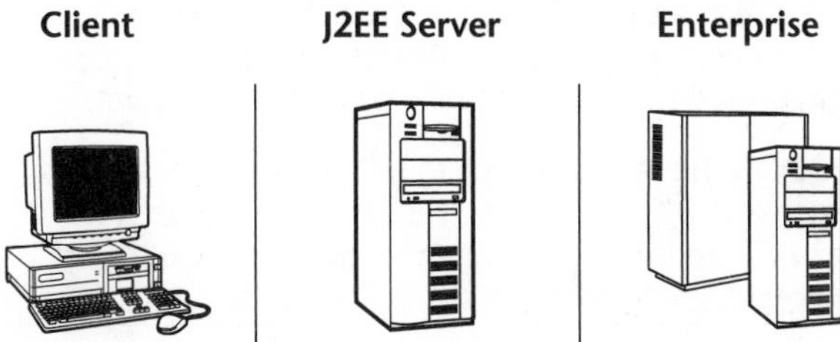

Figure 1.1 J2EE tiers.

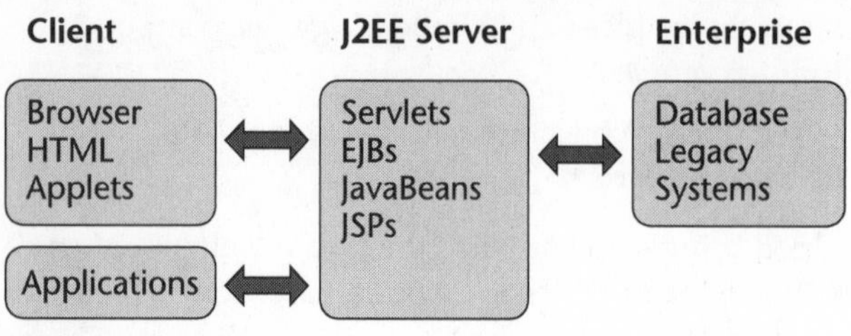

Figure 1.2 J2EE tiers.

J2EE APIs

Java has many APIs that have various versions. Some of the Java API versions are incompatible. The J2EE specification is a roadmap to which versions of the API work together. The J2EE specification lists the versions of the APIs that ensure their compatibility. The J2EE APIs are also referred to as J2EE Services. All J2EE servers need to support this set of APIs. IBM WebSphere Application Server v4 was one of the first application servers to be J2EE certified.

J2EE has both required APIs and optional APIs. The required APIs are very basic, and if you do much Java programming you probably take them for granted. These APIs are significant, because they are general purpose and you can use them in your J2EE applications. An application must support these APIs to be J2EE compliant. They are listed in the following "Required APIs" section. The optional APIs are a mix of different APIs that can solve application-specific problems.

Required APIs

J2EE-compliant applications must take advantage of the following required APIs:

Table 1.1 Required APIs in J2EE-Compliant Applications

API	DESCRIPTION
Hypertext Transfer Protocol (HTTP) and HTTP with SSL (HTTPS)	HTTP and HTTPS are required protocols for J2EE. There are many different protocols, but it is essential to support HTTP to allow Web browser views.
Java Interface Definition Language (IDL)	IDL defines the Java interface to CORBA objects, which is managed by the Object Management Group (OMG; see their Web site at www.omg.org).
Java Database Connectivity (JDBC) Core	JDBC is the Java interface to relational databases such as DB2 and Oracle. JDBC has been around for a while and there are examples in Chapter 18, "Data Access."

Table 1.1 *(continued)*

API	DESCRIPTION
Remote Method Invocation–Internet InterOrb Protocol (RMI-IIOP)	RMI-IIOP allows one object to call a method in an object running on another machine.
Java Naming and Directory Interface (JNDI)	JNDI has two functions. Service providers use JNDI to attach naming and service directory providers. Application component providers use JNDI to access naming and directory services.

Optional APIs

The optional APIs are far more numerous than the required ones, and you may never need to use some of these APIs. Some of the APIs are fairly new and will most likely be updated. Other APIs are very mature and should only have small changes in the future. Table 1.2 lists the optional J2EE APIs and gives a brief description of each.

Table 1.2 Optional APIs with J2EE-Compliant Applications

Java Database Connectivity (JDBC) v2	JDBC updates that allow backward scrolling in a result set and new data types. You can also use Java methods to update a database.
Enterprise JavaBeans (EJB) v2.	Enterprise JavaBeans are designed to encapsulate business objects that can hold data and business rules. This is key J2EE technology that we cover in Chapter 22, " Enterprise JavaBeans, " and Chapter 23, "Entity EJBs." EJBs are similar to JavaBeans, but they work in a distributed environment.
Servlet v2.3.	This is an updated version of the Servet API that has been the workhorse of server programming for quite a while. We cover servlets extensively in Chapters 9, "Making Servlets," and Chapter 10, "Servlets with JavaBeans." Servlets provide server-side functionality to process client requests.
JavaServer Pages (JSP) v1.2.	JavaServer Pages are a key J2EE technology that allows dynamic Web pages. This updated version allows tag libraries. JSPs are covered in Chapter 11, "JavaServer Pages." JSPs provide a way to dynamically generate a response.
Java Message Service (JMS) v1.0.	JMS is an API that permits point-to-point messaging and publish-subscribe messaging.

(continued)

Table 1.2 *(continued)*

Java Transaction API (JTA) v1.0.	JTAs are used with EJBs. They give the transactional demarcation for EJB transactions used by the container.
JavaMail v1.2.	This API makes it easy to email messages and files to email addresses.
JavaBeans Activation Framework (JAF) v1.0.	JAF is used by the JavaMail API and allows support for MIME types.
Java API for XML Parsing (JAXP) v1.1.	JAXP provides an interface for SAX and DOM coding. It also has support for XSLT.
J2EE Connector Architecture v1.0.	This is referred to as an SPI (Service Provider Interface) for transactions with the Enterprise tier (EIS).
Java Authentication and Authorization Service (JAAS) v1.0.	JAAS provides an interface to support user-based security.

All of the APIs in Table 1.2 have separate documentation and examples. They can be a little overwhelming. The best strategy is to start learning one API at a time, even though they can all work together. Even if you don't use all the APIs, you should be aware that they are in J2EE. Take advantage of them when you can. There is no sense in reinventing the wheel. It is best to take advantage of the services that a J2EE server provides.

Packaging

Knowing how a Java application is organized and packaged is very important. Prior to the J2EE specification, the way Java applications were packaged was influenced by the application server vendor or the conventions used by developers. This lack of consistency in packaging resulted in a lot of difficulties with deployed applications. For example, switching application servers was difficult, as was getting the same application to run on different application servers. To solve these problems, packaging requirements were added to J2EE. Tool developers have provided support for these packaging conventions in such platforms as WebSphere Application Server and WebSphere Studio Application Developer.

When you develop a J2EE application, you need to define an Enterprise Archive, or EAR, file to hold the application information. The J2EE packaging conventions manage the Web content part with the HTML and JSP files, and the EJB (Enterprise JavaBeans) part in separate packages. You will learn about EJBs in Chapter 22, "Enterprise JavaBeans," and Chapter 23, "Entity EJBs." For now, you need to know that EJBs are packaged and managed separately from the Web content files. The Web content comprising the servlets, JavaBeans, JSPs, and static Web content, along with a deployment descriptor, are packaged in a Web Archive (WAR) file, as shown in Figure 1.3. The EJB files, along with a deployment descriptor, are placed in a separate JAR (Java Archive) file.

The application deployment configuration is very flexible because it can manage the Web content and the EJB content. This design allows you to combine multiple EJB JARS or Multiple WAR files in an Enterprise Archive.

The EAR, WAR, and JAR files are like the zip files that you are accustomed to using. They compact many files and retain their file path structure. These files can be versioned in a file-based versioning system such as PVCS, CVS, or ClearCase. Most companies deploying commercial software rely on these versioning systems so that they can maintain deployed systems.

After the EAR file is built, it is then deployed to the J2EE server. When you deploy an EAR file to WebSphere AppServer, the files in the EAR and WARs are exploded, or unzipped, on the J2EE server. You can go to the file system, and you will see the files. You will learn more about deployment and how to do it in WebSphere in Chapter 16, "J2EE Application Deployment." The new packaging conventions make it easier to deploy new Java applications, but it creates problems for existing applications. There are many production applications that use JSPs, Servlets, or EJBs from earlier APIs. These applications are deployed using various conventions employed by their developers and architects. Many businesses have resisted migrating working applications to the J2EE packaging for a lack of cost justification. Switching to the J2EE packaging entails the following:

- Upgrading the application server
- Possibly updating other software such as the relational database
- Learning new tools to make the J2EE packaging
- Packaging the application
- Deploying the application
- Testing the application

All of these tasks take time and coordination, which costs money. In today's environment, many mangers feel that "if it is not broken, then don't try to fix it." For this reason it will take a while to migrate existing Java applications to the J2EE packaging.

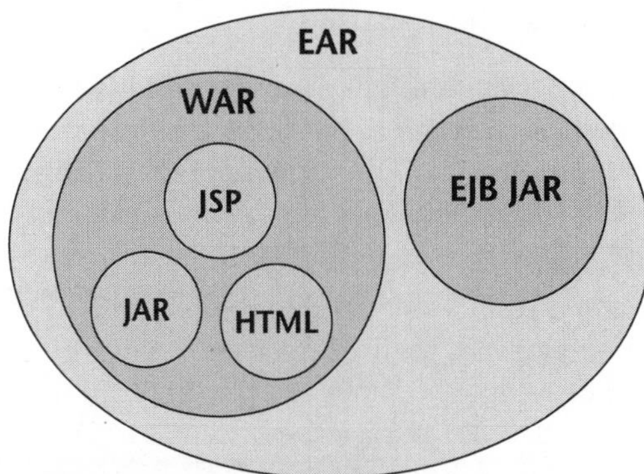

Figure 1.3 J2EE packaging.

Development Roles

Software development projects have a number of different participants. J2EE has formal descriptions for the different roles that people can perform in a Java project. For small Java projects or in one-person consulting companies, one person may need to fulfill all the roles. In large companies these roles may be assigned to separate individuals, sometimes in different departments. Making sure that somebody in the development for each project is assigned to every role is very important.

Role names differ or are combined in the various articles and books discussing J2EE roles. You should try to consistently use the correct role names to avoid any confusion, even if you are fulfilling multiple roles on a project. Six roles are described in the J2EE specification. The following sections discuss each of these roles.

Product Provider

The product provider is anyone who provides software products that implement the APIs and features described in the J2EE specification. A J2EE application can use many different software resources, so product providers are numerous. For example, IBM provides a number of products that support J2EE such as DB2 and WebSphere Application Server. There are many more products providers such as Oracle, BEA, Sun, and Macromedia, to name a few. Sun provides a great catalog of J2EE providers at http://industry.java.sun.com/solutions.

Tool Provider

The tool provider is anyone who provides a software tool that supports the J2EE architecture. Most of the product providers also act as tool providers.

Application Component Provider

The application component provider is anyone who designs and develops components or parts of a J2EE application. There are three types of developers that match three different skill sets for J2EE development, and they are the following:

Enterprise Bean Developer— is a Java coder that designs and develops EJBs that map to a domain model. An Enterprise Bean Developer packages the EJBs in an EJB jar file along with a deployment descriptor. You will learn more about EJBs and how they work using WebSphere in subsequent chapters 22 EJB Basics and 23 EJB Advanced.

Web Component Developer— is usually a Web developer that designs and develops HTML, JSP, CSS files and their graphics for the presentation layer of a J2EE application. The Web component developer is responsible for testing and packaging the Web components, along with a deployment descriptor, in a WAR file. There are a number of chapters in this book, such as Chapter 5, "Web Page Content," Chapter 6, "Linking Web Page Content," and Chapter 14, " Making Slick Web Pages," that cover Web content creation using WebSphere.

Application Client Developer— is a Java coder that designs and develops a Java application to run on the client. The client applications usually use the AWT or Swing Java frameworks for the graphical user interface. The application client developer is responsible for testing and assembling the code into a Jar file, along with its deployment descriptor.

Application Assembler

The application assembler is anyone who takes the application components and assembles them in an EAR file with the deployment descriptor. In practice, this is usually a team leader or project architect. It has long been a goal of software developers to merely gather existing components and assemble them in the desired manner and have a complete application pop out. This works for very simple applications, but for the most part, this is a panacea. Usually, there is not a pure application assembler role on a J2EE project. It is common for either the deployer or the lead developer, who is also an application component provider, to assume the role of application assembler.

Deployer

The deployer is the person responsible for installing and configuring a J2EE application EAR file on a J2EE server. This role has long been a "black art," something few developers ever saw, but somehow magically happened. Chapter 16, "J2EE Application Deployment," is devoted to describing how to deploy a J2EE application. J2EE packaging has enabled Web applications to be deployed in a consistent way, making the deployer's job a lot easier. In large companies, the deployer may not necessarily be a developer, but having a person in that role who is skilled in Web development can help prevent many deployment problems.

System Administrator

The system administrator is the person responsible for setting up the runtime environment, applying maintenance fixes to the run time, starting and stopping the system, and monitoring the system for performance and reliability. In many development shops, the system administrator also serves the role of deployer. J2EE packaging makes deployment a lot easier and more closely links the process of deployment to the runtime environment. Many companies have documented standards for Web applications. The system administrator is responsible for ensuring that the Web application is up and running, and may occasionally run performance testing. The system administrator manages all the maintenance fixes for the J2EE server.

J2EE Runtime

The J2EE architecture describes the different Java components and how they interact. The architecture uses the APIs and packaging described in the J2EE specification. The architecture is flexible and scalable. There has been a lot of work devoted to Model-View-Controller and separating these pieces into different components.

Some Web sites run on a single server. These are usually internal Web sites for a company, with a specific purpose, or Web sites with a very narrow audience such as a local real estate agent's Web site or a local sports club's Web site. These sites are easy to set up and manage, and really do not require all the flexibility that is provided with J2EE. Nevertheless, smaller Web applications should still follow the J2EE architecture to make it easier to maintain and provide the flexibility to grow.

Larger Web applications or ones that have many active users, such as commercial Web sites, can exploit the benefits of J2EE. These installations can have many computers with multiple J2EE servers running the same Web application, or many different Web applications, at the same time.

Containers

J2EE uses the notion of containers to isolate and separate the different components. A J2EE server can manage either a Web container or an Enterprise JavaBean (EJB) container, both of which are described in the following sections. Figure 1.4 shows a common example of how a J2EE server is commonly configured. Keep in mind, however, that there are many variations of J2EE server configurations. The J2EE server is responsible for managing the communications among containers. The container is responsible for the communications within the container.

Web Containers

Web containers run on a J2EE server and hold the Web content. The Java code in the form of Servlets and JavaBeans are usually packaged in a JAR file. The JSP files and other Web files, such as CSS files and graphics files, are also part of the Web application.

There is no exact rule on how to define the function for a given Web container. You would not want every page on a Web site to have a different Web container. There would be too much maintenance and performance overhead with this design. And on the other hand, it may be easier to lump all the Web content files in one Web container, but this design also has some pitfalls.

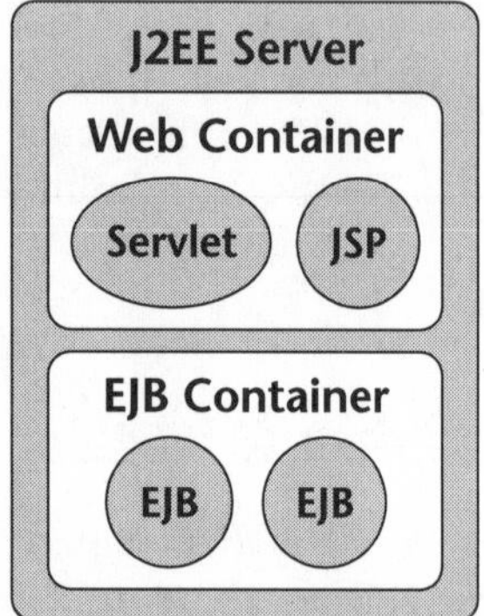

Figure 1.4 J2EE containers.

EJB Containers

Enterprise JavaBeans are designed to encapsulate business objects that can hold data and business rules. EJB class files are grouped together for run time in a JAR file. EJB Jars are deployed to the EJB container on the J2EE server.

Runtime Architecture

All of the material in this chapter so far describes J2EE, but has not shown how a J2EE application works at run time. In this section, we will step through how the basic components work at run time. Figure 1.5 depicts a high-level view of the components and their flows. The following steps are one example of a common execution scenario:

1. A Web page is displayed in a client Web browser.
2. The client user selects a link or presses a button.
3. A request is made to a Uniform Resource Locator (URL) using HTTP.
4. A servlet on a J2EE server receives the request and calls the appropriate business object (EJB or JavaBean).
5. The business object performs the necessary transactions with the Enterprise tier.
6. The business object returns control to the servlet.
7. The servlet forwards the response to a JSP or the HTML code.
8. The resultant HTML is transmitted to the client via HTTP and displayed in the Web browser.

This J2EE runtime scenario can be extended in many different ways. Servlets can forward control to other servlets, and JSPs can include other JSPs. In an actual application there would be many EJBs or JavaBeans. This design pattern provides for good Model-View-Controller separation. We discuss other runtime scenarios in Chapter 11, "JavaServer Pages," and Chapter 19, "Displaying Data."

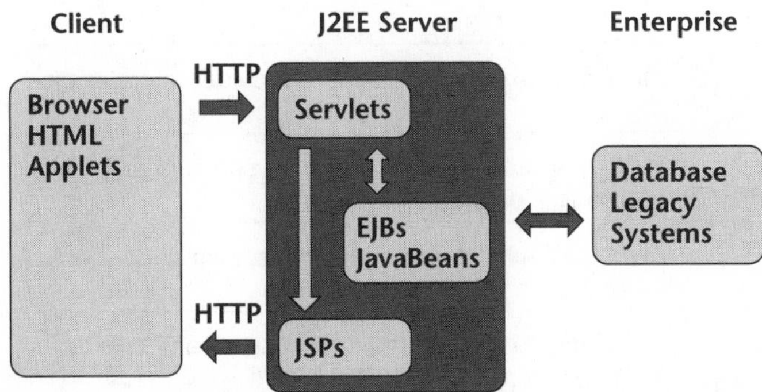

Figure 1.5 J2EE runtime architecture.

Future Enhancements

A number of enhancements are planned for existing Java APIs, and additional APIs that may become part of J2EE. These updates are part of the J2EE Specification, but the APIs and technologies are still fairly new or changing, so they are not required for J2EE conformance. There is a chance that some of these additional APIs will become part of the base J2EE APIs and be required in the future.

New APIs always seem to be added to the Java arsenal. These APIs can come from many sources, but they all share some common features. They must integrate with the existing J2EE APIs, and they must be open and extendable.

The enhancements to J2EE will provide additional breadth and depth to this robust programming framework.

What Is Not in J2EE?

Even though it seems like J2EE covers everything under the sun, there are a few areas that it does not cover. The following list shows some of the items not covered in J2EE:

Other languages— J2EE is a Java specification and is designed for Java programming. It does not include interfaces for C++, Visual Basic, Pascal, or other programming languages, except through JNI (Java Native Interface, a Java API for calling C and C++) or CORBA. You can get more information on CORBA, a generic open interface from OMG, at www.omg.org.

Table 1.3 Additional APIs in J2EE-Compliant Applications

API	DESCRIPTION
Java Database Support Technology (JDBC)	See the description in Table 1.1. Additional support is available for RowSets.
XML Data binding	Used to support XML schemas.
Java Network Launch Protocol (JNLP)	JNLP allows a client to start applications on a server.
Service Provider Interface (SPI)	More APIs that support Service Provider Interfaces.
Java Authorization Contract for Containers (JACC)	JACC involves the interaction between containers and service providers.
Deployment APIs	Additional APIs to support new deployment options for tools.
Management APIs	The ability to imbed Structured Query Language (SQL) directly in Java code.
SQL-Java (SQLJ)	The ability to imbed SQL (Structured Query Language) directly in Java code.

JavaScript— Although JavaScript is a usage of the Java language, the J2EE specification does not cover it. It is very common to use JavaScript for data validation on a client Web browser, so Chapter 12, "JavaScript," covers JavaScript.

Vendor specific APIs— J2EE does not support the OLE, DCOM, or .NET architectures.

Legacy applications— You will still need to maintain legacy applications that run on EIS systems like Cobol. J2EE merely provides access to these resources.

Ways to implement the APIs— There are many different examples in this book on how to use J2EE, but there is no single solution. One size does not fit all. You will have to determine the best ways to implement the J2EE APIs through awareness and experience. These are your best Web development assets.

Summary

In this chapter, you learned about the J2EE architecture and its components. J2EE is a set of Java APIs that work in a client-server environment, delivering robust scalable applications. The key concepts in J2EE are:

- **J2EE architecture—** its tiers and components.
- **J2EE services—** the many APIs and their versions that are available for a J2EE application.
- **Packaging—** the nested structure of an EAR file that contains WAR files and EJB JARs.
- **Roles—** the many formal roles that describe the tasks needed to develop J2EE applications.
- **J2EE runtime—** the different components and how they work at runtime.

J2EE has a lot of functions, and there are many ways to use the different components. By learning about the different components in J2EE and how they work, you are better prepared to solve your application development needs. You have learned enough Java acronyms in this chapter to be able to speak like a true Java programmer, which means that an average person will not understand a word you are saying.

The next chapter covers the WSAD development environment and how to do basic operations on the workbench.

Getting Started

What's in Chapter 2?

This chapter will help you get familiar with the WSAD integrated development environment (IDE). WSAD combines the functions previously provided in VisualAge for Java and WebSphere Studio, but WSAD has a completely different IDE based on the open source Eclipse IDE. This chapter covers the following topics:

- Installation considerations
- Workspace settings
- Using the Help system
  - Cheat sheets
  - Help contents
- IDE essentials
  - Perspectives
  - Views
  - Editors
  - Workbench options

- Working with code
  - Creating projects
  - Importing files
  - Editing code
  - Using code assist
- Running Java code

You will use the IDE and see how to customize it with your preferences. You will get a chance to write a little code and use some of the WSAD features. You will see how to run Java code in the IDE.

Installation Considerations

Installing WSAD is pretty easy, but there are a few things that you should consider before starting the installation. You need to make sure that your system has enough memory and disk space to run efficiently.

Prerequisites

The hardware requirements have not changed much except for the increase in memory and disk space. WSAD will work on a 500-MHz PC with a monitor with a resolution of 1024 by 768. The memory requirements are a minimum of 512 MG of RAM and 950 MB of disk space. You need more disk space for the application files. These are the minimum requirements, and more memory and a faster processor are needed for daily usage.

WSAD works on a variety of operating systems, which include:

- Windows 2000 with fixpack 2
- Windows XP
- Windows NT with fixpack 6a
- Red Hat Linux 7a
- Suse 7a

Once you have the basic hardware and software, you are ready to install WSAD.

Installation Options

When you install WSAD, you can select the custom installation as shown in Figure 2.1. Both WebSphere Application Server v4 and v5 are installed by default. If you are migrating to WebSphere Application Server v5, you may not need to install v4. If you use the Apache server, you should prevent the WebSphere Application Server from installing. The plug-in development is not installed by default, so you need to select these if you intend to use this feature.

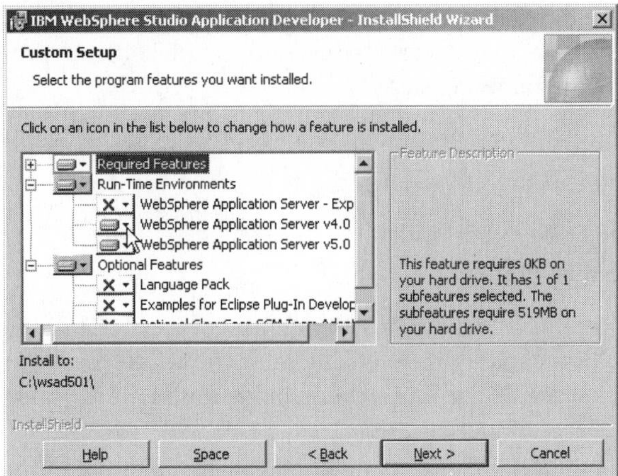

Figure 2.1 Installation options.

Installation takes a little while, so be patient. You should consider using a file base versioning system such as CVS, PVCS, or ClearCase. Chapter 21, "Versioning Code," discusses versioning in WSAD and shows you how to work with CVS as an example. After WSAD is installed, there are a few options for the workspace that are discussed in the next section.

Workspace Settings

WSAD stores data for the IDE and your application-specific files in a directory structure called the workspace. When WSAD starts, you are prompted with a window to specify the workspace as seen in Figure 2.2. This window is a helpful way to switch between multiple workspaces.

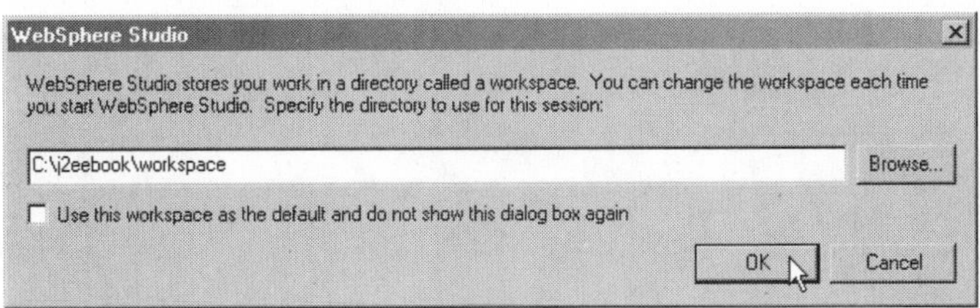

Figure 2.2 Workspace at run time.

You can configure the workspace location with icons on the desktop. This is helpful if you have one workspace or if you have many workspaces for different software projects. Make a WSAD shortcut with the following steps:

1. From the install directory, drag a WSAD (wsappdev.exe) shortcut to the desktop.
2. From the shortcut's popup menu, select Properties.
3. Enter **–data c:\j2eebook –showlocation** as shown in Figure 2.3.
4. Click the OK button to save this setting.

When you double-click the icon on the desktop, it will automatically start and the workspace will use the location c:\j2eebook for its files. The –showlocation parameter displays this workspace directory in the title bar. The location indicator is helpful when you are using two different workspaces at the same time.

Using the Help System

The Help system is automatically installed with the product. It's pretty easy to use and includes a convenient search feature. The two key components to the Help system are Cheat Sheets and Help Contents. The following sections demonstrate how these components work.

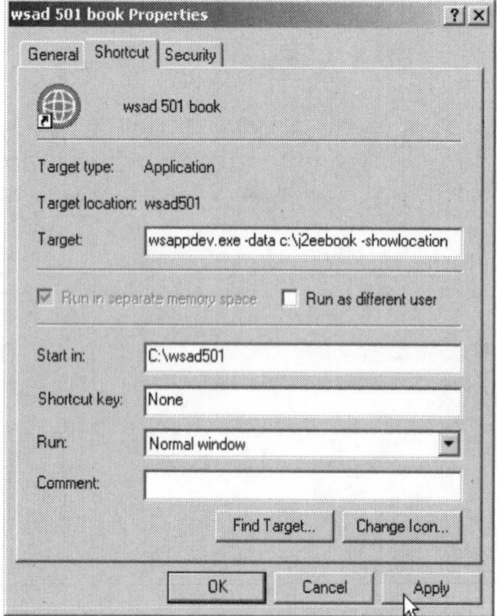

Figure 2.3 Workspace as a property.

Cheat Sheets

Cheat Sheets are a new innovation for the Help system intended to provide a quick reference for common tasks. After starting WSAD, select Help > Cheat Sheets > Create a Web application, and the Cheat Sheets window displays as shown in Figure 2.4. Cheat Sheets provide a quick and easy way to learn how to do basic operations, and they serve as handy reminders. There needs to be more Cheat Sheets for other common tasks; however, you can find more tutorial information in the Help Contents.

Help Contents

The Help Contents is the biggest part of the Help system and it contains a comprehensive collection of Help topics for all of WSAD. The Help content is separated into the following sections:

- Application developer information has specific help on using the Workbench and its various tools.
- Java 2 Standard Edition (J2SE) API reference documentation
- Java 2 Enterprise Edition (J2EE) API reference documentation
- Tool developer help
- WebSphere Application Server network deployment

The Help Contents are packed with information. When you select the Application developer information, the options display as seen in Figure 2.5. These sections closely match the different perspectives provided in WSAD, and they usually contain three sections: Concepts, Tasks, and Reference. Some of the sections have their own samples to help illustrate proper usage.

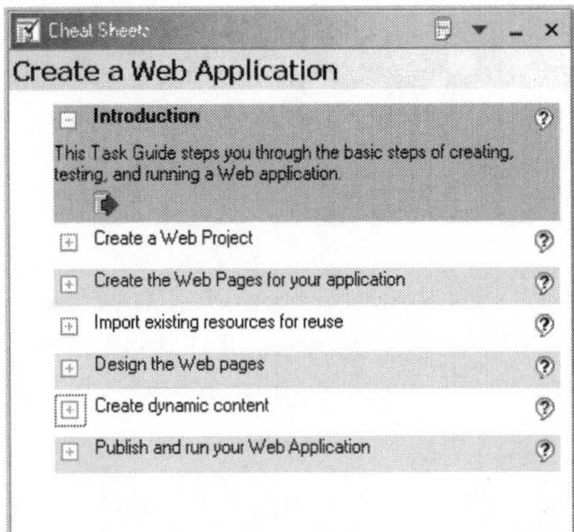

Figure 2.4 Web application Cheat Sheet.

Application developer information
- Product overview
- Getting Started
- Scenarios
- Workbench basics
- Java development
- Visual Editor for Java
- J2EE development
- Web development
- Struts application development
- Application Template Wizard
- EJB development
- XML development
- Web services development
- Relational database tools
- Component test
- Application testing and publishing
- Debugging applications
- Agent Controller
- Application profiling
- Accessibility for special needs
- Other sources of information
- Glossary

Figure 2.5 Application developer help.

IDE Essentials

The WSAD IDE has a number of features that make it different from the earlier WebSphere Studio and VisualAge for Java products. WSAD integrates all the development features for Java code development, such as servlets, applications, and EJBs, with Web content, such as HTML, JSP, XML, and Web artwork. It's great to have a completely integrated development environment, but all the tools can be overwhelming. Once you have mastered the basic concepts of the IDE, you will feel more comfortable with the working environment. The first step is to make a few custom settings.

Setting Options

When you install WSAD, there are a number of options that you should change from the default settings. The options fall into many different categories, and this section will show you a few key settings. You can access the workbench options with the following steps:

1. Select Window > Preferences, and the Preferences windows appears, as shown in Figure 2.6.
2. Under Workbench > Editors, you should change the size of recently opened files list to **9**. This provides a longer list of files to select for editing.

3. Under Debug, you should select the checkbox labeled Remove terminated launches when a new launch is created. This is a handy feature that cleans up the view showing the running threads.
4. Under Java > Code Formatter on the New Lines tab, you can set the style for the format function. You should check the box labeled Clear all blank lines. On the Line Splitting tab, you should set the Maximum line length to **120**. This will tighten up the code and make it easier to read.
5. Select Java > Compiler and the compiler options appear, as shown in Figure 2.7. Compiler errors are reported in the tasks list, and this page allows you to set the type of errors detected. You should change some of the default settings to improve your code. Any changes to these settings cause all the code to be recompiled under the new rules. Change the following setting:
   - Unused imports to Warning. This will help you reduce unneeded import statements.
   - Unused local variables to Warning. This identifies code that can potentially be removed.
   - You may want to change the Usage of deprecated API setting to Ignore. Usually there are a number of deprecated methods in large projects. You can also hide these by ignoring warnings in the Tasks filter.
6. If you intend to use the Visual Editor, select Java > Visual Editor. Select the Show the Visual Editor and Source Editor option as On Separate notebook tabs. This provides more area for the Visual Editor and the Source Editor.
7. Click the OK button to save these changes.

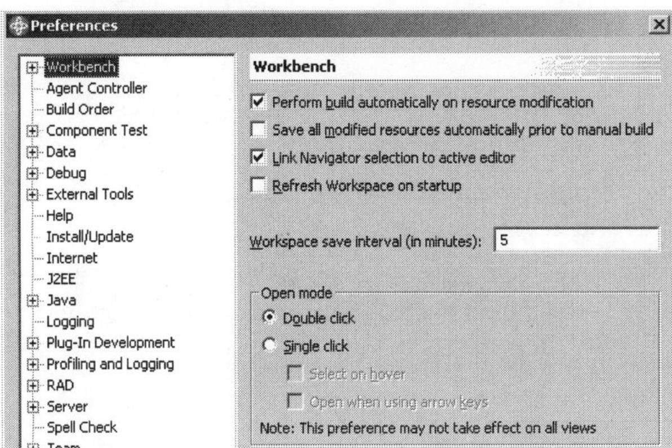

Figure 2.6 Workbench options.

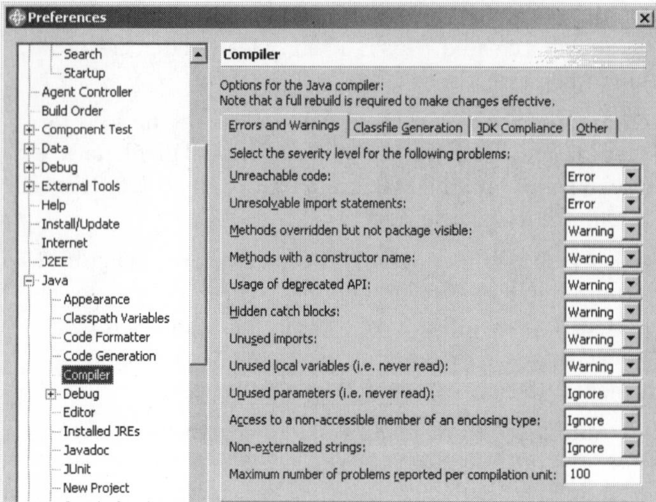

Figure 2.7 Compiler options.

There are a lot more options that you may want to use as you become more familiar with WSAD. You should browse the various option sections and try some of the other settings. You will get a lot more out of WSAD by tuning the tool with your preferences.

Using Perspectives

Perspectives are the special predefined widows that contain views and editors intended for a specific purpose. Along with specific views, each perspective has specific tools on the toolbar or available directly from a popup menu. WSAD has the following perspectives:

- Resource is the simplest perspective that merely shows files, and it has the Navigator, Outline, and Tasks views with no special tools.
- Java has the basic views for simple Java applications, including the Package Explorer, Hierarchy, Outline, and Tasks.
- Web has the J2EE Navigator, Tasks, Servers, and Server configuration views, along with views for creating Web content such as Gallery, Links, and Styles.
- J2EE has the same views as the Java perspective, along with the Servers view and DB Servers view.
- XML has the Outline, Navigator, and Tasks views.
- Server has the Navigator, along with the Servers and Server Configuration views.
- Debug has a lot of views, including Debug, Servers, Outline, Console, Tasks, and Variables.
- Plug-in Development looks like the Java perspective with the addition of the Plugin view.

- Component Test has the Outline and Task views, along with the Definitions view for test cases.
- CVS Repository has the CVS History view and the CVS Repository view.

Even though there are a lot of perspectives, you will most likely only use a couple of perspectives during development. If you have many perspectives open, you can cycle through them using Ctrl-F8. Part of your WSAD learning curve is getting used to working with these perspectives.

Customizing Perspectives

It's easy to customize the IDE. Each view in a perspective can be deleted, added, resized, or moved. These settings are saved with the workspace automatically. You can change the Java perspective by removing the Outline view and adding the Debug view. Let's customize the Java perspective with the following steps:

1. Open the Java perspective by selecting Window > Open Perspective > Java.
2. Click the X on the tab for the Outline view to delete it.
3. Select the menu items Window > Show View > Debug and the Debug view is added to the perspective.

The changes to the perspective should look like Figure 2.8. When you exit WSAD the workspace is automatically saved. The next time you start WSAD the Java perspective will look just the way you customized it. You can save the perspective with a unique name by selecting Window/Save Perspective as. You can get the default perspective back by selecting Window/Reset Perspective. All of these features show how easy it is to customize perspectives.

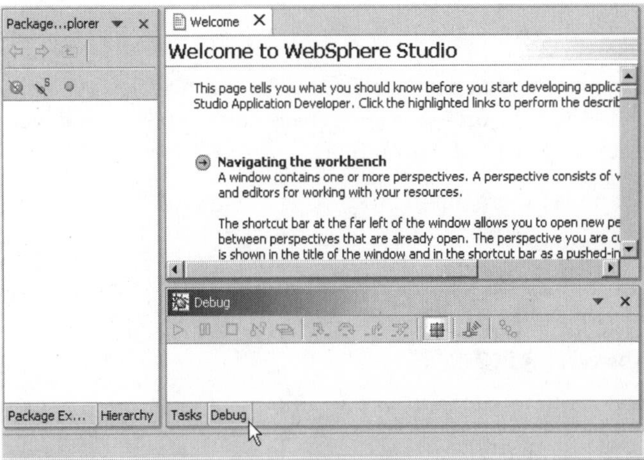

Figure 2.8 Customized Java perspective.

A small icon appears on the left side of the workbench each time that you open a perspective. Figure 2.8 shows the icon for the Java perspective. These icons provide a quick way to navigate to the open perspectives. Keep in mind that you can have multiple perspectives of the same type open at the same time. It can be a little confusing. If this occurs, you can close the unneeded perspectives from the icons.

Fast Views

The views in a perspective can be resized by dragging their borders with the mouse. You can move views that are used often to the area on the left of the workbench with the perspective icons. If you select the Hierarchy tab on the bottom left of the workbench, the Hierarchy view displays. When you drag the Hierarchy view to the left bar with the perspective icons, WSAD makes an icon for the Hierarchy view, as shown in Figure 2.9. This Fast view is associated with the Java perspective, and it displays whenever the Java perspective is displayed.

You can use WSAD to write all different types of J2EE applications. In the next section, you will get acquainted with using the Java Editor.

Writing Java Code

Now that the workbench is set up, you are ready to use WSAD for writing applications. This section briefly introduces you to the basic steps for writing code. You will become familiar with using the IDE and some of its common features. The rest of the book covers different J2EE topics in greater depth and assumes that you are familiar with working in the IDE. First, you will learn about projects, a very important part of the IDE.

Project Types

Code in WSAD is organized in projects that have different types. Each project type has specific folders and runtime files to support a specific type of Java application development. The following projects are provided with WSAD:

- Simple has no runtime and is for organizing files.
- Java has the basic Java runtime.
- Web has the basic Java runtime and server support for HTML, JSPs, and servlets.
- EJB has support for EJBs v1.1 and v2.0.
- J2EE has the Web project runtimes and support for EJBs.
- Server is a separate project for defining test servers.

All the files for an application need to be organized into one or more projects. So, the next step is to set up your first project in WSAD.

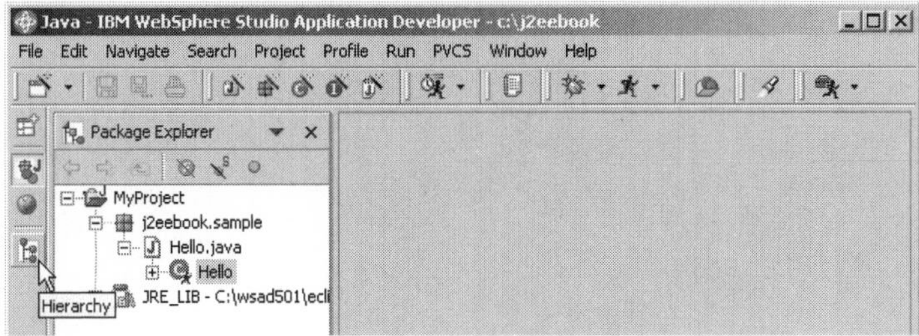

Figure 2.9 Fast views.

Creating a Project

You must have a project for anything that you want to create in WSAD. A Web project has the runtime files for the items in the project. The classpath is limited to the project by default. You can add external JAR files to the classpath and also reference other projects in the workspace. You will make a new Java project and do some basic coding in this chapter. Create a new Java project with the following steps:

1. From the Java perspective, select File > New > Project, and the New Project window displays as seen in Figure 2.10.
2. Select Java and Java Project, and then click the Next button to proceed.
3. The Java Project window displays as seen in Figure 2.11.
4. Enter **MyProject** for the project name.
5. Click the Finish button to create the project.

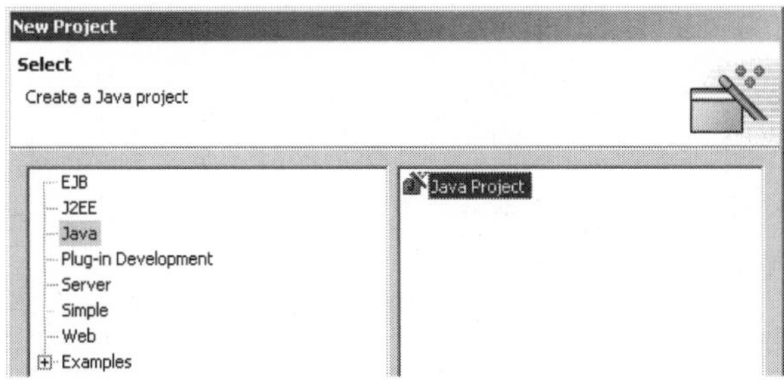

Figure 2.10 New WSAD project.

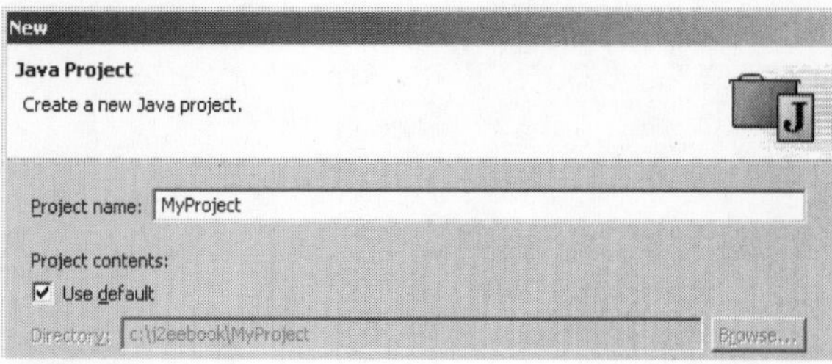

Figure 2.11 New Java project.

Importing Files

You can start working with Java code now that you have a project. You will import a file from the Web site for this book. It is very easy to import code into WSAD, which supports importing many file types, including the J2EE package types such as JARs, WARS, and EARs. Import the JAR file that has a sample Java application with the following steps:

1. Select the MyProject project that you just created. The file will be placed in this project.
2. Select File > Import.
3. Select Zip file from the Import window.
4. Click Next, and The Import Zip file window appears, as shown in Figure 2.12.
5. Select the hello.jar file on the CD-ROM.
6. Make sure the folder is MyProject.
7. Click the Finish button to import the JAR file.

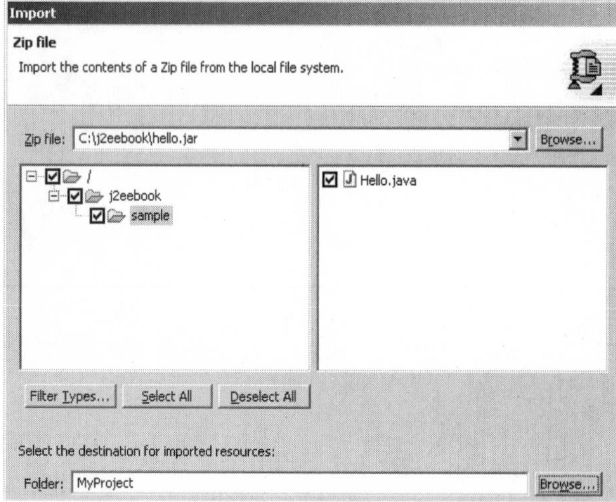

Figure 2.12 Importing a JAR file.

When the code for the Hello class loads into WSAD, a Java Editor is automatically opened, displaying the class. The code should look as follows:

```
package j2eebook.sample;
/**
 * @author drnilsso
*/
public class Hello {
    /**
     * Constructor for Hello.
     */
    public Hello() {
        super();
    }
    public static void main(String[] args) {
    }
}
```

As you can see from the code, the Hello class is very simple. It has a default constructor and a `main()` method that has no content. Nothing will happen when the Hello class runs. You will edit the code to display a message in the console.

Editing Java Code

There are a couple of source editors in WSAD. There is a basic Java Editor. Edit the Hello class with the following:

```
public static void main(String[] args) {
    System.out.println("Hello World");
}
```

Save the code by pressing the Ctrl-s keys. The Hello class displays the message Hello World in the Console view when it runs. So let's test this simple application.

Running Java Programs

WSAD supports running many different types of Java applications. The Hello class is a simple Java class with a `main()` method. It requires no other classes or JAR files, and it does not have any parameters. Run the Hello class with the following steps:

1. Select the Hello.Java file in the Package Explorer.
2. Select the menu items Run > Run as > Java Application.

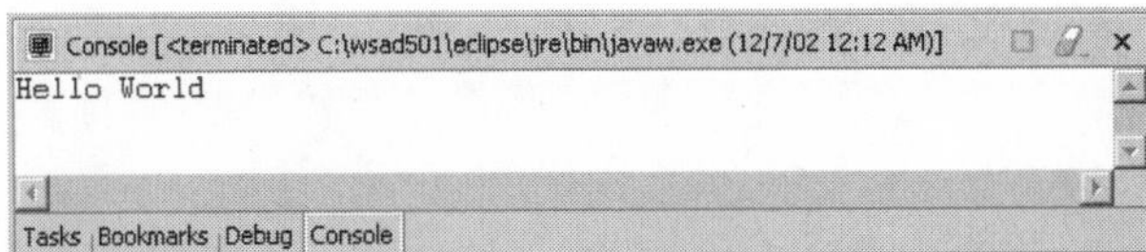

Figure 2.13 Hello World running.

The Hello class runs, the `main()` method executes, and the message Hello World displays in the console as seen in Figure 2.13. If you run the Hello class from a command line, the message displays on the command line. WSAD has a separate Console View to handle the System.out messages.

Using Code Assist

Code assist is a helpful feature that provides hints to code as you are editing. You make a change to the Hello class and use the code assist feature. Add a new output line that displays an argument passed to the class with the following:

1. In the Java Editor for Hello.java, create a new line below the Hello World message.
2. Enter **System.out.println("Welcome "+ar**
3. Invoke code assist by pressing Ctrl-space, and the code assist panel displays, as seen in Figure 2.14. Notice how all the items in the list start with "ar." As you type characters, the list narrows to those items matching what you have typed.
4. Select the args item on the list.
5. Complete the line so it is: **System.out.println("Welcome "+args[0]);**
6. Save the code by pressing Ctrl-s.

Code Assist is very helpful because it shows all the items that are available at a certain point in the code. Code Assist shows the classes and methods that you have defined too. If you do not see a class that you expect, you may need to add an import statement to the code. The Code Assist feature also works when you edit HTML and JSP files. The completed Hello.java file should look as follows:

```
package j2eebook.sample;
/**
 * @author drnilsso
 */
public class Hello {
    /**
     * Constructor for Hello.
     */
    public Hello() {
        super();
    }
    public static void main(String[] args) {
    System.out.println("Hello World");
    System.out.println("Welcome "+args[0]);
    }
}
```

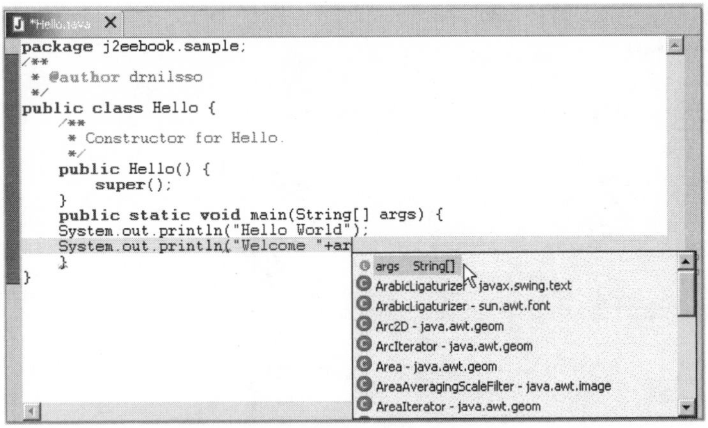
*Hello.java
package j2eebook.sample;
/**
* @author drnilsso
*/
public class Hello {
/**
* Constructor for Hello.
*/
public Hello() {
super();
}
public static void main(String[] args) {
System.out.println("Hello World");
System.out.println("Welcome "+ar
}
}
args String[]
ArabicLigaturizer - javax.swing.text
ArabicLigaturizer - sun.awt.font
Arc2D - java.awt.geom
ArcIterator - java.awt.geom
Area - java.awt.geom
AreaAveragingScaleFilter - java.awt.image
AreaIterator - java.awt.geom

Figure 2.14. Code assist panel.

Running Java Programs with Arguments

The arguments passed through the args[] array can be passed as command-line arguments. In the IDE, these arguments are specified as runtime parameters. Test the updated Hello application with the following steps:

1. Select the Hello.java file.
2. Select the menu item Run > Run..., and the Launch Configurations window appears, as seen in Figure 2.15.
3. Select the Arguments tab.
4. Enter some text for the argument to the Hello class. If the text has spaces, you need to use the quote marks at the beginning and end of the text.
5. Click the Apply button to save this change.
6. Click the Run button to run the code.

The Hello class displays a new message in the console, as seen in Figure 2.16. The previous message is still in the console. You can clear old messages from the console by selecting Clear from the popup menu in the console.

Using Bookmarks

The IDE has a great feature called bookmarks that lets you label places in the code for quick access. You can create bookmarks anywhere in the code, then, you can use the Bookmark view to quickly access any of the bookmark locations.

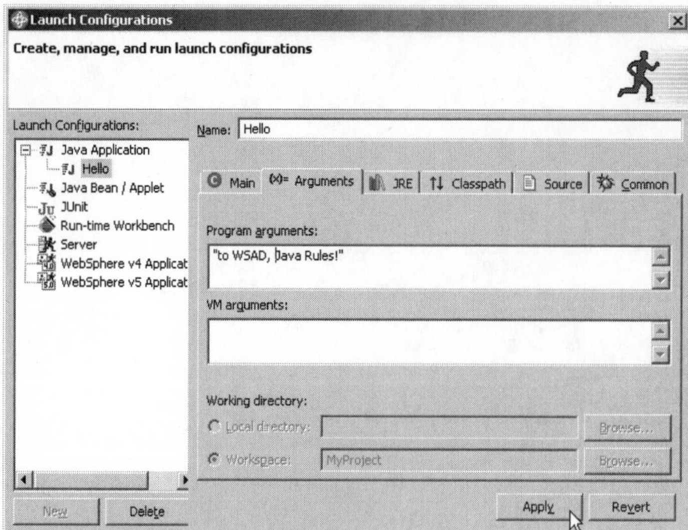

Figure 2.15 Setting a runtime argument.

Adding a Bookmark

You can add bookmarks to any line in the source code. You define a label when you make a bookmark. The label serves as a reminder or hint for the bookmark. You will add a bookmark in the Hello class on the `main()` method with the following steps:

1. Make sure the Hello.java file is still open in the Java Editor.
2. Move the mouse to the left edge of the editor in the gray area next to the main() method.
3. From the popup menu, select Add Bookmark..., and the Add Bookmark window appears, as seen in Figure 2.17.
4. Enter a meaningful label such as **Hello main()**.
5. Click the OK button to save the bookmark.

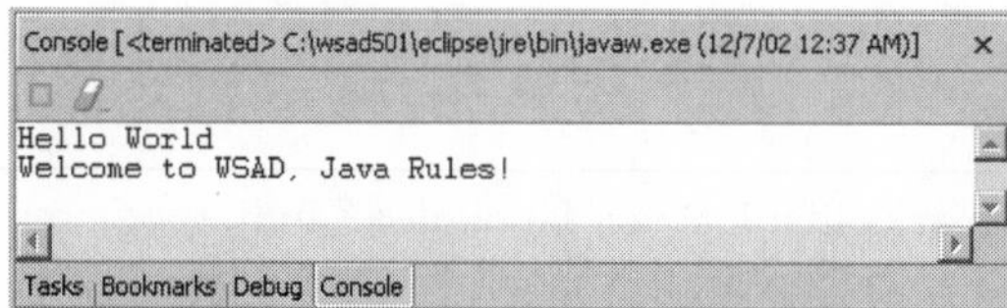

Figure 2.16 Hello World using an argument.

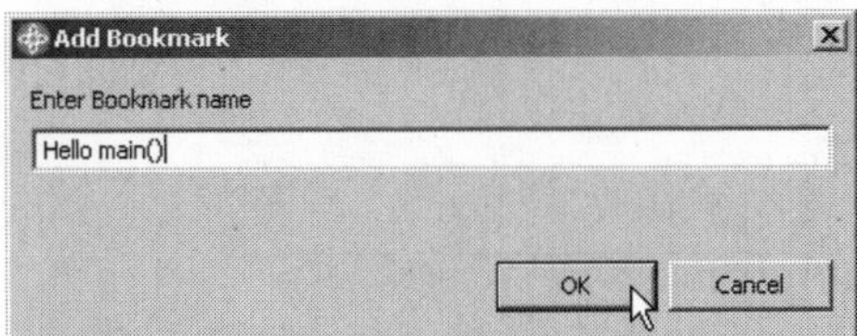

Figure 2.17 Adding a bookmark.

The bookmark appears in the Java Editor, as seen in Figure 2.18. You can use the Bookmarks view to access this class at this point in the code.

Adding the Bookmarks View

The Bookmarks view needs to be displayed to use the bookmarks. The Bookmarks view is not part of the standard perspectives, like the Java perspective, so you must add the view to the perspective. The Bookmarks view is saved with the workbench when WSAD is closed. Add the Bookmarks view with the following steps:

1. Select Window > Show View > Other, and the Show View window appears, as seen in Figure 2.19.
2. Select Basic > Bookmarks.
3. Click OK, and the Bookmarks view displays in the workbench, as seen in Figure 2.20.

The Bookmarks view is another tab at the bottom of the workbench. You can move this view or make it a Fast view. You can test the bookmark by closing the Hello.java file, then double-clicking the bookmark in the Bookmarks view. The Hello.java file is automatically loaded and positioned at the bookmark in the code.

Hello.java

```
package j2eebook.sample;
/**
 * @author drnilsso
 */
public class Hello {
    /**
     * Constructor for Hello.
     */
    public Hello() {
        super();
    }
    public static void main(String[] args) {
    System.out.println("Hello World");
    System.out.println("Welcome "+args[0]);
    }
}
```

Figure 2.18 Bookmark label.

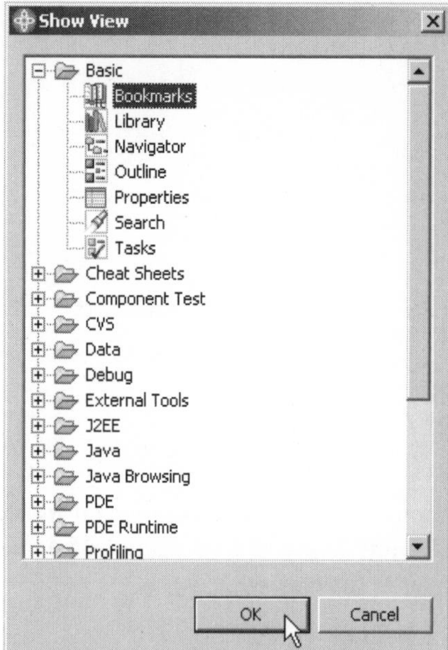

Figure 2.19 Adding a bookmark.

Figure 2.20 Bookmarks view.

Importing VisualAge code

Many WSAD users need to migrate code from VisualAge for Java to WSAD. There are a number of things to consider for a successful migration from VisualAge for Java. Following is a list of items that you should evaluate when you migrate from VisualAge for Java:

- As you will see in Chapter 21, WSAD relies on a separate file-based versioning system like CVS. You will need to install the versioning system and set up the appropriate linkage in WSAD.
- Graphical applications developed in the Visual Composition Editor need special handling. WSAD v5 has a new Visual Editor that lets you paint AWT or Swing applications. The new Visual Editor does not support the connections;

you must do the event coding by hand. If you have classes that use an abstract class that you developed, such as a specialized JPanel or JButton, the classes are not displayed in the Visual Editor. To fix this, you must change the parent class so it is concrete by removing the abstract keyword.

- In VisualAge, you can set the classpath for the entire workspace. In WSAD each project has its own classpath, so you need to set the project dependencies after the code is imported into WSAD.
- There will be some deprecated methods as you move to WSAD and use a more current JDK. But this is a normal situation for most Java programs in transition.
- You will see additional warnings in the code as WSAD identifies unneeded import statements and local variables that are not used.

IBM has dropped support for VisualAge as of May 2003, and WSAD is the replacement product. Migrating from VisualAge for Java to WSAD is not hard, and you can take the opportunity to tune your code a bit. The hardest part of the transition is moving to a file-based versioning system, but on the plus side, all the application files are easily accessible.

Importing WSAD v4 code

WSAD v5 has different structures for its projects than those used in WSAD v4. When you open an existing WSAD v4 workspace with WSAD v5 a warning message appears, as seen in Figure 2.21. WSAD automatically migrates the workspace to the current format, and all the projects should be intact. Some of the file associations are changed, affecting the default editor. For example, the HTML files are associated with the Web browser instead of the Page Designer as they should be. Additionally, Web projects have different subdirectories in v5, and the migration does not convert the old subdirectories. For these reasons, you may want to create new projects in WSAD v5 and import the v4 source code to get the proper project configuration.

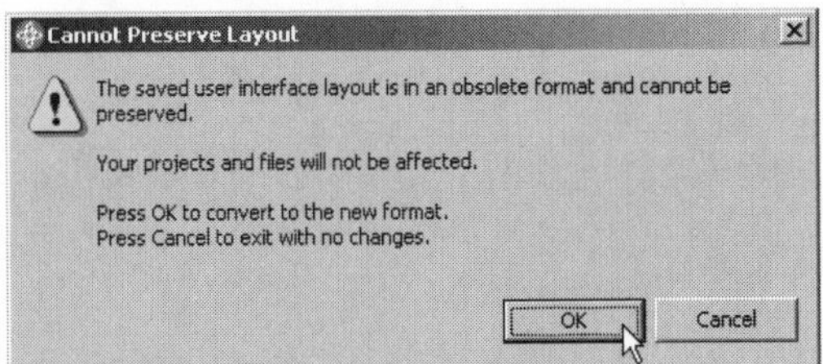

Figure 2.21 WSAD v4 migration.

Summary

WSAD is a very powerful high-end tool set that contains a very tightly integrated development environment. In this chapter, you learned how to do the basic steps required to develop and run Java applications. This chapter covered the following topics:

- Installation considerations
- Workspace settings
- Using the Help system
- IDE essentials
  - Perspectives
  - Views
  - Editors
  - Workbench options
- Working with code
- Running Java code

This chapter gave you a basic understanding of how to effectively use the key elements in the WSAD workbench. You will learn more detailed information as you progress through the book. There are many ways to customize the workbench to your tastes, and there are many other functions to learn.

In the next chapter, you will build a Java application that has a Swing user interface. You will learn how to use the Visual Editor to design applications, and you will add code to handle what happens when a button is pressed.

Making a Simple Java Application

What's in Chapter 3?

This chapter covers the basic foundations for Java application development. WSAD has a number of tools that make it easier to develop Java applications. You will develop a basic Java application and run it using WSAD. In this chapter, you will cover the following:

- Making a Java project
- Creating packages
- Creating classes
- Adding comments
- Using the Visual Editor
- Adding fields
- Adding methods
- Setting class properties
- Testing an application

These steps used for developing Java applications form a basis for the more advanced development in later chapters of this book. You will build a Java Calculator using the Java Swing graphical user interface (GUI) controls. By the end of the chapter the Calculator will be tested and running.

Developing a Java Application

In this chapter, you will become familiar with using WSAD by making a Java application. This application is a GUI application that acts as a calculator. It has the functions to add numbers and clear the display. These basic functions illustrate how to add logic to an application. First, you need to make a Java project for this application. Projects are not part of J2EE, but they are necessary in WSAD. All the code in WSAD is organized into projects that are subdirectories for holding the application files.

Making a Java Project

WSAD has a number of different types of projects that you can make. For Java application development, a Java project will be fine. You will develop this application in the WSAD Java Perspective. Make a Java project with the following steps:

1. If you are not in the Java Perspective, select the menu items Window > Open Perspective > Java.

2. Select the create Java Project button on the toolbar.
3. The New Java Project dialog box appears, as shown in Figure 3.1. Enter **CalcProject** and press the Finish button to create the project.

You can see the new project in the Package Explorer view of the Java Perspective. WSAD created a new subdirectory for this project. WSAD projects help keep your application files organized, but you need to add packages and folders to keep the different file types organized. The project needs a package for the Java code.

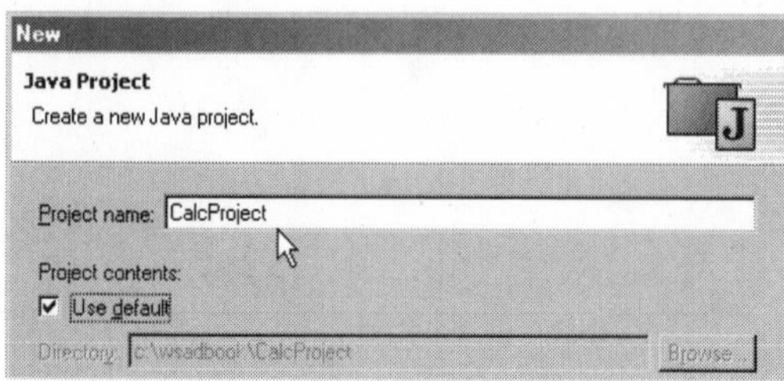

Figure 3.1 Making a project.

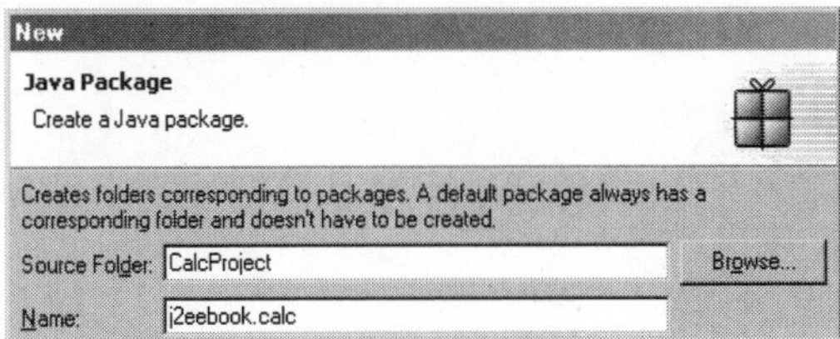

Figure 3.2 Creating a package.

Creating a Package

You need a package to hold the Java class that you are building. Add a new Java package to the CalcProject with the following:

1. Make sure the new CalcProject is selected in the WSAD Package Explorer.

2. Press the Create a Java Package button on the toolbar.
3. The New Java Package window displays as shown in Figure 3.2.
4. Enter **j2eebook.calc** for the package name.
5. Press the Finish button to create the package.

After the project and package are created, they appear in the Package Explorer on the left side of the IDE, as seen in Figure 3.3. You can see that WSAD has included the Java runtime in the project. Although j2eebook.calc looks like one subdirectory, it becomes two subdirectories in WSAD and at runtime. The Java Perspective hides some text files like property files.

Creating a Class

Now that there is a project and a package, you are ready to create a Java class. The application class is named `Calculator`, and it subclasses `JFrame`. Add a new class to the j2eebook.calc package with the following steps:

1. Make sure the j2eebook.calc project is selected in the WSAD Package Explorer.

2. Select the Create a Java Class button from the toolbar, or you could select the menu items File > New > Class.

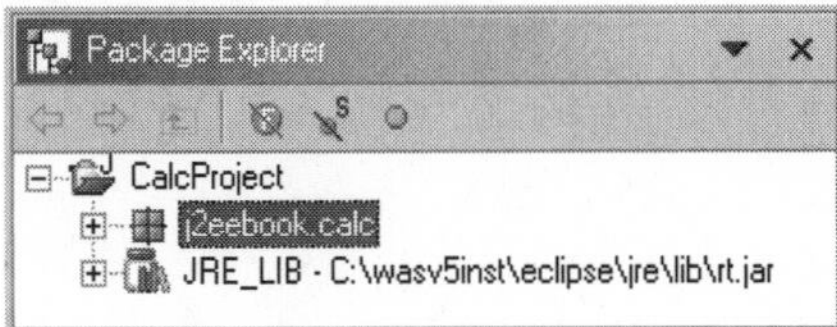

Figure 3.3 Explorer with Project and Package.

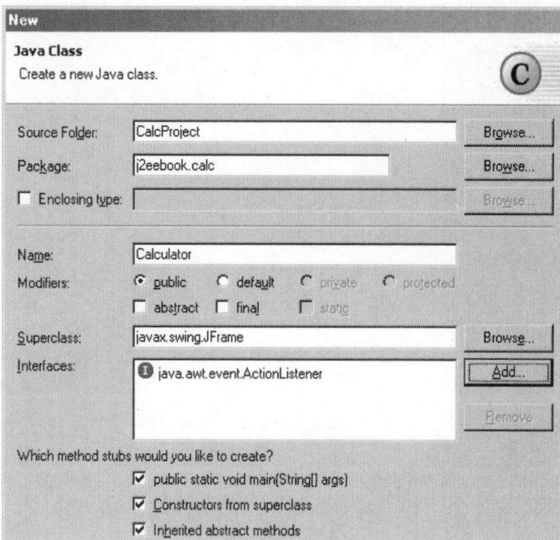

Figure 3.4 New Java class.

3. The New Java Class window appears, as shown in Figure 3.4. Make sure that the Source Folder is CalcProject and the package is j2eebook.calc. Note, you can also use a special version of the wizard for Visual classes by selecting File > New > Visual Class.
4. Enter **Calculator** as the class name.
5. Next, you need to enter the fully qualified name of the superclass. Select the Browse button next to the Superclass field to search for the superclass, and the Superclass Selection window appears, as seen in Figure 3.5. This window makes it easy to select fully qualified class names.

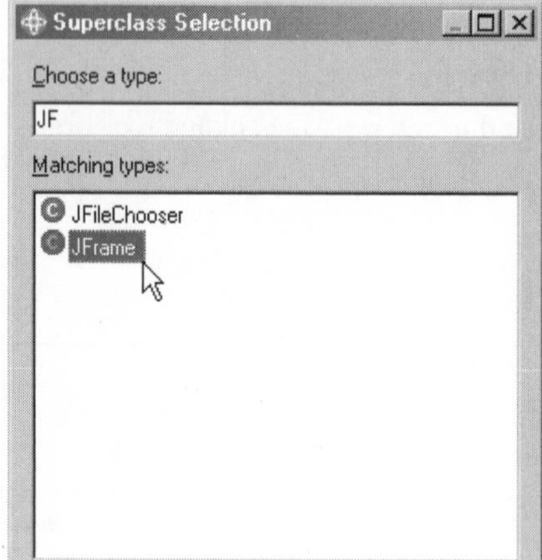

Figure 3.5 Superclass selection.

6. Enter **JF** in the Choose a type field. As you enter characters, the Superclass Selection displays classes that match the characters entered.
7. Select the JFrame class, and press the OK button to close the Superclass Selection window.

You can see that the fully qualified class name `javax.swing.JFrame` is in the Superclass field. The Calculator has two buttons that send an Action event when they are clicked. In order for the Calculator to act on these events, it needs to implement the ActionListener interface. You need to specify the fully qualified name for the ActionListener for the class declaration. Add this interface with the following steps:

1. Press the Add button that is next to the Interface's textarea.
2. Enter **acti** in the Choose interfaces field, and the list of interfaces changes in the Matching types textarea.
3. Select ActionListener from the list, as shown in Figure 3.6, and click the Add button.
4. Click on the OK button to close the Implemented Interfaces Selection window.

There are still a few more items that you need to specify for the wizard to generate the `Calculator` class. There are a few methods that should be implemented that are common conventions for Java applications. Complete the rest of the class information with the following steps:

5. Check the box to generate `public static void main(String[] args)`. This method is needed to run the Java application.
6. Check the box to generate Constructors from superclass.
7. Check the box to generate Inherited abstract methods.
8. When all the information is entered, press the Finish button to create the class.

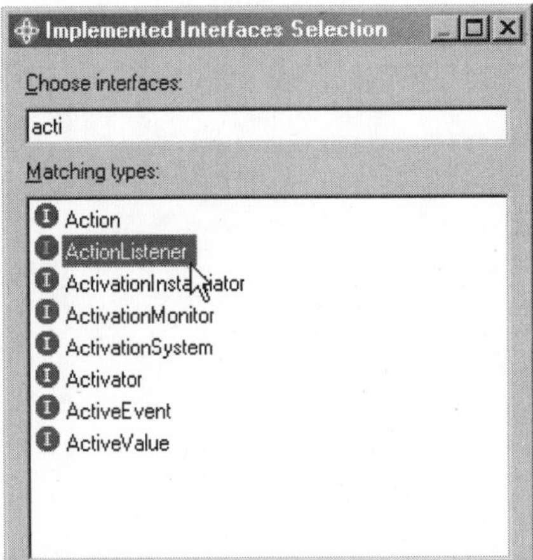

Figure 3.6 Interface selection.

The WSAD Servlet wizard generates the basic code needed for the application. It generated the package statement, the imports, class declaration, constructors, and required methods. The code should look as follows:

```
package j2eebook.calc;
import java.awt.GraphicsConfiguration;
import java.awt.event.ActionEvent;
import java.awt.event.ActionListener;
import javax.swing.JFrame;
/**
 * @author dnilsson
 * To change this generated comment edit the template variable
"typecomment":
 * Window>Preferences>Java>Templates.
 * To enable and disable the creation of type comments go to
 * Window>Preferences>Java>Code Generation.
 */
public class Calculator extends JFrame implements ActionListener {
    /**
     * Constructor for Calculator.
     */
    public Calculator() {
        super();
    }
    /**
     * Constructor for Calculator.
     * @param arg0
     */
    public Calculator(GraphicsConfiguration arg0) {
        super(arg0);
    }
    /**
     * Constructor for Calculator.
     * @param arg0
     */
    public Calculator(String arg0) {
        super(arg0);
    }
    /**
     * Constructor for Calculator.
     * @param arg0
     * @param arg1
     */
    public Calculator(String arg0, GraphicsConfiguration arg1) {
        super(arg0, arg1);
    }
    /**
     * @see java.awt.event.ActionListener#actionPerformed(ActionEvent)
     */
```

```
        public void actionPerformed(ActionEvent arg0) {
        }
        public static void main(String[] args) {
        }
    } @jve:visual-info  decl-index=0 visual-constraint="0,0"
```

You can see a special comment at the end of the code. This comment is used by the Visual Editor to hold positioning information for the objects in the editor. Make sure not to alter or delete this comment. Everything looks good, except for the default comment generated by WSAD. It is easy to fix this default message in the WSAD preferences. Let's fix this setting before you start working on the `Calculator` class.

Adding Comments

All classes should have a comment at the top describing the purpose of the class. Usually the class comments should include the following:

- The author or authors of the class
- A copyright and date or date last changed
- The purpose of the class

All methods, excluding getters and setter, should also have appropriate comments, too. Since methods belong to a class, they do not need an author. However, it is important to include the following:

- The purpose or intent of the method
- The parameters needed for the method and example values
- The return value if it is not a void method

A default comment is generated for methods when you generate the accessor methods, but other comments need to be generated or entered in the Java Editor. WSAD has functions to generate a default comment in your code. Add a comment to the `Calculator` class with the following steps:

1. In the Outline view, select the `Calculator` class.
2. From the popup menu, select Add JavaDoc Comment.

WSAD generates a default comment, as shown in the following code:

```
/**
 * @author dnilsson
 * To change this generated comment edit the template variable
"typecomment":
 * Window>Preferences>Java>Templates.
 * To enable and disable the creation of type comments go to
 * Window>Preferences>Java>Code Generation.
 */
```

This comment has one of the needed comment elements, the author, and fortunately a helpful comment on how to change the default comment. If you don't change this setting now, every time you generate JavaDoc you will get this same comment. In the next section, you will change the default JavaDoc template.

Editing JavaDoc Templates

It is easy to change the default JavaDoc template in WSAD with the following steps:

1. Select Window > Preferences to display the WSAD preferences.
2. Navigate to the Java / Templates section in the tree view in the left view, as shown in Figure 3.7.
3. Select the typecomment template and its default text appears in the Preview view.
4. Edit the default comment by clicking the Edit button.
5. Change the default comments in the Pattern field to include the information that you prefer such as the author, copyright, project, and purpose. Click the OK button to close the Edit template window.
6. Press the Apply button and the OK button to save these changes and close the Preferences window.

Now, all new classes generated by WSAD will get the new comment template. The generated comment in the `Calculator` class needs to be updated. Change the comments in the `Calculator` class code and update the author, copyright, and purpose.

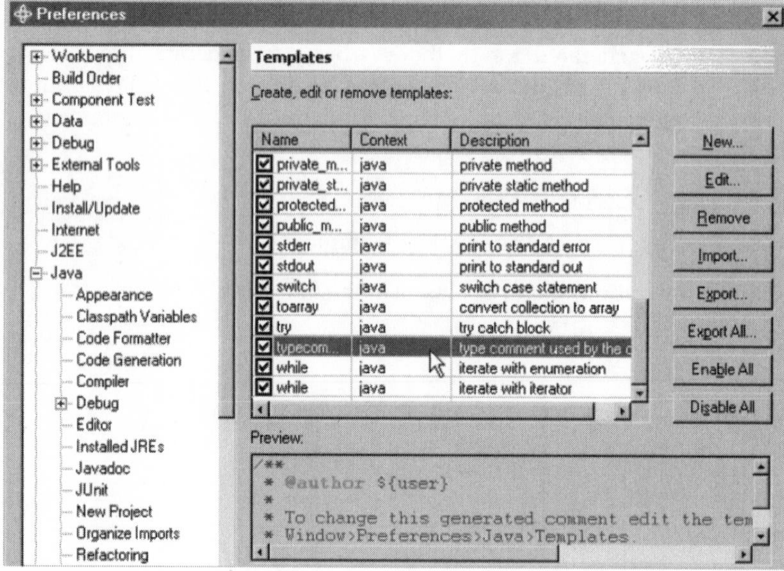

Figure 3.7 Comment template.

Using the Visual Editor

The next step in building the Calculator is to work on the GUI. WSAD has a new tool in version 5 that makes it easy to visually design GUI applications. This is a special editor that can only be used for AWT or Swing user interfaces. It allows you to drag and drop the different GUI components and change their settings through property editors. It does not have the visual connections that VisualAge for Java's Visual Composition Editor has. All the business logic and control flow must be hand-coded. This is not so bad, because even with the VisualAge for Java you had to code the business logic part by hand. The Visual Editor supports round tripping. This is a key benefit; the generated code can be edited and still modified in the Visual Editor.

You do not need to be a Java GUI expert to use the Visual Editor. The Calculator application needs to have the following Swing components:

- A JLabel for the title
- A JTextField for entering the numbers and showing results
- A JButton for the add function
- A JButton for the clear function

Let's start the Visual Editor. First, you must close the Java text editor that opened when the wizard created the class. Open the Visual Editor with these steps:

1. Close the Java editor for the Calculator class by clicking the X next to the Calculator.java tab.
2. Select the Calculator.java file.
3. Open the Visual Editor by selecting from the popup menu Open with > Visual Editor.

Visual Editor Tools

The Visual Editor opens in the Java Perspective, as shown in Figure 3.8. The Visual Editor has a number of features to help you develop GUI applications. The separate distinct areas have the following functions:

- Component Pallets are separated into different groups:
  - Selection contains the Marquee for selecting multiple items in the design area, and the Choose Bean that provides a way to use any Java class in the design area including GUI and Invisible JavaBeans.
  - Swing Containers contain the Swing GUI classes, such as JPanel and JFrame, that can contain or hold Java Swing components.
  - Swing Components contains the Swing GUI component classes such as JButton and JTextField.
  - AWT Controls contains the Abstract Window Toolkit components and containers. These GUI class are more primitive and not as rich in function as the Swing classes.
- The Design area is the place where you can visually design application GUIs.

- The Property Editor allows you to change the values of the components in the Design area. It has buttons to reset properties and to set them to null.
- The Source Editor and Overview tab allow you to add custom code to the GUI class.

The Visual Editor can be used to make new GUI applications or modify existing GUI applications. Even though this tool makes it easier to develop GUIs, you still need to understand good design principles and basically how the different GUI components behave. There are many different GUI components in the JDK, and this example shows how to use the basic ones. There are entire books devoted to explaining how to use the many different GUI components. The Visual Editor uses the J2EE JavaBeans, and you will learn more about this J2EE API in Chapter 7, "Making JavaBeans." Next, you will use the Visual Editor to build the GUI for the Calculator application.

Setting a Layout Manager

First, you need to resize the JFrame and set the layout manager for the JPanel. You can make these changes without writing any code; the Visual Editor generates it for you. Use the Visual Editor to modify the JFrame with the following steps:

1. Select the outside of the JFrame in the design area, then drag a corner diagonally to resize it, as shown in Figure 3.9.
2. Select the gray area inside of the JFrame. This is a JPanel that the Visual Editor automatically creates.

The BorderLayout Manager is set as the default by the Visual Editor. The BorderLayout Manager has five different zones: north, south, east, west, and center. Each of these zones expands and requires additional JPanels to manage components in these zones. There are a number of other layout managers that you can use that come with the JDK. The GridBagLayout and the BoxLayout are very good for organizing components in managed grid, but these layout managers are a bit complex and require you to make a lot of property settings. The FlowLayout Manager is much easier to use and good enough for this application. Change the layout property to FlowLayout as follows:

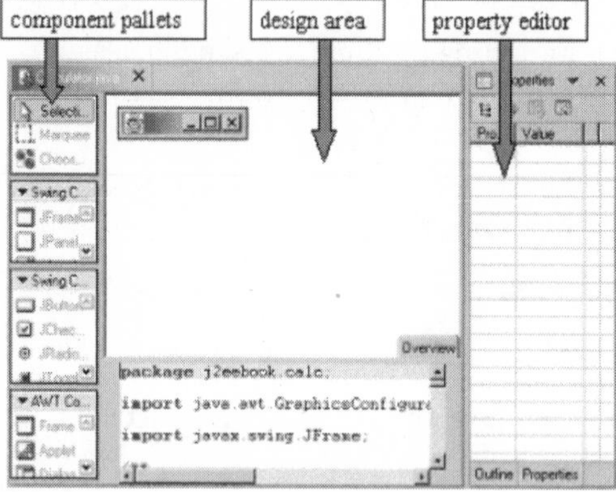

Figure 3.8 Visual Editor areas.

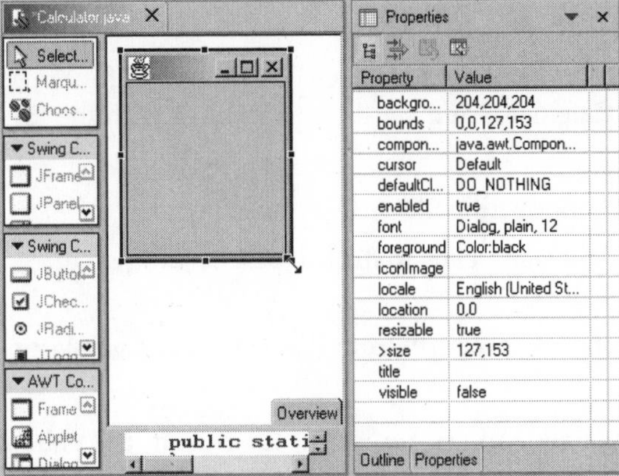

Figure 3.9 Resizing the JFrame.

1. Select the layout property in the Properties area.
2. In the dropdown list, select the FlowLayout as shown in Figure 3.10.

You will not see any visual differences in the JPanel after setting the FlowLayout Manager. The FlowLayout Manager affects how the JPanel positions its components. The FlowLayout Manager positions components at the top center of the container, and subsequent components follow to the right of the first component. If there is not enough room for a component, it is placed on the next row beneath the previous component. The FlowLayout Manager does not fix the components in a certain location, rather they move as the window is resized. This is not the best behavior for a GUI. Using the GridBag or Box layout manger can fix this problem.

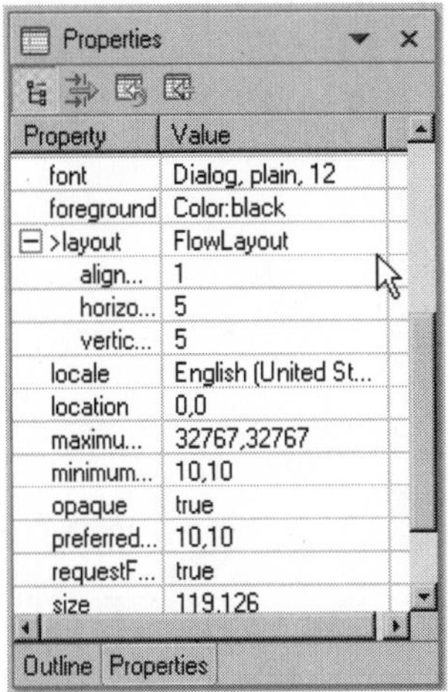

Figure 3.10 Layout property.

Adding Components

Now that the JFrame and JPanel are set, you can add the JLabel, JTextfield, and JButtons. Add these Swing components to the Calculator and set their properties with the following steps:

1. Select a JLabel from the Swing Component pallet.
2. Place the mouse cursor on the JPanel, and click to drop a Jlabel, as shown in Figure 3.11.
3. In the Properties Editor, change the text property from JLabel to **Java Calculator,** as shown in Figure 3.12.

You can add other controls in the same manner. You select them from the pallet, place them on the JPanel, and set their properties. If you want to change a component's location, you can drag it to the desired location and WSAD will handle positioning it. Add the JTextfield and JButton components with the following steps:

1. Place a JTextfield on the JPanel after the JLabel.
2. Change the JTextfield text property to **0**. This field is used to enter numbers for adding and displaying the result. When the Calculator starts, it has an initial value of zero.
3. Place a JButton on the JPanel after the JTextfield.
4. Change the JButton text property to **+**. This is the add button.
5. Place another JButton on the JPanel after the first JButton.
6. Change the JButton text property to **C**. This is the clear button.
7. Press Ctrl-S to save these changes to the source code.

The completed Calculator GUI should look like Figure 3.13. There are a number of properties for each of the components on the Calculator JFrame. You may want to experiment with some of the other properties. For example, you can change the background property of the JPanel to some more interesting color. Remember that the color property is expressed as three numbers representing the mixture of red, green, and blue.

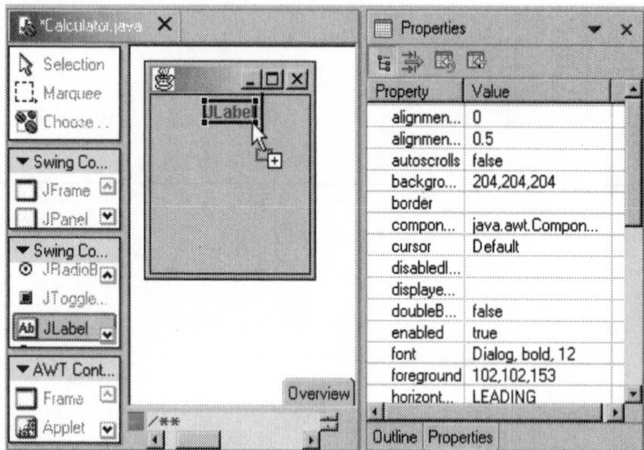

Figure 3.11 Adding a component.

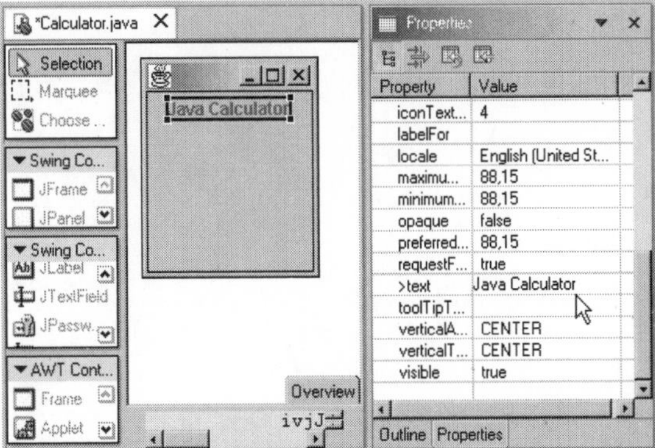

Figure 3.12 Setting properties.

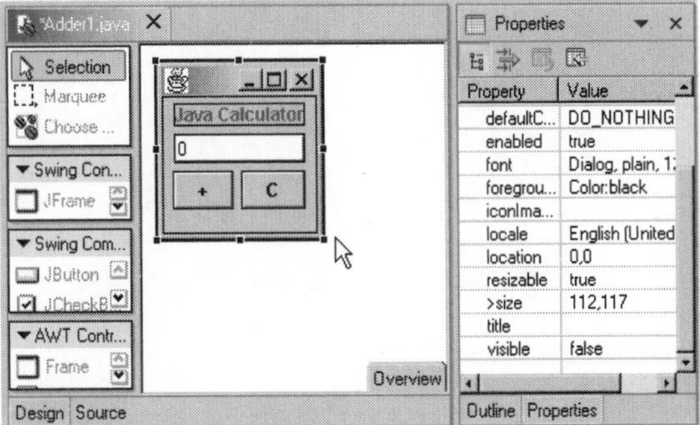

Figure 3.13 Calculator GUI.

The Visual Editor generated all the code for the Calculator GUI, including some code to support the ActionListener for the JButtons. The code for the GUI is complete, but there will need to be more code added to run the Calculator application. You can see a comment at the bottom that holds information for the Visual Editor. The generated code for the Calculator GUI should look as follows:

```
package j2eebook.calc;
/**
 * This class is a Swing GUI frame that has a simple calculator.
 */
public class  Calculator   extends JFrame implements
java.awt.event.ActionListener {
    private javax.swing.JPanel jContentPane = null;
    private javax.swing.JTextField jTextField = null; //
    private javax.swing.JButton jButton = null; //
    private javax.swing.JLabel jLabel = null;
    private javax.swing.JButton jButton1 = null;
    /**
     * Constructor for  Calculator   .
```

```
     */
    public Calculator   () {
        super();
    }
    /**
     * Constructor for Calculator   .
     * @param gc
     */
    public Calculator   (GraphicsConfiguration gc) {
        super(gc);
    }
    /**
     * Constructor for Calculator   .
     * @param title
     */
    public Calculator   (String title) {
        super(title);
    }
    /**
     * Constructor for Calculator   .
     * @param title
     * @param gc
     */
    public Calculator   (String title, GraphicsConfiguration gc) {
        super(title, gc);
    }
    public static void main(String[] args) {
    }
    /**
     * This method initializes this class
     * @return void
     */
    private void initialize() {
        this.setContentPane(getJJContentPane());
        this.setSize(112, 117);
    }
    /**
     * This method initializes jContentPane
     * @return javax.swing.JPanel
     */
    private javax.swing.JPanel getJJContentPane() {
        if (jContentPane == null) {
            jContentPane = new javax.swing.JPanel();
            java.awt.FlowLayout layFlowLayout_1 = new
java.awt.FlowLayout();
            jContentPane.setLayout(layFlowLayout_1);
            jContentPane.add(getJLabel(), getJLabel().getName());
            jContentPane.add(
                getJTextField(),
                getJTextField().getName());
```

```
            jContentPane.add(getJButton(), getJButton().getName());
            jContentPane.add(getJButton1(), getJButton1().getName());
        }
        return jContentPane;
    }
    /**
     * This method initializes jTextField
     * @return javax.swing.JTextField
     */
    private javax.swing.JTextField getJTextField() {
        if (jTextField == null) {
            jTextField = new javax.swing.JTextField();
            jTextField.setSize(56, 19);
            jTextField.setColumns(8);
            jTextField.setText("0");
            jTextField.setSelectionStart(0);
        }
        return jTextField;
    }
    /**
     * This method initializes jButton
     * @return javax.swing.JButton
     */
    private javax.swing.JButton getJButton() {
        if (jButton == null) {
            jButton = new javax.swing.JButton();
            jButton.setText("+");
        }
        return jButton;
    }
    public void actionPerformed(ActionEvent evt) {
        if (evt.getSource() == getJButton()) {
            add();
            //getJContentPane().repaint();
        } else if (evt.getSource() == getJButton1()) {
            clear();
        }
    }
    /**
     * This method initializes jLabel
     * @return javax.swing.JLabel
     */
    private javax.swing.JLabel getJLabel() {
        if(jLabel == null) {
            jLabel = new javax.swing.JLabel();
            jLabel.setText("Java Calculator");
        }
        return jLabel;
    }
    /**
```

```
     * This method initializes jButton1
     * @return javax.swing.JButton
     */
    private javax.swing.JButton getJButton1() {
        if(jButton1 == null) {
            jButton1 = new javax.swing.JButton();
            jButton1.setText("C");
        }
        return jButton1;
    }
} @jve:visual-info  decl-index=0 visual-constraint="0,0"
```

Testing an Application

Now that you have generated the GUI, it would be nice to see it running. You need to edit the code before it can run. The `main()` method and the default constructor need to be changed so that the application will run.

Editing the main()

The `main()` method is the first method that is automatically executed in a Java application. Other Java programs like Servlets do not follow this convention. The generated `main()` method is empty, so nothing happens when the Calculator application is run. The main method needs to make an instance of the Calculator class, have a listener for the window closing event, and then call its `show()` method to display the Calculator. Edit the `main()` method in the source editor to look as follows:

```
public static void main(String[] args) {
    Calculator calc = new Calculator();
    calc.addWindowListener(new java.awt.event.WindowAdapter() {
       public void windowClosing(java.awt.event.WindowEvent e) {
           System.exit(0);
       };
    });
    calc.show();
}
```

The default constructor should call the `initialize()` method that the Visual Editor generated. The initialize method sets up the components in the application. The set up code could go directly in the default constructor, but the amount of code needed to set up more complex applications can be very large. It needs to be called after the call to the `super()` constructor. Edit the default constructor `Calculator()` in the source editor to look as follows:

```
public  Calculator   () {
    super();
    initialize();
}
```

Running an Application

Now that the `main()` method is updated to call the default constructor, and the default constructor is updated to call the initialize() method, you are ready to run the Calculator application. There is a little set up required the first time that you run an application. Run the Calculator application with the following:

1. From the menubar, select the arrow part of the run button.
2. Select Run..., and the Launch Configurations window appears, as seen in Figure 3.14.
3. Make sure that **Calculator** is entered in the Name field.
4. Make sure that the correct project is in the Project field.
5. Make sure that the fully qualified class name is in the Main class field.
6. Press the Apply button to save these changes.

You can see a number of other tabs in Figure 3.15 that let you set additional launch properties. It is very common to pass parameters to an application at runtime. These parameters can be entered on the Arguments tab in the Launch Configurations window.

The JRE and Classpath tabs allow you to modify the runtime configuration for the application. For example, your application may need to reference external classes that are in a JAR file, or you may want to change the order in which JAR files are searched.

The Common tab has a couple of cool features. You can set up a shared configuration on a LAN shared drive. You can also indicate that the application should be displayed on the Run or Debug list in the WSAD IDE. Select the Run checkbox for this application, and click the Apply button.

7. Press the Run button to launch the Calculator application.

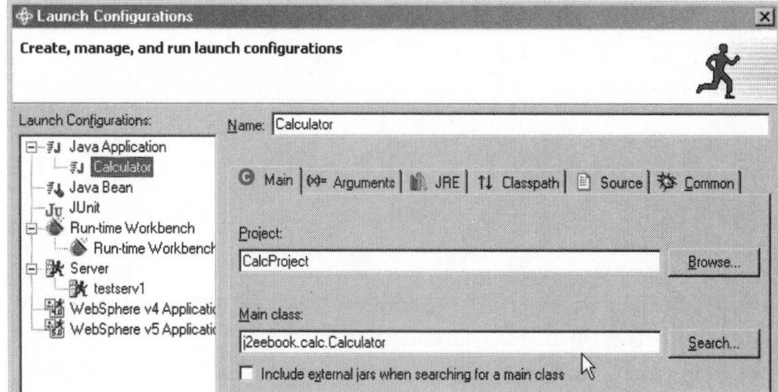

Figure 3.14 Launch configuration.

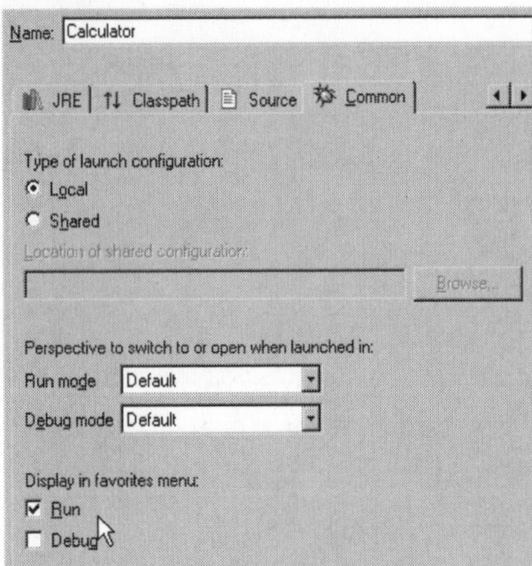

Figure 3.15 Launch favorites.

When the Calculator runs it should look like Figure 3.16. You can enter values and press the buttons, but nothing happens. This test was merely to confirm that the application would start and appear. In order to get the Calculator to work properly, there needs to be some more code added to the Calculator class. Close the Calculator window by clicking the X in the corner of the Calculator window.

Updating the Code

Now that you have tested the GUI, you need to edit the code so that it works properly. The business logic needs to be added to the Calculator to perform the add and clear functions when the appropriate buttons are clicked.

Adding Fields

The Calculator needs a field to hold the value that is being used for adding. There are a number of different types that you could use; for this application you will make a private field named *value* with type float. From the Java source editor, add the field definition at the top of the class:

```
private float value = 0;
```

You should press Ctrl-S to save this change to the source code.

Implementing Events

In order for the Calculator to act when the buttons are clicked, code needs to be added to register the Calculator with the JButtons. There also needs to be code added to sort through the Action events because there are two different buttons that can be pressed.

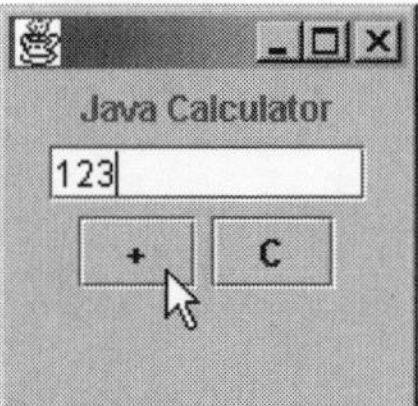

Figure 3.16 Running Java application.

Adding Listeners

You can register or listen for the button clicks by calling the `addActionListener()` method in each of the JButtons. You must pass a reference to the JFrame in the method call. This can be done by passing `this`. The `initialize()` method is a good place to put this code. It is only run once, when the application is started. You will also add a line to the `initialize()` method that has the JFrame dispose, or remove from memory, when the frame is closed. Edit the `initialize()` method in the source editor to look as follows:

```
private void initialize() {
    setDefaultCloseOperation(this.DISPOSE_ON_CLOSE);
    this.setContentPane(getJContentPane());
    this.setSize(112, 117);
    getJButton().addActionListener(this);
    getJButton1().addActionListener(this);
}
```

This is not the best way to implement the listeners. There are a couple of other options available. You could have the JPanel listen for the events. This would be much better because the JPanel could be reused in other applications that needed the calculator function.

Implementing the actionPerformed method

The `actionPerformed()` method is called when the buttons are clicked. There needs to be some code added to the `actionPerformed()` method to sort out the different button calls and route these calls for processing. Edit the `actionPerformed()` method in the source editor to look as follows:

```
public void actionPerformed(ActionEvent e) {
        if (e.getSource().equals(getJButton())) {
            add();
        } else
            if (e.getSource().equals(getJButton1())) {
                clear();
        }
    }
```

The actionPerformed() method acts as a filter and checks the source of the click event. It routes the + button (jButton) to the add() method and the C button (jButton1) to the clear() method. All other button clicks are ignored.

Adding Methods

The Calculator needs two new methods that are referenced in the action-Performed() method. The add method adds the value in the textfield to a field that holds the current value. The clear() method clears the textfield and resets the field that holds the current value to 0. Add the following code for these methods to the Calculator in the Java Editor:

```
public void add() {
    value += Float.parseFloat(getJTextField().getText());
    getJTextField().setText(Float.toString(value));
    getJTextField().repaint();

}
public void clear() {
    value = 0;
    getJTextField().setText(Float.toString(value));
    getJTextField().repaint();

}
```

After entering this code, you should press Ctrl-S to save your changes.

Retesting an Application

Now that the code for the Calculator is complete, it is ready to be tested again. Test it with the following steps:

1. Press the run button to retest the Calculator.
2. Enter **123** in the textfield, as seen in Figure 3.17.
3. Click the + button and the textfield shows the cumulative sum, as seen in Figure 3.18.

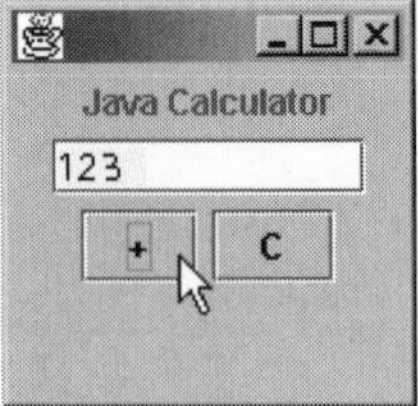

Figure 3.17 Calculator input.

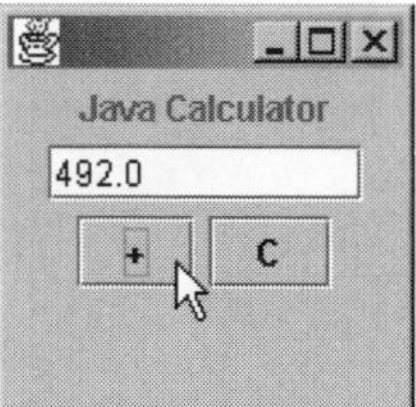

Figure 3.18 Calculator result.

You can try using the clear button, it should clear the textfield. There are a number of improvements that can be made to the Calculator. It would be very easy to put in other calculator functions like subtract, multiply, and divide. It would be easy to add a memory and memory clear function too. The design of this application embedded the business logic in the JFrame. You could place the Calculator math methods in a separate class. This class would provide separation between the Calculator view and the Calculator model or business logic.

There were a number of changes to the generated code so that it would work properly. If you review the completed code, the source for the `Calculator` class looks as follows:

```
package j2eebook.calc;
import java.awt.GraphicsConfiguration;
import java.awt.event.ActionEvent;
import java.awt.event.ActionListener;
import javax.swing.JFrame;
/**
* This class is a Swing GUI frame that has a simple calculator.
 */
public class Calculator extends JFrame implements ActionListener {
    private javax.swing.JPanel jContentPane = null;
    private javax.swing.JLabel jLabel = null;
    private javax.swing.JButton jButton = null;
    private javax.swing.JButton jButton1 = null;
    private javax.swing.JTextField jTextField = null;
    private float value = 0;
    /**
     * Constructor for Calculator.
     */
    public Calculator() {
        super();
        initialize();
    }
    /**
     * Constructor for Calculator.
     * @param gc
     */
    public Calculator(GraphicsConfiguration gc) {
        super(gc);
```

```
}
/**
 * Constructor for Calculator.
 * @param title
 */
public Calculator(String title) {
    super(title);
}
/**
 * Constructor for Calculator.
 * @param title
 * @param gc
 */
public Calculator(String title, GraphicsConfiguration gc) {
    super(title, gc);
}
/**
 * @see java.awt.event.ActionListener#actionPerformed(ActionEvent)
 */
public void actionPerformed(ActionEvent e) {
    if (e.getSource().equals(getJButton())) {
        add();
    } else
        if (e.getSource().equals(getJButton1())) {
            clear();
    }
}
public static void main(String[] args) {
    Calculator calc = new Calculator();
        calc.addWindowListener(new java.awt.event.WindowAdapter() {
        public void windowClosing(java.awt.event.WindowEvent e) {
            System.exit(0);
            };
        });
    calc.show();
}
/**
 * This method initializes this
 * @return void
 */
private void initialize() {
    setDefaultCloseOperation(this.DISPOSE_ON_CLOSE);
    this.setContentPane(getJContentPane());
    this.setSize(146, 140);
    getJButton().addActionListener(this);
    getJButton1().addActionListener(this);
}
/**
* This method initializes jContentPane
* @return javax.swing.JPanel
```

```
    */
    private javax.swing.JPanel getJContentPane() {
        if (jContentPane == null) {
            jContentPane = new javax.swing.JPanel();
                java.awt.FlowLayout layFlowLayout_2 = new
java.awt.FlowLayout();
                jContentPane.setLayout(layFlowLayout_2);
                jContentPane.add(getJLabel(), getJLabel().getName());
                jContentPane.add(
                    getJTextField(),
                    getJTextField().getName());
                jContentPane.add(getJButton(), getJButton().getName());
                jContentPane.add(
                    getJButton1(),
                    getJButton1().getName());
        }
        return jContentPane;
    }
    /**
    * This method initializes jLabel
    * @return javax.swing.JLabel
    */
    private javax.swing.JLabel getJLabel() {
        if (jLabel == null) {
            jLabel = new javax.swing.JLabel();
                jLabel.setText("Java Calculator");
        }
        return jLabel;
    }
    /**
    * This method initializes jButton
    * @return javax.swing.JButton
    */
    private javax.swing.JButton getJButton() {
        if (jButton == null) {
            jButton = new javax.swing.JButton(); jButton.setText("+"); }
        return jButton;
       }
    /**
     * This method initializes jButton1
     * @return javax.swing.JButton
     */
    private javax.swing.JButton getJButton1() {
        if (jButton1 == null) {
            jButton1 = new javax.swing.JButton();
            jButton1.setText("C");
        }
        return jButton1;
    }
    /**
```

```
         * This method initializes jTextField
         * @return javax.swing.JTextField
         */
        private javax.swing.JTextField getJTextField() {
            if (jTextField == null) {
                jTextField = new javax.swing.JTextField();
                    jTextField.setColumns(10);
                    jTextField.setCaretPosition(0);
            }
            return jTextField;
        }
        /**
         * This method adds the value from the textfield.
         */
        public void add() {
            value += Float.parseFloat(getJTextField().getText());
            getJTextField().setText(Float.toString(value));
            getJTextField().repaint();
        }
        /**
         * This method clears the textfield.
         */
        public void clear() {
            value = 0;
            getJTextField().setText(Float.toString(value));
            getJTextField().repaint();
        }
    }  //  @jve:visual-info  decl-index=0 visual-constraint="0,0"
```

Summary

In this chapter, you learned the basics of Java application development in WSAD. You developed a simple Java GUI application and tested it in WSAD. You did the following:

- Created a Java application including a project and package
- Used the Visual Editor to create a Swing GUI
- Modified the generated Java code so the application would run
- Added code to handle the button click events
- Added methods to support the Calculator math functions
- Set the launch configuration
- Tested an application in WSAD

This chapter covered the basic Java development functions in WSAD. There are a lot of improvements that you can make to the Calculator GUI and the business logic. You can use the Visual Editor to experiment with some of these changes.

Debugging in WebSphere Studio Application Developer

What's in Chapter 4?

We shall survey debugging tools and techniques in this chapter that are useful in discovering logic, flow, and other problems in Java programs. Well-designed applications, written by ace programmers, still may exhibit problems during initial testing. In this chapter, we survey the debugging aids available in WSAD. You will learn to do the following:

- Use display statements to trace a problem
- Use WSAD to display locations and results to the console
- Launch a Java application in debug mode
- Set breakpoints using the WSAD debugger
- Inspect and modify live values
- Modify executable code during debugging
- Use the WSAD scrapbook
- Debug remotely
- Set breakpoints on exceptions
- Debug three actual errors using WSAD debug feature

You will import a small Java calculator application designed in a model-view-controller paradigm that uses a mediator design pattern to isolate the view from the core logic. Some parts of the calculator mediator malfunction. WSAD will help us to find and repair two malfunctions in the application mediator logic. The WSAD debugger will assist us in debugging a remote instance of an application to minimize interference with GUI events or to debug on a platform or environment not directly supported by WSAD. Finally, you will use a remote debugging session to identify a third calculator problem.

Introduction to Debugging

Even well-designed applications written by ace programmers, may exhibit problems during initial testing. The ancient standby debugging technique is to display intermediate results on the console. This approach, low-tech though accessible, requires modification of the program unless a fine-grained administrable tracing facility is designed into it. The WSAD Java IDE provides debugging capabilities that don't require modification of the application. The debugger runs in a separate virtual machine (VM) from that of the application, to avoid conflicting interactions. WSAD even enables the debugging target VM to be on another networked computer.

Use System.out.println()

Those with a C or C++ background may have used the `printf()` function to display variable content and to print messages as a program executes. Other languages have similar display capabilities. Programmers may use these to display the execution status of variables or execution location to a console or trace file.

In Java, you may take the same approach with the `System.out.println()` method. You could insert `System.out.println()` messages anywhere in code to send messages to ourselves or to examine variable and state information. The `print()` and `println()` methods are defined in the `java.io.PrintStream` class. These are versatile because they are extensively overloaded, as seen in Table 4.1.

Write a Trace Utility

If you pass a `java.lang.Object` to `println()`, the object's `toString()` method is automatically called to obtain that object's particular string representation. All objects have the `toString()` method defined. The default implementation is defined at the top of the Java class hierarchy in the `Object` class. This default `toString()` method returns a string of the form `className@hashcode`. It is a good programming practice to override the default `toString()` method to supply a custom string representation of objects of classes that are developed.

Simply displaying locations and results is a straightforward technique to obtain information from a program during execution. One downside is that you must have modifiable source code available. Another negative is that you may obscure normal program operation if you are not careful. This uncertainty can be a problem in using other debugging techniques, as well.

Table 4.1 Parameter Types for println()

TYPE
boolean
char
char[]
double
float
int
long
java.lang.String
java.lang.Object

Designing a granular trace capability into an application could mitigate this problem. For example, define four trace levels. Level zero would mean nothing is traced. Thus, level 3 would mean everything is traced. The other levels provide intermediate granularity. A static trace method would require a level parameter and a message string parameter. A global static variable would hold the current trace level set by administrative action. A sample trace utility class follows:

```
package com.rogers60.trace;
/**
 * Implements a granular trace capability.
 * It is not thread-safe. Callers may synchronize
 * on an object to make it thread-safe.
*/
public class Trace {
    public static final int L0 = 0; // Trace nothing
    public static final int L1 = 1;
    public static final int L2 = 2;
    public static final int L3 = 3; // Trace all
    private static int level = L0; // Default: trace nothing
    private static java.io.PrintStream out = System.out;
    /**
     * Sets the current trace level. Does
     * nothing if not given a valid level.
     * @param aLevel int, valid values: L0 <= aLevel <== L3
     */
    public static void setLevel(int aLevel) {
        if (aLevel <= L3 && aLevel >= L0) {
            level = aLevel;
        }
    }
    /**
     * Writes the given string to the trace stream only if
```

```
     * the given level if less than or equal to the current
     * trace level.
     * @param aLevel int
     * @param aMsg java.lang.String
     */
    public static void trace(int aLevel, String aMsg) {
        if (aLevel <= level) {
            StringBuffer buf = new StringBuffer(100);
            buf.append("Trace ").append(level)
                    .append(": ").append(aMsg);
            out.println(buf);
        }
    }
}
```

You would set the desired trace level by calling `Trace.setLevel(Trace.Lx)`. Permanently place `Trace.trace(aLevel, aMsg)` calls at interesting points of the application. The current level is a measure of desired verbosity. You would assign lower levels to trace points that you decide are more important. Higher trace levels would be used at points that provide additional information that could ordinarily cloud the readability of the trace with too much information. Following is a test script that shows how to set the trace level and insert trace calls:

```
package com.rogers60.trace.script;
import com.rogers60.trace.Trace;
/**
 * Exercises class com.rogers60.trace.Trace.
*/
public class ExerciseTrace {
    /**
     * Test script for the Trace facility.
     * @param args java.langString[], contents ignored
     */
    public static void main(String[] args) {
        Trace.setLevel(Trace.L0);
        Trace.trace(Trace.L2, "This shouldn't trace");
        Trace.setLevel(Trace.L2);
        Trace.trace(Trace.L2, "This should trace");
        Trace.trace(Trace.L3, "This shouldn't trace");
        Trace.trace(Trace.L1, "This is my Object: " +
                              new Object().toString());
    }
}
```

The output of this test program follows:

```
Trace 2: This should trace

Trace 2: This is my Object: java.lang.Object@746f9fa0
```

The WSAD Debugger

You have seen how to add to code to aid in debugging. How would you debug code if you could not modify it? WSAD includes a debugger that enables you to detect and diagnose errors in a Java program that is running either locally or on another computer. You may monitor and control the execution of a multithreaded application by setting breakpoints, where you can step into, through, or over Java methods. You may examine the contents of variables while stopped at a breakpoint or you may suspend threads and suspend the launching of subsystems.

Debug Preparation

The debug target need not be modified, but it is helpful to use a coding style that does not place multiple statements on one line. Some of the debugger features, such as breakpoints, operate on a line-by-line basis. In addition, it is helpful to attach source code for supporting JAR files when it is available. Then, you could step through that code, or place breakpoints in it, instead of being constrained to skip over it in the debugger.

Import Sample Projects

Let's use a real program that has actual problems for test purposes. Import the **buggy-calculator-app** and **buggy-calculator-lib** projects found on the Web site for this book. You shall reference code in these projects as you survey debugging in WSAD. The calculator is a Java Swing application shown in Figure 4.1.

You will find and repair three problems in the calculator. Its overall model-view-controller structure is diagramed in Figure 4.2. Class `Calculator` is the view. The controller is the `actionPerformed()` method, which routes events to application logic written in the mediator design pattern.

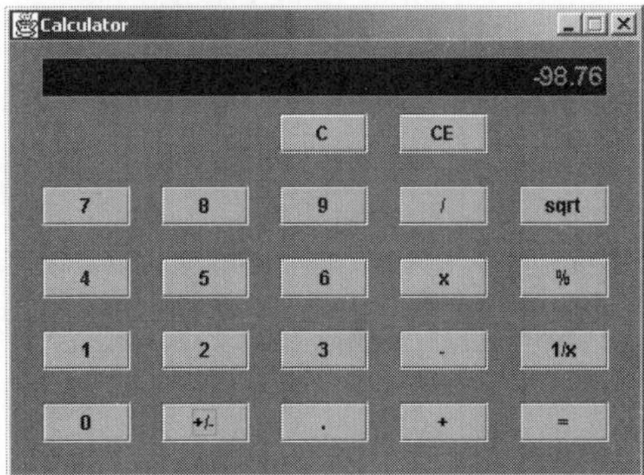

Figure 4.1 Calculator application.

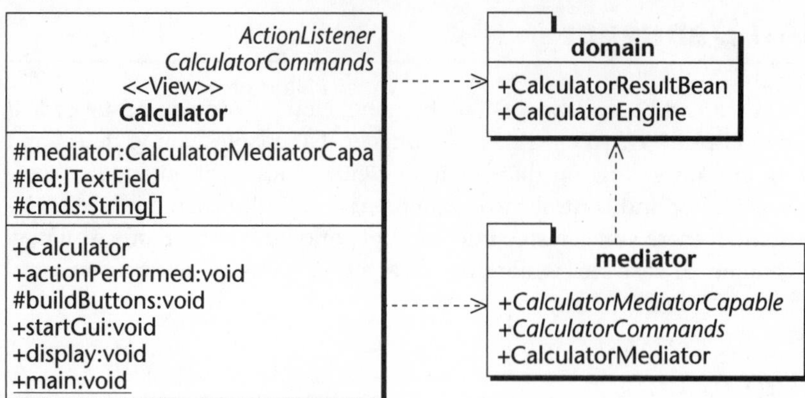

Figure 4.2 Calculator view layer.

The mediator contains the state of the application and dictates its flow. It is diagrammed in Figure 4.3. The mediator is not dependent upon any particular view technology. It is capable of interacting with a Swing class as well as a command-line view, a JavaServer Page, a Java servlet, or a Java applet.

The mediator uses model or domain logic housed in the `CalculatorEngine` class. See Figure 4.4. Methods of this class return a result in a JavaBean suitable for rendering by any kind of Java view technology.

The calculator diagrams should show a high-level concept of the logic. You shall investigate three problems in the mediator in the following sections.

Breakpoints

What exactly is breakpoint? It is a temporary marker that you may logically insert into an application to signal to the debugger to stop thread execution at that point. The insertion does not physically modify the application. The debugging engine works in concert with the VM to implement a breakpoint. An executing thread is suspended as it attempts to pass through an enabled breakpoint. At this point, you may view the stack of nested method calls to reach that point in the thread. Additionally, you may inspect the contents of variables at any level in the stack. You can step over statements, step into or over subsequent methods, resume running until the next breakpoint is reached, or resume running until the logical end of program execution.

An enabled breakpoint displays as a small *blue* circle in the editor marker bar or the Breakpoints view. A blue breakpoint icon means that the breakpoint is unverified. This means that its target class has not successfully been loaded into a Java VM. When it is successfully installed in a class in a VM at run time, it becomes a green circle. You may temporarily disable a breakpoint such that it will not suspend a thread attempting to pass through it. A disabled breakpoint icon is rendered as a *white* circle in the editor marker bar or the Breakpoints view.

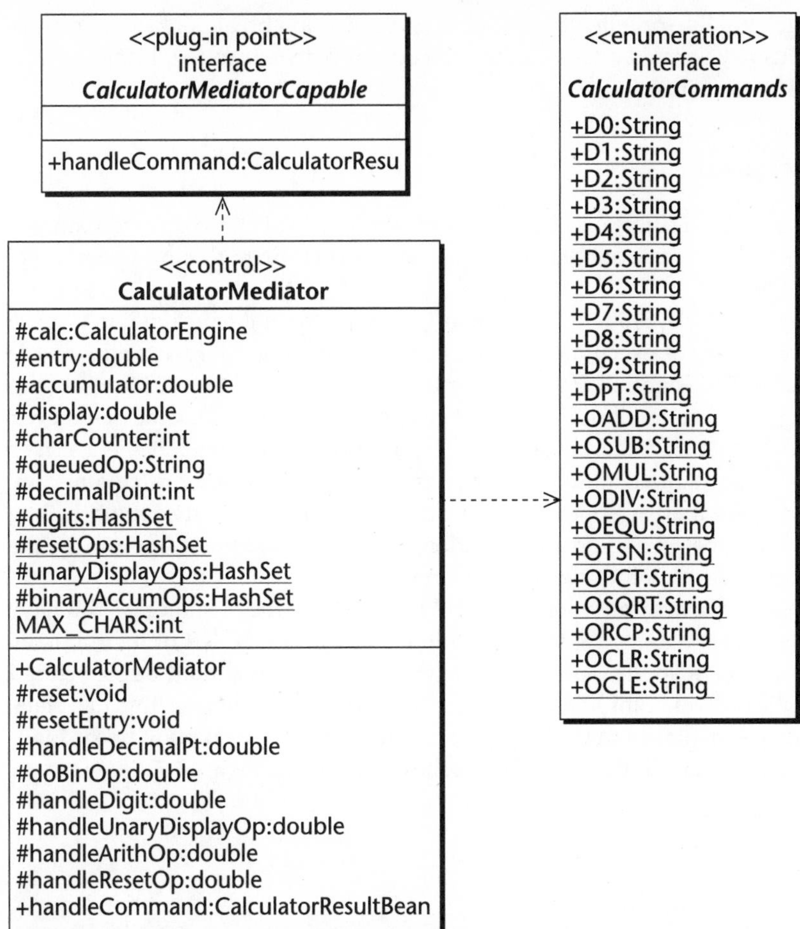

Figure 4.3 Calculator controller/mediator.

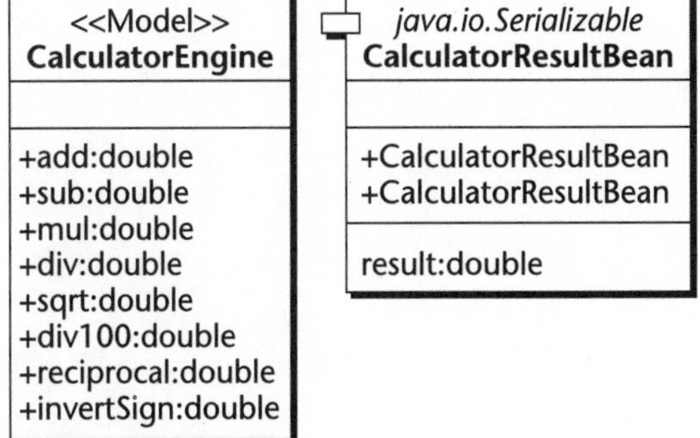

Figure 4.4 Calculator model/domain.

There are general line-oriented breakpoints and exception breakpoints. You can set line breakpoints to be armed after a certain hit count is reached. You will learn how to manage these breakpoints.

Add a Breakpoint

A breakpoint is set on a single executable line of an object. This line-oriented nature is the reason it is better to have one statement per line, aside from this being a good practice for readability.

Add a breakpoint by opening the file where you want to set the breakpoint. Choose the line where you want execution to stop. The vertical bar to the left of the text is called the marker bar. Right-click the marker bar at the desired line, and then choose Add Breakpoint, as seen in Figure 4.5, or you may simply double-click the marker bar at the desired line to add the breakpoint. Try setting a breakpoint in the `main()` method of `bellmeade.calculator.Calculator` in project **buggy-calculator-app**.

A new breakpoint marker appears on the marker bar, directly to the left of the line where you added the breakpoint. In addition, the new breakpoint appears in the Debug Perspective Breakpoints view, as seen in Figure 4.6.

Run the class as a Java application. Why did it not stop at the breakpoint? You have to run it in a separate debugging VM. Use the debug icon to the left of the run icon. Select Debug as a Java application. This time thread execution should be suspended before the enabled breakpoint line of code is executed. The suspended thread's stack frame contents are displayed in the Debug view pane, and the breakpoint line is highlighted in the editor pane in the Debug Perspective, as seen in Figure 4.7.

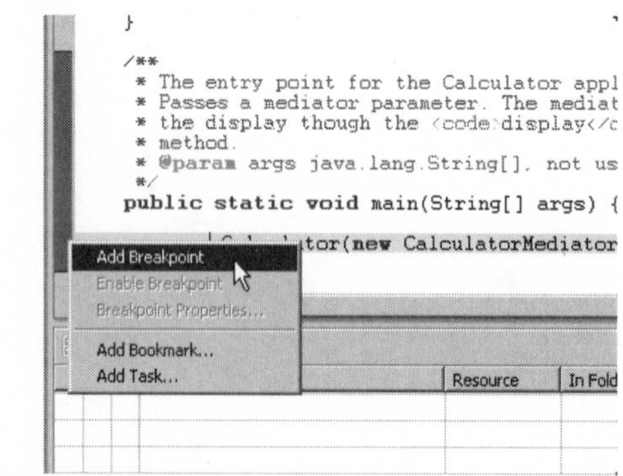

Figure 4.5 Marker bar context menu.

```
Calculator.java
/**
 * The entry point for the Calculator applica
 * Passes a mediator parameter. The mediator :
 * the display though the <code>display</code
 * method.
 * @param args java.lang.String[], not used c
 */
public static void main(String[] args) {
    new Calculator(new CalculatorMediator())
}
```

Figure 4.6 Debug Perspective Breakpoints view.

Whenever you run the code in debug mode and a breakpoint is encountered, the Debug Perspective appears. The behavior may be changed to remain in the Java Perspective, but the editor is positioned to the breakpoint in either perspective. See the stack trace in the Debug view. If the halt was several frames deep, you could select an earlier frame to display its variables and source code.

Select the Variables tab in the Breakpoints pane. The currently scoped variables are shown—in this case only the args variable. The lower-right pane is the Outline view. It shows the variable and method outline of the selected class. Notice the toolbar in the Debug view. Some of its icons are used to step into, stop over, and return from the current location. Hover the pointer over each icon to read its Help.

Press the right-arrow icon to resume the application, and the calculator GUI appears. Close it. The Debug view shows the terminated process. Use the pop-up menu to remove it.

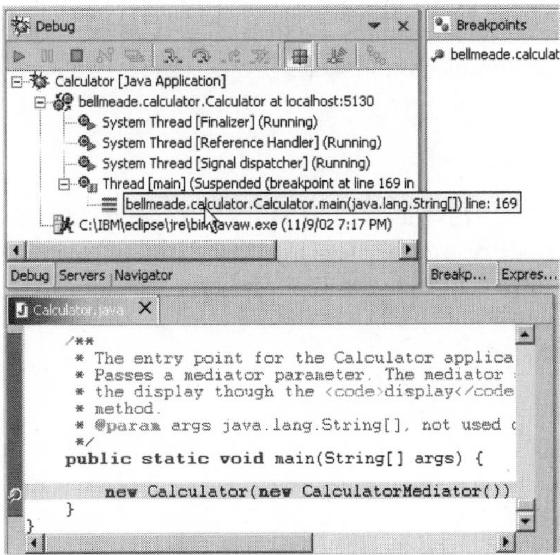

Figure 4.7 Breakpoint halt.

Delete a Breakpoint

You may remove a breakpoint from either the marker bar or the Breakpoints view. Select Remove from the context menu of the marker bar, as seen in Figure 4.8, or select Remove Breakpoint from the context menu of the breakpoint in the Breakpoints view. The breakpoint will disappear from the marker bar and from the Breakpoints view.

You may delete all breakpoints by clicking the Remove All Breakpoints button in the Breakpoints view, or you may select Remove All from the view's context menu. Please know that this command removes all breakpoints in the *entire* WSAD workbench, not just from the active program.

The Go to File menu item in the context menu will cause the editor to display the file that has the breakpoint. The editor will position itself on the breakpoint line.

The Show Qualified Names option menu item is used to toggle the display of fully qualified package names in the breakpoint list for all breakpoints.

Enable and Disable Breakpoints

A breakpoint is enabled when you set it, but you may disable it from having any effect. Why would you do that? You may want to allow execution to pass through the breakpoint until the application reaches a certain state of interest. Then, you could enable the breakpoint to trap the execution the next time it passes through that point.

To disable a breakpoint, use the Breakpoints view to display all breakpoints. Right-click the desired breakpoint to see its context menu. Select the Disable item. Any disabled breakpoint displayed on the marker bar of the editor or the Breakpoints view changes from a blue or green icon to a white icon, indicating that it is not active. Enable a disabled breakpoint by using the same context menu in the Breakpoints view. A disabled breakpoint's context menu shows an Enable item instead of a Disable menu item.

Hit Counts

You may apply a hit count to any breakpoint. This means that a given thread must pass through the breakpoint a specified number of times before the thread is suspended. When you resume the thread, the breakpoint is disabled until you change the hit count, enable the breakpoint, or stop and restart the application in debug mode.

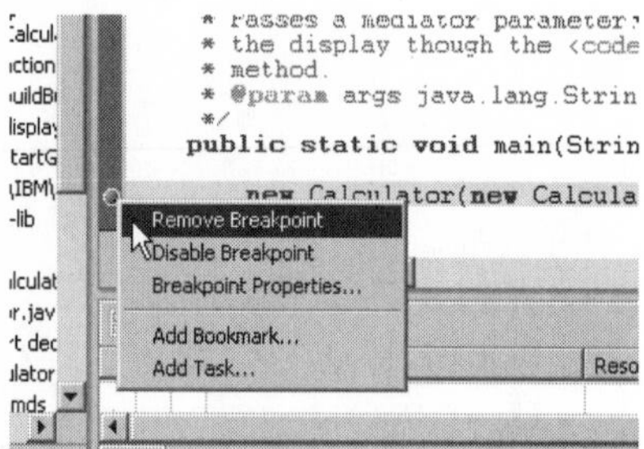

Figure 4.8 Remove a breakpoint with the marker bar.

First, set a breakpoint using either of the approaches described previously. Set it in the body of the `add()` method of `bellmeade.calculator.domain.CalculatorEngine` in project buggy-calculator-lib. Then use the Breakpoints view of the breakpoint to apply a hit count to it. Carry this out by right-clicking the desired breakpoint to obtain its context menu. Select the Hit Count item from the pop-up menu. WSAD displays a dialog for you to enter a hit count in, as seen in Figure 4.9. Enter a count of two. Check the Enable Hit Count option, and then press the OK button.

This breakpoint suspends the thread after it tries to execute through the breakpoint the second time when the thread is running in a local or remote debugging VM. Run the calculator in the debugging VM. Use the calculator to add 2 + 2. Now try to add 3. The calculator thread will be suspended. At this point, the breakpoint icon turns white. Its context menu in the Breakpoints view shows an Enable menu item because the breakpoint is disabled. You may reenable it from the context menu or, the breakpoint will be enabled with the given hit count applied if the target application exits and is restarted in debug mode.

Exception Breakpoints

You can suspend execution of a thread when a given exception is thrown. You can do this at locations where the exception is caught, not caught, or both. Thus, the action is that of a breakpoint that is based upon a thrown exception instead of a location. Let us use an actual coding bug to learn about exception breakpoints in the following section.

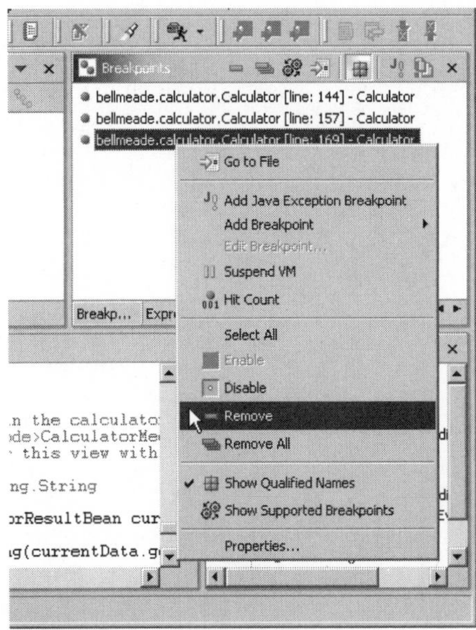

Figure 4.9 Set hit count.

Calculator Bug One: Divide

By now the Breakpoints view should be familiar. Right-click the Breakpoints view, and then use the context menu to remove all breakpoints from WSAD. Execute `bellmeade.calculator.Calculator` from project buggy-calculator-app again. Try a division operation. Does it give correct results? Notice that an exception is thrown in the Console view messages. This is a clue, but what if the developer hadn't displayed the exception. The WSAD debugger can suspend a thread when it encounters an exception. Now, you will cause a breakpoint to suspend a thread when it suffers a particular exception. Break on an exception being thrown by pressing the Add Java Exception Breakpoint icon on the Breakpoints view toolbar, as seen in Figure 4.10.

This presents a dialog that lists available exceptions in the build path. It is a live search list, so you need only type the first few characters of an exception to narrow the list contents. Select the UnsupportedOperation exception, because you know that particular kind of exception was thrown. If you don't know which exception is thrown, you can begin by selecting an ancestor such as `java.lang.Exception`, but this could trap other problems or even "normal" exceptions. Specify whether the exception must by caught, uncaught, or both, as seen in Figure 4.11.

This kind of breakpoint appears differently in the Breakpoints view as seen in Figure 4.12. Notice that its entry states the kind of exception that will cause a break, and the catch conditions under which a thread will suspend.

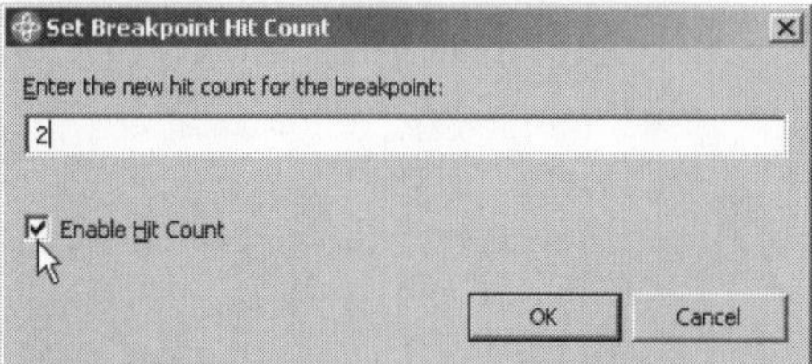

Figure 4.10 Java exception breakpoint.

Figure 4.11 Exception breakpoint dialog.

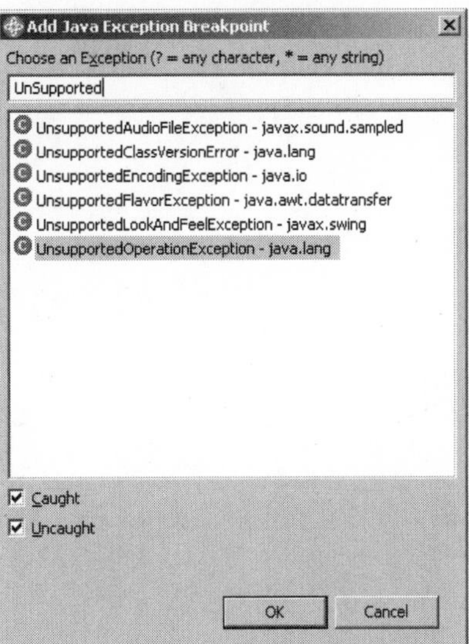

Figure 4.12 Exception breakpoint.

Figure 4.13 shows the context menu of an exception breakpoint. Notice that the catch conditions may be modified after setting the breakpoint. Further notice that the breakpoint may be disabled and reenabled.

If the given exception is thrown during a debug session, the current thread will be suspended with the offending line of code displayed in the editor. Run bellmeade.calculator.Calculator from project buggy-calculator-app in the debugger. Try a division operation again. The thread is suspended in method `CalulatorMediator.doBinOp()`. The Edit view displays the method positioned at the statement that threw the exception. The code follows.

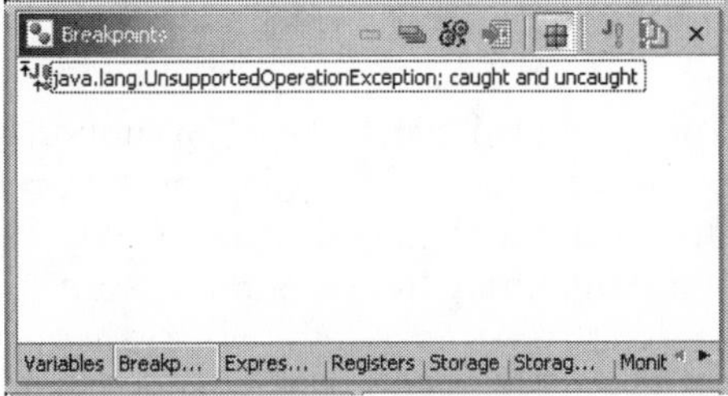

Figure 4.13 Exception breakpoint context menu.

```
/**
 * Returns arg1 aBinOp arg2
 * @param arg1 double
 * @param arg2 double
 * @param aBinOp java.lang.String
 * @return double
 * @throws java.lang.UnsupportedOperationException
 */
protected double doBinOp(
    String aBinOp, double arg1, double arg2) {
    double result;
    if (aBinOp.equals(CalculatorCommands.OADD))
        result = calc.add(arg1, arg2);
    else
        if (aBinOp.equals(CalculatorCommands.OSUB))
            result = calc.sub(arg1, arg2);
        else
            if (aBinOp.equals(CalculatorCommands.OMUL))
                result = calc.mul(arg1, arg2);
            else
                throw (new java.lang.UnsupportedOperationException(
                       "Invalid arithmetic command"));
    return result;
}
```

The problem seems obvious now that you see it. Somebody forgot to code a clause to conditionally call `calc.div()` when the `aBinOp` parameter value is ODIV. If the debug session were resumed, the normal processing of the exception would proceed. Before resuming, insert the following into the source code just prior to the throw clause while the thread is suspended.

```
if (aBinOp.equals(CalculatorCommands.ODIV))
    result = calc.div(arg1, arg2);
else
```

Key Ctrl+S to incrementally compile the change provided that the host VM supports hot code replace. Press the resume arrow now. The exception will display in the Console view because the thread resumed on the throw clause. Try another division operation on the calculator. It works! You repaired the bug during live execution.

TIP If you receive an error message saying that the target VM does not support hot code replace, you need to redeploy the modified class to the debug host VM and then restart the debugging session.

If any thread in the virtual machine had thrown an UnsupportedOperation exception, that thread would have been suspended. You needed only to suspect that the exception was going to be thrown from anywhere, set the appropriate exception breakpoint, and then run the offending application. This kind of breakpoint is a powerful tool for finding the source of an exception when catch processing doesn't reveal enough information to locate the source.

This concludes calculator bug one. There are two more examples that follow.

Thread Suspension and Resumption

Any thread executing in debug mode may be suspended and subsequently resumed. Use the Debug view to select a running thread. Click the Suspend item in its right-click pop-up menu, as seen in Figure 4.14.

There are icons for Suspend and Resume. When a running thread is suspended, its call stack at the point of suspension is displayed beneath its thread name in the thread tree view. WSAD prompts for a source code location if it is not known. If the source code is found, the editor will display the point of suspension in source code form, as if a breakpoint were reached. After all, a breakpoint is merely another means to suspend a thread.You may terminate any thread from its context menu.

Execution Stepping

You have seen several ways to suspend a thread such that the current execution stack displays a frame for each nested method call used to reach the point of suspension. If source code is available to the debug client for a selected stack frame, the editor will show the source at the point of suspension. How can you discover where execution will proceed? You could scatter some breakpoints in likely locations and press the Resume icon in the Debug view toolbar, or you could step the execution forward.

There are four ways to step execution. The first is to run until a selected source code line is reached. This is an alternate way to suspend execution at a line without setting a breakpoint. Simply place the cursor on the target line, then select Run to Line from the pop-up menu. The thread resumes execution, and if the line is reached, the thread is suspended.

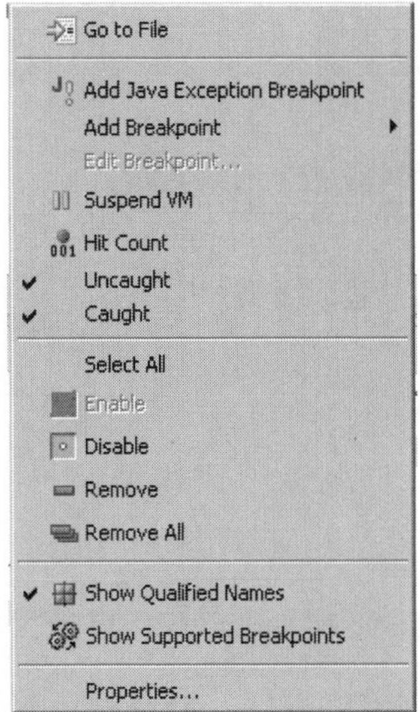

Figure 4.14 Suspend a thread.

The remaining three stepping variations are:

- **Step over.** The thread executes the current line, then is suspended on the next executable line.
- **Step into.** The thread evaluates the next expression on the current line, then is suspended on the first executable line of a method of that expression.
- **Run to return.** The thread evaluates expressions until the next return statement in the current method, and then is suspended on the next executable line of the caller.

In each case you would select, or leave selected, a stack frame in the Debug view. The current line is highlighted in the editor. Then, you would either press the icon that corresponds to the desired action or press a function key for the action, as seen in Table 4.2.

Inspecting Values

The top stack frame of a suspended thread is automatically selected. If you select a stack frame, the variables of the current scope of that stack frame are displayed in the Variables Tree view. You may examine the children of a compound variable by expanding its node. Figure 4.15 shows an alternate means to display a variable by hovering the cursor over it in the editor. This is called value hovering.

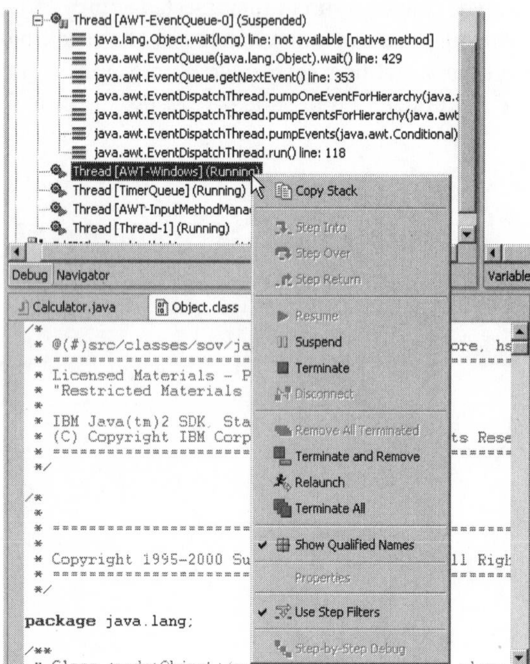

Figure 4.15 Value hovering.

Table 4.2 Execution Stepping Options

STEP VARIANT	TOOLBAR	KEYBOARD
Step Over		F6
Step Into		F5
Run to Return		F7

Evaluating Expressions

The debugger allows you to evaluate an expression that you enter in the context of a stack frame of a suspended thread. During thread suspension, use the following steps:

1. Select the desired stack frame.
2. Enter the desired expression into the Display view or into the editor when it shows modifiable source code.
3. Select (swipe-mark) the expression, then right-click to display its context menu.
4. Choose Display or Inspect.
5. Look for the result in the Display view if you chose Display, or in the Inspector if you picked Inspect.

An example using the Display option with the `CalculatorMediator.doBinOp()` method is seen in Figure 4.16. Try it by placing a breakpoint on the first executable statement of the method and then following the steps listed previously.

Had you chosen the Inspect option, the Inspector view would have displayed an expandable tree view of the result, much as you saw in the Variables view.

TIP Expression evaluation is not supported in class files or inner types.

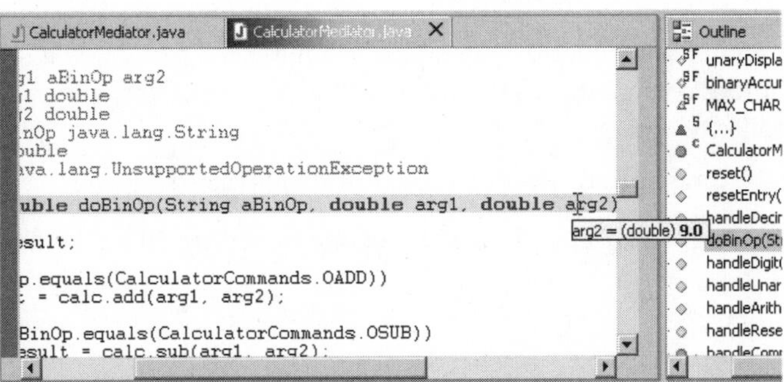

Figure 4.16 Evaluate and display an expression.

Calculator Bug Two: 1/x

The calculator reciprocal 1/x key intermittently returns a result of infinity when you run the version in project buggy-calculator-app. After trying various scenarios, you determine that when you enter a number **2**, for example, and then press the reciprocal key, you receive a good result. However, if you enter an expression such as **1 + 1 =**, and then hit the reciprocal key, the display erroneously shows Infinity.

Each button on the calculator creates an event that is passed to `CalculatorMediator.handleCommand()` in the package `bellmeade.calculator.mediator`. Follow these steps to repair the problem from the debugger:

1. Start the calculator in the WSAD debugger.
2. Open the mediator in the WSAD Java Perspective. Find `CalculatorMediator.handleCommand()`. Place a breakpoint on the first statement in the method body.
3. Disable that breakpoint by using the context menu of the Breakpoints view.
4. Enter **1 + 1 =** in the calculator application.
5. Enable the breakpoint from the WSAD Breakpoints view.
6. Press the reciprocal key on the calculator. The thread suspends. The Debug Perspective shows the breakpoint in the editor. Notice that you may double-click stack frames to see the calling code.
7. Use the Step Over button in the Debug view to step over each if statement until one of them fires, setting current location in its body. This should be the statement that calls the `reciprocal()` method.
8. Use the Step Into button to proceed into the method. The `reciprocal()` method seems basic, but its argument is zero, causing the divide-by-zero = infinity problem. Use Step Over to return.
9. Press the Variables tab. Notice that the code passed an entry argument value of zero to the `reciprocal()` method. The user's concept of action of the 1/x key is to invert the value in the display. The display numeric value is not being passed to the `reciprocal()` method. Let us permanently repair this problem from the debugger.
10. Press `Resume`, then repeat the scenario. When you reach the call to `reciprocal()` method, change the argument to be the `display` variable. Press Ctrl+S to compile the repair.
11. Press the debugger Resume button. The correct result displays: 0.5.

This concludes calculator bug two. You will investigate one more bug when we discuss remote debugging.

The Scrapbook

WSAD has a scrapbook feature that you may use to experiment with Java code snippets. This is useful for understanding how an API, such as an XSL transform, operates before you commit to spreading it throughout an application. A scrapbook page editor is used to enter and evaluate code snippets. You may examine the result as a display string, or show it in the debugger's Inspector view. You can create multiple scrapbook pages. Each runs in its own VM.

- Select project buggy-calculator-app in the Package Explorer. Create a scrapbook page using one of the following alternatives from the workbench window:
- Select the Open the New Wizard button on the upper-left corner of the toolbar. Choose Java from the Tree view left-hand pane, and Scrapbook Page in the right-hand pane, or . . .
- Select File > New Java Scrapbook Page from the main menu, or . . .
- Push the Create a Scrapbook Page button in the workbench toolbar. This button sits just to the right of the Create a Java Interface button.

The Create Java Scrapbook Page wizard appears, as seen in Figure 4.17. Enter or browse to a folder that will contain the new scrapbook page. The file extension `.jpage` will be appended if you do not enter it. When you click the Finish button, the new page will open in a folder.

At this point, you may enter code as you would in a method body. Code assist is available as usual. Evaluate the code by first marking it as you did for evaluating an expression previously, and then display or inspect the results. The scrapbook page persists in the file system as if it were a class.

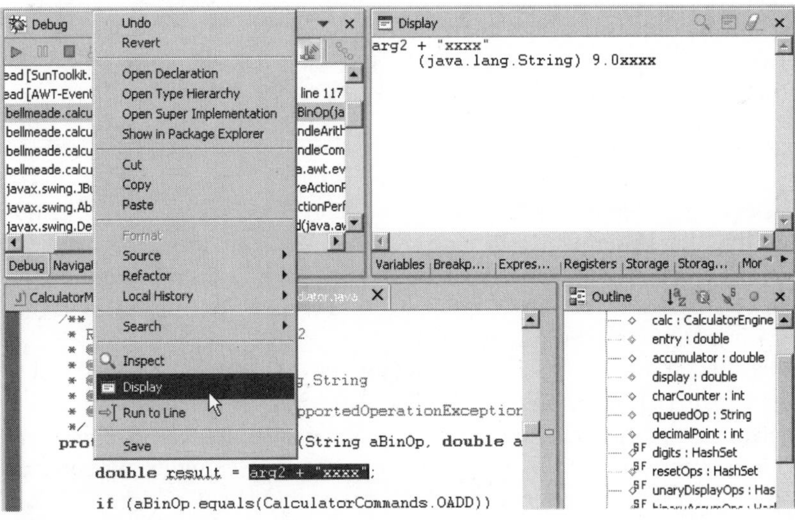

Figure 4.17 Create a scrapbook page.

Remote Debugging

The debugger leverages Java's client-server debugging interface such that the application being debugged may optionally execute in a VM on a separately networked computer. Indeed, even when the target executes with WSAD, it is run in a separate VM for debugging. An IP port is used to communicate with the remote debugging engine. Shared memory is used for local debugging. WSAD attaches to a remote target machine and port through a simple dialog. Thus, WSAD runs the debugger, while the remote machine runs the application and the debugging engine. The only requirement is that the application has access on the remote machine to the files and classes that it needs.

Why use remote debugging? The program that you need to debug may not be able to run on the WSAD machine. Perhaps it is tied to AIX, while WSAD may reside on a Linux or Microsoft Windows system. Moreover, if the program has a GUI, it is easier to debug on a separate machine because user interactions with the debugger do not interfere with user interactions with the target applications. For example, the debugger could obscure the target application window, causing extra repaints that would not happen if the debugger and application were on separate machines.

WSAD as a Debug Client and Server

WSAD uses remote debugging even when you carry out local debugging. Let us explain. You would set breakpoints and debug using WSAD as a debug client. This local debugging task is actually a trivial case of remote debugging, where the debugging server VM and a separate debug client VM actually execute in one WSAD process. The client VM connects to the server VM by using a socket. The client uses this socket for requests of the server during local debugging as well as remote debugging. Let us discuss this more, so that you understand true machine-to-machine remote debugging.

You may see the port address where the WSAD debug server listens. After starting buggy-calculator-app in a local debug session, look at the Debug View. Select the Debug tab. Notice the gears icon node with text resembling the following:

```
bellmeade.calculator.Calculator at localhost:5073.
```

The debug server is listening at IP address and port `locathost:5073` in this instance. Invoke the context menu on this node to inspect its properties. There, you can see the complete command line used to start the debug VM, as seen in Figure 4.18. Notice the `address=localhost:5073` option to `javaw.exe`. This number will generally change each time you start the debug VM.

Could you use this information to connect a remote WSAD process' debug client to this WSAD debug server? The current answer is no. The server only creates one socket instance. The client immediately connects to it, making it unavailable for another client connection. To use a sports metaphor, think of the process as catching its own on-side kick in U.S. football. The kicking team acts as both server and client, making the only ball unavailable to the other team.

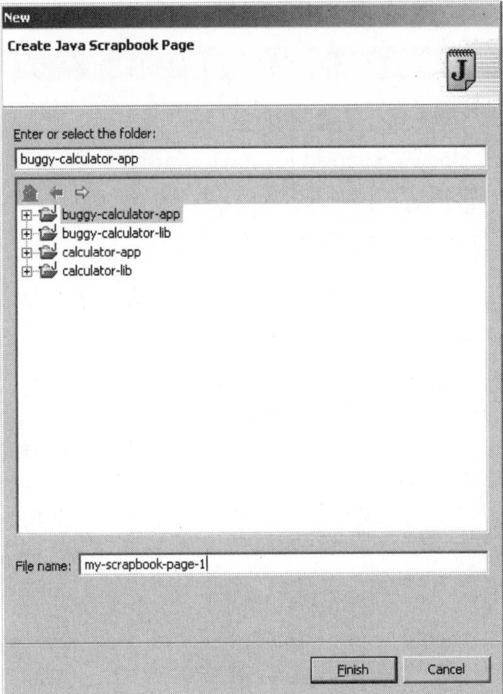

Figure 4.18 Debug process information.

An Arbitrary VM as a Debug Server

If one WSAD process cannot debug another WSAD process' debug target, how is remote debugging carried out? The answer is that the remote application must be started in debugging mode under an independent Java VM. Perhaps the application is hosted on Unix, but the WSAD debug client is on a Windows or Linux system. Remember, when a VM is running in debugging mode, another VM may attach to it to debug its executing application. The WSAD Help Perspective is maddeningly silent about the options that must be supplied to the remote VM, presumably because the options are dependent upon the VM implementation and version. Practically speaking, you find that a common set of options works, as seen in Table 4.3. The port seen in the address suboption may be any unused port that you choose. You must know that number when you attach to the debug VM from WSAD. The `-Xrunjdwp` option, with its suboptions, loads the debugging engine and specifies its connection.

Table 4.3 Debug Mode VM Options

JAVA VM OPTION	COMMENT OR PARAMETER
-Xdebug	Enables debugging support in the VM
-Xnoagent	Disables VM support for sun.tools.debug
-Xrunjdwp: ‡	transport=dt_socket,server=y, address=8888,suspend=n
-Djava.compiler=NONE	Disables the JIT compiler on the classic VM
-classic	Not used for JDK 1.3.1 or later

An explanation of the `-Xrunjdwp` suboptions is seen in Table 4.4.

You may practice remote debugging by running a debug target application using the JRE supplied with WSAD. Start the VM by using a command line having parameters derived from Table 4.3 and Table 4.4. You may create a script for starting a remote debugging application using the JRE supplied with WSAD. A sample Windows script follows. The trailing '\' near the end indicates a single statement that was split for publication. Use `netstat -a` to ensure that the chosen port address is unused. Remember, any unused port address will work, but you need to remember it to pass it to the debug client. The debug target is `bellmeade.calculator.Calculator`. You can debug it remotely after creating a remote debug configuration for it in WSAD. The following is the example script for Windows:

Table 4.4 JDWP Parameters

PARAMETER	EXPLANATION
transport=dt_socket	Specifies that the debugger will use socket transport. It will listen for client connections on the port specified by `address` below.
server=y	Sets the VM to run as a debug server, allowing a debug client to connect to it.
8888	Specify any free port. Use `netstat` address=`-a` to find the ports in use on the debug target machine. This command works on Windows, Linux, and Unix systems.
suspend=n	Specifies that the server does not suspend when it starts. Suspension may be useful when debugging a servlet or EJB that initializes upon load. Specifying 'y' would yield time to set breakpoints before letting execution continue.

```
setlocal
set WSAD="C:\Program Files\IBM\Application Developer"
set PORT=9490
set JAVA_HOME=%WSAD%\JRE
set PATH=%JAVA_HOME%\bin
set CP=%WSAD%\workspace\calculator-app;
set CP=%CP%;%WSAD%\workspace\calculator-lib
set CLASS=bellmeade.calculator.Calculator
java -cp %CP% -Xdebug -Xnoagent \
  -Djava.compiler=NONE \
  -Xrunjdwp:transport=dt_socket,server=y, \
   address=%PORT%,suspend=n %CLASS%
endlocal
```

Let us create a WSAD debug configuration for WSAD to act as a debug client for the Calculator application. Use the following steps:

1. Choose main menu item Run > Debug. The Launch Configurations wizard appears.
2. Select Remote Java Application in the Launch Configurations pane. Press the New button.
3. Click the Connect tab. Name the configuration **remote-buggy-calculator-app**.
4. Use the Browse button to pick project buggy-calculator-app. The remote class files match those in this local project so the local client can properly debug the application
5. Set the Host to the IP address or DNS name of the remote host. Use localhost in this example.
6. Set the Port to the port that the remote VM is listening on. Use 9490 if you are using the start script you created previously. The wizard should resemble that shown in Figure 4.19.
7. The Source and Common tabs should be fine for this configuration. Inspect them to understand the information there, and then press the Apply button. This creates the configuration.
8. You may use this configuration to debug now or at any later time. Press Close to exit the wizard.
9. Invoke the main menu Run > Debug commands to start the WSAD debug client after the debug target server VM is started. The Launch Configurations dialog appears again. This time, select your new remote-buggy-calculator-app configuration and then press Debug.

TIP The Calculator GUI will appear just after you execute the startup script for the debug target server. If the GUI doesn't appear, then there is something incorrect in the startup script you created.

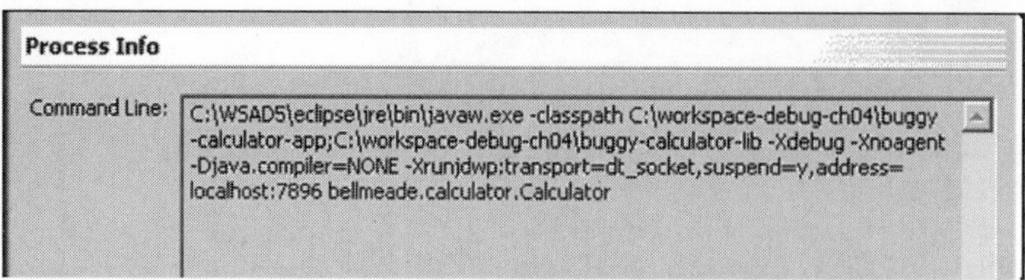

Figure 4.19 Create the remote debug configuration.

The Debug Perspective appears unless you have set other options. You may debug the target as if it were being debugged locally. Remember, local debugging actually uses remote debugging, so there is no difference between local and remote debugging in the WSAD debugger client user interface.

The remote client could be anywhere in the world that has IP connectivity to the server machine and port address. You could start a profoundly remote VM using Telnet or SSH, but you would need a remote colleague to operate any user interface of a truly remote application, or use a remote operation system. Examples are: freely available AT&T Virtual Network Computing utility, Windows Terminal Services, and Unix X-Windows.

You detach from the remote debugging server by using the Disconnect icon in the Debug view toolbar. It is the fourth icon from the left.

Calculator Bug Three: Decimal Point

The calculator mediator maintains the entry value in a primitive double type. Each incoming digit is added to the `entry` variable after multiplying it by 10, unless the user has previously pressed the decimal point. In this case the inbound digit is divided by 10 times the distance from the decimal point, or the number of decimal positions and then added to the display variable. The problem is that entering, say, **1.2**, results in **1.02** being displayed and entered. You choose to use the remote debugger to find this problem to become familiar with this approach. You may need to debug a Java application on a different platform someday. Use the following steps:

1. Start the buggy version of the calculator in a debug VM. Use or adapt buggy-**calc-sun.cmd** or **buggy-calc-ibm.cmd** to run the application in the local machine or a network-attached machine. Note the port number. You need to know it when you work in the WSAD session.

2. You suspect the `handleDigit()` method of the mediator has the problem after rereading the previous explanation of its operation. If you didn't have this knowledge, you could step through the code from a breakpoint in the action handler as you did in bug two. Place a breakpoint at the first statement of `handleDigit()`. Disable it from the WSAD Debug Perspective Breakpoints view.

3. Start a remote debug session of the buggy calculator using the port number from Step 1. It should show as a process in the Debug view of the Debug Perspective.
4. In the calculator, enter **1** followed by **.**
5. Return to WSAD. Enable the breakpoint in the Breakpoints view.
6. Enter **2** in the calculator. The button stays pressed. WSAD suspends the thread at the breakpoint.
7. Display the Variables tab in the Debug Perspective. Expand the *this* node of the **CalculatorMediator**. Observe that the `decimalPoint` variable has a value of 2. It should be 1. This variable tracks the number of fractional positions. You entered the first digit after the decimal point, not the second. You suspect that the test `decimalPoint >= 0` should read `decimalPoint > 0`.
8. Modify the value of `decimalPoint` to be **1** by using the context menu
9. Use Step Over to step through the statements of the method. Observe the variables. Notice that entry assumes the correct value 1.2 due to the modification of the `decimalPoint` value.
10. Press Resume. Observe the correct value in the calculator.

You cannot incrementally repair the error with the debugger code to have it picked up in the remote debugging host because it and WSAD are using identical separate class files. You would normally repair the problem and then export its class in a JAR file to the remote platform. This concludes the final calculator bug.

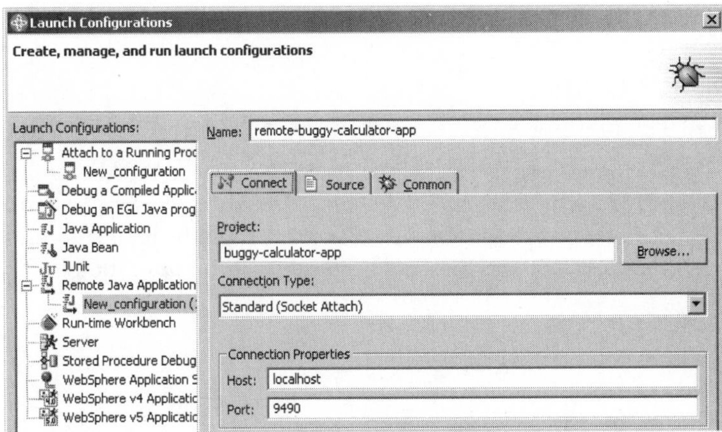

Figure 4.20 Create the launch configurations.

Summary

Flawless code is usually the product of a good, layered design, followed by multiple iterations of testing, problem determination and debugging. A good debugging tool is an important enabler for success. If you need to progress beyond tracing intermediate results, you need a tool that will allow us to halt, inspect, and modify code and variables of any stack frame of any arbitrary thread of execution. WSAD is an excellent debugging tool for Java applications because it implements Sun's standard client/server debugging framework, enabling minimal interference between the debug target server VM and the client's debugging interface. Its standardized client/server design enables remote debugging to VM running on any Java platform. This is a handy feature for cross-platform debugging, or to prevent spurious interactions with the debugger user interface when you investigate problems involving events.

You saw several debugging features of WSAD in this chapter, along with some ad-hoc debugging techniques such as tracing or isolating an algorithm using the scrapbook. This chapter showed how to:

- Use display statements to trace a problem
- Use WSAD to display locations and results on the console
- Launch a Java application in debug mode
- Set breakpoints using the WSAD debugger
- Inspect and modify live values
- Modify executable code during debugging
- Use the WSAD scrapbook
- Debug remotely
- Set breakpoints on exceptions
- Debug three actual programming errors, using debug features in WSAD

Chapter 16, "J2EE Application Deployment," explains how to use the WSAD debugger to carry out debugging procedures using WSAD on server-side Java Servlets and JavaServer Pages. We defer this material until after we cover those technologies and their deployment to a server. We cover the basics of creating a Web application in the next chapter.

Web Page Content

What's in Chapter 5?

Web applications are a key part of the J2EE architecture. The presentation or view layer for Web applications can be static content, which does not change, or dynamic content, which changes. Static content is implemented using Hypertext Markup Language (HTML). Most dynamic pages are created using technologies like JSP that generate HTML at runtime.

In this chapter, you will learn the right way to build HTML pages and gain some of the basic confidence using the WSAD Page Designer. You will build an HTML page and test it with the WebSphere Test Environment. This chapter covers the following concepts:

- HTML structure
- Setting up a Web application
- Creating links
- Using the <TABLE> tag
- Input tags and their various options

All of these topics provide you with the basics for creating good static pages. Even if you are an HTML guru, this chapter shows you how to develop HTML pages in WebSphere Studio Application Developer. The chapter shows you how to create a Web application in WSAD, and it introduces you to some of the editors in WSAD.

HTML Structure

First, we will cover how HTML is structured, and then we will cover some fundamental HTML tags. There are many HTML tags, so we will cover the basic ones in this chapter. An HTML document is identified with the <HTML> tag. The following code shows the smallest HTML file you will ever see:

```
<HTML>
  Example of HTML
</HTML>
```

Web browsers like Internet Explorer and Netscape Navigator are used to display HTML content. You can load an HTML file directly in your browser, or you can call an HTML file on a server. Web browsers are very forgiving, and they will ignore unknown tags and handle missing end tags. The previous simple sample page has the required HTML tags, and it will display correctly in a Web browser.

You can see that the HTML tag is capitalized. This is the original convention, and a lot of tools still use this convention. It does not make any difference to the Web browser if the HTML tags are in lowercase or uppercase, but it is a good practice to be consistent. You will add more tags to the document and build a good, well-formed Web page.

Document Structure

The first improvement to the HTML page is a DOCTYPE identifier. HTML has had a number of revisions, and version 4 is very common. It supports many advanced features like the <FORM> and <FRAME> tags. The HTML standard is published by the World Wide Web Consortium (W3C), and you can get more information about the standard at www.w3c.org. The following tag should be added to the beginning of the Web page as an identifier:

```
<!DOCTYPE HTML PUBLIC "-//W3C//DTD HTML 4.01 Transitional//EN">
```

This <DOCTYPE> tag indicates that this document uses HTML version 4.01. The `EN` at the end of the tag identifies that this page uses the English language and characters.

HTML documents have a basic nesting structure as shown in Figure 5.1. Your HTML documents should have <HEAD> tags and <BODY> tags. These tags separate sections in the Web page with different purposes.

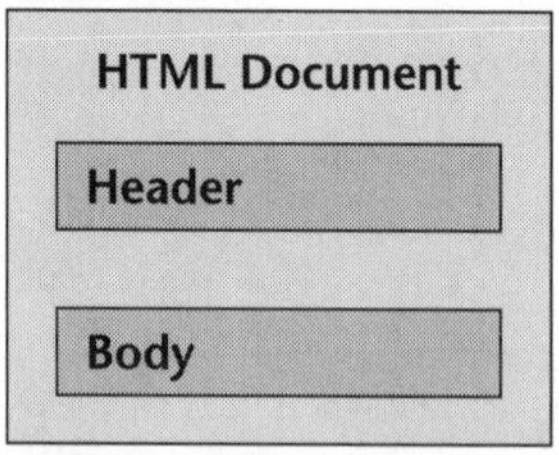

Figure 5.1 HTML document structure.

As with all tags, the <HEAD> and the <BODY> tags have a start and an end. The following code sample shows the addition of the <HEAD> and <BODY> tags to the <HTML> and </HTML> tags:

```
<!DOCTYPE HTML PUBLIC "-//W3C//DTD HTML 4.01 Transitional//EN">
<HTML>
  <HEAD>
     Header tags
  </HEAD>
  <BODY>
  Content goes here.
  </BODY>
</HTML>
```

When this updated version of the Web page is displayed in a Web browser, it looks the same to the user. These additional tags make it easier for the browser to parse the page.

The Header

Although a header is optional, you really should have a header in an HTML document. The information in the header is not shown in the page by the browser, but tags within the header add valuable information to the page. Following is a list of different tags that can be used in the header:

- The <TITLE> tag is important for identifying the page. It is used when creating bookmarks or favorites. Although you can have multiple <TITLE> tags, it makes sense to have only one.
- <META> tags are used for various identifiers for the page. <META> tags are important for search engines and spiders. Spiders or Web crawlers go through Web sites via links.
- <LINK> tags are used for linking external files like Cascading Style Sheet (.css) files.
- JavaScript definitions go in the header. Chapter 12, "JavaScript," covers JavaScript and shows how it is used in the header.
- Additional tags for JSPs are also placed in the header. These are covered in Chapter 11, "JavaServer Pages."

Many amateur Web pages do not have <HEADER> tags. If you look at most commercial Web sites, you will see a number of tags in the header file. There are many different <META> tags that you can add to Web pages, for example:

```
<META name="AUTHOR" content="Your Name" />
```

Notice that there is no </META> tag. The slash (/) at the end of the tag makes it a self-ending tag. Some of the earlier tags in HTML did not have an end tag, so this is an easy way to make the tag have an end. In order to make the HTML easier to parse, tags must have an ending tag or a self-ending mark.

At some time, you may have set a bookmark or favorite in a browser and gotten "home" or blank. This is caused by a common oversight by some Web developers. A simple <TITLE> tag can solve this problem, and it is very easy to add to your Web pages. Remember that this text will show on the favorite's list, so the text should be descriptive and not too long. The following is a sample <TITLE> tag for the Web page:

```
<TITLE>J2EE HTML Example</TITLE>
```

Make sure to put <TITLE> tags on all the Web pages. A user may bookmark any page on the Web site. For searching purposes, the <META> tags should follow the <TITLE> tag. The updated HTML should look as follows:

```
<!DOCTYPE HTML PUBLIC "-//W3C//DTD HTML 4.01 Transitional//EN">
<HTML>
  <HEAD>
     <TITLE>J2EE HTML Example</TITLE>
     <META name="AUTHOR" content="Your Name" />
  </HEAD>
  <BODY>
  Content goes here.
  </BODY>
</HTML>
```

The Body

Between the <BODY> tags is where most of the page content goes. The document body can contain many other tags or elements. In the next chapter, we will show you how to use some basic elements like the <ANCHOR>, <INPUT>, <FORM>, and <TABLE> tags. These basic tags allow you to add most of the required function to a Web page. In Chapter 14, "Making Slick Web Pages," we will cover how to refine the Web page's look.

You can develop HTML in any text-based editor. Many people use Notepad or Wordpad to edit simple HTML pages. We will use WSAD to develop the sample HTML page because WSAD includes a test server. The test server shows the page as it will look when it is deployed to a real browser.

Creating a Web Project

WSAD is organized by projects. You should use the project type that best suits the needs of your application. For this application, you need a Web project that has the necessary structure to develop and test Web applications.

Now, let's try making a Web page in WSAD. Make sure that WSAD is already started. You should also be in the Web Perspective. First, we need to define a new Web project for this HTML page with the following steps:

1. Select File > New > Web Project, and the Create a Web Project window displays, as shown in Figure 5.2.
2. Enter **GolfProject** for the Project name.

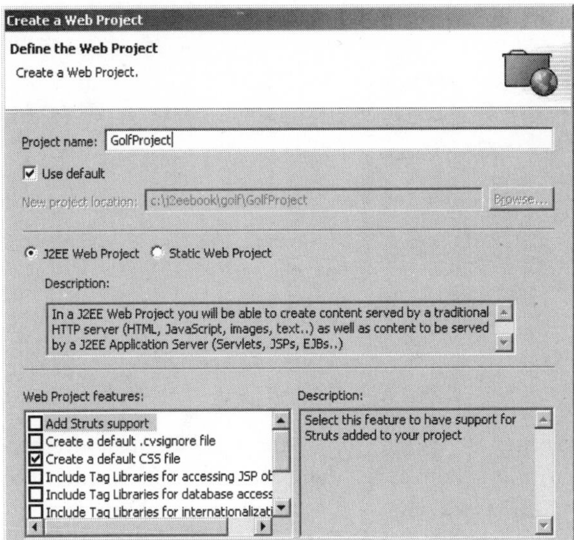

Figure 5.2 New Web project.

3. You can use the default location for code generation.
4. Make sure the J3EE Web Project radio button is selected. This ensures that all the necessary runtime files are added to the project.
5. Make sure the create a default CSS file checkbox is checked. A CSS file is a Cascading Style Sheet that provides a mechanism for easily changing the behavior of the tags.
6. Click the Next button to proceed.

The Create a Web Project J2EE Settings Page appears. You can specify additional information for the J2EE runtime. Complete the following steps as shown in Figure 5.3:

1. Make sure that **New** is selected for Enterprise application project.
2. Change the EAR file from DefaultEAR to GolfEAR.
3. You can use the default location for code generation.
4. The Context root should be GolfProject.
5. Select the J2EE Level 1.3.
6. Press Finish to create the Web project.

You did not need to enter any information on the other pages of the Web Project wizard. These other pages allow you to identify dependent projects and additional runtime classes in JAR files required for this project.

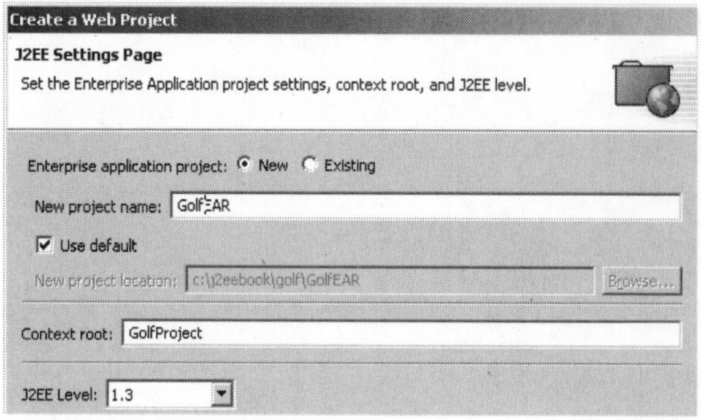

Figure 5.3 New Web project info.

WSAD created the GolfEAR project and the GolfProject, and additional subdirectories and files inside these projects. You will be placing the Web content files under the Web Content subdirectory in the GolfProject. The Web application is a J2EE convention, and it is defined in the web.xml file under the WEB-INF folder. Servlets and JSPs are added to the Web application with entries in the web.xml file. The web.xml file should look as follows:

```
<?xml version="1.0" encoding="UTF-8"?>
<!DOCTYPE web-app PUBLIC "-//Sun Microsystems, Inc.//DTD Web Application
2.3//EN" "http://java.sun.com/dtd/web-app_2_3.dtd">
<web-app id="WebApp">
    <display-name>GolfProject</display-name>
    <welcome-file-list>
        <welcome-file>index.html</welcome-file>
        <welcome-file>index.htm</welcome-file>
        <welcome-file>index.jsp</welcome-file>
        <welcome-file>default.html</welcome-file>
        <welcome-file>default.htm</welcome-file>
        <welcome-file>default.jsp</welcome-file>
    </welcome-file-list>
</web-app>
```

WSAD adds additional Web application information in the ibm-web-ext.xmi file. The generated extension file should look as follows:

```
<webappext:WebAppExtension xmi:version="2.0"
xmlns:xmi="http://www.omg.org/XMI" xmlns:webappext="webappext.xmi"
xmlns:webapplication="webapplication.xmi"
xmlns:xsi="http://www.w3.org/2001/XMLSchema-instance"
xmi:id="WebAppExtension_1"
  reloadInterval="3"
  reloadingEnabled="true"
  additionalClassPath=""
  fileServingEnabled="true"
```

```
    directoryBrowsingEnabled="false"
    serveServletsByClassnameEnabled="true">
      <webApp href="WEB-INF/web.xml#WebApp"/>
</webappext:WebAppExtension>
```

Creating an HTML File

Now that you have a Web project, you are ready to start creating Web content. WSAD lets you import existing HTML files or create new ones. After you have been developing Web content for a while, you will tend to reuse files from previous projects. In this case, we will start with a new HTML file. Make a new HTML file with the following steps:

1. Select the Web Content folder in the GolfProject.
2. Select File > New > HTML/XHTML file, and the New HTML window displays as seen in Figure 5.4.
3. The Folder should be /GolfProject/Web Content.
4. Enter **index** for the File Name.
5. Make sure the Markup Language is HTML.
6. The model is None. In Chapter 17, "Struts," you will use the struts model for HTML.
7. Click the Next button to proceed.
8. The second page of the New HTML wizard displays, as seen in Figure 5.5. Select Use workbench default for the Workbench Encoding.
9. Make sure the Content Type is text/html.
10. The Document Type should be HTML 4.01 Transitional.
11. The file Master.css should be in the Style Sheet field. WSAD fills this field in from the CSS file generated when the project was created.
12. Press the Finish button to generate the HTML file.

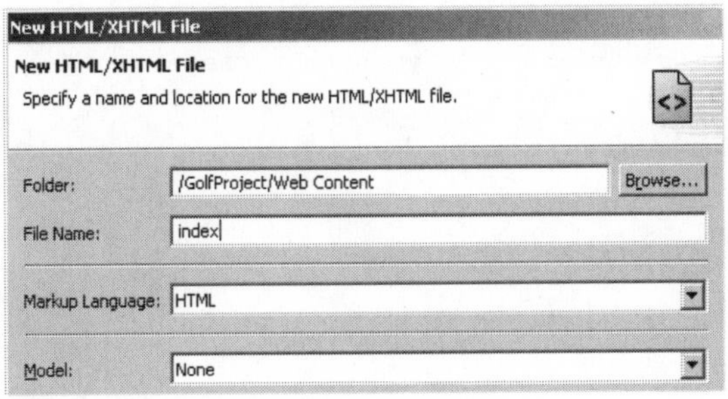

Figure 5.4 New HTML/XHTML file.

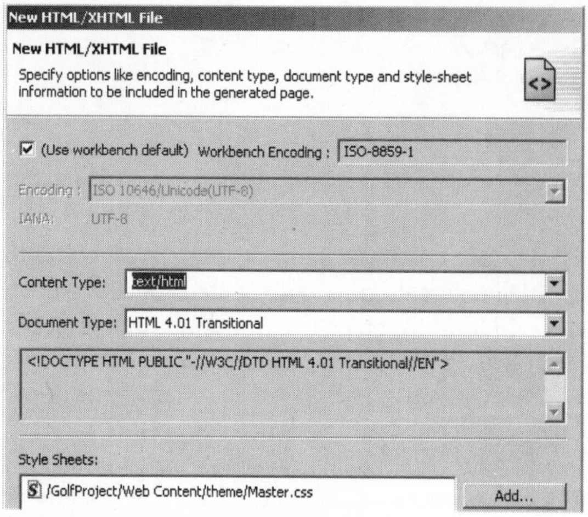

Figure 5.5 Create an HTML file.

After the HTML page is created, the Web Perspective in WSAD should look like Figure 5.6. The Web Perspective has a default editor for HTML and JSP content, which is shown in the top-right section of the window. This editor has three different views, shown by the tabs at the bottom. These views are as follows:

- Design provides a WYSIWYG (what you see is what you get) visual editor.
- Source provides a standard text editor with specific functions to help with HTML development.
- Preview provides a quick preview of the HTML in a browser.

If you switch to the Source tab at the bottom, the HTML source code is displayed in an editor. The HTML code looks like the following:

```
<!DOCTYPE HTML PUBLIC "-//W3C//DTD HTML 4.01 Transitional//EN">
<HTML>
<HEAD>
<META name="GENERATOR" content="IBM WebSphere Studio">
<META http-equiv="Content-Style-Type" content="text/css">
<LINK href="theme/Master.css" rel="stylesheet" type="text/css">
<TITLE>index.html</TITLE>
</HEAD>
<BODY>
Place index.html's content here.
</BODY>
</HTML>
```

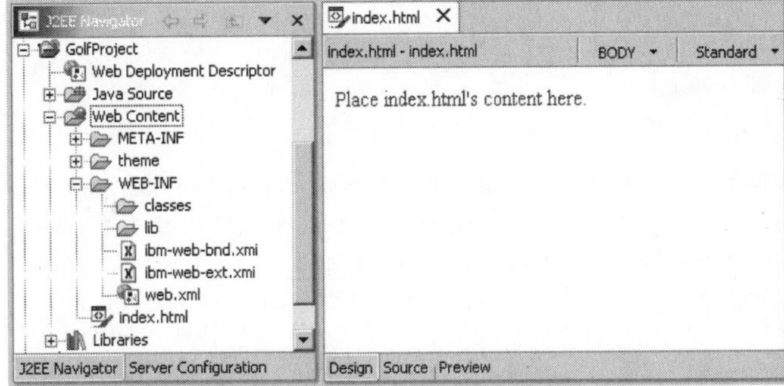

Figure 5.6 New HTML page.

The WSAD generated HTML file has most of the elements that we covered earlier. It starts with the <DOCTYPE> tag. It has an <HTML> tag with nested <HEAD> and <BODY> tags. You can see the <LINK> tag necessary for the CSS file. WSAD even generated a <TITLE> tag, although the HTML filename is used for the title value. This is a good start, but you need to edit the HTML to change some of these tags.

Notice that there is a <META> tag identifying that WebSphere Studio generated the page. This tag is not necessary and you can delete it. Let's modify the HTML with the following steps:

1. Delete the entire <META> tag identifying that the page was generated by IBM WebSphere Studio.
2. Edit the <TITLE> tag data so that it reads `My Golf Page.`
3. Edit the placeholder text after the <BODY> tag so that is reads `Welcome to my Golf Page!`
4. Add the <META> tag identifying you as the author with the following code:

   ```
   <META name="AUTHOR" content="Your Name" />
   ```

5. Save these changes by pressing Ctrl+S.

The HTML code should now look like the following:

```
<!DOCTYPE HTML PUBLIC "-//W3C//DTD HTML 4.01 Transitional//EN">
<HTML>
<HEAD>
<META name="AUTHOR" content="Your Name" />
<META http-equiv="Content-Style-Type" content="text/css">
<LINK href="theme/Master.css" rel="stylesheet" type="text/css">
<TITLE>My Golf Page</TITLE>
</HEAD>
```

```
<BODY>
Welcome to my Golf Page!
</BODY>
</HTML>
```

The HTML file is much better now. If you select the Preview tab, you can see the updated text, but there is a lot left to do. There may be some standard that you use in your Web pages. It would be very good to make a template page in a special project. You could then copy this page and use it to initialize new HTML pages. Even if you start with a special HTML template file, every time that you save an HTML file, WSAD will modify it with some specific tags. These tags are specified in the WSAD preferences, and it is a good idea to modify the default settings. The next section shows you how to make these modifications.

Customizing HTML Settings

You have already customized other preferences in WSAD. This point in development gives us the opportunity to change the way that HTML files are handled.

1. Select Window > Preferences and the Preferences window appears.
2. Select Web and XML Files > HTML Files item in Tree view on the left side of the window, as shown in Figure 5.7.

There are a number of options that you may want to change for HTML files. The second field labeled *Add this suffix* puts a default file extension on html files when they are saved. Some Web developers use .htm for html files, and others use .html. It makes no difference to the Web server; it will handle both file extensions just fine. If you prefer the shorter extension, you should change it here. For the examples in this book, we will use .html.

Notice the option for including the <DOCTYPE> tag. This is included by default, and you should not change it. You may want to change the attribute of the <DOCTYPE> tag if the Web page is not in English.

The check box at the bottom labeled *Insert GENERATOR with META tag* Source is the option that adds the unneeded <META> tag discussed previously. You should uncheck this box. If you leave this GENERATOR checkbox checked, every time that you save an HTML file, WSAD will check for that <META> tag, and if it does not exist, WSAD will generate a new one. Fix this by following these steps:

1. Make sure the Insert GENERATOR with META tag checkbox is unchecked.
2. Press the Apply button so that this change will be saved.
3. Press the Finish button to close this window.

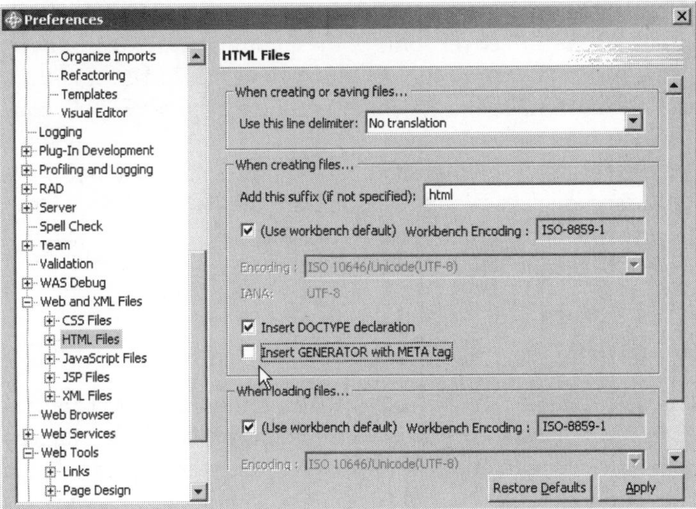

Figure 5.7 Web tool options.

Simple Tables

The HTML sample page we have built so far has a small problem. As the browser window is resized, the text floats and wraps to the next line as the window becomes smaller. This is not very good behavior. It can make the text appear jumbled and difficult to read. Users expect the page to be stable and readable. The <TABLE> tag solves this problem. HTML tables are not just for displaying lists of items in a row and column grid. They are used throughout a Web page to organize and manage the page sections.

Tables are a little complex because they have a number of nested parts, as shown in Figure 5.8. Each of these components is a separate HTML tag, requiring a begin and an end tag. The tags must be nested as shown. Tables, <TABLE>, have a <TBODY>. A <TBODY> has table rows <TR>. Table rows have table data, <TD>, tags.

Figure 5.8 HTML table components.

Tables are very flexible, and there are many attributes that you can set for the table, column, row, or individual cell. We will cover some of the common attributes, but you should experiment with the Attributes Editor in the Design view. The Attributes Editor displays most of the available attributes, and it generates the appropriate HTML code for the settings that you make.

A table can also be nested inside of another table. This nesting allows a Web page designer to better mange the sections of a Web page. Nesting tables is like adding spices to food, a little goes a long way. It is common to see two to four levels of table nesting. It is very hard to manage the Web page when the table nesting is overly complex.

Adding an HTML Table

It is pretty easy to add an HTML table to the Web page. You can use a WSAD generator, or you can just enter the tags in the source editor. I find it faster to enter the tags by hand or clip them from another table in another HTML file. You need to add a single table with a body that has one row with one table data item. This single table will act as an invisible frame for the Web page.

Enter the following tags after the <BODY> tag:

```
<TABLE><TBODY><TR><TD>
```

Enter the following tags before the </BODY> tag:

```
</TD></TR></TBODY></TABLE>
```

The HTML source should look like the following:

```
<!DOCTYPE HTML PUBLIC "-//W3C//DTD HTML 4.01 Transitional//EN">
<HTML>
<HEAD>
<META name="AUTHOR" content="Your Name" />
<META http-equiv="Content-Style-Type" content="text/css">
<LINK href="theme/Master.css" rel="stylesheet" type="text/css">
<TITLE> My Golf Page </TITLE>
</HEAD>
<BODY>
<TABLE><TBODY><TR><TD>
Welcome to my Golf Page!
</TD></TR></TBODY></TABLE>
</BODY>
</HTML>
```

Setting Nowrap in a Table

You are almost ready to test all these changes. The table needs to have an attribute to prevent the text from wrapping to another line. Edit the table attribute with the following steps:

1. From the Design tab, place the tip of the mouse over the dashed line that represents the table.
2. You can double-click it with the mouse, or from the popup menu select Attributes..., and the Attributes editor appears, as seen in Figure 5.9.
3. Uncheck the box *Wrap lines automatically*. This causes the attribute nowrap to be inserted in the cell or <TD> of the Web page.

NOTE The nowrap attribute tag is a little odd. Most tags are a name/value pair like colspan="2". It would be better if the tag were wrap="no", then it would be easier to edit its value than to search for a nowrap tag.

4. Press the OK button to save this change and close the Attributes window.
5. There is one more thing to do. Click the Source tab.
6. Display the popup menu by clicking the right mouse button, and select Format/Document to clean up the HTML source.

On the Source tab, the code should look like the following:

```
<!DOCTYPE HTML PUBLIC "-//W3C//DTD HTML 4.01 Transitional//EN">
<HTML>
<HEAD>
<META name="AUTHOR" content="Your Name"/>
<META http-equiv="Content-Style-Type" content="text/css">
<LINK href="theme/Master.css" rel="stylesheet" type="text/css">
<TITLE>My Golf Page</TITLE>
</HEAD>
```

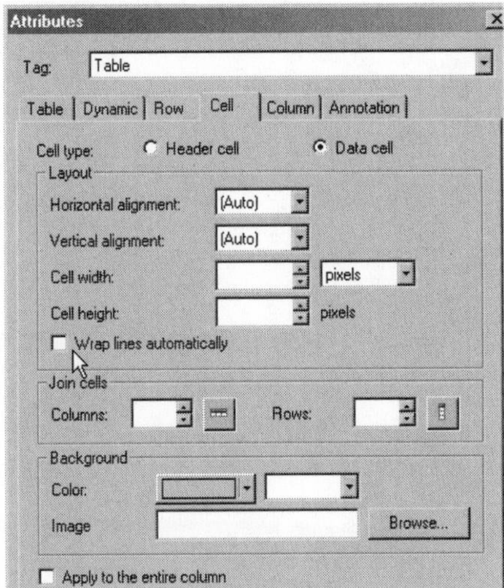

Figure 5.9 Setting cell attributes.

```
<BODY>
<TABLE>
    <TBODY>
        <TR>
            <TD nowrap>Welcome to my Golf Page!</TD>
        </TR>
    </TBODY>
</TABLE>
</BODY>
</HTML>
```

Now that the HTML page is complete, it is ready to be tested. In the next section, you will see how easy it is to test Web page in WSAD.

Testing an HTML Page

Since all the HTML tags are static and are not pointing to any Web resources, you could test this HTML page by loading it in a Web browser. You can view the HTML page on the Preview tab to get a rough idea of how it will look at runtime, but the Preview tab does not handle dynamic tags. To get a true runtime view, you need to run the HTML file with the WSAD test server, using the following steps:

1. Select the index.html file in the Navigator under the GolfProject.

2. From the popup menu, select Run on Server, or you can press the Run on Server button.

First, WSAD saves and compiles the necessary files. As the WebSphere server starts, you see the Publishing dialog, as shown in Figure 5.10. The publishing process and starting the J2EE sever takes a little time, so be patient. Once the server is up and running you may only need to restart or bounce the J2EE server in WSAD. The Console view in the lower right should display *server1 open for e-business*. This console message signals that the WebSphere test application server started correctly.

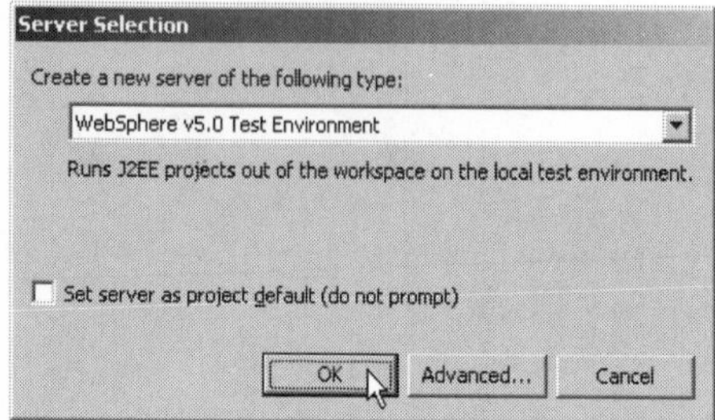

Figure 5.10 Publishing dialog.

After the J2EE server is up and running, the Web page is loaded into an internal Web browser, as shown in Figure 5.11. This internal browser is not a commercial browser, and you should always test your applications on a real commercial Web browser like Internet Explorer or Netscape Navigator. You can use the same URL displayed in the WSAD browser to test it in a real browser. For this page, the URL is http://localhost:9080/GolfProject/index.html.

If you open Internet Explorer or Netscape Navigator and enter the URL for this page, it will appear much as it did in the WSAD browser. It is very productive to use a separate browser to test Web applications. The Web browser in WSAD is a very small window that will not display enough of a Web page to be useable.

Editing Fonts

The page looks OK, but the welcome banner line is very understated. It is very easy to edit fonts in a Web page. Fonts can be changed in the page by using the <FONT> tag and setting specific font attributes such as color or size. You can also use specific tags to change the text physical emphasis. These tags are shown in Table 5.1.

These are all valid HTML tags; they can be used in combination and you will get the expected result. When these tags are used together they must be nested. For example, if you wanted bold and italics, you would use the following:

```
<B><I>This is bold italic text.</I></B>
```

You can set these physical emphasis tags in WSAD from the Design page by first selecting the text, then clicking Format > Physical Emphasis. Although using WSAD to enter physical emphasis may be harder than simply entering the tags in the code, WSAD always generates the tags in the right order. It is also helpful to generate the more uncommon tags.

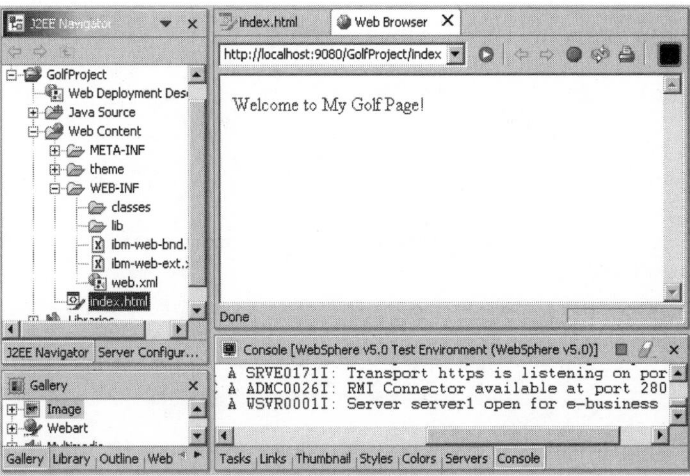

Figure 5.11 Publishing dialog.

Table 5.1 Tags for Editing Fonts

TAG	PURPOSE
<I>	Italics or slanted text
<B>	Bold darker text
<U>	Underline beneath the text
<TT>	Fixed-space font used for showing text that needs alignment such as code
<SUP>	Superscript, which makes the font smaller and raises the text position
<SUB>	Subscript, which makes the font smaller and lowers the text position
<S>	Strikeout, which shows characters with a line through them
<BLINK>	Makes the text flash in some browsers

Of course, it does not make sense to combine some of these tags. Although you can combine <SUP> and <SUB> tags, it does not make sense to use these two tags together.

The welcome text should be bolder and larger. We could use the <B> tag and <FONT> tags, but there is an easier tag to use for this. For this banner text, it is very simple to use the existing heading tags to increase the size. These tags are sometimes called "H" tags. We will use the <H1> tag to add emphasis to the text. The <H1> attributes have default values that can be overridden. You will learn how to do this in the next section. Change the text with the following steps:

1. Flip to the Source tab.
2. Add <H1> before the Welcome text.
3. Add the </H1> end tag after the Page! Text.

The HTML code for the text should look like the following:

```
<!DOCTYPE HTML PUBLIC "-//W3C//DTD HTML 4.01 Transitional//EN">
<HTML>
<HEAD>
<META name="AUTHOR" content="Your Name"/>
<META http-equiv="Content-Style-Type" content="text/css">
<LINK href="theme/Master.css" rel="stylesheet" type="text/css">
<TITLE>My Golf Page</TITLE>
</HEAD>
<BODY>
<TABLE>
    <TBODY>
        <TR>
            <TD nowrap colspan="2"><H1>Welcome to my Golf
             Page!</H1></TD>
```

```
            </TR>
        </TBODY>
    </TABLE>
    </BODY>
    </HTML>
```

You can see how the <H1> tag affects the text by flipping to the Preview tab, as shown in Figure 5.12. The <H1> tag makes the text much larger, and the text color is blue. It is very good to use these types of tags to insure uniformity in your Web site. If you use the separate <FONT> and physical emphasis tags, there is a chance that you may forget to use one of the tags or attributes.

Editing the Web Page's Style

The text of the page looks better, and there are a lot of other changes that could improve the page. There are a number of attributes that you can set for a Web page, and changing the background is very common. Many Web page development tools allow you to change page attributes, and the tools generate code that goes into the Web page. WSAD has a special editor that makes it easy to change the many different page attributes without having to remember the possible tags or their values.

Changing Page Attributes

The background color can be very important for a Web page. Most business Web sites go for a clean look and choose white as a background. Other sites use a careful blending of colors that usually goes with a corporate logo. Some sites even use black as a background, but this forces you to change all the fonts to a light color. These dark sites are usually hard to read, and these color schemes should be avoided. The Master.css file that WASD uses has a white background as a default color. This is very common for Web pages, and you will keep this setting. However, the font tags use a blue-gray color that you will change to a pure blue. We will change this color for our site.

Figure 5.12 <H1> text.

The page background is a page attribute that is reflected in the <BODY> tag. You can look up the correct attribute tags and RGB value in an HTML reference book, or edit the page attributes in WSAD, using an easy editor. Let's try changing the page background to white, using the editor. From the Design tab in WSAD:

1. Select Format > Set Background and Text Colors, and the Page Attribute Editor appears, as seen in Figure 5.13. All the items on this page can be added to the <BODY> tag.
2. Select the Background dropdown list.
3. Select the white box in the color pallet.
4. Press Apply.
5. Press OK to close the Page Attribute Editor.

After the Page Attribute Editor closes, you see the Web page in WSAD and the color has not changed. Let's see what the Attribute Editor did. If you flip to the Source tab you can see that WSAD changed the <BODY> tag to:

```
<BODY bgcolor="#ffffff">
```

This is the right code to get a white background. The #ffffff value for white uses the Red-Green-Blue (RBG) convention for colors. The ff in the tag is hexidecimal for all red, all green, and all blue. It is hard to remember the many different color combinations. Most tools, including WSAD, have color pallets that allow you to pick a color and have it generate the correct RGB value.

The same tag can be used to produce a textured background. This is accomplished with a graphic .gif file. There are many Web sites that have free background .gif files that have a wide variety of textures and colors. If you want to use a .gif file, the tag is as follows:

```
<BODY bgcolor="mybackground.gif">
```

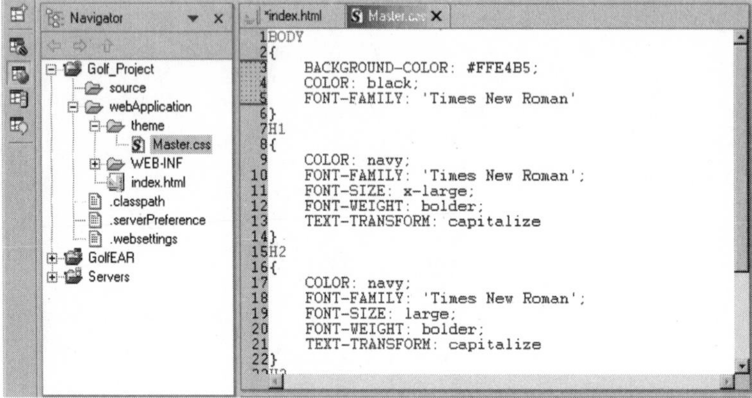

Figure 5.13 Page attribute editor.

You can use the Attribute editor for the page properties to set background .gif file, or use drag and drop. If you drag a .gif file to the Web page, WSAD generates the correct code, but it also copies the .gif file to the subdirectory that has the .html file. If you already have a separate subdirectory with the .gif files for the Web site, you will need to delete this newly copied .gif file and change the reference in the background attribute to point to the separate subdirectory with the .gif files. The drag-and-drop feature is good for small simple sites that don't have a lot of files, but a large site with some structure to the file locations is much harder to modify using drag and drop.

It is also possible to set the various link colors in the <BODY> tag. It is much better to set the body tag attributes in a CSS file and let the CSS file control the styles. You need to reset the code and remove the erroneous bgcolor attribute. Edit the code so that the <BODY> tag does not have any attributes, and save the page. It should be a plain <BODY> tag. Now, we can set the background color in the style sheet.

Editing a Cascading Style Sheet

When you built this page, a Cascading Style Sheet, Master.css, was automatically added to the page. Style sheets are a great way to centrally control the look and feel of a page or an entire Web site. We need to edit the Cascading Style Sheet to get the desired background color for the Web page.

The background color should be the same on each page. By adding a bgcolor attribute to the <BODY> tag of a Web page, you are creating a maintenance problem. If someone decides that the page background should be different, you would need to edit, save, and deploy each page. This would be very tedious, take a lot of time, and is not a very effective way to maintain Web page attributes.

The HTML page has a link to the Master.css file as its Cascading Style Sheet. This file defines default attributes for the HTML tags. Let's use the WSAD editor to change the Master.css file for this page with the following steps:

1. In the GolfProject, go to the Master.css file in the Navigator by opening the Web Content folder and its theme folder, as shown in Figure 5.14.
2. Double-click the Master.css file to edit it, as shown in Figure 5.15. You can see that the BACKGROUD color is FFFFFF, which is hexidecimal for white. You can also see the entry for the <H1> tag and how its color and font attributes are set.
3. Change the H1 COLOR to **#0000FF**, the hex code for blue. As you change the number for the color on the left, the preview HTML file on the right changes to show the new color. You can also select one of your pages to preview with the CSS file.
4. Save this change in Master.css by pressing Ctrl-S.
5. Close the Master.css file by clicking the X next to the Master.css tab.
6. The index.html page appears. Change to the Preview tab to see the changes.

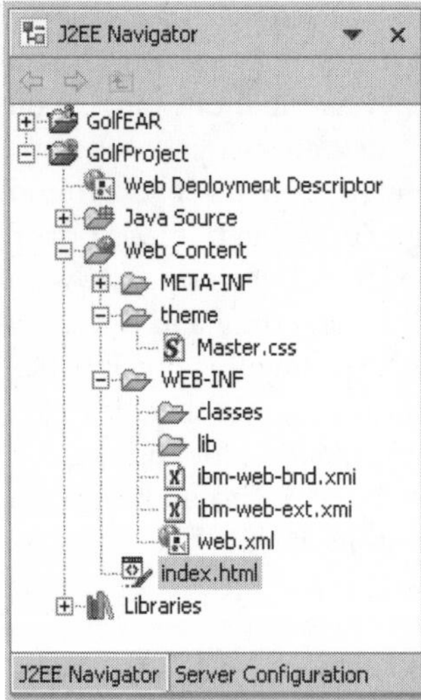

Figure 5.14 Master.css Tree view.

The html page appears as shown in Figure 5.16. You may have to select Refresh from the popup menu to get the correct appearance. You can use this same Cascading Style Sheet on other Web pages, and you will get the same effects.

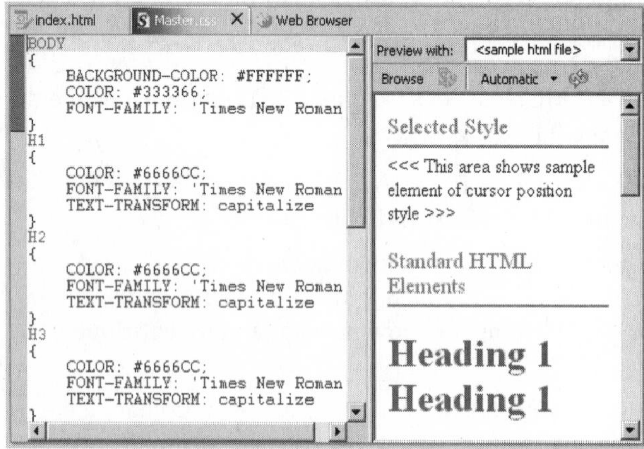

Figure 5.15 CSS Editor.

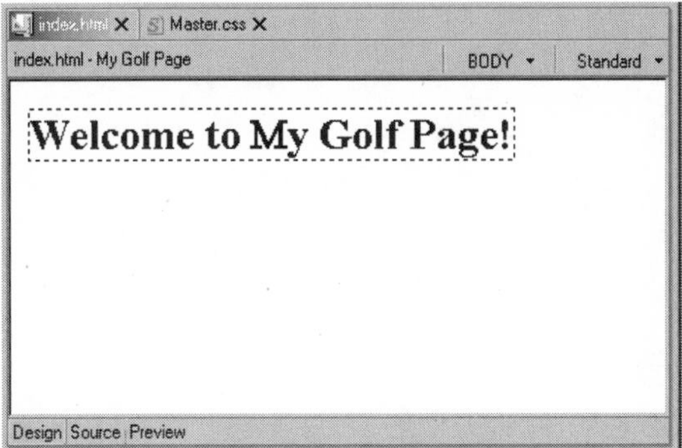

Figure 5.16 Updated Welcome background.

Summary

In this chapter, you learned the basics of HTML and static Web page design. You learned the core HTML tags to start a Web page, and you built a sample page. These elements are essential for the static content in a Web page. The key concepts covered include:

- The basic structure of HTML with the <HEAD> and <BODY> tags
- Basic <META> tags
- Tables <TABLES> and their components
- How to automatically format the HTML code to get proper nesting
- Testing an HTML page
- Physical emphasis types and their tags
- Changing the Cascading Style Sheet values

You used many WSAD tools to develop the static HTML page, such as the HTML wizard, Design page, Editor page, Preview page, Cascading Style Sheet Editor, Page Attribute Editor. These many tools make it easy to develop static pages in WSAD. However, these tools merely generate HTML tags. It is up to you to learn how to use the tags correctly. Also, the tools can sometimes generate useless or unneeded tags.

Many Web pages contain information that does not change very often or is not specific to a certain user or customer. These static informational pages can be a key part of a J2EE application. This chapter showed you the basics of making a good static HTML page. There is a lot more interesting function that you can add to a Web page. In the next chapter, you will see how to add more types of content to the page.

CHAPTER 6

Linking Web Page Content

What's in Chapter 6?

In this chapter, you will build on what you learned about Web pages in the previous chapter. You will learn about additional features that can be added to a good Web page. You will learn how to use the tags necessary for passing data to a server. This chapter covers the following concepts:

- Adding table rows and columns
- Links <A> tags
- Building an HTML Form
    - <FORM> tag
    - <INPUT> tags
    - Comments

All of these topics are essential for good static HTML pages. As in the previous chapter, you will also learn how to use other features in WSAD. You will see the HTML tags generated by WSAD and learn some better ways to use them.

Adding Table Rows and Columns

In this chapter, you will build on the Web page that you started in the previous chapter. The table for this Web page has only one row and one column. Web pages are commonly designed with conventional areas, as seen in Figure 6.1. The top area is referred to as the banner, and it usually contains an identifier for the page. The area on the left is referred to as a button bar or navigation bar and usually contains links to other Web pages. The largest area in the middle is called the main, or body, section of the Web page. This area is the main informational area.

The separation of the Web page into separate sections can be done through tables or through frames. Frames are an advanced feature in HTML, and they have some pluses and minuses. For this Web page, we will use tables. Later in Chapter 14, "Making Slick Web Pages," we discuss how to use frames and what the drawbacks are to using them.

Adding Table Rows

You will add a new row to the main table that will hold the navigation bar and the main display area. The row will have two columns using the <TD> tag. Each of these columns will have its own table that will allow for the most flexibility placing the components. You can make all these changes directly in the HTML source, but it can be a little tricky when you are nesting multiple tables. Use the Visual Design Editor to add a row as follows:

1. Make sure the index.html file is open in the editor. Also, make sure that the Design tab is selected.
2. Select the table on the Web page by moving the mouse over the Welcome... text and clicking the mouse. This makes the table functions available.

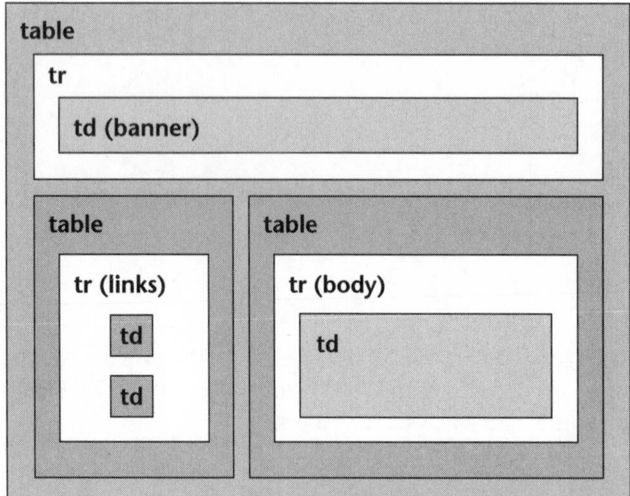

Figure 6.1 Common Web page layout.

3. On the toolbar, click the Add Table Row button. You could instead use the menu selections Table > Add Row > Add Below.

Now, the main table should have another row, as shown in Figure 6.2. This row will hold the navigation bar and the main body sections of the Web page. If you flip to the Source tab, you will see the HTML code that was added to the page. WSAD inserted a table row <TR> with a table data tag <TD>. All the tags have ending tags and are properly indented, as seen in the following code:

```
<BODY>
<TABLE>
    <TBODY>
        <TR>
            <TD nowrap><H1>Welcome to My Golf Page!</H1></TD>
        </TR>
        <TR>
            <TD></TD>
        </TR>
    </TBODY>
</TABLE>
</BODY>
</HTML>
```

You can use the Add Row button to add many rows to a table. There is also the Delete Row button or corresponding menu item to delete table rows. Even though empty rows do not show when the page is displayed in a browser, you should remove them from the page. Extra unneeded tags make the HTML bigger than it needs to be and could make it harder to maintain.

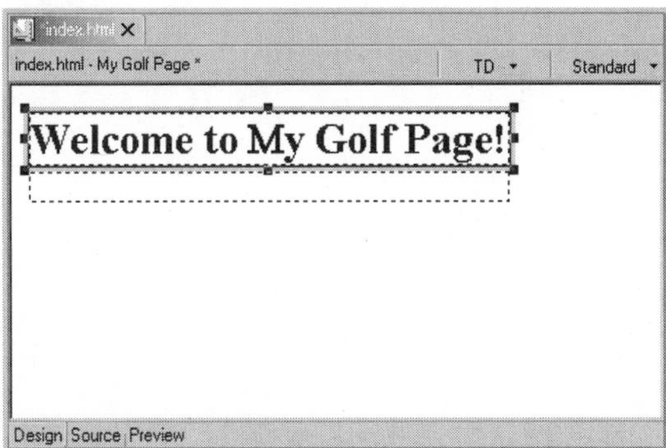

Figure 6.2 New table row.

Splitting Table Columns

You need to split this new row into two columns, one for the navigation bar and one for the main body section. There is no column tag for tables, actually you will be adding a <TD> to the row and changing the first row so that it spans two columns. This will divide the main table into the three sections that we need. Change the Web page with the following steps:

1. From the Design tab, make sure that new empty row in the table is selected.

2. Press the Add Column button. You could instead use the menu item Table > Split Cell into Columns.

The last row is split into two columns, as seen in Figure 6.3. A new column is put into the row by inserting empty <TD></TD> tags. Tables need to be balanced. Each row needs to have the same number of <TD> tags. There are not two columns or two <TD> tags in the first row. WSAD added a `colspan` attribute to the first row, as seen in the following code:

```
<BODY>
<TABLE>
    <TBODY>
        <TR>
            <TD nowrap colspan="2"><H1>Welcome to My Golf
                Page!</H1></TD>
        </TR>
        <TR>
            <TD></TD>
            <TD></TD>
        </TR>
    </TBODY>
</TABLE>
</BODY>
```

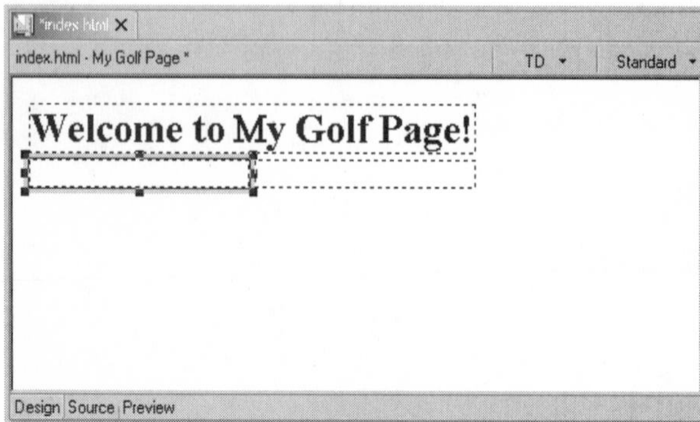

Figure 6.3 Splitting table columns.

It is easy to use the Design editor because it generates the appropriate tags for you. You always have the option of editing the HTML code directly. WSAD is not very good at removing unneeded tags. When you split columns or rows and then delete one of the rows or columns, usually there are unneeded colspan or rowspan tags in the HTML. Although they do not affect the way the HTML is displayed, you should still go back and clean out these erroneous tags.

Cell Attributes

We could jump in and start adding links to the new cell on the left side of the table, but it is better to fix a few table attributes before we start adding the links. The following are the steps to change the attributes:

1. Double-click the new cell in the bottom left of the table, and the Cell Attribute Editor appears, as seen in Figure 6.4.
2. Set the Horizontal alignment to Left.
3. Set the Vertical alignment to Top, which keeps the links in the top of the cell. Without this setting, the default position is in the center of the cell.
4. Uncheck the Wrap lines automatically checkbox.
5. Change the Background Color to light gray. You can enter #cccccc or select light gray from the dropdown list of colors.
6. Click OK to generate the HTML code for these changes.

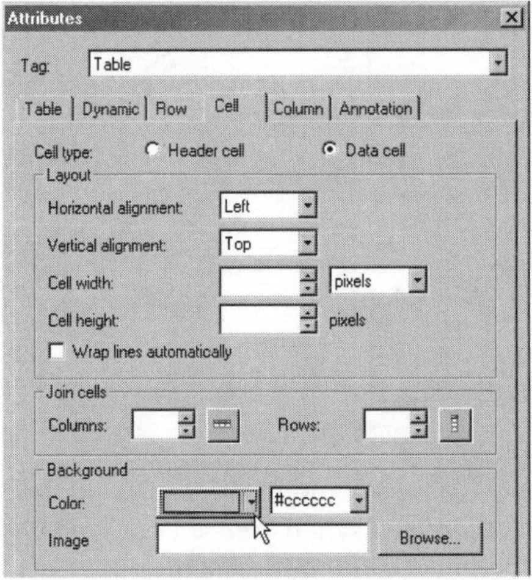

Figure 6.4 Cell attributes.

HTML Links

Links are very common in Web pages. In fact, links were the original reason for HTML. The ability to link text to other text or other documents makes it hypertext. Links can point to other places in the same document, or they can point to a URL on the World Wide Web.

Adding Text

Before we add some links, the Web page needs a brief description for the links. You can simply enter the text in the WSAD Design Editor. Add some text that will describe the links that you will be adding with the following steps:

1. Make sure the bottom-left cell of the table is selected.
2. Enter the text **My Favorite Links:**
3. Press the Enter key two times. This inserts two <BR> tags in the HTML and makes some space between the text and the links that will be added.
4. Press Ctrl-S to save these changes.

The Web page should look like it does in Figure 6.5. The Web page is looking better, but there is still a lot more to add.

Adding Links

The anchor tag is short and simple, <A>, but it has a number of attributes. Anchor tags can link to the following different locations:

- **Files** — allows you to load or view files on a Web browser.
- **URL** — specifies a link to another Web page, which can be on your site or somewhere on the World Wide Web.
- **Label** — allows the user to jump to another part of this document. It is very helpful with very long documents when a user is looking for a specific piece of information.
- **Mail** — specifies an email address. When this link is selected, the browser invokes a dialog for sending an email.

Links are very important to Web pages. External links sometimes change, so they need to be updated occasionally. Internal links are affected when Web sites are reorganized or renamed. Also, you may use a link many times on different Web pages. WSAD has a Links view that shows the links and provides a way to easily correct them. For this Web page, you will hard-code the link URL in the HTML.

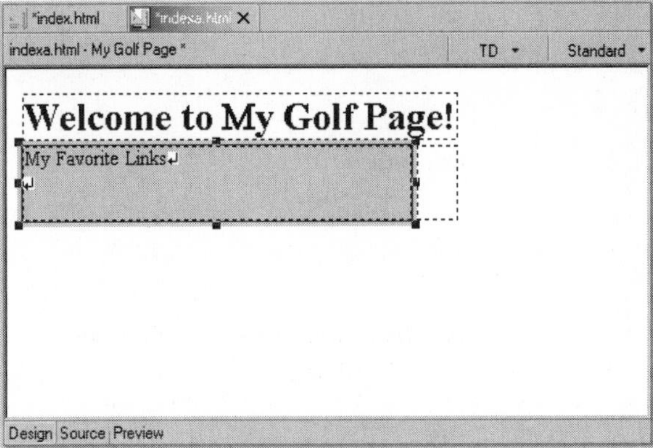

Figure 6.5 Text in HTML.

Using the Anchor Tag

Anchor tags can be entered by hand or generated with WSAD. After you have made your first anchor tag, you will see the HTML code needed for this tag. Creating links in WSAD is very easy when the Link wizard is used. You will add some links to the column on the left side of the Web page. Add a link to the USGA with the following steps:

1. Make sure you are on the Design page, and select the empty cell in the bottom left of the table.
2. Place the cursor at the bottom of the row below the last line break <BR> shown by the symbol.
3. From the menubar, click Insert > Link, and the wizard displays, as seen in Figure 6.6.

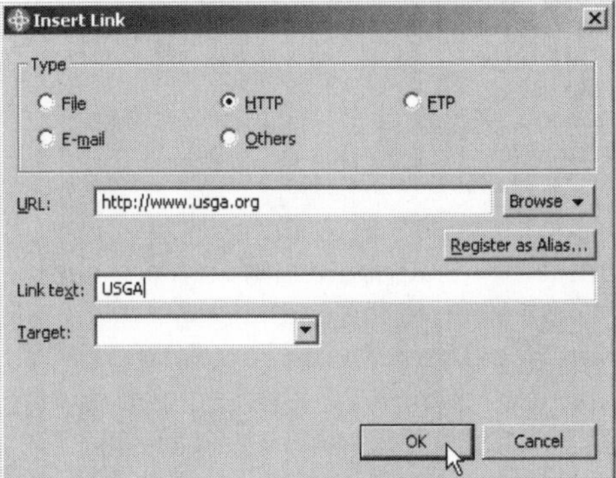

Figure 6.6 Insert Link wizard.

4. Select HTTP for the Type.
5. Enter **http://www.usga.org** as the link address.
6. Enter **USGA** as the Link text.
7. You do not need to specify the target. The response will return to the same window.
8. Click the OK button to create the link, and the Design page should look as shown in Figure 6.7.
9. Change to the Source tab, and format the code from the pop-up menu. Select Format > Document.

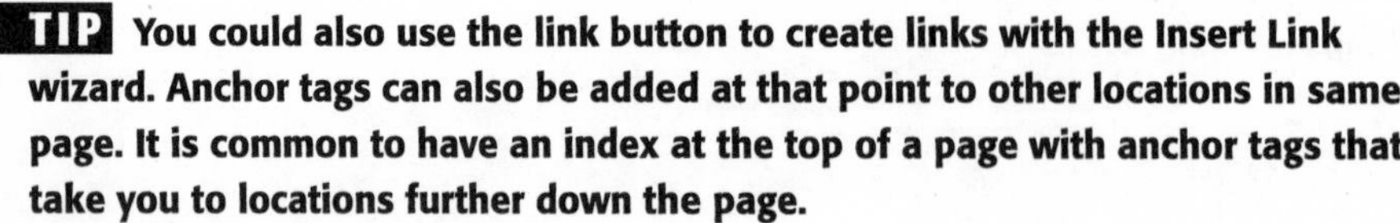

TIP You could also use the link button to create links with the Insert Link wizard. Anchor tags can also be added at that point to other locations in same page. It is common to have an index at the top of a page with anchor tags that take you to locations further down the page.

The text and the link are now in the Web page. The affected code should look as follows:

```
<TABLE>
    <TBODY>
        <TR>
            <TD nowrap colspan="2">
            <H1>Welcome to My Golf Page!</H1>
            </TD>
        </TR>
        <TR>
            <TD nowrap valign="top" align="left" bgcolor="#cccccc">
My Favorite Links<BR>
            <BR>
            <A href="http://www.usga.org/Index.html">USGA</A></TD>
            <TD></TD>
        </TR>
    </TBODY>
</TABLE>
</BODY>
```

The anchor tag has two key aspects. First the `href` attribute is where you set the URL where the link goes. Second, anything placed before the end tag, </A>, will be active for the link. Text or graphics are commonly put before the end tag. You can build a Web page with text links, then go back later and change the text to graphics for a more polished look.

Figure 6.7 Link added.

The Web page needs a few more helpful links. You can use the Link Smart Guide to add these links, or you can edit the HTML source code. Place a blank link between each link with an extra <BR> tag. Add the following links:

LINK URL	LABEL
http://www.weather.com	The Weather
http://www.mapquest.com	Travel Maps

The affected part of the HTML code should look as follows:

```
<TABLE>
    <TBODY>
        <TR>
            <TD nowrap colspan="2">
            <H1>Welcome to My Golf Page!</H1>
            </TD>
        </TR>
        <TR>
            <TD nowrap valign="top" align="left" bgcolor="#cccccc">
My Favorite Links<BR>
            <BR>
            <A href="http://www.usga.org/index.html">USGA</A><BR>
            <BR>
            <A href="http://www.weather.com">The Weather</A><BR>
            <BR>
            <A href="http://www.mapquest.com">Travel Maps</A></TD>
            <TD></TD>
        </TR>
    </TBODY>
</TABLE>
</BODY>
```

Testing Links

Testing the links on a Web page before deploying them for use is always a good idea. It's very easy to make a simple typing error on the link URL that would make the link invalid, or possibly link it to an incorrect URL. Both of these situations would be very bad for the end user because there is usually no way to navigate to the intended feature. Maintaining links is critical to any Web site.

Two types of links are used for testing: internal links and external links. Internal links are those that are local to your machine. Internal testing can help catch links errors before you deploy your files to a server. External links are dependent on resources not on your machine. They link to a resource on local area network (LAN), on an intranet, or on the World Wide Web. Either of these types of links can be full URLs or partial relative URLs. A fully qualified URL includes the protocol, host, and full path for the resource, such as http://my.yahoo.com/mypage.html. A relative URL can be used for resources common to the Web application and usually omits the protocol and host, such as /mypage.html. Internal links are easier to test and resolve using the WSAD test server. You need to be connected to the LAN, intranet, or World Wide Web to test external links.

Let's test the links on the Web page. You must be connected to the World Wide Web to test these links because they point to external URLs. You can flip to the Preview tab and try the USGA (United States Golf Association) link. The WSAD should resolve the link, as shown in Figure 6.8.

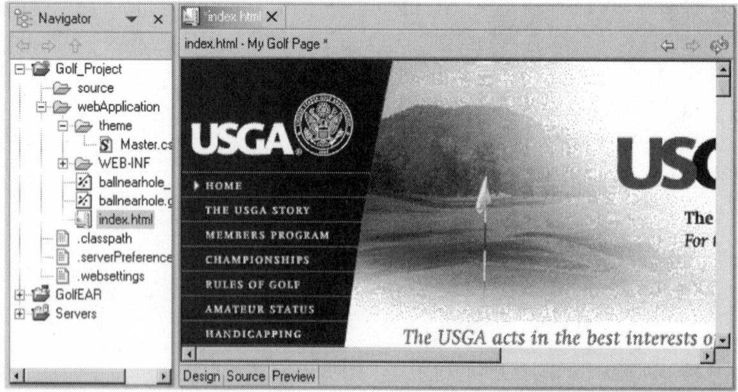

Figure 6.8 Running links.

Building an HTML Form

All the content on the Web page so far has been focused on passing information to the user. In this section, you will learn how to add components that allow the passing of data to the server. In order to pass data to the server, you need to add another tag to the Web page. You will use the HTML <FORM> tag along with <INPUT> tags to pass data to the server.

The <FORM> tag marks an area on the Web page that can have <INPUT> tags to send data to a server. You can add the <FORM> tag and </FORM> tag to the appropriate locations in the HTML code, or you can use WSAD designer to generate the tags. The <FORM> tags do not need to cover the entire Web page. For this page, the <FORM> tags will cover the main body section of the page, as shown in Figure 6.9.

Adding <FORM> Tags

The Golf Web page will have a form for calculating a Golf handicap, which is the number above average that a player usually scores. There are a few different ways to calculate a handicap. For this example, the users will enter their last five scores.

The <FORM> tags are invisible at run time and can be difficult to place in an HTML file. Before you add the <FORM> tags, you will add a title for the form. Add the title and form with the following steps:

1. From the Design tab, select the main body section in the table, as shown in Figure 6.10.
2. Enter **Handicap Calculator**, and press the Enter key, which inserts a <BR> tag.

3. Click the Insert Form button to add a <FORM> to the page. Instead you can select the menu items Insert > Form and Input Fields > Form.

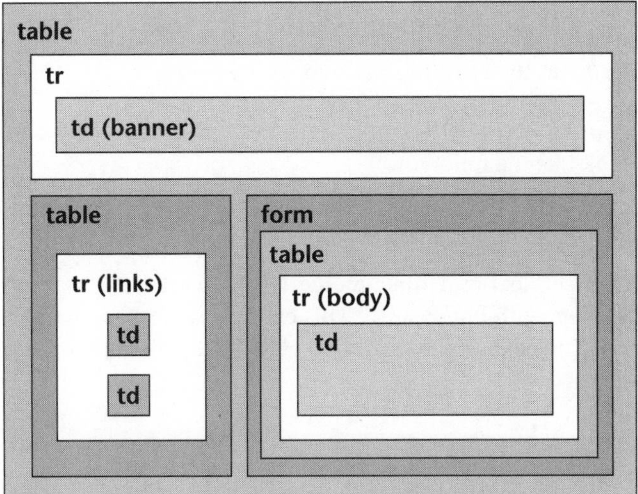

Figure 6.9 Form placement.

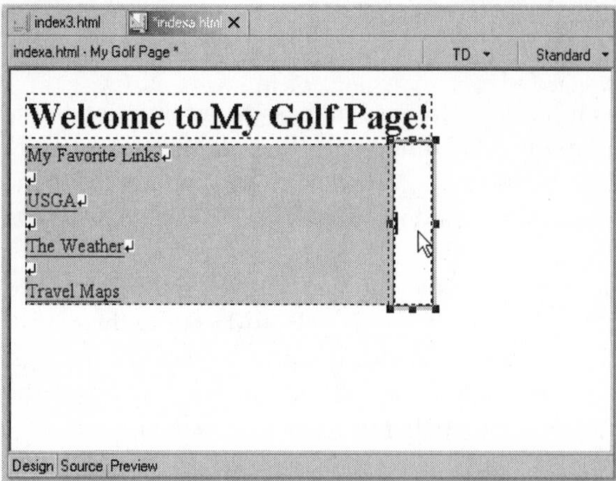

Figure 6.10 Selecting the main body section.

WSAD generates the <FORM> and </FROM> tags in the correct location, and you should see a faint black outline box for the form in the Design editor. This outline is only for development use, and you will not see this box in the Preview tab. If you make a mistake and place the <FORM> tag in the wrong location, you can press Ctrl-Z to undo the change, or change to the Source and remove the tags from the code. It is a lot easier to use the undo function.

The <FORM> tag needs to be linked to the server. The `action` and the `method` attributes need to be set for the <FORM> tag. The `action` attribute references a server resource, which is usually a servlet. For this application, you will use the `GolfAVG` servlet. The *method* attribute is the method that is called in the servlet. For this application, you will call the `doPost` method, so the method value is `post`. Add the action and method attributes to the <FORM> tag with the following steps:

1. Select the Source tab and locate the <FORM> tag.
2. Edit the <FORM> tag and add the attribute **`action = "GolfAVG"`**.
3. Edit the <FORM> tag and add the attribute **`method = "post"`**.
4. Press Ctrl-S to save the changes.

The <FORM> tag should look like the following:

```
<FORM action="/GolfAVG" method="post">
```

There is more discussion on servlets and their methods in Chapter 9, "Making Servlets" and Chapter 10, "Servlets with JavaBeans." This chapter is focused on completing the Web page and form. The next step is to add an HTML table to the form.

Imbedding a Table

The HTML table is a great way to manage the alignment of input components in a form. The table automatically aligns text, input fields, and buttons so that they look good on different browsers on different computers with different screen resolutions. Web pages can have a couple of levels of table nesting to achieve the desired formatting. First, you create the nested table, and then you set its headings and attributes.

Creating a Nested Table

Let's make a nested HTML table inside the HTML form. Add a table to the form with the following steps:

1. From the Design tab, select the form on the Web page, as seen in Figure 6.11.

2. Click the Insert Table button, or you can select the menu item Insert > Table.
3. The Insert Table window displays. This window allows you to set the number of rows and columns for the table. Change the number of rows to **7,** as shown in Figure 6.12.
4. Click the OK button to generate all the tags for the table.

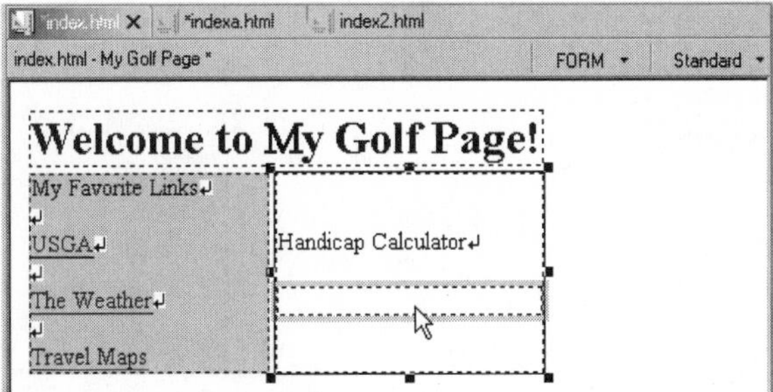

Figure 6.11 Select a form.

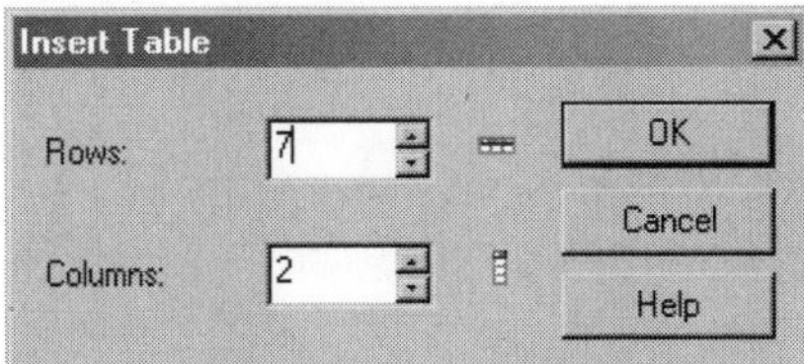

Figure 6.12 Insert a table.

You have added a lot of code to the HTML page. The following HTML code shows the <FORM> tag along with all the rows and columns added to the table:

```
<BODY>
<TABLE>
    <TBODY>
        <TR>
            <TD nowrap colspan="2">
            <H1>Welcome to My Golf Page!</H1>
            </TD>
        </TR>
        <TR>
            <TD nowrap valign="top" align="left" bgcolor="#cccccc">
My Favorite Links<BR>
            <BR>
            <A href="http://www.usga.org/index.html">USGA</A><BR>
            <BR>
            <A href="http://www.weather.com">The Weather</A><BR>
            <BR>
            <A href="http://www.mapquest.com">Travel Maps</A></TD>
            <TD>Handicap Calculator<BR>
            <FORM action="/GolfAVG" method="post">
            <TABLE border="1">
                <TBODY>
                    <TR>
                        <TD></TD>
                        <TD></TD>
                    </TR>
                    <TR>
                        <TD></TD>
                        <TD></TD>
                    </TR>
                    <TR>
                        <TD></TD>
                        <TD></TD>
                    </TR>
                    <TR>
                        <TD></TD>
                        <TD></TD>
                    </TR>
                    <TR>
                        <TD></TD>
                        <TD></TD>
                    </TR>
                    <TR>
                        <TD></TD>
                        <TD></TD>
                    </TR>
```

```
                        <TR>
                            <TD></TD>
                            <TD></TD>
                        </TR>
                    </TBODY>
                </TABLE>
                </FORM>
                </TD>
            </TR>
        </TBODY>
    </TABLE>
</BODY>
```

Modifying Table Headings

This table will be used to enter golf scores. The golf scores will be sent to a server to calculate the average. You will put a heading in the first row of the table. You could simply enter text in the first row, but there is a special tag for headings that we can use. Make the heading with the following steps:

1. Place the mouse over the top-right cell in the new table and double-click the mouse. The Table Attributes editor opens, as seen in Figure 6.13.
2. Select the Cell type **Header cell** radio button.
3. Uncheck **Wrap lines automatically**.
4. Click the OK button to save these changes.
5. Now, enter **Scores** in the header cell.

The code for the header uses the <TH> tag for the table heading. The table heading is automatically centered and bold, unless you change this behavior in the .css file. If you change to the Source tab, you will see the following code for the header that you just completed.

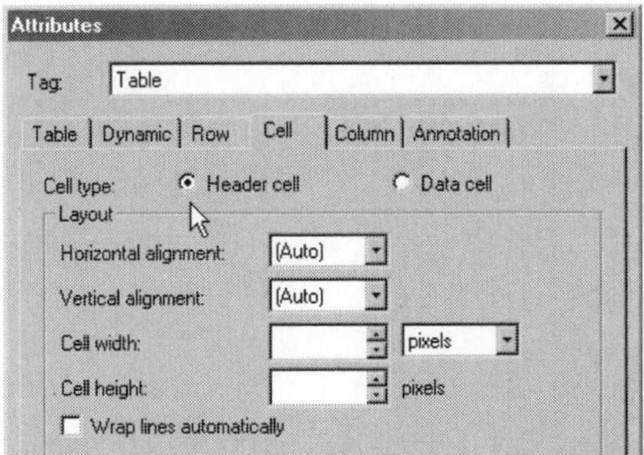

Figure 6.13 Setting cell headings.

```
<FORM action="/GolfAVG" method="post">
 <TABLE border="1">
     <TBODY>
         <TR>
             <TD></TD>
             <TH nowrap>Score</TH>
         </TR>
```

Adding Text

Adding text for the input fields is the easiest step in building a form. This page will average the scores from five rounds of golf. Enter the following text for the table in the indicated cells:

TABLE LOCATION	TEXT TO ADD
Row 2 Column 1	Round1:
Row 3 Column 1	Round2:
Row 4 Column 1	Round3:
Row 5 Column 1	Round4:
Row 6 Column 1	Round5:

The Web page is getting better. The new table with the labels should look like Figure 6.14, as seen from the Design tab. The next step is to add the text fields.

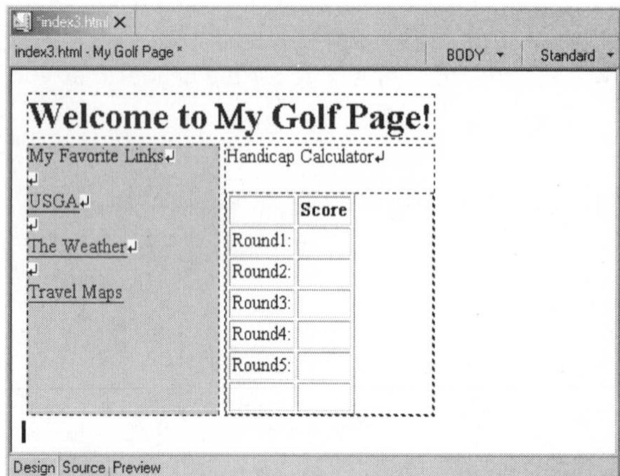

Figure 6.14 Table text.

Input Tags

Many different input tags can be used in a form. By using the appropriate input, you will make Web page much easier to use. Table 6.1 shows the basic input tags.

Each of the input types shown in Table 6.1 uses name/value pairs to pass data to the server. Initially, you will use the test field and the Submit button. Additional components can be used for input like the <TEXTAREA> and the various <SELECT> types.

Text Fields

Text fields are very common in user interfaces. Typically, filling out a Web form requires the user to enter his or her name, email, or other information. For this web form you need five text fields to enter the golf scores. Add text fields with the following steps:

1. From the Design Editor, select the empty cell to the right of Round1.

2. Click on the Insert Text Field button, or else you could select the menu items Insert > Form and Input Fields > Text Field. The Text Field Attribute Editor appears, as shown in Figure 6.15.
3. Each textfield needs a unique name. Set the name to **round1**.
4. Golf scores range from 65 to 120, so there is no reason to enter numbers greater than three digits. Set the Columns to 3 and the Maximum Length to 3.
5. Click the OK button to save the changes.

NOTE Tag names are case sensitive. Be very careful when assigning names to input fields. It is better to use short, lowercase descriptive names. These names need to be read by the server code to get the values that they hold.

Table 6.1 Input Tags

INPUT TAG	USED WHEN
Submit	Buttons that the user will click to pass the data to the server.
Text	Input fields are used to enter text.
Radio	There is a list of options where the user can pick only one of the options.
Checkbox	There is an option or list of options where the user can pick any or all of the options.

6. Repeat these steps and add textfields for Round2 through Round5. Set their names and sizes correspondingly. When you finish, the HTML code should look as follows:

```
<FORM action="/GolfAVG" method="post">
<TABLE border="1">
    <TBODY>
        <TR>
            <TD></TD>
            <TH nowrap>Score</TH>
        </TR>
        <TR>
            <TD>Round1:</TD>
            <TD><INPUT size="3" type="text" maxlength="3"
                 name="round1"></TD>
        </TR>
        <TR>
            <TD>Round2:</TD>
            <TD><INPUT size="3" type="text" maxlength="3"
                 name="round2"></TD>
        </TR>
        <TR>
            <TD>Round3:</TD>
            <TD><INPUT size="3" type="text" maxlength="3"
                name="round3"></TD>
        </TR>
        <TR>
            <TD>Round4:</TD>
            <TD><INPUT size="3" type="text" maxlength="3"
                  name="round4"></TD>
        </TR>
        <TR>
            <TD>Round5:</TD>
            <TD><INPUT size="3" type="text" maxlength="3"
                 name="round5"></TD>
        </TR>
        <TR>
            <TD></TD>
            <TD></TD>
        </TR>
    </TBODY>
</TABLE>
</FORM>
```

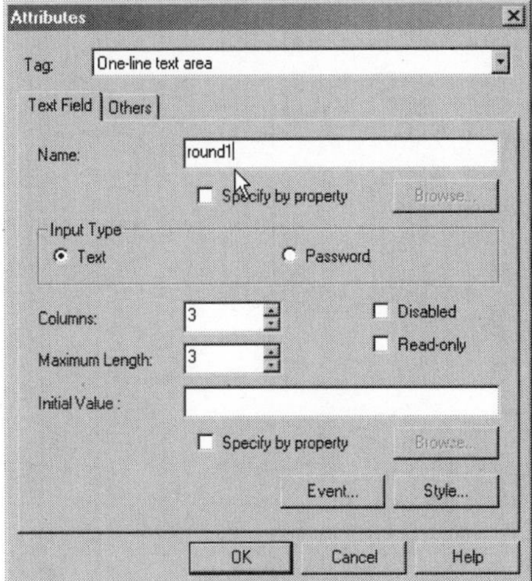

Figure 6.15 Textfield attributes.

WSAD generates all the <INPUT> tags and the necessary attributes for the tags. Everything is indented correctly. Now that all the input fields are on the form, you can add the buttons.

Buttons

Buttons are common in user interfaces for executing commands. HTML input types Submit and Reset make buttons that can be used on a form. There is a default gray system button that is very easy to use, or you can use a graphic button. Commonly, a Web page is prototyped with the simple gray buttons, then graphic buttons are added later.

You will use a Reset button and a Submit button on this Web page. The Reset button automatically clears all the fields on the form. The Submit button calls the URL identified in the <FORM> tag. The HTML form needs a Submit button to pass the data to the server. Add the necessary buttons to the Web page with the following steps:

1. From the Design editor, select the bottom-right cell in the table with the input fields.
2. Click the Insert Submit button, or instead select the menu items Insert > Form and Input Fields > Submit Button. The Button Attributes window appears, as shown in Figure 6.16.
3. Enter **submit** for the Name.
4. Enter **Calculate** for the Label.
5. Click the OK button to generate the HTML code for the Calculate button.
6. Select the bottom-left cell in the table, and add a Reset button named **reset** with a **Reset** label.

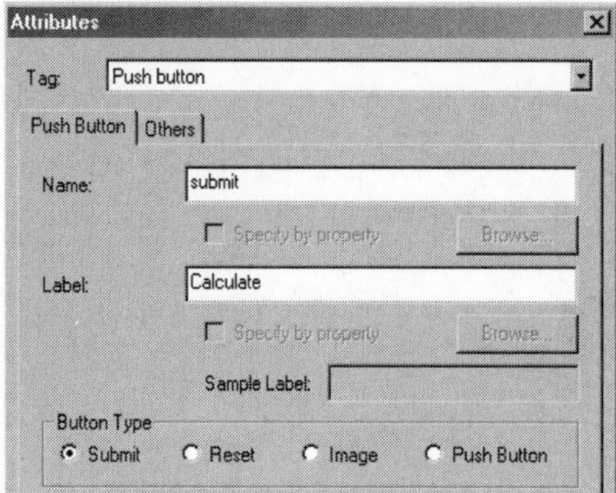

Figure 6.16 Submit button attributes.

After the buttons are added to the Web page, it should look like Figure 6.17. The Web page has all the user interface components for this application. Let's look at the HTML code needed for the buttons. If you change to the Source tab, you will see the following affect code segment for the form:

```
<FORM action="/GolfAVG" method="post">
<TABLE border="1">
    <TBODY>
        <TR>
            <TD></TD>
            <TH nowrap>Score</TH>
        </TR>
        <TR>
            <TD>Round1:</TD>
            <TD><INPUT size="3" type="text" maxlength="3"
                 name="round1"></TD>
        </TR>
        <TR>
            <TD>Round2:</TD>
            <TD><INPUT size="3" type="text" maxlength="3"
                 name="round2"></TD>
        </TR>
        <TR>
            <TD>Round3:</TD>
            <TD><INPUT size="3" type="text" maxlength="3"
                 name="round3"></TD>
        </TR>
        <TR>
            <TD>Round4:</TD>
            <TD><INPUT size="3" type="text" maxlength="3"
                 name="round4"></TD>
        </TR>
        <TR>
            <TD>Round5:</TD>
```

```
            <TD><INPUT size="3" type="text" maxlength="3"
                name="round5"></TD>
        </TR>
        <TR>
            <TD><INPUT type="reset" name="reset" value="Reset"></TD>
            <TD><INPUT type="submit" name="submit"
value="Calculate"></TD>
        </TR>
    </TBODY>
</TABLE>
</FORM>
```

Comment Tags

You should add comments to your HTML just as you do in your code. The HTML comment tag is a lot different from Java comments and any other HTML tags. The start of a comment is <!— and the end comment tag is —>. Everything between the begin and the end tag is ignored by the browser, but remember that the end user can see these comments using the View > Source command in the browser.

Usually, it is helpful to place a comment describing an important block of code. It is also helpful to comment data values that you would have to look up, such as the light gray background #cccccc. When you see the value cccccc, it is difficult to know if it is red, or teal, or some other color. The color value cccccc is a medium gray. For this application, it would be good to comment the intention for the main <FORM> tag. Add the following comment line before the <FORM> tag:

```
<!— Form to capture socres for handicap calculator —>
```

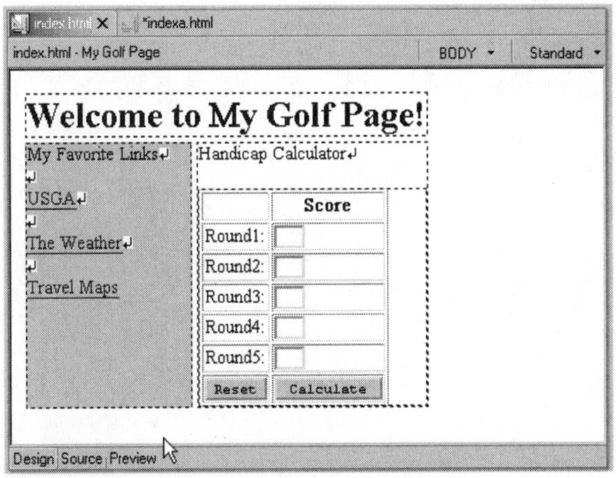

Figure 6.17 HTML buttons.

Summary

In this chapter, you learned more about HTML and static Web page design. You used a number of editors in WSAD and also directly edited HML code. The key concepts covered in this chapter were the following:

- Adding rows and columns to tables
- Adding anchors and links to a Web page
- Setting cell attributes
- Adding forms so that you can pass data to a server
- Imbedding tables
- Using various input fields
- Making HTML comments

This chapter covered how to create the components needed to pass data to the server. In Chapter 10, "Servlets with JavaBeans," you learn how to capture and use this data with J2EE servlets. The basic input tags on an HTML form provide the basis for entering data in a J2EE Web application. There are other user input tags that can improve usability that were not covered in this chapter.

Additional cosmetic refinements can also be added to this page. These changes are covered later in Chapter 14, "Making Slick Web Pages." Chapter 7, "Making JavaBeans," covers developing JavaBeans, another J2EE API. In the J2EE architecture, JavaBeans act as the model and hold the data for the application.

Making JavaBeans

What's in Chapter 7?

You have completed a basic Web page with HTML for the user interface. The tools in WSAD made the development somewhat easy. In this chapter, you will learn about JavaBeans, another J2EE API. You will learn about the different JavaBean features and how to build one using WSAD. You will write some simple Java code for the JavaBean to perform business logic. This chapter covers the following topics:

- JavaBeans basics
  - Properties
  - Methods
  - Events
- Bean types
- Java requirements
  - Introspection
  - Customization
  - Property editors
  - JAR files
- Building JavaBeans in WSAD

Now that you have completed a simple Web application, it's time to look at another Java API. To start J2EE server-side programming, you need to understand JavaBeans. This will help you design and implement good applications and build on what you have already learned. You will learn how to create JavaBeans that you can use in J2EE applications.

JavaBeans Basics

The notion of JavaBeans was introduced in JDK V1.1 to bring some uniformity to Java development. End users of a program using JavaBeans neither know nor have to care that JavaBeans were used. JavaBeans were introduced primarily to assist Java developers by defining a set of conventions to follow when developing classes. There were many changes in JDK V1.1 to support JavaBeans.

The entire AWT (Abstract Window Toolkit) GUI class library was updated to support JavaBeans, including the V1.1 event model. The JFC (Java Foundation Classes) GUI classes were added in JDK 1.2 to give greater functions for GUI interfaces. Because AWT and JFC implement methods supporting the JavaBeans event model, all AWT-based classes inherit these special functions, which support the notification, or messaging, framework in the AWT class library. Implementation of a notification framework enables beans to notify, or send messages to, other beans.

What Are JavaBeans?

JavaBeans are Java classes that conform to the JavaBeans conventions. There are two key requirements for a JavaBean as defined in the specification:

1. A JavaBean should have a default no argument constructor that provides a common way to instantiate it. For example, the `Car` class should have a `Car()` constructor.
2. A JavaBean should be serializable, that is, provide a mechanism to save its data.

JavaBean must also follow a number of conventions. These conventions cover the data for the class known as `properties`, the behavior for the class known as `methods`, and the states of a class known as `events`. The JavaBeans specification describes the standard conventions that should be followed when using properties, methods, and events. These three aspects of a JavaBean are covered in the following sections.

Properties, methods, and events need an access qualifier to follow the conventions. The Java access rules are discussed in the next section.

Access Rules

Access, or visibility, defines who can access or get a reference to information. Java has the same access modifiers for methods and fields as C++. These are part of the Java language, and they are as follows:

- **`Private`** — Access is limited to the class.
- **`Protected`** — Access is limited to the class, all of its subclasses, and all the classes in the same package.
- **`Public`** — Access is not limited.

The following code for the `User` class shows a very common usage of the `public`, `private`, and `protected` access modifiers:

```
public class User {
    private String name;
    protected String id;
}
```

Java allows another type of access when you do not specify an access modifier for the method or variable. This access, called default access, is a very loose level of access control because it is implied. Default access allows any class in the package to have access to the method or variable. You should not rely on default access. Good Java programs have the access modifiers explicitly in the code.

Properties

Properties are the data holders for a JavaBean. They are class fields that support public access so that the field data can be called from other objects. Properties have a field and accessor methods. The field has an access modifier, a type, and a name.

Property Types

JavaBean properties need to have a specific Java type. It can be a primitive type like `int`, `boolean`, and `float`, or it can be one of the common Java classes like `String`, `Vector`, and `Hashtable`. As you develop JavaBeans, you will start to use your own JavaBeans as property types, like Address, Contact, and User.

Property Accessors

JavaBean properties have accessor methods, commonly referred to as getters and setters. You should always use these accessor methods to get or set the values of properties. The following code shows you a sample getter and setter method. Later in this chapter, you will learn how to generate the accessor methods in WSAD.

```
public class User {
    private String name;
    protected String id;
    public String getName(){
        return name;
    }
    public void setName(String newName){
```

```
            name = newName;
        }
    }
```

Special Properties

Properties are designed to be flexible data holders. They are designed this way so that all data holders can be properties and conform to the JavaBean property conventions. To accommodate this capability, there are additional property types and special behaviors that can be added to properties, which are discussed in the following sections.

Indexed Properties

Properties can be associated in a group or list. These group types are called *indexed* properties and are defined as Java arrays. Indexed properties are a little tricky to work with because the accessor methods need additional code to handle arrays. An indexed property needs two accessor methods; one gives access to the array, and the other provides access to the individual elements in the array. The following code sample shows a simple TestBean class that has a `phones` property to hold a list of phone numbers as an indexed property:

```
class TestBean {
    private String[] fieldPhones = null;
/**
 * TestBean constructor comment
 */
public TestBean() {
    super();
}
/**
 * Gets the phones property (String[]) value
 * @return The phones property value
 * @see #setPhones
 */
public String[] getPhones() {
    return fieldPhones;
}
/**
 * Gets the phones index property (String) value
 * @return The phones property value.
 * @param index The index value into the property array.
 * @see #setPhones
 */
public String getPhones(int index) {
    return getPhones()[index];
}
/**
 * Sets the phones property (String[]) value
```

```
     * @param phones The new value for the property
     * @see #getPhones
     */
    public void setPhones(String[] phones) {
        fieldPhones = phones;
    }
    /**
     * Sets the phones index property (String[]) value
     * @param index The index value into the property array
     * @param phones The new value for the property
     * @see #getPhones
     */
    public void setPhones(int index, String phones) {
        fieldPhones[index] = phones;
    }
```

As you can see from the code, indexed properties are similar to simple properties in many ways. There is a setter and getter for the phones property, and also a setter and getter for the phones index that has an additional parameter for the index. The setter and getter for the indexes could have try/catch blocks to handle errors, because it is very easy to get an array out of bounds error when using indexed properties.

Indexed properties were introduced back in JDK 1.1 before the additional Java collection classes were added. It is more common and easier to use classes like a `Hashtable`, `Vector`, or `Enumeration`. The indexed properties imply a required, or fixed, order for the data that they hold, and in many cases this is inconvenient for accessing items in the index. Also, an array is a fixed Java type and can only hold items of that type. The only way around this limitation is to always use `Object[]` arrays. It is good to know about indexed properties, but for these reasons their usage is not very common.

Bound Properties

Bound properties are special properties that signal an event whenever they change. Properties should be changed by calling their setter method, so Bound properties should signal the `propertyChangeEvent` in the setter method. The `property ChangeEvent` takes three parameters, a String name, the old value, and the new value. The following code example shows how the set name method would be changed to fire the `propertyChangeEvent`:

```
    public void setName(String name) {
        String oldValue = fieldName;
        fieldName = name;
        firePropertyChange("name", oldValue, name);
    }
```

Bound properties fire Java Events, and these are described in greater detail in the "Events" section. Events are part of the JavaBeans specification, so bound properties follow these conventions. The events will always fire, if there are any event listeners, they will be triggered by the event.

Constrained Properties

Constrained properties are similar to bound properties in that they also signal an event whenever they change properties, but constrained properties fire the `property ChangeEvent` before the property is changed. The following code sample shows how the `setName()` method would be changed to be constrained:

```
public void setName(String vane) throws java.beans.PropertyVetoException
{
    fireVetoableChange("eventid", fieldName, name);
    fieldName = Name;
}
```

You can see in the code that a constrained property fires a `Vetoable` Event. A `Vetoable` Event does not change if the listeners veto the change. The Event is fired before the property is changed. This type of Event is very rarely used, but it is part of the JavaBeans specification.

The classic example for a constrained property is the numeric-only textfield. When keys are pressed there is a listener for the key events. If the keys are not numeric, then the property change is vetoed. This behavior is easier to implement by subclassing a `TextField` and handling key Events. This technique is simpler than managing `Vetoable` Events.

Combined Properties

These different property conventions are not mutually exclusive. You can make various combinations such as a bound and constrained property.

Methods

Methods are the actions or functions that a Java class can perform. These are the `public` methods that can be called by other classes. This excludes the `private` and `protected` methods in a class. A JavaBean may have `private` or `protected` methods, but these methods are not visible to other Java classes. Only the `public` methods are considered part of the JavaBean interface.

By convention method names should start with a lowercase character. Method names should be verbs expressing an action such as save or find. Method names can be more descriptive such as `findItemsByKey()` or `saveItemsUsingProfile()`. Thus, you should use descriptive names, but try not to make them look like a paragraph. Method names that are 10 to 30 characters long can be descriptive and still be readable. If the method names are too long, reading the code can be difficult. You should rely on the package name to do some of the description of methods.

JavaBean methods, like other Java methods, need the following:

1. Qualifiers that include `public`.
2. A return type. This can be a primitive, such as `int`, or a class, such as `Customer`. If there is no return type you would use the Java reserved `void`.

3. A method name that conforms to the guidelines already discussed.
4. Optional parameters. The parameters have a Java type and a local name. If there are no parameters you use empty parentheses `( )`.
5. And finally, the method body. This is the code that runs when the method is called and it is enclosed by braces `{ }`.

The following are three different examples of JavaBean methods. The `paint()` method is an action method, the `setGroups()` method is a setter method, and the `getApproved()` method is a getter method:

```
/**
 * Paints a green square
 * @return void
 * @param Graphics
*/
public void paint(Graphics g) {
      g.setColor(Color.green);
      g.fillRect(20,20,20,20);
}
/**
 * Sets the approvedComplete property (java.lang.String) value
 * @return void
 * @param Hastable for the new groups
/
public void setGroups(java.util.Hashtable newGroups) {
    groups = newGroups;
}
/**
 * Gets the approved property (java.lang.String) value
 * @return The approved property value
 * @see #setApproved
 */
public java.lang.String getApproved() {
    if (approved == null){
      setApproved(Integer.toString(Integer.parseInt(getApproval()));
    }
    return approved;
}
```

Events

Events generally indicate that a component in a program has reached a certain state or that a certain externally generated action has taken place. Events usually happen at an unpredictable moment in time. It is not necessary for the program to wait for the event to occur. However, when the event occurs, the program should be notified and respond appropriately.

You should not confuse events with Java Exceptions, even though on the surface they appear quite similar. Exceptions have a completely different execution path and occur as the result of an error. Once an exception is thrown, the calling stack of the program is unwound until some component handles the exception in a catch block, or the program abnormally terminates. In contrast, if an event is signaled and no component is listening for it, nothing happens.

Types of Events

Events are raised or signaled by one class, and another class can listen for these events. This is a key mechanism by which the user interface calls or communicates with the business logic of an application. Events are Java classes and they have a distinct type.

There are a number of events that are very common to computer operations that deal with user input from the keyboard or mouse. The following are some examples of these events that Java classes signal:

`key`	When a key is pressed
`mouse`	When the mouse is clicked or moved
`focus`	When a different item in the user interface is selected
`propertyChange`	When any data changes in a class

Data changes result in a number of events occurring in the system. The following are some examples of these types of events:

`connection`	When a database connection changes
`propertyChange`	When data changes in a class
`servlet`	When a Servlet changes as part of WebSphere

You can create your own events to use in programming with JavaBeans. For example, if you have a bean that represents a disk file, it should raise an end-of-file event to signal that there is no more data to be read. If the bean representing a fuel tank changes state to almost empty, an event should be fired to turn on a light and warn the driver to get fuel.

The Java event model is said to be delegation based. In the delegation model, there are event sources and event listeners. Listeners are responsible for registering their interest in an event with the source of the event. When the event occurs, the source informs all listeners, which can then act on the event according to their own needs.

JavaBeans events happen between classes running in a single JVM (Java Virtual Machine). There are other Java APIs that need to be used if a JavaBean needs to send a message to another JavaBean running in another JVM. This can be a very common requirement for Web applications running on multiple servers, and it can be solved with Enterprise JavaBeans, which we will cover in Chapter 22, "Enterprise JavaBeans," and Chapter 23, "Entity EJBs."

Types of Beans

A single Java class is a JavaBean, but there are different types of JavaBeans, namely GUI beans and invisible beans. For more information, see the "GUI Beans" and "Invisible Beans" sections, which follow. Examples of primitive beans from the Java class library are Button, which is a GUI bean, and date, which is an invisible bean. You can change the settings and default properties of primitive beans in the Java Visual Editor.

Beans can be combined to create composite beans. When you combine two or more invisible beans, you have a composite invisible bean. For example, if you were building the invisible component of a Clock bean, you would combine the Timer and Date invisible beans in a composite invisible bean named Clock. The Clock bean would supply the services you would expect from such a bean, like setting and getting the time and date.

You create a composite GUI bean when you combine a GUI bean with one or more other beans. For example, you can combine an invisible Timer and Alarm JavaBeans with a user interface bean that displays the time and date and has buttons to perform the various clock functions. You could call this bean a `ClockView`, as seen in Figure 7.1. In fact, the clock could have multiple views such as digital, analog, or a combination of both, where the date is shown in digital format and the time, as a traditional clock with hands moving.

GUI Beans

GUI beans are user interface controls in the AWT or JFC class libraries such as Button, TextField, and JFrame. The WSAD Visual Editor generates Java code for GUI beans. GUI beans supplied with the Visual Editor are sometimes called controls or widgets. The terms controls and widgets come about because the higher-level definitions in Java AWT and JFC essentially map to the underlying graphical API for each windowing system running Java. When talking about GUI beans in this book, we will refer to them as beans or controls interchangeably.

GUI beans are subclasses of `Component`, which is an abstract base class in the Java class library. The `Component` class sets the base behavior for user interface controls and for the `Container` class. You can see this inheritance relationship in Figure 7.2.

Figure 7.1 ClockView composite GUI part.

Figure 7.2 Button inheritance hierarchy.

Finding Beans

One of the hardest things to learn when programming in Java is all the different classes that come with the JDK. You may want to search for other JavaBeans in the workspace when you are developing Java programs. Let's try searching for *JApplet* with the following steps:

1. Select the Search button on the toolbar and the Search dialog appears.
2. Press the Java Search tab, as seen in Figure 7.3.
3. Enter **JApplet** in the Search Expression field.
4. Select the Type radio button in the Search For area.
5. Select the Declarations radio button in the Limit To area.
6. Press the Search button to begin the search.

If there are no matches to the search string, a short message *Search (0) matches found* appears in the title bar of the Search panel. This message is a bit subtle, so be careful because you may think WSAD is still searching. Also, take care not to waste time searching the entire workspace for a common class reference. You can always use the Cancel button to end a search that is out of control. Once the Search panel opens, as shown in Figure 7.4, you can view the declaration and methods in the Java JApplet class.

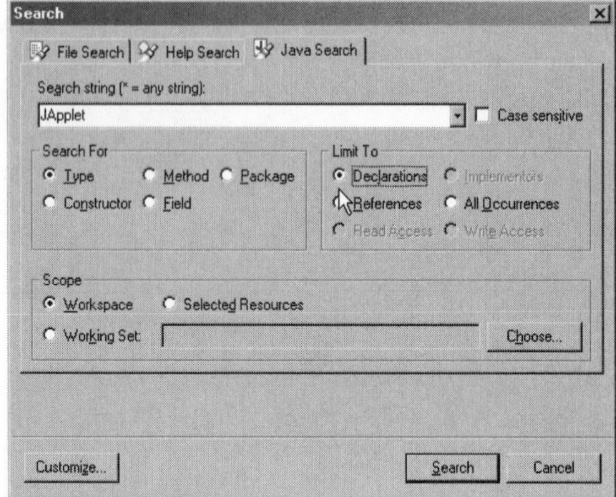

Figure 7.3 Search dialog.

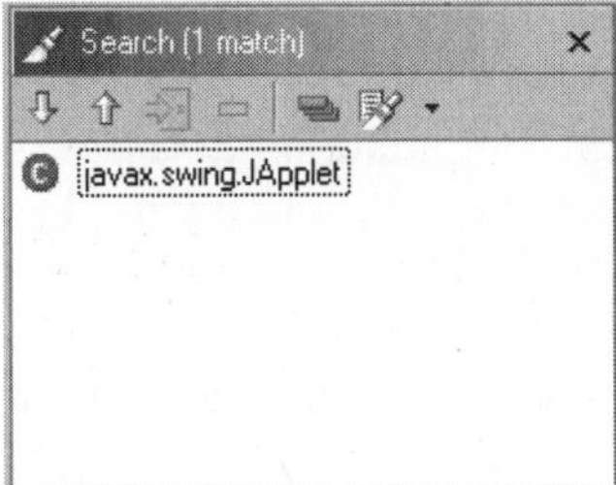

Figure 7.4 Search results.

Frequently, you will be looking for a method or a class that is referenced in many places. When a list is returned from the search, you usually open a view or browser to inspect the class in detail. Open a view for the JApplet by selecting the JApplet in the Search panel, and from its popup menu selecting the Open Type Hierarchy menu item. The Class browser opens; select the Hierarchy tab on the view, and you can see the extensive hierarchy tree, as shown in Figure 7.5.

NOTE **Be careful when searching. You should try to scope the search as much as possible to save time. It is a good idea to look for declarations. Also, there are usually many references in the workspace, and you can scope the search to the project or package to speed things up.**

Now that you have found the JApplet class, you can browse its definition and learn more about the class and its superclasses. If you ever need to find out information about a bean, the search feature in the IDE is a fast way to get to that information. It will also verify whether the class is loaded in the workspace and available for use.

TIP **Search window keeps previous searches. You can run multiple searches and go back to a specific search by using the dropdown box in the Search Expression box. When you select the previous search, it even remembers the other settings like the Search For and Limit To items.**

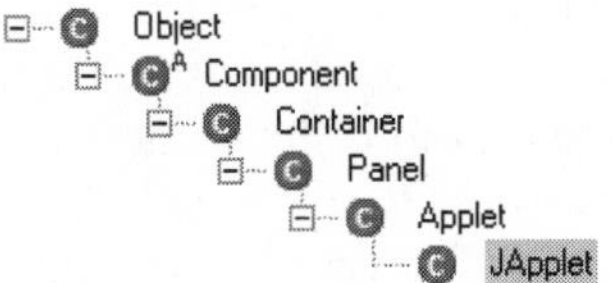

Figure 7.5 JApplet hierarchy.

Invisible Beans

Invisible beans contain business logic, such as mathematical computations, data access functions, and application logic. For Web applications, JavaBeans are primarily used as data holders. They usually have a number of specific properties for that class and a few common methods for retrieving, saving, and validating the JavaBean. You can put business methods in JavaBeans, but frequently companies rely on business logic on a mainframe or code in stored procedures.

The Java classes come with a number of invisible beans that are very helpful in building applications. Most of these beans are designed for general-purpose use, and in many cases, they need to be subclassed to add application-specific functions.

Other JavaBean Requirements

There are a number of JavaBean APIs that are intended for use by Java tool developers. These APIs can also be used by application developers, and they provide some really cool functions. This section covers these JavaBean APIs so that you will be more familiar with what they do and how to use them.

Introspection

Introspection is a pretty fancy term for the JavaBean requirement for a class to be self-describing. The JavaBeans specification provide for the Introspection APIs that give access to all the public information about a class. Introspection is very helpful at development time and can also be used at runtime. It was designed so that Java tool providers can make development tools for developing JavaBeans.

How Introspection Works

Introspection sounds like something magical, but it is works primarily through the JavaBean conventions already discussed in this chapter. The `Introspector` class provided in the JDK has the functions that allow you to access a JavaBean's properties, methods, and events. The `Introspector` class uses the `getBeanInfo()` method, which returns a special class that explicitly describes a JavaBean. The `BeanInfo` class gets the JavaBean features with the `getPropertyDescriptors()`, `getMethodDescriptors()`, and `getEventDescriptors()` methods. Each of these methods returns an array that includes the properties, methods, and events for the JavaBean.

`BeanInfo` classes can contain a lot of other information about a JavaBean's features. There are utility methods that specify the following values:

- Hidden
- Expert
- DisplayName
- ShortDescription

If there is no BeanInfo class, the Introspector class uses the reflection API to get information about the class. Every class has a getClass() method that returns the Class class, which describes the class. The Introspector class can call the Class class and get its methods. The Introspector class then analyzes the methods for those matching the JavaBean conventions for properties, methods, and events. Any getter or setter method implies a property. The other public methods are JavaBean methods. The Introspector class must do this for the class and all of its parent classes to ascertain the JavaBean features.

Customization

The JavaBeans specification requires that JavaBeans can be customized or changed during development. There are a number of Java APIs that permit this customization. These APIs were primarily designed for Java development tool providers.

Property Editors

The JavaBeans specification provides for special property editors to visually edit JavaBean properties. These editors are provided by tool developers and are meant to make it easier to develop JavaBeans. The AWT and JFC classes have a lot of property editors that you can use in WSAD.

The WSAD Java Visual Editor uses property editors extensively. These editors are purely convenience mechanisms that can make it easier to set many properties. The property editors are associated with a certain Java type such as String or Font. When that property used a type, it gets the property editor for that type.

You can create your own property editors for your JavaBeans. If you have an Invoice class with a region property, that takes values of northeast, southeast, central, northwest, and south. You could make a RegionPropertyEditor that only accepts these values during development. Usually custom property editors extend JPanel, and they need to implement the interface PropertyEditor. By implementing the PropertyEditor interface, the custom property editor must implement the following methods:

- addPropertyChangeListener
- removePropertyChangeListener
- getAsText()
- getCustomEditor()
- getJavaInitializationString()
- getTags()
- getValue()
- isPaintable()
- paintValue()
- setAsText()

- setValue()
- supportsCustomEditor()

That's a lot of methods to code, but it is necessary to easily change more complex properties. You can see some good examples of this in the FontEditor and the ColorEditor. These editors make it very easy to set these properties during development. Remember that these classes have no purpose in most applications and should be excluded from the runtime files.

JAR files

Java Archive (JAR) files are defined in the JavaBeans specification to help with deploying Java code at run time. A JAR file is essentially a zip file that includes a manifest file and certain runtime files. It is very common to group similar functions into a JAR for convenience. For example, it would be good to group the database access classes in a common JAR file. JAR files and J2EE packaging is covered in greater depth in Chapter 16, "J2EE Application Deployment." Just keep in mind that JAR files are merely zip files used for Java packaging.

Building JavaBeans

Talking about JavaBeans and building JavaBeans are two different things. You can build JavaBeans by typing Java code or by using the WSAD wizards. In this section, you will use WSAD to build a JavaBean for the Golf Web page. First, you will learn about Java packages.

Java Packages

Packages are Java language elements and represent a logical group of classes that provide related services. Package names make up the directory structure of the classes they contain. Naming conversions are still evolving, but there are many common best practices. The current trend is that package names be in all lowercase alphabetic characters. Usually, when developing commercial packages, the company's Universal Resource Locator (URL) is used to make up the start of the package name. The URL is used backwards; for example, IBM's URL is www.ibm.com, and any package names originating from IBM start with com.ibm.

NOTE There is almost always an exception to the rule, and that goes for naming conventions as well. You may see some old packages COM.ibm.xxx, with COM in uppercase letters. This convention has changed for new packages, starting around October 1997.

You should choose package names carefully, because changing package names later can be time-consuming. As a common convention, the package names follow the convention:

com.companyname.project.packagetype.subtype

There is nothing that prevents you from following this convention, although WSAD warns you with a *Discouraged package name* error. Using uppercase or special characters will only make it difficult to deploy your applications, so it is not worth it to have creative package names. When it comes time to deploy your program, packages can be exported out of the WSAD environment in a single step. You will see these packages become subdirectories on the runtime server.

When you refer to objects and methods, you refer to them by name. This name can be either unqualified or fully qualified, which includes the specific packages that contain the referenced item. Fully qualified names can be very long, so it is common to use unqualified names. When you move a bean to another package, the unqualified names become out of scope. For most of the examples in this book, we use the shorter unqualified names. WSAD will detect if there is a conflict in the code when using these unqualified names.

You need to create packages in WSAD before you start making JavaBeans. If you don't make any packages, the JavaBeans will be placed in the default package, which means that JavaBean classes are not organized in a subdirectory. All classes should be in a package to avoid duplication of classes in another project. For example, there may be two Customer classes, one is for retail customers and one is for commercial customers. The classes can be separated as `com.mycompany.retail.Customer` and `com.mycompany.commercial.Customer`.

WSAD automatically creates a Java Source folder in the Web project to hold the source code for the Web application. This is the location where you create the packages for the classes. Create a the package for this project with the following steps:

1. Select the source subdirectory under the GolfProject.
2. From the pop-up menu, select New > Other....
3. Select Java and Java Package, then press Next.
4. Enter **j2eebook.golf.domain** for the Package, as shown in Figure 7.6.

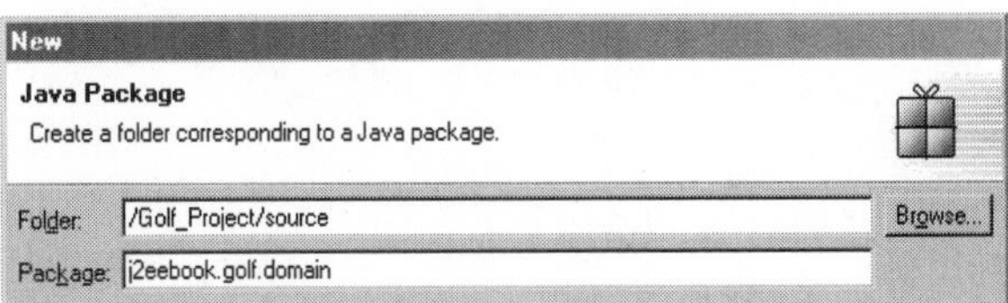

Figure 7.6 New package.

You will see the subdirectories **j2eebook**, **golf,** and **domain**, which WSAD created under the `source` directory, as shown in Figure 7.7. It is common to group JavaBeans in the same subdirectory. Since JavaBeans frequently represent domain objects, it is appropriate to use domain for their package name. Other domain JavaBeans should go in this same package. Other classes with different responsibilities should go in different packages.

Creating a JavaBean

Now that you have a package, you are ready to make a JavaBean. The JavaBean for the Golf Web page needs a number of properties. First, let's make the new class, and then you will add the properties.

1. Select the `domain` package that you just created in the `GolfProject`.
2. From the pop-up menu, select New > Other....
3. Select Java > Java Class, then press Next, and the New Class wizard displays, as seen in Figure 7.8.
4. Enter **GolfData** for the Name.
5. Make sure that the Superclass is `java.lang.Object.` This is the default superclass, but it must be shown in the WSAD wizard.
6. Select the checkbox **Constructors from superclass**. This generates a default no argument constructor for the JavaBean.
7. Press the Finish button to generate the JavaBean.

You can see the code generated for the GolfData JavaBean in the following example:

```
package j2eebook.golf.domain;
public class GolfData {
    /**
     * Constructor for GolfData
     */
    public GolfData() {
        super();
    }
}
```

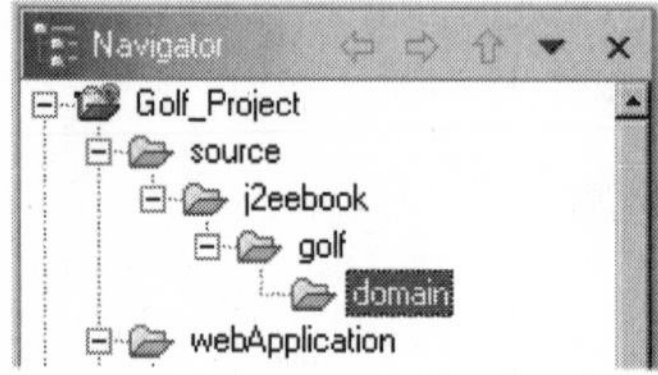

Figure 7.7 Package subdirectories.

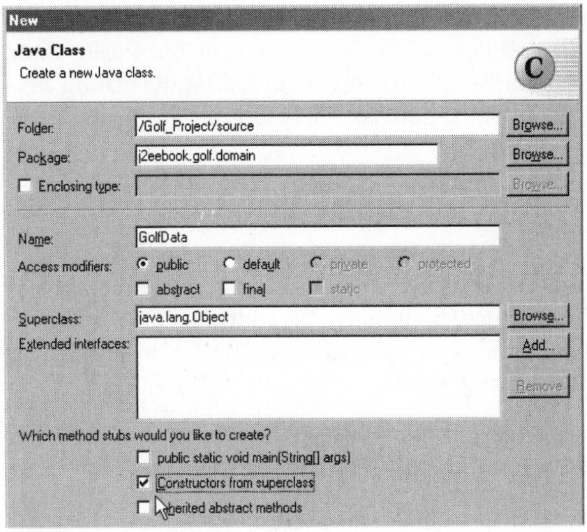

Figure 7.8 New Class wizard.

WSAD generated the package statement, the class declaration, the default constructor, and all the needed braces {} with the proper indenting in the code. Now that you have a class, you can start adding properties.

Making Properties

Once you have a JavaBean, you can add its properties and methods. The GolfData bean needs fields for the user's name as a `String`, an ID as a `String`, a list or `Vector` for the golf scores, and a `boolean` field to indicate that the JavaBean is valid. Add these fields to the code by editing the `GolfData` class. All fields should be private and can be initialized. You need to add an import statement for the Vector. The code should look like the following:

```
package j2eebook.golf.domain;
import java.util.*;

public class GolfData {
private String username;
private String userid;
private Vector scores;
private boolean valid;
    /**
     * Constructor for GolfData
     */
    public GolfData() {
        super();
    }
}
```

Fields are declared at the top of a class before the methods and after the class declaration. Some people always initialize all fields. This is usually safe, but it can waste processor time and memory. There is further discussion about field initialization covered in the section that discusses lazy initialization. For this example, you will not initialize the fields.

Getters and Setters

Since the fields for the properties are private, the properties need accessor methods to get and set the data. You can type the accessor methods in the code or generate them in WSAD. The IDE has a tool to generate the getter or setter for a field. Create accessor methods using the IDE tool with the following steps:

1. Select Perspective > Open > Java, and the Java Perspective displays.
2. Select the username property in the Outline panel.
3. From the pop-up menu, select Generate Getter and Setter.
4. The Generate Getter and Setter window displays, as seen in Figure 7.9. Select all the methods for generation.
5. Click the OK button to generate the code.

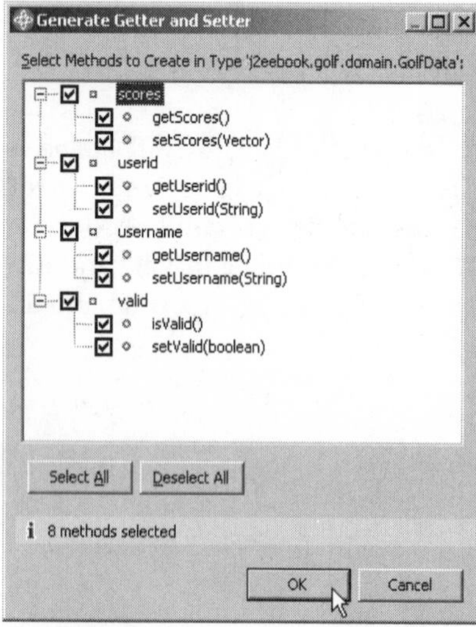

Figure 7.9 Generating accessors.

After the code has been generated for all the properties, the code for the GolfData JavaBean should look like the following:

```
package j2eebook.golf.domain;
import java.util.*;
public class GolfData {

private String username;
private String userid;
private Vector scores;
private boolean valid;

    /**
     * Constructor for GolfData
     */
    public GolfData() {
        super();
    }
    /**
     * Gets the username
     * @return Returns a String
     */
    public String getUsername() {
        return username;
    }
    /**
     * Sets the username
     * @param username The username to set
     */
    public void setUsername(String username) {
        this.username = username;
    }
    /**
     * Gets the userid
     * @return Returns a String
     */
    public String getUserid() {
        return userid;
    }
    /**
     * Sets the userid
     * @param userid The userid to set
     */
    public void setUserid(String userid) {
        this.userid = userid;
    }
```

```
    /**
     * Gets the scores
     * @return Returns a Vector
     */
    public Vector getScores() {
        return scores;
    }
    /**
     * Sets the scores
     * @param scores The scores to set
     */
    public void setScores(Vector scores) {
        this.scores = scores;
    }
    /**
     * Gets the valid
     * @return Returns a boolean
     */
    public boolean getValid() {
        return valid;
    }
    /**
     * Sets the valid
     * @param valid The valid to set
     */
    public void setValid(boolean valid) {
        this.valid = valid;
    }
}
```

It may seem like you are adding unneeded code by having a getter and a setter for each property. But methods are not very costly, and they are easy to make in WSAD. So if you are ever tempted to directly access a field for data, remember to use getter and setter methods instead. It makes the code easier to read and maintain.

Refactoring

The term refactoring is now in widespread use. It is a colorful way to describe reworking code to fix design flaws that you did not have time to fix earlier. Refactoring code usually increases performance, and it is a natural part of good iterative object-oriented development. WSAD uses the term refactor for the simpler, but necessary, tasks of renaming and moving items in the IDE. You can always make these kinds of changes by directly editing the code, the refactor function provides another way to manage your code elements, and sometimes it can be a lot faster when there are extensive changes.

The `valid` property is a boolean property and will most likely be used in `if` statements. The setter method `setValid()` is fine, but the getter method `getValid()` that WSAD generated for the `valid` property should be changed. It is a JavaBean convention to start boolean getter method names with `is` instead of `get`. Rename the `getValid()` method with the following steps:

1. Select the `getValid()` method in the Outline pane.
2. From the pop-up menu on the main menubar, select Refactor > Rename.
3. The Rename window displays, as shown in Figure 7.10. Enter **isValid** for the new name.
4. You could press the Finish button and complete the renaming, but instead press the Next button to see additional functions provided for renaming.
5. The Rename window displays, as shown in Figure 7.11, and it displays references to the method that is being renamed in the Changes to be preformed pane. You can select the method references that you don't want to change. Be careful with this function, because you may not want all references to this method renamed to the new name.
6. You want to change all the references to the `isValid()` method, so press the Finish button to complete the renaming.

The `Refactor/Rename` function is helpful when you need to rename a method and change its references. If you have a fairly unique method or one that is not widely used, you can easily change the method name in the Java Editor. The Refactor function also has the option to pullup a method or move it to a superclass. This is a very common refactoring activity and will improve your code.

Lazy Initialization

At runtime, the JVM places default values in uninitialized primitive fields. For example, an `int` is set to 0. But classes are not initialized, so fields that are classes will return a null if not initialized. You can initialize the fields by running a constructor, but this may be very wasteful. Also, you may not know which constructor to run during initialization.

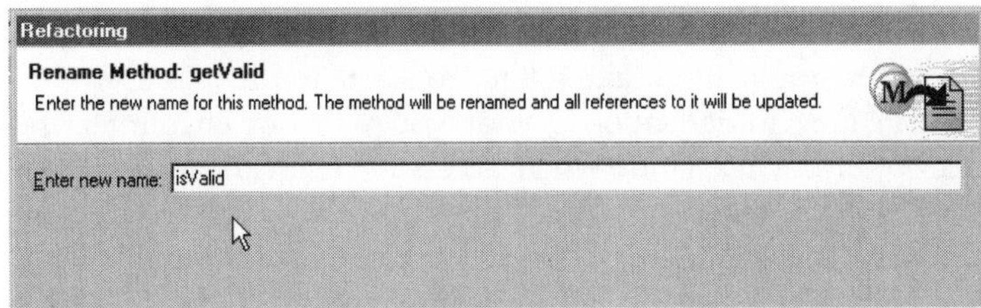

Figure 7.10 Renaming a method.

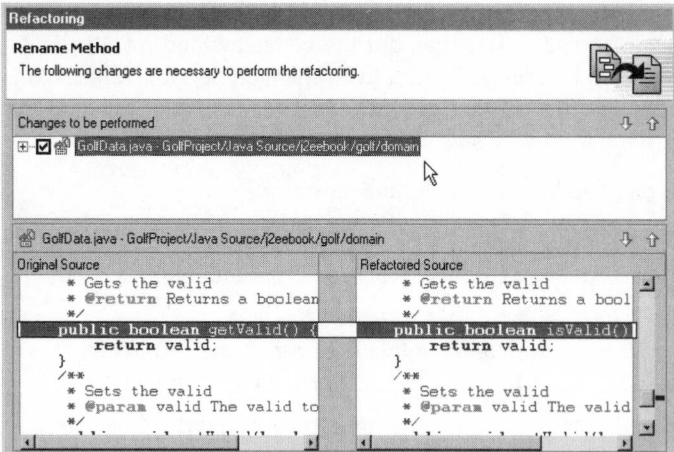

Figure 7.11 Renaming references.

There is a common design pattern for adding lazy initialization to a getter method. By adding a simple `if` statement to the getter, you can change a simple getter so that it always returns a valid Object and not a null reference. The following code sample shows the `if` statement added to the getter method for the username property:

```
/**
 * Gets the username
 * @return Returns a String
 */
public String getUsername() {
    if (username == null){
        username = new String();
    }
    return username;
}
```

Lazy initialization provides a number of benefits. If your application has a number of classes, lazy initialization defers the creation of classes until they are called by a getter method. This improves application startup time and reduces unnecessary overhead. If you don't use lazy initialization, you could instead initialize all fields with the default constructor. This will make the application take longer to start, and it will use more memory. Another benefit to lazy initialization is that you will not encounter the dreaded null pointer exception, at least not when accessing a JavaBean property. It is very common to string Java statements together into a compound statement like `customer.getAddress().getCity()`. The `getCity()` method is invalid if `getAddress()` returns a null pointer. Lazy initialization prevents this type of runtime error.

Making Methods

You already made JavaBean methods when you created the getter and setter methods for the properties. Just like other JavaBean features, methods can be entered in the Java Editor. Any of the public methods in a JavaBean can be accessed by other classes. Remember that methods should start with a lowercase character, and they should be verbs or action words like save or create.

Edit the `isValid()` method to follow the business rules. The GolfData JavaBean is valid if all the properties have values. You can add an `if` statement to the `isValid()` method that tests the `getUsername()`, `getUserid()`, and `getScores()` values. The code for the method should look as follows:

```
/**
 * Tests the bean for valid values
 * @return Returns a boolean
 */
public boolean isValid() {vc
    if (getUsername().length() > 0
        && getUserid().length() > 0
        && !(getScores().isEmpty())) {
        return true;
    } else {
        return false;
    }
}
```

There are a few tools in WSAD that can help generate specialized code. But when it comes to writing business logic, this task is mainly left to the coder and their keyboard. So, all the public methods that you make in the class are JavaBean methods.

Using Events

Events are the most complex of the JavaBean features because they require a number of methods to use. Many of the user interface events are grouped together in the `ActionEvent`. By convention, event classes end with *`Event`* so their purpose is clear. Also, the events use other classes, and the root class name is used for these classes, too. The `ActionEvent` has a corresponding `ActionListener` interface class. When a class implements the `ActionListener`, it must add the `actionPerformed(Event evt)` method.

The following code shows part of the `EventTester` class, which has a button named jButton1. The `EventTester` class implements the `ActionListener` interface, so it has the `actionPerformed(event)` method. The `actionPerformed` method is called when the Submit button is clicked.

```
import javax.swing.*;
import java.awt.event.*;

public class EventTester extends JPanel implements ActionListener {
```

```
    private JButton jButton1 = new JButton("Submit");

    // more code ...

    public void actionPerformed(java.awt.event.ActionEvent evt) {
        if (evt.getSource() == getJButton1()) {
            //then do something...
        }
    }

    // more code ...

    public void initialize() {
        getJButton1().addActionListener(this);
    }
}
```

The `actionPerformed` method is passed an event object that is used to determine the source of the event. The `actionPerformed` method can receive messages from other objects, so the first operation is to have an `if` statement to determine that JButton1 was the source of the click. This is where you place the code for the behavior of the Submit button. You can call methods, set data values, and even fire other events.

In order for the `EventTester` to receive the messages from the JButton, the class must register itself for these events. The `initialize()` method does this work by calling the `addActionListener()` method and passing itself as the `this` parameter. This registration must be run before any events from the JButton can be received. There is also a `removeActionListener()` method that allows you to turn off, or deregister, these events.

When using JavaBean events, you will have many different methods to handle all the different events that occur. You may not care about some events, but when you implement a `Listener` interface, you must implement all the methods defined in the interface. For example, if you use the `MouseListener`, you will have to implement five methods:

- mouseClicked
- mouseEntered
- mouseExited
- mousePressed
- mouseReleased

If you do not have any function for a given event to perform, you merely implement the method with no code between the braces { }.

Custom Events

You may need to design your own Java events for business functions. Say for example, you need to signal if an inventory amount is low. This can be handled by creating an `InventoryLowEvent` and adding the appropriate listener to your code. To create the `InventoryLowEvent`, you can simply extend the existing event framework by subclassing. If you want to make your own events, you will need to implement the following interface and classes:

- Event listener interface
- Event object class
- Event multicaster class

You will also need to define the following methods:

- addInventoryLowListener()
- removeInventoryLowListener()
- fireInventoryLow()

The listeners use the first two methods to add themselves to and remove themselves from the list of interested objects. The bean uses the last method to indicate that the inventory is low.

Summary

This chapter covered the main features of JavaBeans, a key J2EE specification. JavaBeans are an important part of the J2EE model-view-controller architecture. They serve as the data holders for Web applications and the graphical (MVC) user interface classes for client applications. In this chapter, you learned about the following:

- JavaBeans basics—properties, methods, and events
- JavaBean types
- Introspection
- Customization
- Building JavaBeans in WSAD, including creating properties and methods
- Refactoring and renaming elements in WSAD

The Java coding conventions listed in the JavaBeans specification makes it easier to program J2EE applications. By following these conventions, you will be developing standard durable classes in the J2EE architecture. In the next chapter, you will learn how to test JavaBeans using JUnit. Then, you will add to the Web application and learn how to use JavaBeans with servlets.

Unit Testing with JUnit

What's in Chapter 8?

This chapter surveys unit testing using the JUnit plug-in for WSAD. JUnit is a unit-testing technology from the Apache organization. It is not a part of the J2EE standard. We will discuss:

- The philosophy of unit testing
- JUnit background and terminology
- Writing a simple test case
- Several approaches to writing a suite of tests
- The textual and Java Swing versions of the JUnit TestRunner
- Finding and repairing three real problems in the Calculator application

Unit testing is beneficial for identifying coding problems and regression problems early and at the origin, where they are easy to repair. The WSAD JUnit plug-in enables a unit test to be executed through the JUnit framework as if it were a simple application. JUnit test cases are easy to code.

It follows from the previous three assertions that each application logic class should be paired with a unit test class for its lifetime. The test should be run every time the class or a related class changes.

This chapter presents a rationale for these assertions. This leads to a session where we will revisit one of the problems in the buggy Calculator application. Here, you will investigate how JUnit can be used to certify that a feature is working correctly, or to narrow the location of any bug detected.

Unit Testing

There are several classifications of program testing, which range from system integration testing through functional testing down to unit testing—the subject of this chapter. Unit testing involves ensuring code correctness at the most fundamental level. Initial unit testing is done by the programmer who wrote the code. In the past, at best, unit testing merely consisted of a simple exercise of the code. At worst, unit testing was deferred until the code feature was combined with other features. This kind of testing is called functional testing. It is necessary, but good unit testing should precede functional testing.

Praxes

"Praxis" means a rule-of-thumb. We assert the following praxes with respect to unit tests:

- Praxis 1: Every application logic class should be paired with a unit test class.
- Praxis 2: Pairing should be for the life of the test target.
- Praxis 3: Each test should be easy to code and run.
- Praxis 4: Each test should be run after a change to its test target. This should be part of the development and maintenance organizations' processes.

JUnit

Notice that the third praxis—number 3—is an enabler for the other praxes. How do you make each test easy to code and run? The answer is to use a framework. You will use JUnit as the testing framework because it is Java based, it has a WSAD plug-in, and it is freely available under IBM's Common Public License Version 0.6.

A JUnit test case is run under a *TestRunner* provided by the framework. There are variants of the TestRunner that accommodate a choice of a GUIs or a textual user interface.

Failures

A simple assertion call results in a test pass or failure. You anticipate the possibility of the failure by inserting an assertion or fail call. The TestRunner displays failures and errors. You may choose from an assortment of overloaded methods such as `assertEquals()`, `assertNull()`, `assertNotNull()`, `assertFail()`, `assertTrue()`, or `fail()`.

Errors

You now know the meaning of failure. What distinguishes an error from a failure? An error is unanticipated, unlike a failure, which is anticipated by an assertion. An error could be a spurious ArrayIndexOutOfBounds exception or a ClassCastException.

If you anticipate a given error, you could test for it with an assertion, or call `fail()` from a catch block. This would convert it into a failure on the results summary.

WSAD JUnit Plug-In

WSAD integrates nicely with JUnit. This makes it more likely that you will adhere to the fourth praxis. Previous WSAD releases required you to find and install the JUnit plug-in. WSAD and WSED release 5 ship with the JUnit plug-in already installed and ready for use. Thus, you are ready to write and run test cases.

Write a Test Case

Writing a test case is simple. Follow these general steps:

1. Create a test case class as a subclass of `junit.frameworkTestCase.`
2. Supply a constructor that takes a test name string parameter, passing it to the super class.
3. Add an instance variable for each component of the test target.
4. Optionally override `junit.framework.TestCase.setup()` to initialize the fixture, as needed.
5. Optionally override `junit.framework.TestCase.tearDown()` to release fixture resources.
6. Write a test for each functional unit of the fixture. Use one of the TestCase.assertXxx()methods to assert correct operation of its functional unit. WSAD code assist will show you the choices.

Now, you will create a simple test case. You will use it to test a simple JavaBean. You will formulate a JUnit Hello World in the following steps:

1. Create a WSAD project called buggy-simple.
2. Create package within that project named bellmeade.simple.
3. Make a class within package bellmeade.simple named SimpleBean.
4. Create two fields in the class: `String firstName` and `String lastName`.
5. Use the pop-up menu on the fields in the Outline view to generate getters and setters for each of them.

The code for the test bean follows:

```
package bellmeade.simple;
/**
```

```
 * A simple Java Bean used as a unit test demo
*/
public class SimpleBean {
    private String firstName;
    private String lastName;
    public String getFirstName() {
        if (firstName == null)
            firstName = "";
        return firstName;
    }
    public void setFirstName(String aFirstName) {
        firstName = aFirstName;
    }
    public String getLastName() {
        if (firstName == null)
            firstName = "";
        return firstName; // @
    }
    public void setLastName(String aLastName) {
        lastName = aLastName;
    }
}
```

Now, you will build a test case for the JavaBean using the following steps:

1. Make a WSAD project named **buggy-simple-test**.
2. Create package bellmeade.simple.test within that project.
3. Use the project's popup menu to open the properties of buggy-simple-test.
4. Select **Java Build Path** from the left-hand property pane.
5. Choose the Libraries tab.
6. Press Add Variable, and choose variable **JUNIT**, and then press OK. See Figure 8.1.
7. Check that the junit.jar file appears in the Libraries build path list, as seen in Figure 8.2, and then press OK.

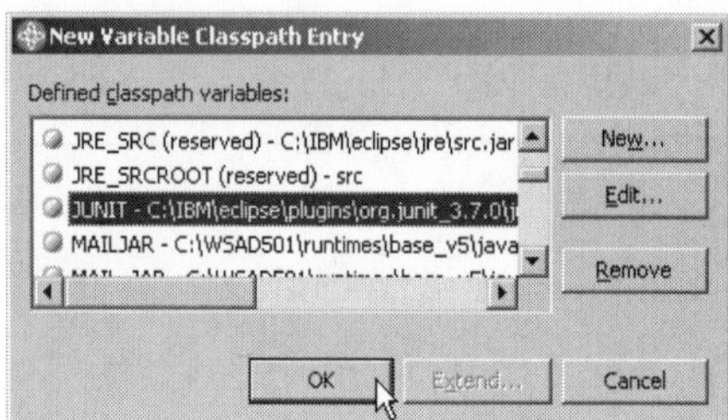

Figure 8.1 JUNIT JAR variable.

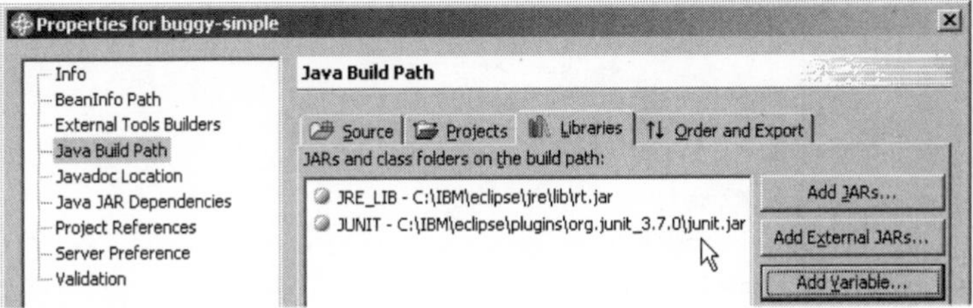

Figure 8.2 JUnit JAR on Java build path.

8. Create package bellmeade.simple.test. It is named after the test target package name, but suffixed with **.test**. It will contain the test counterparts to the application classes.
9. Make a class named SimpleBeanTest in the bellmeade.simple.test package, extending TestCase. Use the New Class wizard, as shown in Figure 8.3. Ensure that Constructors from Superclass is checked. Press Finish.
10. Use content assist to add needed import statements.
11. Add the following field to the class:

```
private SimpleBean target = new SimpleBean();
```

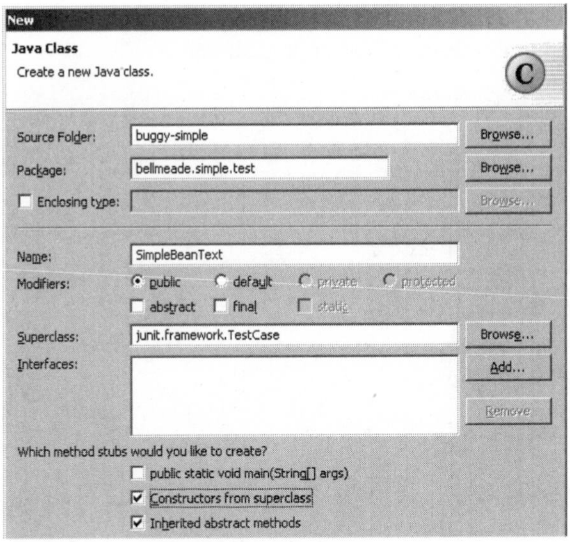

Figure 8.3 Create JUnit test class.

12. Add a test case method for the firstName property:

```
/**
 * Tests the firstName property
 */
public void testFirstName() {
    String name = "Ellwood";
    target.setFirstName(name);
    this.assertEquals(name, target.getFirstName());
}
```

13. Add a similar test for property lastName, by copying and pasting the testFirstName method, changing **first** to **last**, and changing **Ellwood** to **Suggins**.
14. Select the test class in the Package Explorer, and then pick Run As > JUnit Test from the main menu.
15. The results on the Hierarchy tab should appear as shown in Figure 8.4.

Now, break the logic of the test bean. Change it to erroneously return firstName instead of lastName from method `getLastName()`. Rerun the test. The results hierarchy appears in Figure 8.5. Notice the expected failure "X" next to testLastName.

This test found a problem caused by doing a copy-and-paste operation without completely modifying the pasted target. Some of us have made similar errors. This problem caused no compiler error, but would have caused strange results in clients of the JavaBean. It is more productive to catch the error early, in its own code layer, than to try to troubleshoot a strange problem in the application logic layer.

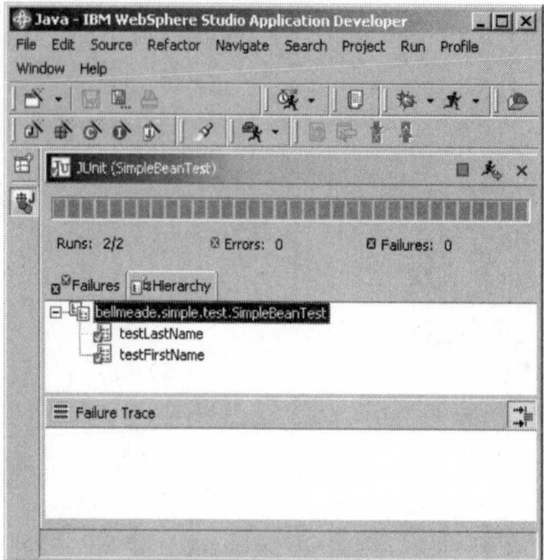

Figure 8.4 Successful test.

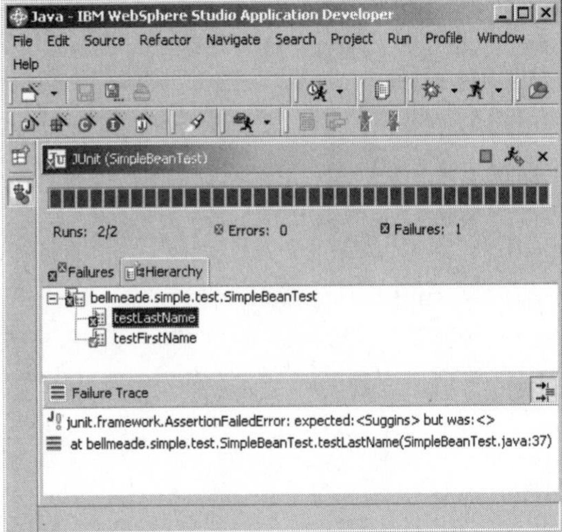

Figure 8.5 Test failure detected.

Build a Test Suite

You would usually have multiple tests. How can you combine them to run as a batch? JUnit provides a `junit.framework.TestSuite` class that raises the option of combining unit tests manually, or combining them automatically through the seeming magic of Java reflection. Both approaches have merit. With either approach, you can compose a suite of test cases, individual tests from test cases, or even suites of suites.

Each approach starts with the same boilerplate. Create a class that extends `junit.framework.TestCase` exactly as you did before. Name it `SimpleTestSuite`. Be sure to create a constructor that takes a `String` argument. It should resemble the following code:

```
package bellmeade.simple.test;
import junit.framework.*;
import bellmeade.simple.test.*;
/**
 * A JUnit test suite
*/
public class SimpleTestSuite extends TestCase {
    /**
     * Constructor for TestSuite
     */
    public SimpleTestSuite(String arg0) {
        super(arg0);
    }
}
```

Notice that the suite is directly executable, having a main() method. The `main` method passes the suite to `junit.textui.TestRunner`, the textual user interface version of the JUnit TestRunner. This is a useful approach in running the suite as part of a build verification process, for example. There is more about this in the section entitled "Textual TestRunner."

Manual Creation

Now, you will enhance the boilerplate into a test suite by manually adding the tests, by name string, that you wish it to include. Add the following method to the class to have it extract and run the tests from the simple test case you just wrote:

```
/**
* Returns a TestSuite
*/
public static TestSuite suite() {
    TestSuite suite = new TestSuite();
    suite.addTest(new SimpleBeanTest("testFirstName"));
    suite.addTest(new SimpleBeanTest("testLastName"));
    return suite;
}
```

Use the WSAD Run As > JUnit Test Application to execute the new test suite. The results should look familiar. The framework used the `suite()` method to find and execute tests. The advantage of constructing a suite this way is the complete freedom to mix and match tests to compose a suite. The disadvantage is the potentially large amount of manual entry needed to construct some suites, with the attendant possibility of missing a test. Use this manual approach when you want the suite to contain a subset of the available tests.

Reflection

Instead of manually entering tests, you could leverage the Java reflection API through the JUnit framework. The framework will automatically extract a suite from a test case. This is often the preferred approach. Simply pass the class of a test case to the `TestSuite` constructor. The framework will extract every method of the test case that starts with `test`. Change the `suite()` method to look like the following:

```
/**
 * Returns a TestSuite
 */
public static TestSuite suite() {
    TestSuite suite = new TestSuite(SimpleBeanTest.class);
    return suite;
}
```

Again, execute the suite using WSAD plug-in TestRunner. You should see the same results, but with less coding effort. That is one advantage. Another is less exposure to an error causing accidental omission of a test. A disadvantage could be that only one test case can join the suite, but is this true? If you add the `suite()` method shown previously to the class `SimpleBeanTest`, it can extract its own tests into a suite. Then, you can modify the `suite()` method in your test suite to add that suite to it, as follows:

```
/**
 * Returns a TestSuite
 */
public static TestSuite suite() {
    TestSuite suite = new TestSuite();
    suite.addTest(SimpleBeanTest.suite());
    return suite;
}
```

An alternate implementation follows:

```
/**
 * Returns a TestSuite
 */
public static TestSuite suite() {
    TestSuite suite = new TestSuite();
    suite.addTestSuite(SimpleBeanTest.class);
    return suite;
}
```

Notice how you can easily add suites and tests to a master suite in an open-ended manner.

Run a Test Suite

You have previewed how to run a test suite in the TestRunner supplied by the JUnit support in WSAD. Let us look at a textual counterpart.

Textual TestRunner

The textual or character-mode or non-GUI version of the TestRunner displays results on the console. You can make a suite or test case execute as a standalone application by adding the following method, as you did previously in the test suite:

```
/**
 * Executes this suite as a standalone application using
 * the text UI version of TestRunner.
 */
public static void main(String[] args) {
    junit.textui.TestRunner.run(suite());
}
```

Try executing SimpleTestSuite as a Java Application instead of a JUnit Test Application. A typical transcript result could resemble the following:

```
. .F.
Time: 0.047
There was 1 failure:
1) testLastName (bellmeade.simple.test.SimpleBeanTest)
junit.framework.AssertionFailedError: expected:<Suggins> but was:<>
    at bellmeade.simple.test.SimpleBeanTest.testLastName
(SimpleBeanTest.java:37)
    at bellmeade.simple.test.SimpleTestSuite.main
(SimpleTestSuite.java:47)
FAILURES!!!
Tests run: 2,  Failures: 1,  Errors: 0
```

This is useful for automated testing outside of WSAD. For example, an Apache ANT script could execute the suite using the textual TestRunner.

Test the Buggy Calculator

Let us put simple testing aside in favor of a real example. First, check that you imported the buggy-calculator-app, buggy-calculator-lib, and calculator-test projects from the book Web site. You must not forget to add the reference to JUNIT JAR variable to the buggy-calculator-app, buggy-calculator-lib, and calculator-test projects in the calculator-test properties' Java build paths. The calculator is a layered application having a view class, a mediator class, and a simple stateless domain class. The tests, as well as the bugs, have been placed on the book Web site; these are actual bugs that arose during application development.

Run the calclulator.test.CalculatorTestSuite as a Java application. Ensure that the build path includes the project buggy-calculator-lib. A reformatted, abridged version of the console follows.

```
..........F.F.F.F.F.E..F.F.
Time: 0.131
There was 1 error:
1) test5(bellmeade.calculator.test.CalculatorMediatorTest)
    *** stack trace removed ***
There were 7 failures:
test10(bellmeade.calculator.test.CalculatorMediatorTest)
   junit.framework.AssertionFailedError:
       expected:<0.25> but was:<Infinity>
    at
    *** stack trace removed ***
test9(bellmeade.calculator.test.CalculatorMediatorTest)
   junit.framework.AssertionFailedError:
        expected:<36.0> but was:<3.6>
```

```
    at
    *** stack trace removed ***
    *** failures 3 through 7 removed ***
FAILURES!!!
Tests run: 19,  Failures: 7,  Errors: 1
```

There are seven failures and one error. You could attack the problems in buggy-calculator-lib using the unabridged information from the console, but many of us have better cognitive powers when information is presented more graphically.

Swing TestRunner

Now, you will return to using the GUI version of the TestRunner to attack the failures and error in the calculator application. Select package TestSuite in the project calculator-test, after making sure that its build path points to the project buggy-calculator-lib, not the project calculator-lib. Use the main menu item Run As > JUnit Application to execute the suite in the TestRunner.

The Console view results should resemble Figure 8.6 when you choose the Hierarchy tab. The results look dismal. How will you repair so many problems? Fortunately, a single defect often fails multiple tests. You will attack the error, and then go after the failures.

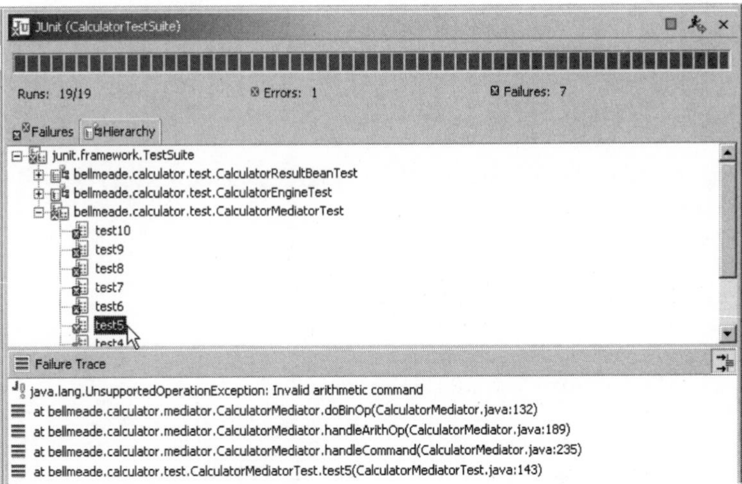

Figure 8.6 Test suite results.

If you select a failure or an error node in the hierarchy, you will see problem details in the lower pane of the results. You have selected the single error (as distinguished from any of the seven failures). This error was caused by an exception thrown in the class `CalculatorMediator` during test5. Notice the stack trace that names the method, `doBinOp()`, that threw the exception. The test code follows:

```
/**
 * Assert that 7/4 returns 7/4, while asserting the intermediate
 * steps.
 */
public void test5() {
    CalculatorResultBean result;
    calc.handleCommand(calc.OCLR);
    result = calc.handleCommand(calc.D7);
    this.assertEquals(7d, result.getResult(), TOLERANCE);
    result = calc.handleCommand(calc.ODIV);
    this.assertEquals(7d, result.getResult(), TOLERANCE);
    result = calc.handleCommand(calc.D4);
    this.assertEquals(4d, result.getResult(), TOLERANCE);
    result = calc.handleCommand(calc.OEQU);
    this.assertEquals(7d/4d, result.getResult(), TOLERANCE);
}
```

This test feeds an arithmetic operation to the calculator, testing for expected results. The CalculatorMediator routes binary operation requests to its `doBinOp()` method. One of the tests triggered an exception in the method. Let us examine the `doBinOp()` method:

```
/**
 * Returns arg1 aBinOp arg2
 * @param arg1 double
 * @param arg2 double
 * @param aBinOp java.lang.String
 * @return double
 * @throws java.lang.UnsupportedOperationException
 */
protected double doBinOp(String aBinOp, double arg1, double arg2) {
    double result;
    if (aBinOp.equals(CalculatorCommands.OADD))
        result = calc.add(arg1, arg2);
    else if (aBinOp.equals(CalculatorCommands.OSUB))
        result = calc.sub(arg1, arg2);
    else if (aBinOp.equals(CalculatorCommands.OMUL))
        result = calc.mul(arg1, arg2);
    else
        // @
        throw (new java.lang.UnsupportedOperationException(
            "Invalid arithmetic command"));
    return result;
}
```

After examination, it appears that it needs to test for a divide request, ODIV. The method throws the exception if it is handed a request that it cannot understand. Replacing the “@” comment with the following statement fixes the problem.

```
if (aBinOp.equals(CalculatorCommands.ODIV))
    result = calc.div(arg1, arg2);
else
```

Naturally, you would run the test again to ensure that the problem was fixed and no new failures resulted. Now let us attack the failures, one by one. Let's look at one of the seven failures, as seen in Figure 8.7. Choose the lowest-numbered test first. The test names are numbered in execution order. Perhaps a fix for that problem will propagate favorably to the higher-numbered tests.

You can find that test2 of test case CalculatorMediatorTest reported that it expected a result of *3.1* but received *3.01*. The lower pane shows that this test failed on line 77. The test is shown with the statement corresponding to line 77 highlighted.

TIP You may use the WSAD context menu Go to Line command to position the editor to a line in the editor.

```
/**
  * Assert that entering 3,14 returns 3,14 while asserting the
  * intermediate steps.
  */
public void test2() {
    CalculatorResultBean result;
    calc.handleCommand(calc.OCLR);
    result = calc.handleCommand(calc.D3);
    assertEquals(3d, result.getResult(), TOLERANCE);
    result = calc.handleCommand(calc.DPT);
    assertEquals(3d, result.getResult(), TOLERANCE);
    result = calc.handleCommand(calc.D1);
    assertEquals(3.1d, result.getResult(), TOLERANCE);
    result = calc.handleCommand(calc.D4);
}
```

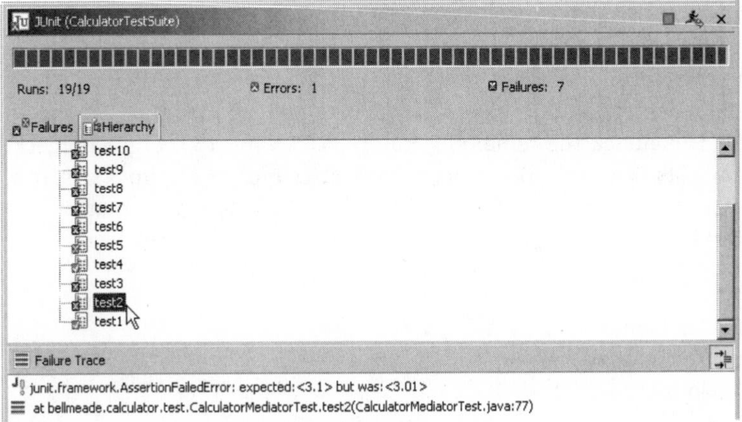

Figure 8.7 Example of a detected failure.

It appears that there is a problem maintaining the decimal point position. Investigation of the handling the decimal point in the `CalculatorMediator` class seems prudent. Each digit is separately passed to the mediator from the presentation layer. In the mediator, it becomes part of an accumulated double held internally. The decimal point is passed in this manner as well, and it is used to modify how digits are accumulated. Let us look at the digit handler shown in the following code snippet:

```
/**
 * Handles a digit
 * @param aDigitCommand java.lang.String
 */
protected double handleDigit(String aDigitCommand) {
if (charCounter < MAX_CHARS) {
        double digit = Double.parseDouble(aDigitCommand);
        if (decimalPoint >= 0) {  //@
            for (int dp = decimalPoint++; dp > 0; --dp)
                digit /= 10;
            entry += digit;
        } else {
            entry *= 10.0d;
            entry += digit;
        }
            charCounter++;
        }
    return entry;
}
```

Look at the place where the decimal point is processed. It seems to be off by one place, according to the test result that showed the decimal point. Change

```
if (decimalPoint >= 0)
```

to the following:

```
if (decimalPoint > 0)
```

Save the file, and then rerun the test suite. Afterward, conditions greatly improve as you observe that six entire test failures have disappeared, as seen in Figure 8.8.

That was easy. Let us attack the remaining failure. You want to see green checkmarks indicating all tests pass with no errors! The failure trace in Figure 8.11 shows that test10 of class `CalculatorMediatorTest` received *Infinity* when it expected a real number. The test is reproduced as follows:

```
/**
 * Assert that the reciprocal of 1+3 is 0.25 , using the
 * addition and reciprocal commands
 */
public void test10() {
    CalculatorResultBean result;
    calc.handleCommand(calc.OCLR);
    result = calc.handleCommand(calc.D1);
```

```
        assertEquals(1d, result.getResult(), TOLERANCE);
        result = calc.handleCommand(calc.OADD);
        assertEquals(1d, result.getResult(), TOLERANCE);
        result = calc.handleCommand(calc.D3);
        assertEquals( 3d, result.getResult(),TOLERANCE);
        result = calc.handleCommand(calc.OEQU);
        assertEquals( 4d, result.getResult(),TOLERANCE);
        result = calc.handleCommand(calc.ORCP);
        assertEquals(0.25d, result.getResult(), TOLERANCE);
    }
```

This test requests the mediator to take the reciprocal of the sum of two numbers. The result was *infinity*. You know that the reciprocal command seems to work correctly because other tests of it passed. It seems to fail when another operation precedes it—in this case, addition. Let's examine the code that carries out reciprocal operations.

```
    /**
    * Handles a unary (one-arg) arithmetic operation
    * on the current display. Displays entry result.
    * @param aDisplayOp java.lang.String
    * @throws java.lang.UnsupportedOperationException
    */
    protected double handleUnaryDisplayOp(String aDisplayOp) {
        if (aDisplayOp.equals(CalculatorCommands.OTSN)) {
            entry = calc.invertSign(display); // @
        } else
            if (aDisplayOp.equals(CalculatorCommands.ORCP)) {
                entry = calc.reciprocal(entry); // @
            }
        if (aDisplayOp.equals(CalculatorCommands.OSQRT)) {
            entry = calc.sqrt(display);
        }
        return entry;
    }
```

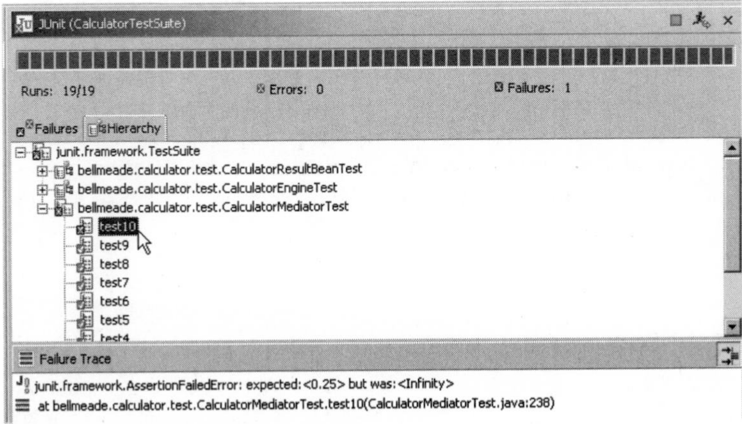

Figure 8.8 Single remaining failure.

The mediator keeps the calculator state in three `double` variables: `accum`, `entry`, and `display`. The `accum` variable holds the accumulated result. The `entry` variable holds the entry used for binary operations such as addition. The `display` variable holds the value presented to the user at any point.

The reciprocal operation is supposed to divide the numeric constant value one by the *displayed* value. You notice that the reciprocal operation is instead dividing the *entry* value by one. The entry value doesn't always match the display value. It is zero after a binary operation has been completed. The result of the binary operation is copied to the display variable. It is clear that it should divide one by the `display` variable value, since the user sees that effect. Change the line that reads:

```
entry = calc.reciprocal(entry);
```

to the following:

```
entry = calc.reciprocal(display);
```

Save the file, and then rerun the test, and there should be no errors. Notice the sign inversion logic just above the reciprocal in the code that you repaired. It has the same problem as the reciprocal, yet the tests passed. Why is this? There was no JUnit test for the sign inversion operation. You need to supply a test, fix the problem, and then rerun the test suite to ensure that the problem is fixed, and that no regressions occurred.

Concluding Remarks

The textual TestRunner is useful for batched or scripted test automation. The Swing version makes it easier for programmers to accept this philosophy and leverage unit testing to stop bugs before they are incorporated into a build. This is important because problems are often easier to repair earlier, when pinpointed to the offending components before integration exhibits hard-to-find problems. If you enforce a policy of rerunning these tests whenever a component is modified, you will reduce regressions. Once you acquire the habit of writing these tests as you write the corresponding components, you will find that writing unit tests takes little time and has a big payback.

Unit test technology makes it easier to adopt a policy of pairing a test case with each application class. JUnit is not suitable for testing some kinds of code. It cannot test private methods or inner classes. It cannot directly test Java servlets. There are follow-on frameworks that enable these kinds of tests. JUnitX and HttpUnit, respectively, address these two issues. At this time, IBM supplies no WSAD plug-in for these derivative test frameworks, but they can be used externally against files residing in a WSAD workspace directory tree.

Summary

This completes the survey of unit testing using the integrated JUnit within WSAD. JUnit is a unit testing technology from the Apache organization. It is not a part of the J2EE standard. JUnit provides a lot of benefit for a small effort. You may feel more assured that code is functioning if it passes when a suite of tests is run against it at any arbitrary time. Of course, you must adhere to a philosophy that says the test is as important as the target code and that the two will remain paired for the duration of their life cycle.

In this chapter, we introduced unit testing through the WSAD integrated JUnit feature. It covered the following major items:

- The philosophy of unit testing
- JUnit background and terminology
- Writing a simple test case
- Several approaches to writing a suite of tests
- The textual and Swing versions of the JUnit TestRunner
- Finding and repairing three real problems in the calculator application

We will move on to the subject of Java servlets in Chapter 9, "Making Servlets."

CHAPTER 9

Making Servlets

What's in Chapter 9?

In this chapter, you will learn about server-side programming using Java servlets. Servlets are an important part of the J2EE architecture and Web applications. In the model-view-controller design, servlets play the role of the controller. In this chapter, you will learn about servlets and how to use them in a Web application. You will build a servlet and test it in the WSAD. This chapter covers the following concepts:

- Defining a servlet
- How servlets work
  - Life cycle methods
  - Request object
  - Response object
- Building a servlet
  - Writing to the response
  - Reading from the request
  - Transferring control
- Running servlets

You will build your first servlet and test it in the WSAD test environment. This servlet will provide HTML content for the response to the browser. You will learn how to read parameters from a request and add these parameters to the response. You will also see how a Web application definition is managed in the WSAD web.xml file.

What Is a Servlet?

A servlet is a standard server-side Java program that extends the function of a Web server. When the Web server gets a request for a servlet (through a URL), it loads the servlet into the server machines' memory (if it is not already loaded) and executes the servlet. When the servlet completes its task, it sends any generated output back to the Web browser. You can write servlets for administrative purposes, such as managing Web server log files or for sending alert emails to administrators. However, what is more interesting and more pervasive is the use of servlets in information systems (IS) applications that run on the Web.

Servlets typically interface to existing JavaBeans or Enterprise JavaBeans (EJBs), which then utilize a database or transactional system to perform the real work. As we have previously discussed, this book breaks down robust applications into layers and follows the model-view-controller (MVC) design pattern. Servlets act as the controller layer for applications that run on the Web. Servlets serve as the glue between ordinary HTML view and the JavaBeans or EJBs that serve as the model. Servlets can then add additional function to the overall Web application by providing session management, user authentication, and user authorization.

Why Use Servlets?

At this point, you might be thinking, "I can use CGI and Perl, why should I use Java servlets?" CGI stands for Common Gateway Interface and was defined as a mechanism for integrating programs written in C/C++, Perl, and other languages with a Web server. The simple answer is that servlets offer a better way to develop server-side function than CGI. In most Web applications that use servlets, the client code (HTML) accesses the servlets in the same way that it would access a Perl script through CGI. Thus, using servlets does not in any way impact how HTML developers do their job.

Servlets offer advantages over standard CGI mechanisms in the areas of portability, performance, and security. Since Java is "write once, run anywhere" your server-side programs are platform independent. Additionally, servlets can take advantage of prepackaged component technologies through the use of JavaBeans and EJBs.

Servlets offer better performance than standard CGI. Once the Web server loads a servlet into the server memory, it stays there and listens for requests. When a request arrives, a new Java thread is automatically created and the servlet code is executed in that thread. Java threads are lightweight and their creation is far more efficient than standard CGI, which creates a new operating system process for each request. Since a servlet remains resident in memory, connections to databases can remain open. An intelligent servlet can create pools of database connections and manage those between concurrent users to further improve performance over standard CGI. IBM WebSphere provides a connection manager object to create and manage pools of connections to JDBC databases. Additionally, servlets provide a Session object that you can use to maintain session information, across multiple accesses by the same user, to the servlets on a Web server. Use of the Session object can reduce the need to retrieve the same information over and over again each time a user accesses a server-side application. Sessions can be setup to expire or to persist indefinitely.

Servlets offer better security than standard CGI. Since a servlet runs within the Web server context and under the control of the Web server, you can use authentication and authorization features of the Web server. Additionally, the JDK includes the java.security and java.security.acl packages, which offer Java Interfaces for creating authentication and authorization functions. IBM WebSphere provides an implementation of the Java Interfaces in the java.security and java.security.acl packages as well as administrative screens for maintaining access control lists.

The overall architecture of a servlet appears in Figure 9.1.

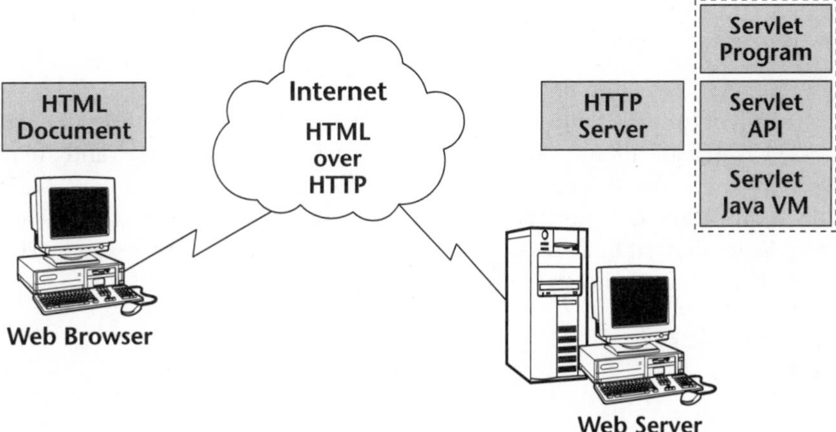

Figure 9.1 Servlet architecture.

Basic Servlet Concepts

Servlets give a server-side programmer the basic building blocks for creating controllers for Web-based applications. To understand servlets, you need to know something about the servlet API, life cycle, requests, responses, HttpServlet class, and how to use PrintWriters.

The Servlet API

The Servlet API resides in two packages, javax.servlet and javax.servlet.http. These packages define all of the Java interfaces and classes needed to begin creating servlets. The javax.servlet package defines the basic classes for servlets, including `GenericServlet`, `ServletInputStream`, and `ServletOutputStream`. All servlets must eventually inherit from the class `GenericServlet`. The javax.servlet package appears in Figure 9.2.

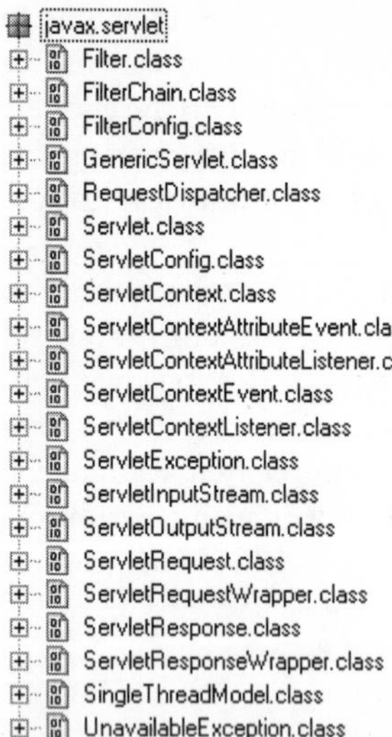

Figure 9.2 javax.servlet package.

The javax.servlet.http package defines classes that are useful in supporting HTTP functions. Servlets that are intended to act like a CGI program use the classes and interfaces in this package. The `HttpServlet` class provides Java methods for HTTP requests such as `POST` and `GET`, and it is the basis for most of the controller code in Web applications. Note that `HttpServlet` is a subclass of `GenericServlet`. The javax.servlet.http package is shown in Figure 9.3.

javax.servlet.http
Cookie.class
HttpServlet.class
HttpServletRequest.class
HttpServletRequestWrapper.class
HttpServletResponse.class
HttpServletResponseWrapper.class
HttpSession.class
HttpSessionActivationListener.class
HttpSessionAttributeListener.class
HttpSessionBindingEvent.class
HttpSessionBindingListener.class
HttpSessionContext.class
HttpSessionEvent.class
HttpSessionListener.class
HttpUtils.class
NoBodyOutputStream.class
NoBodyResponse.class

Figure 9.3 javax.servlet.http package.

Servlet Life Cycle

The servlet life cycle defines the process used to load the servlet into memory, execute the servlet, and then unload the servlet from memory. A Web browser requests a servlet through a URL. The URL can be on the location line of the Web browser, or it can be a link embedded in the HTML document being viewed. A default servlet URL appears as http://host/servlet/com.packagename.SimpleServlet. The host is defined as a machine and a port that is assigned in the server configuration. For example, when testing in WSAD the host is usually localhost:9080. The keyword servlet lets the Web server know that the request is for a servlet and not an HTML page or CGI program. The fully qualified name com.packagename.SimpleServlet, in this example, is the class name of the desired servlet. Usually a short name or alias is used for the servlet. The servlet alias is defined in the Web application definition located in the web.xml file. The servlet alias maps the fully qualified name to a shorter name. The URL for calling the same servlet with an alias would be http://host/SimpleServlet.

NOTE When testing in WSAD with the WebSphere test environment, you do not need the keyword servlet in the URL when there is a servlet alias. WSAD automatically makes an alias for the servlet when you use the Servlet wizard to make the servlet.

To create a servlet, you must create a subclass of the `GenericServlet` class or one of its subclasses. When your servlet is first requested, the Web server loads the requested servlet class and all of the associated classes into memory on the Web server. Control then passes to the `init()` method in the servlet. GenericServlet provides an empty `init()` method. If you wish to perform initialization tasks, such as connecting to a database, you need to provide an `init()` method in your subclass. The `init()` method receives only one call, and that is immediately after the Web server loads your servlet into memory.

Each time the servlet is requested (including the first time after the `init()` method is called) a new thread is created, and that thread executes over the `service()` method. GenericServlet provides an empty `service()` method. You must override this method if want to do any real work. Since the `service()` method is called in its own thread, the Web server is free to take additional requests for the same servlet or another servlet, which it executes in another thread. The `service()` method is where the work of the servlet is accomplished. You should note that since the `service()` method is always executed inside a new thread, you must be careful to ensure that everything done in the `service()` method is thread-safe (reentrant).

At some later time, when the Web server deems it necessary, the `destroy()` method of the servlet is called, and then the servlet is unloaded from the server's memory. If the servlet has a `destroy()` method, it is automatically called. Common tasks performed by the `destroy()` method include disconnecting all database connections, closing all files, and other administrative items.

The complete life cycle of a GenericServlet appears in Figure 9.4.

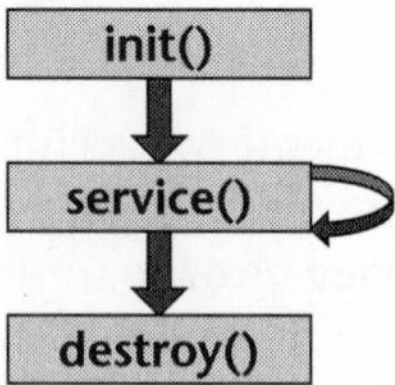

Figure 9.4 Servlet life cycle.

HttpServlet

While GenericServlet provides the basic behavior of a servlet, a mechanism for handling HTTP requests is necessary for common Web applications. The HttpServlet, which is a subclass of GenericServlet, provides the additional behavior for handling HTTP requests. HttpServlet provides Java methods for each of the HTTP request methods. While all of the HTTP methods are supported, the `GET` and `POST` methods are the most prevalent. The HttpServlet provides the `doGet()` and `doPost()` Java methods to handle the HTTP `GET` and `POST` methods.

When an HttpServlet is requested via a URL, the `service()` method reads the HTTP header and determines which HTTP method to call. The `service()` method, in turn, routes the request to the appropriate method, which is usually the `doGet` or `doPost`. The `doGet()` method is usually called through a link on an HTML page or directly called via a URL. The `doPost()` method is usually called when a button is pressed on an HTML form. Most servlet programming is done by overriding the `doGet()` or `doPost()` methods.

Request and Response Parameters

When the `service()`, `doGet()`, `doPost()`, or other methods are called, two parameters are always passed. These parameters represent the request information from the Web browser and the response information that is returned to the browser. The request and response are Java classes with these responsibilities:

ServletRequest — This provides the servlet with the ability to access the requested information such as parameters, session information, HttpServletRequest information on the HTTP header, and cookies.

ServletResponse — This provides the servlet with facilities to create a response document for the Web browser. You can set the content type and write data in the form of the specified content type to an encapsulated PrintWriter object. The PrintWriter is the channel by which the servlet communicates with the Web browser.

Most of servlet programming is reading information sent in the request, acting upon this information, then placing content in the response.

Servlet Packaging

The servlet classes were initially packaged in a separate Java Server Development Kit (JSDK) that contained all of the classes to develop and test servlets. The servlet classes are now bundled in with J2EE, so you get them when you install the J2EE SDK (Server Development Kit) or WSAD. In order to run servlets, you need an application server such as WebSphere or Apache Tomcat.

WebSphere Application Server

The servlet classes in the JDK from Sun provide all of the necessary classes to develop servlets and a servlet-only Web server. The IBM WebSphere Application Server product provides additional functions for running server-based J2EE applications. The following is a short list of features that the IBM WebSphere product provides:

- All of the function needed to run servlets
- The IBM Connection Manager for managing database connections
- JavaBeans for accessing data from JDBC databases
- An implementation of the `java.security` and `java.security.acl` interfaces
- An administration console that allows users, groups, and ACLs (Access Control List) to be created and maintained
- An administration console that allows easy manipulation of the many .properties and files associated with servlets
- The ability to mark servlets to be preloaded when the Web server starts instead of waiting for the first request for those servlets
- A site access monitor that allows an operator to view servlet activity in real time
- The ability to dynamically reload modified servlets without rebooting the Web server machine
- An implementation for the JavaServer Pages (JSP) specification

WSAD lets you run the WebSphere Application server inside WSAD during development. You can test servlets as you build them, and you can even set breakpoints in servlets, helping you with debugging. In WSAD V5, you can work on projects that use different versions of WebSphere. This is a really cool feature. The development tool is not directly tied to the runtime environment.

Servlet Role in J2EE

Servlets are the controllers in the model-view-controller design of the J2EE Web architecture, as shown in Figure 9.5. Servlets play a key role in the architecture as they collaborate with other J2EE components. There are many different components in this architecture, but you can use servlets in a simpler design.

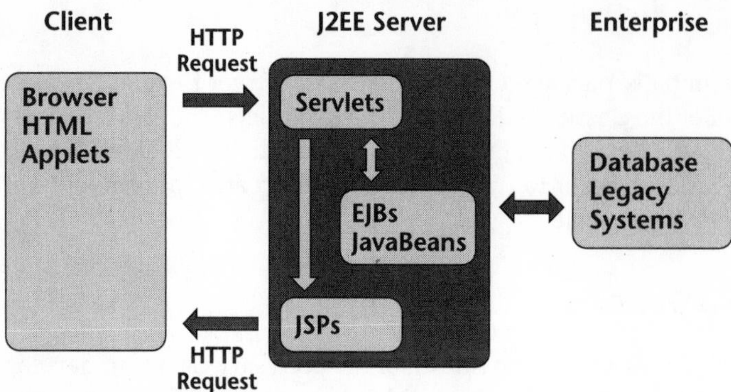

Figure 9.5 J2EE architecture.

Simple Servlet Design

Before the J2EE Web architecture was formalized, servlets were used in a very simple design. This usage is shown in Figure 9.6. A client calls a servlet on a server. The servlet reads the request and can dynamically provide specific content for each request. This was a big leap forward for Java server-side programming. As a means to learn how servlets work, you will use this design in this chapter. After you have learned how to use JavaBeans with servlets and JavaServer Pages, you will be able to implement the full architecture.

There are a few key drawbacks with this use of servlets. It is very difficult to place HTML tags in Java code. Any change to the servlet requires a Java programmer to code, test, and deploy the servlet in order to see the changes. Most Web pages are primarily static, with parts that are dynamic. Even static changes to a servlet Web page require the same Java development steps. Additionally, there are many great tools for developing Web pages and editing HTML that cannot be used when servlets generate the HTML. You will learn how to handle this problem with JavaServer Pages in Chapter 11, "JavaServer Pages."

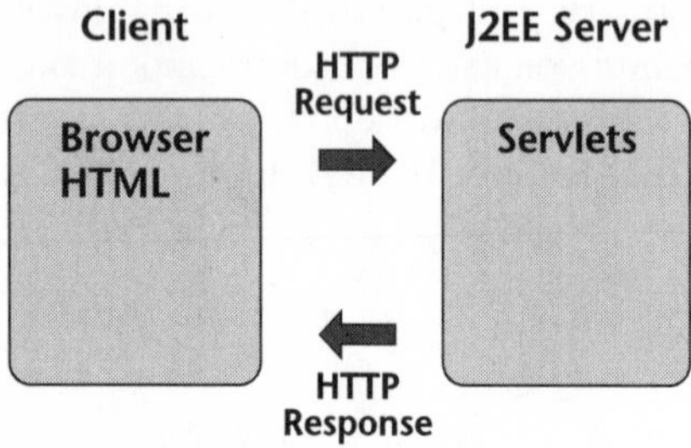

Figure 9.6 Simple servlet.

Making Your First Servlet

For your first servlet, you will develop a servlet for the Golf Web site started in Chapter 5, "Web Page Content." This servlet is named GolfAVG, it subclasses the HttpServlet, and implements the following methods:

- doPost()
- doGet()
- init()
- destroy()

First you will add some code to the `doGet()` method to test the servlet `GET` requests. This is a good way to learn how servlets operate. You will add trace code to both the `init()` and `destroy()` methods. It is not required that a servlet implement the `init()` and `destroy` methods, but they are helpful methods that are part of the servlet life cycle. You will continue to add more function to the GolfAVG servlet in the next chapter, "Servlets with JavaBeans." In that chapter, you will modify the `doPost()` method to hand requests from the Golf Web page.

Making a Package

The servlet goes in the same GolfProject that you have been using in the previous chapters. Since servlets act as controllers, it is a good idea to group servlets together in a common package. It is common to see servlets or the controller as the package name for servlets. The root packages j2eebook.golf remain the same; that way, the servlet is separate from the JavaBeans, yet only one subdirectory away. Create the new package with the following steps:

1. From the Java Perspective, Select the **Java Source** folder in the GolfProject.
2. Select the Create a Java Package button, or instead you can select the menu items File > New > Package, and the new Java Package window displays as shown in Figure 9.7.
3. Ensure that the Source Folder is GolfProject/Java Source.
4. Enter **j2eebook.golf.controller** for the Name.
5. Click the Finish button to create the package.

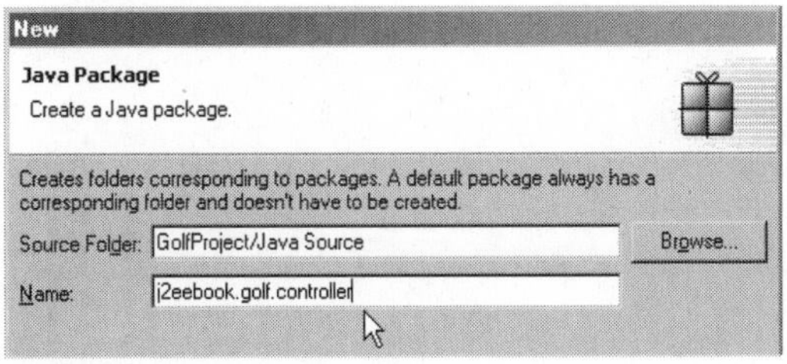

Figure 9.7 New package.

Creating a Servlet

Now that there is a package, you are ready to start creating a servlet. WSAD has a great wizard that you can use to create servlets. You can also make servlets by creating a class and adding the proper code in the source editor. After you have made a few servlets, you may end up using existing servlets as templates for new ones. Create the GolfAVG servlet with the following steps:

1. From the Web perspective, select the Java package **j2eebook.golf.controller** that you just created.
2. Select the Create a Java Servlet Class button, or instead you can select the menu items File > New > Servlet.
3. Enter **GolfAVG** for the Class Name, as shown in Figure 9.8. Be careful because the class name is case sensitive.
4. Click the Next button to continue with the servlet specifications.

When the second page in the New Servlet wizard displays, enter additional information for the servlet as follows:

1. Select the `init()` method checkbox.
2. Select the `destroy()` method checkbox.
3. Select the **Constructors from superclass** checkbox.
4. Make sure the `doPost()` and `doGet()` methods are checked.
5. Click the Finish button to create the servlet.

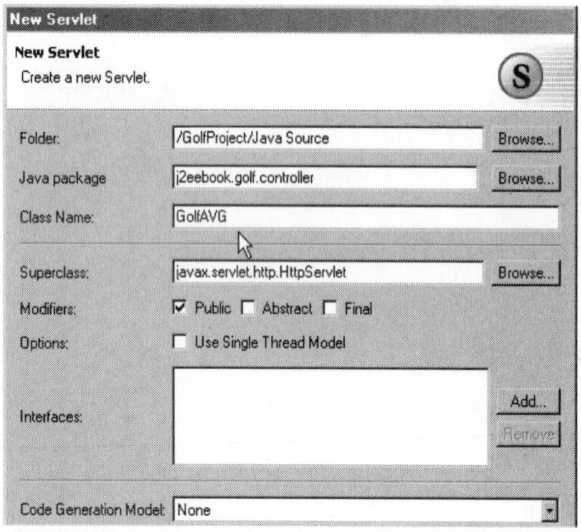

Figure 9.8 New servlet.

The New Servlet wizard closes, and the generated servlet displays in the IDE Source Editor. Let's take a minute to review what the wizard generated. The servlet had the correct import statements. The class includes a default constructor. The `doGet()`, `doPost()`, `init()`, and `destroy()` methods are created but they have to be completed. The generated servlet code should look as follows:

```
package j2eebook.golf.controller;
import java.io.IOException;
import javax.servlet.ServletException;
import javax.servlet.http.HttpServlet;
import javax.servlet.http.HttpServletRequest;
import javax.servlet.http.HttpServletResponse;
/**
 * @version     1.0
*/
public class GolfAVG extends HttpServlet {
    /*
    * Constructor
    */
    public GolfAVG() {
        super();
    }
    /*
    * @see GenericServlet#destroy()
    */
    public void destroy() {
    }
    public void doGet(HttpServletRequest req, HttpServletResponse resp)
        throws ServletException, IOException {
    }
    public void doPost(HttpServletRequest req, HttpServletResponse resp)
        throws ServletException, IOException {
    }/*
    * @see GenericServlet#init()
    */
    public void init() throws ServletException {
    }
}
```

The generated code for the GolfAVG servlet has the `doGet()` and a `doPost()` methods. Both of these methods are passed an HttpServletRequest with a local variable req, and an HttpServletResponse with a local variable resp. It is common to see the HttpServletRequest spelled out as request and the HttpServletResponse as response. The longer names are easier to read and less likely to be confused, since req and resp look a lot alike. The shorter names are popular because they take up less screen space and they are faster to type. Whatever names you end up using, you should be consistent and use the same convention throughout your code. For the servlet samples, we will use the convention generated by WSAD.

Editing a Servlet

The generated code is a good start, but it is only a start. You need to code all the logic in the servlet methods. First, you will add a little code to the `doPost()` method to test the servlet. This code will display a very simple Web page.

Writing to the Response

The Response object, that comes as a parameter in the servlet call, contains the services that allow you to create the content that is sent back to the browser. The ServletResponse is a Java interface that provides the many methods as seen in Figure 9.9. The `getWriter()` method in the Response provides a reference to Java PrintWriter. It is good form to use the `setContentType()` method when writing to the PrintWriter. The GolfAVG servlet, just like other HttpServlets, uses the `HttpServletResponse` that subclasses the `ServletResponse` Interface.

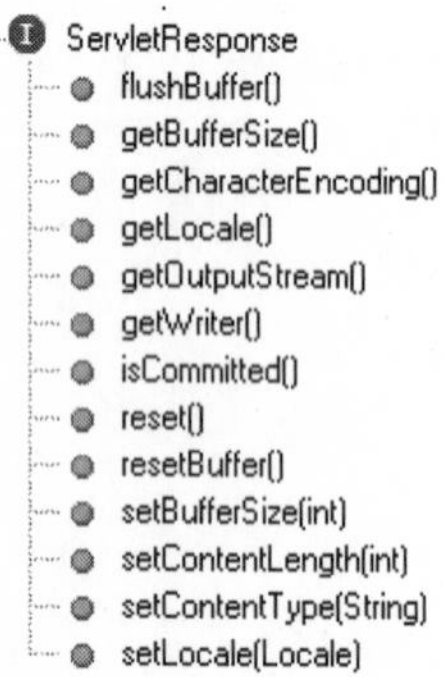

Figure 9.9 Response methods.

Using the PrintWriter

As mentioned earlier in this chapter, usually servlets should not have hard-coded HTML tags in them. But in this case we will make an exception to illustrate how a servlet works. You will use the `getWriter()` method in the Response to set a local variable as a `PrintWriter` type. The Java `PrinterWriter` class is in a different package, so you need to change an import statement in the GolfAVG servlet. Using the Source Editor, add the following import statement to the top of GolfAVG servlet:

```
import java.io.PrintWriter;
```

The servlet, acting as the controller, should sort through different requests and route them to the appropriate JavaBeans. The `doGet()` method is called when a servlet is referenced in a URL, and the code for sorting the requests would go in this method. You will add a new method that can provide an HTML response to the browser. It will be easier to update the servlet by placing this code in a separate method instead of placing all the code in the `doGet()` method. Edit the GolfAVG servlet in the Source Editor and add the `displayMessage()` method as follows:

```
public void displayMessage(HttpServletResponse resp, String message)
throws IOException {
    // Obtain the output stream from the response
    PrintWriter out = resp.getWriter();
    // print a simple html page in the printwriter
    out.println("<html><body><h2> " + message);
    out.println("</h2></body></html>");
}
```

This code will display a very simple Web page in the same browser that made the request. There is more code that could be added for good style and completeness. The content type should be set in the response so that the browser knows how to display the contents. In this case, you are sending HTML back to the browser, and it has no problems handling this content. You can explicitly set the content type with the following code:

```
    resp.setContentType("text/html");
```

When the `displayMessage()` method runs, the PrintWriter buffer is automatically flushed and closed. You can explicitly put this in the code with the following:

```
    out.flush();
    out.close();
```

Updating the doGet() Method

The `doGet()` method needs to be updated to call the `displayMessage()` method. You will pass the resp as the Response and the String message **Hello World!** Edit the `doGet()` method to look as follows:

```
public void doGet(HttpServletRequest req, HttpServletResponse resp)
    throws ServletException, IOException {
    // display HTML message
    displayMessage(resp, "Hello World!");
}
```

You could test the servlet now, but there are a few other updates you should make to the servlet. After you add a little code to the `init()` and `destroy()` methods, you will be ready to test the GolfAVG servlet.

Servlet Tracing

It is very common to load values into a servlet when it starts. This can be handled easily with the `init()` method. The same is true for the `destroy()` method, which is implicitly called when the servlet is finished and about to be removed from memory. The designers of the servlet API could have used a better name than `destroy()` for this method. The terms wrapup, finish, or last would probably been much easier to remember. If you do not need to have the servlet run special code when it starts or ends, you can merely omit these methods from your servlet class.

It will be helpful to put a little trace code in the GolfAVG servlet. If you print a message to the console in these methods, you will have a trace message when the servlet starts and ends. Edit the `init()` and `destroy()` methods in the Source Editor as follows:

```
public void init() throws ServletException {
    System.out.println(
        new java.util.Date()+ " " + getServletName() + " started");
    }
public void destroy() {
    System.out.println(
        new java.util.Date() + " " + getServletName() + " stopped");
    }
```

Save your changes to the GolfAVG servlet code, and you will be ready to start testing the code.

Testing a Servlet

There is enough code in the GolfAVG servlet to run a quick test. It is very easy to use the default WSAD test server and built-in Web browser to run this test. Test the GolfAVG servlet with the following steps:

1. From the Web Perspective, select the GolfAVG servlet.

2. Press the Run on Server button.

```
Console [WebSphere v5.0 Test Environment [WebSphere v5.0]]
[GolfProject] [/GolfProject] [Servlet.LOG]: JSP 1.2 Processor: ini
[GolfProject] [/GolfProject] [Servlet.LOG]: SimpleFileServlet: ini
[GolfProject] [/GolfProject] [Servlet.LOG]: InvokerServlet: init
Transport http is listening on port 9,080.
Transport https is listening on port 9,443.
SOAP connector available at port 8880
RMI Connector available at port 2809
Server server1 open for e-business
[GolfProject] [/GolfProject] [Servlet.LOG]: GolfAVG: init
20:12:56 PDT 2002GolfAVG started
Tasks Properties Links Thumbnail Styles Colors Servers Search Package Explorer Console
```

Figure 9.10 WebSphere test server console.

WSAD automatically runs the servlet on a configured server. Since a server has not been configured, WSAD automatically configures a WebSphere v5 Test Server. It takes a little while for the server to start, so be patient. When the server is started, the message `Server server1 open for e-business` displays in the console at the bottom of the IDE, as seen in Figure 9.10.

NOTE If the console gets cluttered with a lot of messages, you can clear the console from the pop-up menu item Clear, or by clicking the Clear Console button.

The window with the Console has another tab that allows you to manage test servers. Click the Servers tab, and the WebSphere v5.0 Test Environment server appears in the Servers window, as shown in Figure 9.11. The window shows that the server is synchronized and started. You can stop and restart this server from this window, using the buttons in the upper-right corner. If you make extensive changes to your servlets or their supporting classes, you may need to restart or bounce the test server for these changes to take effect on the test server.

The WebSphere test server called the GolfAVG servlet and the `doGet()` method ran. The HTML content is returned to the WSAD Web browser. You should see a new tab next to the GolfAVG.java tab. Click this tab, and the HTML document should appear in the WSAD Web browser, as shown in Figure 9.12. The Hello World text appears in large bold characters because of the <h2> tag used in the HTML. You can see the URL used to call the servlet as http://localhost:9080/GolfProject/GolfAVG. While the test server is running, you can use this same URL in a real browser such as Internet Explorer or Netscape Navigator.

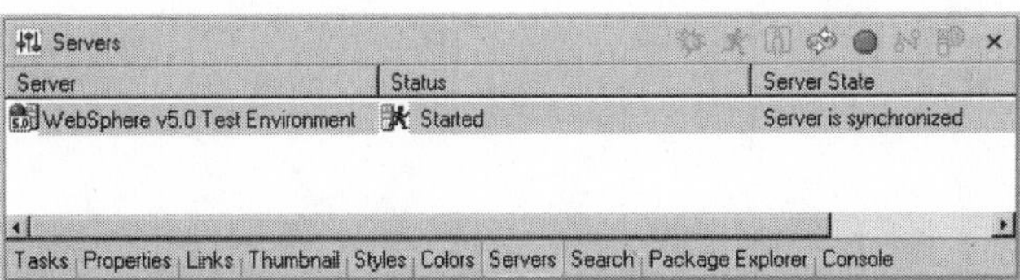

Figure 9.11 Server view.

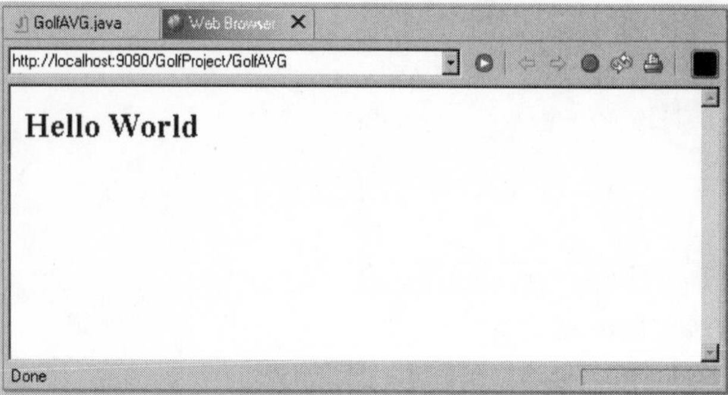

Figure 9.12 Servlet test.

The Web Application Definition

You may be wondering how WSAD was able to run the servlet automatically. There is a checkbox **Add to web.xml** in the Servlet wizard second page that automatically registers the servlet in the Web application definition. The file that contains the Web application definition is in the J2EE Navigator window a few levels below the Web Content directory, as shown in Figure 9.13. This is an XML file, and it has configuration information for the J2EE application server.

Double-click the web.xml file to view its contents. The Web Deployment Descriptor window displays, as shown in Figure 9.14. You can also double-click the Web Deployment Descriptor item, the first item in the GolfProject folder, to view the Web application definition. This is a nice editor for viewing and changing the many different configuration options for a Web application. This editor has separate views that can be accessed using the tabs at the bottom.

Figure 9.13 Web application configuration.

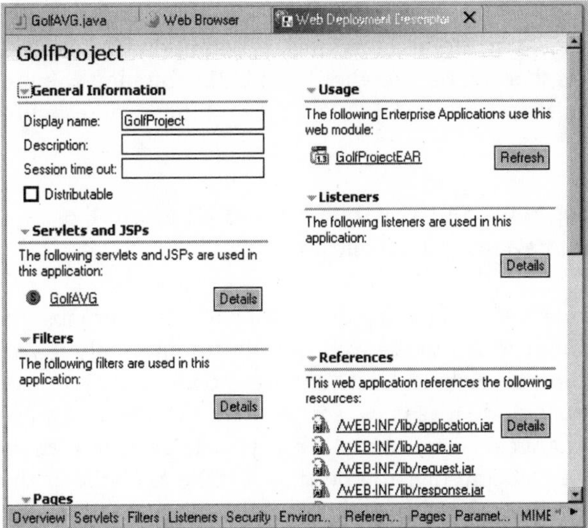

Figure 9.14 Web Deployment Descriptor viewer.

Click the Source tab to see the XML file. The file appears in the Web Deployment Descriptor window and should look as follows:

```
<?xml version="1.0" encoding="UTF-8"?>
<!DOCTYPE web-app PUBLIC "-//Sun Microsystems, Inc.//DTD Web Application
2.3//EN" "http://java.sun.com/dtd/web-app_2_3.dtd">
<web-app id="WebApp">
  <display-name>GolfProject</display-name>
  <servlet>
    <servlet-name>GolfAVG</servlet-name>
    <display-name>GolfAVG</display-name>
    <servlet-class>j2eebook.golf.controller.GolfAVG</servlet-class>
  </servlet>
  <servlet-mapping>
    <servlet-name>GolfAVG</servlet-name>
    <url-pattern>/GolfAVG</url-pattern>
  </servlet-mapping>
  <welcome-file-list>
    <welcome-file>index.html</welcome-file>
    <welcome-file>index.htm</welcome-file>
    <welcome-file>index.jsp</welcome-file>
    <welcome-file>default.html</welcome-file>
    <welcome-file>default.htm</welcome-file>
    <welcome-file>default.jsp</welcome-file>
  </welcome-file-list>
</web-app>
```

You can see the GolfAVG <servlet> and <servlet-mapping> sections in the XML file. The servlet has its servlet-name, display-name, and servlet-class definition. The servlet-mapping defines the servlet aliases that can be referenced in a URL. You may want to have different or additional servlet aliases for the URL. You can edit these values without affecting the servlet code.

NOTE If you pick other options in the Servlet wizard, such as Struts or other taglibs, the Web application will have additional entries.

You can directly edit the XML file instead of using the editors on the other tabs. As you create other servlets, they can be added to the web.xml file automatically if you use the Servlet wizard. If you import servlets or create servlets from copies, you will need to update the web.xml file to include these new servlets. WSAD does not automatically update this file for all changes. For example, when you delete a servlet, its definition is not removed from the web.xml file. You need to edit the XML file or the Servlet page and remove the servlet from the Web application definition. It technically does not hurt to have erroneous servlets listed in the Web application definition, but they should be removed so that the web.xml file is accurate.

Rerunning a Servlet

WSAD prompts you to select a server when you run the GolfAVG servlet again. When you select the Run on Sever button, the Server Selection window appears, as shown in Figure 9.15. You must select an appropriate server, which is the WebSphere v5.0 Test Environment.

There is a checkbox at the bottom of the Server Selection window that can help you test servlets. The option to **Set this server as the preferred server** makes it easier to retest the servlet. The selected server becomes the default and automatically starts when you want to run the servlet.

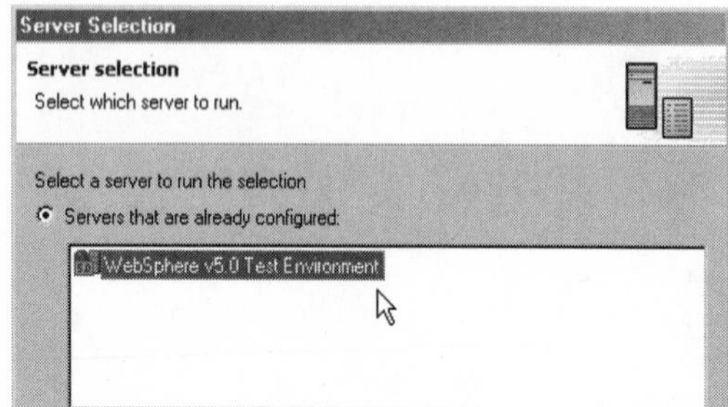

Figure 9.15 Server selection.

If you want to change this default setting later, you can do that through the Project Properties. You can change the server settings with the following steps:

1. Select the **GolfProject** in the J2EE Navigator.
2. From the pop-up menu, select **Properties**.
3. Select **Server Preference** in the tree view on the left, as shown in Figure 9.16.

You can change the default server on the Properties window for a project. You can also set it so that the prompting window does not appear. This will make testing servlets in WSAD a bit easy to start.

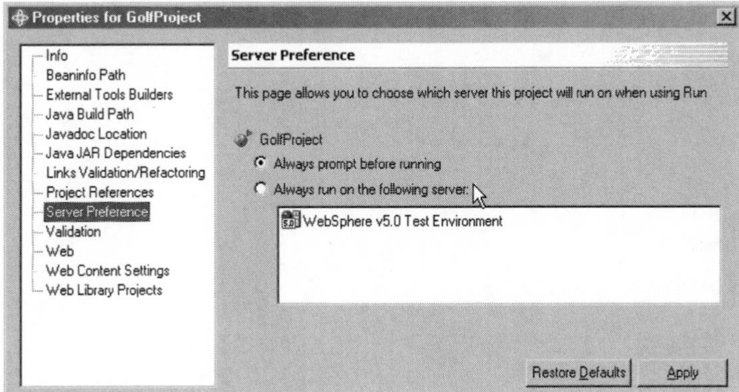

Figure 9.16 Project properties.

Using the Request

In order to read the items entered on the Golf Web page, you need to use the Request object that is also passed on the call to the servlet. There are many helpful methods in the ServletRequest interface, as seen in Figure 9.17. The methods cover two basic functions, namely information about the request and the data that is passed in the request. The ServletRequest uses the Java naming standards for methods with the familiar getter and setter methods for the different attributes.

Values on a Web page can be passed to a J2EE server by using named parameters as part of a URL or by parameters on an HTML form. First, you will see how to use parameters in a URL with an example in this chapter. You will learn how to handle parameters from forms in the next chapter, "Servlets with JavaBeans." Both techniques are commonly used in J2EE Web applications.

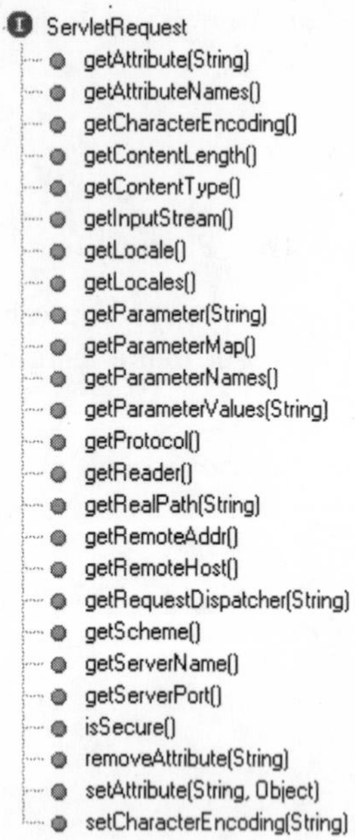

ServletRequest
- getAttribute(String)
- getAttributeNames()
- getCharacterEncoding()
- getContentLength()
- getContentType()
- getInputStream()
- getLocale()
- getLocales()
- getParameter(String)
- getParameterMap()
- getParameterNames()
- getParameterValues(String)
- getProtocol()
- getReader()
- getRealPath(String)
- getRemoteAddr()
- getRemoteHost()
- getRequestDispatcher(String)
- getScheme()
- getServerName()
- getServerPort()
- isSecure()
- removeAttribute(String)
- setAttribute(String, Object)
- setCharacterEncoding(String)

Figure 9.17 Request methods.

Reading Parameters from a URL

To read data passed on a URL from a Web page, you need to use the Request object that is passed along with the Response object in the `doGet()` method. The `getParameter(tag)` method in the Request returns an object that matches the tag name specified in the request. The values passed from a Web page come as Java Strings. You will need to convert the Strings to the desired type for further work. For example, we will need to convert the golf scores to an `Integer` or an `int` in order to do calculations.

There is no guarantee that the expected parameter is in the Request. You should always check if the returned value is null, which indicates that no value is found. You will use an if-else statement to handle this processing. If there is no value, the method returns an empty string. You can place this code in a new method called `readParameter()`. In the Source Editor for the GolfAVG servlet, create the new `readParameter()` method with the following code:

```
public String readParameter(HttpServletRequest req, String tag) {
    String param = (String) req.getParameter(tag);
    if (param != null) {
        return param;
    } else {
        return "";
    }
}
```

Now, you need to modify the doGet() method to read the user parameter and display the user in the HTML message. First the doGet() method calls the readParameter() method and saves the returned value in a temporary String. Then temporary String is passed as part of the message in the displayMessage() method. Now, edit the doGet() method to look as follows:

```
public void doGet(HttpServletRequest req, HttpServletResponse resp)
    throws ServletException, IOException {
    // read the user parameter
    String user = readParameter(req, "user");
    // display HTML message
    displayMessage(resp, "Hello World!<br><br>Welcome " + user);
}
```

Make sure that you save the GolfAVG servlet code. You can press CTRL-S to save the code changes. You are ready to test the updated servlet.

Passing Parameters in a URL

Parameters are passed at the end of a URL. A question mark (?) is placed after the servlet name as a delimiter for the parameter. The parameter name follows the question mark with an equals sign (=) and the actual parameter value. For example, a valid car parameter would be ?car=bmw. Parameter values may contain spaces, and there is a special convention to handle this. You must replace spaces in parameter values with a plus sign (+). Another example of a valid car parameter is ?car=bmw+330ic. When the value is read in the servlet using the getParameter() method, the plus sign is automatically removed, and the result would be **bmw 330ic**.

There are a few rules with parameter names. First parameter names are case sensitive. The following represent three distinctly different parameters: firstname, firstName, and FirstName. It is a good idea to adopt some standard naming conventions for parameter names. It is a good practice to keep parameter names in lowercase and fairly short. On a large project, you need to make sure that all developers are using the same conventions for parameters names. This will help ensure that independently developed modules can work together.

The updated servlet can take user as a parameter. You can add ?user=YourName to the servlet URL, and YourName will appear in the servlet response. Test the updated servlet in the Web Browser with the following steps:

1. Select the Web Browser tab in WSAD.
2. Make sure the URL is http://localhost:9080/GolfProject/GolfAVG.
3. At the end if the URL, add **?user=Firstname+LastName**.
4. The URL should look like: http://localhost:9080/GolfProject/GolfAVG?Dale+Nilsson.

5. Click the Serve the Selected URL button to test the servlet, and the information in the browser is displayed as shown in Figure 9.18.

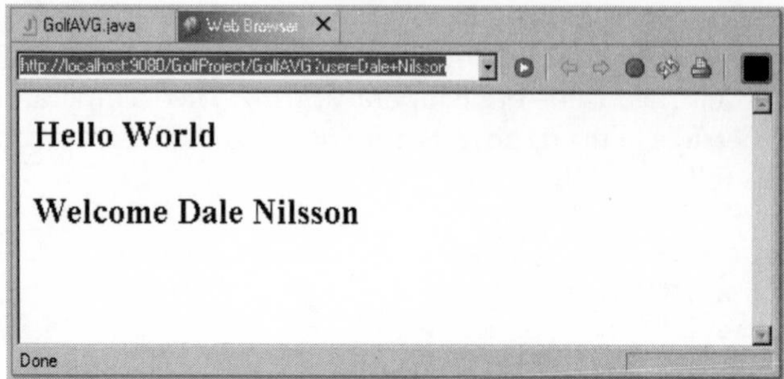

Figure 9.18 Passing parameters in a URL.

You can experiment with passing different values as the user parameter. You can also try changing the name of the parameter to something else like User and see what happens.

If there are errors in the servlet, you will need to fix those errors before you can test the servlet. The completed servlet should look as follows:

```
package j2eebook.golf.controller;
import java.io.IOException;
import javax.servlet.ServletException;
import javax.servlet.http.HttpServlet;
import javax.servlet.http.HttpServletRequest;
import javax.servlet.http.HttpServletResponse;
import java.io.PrintWriter;
public class GolfAVG extends HttpServlet {
    /*
    * Constructor
    */
    public GolfAVG() {
        super();
    }
    /*
    * @see GenericServlet#destroy()
    */
    public void destroy() {
        System.out.println(
            new java.util.Date() + " " + getServletName() + " stopped");
    }
    public void doGet(HttpServletRequest req, HttpServletResponse resp)
        throws ServletException, IOException {
        // read the user parameter
        String user = readParameter(req, "user");
        // display HTML message
        displayMessage(resp, "Hello World!<br><br>Welcome " + user);
    }
    public void doPost(HttpServletRequest req, HttpServletResponse resp)
        throws ServletException, IOException {
    }
    /*
```

```
    * @see GenericServlet#init()
    */
    public void init() throws ServletException {
        System.out.println(
            new java.util.Date() + " " + getServletName() + " started");
    }
    /*
    * display an HTML message
    */
    public void displayMessage(HttpServletResponse resp, String message)
        throws IOException {
        // Obtain the output stream from the response
        PrintWriter out = resp.getWriter();
        // print a simple html page in the printwriter
        out.println("<html><body><h2>" + message);
        out.println("</h2></body></html>");
    }
    /*
    * read a parameter from the request
    */
    public String readParameter(HttpServletRequest req, String tag) {
        String param = (String) req.getParameter(tag);
        if (param != null) {
            return param;
        } else {
            return "";
        }
    }
}
```

Redirecting a Web Page

There is another helpful method in the response that a servlet can use to control flow. The `sendRedirect(URL)` method. When a servlet calls the `sendRedirect(URL)` method, control is passed indirectly to the URL that is a parameter to the method. The redirect actually returns to the browser, creates a new response, and goes to the specified URL. This routing occurs even if the URL resource is local, such as an HTML file or JSP on the same server, as shown in Figure 9.19.

The code in the GolfAVG `doGet()` method was good for an example, but it needs to be updated to finish the servlet. It would be better if the `doGet()` method would redirect to the golf Web page. Use the source editor and edit the `doGet()` method in the GolfAVG servlet as follows:

```
public void doGet(HttpServletRequest req, HttpServletResponse resp)
    throws ServletException, IOException {
    // redirect to golf web page
    resp.sendRedirect("index.html");
}
```

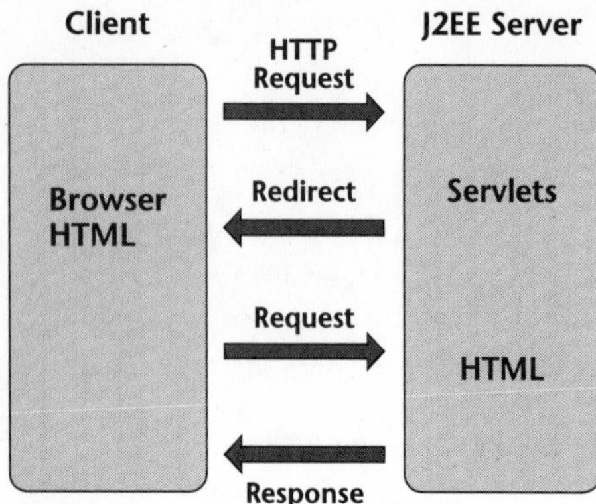

Figure 9.19 Response redirect.

Filters

The v2.3 Servlet API has a new Interface, called `Filter` that is intended to be used with servlets. A filter can intercept the initial call to a Web resource and act as a switch for an existing Web application. This provides a quick way to modify a Web application without changing the servlets that are already tested and deployed. The `Filter` Interface has the following methods:

- **init** — automatically runs when the filter starts. This method is good for initialization code.
- **doFilter(ServletRequest, ServletResponse, FilterChain)** — handles the requests and may be part of a chain of filters.
- **destroy** — automatically runs when the filter closes. This method is good for cleanup code.

Summary

In this chapter, you learned the basics of servlets and J2EE server-side programming. Servlets focus on controlling the program flow. They are an important part of the J2EE architecture and they take advantage of the many strengths already provided by Java. The key concepts covered include:

- The servlet life cycle
- Using the ServletRequest
- How the `doGet()` method is used
- Testing servlets

- How to manage the Web application definition in the web.xml file
- Using the Servlet Response
- Redirecting flow using the Response `sendRedirect()` method

There are tons of ways to use servlets, and this chapter only shows some of the basic uses. Server-side Java is an important area of Java development and a key J2EE component. There are a lot of design issues related to servlets and ensuring adequate performance. In the next chapter, you will build on what you have learned and use JavaBeans with servlets.

Servlets with JavaBeans

What's in Chapter 10?

In this chapter, you will incorporate the work from the previous few chapters. You will modify a servlet to read the data from an HTML page and store it in a JavaBean. The JavaBean will have the logic to average the values in a vector. You will test the servlet and fix a design error. This chapter covers the following topics:

- Reading parameters from a Web page
- Checking the session
- Working with a session
- Adding attributes to a session
- Using JavaBeans
- Centralizing references

Servlets with JavaBeans allow you to place data and business logic in a JavaBean. You will build on the concepts covered in the previous chapter, where you learned how to read parameters in a servlet from a URL. In this chapter, you will learn how to read parameters from an HTML form and store the values in a Javabean. You will create methods that use the data in the JavaBean and learn how to debug servlets. Finally, you will learn how to place strings in a separate class as a common technique for centralizing references.

Reading Parameters from a Web Page

You can use the same server code that you used for reading parameters from a URL to read parameters from a Web page. You will add a new method to the GolfAVG servlet that calls the existing readParameter() method and stores the values in the GolfData JavaBean.

The Golf Web page created in Chapter 5, "Web Page Content," and Chapter 6, "Linking Web Page Content," is used as the input page for the data. The HTML for the page should looks as follows:

```
<!DOCTYPE HTML PUBLIC "-//W3C//DTD HTML 4.01 Transitional//EN">
<HTML>
<HEAD>
<META name="AUTHOR" content="Your Name" />
<META http-equiv="Content-Style-Type" content="text/css">
<LINK href="theme/Master.css" rel="stylesheet" type="text/css">
<TITLE>My Golf Page</TITLE>
</HEAD>
<BODY>
<TABLE>
  <TBODY>
    <TR>
      <TD nowrap colspan="2">
      <H1>Welcome to My Golf Page!</H1>
      </TD>
    </TR>
    <TR>
      <TD nowrap valign="top" align="left" bgcolor="#cccccc">
          My Favorite Links<BR>
      <BR>
      <A href = "http://www.usga.org/index.html"> USGA</A><BR>
      <BR>
      <A href="http://www.weather.com">The Weather</A><BR><BR>
      <A href="http://www.mapquest.com">Travel Maps</A></TD>
      <TD>Handicap Calculator<BR>
      <!-- form to capture scores for handicap calculator -->
      <FORM action="/GolfProject/GolfAVG" method="post">
      <TABLE border="1">
        <TBODY>
          <TR>
            <TD></TD>
            <TH nowrap>Score</TH>
          </TR>
          <TR>
            <TD>Round1:</TD>
            <TD><INPUT size="3" type="text" maxlength="3"
name="round1"></TD>
          </TR>
          <TR>
            <TD>Round2:</TD>
```

```
                <TD><INPUT size="3" type="text" maxlength="3"
name="round2"></TD>
              </TR>
              <TR>
                <TD>Round3:</TD>
                <TD><INPUT size="3" type="text" maxlength="3"
name="round3"></TD>
              </TR>
              <TR>
                <TD>Round4:</TD>
                <TD><INPUT size="3" type="text" maxlength="3"
name="round4"></TD>
              </TR>
              <TR>
                <TD>Round5:</TD>
                <TD><INPUT size="3" type="text" maxlength="3"
name="round5"></TD>
              </TR>
              <TR>
                <TD><INPUT type="reset" name="reset" value="Reset"></TD>
                <TD><INPUT type="submit" name="submit"
value="Calculate"></TD>
              </TR>
            </TBODY>
          </TABLE>
          </FORM>
          </TD>
        </TR>
    </TBODY>
</TABLE>
</BODY>
</HTML>
```

The Golf Web page has an HTML <Form> tag with input fields for the golf scores and a submit button labeled Calculate. The five input fields are named round1, round2, round3, round4, and round5 using the name attribute in the tag. The parameters are read in the servlet using these names, and they are case sensitive. It is very important to choose names that can be easily understood and not reuse generic names like data1.

Reading Form Parameters

You will build on the GolfAVG servlet that you built in Chapter 9, "Making Servlets," which read parameters from a URL. The `doGet()` method and the `doPost()` method are changed from Chapter 9. Here, the `doGet()` method is used to display the HTML page, and the `doPost()` method is used to collect the parameters. In Chapter 9, the input parameters are passed in the query string when the `doGet()` method was called. You will be adding new methods and working primarily with the `doPost()` method that is called when a form button is clicked. The GolfAVG servlet should look as follows:

```
package j2eebook.golf.controller;
import java.io.IOException;
import javax.servlet.ServletException;
import javax.servlet.http.HttpServlet;
import javax.servlet.http.HttpServletRequest;
import javax.servlet.http.HttpServletResponse;
import javax.servlet.http.HttpSession;
import java.io.PrintWriter;
import j2eebook.golf.domain.GolfData;
import java.util.*;
public class GolfAVG extends HttpServlet {
    /*
    * Constructor
    */
    public GolfAVG() {
        super();
    }
    public void destroy() {
        System.out.println(
            new java.util.Date() + " " + getServletName() + " stopped");
    }
    public void doGet(HttpServletRequest req, HttpServletResponse resp)
        throws ServletException, IOException {
        // redirect to golf web page
        resp.sendRedirect("index.html");
    }
    public void doPost(HttpServletRequest req, HttpServletResponse resp)
        throws ServletException, IOException {
    }
public void init() throws ServletException {
        System.out.println(
            new java.util.Date() + " " + getServletName() + " started");
    }
// display an HTML message
    public void displayMessage(HttpServletResponse resp, String message)
        throws IOException {
        // Obtain the output stream from the response
        PrintWriter out = resp.getWriter();
        // print a simple html page in the printwriter
        out.println("<html><body><h2>" + message);
        out.println("</h2></body></html>");
    }
// read a parameter from the request
    public String readParameter(HttpServletRequest req, String tag) {
        String param = (String) req.getParameter(tag);
        if (param != null) {
            return param;
        } else {
            return "";
        }
    }
}
```

You need to create a new method in the GolfAVG servlet to read these five scores and store them in a Java Vector. The `readScores()` method is passed the HttpServlet-Request as a parameter, because the values from the input fields on the HTML form are in the request. The input field values are accessed with the `getParameter()` method and located by their name. The `getParameter()` method returns a `null` if there is no parameter found. Add the new `readScores()` method to the GolfAVG Servlet with the following code:

```
// read golf scores from the request
public Vector readScores(HttpServletRequest req) {
    Vector scores = new Vector();
    for (int i = 1; i < 6; i++) {
        String param = (String) req.getParameter("round" + i);
        if (param != null) {
            scores.addElement(param);
        }
    }
    return scores;
}
```

Notice the `if` statement in the `for` loop of the `readScores()` method that tests if the parameter is `null`. This test prevents a programming error. If one of the textfields is not properly labeled, the parameter would be null. The scores Vector takes an Object in the `addElement()` method. You cannot add null Objects to a Vector.

The `readScores()` method needs to be linked to the servlet processing. You need to modify the `doPost()` method that gets called when the Calculate button is pressed on the Golf Web page. The `doPost()` method calls the new `readScores()` method and the existing `displayMessage()` method to display the scores read by the server. Edit the `doPost()` method in the GolfAVG servlet to look as follows:

```
public void doPost(HttpServletRequest req, HttpServletResponse resp)
    throws ServletException, IOException {
    displayMessage(resp, "You entered the following scores:<br><br>"+
readScores(req).toString());
}
```

Testing HTML Form Parameters

You can test the code that you have written even though the implementation is not finished. Now, test the Golf Average application with the following steps:

1. Select the index.html file in the J2EE Navigator under GolfProject > Web Content.
2. From the pop-up menu, select Run on Server. It will take a little while for the WebSphere Test Environment to start, if it is not already running.
3. The Web page displays in the browser, as seen in Figure 10.1. Enter numbers for each score, and click the Calculate button.

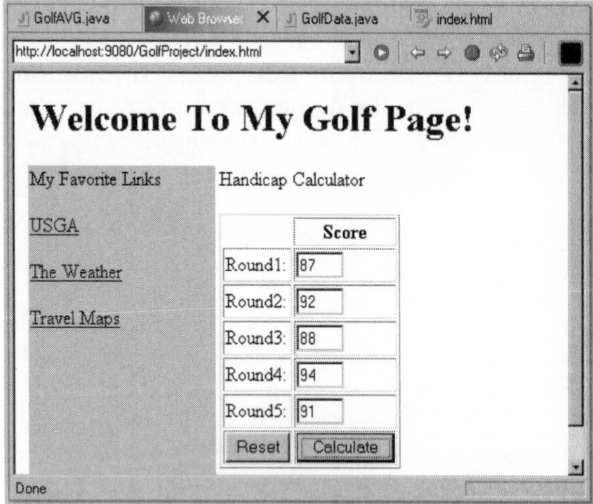

Figure 10.1 Entering test data.

4. The parameters are passed to the GolfAVG servlet calling the `doPost()` method. The servlet returns the HTML response shown in Figure 10.2.

The values displayed in the response are the result of the Vector's `toString()` method and it shows brackets at the beginning and end of the Vector. You could improve the display and remove the brackets with a `while()` loop that iterates through the Vector and display the elements individually. This chapter is not focused on how the response looks; rather it covers how to save the data in a JavaBean. In the next chapter, "JavaServer Pages," you will see how to improve the way the response looks.

Working with a Session

The use of Sessions is very important in J2EE programming. This section discusses the HttpSession and shows you how to use it with servlets. You will modify the servlet and place the JavaBean to hold the data from the Web page for the session.

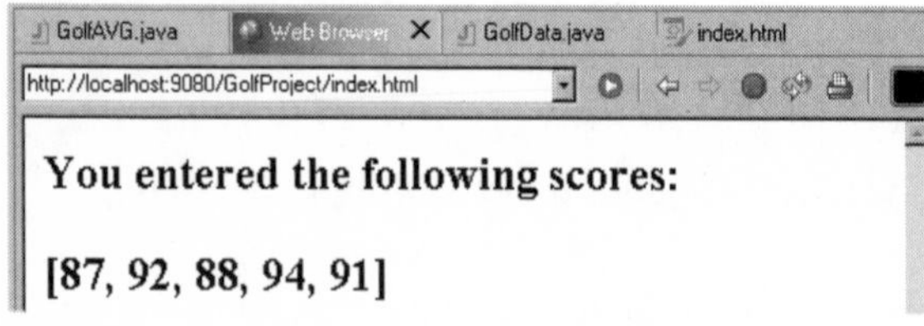

Figure 10.2 Testing HTML form parameters.

What Is a Session?

A session is another interface that is part of the J2EE Servlet API. The session carries the application data that is not in the URL. A lot of servlet programming is reading attributes from the request, processing business logic, and then returning HTML in the response.

Session ID

The session has a unique ID that is created during the request to the server. This unique session ID allows multiple client browsers to call the same servlet URL, as shown in Figure 10.3. The response processing is then returned to the same client browser. This works whether the browsers are on the same client or on different clients.

Session Methods

There are many methods in the HttpSession interface, as shown in Figure 10.4. The key methods that you will be using are the `getAttribute()`, `getAttributeNames()`, `removeAttribute()`, and `setAttribute()` methods. These methods replace the older deprecated `getValue()`, `getValueNames()`, `removeValue()`, and `putValue()` methods that act the same as their new replacements. The `getAttribute()` and `setAttribute()` methods are used to retrieve and place objects in the session. You will add a JavaBean as an attribute to the session using these methods. The next section covers attributes in greater detail.

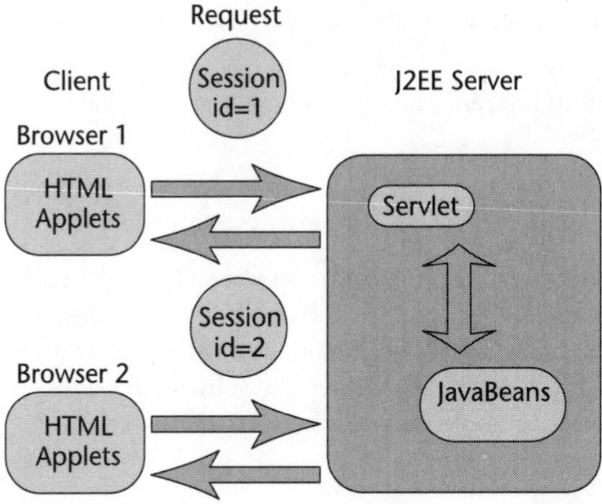

Figure 10.3 Passing a session ID.

HttpSession
- getAttribute(String)
- getAttributeNames()
- getCreationTime()
- getId()
- getLastAccessedTime()
- getMaxOnactiveOnterval()
- getServletContext()
- getValue(String)
- isNew()
- putValue(String, Object)
- removeAttribute(String)
- removeValue(String)
- setAttribute(String, Object)
- setMaxInactiveInterval(int)

Figure 10.4 HttpSession methods.

Making a session

The session has three different ways to use its getter methods with the request, and they are as follows:

request.getSession() — A session reference is returned if a session exists, or else a null is returned.

request.getSession(false) — A session reference is returned if a session exists, or else a null is returned.

request.getSession(true) — A session reference is returned if a session exists, or else a new session is constructed and returned. This getter always returns a session.

Each getter can be used in a different situation. It is common to use the third variation in a logon servlet for the first time a user visits the Web application. Subsequent calls to the Web application would use the first or second getter variation. You can assume that the user is not logged on or the session has timed out if the getter does not return a reference. You can rely on variation three for sites that do not rely on logging into the Web application.

Session Attributes

A request contains a session that can hold many attributes, as shown in Figure 10.5. It is better to put a few well-designed classes in the session than to scatter a lot of different diverse objects. The `getAttribute()` method returns an object. You need to know the object type and cast it in your code before accessing any of its methods. Conversely, the `setAttribute()` method takes a name and an object as parameters. When the `setAttribute()` method is called to add attributes to the session, the object is implicitly cast to a Java object.

NOTE **You cannot directly store primitive data like an int or a float in a session. The attribute getter and setter methods only handle Objects. If you need to save primitive data you will need to save it in its wrapper class such as Integer or Float.**

Session attributes are saved as a name/value pairs. The names are Strings that can hold any text value, including spaces and many special characters. The names should be descriptive but not too long. You need to take special care because the attribute names are case sensitive. The values are Java Objects and can be a simple String, a list object like a Vector or a Hashtable, or a complex object like Customer, which has a name, address, ID, profile, current balance, buying history, and other information.

An example of a request with attributes is shown in Figure 10.6. The session has three parameters:

1. A user attribute with the value Karl.
2. A car attribute with the value Porsche.
3. A golfdata attribute with a Vector of values starting with 80, 84, 88.

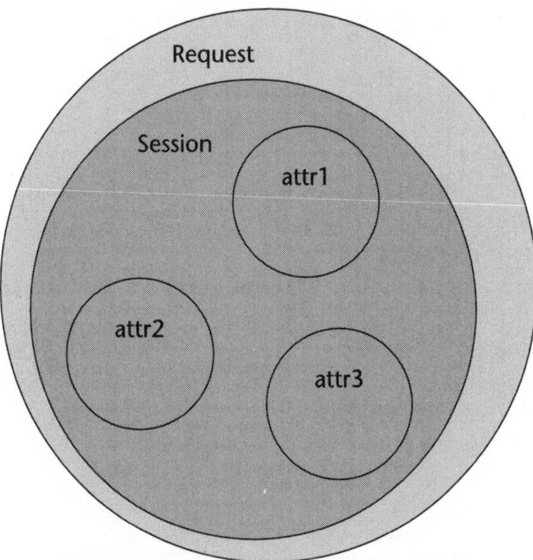

Figure 10.5 Request with session and attributes.

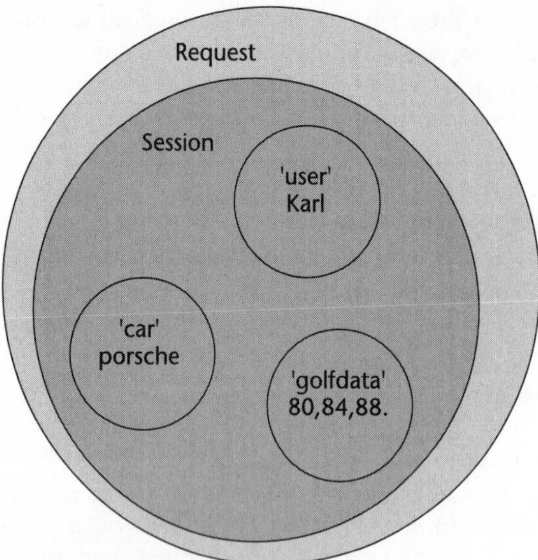

Figure 10.6 Request with session and specific attributes.

All of these attributes are stored as Java Objects. The session acts as a data holder for information specific to this session. The data will stay in the session until the browser is closed, the session times out on the server, or instructions in a servlet use the `removeAttribute()` method. As a servlet developer, you need to account for the number of users and the size of the information that is stored in the session. Web sites that have a lot of users usually set a short session timeout such as 5 minutes or less. The session remains active as long as the user is clicking links or buttons that call the Web site.

Adding JavaBeans to the Session

The JavaBean acts as a data holder for in the Web architecture, as shown in Figure 10.7. A reference to the JavaBean is added as an attribute to the session. The data is kept in the session because the servlet is stateless and should not hold on to data for a specific client. This is how you can have one servlet serving many clients.

You will build on the code already in the servlet by adding a new method called `calcScores()`. This new method creates a GolfData JavaBean and adds it to the session with the name golfdata. The method takes the request as a parameter so that it can get a reference to the session. Then the `calcScores()` method calls the existing `readScores()` method and stores the scores in the JavaBean. The `calcScores()` method should look as follows:

```
/ load golf scores from the request
public Vector loadScores(HttpServletRequest req) {
    // get the session
    HttpSession session = req.getSession(true);
    // make a GolfData bean
    GolfData data = new GolfData();
    // add GolfData to the session
```

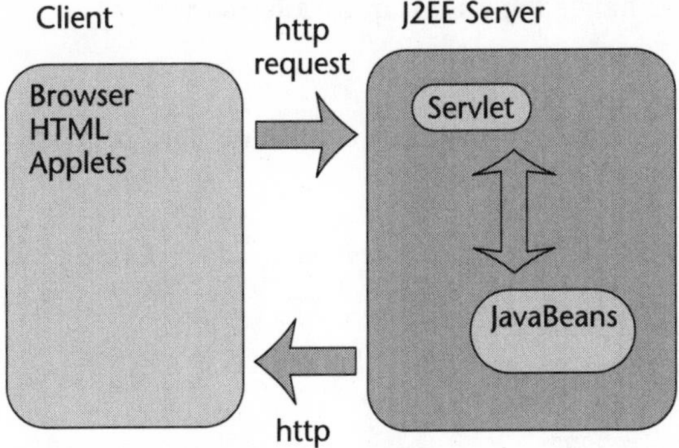

Figure 10.7 Servlet and JavaBean.

```
        session.setAttribute("golfdata", data);
        // read the scores into the GolfData bean
        data.setScores(readScores(req));
        return data.getScores();
    }
```

Add another utility method, named `avgScores()`, to average the numbers in a Vector. This method should take a Vector as a parameter and return a float as the average. Edit the code and add the `avgScores()` method as follows:

```
    // calculate an average from a vector
    public float avgScores(Vector numbers) {
        // loop through the Vector and calculate the average
        int sum = 0;
        for (int i = 0; i < numbers.size(); i++) {
            sum += Integer.parseInt((String) numbers.elementAt(i));
        }
        float avg = sum / numbers.size();
        return avg;
    }
```

The `doPost()` method needs to be modified to use this new code. The `doPost()` method should do the following:

1. Call `loadScores()` and save the returned Vector in a local variable.
2. Call `avgScores()` passing the returned Vector. The averages should be saved in a local variable.
3. The `displayMessage()` method should be called passing the response and a message. The message should include the Vector of scores entered, the average, and the handicap. To simplify calculations, the handicap is the average minus 72.

NOTE **Calculating golf handicaps has a number of rules that would make the code for this example application more complex. Later in the chapter, you will move the average calculation to the GolfData JavaBean where the logic should**

reside. It would not be difficult to enhance the handicap calculation with a method in the JavaBean.

Using the Java Editor, modify the `doPost()` method in the GolfAVG servlet as follows:

```
public void doPost(HttpServletRequest req, HttpServletResponse resp)
    throws ServletException, IOException {
// load the scores and calculate the average
    Vector scores = loadScores(req);
    float avg = avgScores(scores);
    // display the data in the response
    displayMessage(resp, "You entered the following scores:<br><br>"
    + scores + "<br><br>Your average is " + avg
    + "<br><br>Your handicap is " + (avg - 72));
}
```

Testing Servlets with JavaBeans

There is enough completed to test the updated Golf Web page. You can run the Web page, enter data, and see the updated response with the average and handicap for the scores. The Web page is already configured to run on a test server. Test the updated Web page with the following steps:

1. Select the index.html file for the Golf Web page in the J2EE Navigator.
2. From the pop-up menu, select Run on Server.
3. The Golf Web page displays as shown in Figure 10.8. Enter data for all the golf scores, and click the Calculate button.

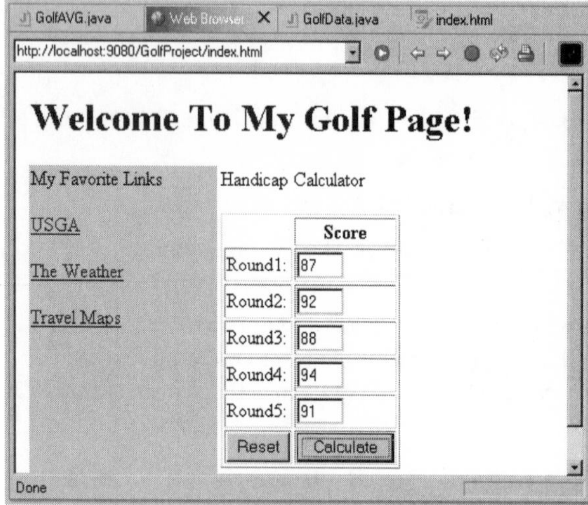

Figure 10.8 Entering test data.

Figure 10.9 Entering data on a form.

The response page shows the same information as before along with the average and handicap, as shown in Figure 10.9. All of these values are stored in the GolfData JavaBean. You will learn how to get values out of the JavaBean in the next section.

Retrieving JavaBeans from the Session

Now that there is a JavaBean reference in the session, you need to be able to retrieve the JavaBean from the session so that you can access the JavaBean in another servlet or use the JavaBean in another method. You can do this by calling the `getAttribute()` method in the session and passing the desired attribute tag. You use the "golfdata" String to get the GolfData JavaBean in the session. The `getAttribute()` method returns an Object, so this must be cast to the desired type. For this case, it needs to be cast to GolfData. Make these changes to the `loadScores()` method so that it looks as follows:

```
// load golf scores from the request
public Vector loadScores(HttpServletRequest req) {
    // get the session
    HttpSession session = req.getSession(true);
    // get the GolfData bean
    GolfData data = (GolfData) req.getAttribute("golfdata");
    if (data == null) {
        // make a GolfData bean
        data = new GolfData();
        // add GolfData to the session
        session.setAttribute("golfdata", data);
    }
    // read the scores into the GolfData bean
    data.setScores(readScores(req));
    return data.getScores();
}
```

Notice the `if` statement in the `loadScores()` method. There is no JavaBean in the session the first time this servlet is called, so the `if` statement handles this case and creates a new GolfData JavaBean and adds it to the session. The servlet uses the existing JavaBean if it exists in the session. This design pattern for retrieving objects from the session is very common. The code would function the same if it created a new JavaBean every time it is called, but this may destroy information that other servlets placed in the JavaBean. It also is better to reuse existing JavaBeans for large classes that may take a while to construct.

If you rerun the Golf Web page and pass numbers to the Golf servlet as you did previously, you should get the same result. Internally, the servlet is reusing the GolfData JavaBean that is in the session.

Adding Logic to JavaBeans

The GolfData JavaBean currently has code to hold data. It is a better design to have the JavaBean do the calculations and remove this business logic from the servlet. You can add additional methods to the JavaBean to perform other functions. You will move the `avgScores()` method from the servlet and change the `doPost()` method to reference the `avgScores()` method.

There are a few ways to move classes in WSAD, but the options for moving methods are limited. Use the cut-and-paste function in the Java Editor or the Outline view in the Java perspective, and move the `avgScores()` method from the GolfAVG servlet to the GolfData JavaBean. Make sure to save both the servlet and the JavaBean after making these changes.

You need to modify the `doPost()` method to get a reference to the GolfData JavaBean in the session, and then store the scores in the JavaBean. Change the GolfAVG `doPost()` method to look as follows:

```
public void doPost(HttpServletRequest req, HttpServletResponse resp)
     throws ServletException, IOException {
     // load the scores and calculate the average
     Vector scores = loadScores(req);
     GolfData data = (GolfData)
     req.getSession(true).getAttribute("golfdata");
     float avg = data.avgScores(scores);
     // display the data in the response
     displayMessage(resp, "You entered the following scores:<br><br>"
     + scores + "<br><br>Your average is " + avg
     + "<br><br>Your handicap is " + (avg - 72));
}
```

Save the GolfAVG servlet after making this change. If you retest the Golf Web page, you should get the same results you saw in Figure 10.9. You did not add any new function; you merely moved the function from the servlet to the JavaBean. This is a form of refactoring, which is defined as moving code to improve the design or to get better reuse.

Debugging Servlets

Chapter 4, "Debugging in WebSphere Studio Application Developer," covered testing and debugging Java applications. This section covers servlet testing and debugging, now that you have a solid understanding of servlets. Debugging servlets is a lot like debugging Java applications with a few differences. First. you will add a little code to detect errors, then you will use the debugger to isolate an error, and finally you will apply a fix for the error.

Handling Servlet Errors

There are two types of runtime errors that can occur: errors that result from programming mistakes and errors that result from user input. Programming errors can happen when null references are returned and loops end abnormally. User input errors can happen if users enter invalid data such as negative numbers or characters for scores. Both errors can be managed using Java Exceptions.

The Java runtime throws Exceptions under many different circumstances. If there is no number entered for a score or if an alphabetic character is entered, the `avgScores()` method will throw an exception. The code that converts an input number to an int using `Integer.parseInt()` throws a NumberFormatException, and there is no code to catch the Exception. As a good practice, the `doPost()` and the `doGet()` methods should have a `try/catch` block to handle Exceptions that may be thrown during execution.

As a review, Java has a construct for catching errors that uses three Java reserved words, namely `try`, `catch`, and `finally` as shown in Figure 10.10. The `try` must be followed by at least one `catch`, and the `finally` statement is optional. Processing starts in the `try` statement. If any Exceptions are thrown, processing is transferred to the `catch` statement. The `catch` is designed to filter and handle different Exceptions. The example in Figure 10.10 shows the `catch` statement handling `Exception`, the parent class for all exceptions. There are other errors that are not caught by the `Exception` class. To handle all errors you would need to use catch(Throwable) instead. There can be multiple catch statements that handle exceptions starting with the most specific finishing with the most general exception, which is the Exception class.

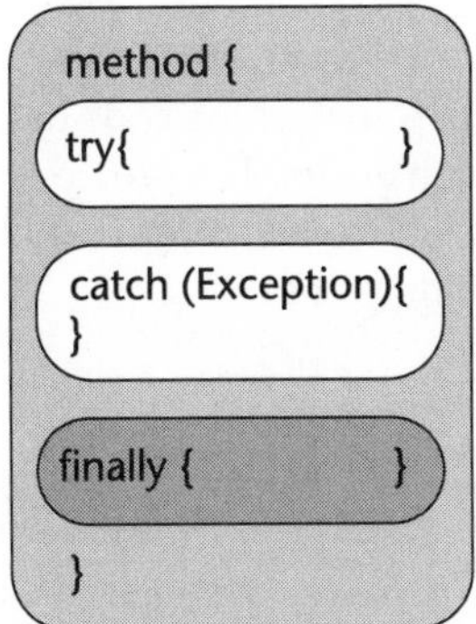

Figure 10.10 Response displaying average.

It is very easy to modify the `doPost()` method and add a `try/catch` block. You can use multiple `try/catch` blocks to isolate specific errors, but this `doPost()` is fairly simple, and adding one `try/catch` block is a lot better than not having one at all. In the `catch` statement, you will add a System.out message that prints in the console. You can employ more elaborate logging techniques, but this is good for a start. You will also add an error message that displays in the catch. Make these changes to the `doPost()` method so that it looks as follows:

```
public void doPost(HttpServletRequest req, HttpServletResponse resp)
     throws ServletException, IOException {
     try {
          // load the scores and calculate the average
          Vector scores = loadScores(req);
          GolfData data+ = (GolfData)
            req.getSession().getAttribute("golfdata");
          float avg = data.avgScores(scores);
          // display the data in the response
          displayMessage(resp,
          "You entered the following scores:<br><br>"
          + scores + "<br><br>Your average is "
          + avg + "<br><br>Your handicap is "
          + (avg - 72));
     } catch (Exception e) {
          System.out.println("GolfAVG Exception in doPost() " + e);
displayMessage(resp,"An error occurred.<br><br>Press the
browser back button and check that all the scores have valid numbers.");
     }
}
```

Using `try/catch` blocks in your code is very important for handling errors. Both the `doGet()` and `doPost()` methods should have `try/catch` blocks to manage exceptions. You are ready to test and debug the servlet now that the code has a `try/catch` block. The next section shows you how to use the WSAD debugger to step through a running servlet.

Starting a Debug Server

When you are testing with a Web server, the server must be started as a debug server. If the server is a standard server and not a debug server, breakpoints in the code are ignored and the code runs without permitting you to step through errors. The previous testing was done using a standard test server, so this server needs to be stopped and restarted as a debug server. Stop the test server with the following steps:

1. Select the Servers tab at the bottom of the Workbench.
2. In the Servers view, select the WebSphere Test Environment, and click the Stop the server button, as shown in Figure 10.11.
3. It takes a little time to stop the server. As the server stops, it passes messages to the console. WSAD automatically switches to the Console view. You will see the message *`Server server1`* stopped in the console when the server is stopped.

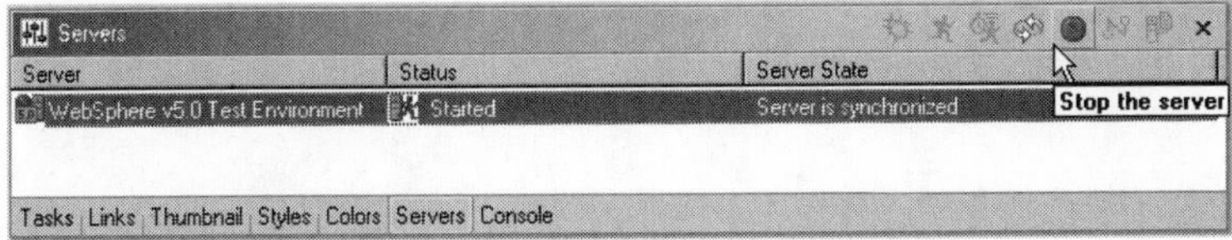

Figure 10.11 Try catch block.

The next step is to start the test server in debug mode. There are a few different ways to start a server; this time, you will use the Servers view. Start the server as follows:

1. Click the Servers tab to display the available servers, as shown in Figure 10.12.
2. Click on the Bug icon and WSAD starts the server in debug mode.

Once the WebSphere Test Environment is started in debug mode, you can start debugging servlets. The following section takes you through the steps to debug a servlet.

Debugging a Servlet

When the WebSphere Test Environment starts, WSAD automatically displays the Debug Perspective. The details of using the Debug Perspective are covered in Chapter 4, "Debugging in WebSphere Studio Application Developer." You need to be familiar with the step-into and step-over functions in the debugger for this section. Start testing the Golf Web application with the following steps:

1. Select the Web Browser tab. If the tab is not displayed, you need to switch to the Web Perspective, select the index.html file, and from the pop-up menu select Debug on Server.
2. The Golf Web page displays. Enter values for Round1, Round2, Round3, and Round4, as shown in Figure 10.13. Make sure to leave Round5 empty.
3. Click the Calculate button on the Web page, and the Step-by-Step Debug window appears. Click the OK button to proceed.
4. The response indicating that an error occurred is shown in Figure 10.14.

Processing starts when the servlet `doPost()` is called by the Calculate button. The `catch` clause in the `doPost()` method catches an Exception and displays an error in the response. Now, you can step through the code and isolate the error. After you isolate the error, you can modify the code to prevent this error from occurring.

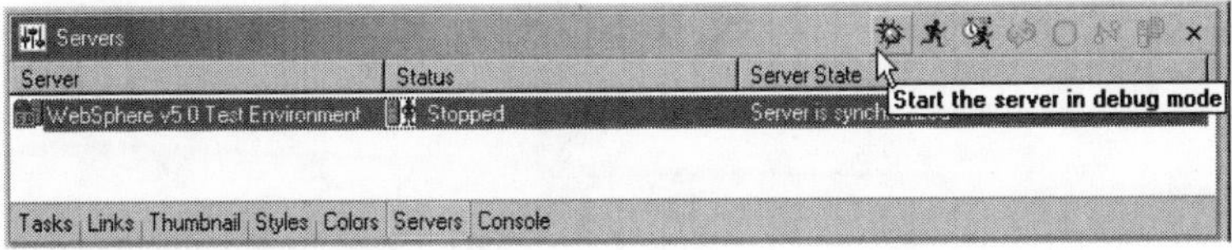

Figure 10.12 Stopping a server.

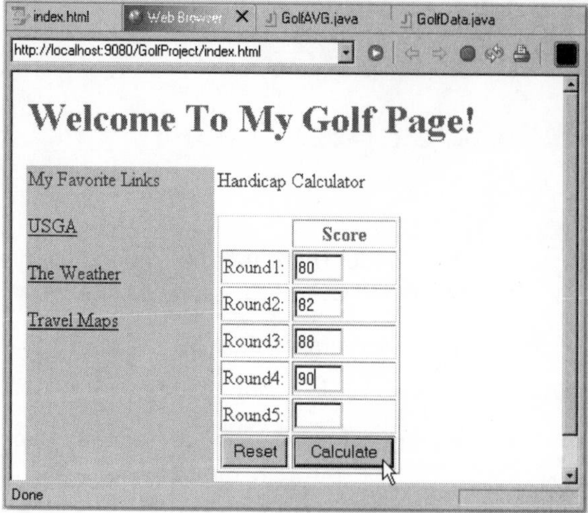

Figure 10.13 Starting a debug server.

Setting breakpoints

You must set breakpoints in the code in order to halt execution and step through code to locate errors. There is a small blue-green strip on the left side of the Source view that allows you to set breakpoints. The breakpoint is only used at development time and is shown as a small teal ball in the breakpoint strip. To catch the entry point of the servlet, you can place a breakpoint in the `doPost()` method. Place a breakpoint at the beginning of the `doPost()` method as shown in Figure 10.15.

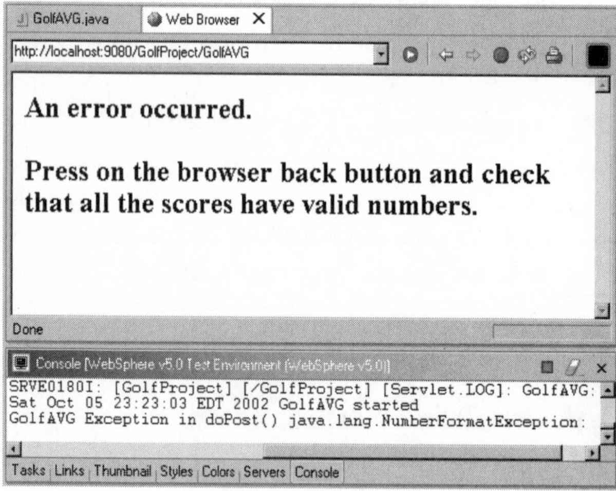

Figure 10.14 Entering invalid data.

```
index.html   Web Browser   GolfAVG.java   GolfData.java
/*
 * @see HttpServlet#doPost(HttpServletRequest req, Ht
 */
public void doPost(HttpServletRequest req, HttpServ
    throws ServletException, IOException {
    try {
        // load the scores and calculate the average
        Vector scores = loadScores(req);
        GolfData data =
            (GolfData) req.getSession().getAttribute
        float avg = data.avgScores(scores);
        // display the data in the response
        displayMessage(resp,
            "You entered the following scores:<br><b
                + scores + "<br><br>Your average is
                + avg + "<br><br>Your handicap is "
```

Figure 10.15 Viewing error message.

Now that the debug server is running and there is a breakpoint in the servlet, you are ready to step thru the code with the following steps:

1. Click the Web Browser tab and bring up the Golf Web page on http://localhost:9080/GolfProject/index.html.
2. On the Golf Web page, enter numbers for all but one of the golf scores.
3. Click the Calculate key.
4. The Step-by-Step Debug window displays, as shown in Figure 10.16. Click the OK button to close this window and continue.

Step-by-step debugging is only supported in the WebSphere v5 Test Environment. It allows you to skip Web objects as they are loaded for debugging. Every time a Web object is loaded you are prompted with a window like the one in Figure 10.16. This window lets you skip or step into the object that is loading. This can be a very helpful feature that allows you to skip code that is stable or that may be unaffected by your latest changes.

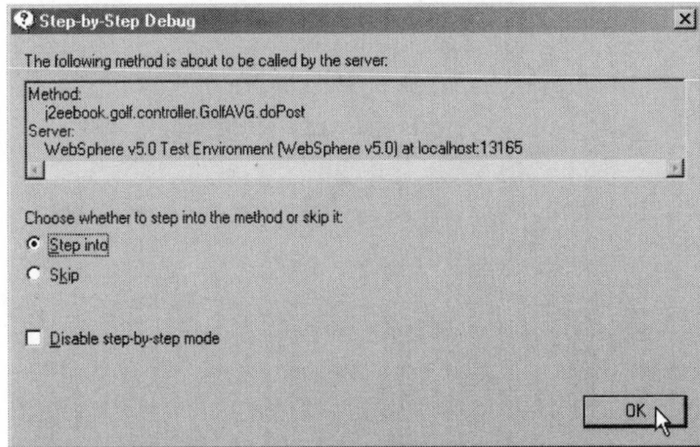

Figure 10.16 Setting a breakpoint.

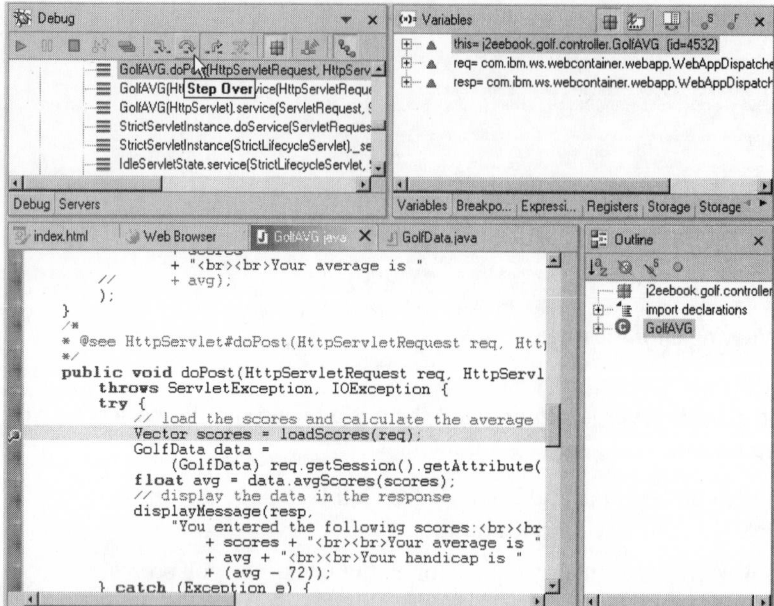

Figure 10.17 Debugging message.

Execution stops at the breakpoint that you placed in the `doPost()` method, as shown in Figure 10.17. The upper-left corner of the Debug Perspective has the debug functions. You may need to click the Debug tab to see these functions because this space is shared with the Server view.

Step through the code until the Exception is thrown. You can see that the `addScores()` method throws a NumberFormatException. This happens because the code that converts the input data to an `int` using the `Integer` class can not convert a blank. The Number FormatException is thrown, and it is up to the developer to handle it in the code.

NOTE You can select the Add Java Exception Breakpoint button in the breakpoints tab in the upper-right section of the Debug Perspective. This function allows WSAD to look for specific Exceptions during debugging. It can be very helpful to look for common Exceptions like the NullPointerException. It should be named NullReferenceException, because Java does not have pointers like C++ does.

You can fix the `readScores()` method so that it does not place empty strings in the scores vector. The code is already checking if a score parameter is null when the parameter value is read. You can add another check to see if the length of the value equals zero. Make this change to the `readScores()` method so that it looks as follows:

```
// read golf scores from the request
public Vector readScores(HttpServletRequest req) {
    Vector scores = new Vector();
    for (int i = 1; i < 6; i++) {
        String param = (String) req.getParameter("round" + i);
        if ((param != null) && (param.length()>0)) {
            scores.addElement(param);
        }
    }
    return scores;
}
```

Make sure to save your changes. Try retesting the Web page. Run the index.html file and omit one of the scores as before. The response page should display the scores read, the average, and the handicap with no errors. The NumberFormatException is thrown if the user enters invalid characters for the score such as **9A** or **8/**. These errors are caught by the `catch()` in the `doPost()` method, and an error message is displayed to the user.

Centralizing References

The Golf Web page and the GolfAVG servlet work fine, but there is another item that can be improved. The text references used in retrieving the parameters from the request and in referencing the JavaBean in the session are hard-coded Strings in the servlet code. These references are case sensitive and should be centralized for the following reasons:

Maintenance — By having the Strings in one place, when you update the centralized reference all the methods that use that reference are updated.

Consistency — With all the tags in one location, it is easy to find and use common tags.

Uniqueness — When you need to create a new tag for a different attribute, you can see the existing tags and choose one with a distinct name.

Externalization — Hard-coded strings should be externalized into a property file so that the Strings can be changed without affecting the code or requiring a recompile.

As you add more functions with additional servlets and Web pages, you will need to use these hard-coded names again. You can use the code assist function (Ctrl-Space) to find tags while you are coding.

Creating a Class for Tags

The attribute names placed in the session are called many different things such as tags, names, and labels. You should make a new class with a short name that can hold the String names, and then you can modify the GolfAVG servlet to use these static variables. Create a new Java class named Tags with the following steps:

1. From the Java Perspective, select File > New > Class, and the new Java Class window appears, as seen in Figure 10.18.
2. Make sure the Source folder is GolfProject/Java Source.
3. Make sure the package is j2eebook.golf.domain.
4. Enter **Tags** for the name.
5. Check the **abstract** checkbox. Making the class abstract prevents developers from making multiple instances of this class.
6. The class should have **java.lang.Object** as the Superclass.
7. Make sure that the checkboxes public static void main(), Constructors from superclass, and Inherited methods from superclass are not checked. This class only holds data and does not have any methods.
8. Click the Finish button to create the class.

The `Tags` class is created, and it is displayed in the Java Editor. You are ready to start adding static variables for the hard-coded Strings.

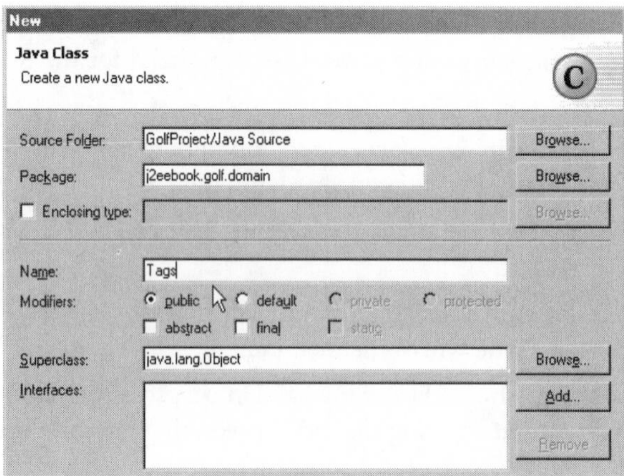

Figure 10.18 Stepping through debugging.

Creating Static Variables

Java has the key word static that allows other classes to call a variable without making an instance of the class. This saves time and memory because the `Tags` class could have many different Strings in it, and there are many different classes that would eventually use it. The variables should also be `public` to allow other classes to reference the variable, and the variables should be `final` because other classes will not change them. By convention, these static variable names are all capitalized. That way they are not confused with classes or other variables. The variables can use underlines as separators between words, but they should not look like sentences.

You need two public static final variables for the Golf Web application. One to represent the parameter String named **round,** and the other for the session attribute named **golfdata.** Edit the `Tag` class in the Java Editor and add these two variables, as shown in the following:

```
package j2eebook.golf.domain;
public abstract class Tags {
    public static final String SCORE = "round";
    public static final String GOLFDATA = "golfdata";
}
```

Remember to save the Tags code by pressing Ctrl-S. These new variables are not visible to the other classes until the code has been saved.

Updating References

The servlet code needs to be updated to use these new static variables instead of the hard-coded Strings. You need to edit the `readScores()` and `loadScores()` methods in the servlet as follows:

```
// read golf scores from the request
public Vector readScores(HttpServletRequest req) {
    Vector scores = new Vector();
    for (int i = 1; i < 6; i++) {
        String param = (String) req.getParameter(Tags.SCORE+ i);
        if ((param != null) && (param.length()>0)) {
            scores.addElement(param);
        }
    }
    return scores;
}
// load golf scores from the request
public Vector loadScores(HttpServletRequest req) {
    // get the session
    HttpSession session = req.getSession(true);
    // get the GolfData bean
    GolfData data = (GolfData) req.getAttribute(Tags.GOLFDATA);
    if (data == null) {
        // make a GolfData bean
```

```
            data = new GolfData();
            // add GolfData to the session
            session.setAttribute(Tags.GOLFDATA, data);
        }
        // read the scores into the GolfData bean
        data.setScores(readScores(req));
        return data.getScores();
    }
```

Save these changes and retest the Golf Web page. You should get the same results as you did before. The function of the Web page did not change; there are only a couple of centralized references that other servlets can use. The completed servlet should look as follows:

```
package j2eebook.golf.controller;
import java.io.IOException;
import javax.servlet.ServletException;
import javax.servlet.http.HttpServlet;
import javax.servlet.http.HttpServletRequest;
import javax.servlet.http.HttpServletResponse;
import javax.servlet.http.HttpSession;
import java.io.PrintWriter;
import j2eebook.golf.domain.GolfData;
import j2eebook.golf.domain.Tags;
import java.util.*;
public class GolfAVG extends HttpServlet {
    /*
    * Constructor
    */
    public GolfAVG() {
        super();
    }
    public void destroy() {
        System.out.println(
            new java.util.Date() + " " + getServletName() + " stopped");
    }
    public void doGet(HttpServletRequest req, HttpServletResponse resp)
        throws ServletException, IOException {
        // redirect to golf web page
        resp.sendRedirect("index.html");
    }
    public void doPost(HttpServletRequest req, HttpServletResponse resp)
        throws ServletException, IOException {
        try {
            // load the scores and calculate the average
            Vector scores = loadScores(req);
            GolfData data =
                (GolfData) req.getSession().getAttribute("golfdata");
            float avg = data.avgScores(scores);
            // display the data in the response
            displayMessage(resp,
```

```
                "You entered the following scores:<br><br>"
                    + scores + "<br><br>Your average is "
                    + avg + "<br><br>Your handicap is "
                    + (avg - 72));
        } catch (Exception e) {
            System.out.println("GolfAVG Exception in doPost() " + e);
            displayMessage(resp,"An error occurred.<br><br>Press on the
browser back button and check that all the scores have valid numbers.");
        }
    }
    public void init() throws ServletException {
        System.out.println(
            new java.util.Date() + " " + getServletName() + " started");
    }
    // display an HTML message
    public void displayMessage(HttpServletResponse resp, String message)
        throws IOException {
        // Obtain the output stream from the response
        PrintWriter out = resp.getWriter();
        // print a simple html page in the printwriter
        out.println("<html><body><h2>" + message);
        out.println("</h2></body></html>");
    }
    // read a parameter from the request
    public String readParameter(HttpServletRequest req, String tag) {
        String param = (String) req.getParameter(tag);
        if (param != null) {
            return param;
        } else {
            return "";
        }
    }
    // read golf scores from the request
    public Vector readScores(HttpServletRequest req) {
        Vector scores = new Vector();
        for (int i = 1; i < 6; i++) {
            String param = (String) req.getParameter(Tags.SCORE + i);
            if ((param != null) && (param.length()>0)) {
                scores.addElement(param);
            }
        }
        return scores;
    }
    // load golf scores from the request
    public Vector loadScores(HttpServletRequest req) {
        // get the session
        HttpSession session = req.getSession(true);
        // get the GolfData bean
        GolfData data = (GolfData) req.getAttribute(Tags.GOLFDATA);
        if (data == null) {
            // make a GolfData bean
```

```
                data = new GolfData();
                // add GolfData to the session
                session.setAttribute(Tags.GOLFDATA, data);
            }
            // read the scores into the GolfData bean
            data.setScores(readScores(req));
            return data.getScores();
        }
    }
```

You can retest the Golf Web page, and you should get the same results as before. The references to the attribute name and the parameter name are in a separate class that other classes can use. This technique saves development time and reduces errors.

Summary

In this chapter, you learned a lot more about servlets. You built on what you learned in the previous chapter on basic servlets. You changed the Web application to read data from an HTML form, store it in a JavaBean, and place the bean in a session. This is an important J2EE pattern that you can use repeatedly. The key concepts covered include:

- Reading parameters from an HTML form
- Storing parameters in a JavaBean
- Accessing the HttpSession
- Getting and setting attributes in the HttpSession
- Testing and debugging servlets using a debug server
- Centralizing references into a separate class with static variables

The example Web application in this chapter provides a realistic glimpse of how to use servlets and JavaBeans. You could easily add additional logic functions to the JavaBean and additional error handling to the servlet. The response page can be improved by using JavaServer Pages, which is covered in the next chapter.

JavaServer Pages

What's in Chapter 11?

In this chapter, you will learn about JavaServer Pages, a key J2EE API. JavaServer Pages (JSPs) provide a clean way to create dynamic content. JSPs provide the view part of model-view-controller architecture. You will learn how to develop JSPs and integrate them using J2EE design patterns. This chapter covers the following topics:

- Defining a JSP
- How JSPs work
  - JSP tags
  - Scriptlets
  - Expressions
  - Directives
  - Declarations
  - Comments
- Creating a JSP
- Running JSPs

- Using JavaBeans with JSPs
- Debugging JSPs
- JSP v2.0 changes

This chapter teaches you the basics of JSPs and gets you started building a JSP for the sample Web application. You will build on what you have learned in the previous chapters and see how JSPs are called by servlets and how JSPs are used to display the data held in JavaBeans. Let's start by describing JSPs and how they work.

What Is a JSP?

JSPs are a great way to add dynamic content to HTML pages. The JSP API includes script tags that you use with HTML tags, as shown in Figure 11.1. JSP tags use Java so you have all the benefits and strengths of Java. These special tags are transformed by the server into HTML at runtime.

JSPs are significantly different from JavaScript, and they serve different purposes. JavaScript is Java code that runs on the browser using the browser JVM. For this reason, JavaScript can behave differently on different browsers. JavaScript is primarily helpful for user interface manipulation like pop-up menus and textfield constraints. JSP is Java code that runs on the server, so the results are consistent when they are called by different browsers. JSP code provides a convenient way to pass data back to an HTML form.

Figure 11.1 JSP and HTML tags.

How JSPs Work

It is important to understand how JSPs work at runtime. A JSP is converted to a servlet at runtime. The JSP compile process, shown in Figure 11.2, only happens the first time the JSP is called. The JSP is translated, compiled, and then run to produce the HTML for the response. On a real production server, you do not notice the first time a servlet is called, but when you test JSPs in WSAD the page compilation has a noticeable delay.

A JSP at runtime is actually a specialized servlet. The JSP engine in WebSphere generates a servlet with a `jspInit()`, a `jspService()`, and a `jspDestroy()` method. The compiled servlet is saved on the server as a .class file. The `jspInt()` method is executed and then the `jspService` method is executed. The JSP is available in memory to service other requests.

A JSP servlet is cached after it is run for the first time. Every subsequent call is much faster, as shown in Figure 11.3. The JSP is located in the application server. The `jspService()` method runs generating the necessary HTML code for the response. This improves performance, and it is a key advantage for using JSPs. The JSP is recompiled if a new JSP is placed on the server, even if the JSP has the same code. The JSP engine recompiles the JSP when the source file date changes. Updating JSPs files is similar to updating HTML files since it does not require the application server to be restarted.

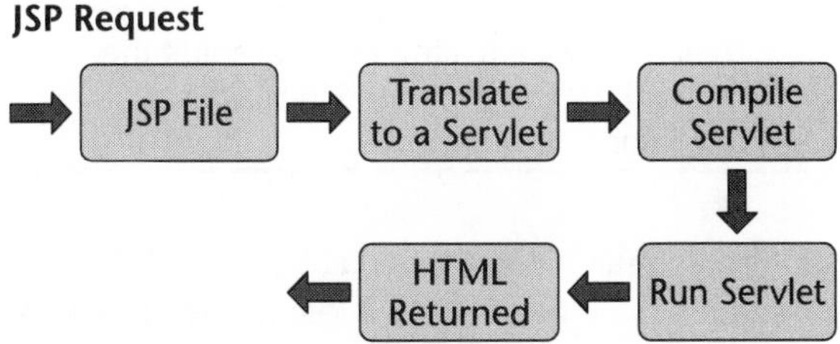

Figure 11.2 JSP first invocation.

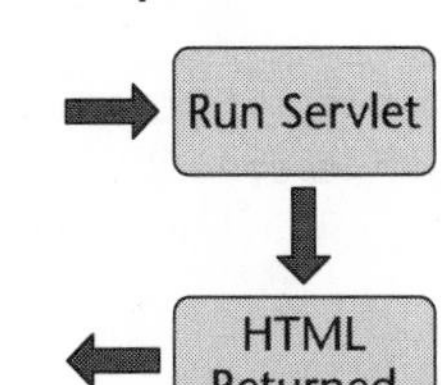

Figure 11.3 JSP subsequent invocation.

JSPs Pros and Cons

JSPs allow you to mix standard HTML tags with special tags that contain Java code. This is a very powerful technology with many benefits, but it brings with it some drawbacks, too. The following table illustrates these pros and cons.

Table 11.1 JSP Pros and Cons

BENEFIT	DRAWBACK
The ability to use Java for dynamic content with HTML. You can program using virtually any Java code.	The HTML file becomes a lot more complex and harder to read. It is tempting to put business logic in the JSP and not in JavaBeans or EJBs where it should be.
JSPs are compiled on the server so they can run faster.	The compiled files are saved on the server disk.
You can use standard HTML tools to develop JSPs.	Some tools do not recognize JSP tags and give erroneous errors.
JSPs allow servlets to have only control code. This means that servlets should not have hard-coded HTML tags.	JSP Java code is harder to debug because it is in a file that most Java compilers cannot handle.
The client browser receives plain HTML tags. Any business logic is contained on the server.	Need extensive testing to ensure that the proper HTML is generated in various conditions.

Although it may appear that there are as many drawbacks as benefits, JSPs truly provide an excellent way to handle dynamic page generation. Most of the drawbacks can be minimized by establishing consistent coding standards and conventions for your JSPs.

JSP Tags

JSP tags are composed of a percent sign and optional special characters, to form the tag. These special tags are parsed and converted to different types of servlet code. There are five JSP tags with five distinct uses. These tags are described in the following sections.

Scriptlets

A JSP scriptlet is a very commonly used tag. You place any executable Java code in a scriptlet. In practice, scriptlets are used mainly for Java logic like `if` statements and `for` or `while` loops. Scriptlets should be used sparingly and should not contain business logic. A JSP scriptlet tag is used as follows:

```
<sometag>
    <% scriptlet %>
</sometag>
```

Expressions

A JSP expression is much like a scriptlet. An expression contains Java code that is automatically converted to a Java String by calling the object's `toString()` method. The developer can take advantage of this by implementing a `toString()` method, which generates the desired string to be displayed in the page. Expressions are commonly used to display values in textfields and to indicate the selected items in lists. It is also very common to use expressions to display status messages to the user. A JSP expression tag looks like a scriptlet with the addition of an equal sign, and it is used as follows:

```
<sometag>
    <%= expression %>
</sometag>
```

Directives

A JSP directive is used to set values that apply to the page. There are three types of directives:

- **page** — Provides a way to specify the various tags that go in the heading part of the HTML.
- **include** — Allows a way to include other files in the JSP. This is very helpful for adding a common header or footer to a Web page, such as a copyright statement.
- **taglib** — Allows you to specify custom JSP tag libraries that are used on a page. Chapter 17, "Struts," covers taglibs in greater detail.

JSP directives should be placed in the HTML <HEAD> and </HEAD> tags. A JSP directive tag uses an ampersand as an identifier, and it is used as follows:

```
<sometag>
    <%@ directive %>
</sometag>
```

Declarations

A JSP declaration is a special tag for declaring Java items for the JSP servlet; it uses a percent sign with an asterisk. You should refrain from using this tag because it can open up a host of maintenance issues. Although you can declare classes with behavior in a JSP, it does not fulfill the MVC separation of responsibilities. As with JSP directives, declarations should be placed at the beginning of the JSP file within the HTML <HEAD> and </HEAD> tags. A JSP declaration tag is used as follows:

```
<sometag>
    <%! declaration %>
</sometag>
```

Comments

Remember that JSPs dynamically generate HTML at runtime using Java code. So it is a good practice to comment your code to help both maintenance and debugging. There are a number of ways to place comments in JSPs, as in the following:

- HTML comments are displayed in the HTML source and are implemented as <!-- comment -->.
- JSP comments are not displayed in the HTML source and are implemented with a special JSP comment tag as <%-- a comment --%>. JSP comments are helpful for commenting JSP tags during development so they do not get executed.
- JSP scriptlets are not displayed in the HTML source and are implemented as <% // a comment %>.

JSP Standard Actions

As the JSP specification evolved, it became evident that there had to be a better way to implement new JSP functions. The special tags can be hard to read and easy to misread, and JSPs are intended to be easy to read and maintain. Table 11.2 lists the standard JSP action tags and how they are used. The tags provide a simpler way to specify commonly used functions than could be done using scriptlets or expressions.

Table 11.2 JSP Action Tags

ACTION	DESCRIPTION
<jsp:useBean>	The useBean action is an essential tag that provides a reference to a JavaBean that is in the Session object. It has the following attributes: • id ="idName" is the String id used to locate the JavaBean in the Session. • scope="page/request/session/application" sets the duration of the JavaBean reference. For page, the reference is kept while the page is active. For request, the reference is kept while the request is active. For session, the reference is kept until the Session is invalidated or times out. For application, the reference is kept until the Web application is restarted. Usually, you will use scope="session". • class="classname" specifies the fully qualified class name that is used to cast the JavaBean from the object in session. • beanName="aName" defines a local variable for the JavaBean reference. This is optional because the id attribute usually is sufficient.

Table 11.2 *(continued)*

ACTION	DESCRIPTION
<jsp:getProperty	The getProperty is a very common action that retrieves a value from a JavaBean, and it has the following attributes: • name ="idName" is the name of the JavaBean with the desired property. The bean name value must match the identifier specified in the useBean action. • property="propName" which identifies the JavaBean property that is retrieved.
<jsp:setProperty	The setProperty action places a value into a JavaBean, and it has the following attributes: • name ="idName" is the name of the JavaBean with the desired property. The bean name value must match the identifier specified in the useBean action. a property expression including: • property="propName" which identifies the JavaBean property that is set. • value="aValue" is the actual value set. • param="paramName" specifies the Request parameter that you want to pass to the JavaBean property.
<jsp:include >	The include action dynamically inserts HTML or JSP pages with a parameter page="URI".
<jsp:forward>	The forward action provides the same function as the servlet request dispatcher forward() method. It has a parameter page="URI" that specifies the target servlet or JSP. The forward action can nest <jsp:param> tags that have name and value attributes. This allows the JSP to pass the Request objects when it forwards control.
<jsp:plugin>	The plugin action allows the JSP to require a browser plug-in. It generates an HTML <EMBED> tag or <OBJECT> tag.
<jsp:body>	The body action is used to generate tags for XML.
<jsp:attribute>	The attribute action is used with the body action to specify attributes for XML.
<jsp:invoke>	The invoke action is a special action used only in tag files.

The getProperty and setProperty actions are dependent on the useBean action. Usually these actions are not used together. The setProperty action can be used in a data input screen and the getProperty action is used in a results page. The JSP patterns in the next section describe how to use the common actions.

JSP Patterns

This section covers the key design patterns for JSPs before you start making them. A JSP can be very simple and provide all the model, view, and controller function, as shown in Figure 11.4. This pattern is called model one, and it can provide a good solution for basic reporting type JSPs or data input pages. Having all the code in one file can prevent errors that can happen when passing data to other objects. Model one is best when using special tag libraries specified in JSP v1.1 and v1.2. These libraries allow custom tags that are more readable and easier to use than Java code in scriptlets.

There are some disadvantages to the JSP model one design. The JSP has all the model, view, and controller code so it can become large and hard to maintain. The JSP would need to have a lot of error detection and correction code, including `try/catch` blocks. It is difficult to reuse code and is limited to cut and paste or JSP includes.

A variation of model one is shown in the Figure 11.5. This model uses a JSP for the view and controller and utilizes a JavaBean or EJB for the data access. This pattern is easier to maintain and enhance because the JavaBeans or EJBs can hold the business logic and the JSP can focus on providing the view. You will learn more about EJBs in Chapter 22, " Enterprise JavaBeans," and Chapter 23, " Entity EJBs."

The other pattern for JSPs is model two, shown in Figure 11.6. This should look familiar because it is the design pattern that is used extensively in this book. Model two has a number of strengths because the model-view-controller separation is clearly divided between different J2EE types. This is a very flexible and extensible design that provides for good performance and a chance for code reuse.

The J2EE design patterns are very flexible and a large system may use all three models. Chapter 19 has additional information covering JSP model one and model two.

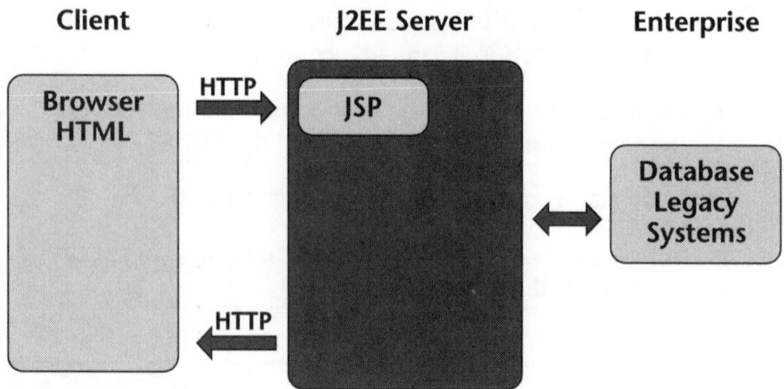

Figure 11.4 JSP model one.

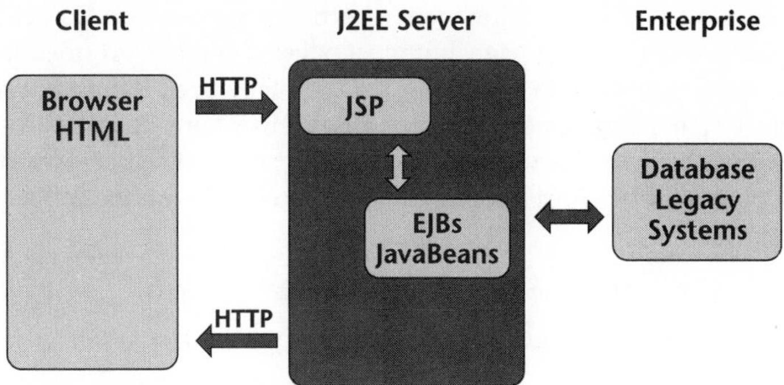

Figure 11.5 JSP model one with JavaBeans and EJBs.

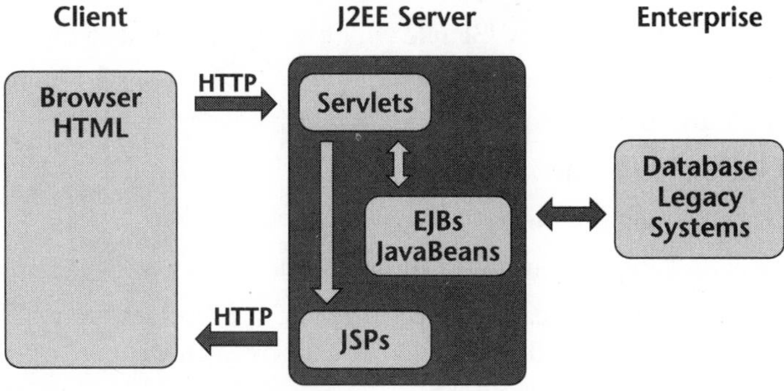

Figure 11.6 JSP model two.

Working with JSPs

In the previous chapter, "Servlets with JavaBeans," the GolfAVG servlet provided an HTML response page and an HTML error page. Both of these pages can be improved a lot by using JSPs. First, you will create a new JSP page that replaces the hard-coded HTML in the servlet that provides the response.

Creating a JSP Page

At this point, you know a lot about JSPs, so it is high time that you started making them. You can hand build JSPs or you can use the wizard in WSAD to help. For your first JSP, let's use the wizard to create a JSP. You will create a JSP under the GolfProject named golfScores.jsp. A JSP needs to have the .jsp extension in its filename. The New JSP wizard allows you to select a number of options for a JSP and then generates the necessary code. The wizard makes an initial JSP that needs to be edited for application-specific code. After you have a few JSPs developed in a large system, it is very common to copy an existing JSP and modify it for a specific use.

The initial page for the Golf Web application went directly under the Web Content folder. That is a good place for the starting page, but most pages should be grouped in separate folders just as the servlets are in separate packages. However, there are no hard-and-fast standards for page organization. Many of the conventions practiced are dictated by the major HTML development tools. You will first make a folder named pages under the Web Content folder. Start making the golfScores JSP with the following steps:

1. From the Web Perspective, select the Web Content folder.
2. Select File/New/Folder, and the New Folder window appears.
3. Enter **pages** for the Folder Name.
4. Click the Finish button to create the folder.
5. From the Web Perspective, select the pages folder that you just created.
6. Select File>New>JSP File and the New JSP File window appears, as seen in Figure 11.7.
7. Make sure that the Folder is /GolfProject/Web Content/pages.
8. Enter **golfScores** for the File Name.
9. Make sure that the Create as JSP Fragment check box is not checked.
10. Press the Next button to accept these values and proceed.
11. The second page of the wizard appears, as seen in Figure 11.8, and lets you specify tag libraries for the JSP, but this JSP will not use any tag libraries.
12. Press the Next button to skip this page and proceed.
13. The third page of the wizard appears, as seen in Figure 11.9, and lets you specify options for a JSP page directive.
14. A page directive is not required in a JSP, but it is good form to have one. Make sure the Generate a Page Directive check box is checked.

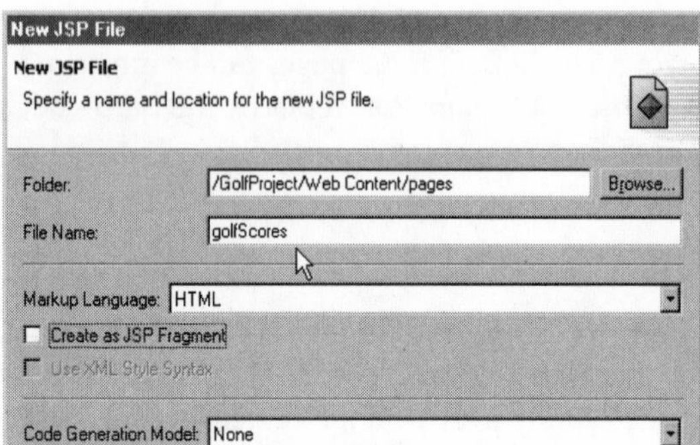

Figure 11.7 JSP wizard page 1.

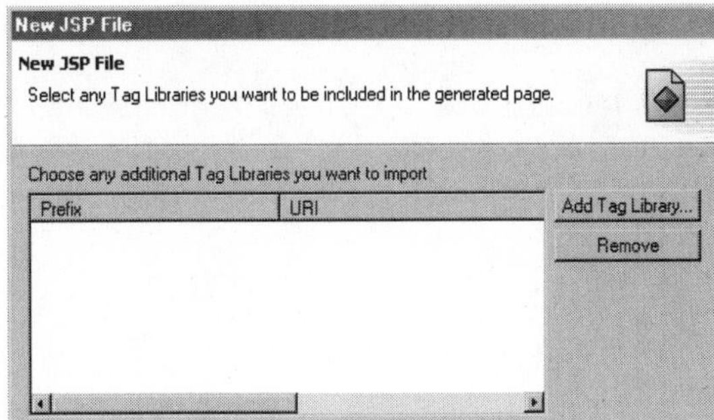

Figure 11.8 JSP wizard page 2.

15. Make sure that Language is checked and **Java** is listed as the language in the drop-down list.
16. Press the Next button to accept these values and proceed.
17. The fourth page of the wizard appears, as seen in Figure 11.10, and specifies information used in the <HEAD> tag.
18. The encoding values are used in a page directive. Make sure the **Use workbench default** check box is checked.
19. The Content Type and Document Type are used in meta tags. Make sure that the Document Type is set to **HTML 4.01 Transitional**.
20. Make sure the Style Sheet is /GolfProject/Web Content/theme/Master.css.
21. Press the Next button to accept these values and proceed.

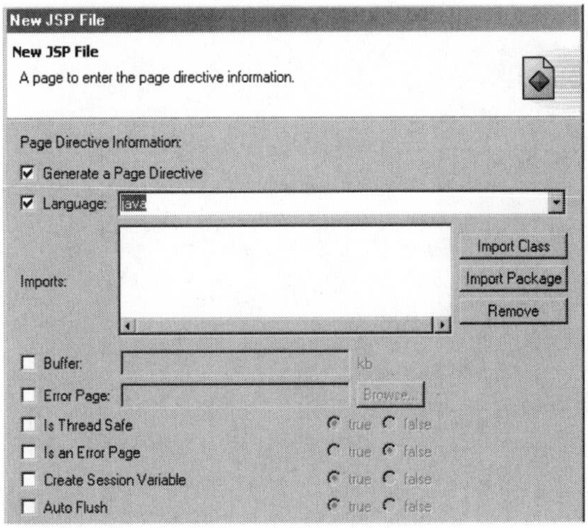

Figure 11.9 JSP wizard page 3.

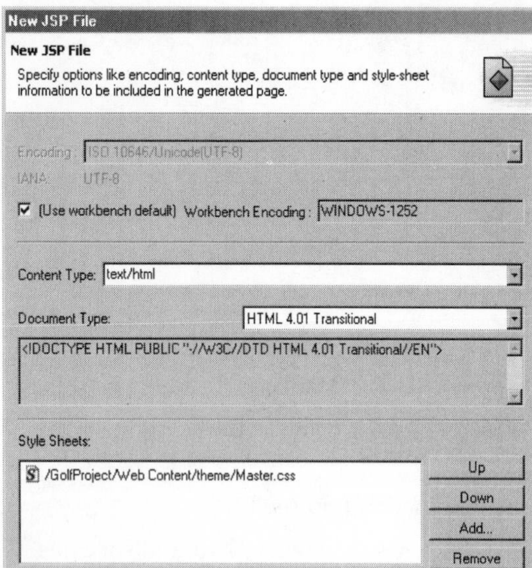

Figure 11.10 JSP wizard page 4.

22. The fifth page of the JSP wizard appears allowing you to specify items for the generated servlet, as seen in Figure 11.11. The wizard can generate method stubs for a `init()`. You can set the servlet name, initial parameters values, and mappings.
23. Keep the defaults for this JSP. Press the Finish button to accept these values and generate the JSP.

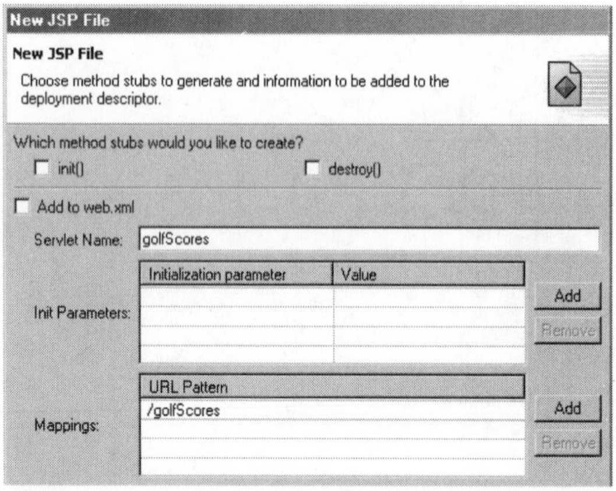

Figure 11.11 JSP wizard page 5.

There are a lot more items that can be specified for a more complex JSP. Anything that is not specified in the wizard can always be added in the JSP later. After the code is generated, it is displayed in the page designer and should looks as follows:

```
<!DOCTYPE HTML PUBLIC "-//W3C//DTD HTML 4.01 Transitional//EN">
<HTML>
<HEAD>
<%@ page
language="java"
contentType="text/html; charset=WINDOWS-1252"
pageEncoding="WINDOWS-1252"
%>
<META http-equiv="Content-Type"
    content="text/html; charset=WINDOWS-1252">
<META name="GENERATOR" content="IBM WebSphere Studio">
<META http-equiv="Content-Style-Type" content="text/css">
<LINK href="../theme/Master.css" rel="stylesheet"
    type="text/css">
<TITLE>golfScores.jsp</TITLE>
</HEAD>
<BODY>
<P>Place golfScores.jsp's content here.</P>
</BODY>
</HTML>
```

Adding Simple JSP Tags

You could test the generated JSP, but it does not have any dynamic tags. The only JSP tag is the page directive that defines the language, content type, and page encoding for the JSP. It is very easy to place the current date on the Web page using the Java Date class. The date can be easily formatted with a Java SimpleDateFormatter class. You can test the JSP after you add some simple JSP tags.

Let's start by adding some simple JSP tags. You will replace the placeholder text generated by the JSP wizard with a title that includes the current date and time. To accomplish this, you will use a JSP declaration and a JSP expression. The JSP declaration defines a SimpleDateFormatter that can convert the current date into the desired format. The JSP expression takes a new Java Date class as a parameter and returns a formatted string for the title. Edit the golfScores JSP and replace the following generated text:

```
<P>Place golfScores.jsp's content here.</P>
```

With the following code:

```
<%!java.text.SimpleDateFormat sdf = new
java.text.SimpleDateFormat("KK:mm' on 'MMMMMM dd"); %>
<P>Golf Scores at <%= sdf.format(new java.util.Date()) %></P>
```

Save the pages after making the changes.

Running a JSP

Running a JSP is just like running any other Web component. In WSAD, you can select a JSP and run it on any configured server. Let's test this JSP to make sure it works properly with the following steps:

1. Select the golfScores.jsp file in the J2EE Navigator.
2. From the pop-up menu, select Run on Server and the JSP is compiled and appears as shown in Figure 11.12. Of course, you will see the current date of your machine when you run the test.

If you have problems running the JSP, you may need to close the Web browser in WSAD and restart the test server. In some cases, you may need to close WSAD and restart it if you are not able to restart the server. The server has a specific TCP/IP port that it listens on. When you are doing a lot of testing, the test server sometimes does not release the port.

These JSP tags are helpful, but there are a lot of items that need to be added to the response page. Next, you will add a number of HTML tags to the page, then incorporate additional JSP tags for the dynamic content.

Adding HTML to a JSP

JSPs tend to be mostly HTML tags with a few JSP tags for the dynamic content. The next step is to add the necessary HTML tags for the response page. You will add an HTML table with two columns and five rows to manage the page formatting. The table will have a title, the scores entered by the user, the average, the handicap, and a button to return to the main Web page. Use the Design tab to create the HTML page shown in Figure 11.13 with the following steps:

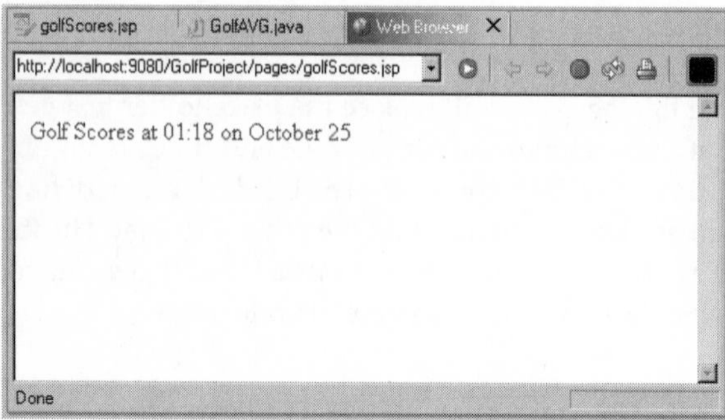

Figure 11.12 Running a JSP.

1. Add a table with two columns and five rows.
2. Set the table to be transparent by setting the border to 0.
3. Join the two columns in the first row. This makes the HTML code `<td colspan="2">`.
4. Click the bold button to make the text in the row bold.
5. Join the two columns in the last row so there is one column.
6. From the Source Editor, move the title with the JSP expression that formats the date to the first row.
7. Go back to the Design page and enter **Scores:** in the first column of the second row.
8. Enter **Average:** in the first column of the third row.
9. Enter **Handicap:** in the first column of the fourth row.
10. Place an HTML <form> in the last row of the table.
11. Set the form action to /GolfProject/GolfAVG. This calls the GolfAVG servlet.
12. Set the form method to **Get**.
13. Place a submit button on the form in the last row.
14. Set the button name to **home** and its label to **Home**.
15. Save these changes.

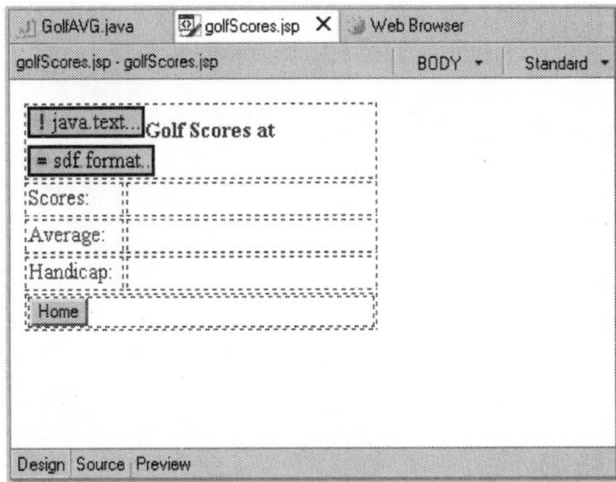

Figure 11.13 JSP with HTML.

After you have saved the code for the golfscores.jsp file, the code should look as follows:

```
<!DOCTYPE HTML PUBLIC "-//W3C//DTD HTML 4.01 Transitional//EN">
<HTML>
<HEAD>
<%@ page language="java"
contentType="text/html; charset=WINDOWS-1252"
pageEncoding="WINDOWS-1252" %>
<META http-equiv="Content-Type"
    content="text/html; charset=WINDOWS-1252">
<META name="GENERATOR" content="IBM WebSphere Studio">
<META http-equiv="Content-Style-Type" content="text/css">
<LINK href="../theme/Master.css" rel="stylesheet" type="text/css">
<TITLE>golfScores.jsp</TITLE>
<jsp:useBean class="j2eebook.golf.domain.GolfData" id="golfdata"
scope="session"/>
</HEAD>
<BODY>
<TABLE border="0" width="250">
    <TBODY>
        <TR>
            <TD colspan="2"><B><%!java.text.SimpleDateFormat sdf = new
java.text.SimpleDateFormat("KK:mm' on 'MMMMMM dd"); %>
            Golf Scores at <%= sdf.format(new java.util.Date()) %>
            </B></TD>
        </TR>
        <TR>
            <TD>Scores:</TD>
            <TD></TD>
        </TR>
        <TR>
            <TD>Average:</TD>
            <TD></TD>
        </TR>
        <TR>
            <TD>Handicap:</TD>
            <TD></TD>
        </TR>
        <TR>
            <TD colspan="2">
            <FORM><INPUT type="submit" name="home" value="Home"></FORM>
            </TD>
        </TR>
    </TBODY>
</TABLE>
</BODY>
</HTML>
```

NOTE **JSP tags frequently add HTML attribute values. You may need to use the Java convention for special character using the \" to represent the quote. All attribute values should be enclosed by quotes. A sample JSP with a JavaBean named displayinfo that holds a columns span value would look as follows:**

```
<td <%="colspan=\""+displayinfo.getcols()+\"%>>
```

At runtime, the JSP code would generate the following:

```
<td colspan="3">
```

The JSP file is ready for more JSP tags. In the next section, you will add a useBean tag, which allows the JSP to reference JavaBeans in the Session. With this reference, the JSP can call methods in the GolfData JavaBean and display data from the bean.

Using the useBean Tag

The JSP does not have any special tags to use data from the servlet. The GolfAVG servlet put a reference to the GolfData bean in the Session. The JSP can access Java Beans in the Session by using the useBean tag, which has a number of parameters. The parameters for this tag are:

id — Specifies the name used to identify the JavaBean in the session. This value must match the name used to place the JavaBean in the session with the `setAttribute()` method.

class — Specifies the fully qualified name for the bean class.

scope — Specifies the scope for the reference with possible values of page, request, session, and application.

type — Specifies a type for the bean. This attribute allows the bean reference to be cast to a different type from its original type.

Adding a useBean Tag

The Design page has a cool function that automatically generates the useBean tag. You can select the desired JavaBean in the J2EE navigator view and drag it with the mouse to the JSP Design page. This drag-and-drop function works for either the .java file or the .class. In WSAD v4, you must use the .class file for this drag-and-drop function. WSAD makes a useBean tag for the JavaBean, but it is missing some of the attributes that you may need like scope, class, and id. It is easier to create a useBean tag using the WSAD wizard because you can specify these attributes for the tag. Add a useBean tag with the following steps:

1. From the Design tab, place the cursor at the top of the Web Page. The useBean tag will be generated at the current cursor location.
2. Select the JSP > Insert Bean... menu items, and the Insert JSP Bean dialog appears, as shown in Figure 11.14.
3. Enter **golfdata** for the ID. Be careful because this value is case sensitive.
4. Use the Browse button to select the fully qualified Class j2eebook.golf.domain.GolfData.
5. Select **Session** for the Scope.
6. The Type does not need to be changed, so leave this field blank.
7. Press the OK button to generate the tag.

The wizard generates a useBean tag with the items specified in the wizard. You can use the Attribute Editor to change the JavaBean in the JSP, or you can edit the generated code. Next, you will check the useBean tag and modify it.

Editing a useBean Tag

You should look at the generated useBean tag to verify that the code has the desired values. The useBean tag needs to be placed in the JSP before it is referenced. The tag is inserted wherever the cursor was located in the Design view. You can place the useBean tag between the <HEAD> tags. This ensures that the bean is found before it is referenced in the HTML body.

NOTE When the useBean tag is generated by dragging the class GolfData Java Bean from the Navigator view to the Design view, the following code is generated:

<jsp:useBean class="j2eebook.golf.domain.GolfData"></jsp:useBean>

Although this useBean tag has the correct class tag, it is missing the id attribute and scope attribute. You need to edit the generated code and add the necessary attributes if you use the drag-and-drop method.

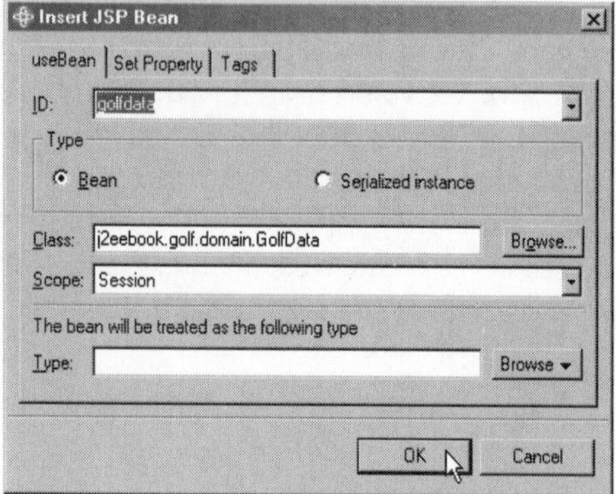

Figure 11.14 Inserting a JSP Bean.

The useBean tag needs an id attribute, and it should have a scope attribute. The useBean is an empty tag since it only has attributes and there is no data used before the end </jsp:useBean> tag, so it is good to make the useBean self-ending. Edit the useBean tag to look as follows:

```
<jsp:useBean class="j2eebook.golf.domain.GolfData" id="golfdata"
scope="session"/>
```

Save this change to the code. You can reference the JavaBean attributes now that the JSP has a reference to a JavaBean. In the next section, you will learn how to pass control from a servlet to a JSP. The JSP, in turn, dynamically generates the response that goes back to the client browser.

Updating the Servlet

The servlet needs to be updated to call the golfScores JSP as the response in the `doPost()` method. The code that currently calculates the average score and handicap needs to be moved to the JavaBean. The servlet will not have any hard-coded HTML tags; the response view is handled by the JSP. The servlet loads scores from the HTML input page into the GolfData JavaBean, then forwards the control to the golfScores.jsp file using a relative URL. Edit the GolfAVG servlet to include these changes as follows:

```
public void doPost(HttpServletRequest req, HttpServletResponse resp)
    throws ServletException, IOException {
    try {
        // load the scores
        loadScores(req);
getServletContext().getRequestDispatcher("pages/golfScores.jsp").  ⮐
forward(req, resp);
    } catch (Exception e) {
        System.out.println("GolfAVG Exception in doPost() " + e);
        displayMessage(resp,"An error occurred.<br><br>Press the  ⮐
browser back button and check that all the scores have valid numbers.");
    }
}
```

The servlet is much simpler than before. The hard-coded HTML for the response is removed. The servlet does not have any of the calculation function. The servlet design is much cleaner; it fulfills its role as a controller.

Updating the JavaBean

The data for information for the calculation of the average score and handicap needs to be placed in the GolfData JavaBean. Edit the GolfData class and add the following methods in the Java Editor:

```
/**
 * Returns the average.
 * @return float
```

```
 */
public float calcAverage() {
    return avgScores(getScores());
}
/**
 * Returns the handicap.
 * @return float
 */
public float calcHandicap() {
    return calcAverage() - 72;
}
```

Save the JavaBean code. The JSP can reference these new methods in the JavaBean. In the next section, you will update the JSP to call these methods using the getProperty tag and expressions.

Calling JavaBean Methods

With the useBean tag in the JSP and the new methods in the GolfData JavaBean, you can add the necessary JSP tags to display the scores, the average, and the handicap. First, you will use a getProperty tag and then a JSP expression. You can enter these tags in the Design view or you can add the code directly to the JSP. Add a JSP getProperty tag with the following steps:

1. In the Design view, select the column next to the **Scores:** label.
2. Select the menu items JSP > Insert Get Parameter, and the Insert JSP Get Parameter window appears, as shown in Figure 11.15.
3. Select the golfdata bean, and then select the **scores** property.
4. Click the OK button to generate the JSP tag.
5. Go to the Java Editor, and you will see the following generated code:

```
<TD nowrap width="181"><jsp:getProperty name="golfdata"
property="scores" /></TD>
```

The average score and handicap can be displayed using a JSP expression that calls the appropriate JavaBean methods. Update the JSP with the following changes:

1. In the Java Editor, select the column next to the **Average:** label, and enter the following JSP expression between the <td> tags: **<%= golfdata.calcAverage()%>**.
2. In the column next to the **Handicap:** label, enter the following JSP expression between the <td> tags: **<%= golfdata.calcHandicap()%>**.
3. Save these changes to the JSP.

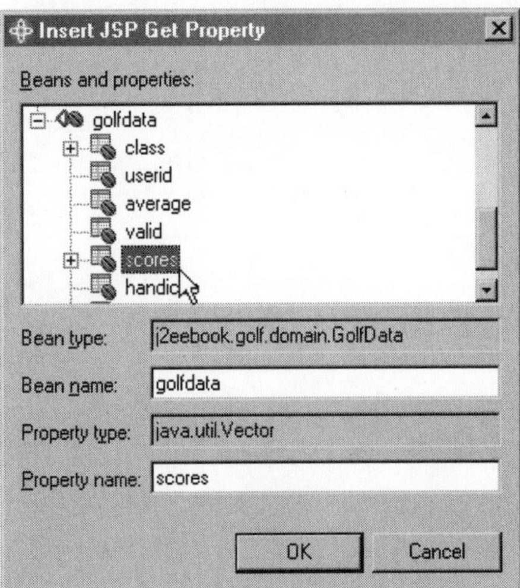

Figure 11.15 Accessing a property.

The next step is to test the changes by running the Web application. The input index.html file passes data to the servlet that loads the data into the GolfData JavaBean and displays the response in the golfScores.jsp file.

Testing the Completed JSP

It would be good to run another test of the Web page to see if it works. Test the Golf Web page with the following steps:

1. Start the Web page by selecting the index.html file, and from the popup menu select Run on Server.
2. When the Golf Web page appears, enter 99, 88, 89, 86, and 78 for the scores.
3. Click the Calculate button.

The scores are passed to the GolfAVG servlet, loaded in the GolfData JavaBean, and forwarded to the golfScores JSP. The JSP is compiled, and it displays the values, as shown in Figure 11.16.

The JSP replaces the function that used to be done by hard-coded HTML tags in the GolfAVG servlet. It is a lot easier to make changes the view now that it is in a JSP. It would look better if the golf scores did not have the brackets around them. The JSP can be updated with a Java loop to display the golf scores dynamically.

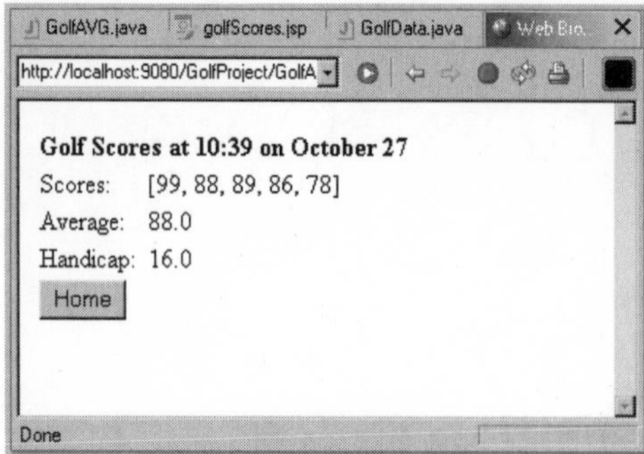

Figure 11.16 Running JSP.

Loops in JSPs

The use of Java code in JSPs to produce dynamic loops is very powerful. It is very common to use `for` loops and `while` loops to dynamically create HTML tables. Let's modify the golfScores.jsp to display the golf scores in separate rows. Use a `for` loop in a JSP scriptlet and replace the getProperty tag with a JSP expression to display the golf score elements. Make these changes as shown in the following section of the JSP file:

```
<BODY>
<TABLE border="0" width="250">
    <TBODY>
        <TR>
            <TD colspan="2"><B><%!java.text.SimpleDateFormat sdf =
new java.text.SimpleDateFormat("KK:mm' on 'MMMMMM dd"); %>
            Golf Scores at <%= sdf.format(new java.util.Date()) %>
            </B></TD>
        </TR>
        <% for (int i=0; i < golfdata.getScores().size(); i++) { %>
        <TR>
            <TD>Score <%=i+1%>:</TD>
            <TD><%= golfdata.getScores().elementAt(i) %></TD>
        </TR>
        <% } // end while loop %>
        <TR>
            <TD>Average:</TD>
            <TD><%= golfdata.calcAverage()%></TD>
        </TR>
        <TR>
            <TD>Handicap:</TD>
            <TD><%= golfdata.calcHandicap()%></TD>
```

```
            </TR>
            <TR>
                <TD colspan="2">
                <FORM action="/GolfProject/GolfAVG"><INPUT type="submit" ⮐
name="home" value="Home"></FORM>
                </TD>
            </TR>
        </TBODY>
</TABLE>
</BODY>
```

Save the updated code. Notice the end of the `for` loop. It is a JSP scriptlet with the close brace indicating the end of the `for` loop. This is a very common usage in JSP code, and it is a little tricky when there are nested loops. Rerun the Golf Web page and the response should look like Figure 11.17. The JSP dynamically generates an HTML row for each score.

The response page is much cleaner than when the HTML code came from the servlet. The JSP can be easily enhanced with additional function or user interface refinements. If you do not get these results, refer to the following code for the updated JSP:

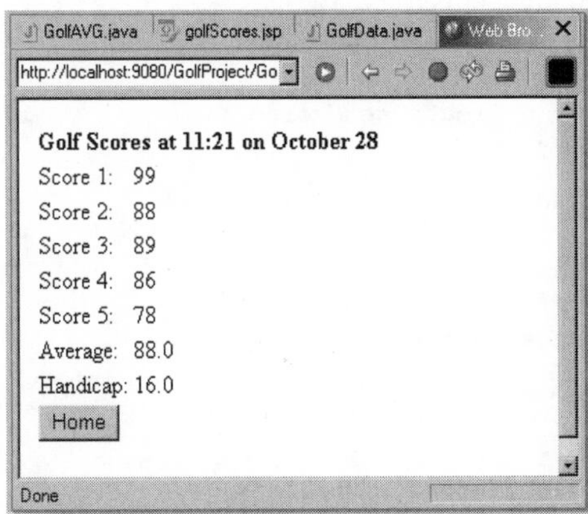

Figure 11.17 JSP loop.

```
<!DOCTYPE HTML PUBLIC "-//W3C//DTD HTML 4.01 Transitional//EN">
<HTML>
<HEAD>
<%@ page language="java"
contentType="text/html; charset=WINDOWS-1252"
pageEncoding="WINDOWS-1252" %>
<META http-equiv="Content-Type"
```

```
    content="text/html; charset=WINDOWS-1252">
<META name="GENERATOR" content="IBM WebSphere Studio">
<META http-equiv="Content-Style-Type" content="text/css">
<LINK href="../theme/Master.css" rel="stylesheet" type="text/css">
<TITLE>golfScores.jsp</TITLE>
<%-- get the GolfData bean from the Session --%>
<jsp:useBean class="j2eebook.golf.domain.GolfData" id="golfdata"
    scope="session" />
</HEAD>
<BODY>
<TABLE border="0" width="250">
    <TBODY>
        <TR><%-- create a date formatter --%>
            <TD colspan="2"><B><%!java.text.SimpleDateFormat sdf = 
new java.text.SimpleDateFormat("KK:mm' on 'MMMMMM dd"); %>
            <%-- display the current date from the server --%>
            Golf Scores at <%= sdf.format(new java.util.Date()) %> 
</B></TD>
        </TR>
        <%-- iterate through the scores Vector placing each on a new 
row--%>
        <% for (int i=0; i < golfdata.getScores().size(); i++) { %>
        <TR>
            <TD>Score <%=i+1%>:</TD>
            <TD nowrap width="181"><%= golfdata.getScores(). 
elementAt(i) %></TD>
        </TR>
        <% } // end while loop %>
        <TR>
            <TD>Average:</TD>
            <TD width="181"><%= golfdata.calcAverage()%></TD>
        </TR>
        <TR>
            <TD>Handicap:</TD>
            <TD width="181"><%= golfdata.calcHandicap()%></TD>
        </TR>
        <TR>
            <TD colspan="2">
            <FORM action="/GolfProject/GolfAVG"><INPUT type="submit" 
name="home"
                value="Home"></FORM>
            </TD>
        </TR>
    </TBODY>
</TABLE>
</BODY>
</HTML>
```

JSPs Implicit Objects

Since JSPs are servlets at runtime, they automatically have all the objects normally associated with a servlet like the Request, Response, Session, and PrintWriter. These objects are automatically provided through implicit variables, as shown in Table 11.3. All these variables can be used directly in any JSP tag, making it a lot faster and easier than using an HttpServlet.

Table 11.3 Implicit Objects

OBJECT REFERENCE	TYPE
out	JspWriter
page	Object
request	HttpServletRequest
response	HttpServletResponse
session	HttpSession
application	ServletContext
config	ServletConfig

Debugging JSPs

Solving runtime errors in JSPs can be a little tricky. The first step in debugging a JSP is viewing the HTML source displayed in the browser. You can then examine the JSP source for a possible error. This technique works well when you are familiar with the JSP code and the application design. Sometimes you may need to step through the JSP as it runs. A JSP can be debugged in the WSAD debugger. Remember that JSPs become servlets at runtime. You can step through the code when the generated servlet runs.

There are two ways to trigger the debugger for JSPs. You can set a breakpoint in the JSP source code, or you can have the debugger watch for specific exceptions. The Source Editor has a column on the left that allows you to set breakpoints. Figure 11.18 shows a breakpoint being placed in the golfScores.jsp file. You need to select a JSP tag, and then the column on the left shows the lines that can have a breakpoint. You cannot place a breakpoint on a line that only has HTML tags.

```
GolfAVG.java    golfScores.jsp  X   GolfData.java    Web Browser
golfScores.jsp
<TITLE>golfScores.jsp</TITLE>
<jsp:useBean class="j2eebook.golf.domain.GolfData" id="golfdata"
    scope="session" />
</HEAD>
<BODY>
<TABLE border="0" width="250">
    <TBODY>
        <TR>
            <TD colspan="2"><B><%!java.text.SimpleDateFormat sdf = ne
            Golf Scores at <%= sdf.format(new java.util.Date()) %> </
        </TR>
        <% for (int i=0; i < golfdata.getScores().size(); i++) { %>
        <TR>
            <TD>Score <%=i+1%>:</TD>
            <TD nowrap width="181"><%= golfdata.getScores().elementAt
        </TR>
        <% } // end while loop %>
        <TR>
            <TD>Average:</TD>
            <TD width="181"><%= golfdata.calcAverage()%></TD>
        </TR>
        <TR>
            <TD>Handicap:</TD>
Design Source Preview
```

Figure 11.18 Breakpoints in a JSP.

When the JSP runs, you are prompted for the debugger with a window, as seen in Figure 11.19. Notice that the window shows the JSP named _golfScores and the method named `_jspService`. When you select the OK button, the Debug Perspective displays, and you have all the debug functions that you can use on any other Java code. Remember that the test server needs to be started in debug mode for the breakpoints to work.

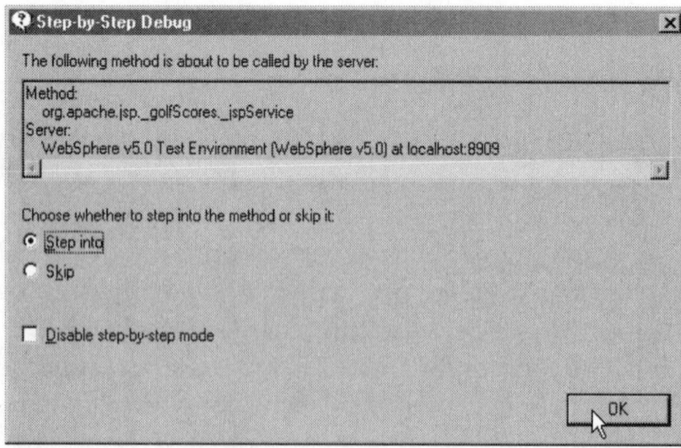

Figure 11.19 Breakpoint window.

JSP 2.0 Changes

The JSP specification has evolved from the initial v.09 to v1.2, which WebSphere supports. JSPs are evolving to be primarily text tags that hide the Java code. JSP 2 has a lot of additions for XML and tag library usage along with a lot of clarification in the documentation. JSP 2.0 adds the Expression Language (EL), which goes a long way toward replacing many expressions and scriptlets.

New JSP Standard Actions

As the JSP specification evolved, it became evident that there had to be a better way to implement new JSP functions. The special tags can be hard to ready and easy to misread, and JSP are intended to be easy to ready and maintain. These actions follow the intent of JSPs by providing readable actions for commonly used functions. The new actions provide extended functions for XML and tab library definition. Following is a list of the new tags:

- <jsp:invoke>
- <jsp:doBody>
- <jsp:root>
- <jsp:directive.root>
- <jsp:directive.include>
- <jsp:declaration>
- <jsp:scriptlet>
- <jsp:expression>
- <jsp:element>
- <jsp:text>

It is much easier to understand <jsp:scriptlet someCode/> than the older <% someCode %> syntax. The new action tags conform to the XML standard, which requires an end tag. This allows JSPs to be well formed and work better with parsers.

Expression Language

The JSP 2.0 specification defines the EL as having three variations, as shown in Table 11.4. The EL brings a more readable format to functions that previously needed Java-specific syntax in a scriptlet or expression. These are new enhancements to the JSP specification and are not fully supported in WSAD v5.0.

Table 11.4 JSP Expressions

EXPRESSION	DESCRIPTION
<label:tag value="${expression}"/>	This tag has one Java expression and returns the attribute's expected type.
<label:tag value="${express1} aString${express2}"/>	This tag has multiple Java expressions and Strings. It is evaluated from left to right, concatenating the values into a String, and returns the attribute's expected type.
<label:tag value="aValue"/>	The value attribute returns a Java String.

New Implicit Objects

The JSP 2 specification adds more implicit objects to the existing objects already discussed. The objects make it easier to access parameters and parameter values from various sources. Following is a list of those objects:

- pageContext
- pageScope
- requestScope
- sessionScope
- applicationScope
- param
- paramValues
- header
- headerValues
- cookie

Summary

In this chapter, you learned about JavaServer Pages and how to link them in a Web application. JSPs introduce new tags that are placed within static HTML tags. The JSP tags provide dynamic values to static Web pages. This ability to create dynamic content is great for displaying data and can also be used to customize an HTML page with special colors, style sheets, or graphics. In this chapter, you learned about:

- How JSPs are compiled as servlets by the application server, then run, and the generated HTML returned to the client
- The different JSP tags types and how they are used including:

  <% Scriplets %>

  <%= Expressions %>

  <%@ Directives %>

  <%! Declarations %>

  <%-- Comments --%>
- Using a JSP tag to reference a JavaBean held in the session
- Using JSP tags to call JavaBean methods and dynamically display values in an HTML response
- Using JSP tags to dynamically generate variable-length data with a loop
- How to debug JSP code

JSP tags are very flexible, and they fulfill a key role in the J2EE architecture. Chapter 19, "Displaying Data," has more examples of JSPs and how they can be used. In this chapter, JSP tags were used to generate HTML. JSPs tags can also be used to generate or transform XML tags. In the next chapter, "JavaScript," you will learn how to use JavaScript in a Web application. JavaScript is not a J2EE API; however, it is a very helpful tool that can make the HTML Web pages a lot better.

CHAPTER 12

JavaScript

What's in Chapter 12?

This chapter provides an introduction to using client-side JavaScript in Web applications. This chapter covers the following topics:

- A brief history of JavaScript, including the ECMA-262 standard
- Basic syntax
- A description of objects, properties, methods, events, operators, and functions
- When not to use JavaScript in Web applications
- The cross-browser problem
- Best practices
- Using WSAD to create scripts and connect events to them
- How to create visual effects on images, hover help, alert boxes, and print

This chapter does not serve as a JavaScript reference, but it does show practical uses for JavaScript in Web applications that do not cause the application to depend upon the script for operation.

This chapter is concerned with enhancing the client-side usability of a Web application. It is tempting to move part of the application logic into the browser. We shall argue that this has a number of shortcomings. Let us first define JavaScript.

What Is JavaScript?

JavaScript is an interpretive object-oriented language that is popular for client-side scripting in Web browsers. Microsoft uses a version called JScript in its Windows Script Host provider, and as a server-side scripting language in Active Server Pages technology. We shall confine our JavaScript discussion to the Web browser aspect of JavaScript in J2EE applications.

Is JavaScript a lightweight version of Java? JavaScript has little in common with Java except for the first two syllables of its name. Historically, JavaScript was born when Netscape added a basic scripting capability to its Navigator Web browser. The language was called LiveScript. Soon, Java emerged as the latest hot computer language. Netscape responded by adding Java applet capability to Navigator release 2. They renamed LiveScript to JavaScript, presumably to ride on the coattails of Sun's popular new language. It didn't seem to matter that Java and JavaScript were each entirely different languages, but some of us technical people were confused at first.

Other vendors embraced JavaScript, but it wasn't standardized. Successive releases of Microsoft Internet Explorer, and Netscape Navigator supported different versions of JavaScript (or JScript) at different times, and on different platforms. In 1997, an international standards body named ECMA (European Computer Manufacturers Association) finally produced a standard for JavaScript called ECMA-262, also called ECMAScript.

There was some natural time lag before browser releases incorporated the ECMA-262 standard. Netscape 6 claims to be 100 percent ECMAScript-compliant. The open-source browser, Mozilla, has a compliant ECMA-262 JavaScript engine. Some open-source browsers, such as the Gnome Galeon browser, use the Mozilla engine and comply with ECMA-262. If you confine your scripts to an ECMA-262 set, many browsers will operate with it properly. If a Web application targets the Internet, you may have to jump through a few hoops to adjust to down-level browsers. The extra effort required is one reason why a Web application should be designed to function correctly, independently of whether client-side scripting operates.

Characteristics of JavaScript

How does JavaScript enhance a Web browser? We said that JavaScript is an *object-oriented* language. JavaScript-enabled Web browsers have an object model that is exposed to scripts embedded within HTML tags. The <script language="text/javascript"> tag declares a JavaScript element within an HTML document. Its document, forms, frames, windows, and events may be manipulated by embedded script. These items are exposed as objects to JavaScript code.

The JavaScript source within the script element should be enclosed in HTML comments so that script-ignorant browsers do not try to process it. A script-aware browser will ignore the HTML comments within a script element. How do you indicate JavaScript comments? Use the Java or C++ double slash `//`, to indicate that everything to its right is to be ignored, or use the Java or C++ `/* stuff */` form of comment flag to indicate that the "stuff" should be ignored. This kind of comment may span lines.

A script element placed within an HTML <HEAD> section is available for execution by the time the <BODY> tag starts loading. Thus `<body onLoad="initFunction()" >` would call an author-defined initialization function defined in a script element child of the header element during loading of the body element. Notice that the function call is itself JavaScript. If the initialization were shot, it could all be carried out in the onLoad reference. An onUnload event handler for the body could show a goodbye message when the body is unloaded. The following HTML page source shows a body onLoad handler in a script element and a body onUnload handler inline. The intrinsic `alert()` function is used to greet the user during page entry and exit. The parentheses indicate that `alert()` is a function, not a variable, object, method, or property. The result of executing the onLoad is seen in Figure 12.1. A similar goodbye message appears when the application closes.

```
<html>
  <head>
    <title>onLoad and onUnload Handlers</title>
      <script type="text/javascript">
        <!--Begin
        function init() {
          alert("Welcome to Script-World!")
        }
        // End -->
      </script>
  </head>
  <body onLoad="init()"
        onUnload="alert('Goodbye from Script-World')">
    <h1>Script-World</h1>
  </body>
</html>
```

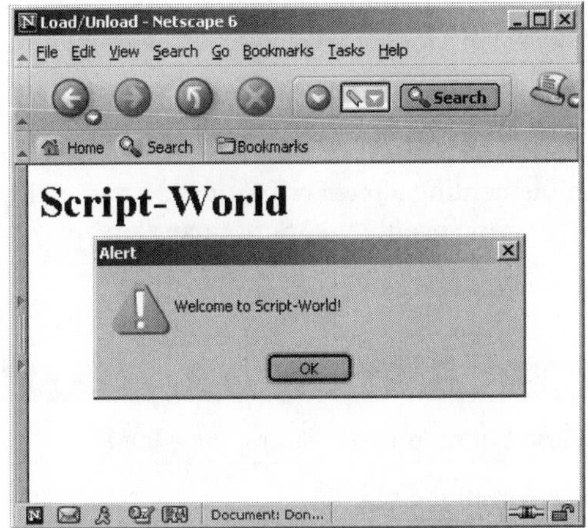

Figure 12.1 Alert from onload event.

Notice that there are no Java-style semicolons at the end of the JavaScript statements. It's okay to use them if doing so is a habit, but they are not mandatory. The parser treats the new-line character as white space so that it is okay to split long lines into multiple lines.

Properties and Methods

The previous example showed how to handle a couple of events. It didn't show much about the browser's object model. Each browser object has properties that you may access or modify from a script. You may attach an identifying name to any tag to enable you to manipulate it by name. Each object has behaviors known as methods. For example, a button has a `click()` method. The parentheses signify that click is a method, not a property. Think of a method as a verb and a property as a noun.

Use dot separators to compose hierarchical references to objects, properties, or methods. The following are some examples of object references to methods:

```
arg.charAt(i)
document.myform.myfunc()
window.open("names.html", "nameWin", "width=50,height="200")
```

Here are examples of references to properties of objects:

```
window.event.keycode
myform.namelist.selectedIndex
document.all.glowtext.style.filter
```

Events

Previously, you saw an example of handling onLoad and onUnload events in a body element. Many document objects generate events in response to user interactions. Examples are a mouse movement over an image, pressing a key, or pressing a form's Submit button. A JavaScript function handles an event by being called in response to the event. All events have a built-in default handler. You need only handle events that you want or need to filter. You can do this by implementing a JavaScript function named for the event prefixed by *on*. Table 12.1 shows common event JavaXScript handlers.

Table 12.1 Common EventHandlers

EVENT HANDLER	EVENT MEANING
onAbort()	Browser Stop button pressed during page load
onBlur()	Focus moved from the object
onChange()	User changed the object
onClick()	User clicked on the object

Table 12.1 *(continued)*

EVENT HANDLER	EVENT MEANING
onError()	JavaScript suffered an error
onFocus()	Object connected to the keyboard
onLoad()	Object finished loading
onMouseOver()	Mouse pointer passed over the object
onMouseOut()	Mouse pointer left the object
onSelect()	Object contents selected
onSubmit()	Form submitted
onUnload()	Window exited

Types, Variables, and Operators

A variable holds one or more values. Most languages allow variables of intrinsic types, defining operators to carry out built-in kinds of work. The type of the variable dictates the interpretation of the value. Table 12.2 lists the common JavaScript types.

Declare a variable by using the var keyword followed by a unique name, as in the following example:

```
var myVar
```

Table 12.2 JavaScript Types

TYPE	MEANING	EXAMPLE
Boolean	true or false	true // true or false allowed values
Function	Return value of a function	function sq(arg) { return arg * arg }
Null	Nothing	var aNull // Initial value is null
Number	Subject to arithmetic functions and operations	2.9 // Integer or floating point
Object	Entity having methods and properties	screen, window, document
String	Text that may be manipulated	"Quoted characters"

A variable contains one or more types. For instance, a variable containing a literal 2.5 could be used in a string expression or a numeric expression. An expression is composed of a mix of JavaScript operands. These may be literals, functions, or variables, each exhibiting a type. Operators reduce an expression to a single value having one or more types.

A number of restrictions constrain variable naming. For example, a variable name is case sensitive, and it may not start with a digit nor contain punctuation or spaces. It cannot be any of the 24 JavaScript reserved words. ECMA-262 adds 10 more words that are reserved. See the file Ecma-262.pdf in the book Web site for a list of these words. This issue is compounded by the fact that 26 Java reserved words are also prohibited from use. For example, `goto` is not allowed, even though neither JavaScript nor Java will probably ever use it. That's not the end of the restrictions on names. None of the intrinsic object, function, or event names should be used as variable names, no matter which character case is used. Some browsers, such as Internet Explorer, are case insensitive. Thus, neither, `window` nor `Window` should be used as a variable identifier.

Previously, we said that operators are used to reduce an expression containing operands to a value. Some operators consume two operands; others simply modify the value of one operand. The JavaScript operators are shown in Table 12.3.

Assignment and Comparison

Placing a value into a variable is called assigning a value. Use the assignment operator for setting a value. JavaScript, like Java and C++, has a simple assignment operation and added assignments that are shortcuts for carrying out an operation and assigning the result to a variable. See Table 12.4 for the JavaScript assignment operations.

Comparison operations use a set of two-operand operators plus one single-operand operator. The type of the result of a comparison is a `boolean` type. Table 12.5 shows the JavaScript comparison operations.

Table12.3 Simple Operators

OPERATOR	OPERANDS	DESCRIPTION
a + b (numeric)	2	Add a and b
s + v (string)	2	Concatenate a and b
a – b	2	Subtract b from a
a * b	2	Multiply a by b
a / b	2	Divide a by b
a % b	2	Remainder of a / b
a++, ++a	1	a = a + 1
a++, ++a	1	a = a – 1
-a	1	a = –a

Table 12.4 Assignment Operations

ASSIGNMENT	MEANING
a = b	Put value of b into a
a += b	a = a + b
a -= b	a = a – b
a *= b	a = a * b
a /= b	a = a / b
a %= b	a = a % b // a modulo b

Looping and Flow

JavaScript uses the same looping and flow statement control syntax as Java, except that the trailing semicolon (;) is optional at the end of a statement. Curly braces enclose compound statements as they do in Java.

Functions

Invoke a user-defined function or an intrinsic function by using its name, including the parentheses. Include any required actual parameters in the parentheses, separated by commas. Any function may be used in an expression. All functions return a value, but not all functions return a non-null value. A literal, a variable, or a complex expression may be passed as an argument to a function.

Table 12.5 Comparison Operations

COMPARISON	TRUE IF:
a == b	a and b are equal
a != b	a and b are not equal
a > b	a greater than b
a >= b	a greater than or equal to b
a < b	a less than b
a <= b	a less than or equal to b
a && b	both a and b are true
a || b	either a or b is true
!a	a is false, else returns true

A user-defined function contains executable JavaScript statements. It is declared as follows:

```
function noEmailAddress() {
  alert("You must supply an email address")
}
```

A function may be declared as having parameters. Actual parameter values are copied to formal parameters named within the parentheses that follow the name. The following is an example:

```
function max(arg1, arg2) {
  if (arg1 > arg2)
    return arg1
  else
    return arg2
}
```

The reserved word identifier restrictions on variables apply to user-defined functions and their formal parameter identifiers.

Browser Object Model

Each server or browser that implements JavaScript supplies an object model that completes the object model defined by ECMA-262. Each browser exposes the operational parts of the rendering process and user interface in an object model that extends the ECMA-262 object model. This means that you almost need to learn two languages: JavaScript itself and the object model of the browser. To script a client means to manipulate this object model in an HTML page using script—JavaScript in this case.

The object model is documented by the browser vendors. Netscape, Mozilla, and Microsoft each have documents about their browser object model, which is referred to as DOM (Document Object Model). The World Wide Web Consortium (W3C) has standardized the DOM for use with XML and HTML.

WSAD helps you author scripts with the advantage of having a structured scripting tool. Only the proper objects, properties, and methods for this version of JavaScript are available to drag from a visual tree into the script.

JavaScript in Web Applications

JavaScript in Web applications is a two-edged sword, as is the case with many technologies. You need to consider a number of advantages, disadvantages, and best practices in any application of JavaScript.

Advantages

The following are potential advantages of using client-side JavaScript in a Web application:

- Offloads some of the centralized application processing to the client.
- Provides prevalidated form entries without needing extra round trips to the server to prompt the user into correcting form entries.
- Provides tools such as WSAD that make embedding workable JavaScript into HTML and JSPs easier and safer than using the Notepad approach.
- Provides extra visual clues and usability devices for a thin browser client. One example is hover help for input fields.

Disadvantages

Now, let us look at the downsides of JavaScript:

- Offloading application processing to the client creates a maintenance issue. It breaks encapsulation and clean layer separation by fragmenting middle-tier processing partially into the presentation layer.
- The various levels of the browser object model and JavaScript constitute a Tower of Babel. A set of various components trying to communicate across standards and release levels is difficult at best, and impossible at the worst. This causes the programmer to take heroic coding and testing measures.
- A bug or incompatibility with a particular browser exposes the application to failure.
- End users can see the application code. Worse, they can modify it. Use of an external imported script file is no help because end users can see its contents in their browser cache or simply access the file from a URL.
- Too much script, mixed with HTML, presents readability issues. Generated code, such as that from WSAD, while tested, may be voluminous because of browser-specific paths.

Best Practices

With JavaScript, the disadvantages appear to outweigh the advantages, but JavaScript has potential that is difficult to ignore. Some judgment is needed to decide when to apply JavaScript and for what purposes. Assume the following praxes for applying JavaScript to Web applications:

- Praxis 1: Ensure that the Web application operates correctly when JavaScript is disabled.
- Praxis 2: Judiciously apply usability aids such as rollover effects and hover help.
- Praxis 3: Strive to use generated snippets and boilerplate from a tested tool such as WSAD.
- Praxis 4: Prevalidate form fields in the browser; note, however that the server should do field validation that works even when JavaScript is turned off.

The last, praxis 4 is a valuable use of JavaScript in a Web application. Remember to test that the application operates correctly without it. The second praxis—applying usability aids judiciously—can increase the usability and user acceptance of an application if you do not create a huge mass of script in your pages. Why carry out local validation at all? Because it reduces the number of trivial server round trips, increasing end-user satisfaction when they find that the application is responsive.

WSAD as a JavaScript Tool

Praxis 3 presents some interesting opportunities because an authoring tool can alleviate some of the hoops that you must jump through to accommodate disparate browser support. For instance, if you want a rollover effect on an image, you need different processing paths for Netscape 4, Netscape 6, any other Mozilla-based browser, and Internet Explorer. An image rollover effect is an example of a task that follows a set pattern, however convoluted it may be for differing browsers. This means that a good tool, such as WSAD, can use a template to generate JavaScript code.

Image Rollover Using WSAD

Let us try a concrete example of praxis 2. You will use WSAD to generate an HTML page having an image that changes when the mouse passes over it. Use the following steps:

1. Create a J2EE Web project named rollover in WSAD. Let its Enterprise Application project name default to DefaultEAR.
2. From the Web perspective, create an HTML file in Web Content folder by using the context menu item New > HTML/XHTML File. Name the file **rollover.html**. Let the wizard supply defaults for the rest of the attributes.
3. Open rollover.html in the Design view. You only need to edit this file, so open the WebArt Designer.
4. Select Tools > WebArt Designer from the main menu.

5. Select the Rollover button on the WebArt Gallery tab.
6. Select image pair labeled 01c. Look for the word "Home" on the graphic.
7. Press the small button at the bottom of the page, labeled Insert.

The image pair appears on the canvas with the Create Rollover dialog. Use it to set the two images that compose a rollover image as follows:

8. Draw a selection box around the top image on the canvas, and then press the left-hand Select button in the Create Rollover dialog. The image appears in the first and last image panes.
9. Draw a selection box around the bottom image on the canvas, and then press the second Select button in the Create Rollover dialog. The image appears in the middle panes, as seen in Figure 12.2.
10. When satisfied with the image sequence, press the Save Rollover button on the Create Rollover dialog. This invokes the Rollover wizard.
11. Press Next, then Finish. The Save Rollover Image Files dialog appears. Use it to save the HTML and two image files in a work directory outside of WSAD. Enter **rollover** in the File Name field, and then press Save.
12. Close the Create Rollover dialog and the WebArt Designer. There is no need to save the canvas when prompted.

Use a browser to open the saved rollover.htm from the external work directory. Move the mouse over the image to see the rollover action provided by generated JavaScript. Figure 12.3 shows the image when the pointer has not entered it. Figure 12.4 shows the image as the mouse rolls over it.

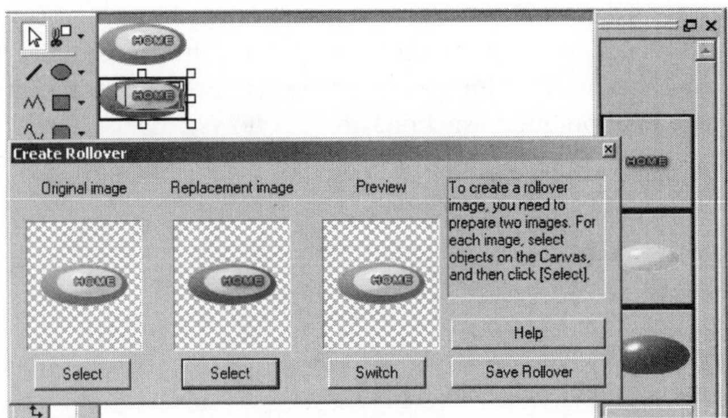

Figure 12.2 Create a rollover Image.

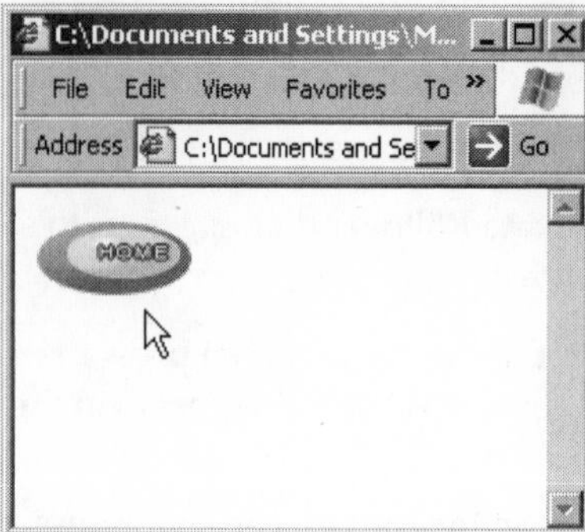

Figure 12.3 Image's normal state.

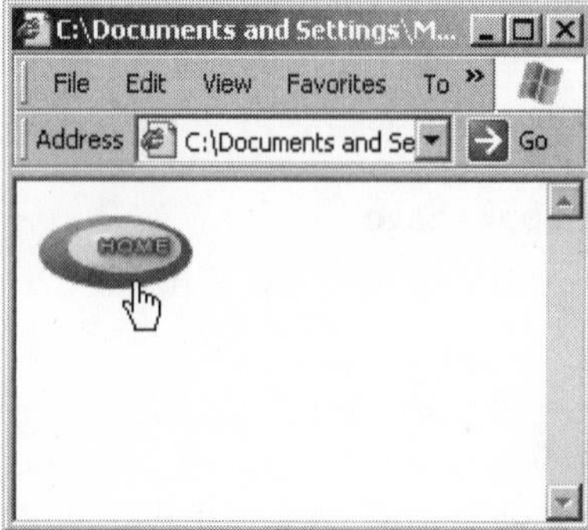

Figure 12.4 Rollover rendition of image.

Open the Source view of the browser. This rollover effect is created by client-side script, so all of the source code is exposed to the end user. Notice that considerable code, including browser type-checking and image swapping has been generated in two script elements. The image manipulation functions are as follows:

```
<SCRIPT language="JavaScript">
<!--HPB_SCRIPT_ROV_50
//  Licensed Materials - Property of IBM
//  (C) Copyright IBM Corp. 1998, 2001 All Rights Reserved.
//  US Government Users Restricted Rights -
//  Use, duplication or disclosure restricted
//  by GSA ADP Schedule Contract with IBM Corp.
//
// HpbImgPreload:
function HpbImgPreload(){
  var appVer=parseInt(navigator.appVersion);
  var isNC=(document.layers && (appVer >= 4));
  var isIE=(document.all    && (appVer >= 4));
```

```
  if (isNC || isIE) {
    if (document.images) {
      var imgName = HpbImgPreload.arguments[0];
      var cnt;
      swImg[imgName] = new Array;
      for (cnt = 1; cnt < HpbImgPreload.arguments.length; cnt++) {
        swImg[imgName][HpbImgPreload.arguments[cnt]] = new Image();
        swImg[imgName][HpbImgPreload.arguments[cnt]].src =
          HpbImgPreload.arguments[cnt];
      }
    }
  }
}
// HpbImgFind:
function HpbImgFind(doc, imgName){
  for (var i=0; i < doc.layers.length; i++) {
    var img = doc.layers[i].document.images[imgName];
    if (!img) img = HpbImgFind(doc.layers[i], imgName);
    if (img) return img;
  }
  return null;
}
// HpbImgSwap:
function HpbImgSwap(imgName, imgSrc) {
  var appVer=parseInt(navigator.appVersion);
  var isNC=(document.layers && (appVer >= 4));
  var isIE=(document.all    && (appVer >= 4));
  if (isNC || isIE) {
    if (document.images) {
      var img = document.images[imgName];
      if (!img) img = HpbImgFind(document, imgName);
      if (img) img.src = imgSrc;
    }
  }
}
var swImg; swImg=new Array;
//-->
</SCRIPT>
```

Notice the `HpbImgPreload()` and `HpbImgFind()` functions. The function named `HpbImgSwap()` actually carries out the image change replacement. The image is rendered within an HTML anchor tag that handles pointer events by calling the `HpbImgSwap()` function.

There is code to check for browser vendor and version number. It would be a tall order for every Web author in the World to keep writing this kind of code error-free. WSAD wrote it once and simply reuses it. If a new browser version behaves differently, this code would possibly break. First, you can assume that new browsers will comply with ECMA-262, and the W3C DOM, so that all browsers will converge to common JavaScript behavior. Second, that failures do not prevent the Web page from rendering or behaving correctly in a Web application. It is possible to crash a browser with a malignant script. WSAD has generated well-tested code with paths for browsers that support ECMA-262. The worst that may happen is that the image will not change. This shouldn't break a Web application.

From which events is the actual rollover effect initiated? Look below the second script in the <BODY> tag area. Notice the onmouseout and onmouseover event handlers on the <A> anchor element that surrounds the <IMG> element for the house. The handlers each call the `HpbImgSwap()` function to replace the image. A representative HTML snippet follows:

```
<A href="#" id="_HPB_ROLLOVER1"
      onmouseout="HpbImgSwap('_HPB_ROLLOVER1', 'image1.gif');"
      onmouseover="HpbImgSwap('_HPB_ROLLOVER1', 'image2.gif');">
  <IMG src="b015icn.gif" width="32" height="32"
       border="0" name="_HPB_ROLLOVER1"
</A>
```

Elaborating Rollover Effects

You could elaborate a rollover effect by changing other images or the colors of parts of a presentation area. For example, you could implement a live table of contents by highlighting lines or images of document parts as the pointer rolls over them. Each highlighted image could have a normal HTML hyperlink attached to it.

This example used the WebArt Designer to create a rollover effect with a boilerplate HTML file and two image files in a work directory. If you wanted to create several rollover images, you could manually paste the script elements into the working HTML or JSP in the Design view, perhaps using a table element to control relative layout. You must remember to include a call to HpbImgPreload() for each rollover image in use. You would also insert actual hyperlink targets into the anchor element encompassing each element. A simple example is included in the Chapter 9 resources on the book Web site. The example implements a rollover button bar as shown in Figure 12.5.

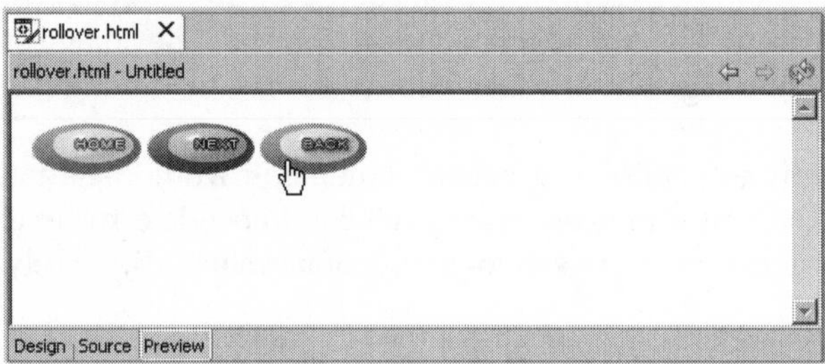

Figure 12.5 Rollover button bar example.

Creating JavaScript in WSAD

You created an image effect entirely based upon JavaScript generated by WebArt Designer without writing or editing a single line of code. But you would need to manually incorporate it into a working Page Designer page. WSAD can help insert script with function templates. It lets you select and drag objects, methods, or properties from a tree view to a <SCRIPT> element, ensuring that you use the correct object model. It has a selection of predefined snippets, including an image swap snippet that you could use to create your own rollover images without needing WebArt Designer.

Now, you will make another client-side script effect by creating a scrolling message in the status bar. You will not need to edit any JavaScript in this exercise. The following are the steps to obtain scrolling text in the status line:

1. Create a new Web project named scroll.
2. Create an HTML page name scroll.html in the Web Content folder. Ensure that it is open in Page Designer.
3. Use the main menu Insert > Paragraph > Heading 1 item to replace the dummy content. Overtype the boilerplate text with **Scrolling Message Demonstration.**
4. Open the Library view by choosing main menu Window > Show View > Library. You may need to choose Window > Show View > Other, depending upon the current perspective.
5. Expand the JavaScript UI node in the Library view. A list of script snippets appears.
6. Select Display a scrolling message on the status line, on the pop-up menu. Invoke its context menu. Choose Insert.
7. The Insert Template appears. It shows the source code for the snippet and allows you to set two variables. Set the delay variable to 100. The implied units are milliseconds. Enter a message like **This is a scrolling message**. The template should resemble Figure 12.6.
8. Press Insert. Save the file.
9. The `function _ScrollStatus(msg, delay)` definition appears in the <HEADER> section. It is called in the <BODY> section.
10. Press the Preview tab to check the operation of your handiwork. The message scrolls from right to left on the status line at the bottom, as expected. See the status line in Figure 12.7.

You still have not written an explicit line of JavaScript. Eventually, you will have to type something into a script. You may drag properties and methods of object definitions into a <SCRIPT> element to compose a custom script. Then, you would flesh out conditional constructs or parameters to suit your own implementation. We discuss practical applications of JavaScript for Web applications in the following sections.

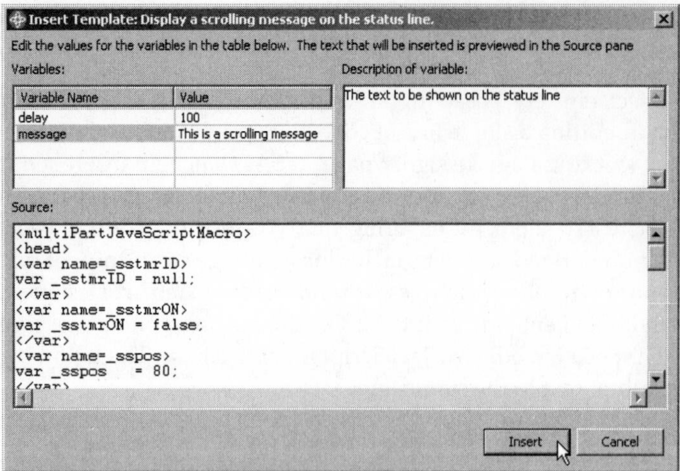

Figure 12.6 Scrolling message function.

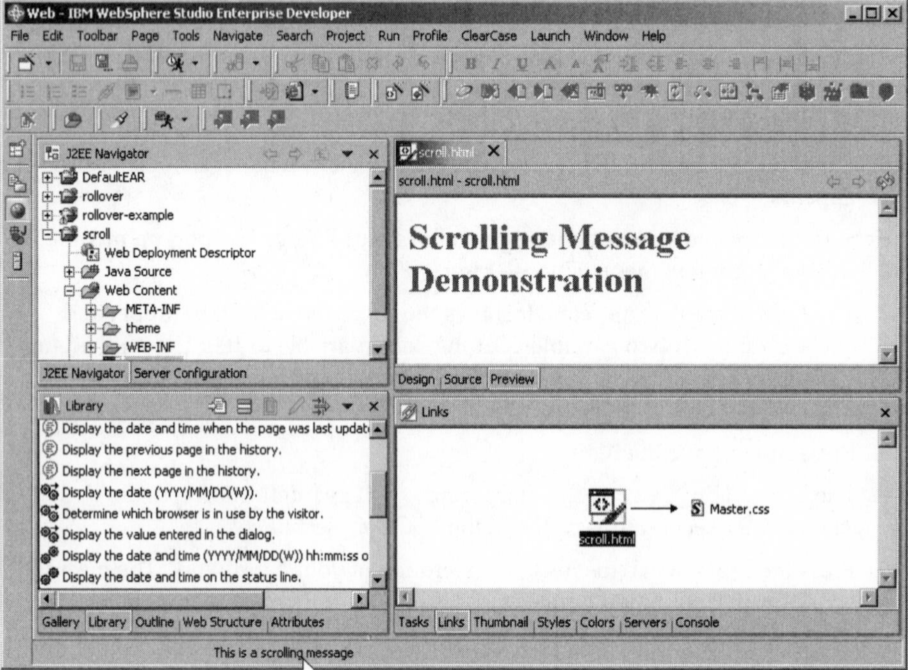

Figure 12.7 Scrolling message on status line.

Applied JavaScript

Let us survey a few practical areas of applied JavaScript in the following sections.

Field Validation

In this section, you will learn how to use JavaScript for client-side form field validations—the focus of praxis 4. Remember, the server-side should carry out its own field validation and be able to prompt the user for corrections, even with JavaScript turned off. Usually, client-side field validation is much less rigorous than the server-side validation. Often, it is enough to check for missing entries, not to validate their contents. It's possible to use JavaScript regular expression processing to check the format of data such as email addresses or IP addresses.

Now, you will do a simple form validation that only checks for field omissions. You will create a form consisting of two input fields and a Submit button. Next, you will create a validation function, and then call it from the form's onSubmit event. If either text field is blank, an alert box will ask the user to enter the missing value.

The following are the steps to follow to check for field omissions:

1. Create a Web project named form.
2. Create an HTML page in the project's Web Content folder named form.html.
3. In the Design view select the dummy text so that it will all be replaced. Pick the main menu items Insert > Form and Input Fields > Form.
4. Enter **Last Name** into the form.
5. Use the menu items Insert > Form and Input Fields > Text Field to insert a text field. Its name should be lastname. Add a normal line break by typing **Ctrl+Enter**.
6. Type **First Name** into the form on the new line.
7. Use the menu items Insert > Form and Input Fields > Text Field to insert a text field. Its name should be firstname. Add a normal line break by typing **Ctrl+Enter**.
8. Use the menu items Insert > Form and Input Fields > Submit Button to insert a submit button. Label it Submit Name. Add a normal line break by typing **Ctrl+Enter**.
9. Use the menu item Insert > Script to insert a script element. Leave the script element selected.
10. Use the context menu on the script element to view its attributes. Enter the following function in the attributes Script pane:

```
function validate(f) {
  if (f.lastname.value.length < 1) {
    alert('Please enter your last name.');
    return
  }
  if (f.firstname.value.length < 1) {
    alert('Please enter your first name.');
    return
  }
}
```

11. Click the Source tab of the Designer view. Add an onsubmit event handler to call the validate function with itself as an argument. Use the following source:

```
<FORM onsubmit="validate(this)">
```

12. Save your work. Select the Design tab.

Select the Preview tab to experiment with the form. If you click the Submit Name button, an alert for a missing field appears, as seen in Figure 12.8.

The following is the code extracted from within the <BODY> element.

```
<FORM onsubmit="validate(this)">
Last Name: <INPUT size="25" type="text" maxlength="25" name="lastname">
<BR clear="">
First Name:
<INPUT size="25" type="text" maxlength="25" name="firstname"><BR>
<BR clear="">
<INPUT type="submit" name="submitname" value="Submit Name"><BR>
<SCRIPT language="JavaScript">
<!--
// Drag the item from the left window and
// drop it here. Or, click the right mouse button
// and select 'Insert to Script' from the context menu.
// The code is inserted at the current cursor position.
function validate(f) {
  if (f.lastname.value.length < 1) {
    alert('Please enter your last name.');
    return
  }
  if (f.firstname.value.length < 1) {
    alert('Please enter your first name.');
    return
  }
}
//-->
</SCRIPT></FORM>
```

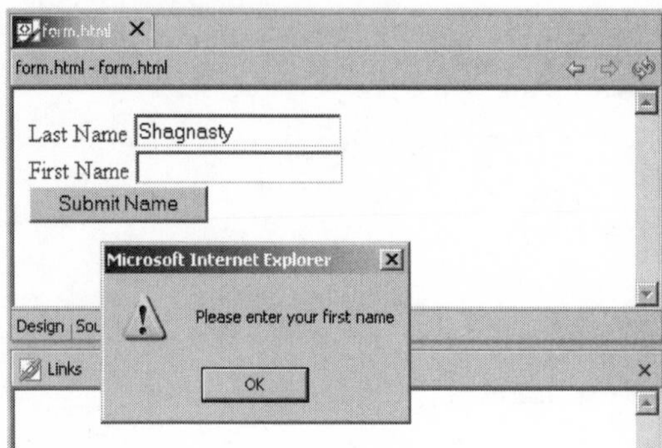

Figure 12.8 Validation pop-up.

Hover Help

We have discussed how onMouseover and onMouseout are used to create image rollover effects. Hover help, also known as tooltips, is another form of rollover effect, except that it pops up a text window instead of changing display characteristics. That text window causes a few cross-browser headaches. Internet Explorer displays hover help easily. Netscape 4 requires additional effort. You manipulate a floating <DIV> element using Netscape layers to create a hover help pop-up window. In addition, you have to put onMouseover and onMouseout into an <A> element or an <AREA> element because the events won't fire without at least a dummy `href` attribute. You had WSAD create the browser test. The event handler functions are called `hoverOn()` and `hoverOff()`. Notice the <DIV> element after the script. This is manipulated to create a pop-up window for Netscape hover help. Notice that the purpose of most of the code is to accommodate Netscape. The following is one of the shorter cross-browser hover help implementations:

```
<BODY>
<SCRIPT language="JavaScript">
<!--
// Globals: IE or Netscape. What version?
var ns = (navigator.appName.indexOf("Netscape")  >= 0);
var ie = (navigator.appName.indexOf("Microsoft") >= 0);
var vr = parseInt(navigator.appVersion);
// Called by onMouseOver handler
function hoverOn(obj, ev, txt) {
  if (ns) {
    document.hoverhelp.document.write(
      '<layer bgColor="white" style="border:1px '
      + 'solid black;font-size:12px;">' + txt + '</layer>')
    document.hoverhelp.document.close()
    document.hoverhelp.left = ev.pageX + 5
    document.hoverhelp.top = ev.pageY + 5
    document.hoverhelp.visibility = "show"
  }
  if (ie) {
      obj.title = txt
  }
}
// Called by onMouseout handler does nothing if IE
function hoverOff() {
  if (ns) {
    document.hoverhelp.visibility="hidden"
  }
}
//-->
</SCRIPT>
<div id="hoverhelp" style="position:absolute;visibility:hidden"></div>
```

Try the following steps to adapt the example you made for form validation:

1. Open the example in the Web Perspective. Show the page Design view.
2. Enter two line breaks between the labels and the input fields. This is only to expand the visual space for the pop-up.
3. Select each label and then use the menu items Insert > Link to make each label a hyperlink. Use # as a dummy URL.
4. Right-click each label to add calls to `hoverOn(this, event, "Help text")` and `hoverOff()` in response to onMouseover and onMouseout, respectively, as seen in Figure 12.9. Use appropriate help text for each field.

When finished, go to the Preview pane. Yellow hover help windows should appear as the pointer is moved across the labels. See Figure 12.9. Test it with a browser by opening form.html from the workspace directory as a file.

External .js Files

Many times JavaScript functions may be reused across pages by having each page reference a single external copy, reminiscent of a C++ "#include" file. The maintenance and page source readability benefits are obvious. External JavaScript files are usually named with a .js file extension. To use an external .js file, simply reference it in the <SCRIPT> tag as follows:

```
<SCRIPT language="JavaScript" type="text/javascript"
        src="validate.js">
```

Do not fall into the trap of believing that you can hide external script from users. If the page can load the script, then users see it in the browser cache, or they may load it directly from a URL. Do use external files to consolidate common scripts.

Page Print

It is questionable to rely on browser navigation and action buttons to participate in an application. Pages should present everything needed for the user to interact with the application. What if you want to invite a user to print an order confirmation? The browser has a print button or print menu item, but the page should invite the user to print it directly. A JavaScript example of a page that prints itself in response to a form submit request follows. Use following steps to add it to form.html:

1. Use the menu item Insert > Script to place a second script element beneath the Submit button.
2. Display the script element attributes.
3. Type the following into the Script pane of the attributes:

```
if (window.print) {
    document.write('<form>Please '
    + '<input type=button name=print value="Print" '
    + 'onClick="javascript:window.print()">
    for your    records!</form>');
}
```

4. Save the page.

The rendered page is shown in Figure 12.10 in an external browser. The Windows print dialog appears when the form button is clicked. If the browser were running on another operating system, the print dialog for that OS would be invoked instead.

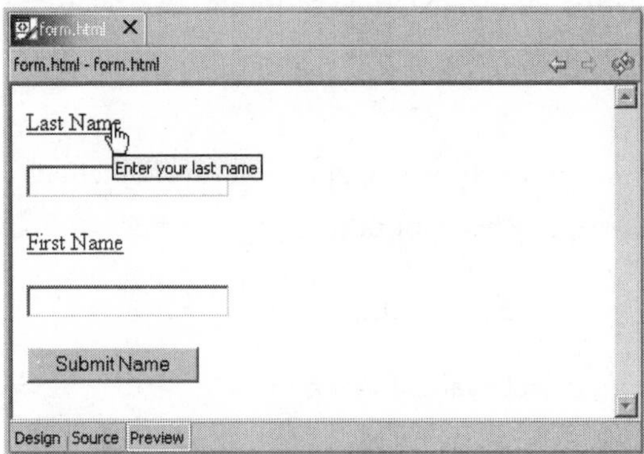

Figure 12.9 Hover help preview.

Figure 12.10 Self-printing Web page.

Summary

JavaScript is useful for client-side scripting, but its use should be limited to visual effects to enhance the usability of a Web application. This includes client-side field validation if the script does not materially participate in application logic. The application should function properly when JavaScript is turned off in the browser. In particular, the application should do rigorous form field validation at the server, returning to the user for corrections if necessary. Of course, the client script shouldn't prevent the application from running properly either. For example, a JavaScript validation bug could prevent valid form entry. Users could turn off JavaScript as a work-around for such an emergency.

This chapter discussed the use of JavaScript to enhance the user interface of Web applications without making the application logic depend on scripting. We covered:

- A brief history of JavaScript, including the ECMA-262 standard
- Basic syntax
- A description of objects, properties, methods, events, operators, and functions
- When and when not to use JavaScript in Web applications
- The cross-browser problem
- Best practices
- Using WSAD to create scripts and connect events to them
- How to make visual effects on images, hover help, alert boxes, and print

In the next chapter we shall discuss how to use inheritance with Java applications.

Using Inheritance

What's in Chapter 13?

You have already used Java inheritance in previous chapters. The lab in Chapter 3, "Making a Simple Java Application," and the lab in Chapter 9, "Making Servlets," subclasses HttpServlet. In this chapter, you will create an abstract class that has common behavior for other classes. You will also create a Java Interface that ensures that classes conform to a specific design. This chapter covers the following topics:

- Inheritance types
- Refactoring classes
  - Creating and using abstract classes
  - Creating and implementing interfaces
- Best practices using inheritance

These topics are very important for good object-oriented development. Proper use of inheritance improves the code maintainability, reduces the code size, and provides for code reuse. In this chapter, you will add an abstract class and a Java Interface to a Web application.

Types of Inheritance

Java has two ways to achieve inheritance using the key words `abstract` or `interface`. These two methods have some similarities and some differences. Both abstract classes and interfaces define behavior for other classes and neither can be instantiated. The next sections review both of these inheritance mechanisms in Java.

Abstract Classes

Abstract classes are an important part of Java that allow you to define parent classes. Abstract classes must have at least one abstract method, and they can also have fully implemented methods. Conversely, any class with one or more abstract methods is itself considered abstract. Any abstract method defined in an abstract class must be implemented with code in a concrete subclass. Sometimes the implementation is stubbed out with only braces, { } providing an empty expression that has no executable code. The Java compiler requires these stubbed out methods, even though they do nothing at runtime.

The JDK comes with a lot of abstract classes that get used implicitly when you subclass them. You used the `SimpleDateFormat` in Chapter 11, "JavaServer Pages." As you can see in Figure 13.1, the `SimpleDateFormat` class has three parent classes, including two abstract classes. The `SimpleDateFormat` class gets all the behavior, methods, and data, defined in the `Object`, `Format`, and `DateFormat` classes automatically.

Interfaces

A Java Interface provides a convenient way to define common behavior. Interfaces only declare method signatures and do not have any implementation code in the methods. Interfaces are frequently used to define a common API for certain classes. The J2EE API uses a lot of Java Interfaces. Chapter 3, "Making a Simple Java Application," shows how the Java event framework uses the listener interface.

Interfaces allow Java classes to get some of the benefits that are restricted with single inheritance. A class can only have one parent class, but it can implement many Interfaces. Interfaces can be subclassed using other Interfaces as parents. This relationship is used in the J2EE API with the HttpJspPage, as seen in Figure 13.2. This is the most common form of inheritance that Interfaces use.

It is a very common requirement to store, or persist, data that is held in a JavaBean. You can use an Interface to define the persistent access methods for the JavaBean to use. The implementation of the methods is still needed in the JavaBean, but the Interface ensures that the JavaBean follows a common API.

Figure 13.1 Abstract chain.

Figure 13.2 Interface chain.

Refactoring

J2EE applications are usually developed with an iterative development process. At the beginning of each iteration, the object model is assessed, and potential abstract classes and interfaces are identified. Refactoring code is the process of consolidating or converting code to a more efficient design. You may find common code patterns that can be placed in a parent class. A servlet could have some general-purpose methods for reading from the request, validating the user, or processing errors that could be used by other servlets. The JavaBeans used in an application may need to be saved in and retrieved from a database. The JavaBeans should use a common access API for saving and retrieving the data. An Interface can easily provide this function.

Determining Inheritance Type

You will use the classes from the Golf Web application developed in previous chapters for this effort. This is a simple application, but it has all the basic elements of a Web application. The Golf Web application has a servlet and a JavaBean, along with Web content such as an HTML file and a JSP file. Usually, similar components in a Web application have some common function that can be shared. The servlets will have common methods for accessing the request and preparing items for the response. The domain JavaBeans may need to be stored in an external form such as a relational database. You can use Interfaces to achieve this in a consistent manner.

You will modify the Golf Web application to use both types of inheritance. You will use an abstract servlet to hold common code for the GolfAVG servlet, and you will use an Interface to define the persistent methods for the GolfData JavaBean. These are good examples of how you can use inheritance in your Java applications. You may also need to use a parent abstract class for the JavaBeans, and the servlets could implement some type of interface.

Defining a Parent Class

You will make a new abstract class that provides functions for other servlets like the GolfAVG servlet developed in Chapters 9 through 11. The GolfAVG servlet has a number of methods that can be used by other servlets such as the default implementation for the `init()` and `destroy()` methods. The `readParameter()` and `displayMessage()` methods are also general-purpose methods, and they could be useful for other servlets.

WSAD handles renaming the constructor when it copies a class. Copying the GolfAVG servlet and giving it a new name is a quick way to achieve the desired result. Create a new BaseServlet with the following steps:

1. Select the GolfAVG servlet in the J2EE Navigator.
2. From a pop-up menu select Copy, and the class is saved in the Clipboard.
3. From a pop-up menu select Paste to copy the class.
4. WSAD displays the Name Conflict window, as seen in Figure 13.3. Enter **BaseServlet** for the new name and click the OK button, and WSAD creates the new servlet.

The BaseServlet should be in the j2eebook.golf.controller package, as shown in Figure 13.4.

The BaseServlet should be placed in a separate common package if you want servlets in different Web applications to use the BaseServlet. Now the new BaseServlet needs to be modified so that it has the common methods that can be shared among other servlets. Make the following changes to the BaseServlet code:

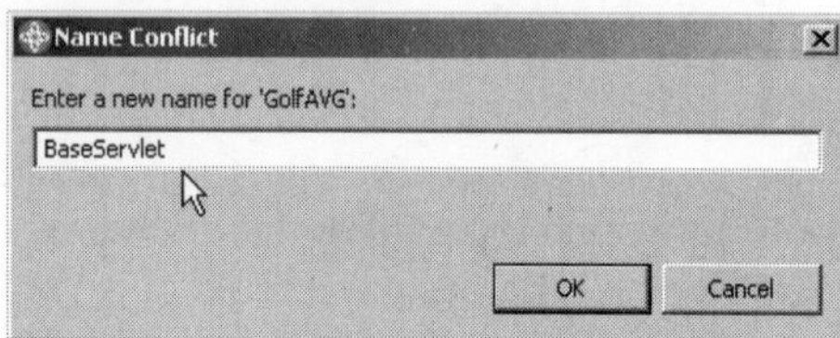

Figure 13.3 Copy and rename servlet.

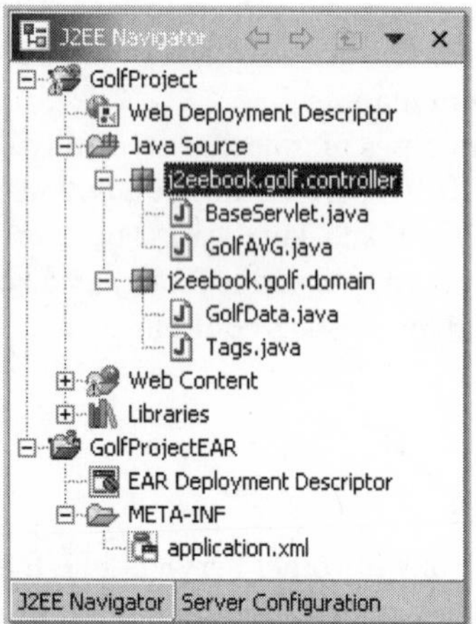

Figure 13.4 J2EE Navigator.

5. Keep the `init()`, `destroy()`, `readParameter()`, and `display Message()` methods and delete the other methods.
6. Delete the following import statements that are not needed:

   import j2eebook.golf.domain.GolfData;

   import j2eebook.golf.domain.Tags;

   import java.util.*;
7. Add the key word **abstract** to the class definition.
8. BaseServlet should look as follows:

```
package j2eebook.golf.controller;
import java.io.IOException;
import javax.servlet.ServletException;
import javax.servlet.http.HttpServlet;
import javax.servlet.http.HttpServletRequest;
import javax.servlet.http.HttpServletResponse;
import javax.servlet.http.HttpSession;
import java.io.PrintWriter;
/**
 * @version     1.0
 * @author
 */
public abstract class BaseServlet extends HttpServlet {
    /*
    * Constructor
    */
    public BaseServlet() {
        super();
    }
    /*
    * @see GenericServlet#destroy()
    */
    public void destroy() {
        System.out.println(
            new java.util.Date() + " " + getServletName() + "        ⮐
stopped");
    }
    /*
    * @see GenericServlet#init()
    */
    public void init() throws ServletException {
        System.out.println(
            new java.util.Date() + " " + getServletName() + "        ⮐
started");
    }
```

```
    /*
    * display an HTML message
    */
    public void displayMessage(HttpServletResponse resp, String ⮐
message)
        throws IOException {
        // Obtain the output stream from the response
        PrintWriter out = resp.getWriter();
        // print a simple html page in the printwriter
        out.println("<html><body>" + message);
        out.println("</body></html>");
    }
    /*
    * read a parameter from the request
    */
    public String readParameter(HttpServletRequest req, String tag) {
        String param = (String) req.getParameter(tag);
        if (param != null) {
            return param;
        } else {
            return "";
        }
    }
}
```

The BaseServlet does not need to be added to the Web application definition in the web.xml file. The BaseServlet will not be directly called in the Web application; rather it is used by its child servlets. The next step is refactoring the original GolfAVG to use the abstract BaseServlet class.

Refactoring a Class

The GolfAVG servlet needs a number of changes to use the BaseServlet. The class declaration needs to be changed, the methods that are in the parent BaseServlet need to be deleted, and a few import statements need to be removed. Modify the GolfAVG servlet with the following steps:

1. Delete the `init()` and `destroy` methods.
2. Delete the `readParameter()` and `displayMessage()` methods.
3. Delete the following import statements, which are not needed:
    a. import javax.servlet.http.HttpServlet;
    b. import java.io.PrintWriter;
4. Change `extends HttpServlet` to `extends BaseServlet`.
5. Save these changes to the code.

These changes simplify the GolfAVG servlet, reducing it to the code that is required to meet its specific needs. The generic code for reading parameters from the request and sending a message in the response is located in the parent class. The completed code for the GolfAVG servlet should look as follows:

```
package j2eebook.golf.controller;
import java.io.IOException;
import javax.servlet.ServletException;
import javax.servlet.http.HttpServletRequest;
import javax.servlet.http.HttpServletResponse;
import javax.servlet.http.HttpSession;
import j2eebook.golf.domain.GolfData;
import j2eebook.golf.domain.Tags;
import java.util.*;
/**
 * @version     1.0
 * @author
 */
public class GolfAVG extends BaseServlet {
    /*
    * Constructor
    */
    public GolfAVG() {
        super();
    }
    /*
    * @see HttpServlet#doGet(HttpServletRequest req, HttpServlet
Response resp)
    */
    public void doGet(HttpServletRequest req, HttpServletResponse resp)
        throws ServletException, IOException {
        // redirect to golf web page
        resp.sendRedirect("index.html");
    }
    /*
    * @see HttpServlet#doPost(HttpServletRequest req,
HttpServletResponse resp)
    */
    public void doPost(HttpServletRequest req, HttpServletResponse resp)
        throws ServletException, IOException {
        try {
            // load the scores and calculate the average
            loadScores(req);
            getServletContext().getRequestDispatcher(
                "pages/golfScores.jsp").forward(
                req,
                resp);
        } catch (Exception e) {
            System.out.println("GolfAVG Exception in doPost() " + e);
            displayMessage(
```

```
                resp,
                "An error occurred.<br><br>Press on the browser back ⮐
button and check that all the scores have valid numbers.");
            }
        }
        /*
        * read golf scores from the request
        */
        public Vector readScores(HttpServletRequest req) {
            Vector scores = new Vector();
            for (int i = 1; i < 6; i++) {
                String param = (String) req.getParameter(Tags.SCORE + i);
                if ((param != null) && (param.length() > 0)) {
                    scores.addElement(param);
                }
            }
            return scores;
        }
        /*
        * load golf scores from the request
        *
        */
        public Vector loadScores(HttpServletRequest req) {
            // get the session
            HttpSession session = req.getSession(true);
            // get the GolfData bean
            GolfData data = (GolfData) session.getAttribute(Tags.GOLFDATA);
            if (data == null) {
                // make a GolfData bean
                data = new GolfData();
                // add GolfData to the session
                session.setAttribute(Tags.GOLFDATA, data);
            }
            // read the scores into the GolfData bean
            data.setScores(readScores(req));
            return data.getScores();
        }
    }
```

The next servlet for this Web application can extend the BaseServlet and use the same common methods as the GolfAVG servlet. All the child servlets benefit when changes or bug fixes are made to the methods in the BaseServlet. You will see how to refactor code using a Java Interface in the next section.

Defining an Interface

You will use the GolfData JavaBean to see how to implement an interface. In the current Web application the GolfData JavaBean is only used as a data holder at runtime. The JavaBean would need methods to allow it to store, or persist, its data. Usually this would be handled with `save()` and `retrieve()` methods. You can ensure that all the JavaBeans access data externally in a consistent manner by using a Java Interface that defines these methods.

First, you will create a new Interface named Persistent using a WSAD wizard. Then, you will modify the generated Interface code and add the necessary method definitions for the Interface. Create the new Interface with the following steps:

1. Select the javabook.golf.domain package in the J2EE Navigator.
2. Select the menu items File > New > Other > Java > Interface.
3. Click the Next button and go to the second page, as shown in Figure 13.5.
4. Make sure that the Project is GolfProject/Java Source.
5. Make sure the Package is j2eebook.golf.domain.
6. Enter **Persistent** for the interface name.
7. Make sure the modifiers or radio button is public.
8. Click the Finish button to create the Interface.

There is not very much code created for an Interface. Interfaces do not have constructors, so there is only the Interface definition. WSAD generates the code for the Interface as follows:

```
package j2eebook.golf.domain;
/**
 * @author dnilsson
 *
*/
public interface Persistent {
}
```

Now, you can add method definitions to the Interface that meet its desired intent. This interface needs the generic methods that can be shared with other JavaBeans. There will not be any real code that runs in the methods, only the method signatures.

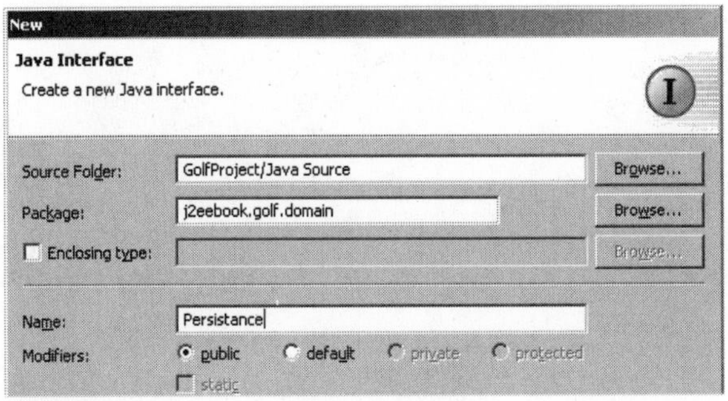

Figure 13.5 New Interface details.

Adding Interface Methods

The new Interface needs the method definitions for this type of behavior. The Persistent Interface needs methods to save an object, retrieve an object, and validate an object. Edit the code for the Persistent Interface and make these changes with the following steps:

1. Add a method definition named **`retrieve`** that has no parameters and returns an `Object`.
2. Add a method definition named **`save`** that has an `Object` as a parameter and returns `void`.
3. Add a method definition named **`isValid`** that has no parameters and returns a `boolean`.
4. Save the changes to the code.

The updated code for the Persistent Interface should look as follows:

```
package j2eebook.golf.domain;
/**
 * @author drnilsso
 *
 */
public interface Persistent {

/**
 * retreives JavaBean data
 *
 */
public Object retreive();

/**
 * stores JavaBean data
 */
public void save(Object saveObject);

/**
 * validates a JavaBean
 */
public boolean isValid();

}
```

This Interface can be used by any class that needs to be stored and retrieved no matter what mechanism is used to store the data. Let's use this Interface with the GolfData JavaBean.

Implementing an Interface

The GolfData JavaBean is only used as a data holder in the current Web application. It can be modified to use the Persistent Interface and have the ability to save and retrieve data from an external source. It is very easy to find and generate the required methods in WSAD. Modify the GolfData JavaBean with the following steps:

1. Change the class declaration to include **implements Persistent.**
2. Save the changes to the code.

The `GolfData` class must implement the methods defined in the Persistent Interface. WSAD marks a red x next to the `GolfData` class, indicating there are errors. In the Tasks view, WSAD shows that the `GolfData` class needs to implement the `save()` and `retrieve()` methods. You could copy the methods from the Persistent Interface or use a special generator in WSAD to get these methods. Let's fix the code with the following steps:

3. Make sure that you have selected the `GolfData` class by double-clicking on it in the J2EE Navigator.
4. Select the menu items Source > Override Methods..., and the Override Methods window appears, as seen in Figure 13.6.
5. Make sure that the `isValid()`, `retrieve()`, and `save()` methods are checked.
6. The class does not need any methods from the object, so it should be unchecked.
7. Click the OK button, and WSAD generates methods required by the Persistent Interface.

The `GolfData` class has the new methods as stubs with no content. When the methods are called nothing happens. You need to complete the implementation for each method to get the `save()` and `retrieve()` methods to behave as desired. The completed `GolfData` class should look as follows:

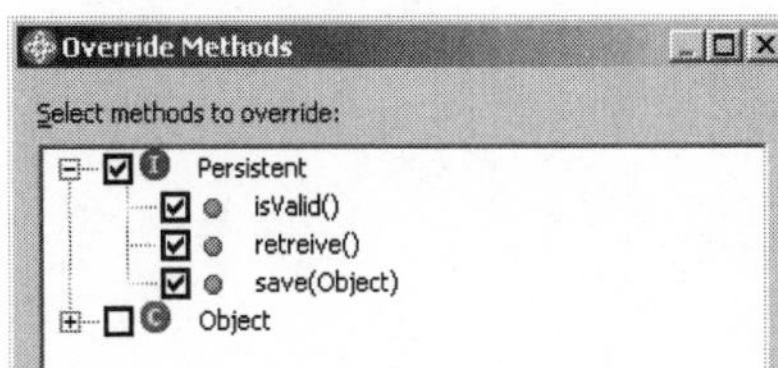

Figure 13.6 Overriding methods.

```
package j2eebook.golf.domain;
import java.util.*;
public class GolfData implements Persistent{
    private String username;
    private String userid;
    private Vector scores;
    private boolean valid;
    /**
     * Constructor for GolfData
     */
    public GolfData() {
        super();
    }
    /**
     * Gets the username
     * @return Returns a String
     */
    public String getUsername() {
        return username;
    }
    /**
     * Sets the username
     * @param username The username to set
     */
    public void setUsername(String username) {
        this.username = username;
    }
    /**
     * Gets the userid
     * @return Returns a String
     */
    public String getUserid() {
        return userid;
    }
    /**
     * Sets the userid
     * @param userid The userid to set
     */
    public void setUserid(String userid) {
        this.userid = userid;
    }
    /**
     * Gets the scores
     * @return Returns a Vector
     */
    public Vector getScores() {
        return scores;
    }
    /**
     * Sets the scores
     * @param scores The scores to set
     */
```

```
    public void setScores(Vector scores) {
        this.scores = scores;
    }
    /**
     * Gets the valid
     * @return Returns a boolean
     */
    public boolean isValid() {
        return valid;
    }
    /**
     * Sets the valid
     * @param valid The valid to set
     */
    public void setValid(boolean valid) {
        this.valid = valid;
    }
    /*
    * calculate an average from a vector
    */
    public float avgScores(Vector numbers) {
        // loop through the Vector and calculate the average
        int sum = 0;
        for (int i = 0; i < numbers.size(); i++) {
            sum += Integer.parseInt((String) numbers.elementAt(i));
        }
        float avg = sum / numbers.size();
        return avg;
    }
    /**
     * Returns the average.
     * @return float
     */
    public float calcAverage() {
        return avgScores(getScores());
    }
    /**
     * Returns the handicap.
     * @return float
     */
    public float calcHandicap() {
        return calcAverage() - 72;
    }

    /**
     * @see j2eebook.golf.domain.Persistent#retrieve()
     */
    public Object retreive() {
        return null;
    }
    /**
     * @see j2eebook.golf.domain.Persistent#save(Object)
```

```
    */
    public void save(Object saveObject) {
    }
}
```

This sample is only meant to illustrate how to organize classes by utilizing inheritance. There is quite a bit to learn about coding persistence. Chapter 18, "Data Access," covers persistence and data access and provides a sample application. The following section shows how to use a special WSAD for refactoring methods.

Refactoring Methods

After an abstract parent class has been created, you may need to move other methods to the abstract class. As you saw in the previous example, refactoring code entails copying methods, deleting methods, and updating import statements. You can do this very easily in WASD with the Refactoring wizard. Let's see how this works using the GolfAVG servlet. Use the following steps to move the GolfAVG servlet `readScores()` method to a parent class:

1. Select the GolfAVG servlet `readScores()` method. The Outline view is good for this.
2. Select the menu item Refactor > Pull Up..., and the Refactoring start window appears, as shown in Figure 13.7. This window shows the parent class BaseServlet and gives its source code on the right.
3. Click the Next button to proceed. The Refactoring summary window appears, as shown in Figure 13.8.

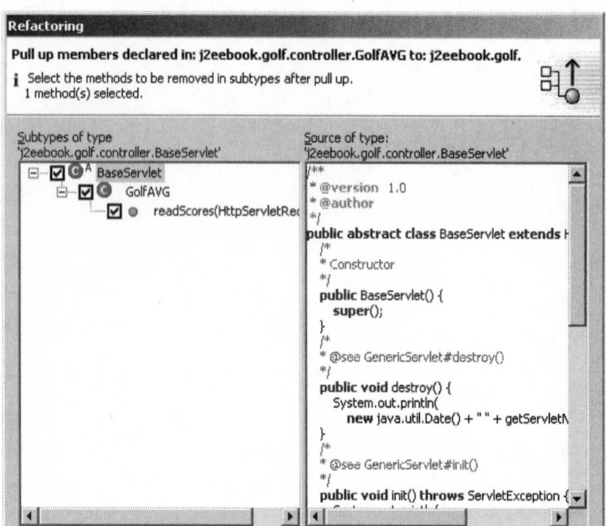

Figure 13.7 Refactoring Start.

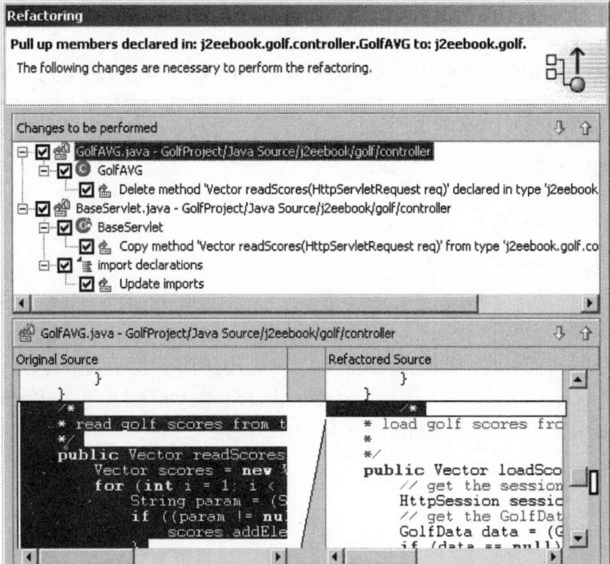

Figure 13.8 Refactoring summary.

The Refactoring summary window shows all the tasks that will happen in the Changes to be performed panel. There is also a view of the original and refactored source code at the bottom. If you click the Finish button, all the changes are performed and the method is placed in the parent class.

The Refactoring wizard is a handy way to move methods to a parent class. You can always make these changes by hand, but the wizard can move multiple methods, and it does all the cleanup work too. A lot of good inheritance usage comes from experience and good object-oriented design. The following section provides some techniques for using inheritance in your Java applications.

Best Practices

A number of best practices should be followed when refactoring classes by using Interfaces and abstract classes. When you see identical sections of code in different classes, it is a telltale sign of using inheritance. It is better to try and implement inheritance in the initial design, but during the iterative development process, it is inevitable that new inheritance patterns will emerge. Nothing is as good as experience, but the following sections discuss some issues that need to be considered when refactoring code and using inheritance.

Code Reduction

Good use of inheritance can reduce the amount of code in a system. For example, a lot of code can be saved if most of the servlets in a system have their own code to read from the request or validate a user. If you refactor this code and place it into an abstract parent class, each servlet can reuse the common code.

Over Layering

Abstract methods must be implemented by a concrete class. Be careful not to define a number of abstract methods in the parent class and then implement the abstract methods in another abstract child class. This defeats the intent of abstract methods and adds unneeded layers to the code. It is a good idea to review the abstract classes in a system and remove those that do not add additional behavior for multiple classes.

Package Placement

The abstract classes and Interfaces may be in the working package of the application to start. As the system evolves and matures, more classes may use the abstract classes and Interfaces. This can cause an artificial dependency on a package that should not exist. When this occurs, you need to move the generalized abstract classes and Interfaces to a separate package. This can usually be done with other refactoring work in an iteration.

Build Issues

WSAD, just as VisualAge for Java, organizes Java code in projects; you should place general-purpose abstract classes and Interfaces in a separate project. This helps eliminate problems with interdependencies when the projects are compiled. Each project has a build order defined for the project. Projects with classes and Interfaces that have no dependencies should be compiled first in the project build order, with dependent classes following later.

Summary

In this chapter, you learned how to use inheritance to improve your applications. This chapter covered abstract classes and Interfaces with examples of how to use these in a Web application. The chapter included the following topics:

- The different inheritance types and how they work
- How to refactor classes
- Creating and using abstract classes
- Creating and implementing Interfaces
- The best practices for using inheritance

Refactoring code is a common process in J2EE development. Software is developed iteratively when the analysis for the total system is incomplete. Experienced developers can foresee some inheritance uses during design, but there is always room for improvement as the software is developed. The tools in WSAD can help make the process of refactoring code much faster and easier. The next chapter covers a number of techniques to spice up a Web page including images, sound, and frames.

Making Slick Web Pages

What's in Chapter 14?

This chapter covers a number of topics all aimed at improving the fit and finish of a Web page. Most of the focus so far has been on J2EE APIs and working in WSAD. You will learn many different techniques for improving how a Web page appears. Each of these techniques can be used independently, or they can be combined on the same page. This chapter covers the following topics:

- Using framesets
- Adding pictures
- Creating a logo
- Making a navigation bar
- Incorporating sound
- Showing the weather

This diverse set of topics will be used to improve the Golf Web application developed in earlier chapters of this book. These techniques will transform the Web page that is a little rough looking into one with a lot more eye appeal.

Framesets

Framesets let you combine different HTML files into frames that can have different scrolling behavior. They provide some of the viewing behavior that is common in client-based applications like the ones written with the Java Swing controls. In this chapter, you will learn about frames and you will build a Web page that uses frames.

How Framesets Work

Framesets have frame HTML tags that specify the HTML files contained in the frameset. The <FRAME> tag has many attributes that let you control the spacing and scrolling. Figure 14.1 shows an example of a simple frameset with two frames, a navigation frame and a main frame. Each frame should have a unique name. Anchor tags can use the frame name as a parameter to the target attribute, for example:

```
<a href="/nextpage.jsp" target="main">Next</a>
```

This code calls the nextpage JSP, which sends the response back to the frame named main. If there is no frame named main, a new browser window opens to display the response. It can be very helpful to have a navigation bar constantly on the left or top of the Web page that allows the users to select different links that change the main content area.

You can nest framesets for a more complex user interface design. Figure 14.2 shows a sample HTML page containing Frameset1, which is split horizontally. The lower child frameset, Frameset2, is a nested frameset that is split vertically, with a navigation bar on the left and a main display area on the right. In this example, the banner frame could be fixed and nonscrolling, while the child frames in Framset2 could scroll either vertically or horizontally.

A frameset can seem a little tricky to build until you have had a chance to make one. In the next section, you will make a frameset like the one shown in Figure 14.1. In the following sections, you will add the frames to the frameset and complete the Web page.

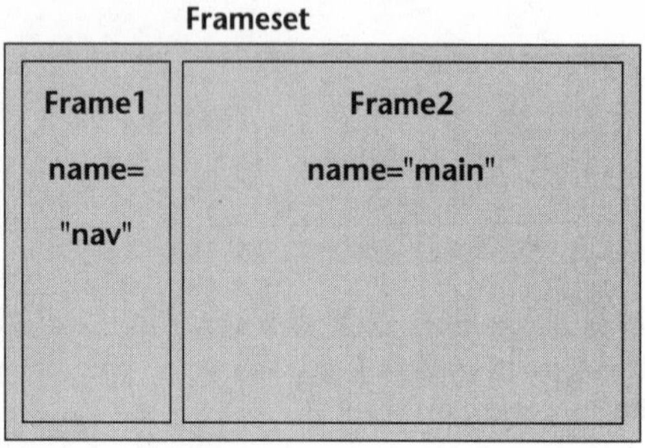

Frameset

Frame1

name=

"nav"

Frame2

name="main"

Figure 14.1 Basic frameset.

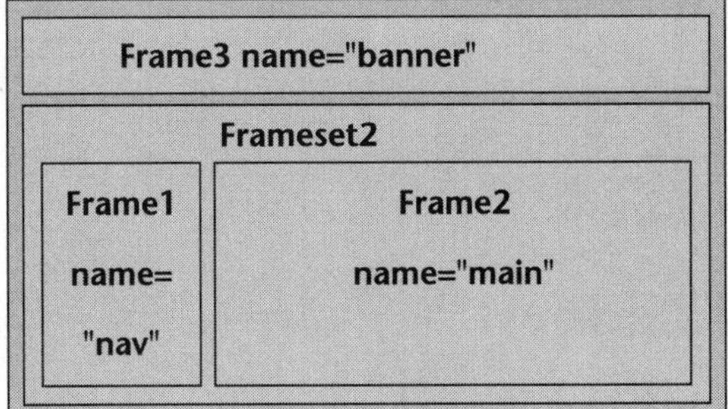

Figure 14.2 Nested framesets.

Using Framesets

Let's make a Web page that uses a frameset. You can hand-code the frameset page or use an automated tool, as with most tasks in WSAD. You will make an HTML page called golfframe that has the <FRAMESET> tags. The frameset has two frames, one used for a navigation bar and one used for a main display area. The Web page will be built in the same GolfProject that was used in previous chapters in this book. Keep in mind that when WSAD generates a frameset, it also generates the two HTML pages for the frames. Create a new HTML page with the following steps:

1. Select the **pages** folder in the GolfProject.
2. Select the menu items File > New > HTML file, as shown in Figure 14.3.
3. Make sure the folder is /GolfProject/Web Content/pages.
4. Name the new HTML file golfframe.
5. Make the Markup Language **HTML**.
6. Make the Code Generation Model **None**.
7. Click the Finish button to generate the HTML page.
8. Delete the placeholder text Place golfframe's content here that WSAD placed in the HTML page. Make sure that the paragraph tags, <p> and </p>, are deleted.
9. Save the golfframe page.

Now, that there is a basic HTML page, you are ready to create the frameset. WSAD can automatically create the frameset and its two child HTML files. The golfframe will be split vertically so there is a navigation bar on the left. Create the frameset with the following steps:

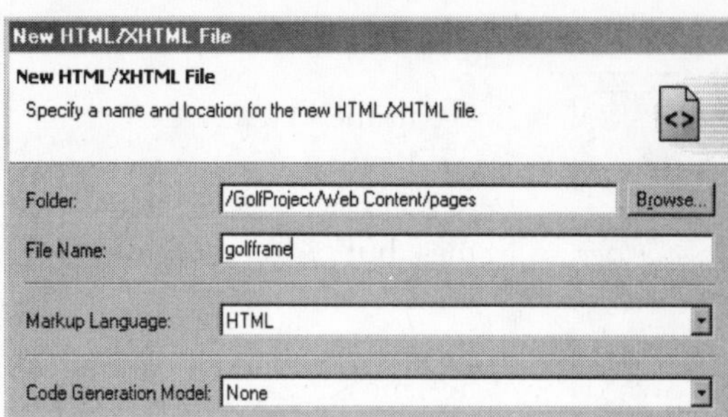

Figure 14.3 New HTML page.

1. Select the menu items Frame > Split Frame > Split Vertically, and the Split Frame dialog displays.
2. Select the radio button labeled **In the frameset parent**.
3. Click the OK button to create the frameset and generate the child HTML files.
4. Save the golfframe.html file.
5. You are prompted by WSAD to specify the child HTML filenames and locations.
6. WSAD created two child HTML files, named newpage1 and newpage2. These names are not very descriptive. Change newpage1.html to **nav.html** and make sure that it is saved under the **pages** subdirectory. Change newpage2.html to **main.html** and make sure that it is saved under the **pages** subdirectory, too.

TIP You cannot use CTRL-Z to undo the frameset. You may want the page split horizontally or the HTML file to be one of the child files. If you make a mistake when creating the frameset, just close the editor in WSAD without saving the changes. You can try creating the frameset again another time.

The Page Designer is a little tricky to use for editing framesets. The Page Designer displays the frameset file in one view and the child HTML files in another view.

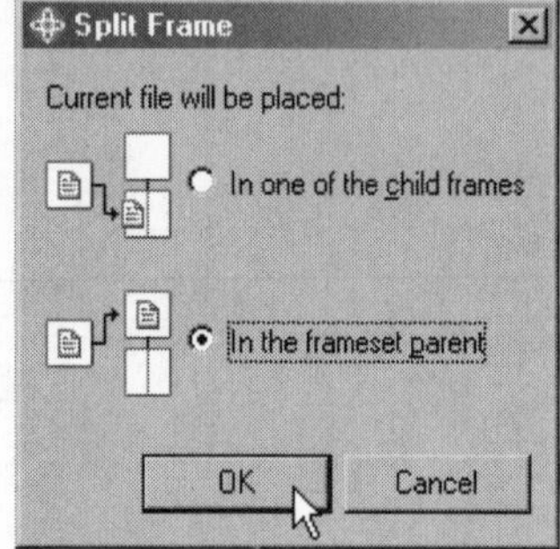

Figure 14.4 Split Frame window.

Frameset Attributes

The generated frameset is a good start, but you need to edit the <FRAMESET> tag to get the desired result for your Web page. The golfframe is displayed in the Design tab as shown in Figure 14.5. The Design tab of the Page Designer cannot be used to set the frameset attributes. You can adjust the size of the frames, but this can only be done using percents of the frameset, and this is not very accurate.

You will edit the generated code for the golfframe and set the size of the two columns that hold the child frames. You will also provide a message for older browsers that do not support frames. Select the Source tab, and the generated code for the golfframe should look as follows:

```
<!DOCTYPE HTML PUBLIC "-//W3C//DTD HTML 4.01 Frameset//EN">
<HTML>
<HEAD>
<META http-equiv="Content-Type"
    content="text/html; charset=WINDOWS-1252">
<META name="GENERATOR" content="IBM WebSphere Studio">
<META http-equiv="Content-Style-Type" content="text/css">
<LINK href="../theme/Master.css" rel="stylesheet" type="text/css">
<TITLE>golfframe.html</TITLE>
</HEAD>
<FRAMESET cols="50%,50%">
    <FRAME src="nav.html">
    <FRAME src="main.html">
    <NOFRAMES>
    <BODY>
    </BODY>
    </NOFRAMES>
</FRAMESET>
</HTML>
```

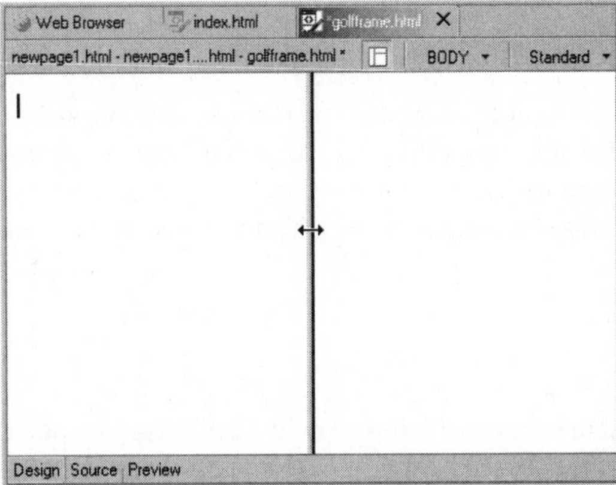

Figure 14.5 Frameset resizing.

If this code does not appear, you may be viewing one of the other frameset files. A frameset displays the two child frames in the Page designer. There is a view to see the frameset source, but it can be a little tricky switching views. You can avoid these problems by opening the golfframe.html file in the Source Editor that does not have a visual component.

Adjusting the Frame Size

The size of the child frames is managed by the frameset. The child frames are in columns, so the cols attribute sets the size of the child frames. The size can be set as a percent or in pixels. For this frameset, the first column will be 150 pixels and the second column takes the rest of the space, so it is set to *. Additionally, the frameset border attributes can be set. The frameset can have a slick look if you use zero for the borders. Make these changes to the <FRAMESET> tag as follows:

```
<FRAMESET cols="150,*" border="0" frameborder="0">
```

Handling No Frames

Old browsers that do not handle the HTML <frameset> tag cannot display the frameset. The <NOFRAMES> tag holds the tags that are displayed when the browser does not handle frames. You need to provide an error message if an old browser is detected. Add a helpful error message between the <body> tags to assist users with old Web browsers as follows:

```
<p>You must have a Browser that supports frames to view this page.</p>
```

Save the golfframe code after making these changes. The next step is to set the individual attributes for each child frame.

Frame Attributes

Each frame within the frameset has its own set of attributes and values. It is important to set a unique name to each frame for addressability. You will see how the frame names are used when the links are made in the navigation bar. The frame can have optional attributes that control the frames scrolling behavior. You will set the navigation bar so that it does not scroll.

Setting the Name

Each frame needs a unique name that is used as an attribute of the name tag. The name is used to identify the frame, and it is used in links on other Web pages to specify the target. You will see how this works when you make the navigation bar. Edit the code for the golfframe and add name attributes to the <FRAME> tags as follows:

```
<FRAME src="nav.html" name="nav">
<FRAME src="main.html" name="main">
```

Controlling Scrolling

Frames automatically scroll both vertically and horizontally so the user can view their contents. The banner or navigation frame can be designed so that everything displays and scrolling is not needed. The resizing bar can be removed to make a clean look for the Web page. Add the following attributes to the <FRAME> tag for the navigation bar:

```
scrolling="NO"
noresize="true"
```

Save the updated code. These parameters give the Web page a nice clean look and still permit the main frame area to scroll. This is all that is needed for the golfframe.html file. Usually, the outside HTML file with the frameset is rather small and does not change very much. This file can be a JSP that dynamically sets the frame values based on different criteria such as a user profile or a certain transaction.

Completed Frameset

A lot of changes have been made to the initial frameset code. Attributes were set in the <FRAMESET>, <FRAME>, and <NOFRAMES> tags. When the code is complete, the golfframe.html file should look as follows:

```
<!DOCTYPE HTML PUBLIC "-//W3C//DTD HTML 4.01 Frameset//EN">
<HTML>
<HEAD>
<META http-equiv="Content-Type"
    content="text/html; charset=WINDOWS-1252">
<META name="GENERATOR" content="IBM WebSphere Studio">
<META http-equiv="Content-Style-Type" content="text/css">
<LINK href="../theme/Master.css" rel="stylesheet" type="text/css">
<TITLE>golfframe.html</TITLE>
</HEAD>
<FRAMESET cols="150,*" border="0" frameborder="0">
    <FRAME src="nav.html" name="nav" scrolling="NO" noresize="true">
    <FRAME src="main.html" name="main">
    <NOFRAMES>
    <BODY>
    <p>You must have a Browser that supports frames to view this
page.</p>
    </BODY>
    </NOFRAMES>
</FRAMESET>
</HTML>
```

Frameset Drawbacks

Framesets provide a great way to manage the way an HTML page scrolls; however, there are a few drawbacks to using framesets that you need to consider. These drawbacks are:

- Old browsers do not support frames, but the <NOFRAMES> tag gives a helpful message.
- There is a big problem with search engines and framesets. Search engines return a link to a Web page, but in the case of frames the link is to a part of the Web page. The link is to the page and does not include the target frame name. When you click on a link returned by a search engine, the page is displayed in the current frame. This can cause a large HTML file to be displayed in a small frame. Also, the page usually looks strange because it is only a part of a larger page.
- Navigation issues arise because form tags cannot set a target frame. The response to an HTML form submit is returned to the same frame. This can force a larger report to display in the smaller navigation bar. You can get around this problem by using JavaScript for the submit function, but this introduces performance and maintenance issues.

For these reasons, framesets are not widely used on the commercial Web sites that you see on the Internet. Framesets are still a helpful tool that you can use to build Web applications, especially for solutions that do no use search engines. Many applications designed to run on company intranets fit this profile.

Adding Pictures

It is really easy to make a Web page more interesting with a few graphics. Digital cameras and scanners are very common now, so it is easy to get a suitable picture for a Web page. In this section, you will learn about the image HTML tag and use it to add a picture to a Web page.

Preparing the Web Page

You will add the pictures to the main.html file created in the previous section. This page needs an HTML table to manage its layout. Insert a table with one column and two rows. The table should not have a border, and its width should be 100 percent. The modified code for the main.html file should look as follows:

```
<!DOCTYPE HTML PUBLIC "-//W3C//DTD HTML 4.01 Transitional//EN">
<HTML>
<HEAD>
```

```
<META http-equiv="Content-Type" content="text/html; charset=WINDOWS-1252">
<META name="GENERATOR" content="IBM WebSphere Studio">
<META http-equiv="Content-Style-Type" content="text/css">
<TITLE>main.html</TITLE>
</HEAD>
<BODY>
<TABLE border="0" width="100%">
    <TBODY>
        <TR>
            <TD></TD>
        </TR>
        <TR>
            <TD></TD>
        </TR>
    </TBODY>
</TABLE>
</BODY>
</HTML>
```

Now you are ready to add a couple of pictures to the Web page. You will cerate a logo and add it to the page. Then, you will import a picture and add it to the Web page.

Creating a Logo

The original Golf Web page had a large font for the title or logo on the screen. WSAD has a great tool for creating logos with many different eye-catching effects. You will create a logo for the new Web page using the WebArt Designer. You will add an existing logo from the WSAD gallery and change its text and a few of its settings. Create a logo with the following steps:

1. Create a new folder under the Web Content folder, named pics, to hold the image, or picture files. It is a good idea to keep the pictures separate from other Web content. They usually don't change as often and usually they utilize different editors.
2. Select the first row in the table of main.html.
3. Select the Gallery tab in the lower-left corner, then select the 015.mif file, as shown in Figure 14.6.
4. Select the blue Welcome Logo 015.mif file and drag it to the pics folder under the Web Content folder for the GolfProject.
5. Select the 015.mif file in the pics folder, and from the pop-up menu, select Open with...> WebArt Designer, and the WebArt Designer window appears.
6. Double-click on the Welcome image, and the Edit Logo Object window appears.
7. On the Text tab, change the text to be **Welcome to My Golf Page**, as shown in Figure 14.7.

8. Select the gradation gallery, as shown in Figure 14.8, and select the **blue01** pattern.
9. On the General tab, set the width to **400**, as shown in Figure 14.9.
10. Close the Edit Logo Object window.

The WebArt Designer is a fast and easy tool that makes custom graphics with special effects for words. There are a lot of different effects and color options in the WebArt Designer that you can try. The new logo for the Golf Web page is fine with these settings.

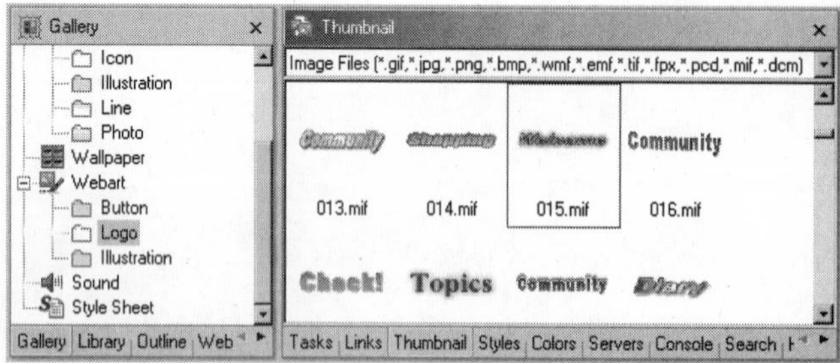

Figure 14.6 Logo Gallery.

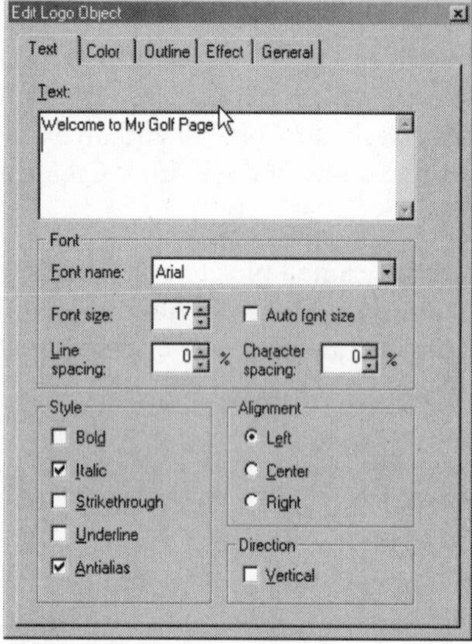

Figure 14.7 Logo text.

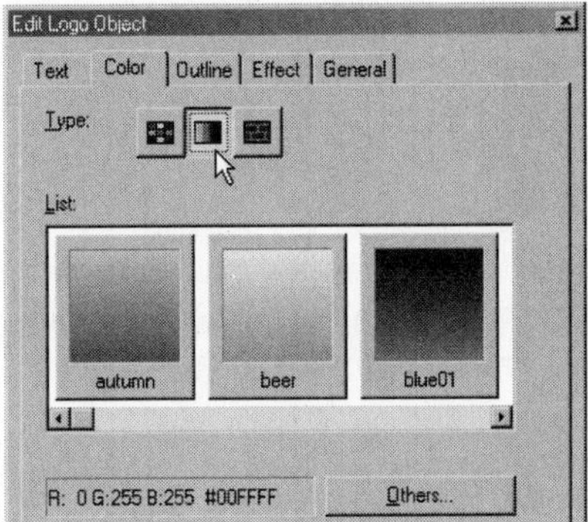

Figure 14.8 Setting color gradation.

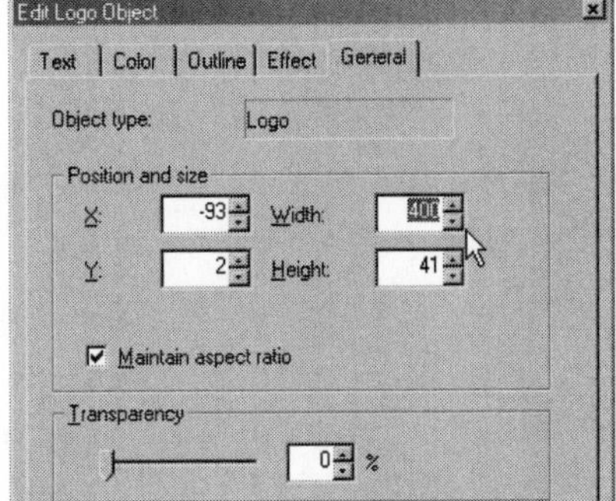

Figure 14.9 Setting the logo size.

The next step is to save the new logo so that it can be used in the Web page. You can save the updated 015.mif file, but this file is used by the WebArt Designer for development and is not the right file to use in a Web page. The WebArt Designers has a special wizard the exports items for use on the Web pages in the required formats. Save the new logo with the following steps:

1. Select the menu items File > Save Wizard for Web....
2. Make sure that the radio button **Save the selected objects** is selected, and press the Next button.
3. On the second page, make sure that the selected format for the image is **GIF**. Press the Next button.
4. Accept the default values on the third page, and click the Finish button.
5. When you are prompted for a name for the file, save the file as **c:\welcome.gif**.
6. Close the WebArt Designer when you are finished.
7. Import the welcome.gif file into the pics folder that you created earlier. It is a good idea to keep all the files for the Web application together.

You can now update the Web Page with the new logo. You will use the image tag to add the logo and another picture to the main.html file.

Using Images

The key to using pictures in HTML pages is the image tag. The tag is actually an abbreviated name starting as <IMG ...>, and it does not require an end tag. There are many attributes that you can use with the image tag. They are the following:

- **border** — This is usually set to 0.
- **scr** — This defines the source file location for the image is required. For Web applications, the location is usually a relative URL.
- **width** — This is the size in pixels for the width that is required.
- **height** — This is the size in pixels for the height that is required.
- **alt** — This provides a text value that appears if the image cannot load or if the browser has disabled images.
- **name** — This is optional and usually not needed.
- **vspace** — This is an optional tag that gives vertical spacing around the image.
- **hspace** — This is an optional tag that gives horizontal spacing around the image.

You can hand-code the image tag or you can use the Page Designer in WSAD to generate the image tag. You will import a picture for the Web page and add it to the pics folder. This is a golf picture that will jazz up the Web page and give it some visual interest. Add the picture to the Web page with the following steps:

1. Import the file onedge.jpg from the Web site for this book and add it to the pics folder.
2. Drag the welcome.gif logo file to the main.html file in the first row of the table.
3. Drag the onedge.jpg file to the main.html file in the row below the logo.
4. Center the image by setting the column horizontal alignment attribute `align="center"`.

The main.html file should look like Figure 14.10. JPG (pronounced jay-peg) files are commonly used for photographs. They hold many colors in an efficient format. The picture can be resized, and the background color can be changed. The initial page for the Golf Web application looks a lot better.

WSAD generated image tags for the logo and the picture. You can see the generated <IMG> tags on the Source tab. WSAD did not generate the `alt` attribute for the image tag. This attribute is used if a picture cannot be loaded or if the browser has image loading turned off. You can add the `alt` attribute in the Attribute Editor or directly into the source code. Add the `alt` attribute with the following steps:

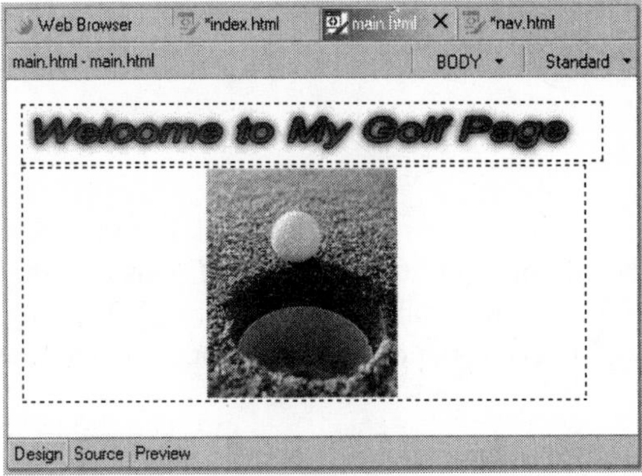

Figure 14.10 Main.html with images.

1. Select the Source tab for the main.html file.
2. Enter an alt="welcome to my golf page" attribute for the welcome.gif image tag.
3. Enter an alt="ball on edge" attribute for the onedge.jpg image tag.
4. Save the code.

The main.html file looks better with the image files. The code should look as follows:

```
<!DOCTYPE HTML PUBLIC "-//W3C//DTD HTML 4.01 Transitional//EN">
<HTML>
<HEAD>
<META http-equiv="Content-Type" content="text/html; charset=WINDOWS-
1252">
<META name="GENERATOR" content="IBM WebSphere Studio">
<META http-equiv="Content-Style-Type" content="text/css">
<TITLE>main.html</TITLE>
</HEAD>
<BODY>
<TABLE border="0" width="100%">
    <TBODY>
        <TR>
            <TD><IMG border="0" src="../pics/welcome.gif" width="379"
height="36" alt="welcome to my golf page"></TD>
        </TR>
        <TR>
            <TD align="center">
            <IMG border="0" src="../pics/onedge.jpg" width="131"
height="152" alt="ball on edge" align="middle"></TD>
        </TR>
    </TBODY>
</TABLE>
</BODY>
</HTML>
```

The previous Golf Web page had everything on one page, including the Golf handicap calculator. Next, you will make a new page for the handicap calculator that can be displayed in the main frame area.

Making the Handicap Page

The index.html page had the handicap calculator built into it. Instead of remaking that entire page, you will make a new HTML page with a table and copy the HTML code for the handicap calculator to the new page. Create a handicap calculator page with the following steps:

1. Create a new HTML file named handicap.html.
2. Place an HTML table with one column and one row in the page, and set its border to 0.
3. Open the index.html file for the Golf Web page in the Source Editor.
4. Copy the code for the handicap calculator to the Clipboard. This code starts with <TD>Handicap Calculator ... and ends with </FORM></TD>.
5. Paste this code in the handicap.html file and replace the existing <TD></TD> tags inside the table.
6. Save the code.

The new HTML file will be called by a link on the navigation bar and displayed in the frame named main. The code of the handicap.html file should look as follows:

```
<!DOCTYPE HTML PUBLIC "-//W3C//DTD HTML 4.01 Transitional//EN">
<HTML>
<HEAD>
<META http-equiv="Content-Type"
    content="text/html; charset=WINDOWS-1252">
<META name="GENERATOR" content="IBM WebSphere Studio">
<META http-equiv="Content-Style-Type" content="text/css">
<LINK href="../theme/Master.css" rel="stylesheet" type="text/css">
<TITLE>handicap.html</TITLE>
</HEAD>
<BODY>
<TABLE border="0">
  <TBODY>
    <TR>
      <TD><B>Handicap Calculator</B><BR>
      <!-- form to capture scores for handicap calculator -->
        <FORM action="/GolfProject/GolfAVG" method="post">
        <TABLE border="1">
          <TBODY>
            <TR>
              <TD></TD>
                <TH nowrap>Score</TH>
```

```
            </TR>
            <TR>
              <TD>Round1:</TD>
              <TD><INPUT size="3" type="text" maxlength="3"
name="round1"></TD>
            </TR>
            <TR>
              <TD>Round2:</TD>
              <TD><INPUT size="3" type="text" maxlength="3"
name="round2"></TD>
            </TR>
            <TR>
              <TD>Round3:</TD>
              <TD><INPUT size="3" type="text" maxlength="3"
name="round3"></TD>
            </TR>
            <TR>
              <TD>Round4:</TD>
              <TD><INPUT size="3" type="text" maxlength="3"
name="round4"></TD>
            </TR>
            <TR>
              <TD>Round5:</TD>
              <TD><INPUT size="3" type="text" maxlength="3"
name="round5"></TD>
            </TR>
            <TR>
              <TD><INPUT type="reset" name="reset" value="Reset"></TD>
              <TD><INPUT type="submit" name="submit"
value="Calculate"></TD>
            </TR>
          </TBODY>
        </TABLE>
      </FORM>
      </TD>
    </TR>
  </TBODY>
</TABLE>
</BODY>
</HTML>
```

If you change to the Design view, the handicap.html file should look like Figure 14.11.

You can start working on the navigation bar now that the main page is complete. The navigation bar is a separate HTML file that goes in the frame named nav. The index.html file had a navigation area, but there are a number of ways to improve this design for the navigation bar. This navigation bar will be in a table, have its own style sheet, and be much easier to enhance and maintain.

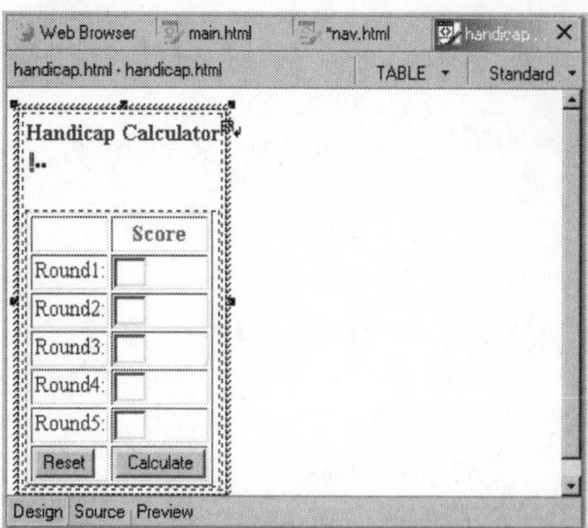

Figure 14.11 Completed handicap.html file.

Making a Navigation Bar

The left frame in the frameset is designed for a navigation bar which is a column of buttons that provide links to other Web pages. These pages may be part of the Web application, or they may link to external pages on the Web. The links on the navigation bar can send the response to the current frame, a different frame, the parent frame, or a new browser window. Now, you will build a navigation bar for the Golf Web page.

Building a Table

The first step in building the navigation bar is to create an HTML table in nav.html. Next, you will make rows for the navigation links and place the appropriate links in the rows. Start building the navigation bar with the following steps:

1. Open the nav.html file in the editor.
2. Add a new HTML table with one column and ten rows.
3. Each row should have the `nowrap` attribute and `align="left"` attribute.
4. Set the table border to `0`.
5. Enter the text **My Favorite Links** in the first row and make it bold.
6. The links will be on rows 3, 5, 7, and 9. In each of these rows, make the row color blue by setting the attribute `bgcolor="#ff0000"`.

The initial navigation bar should look like Figure 14.12. It has the basic shape required for the Web page. It has nice colors, and the links can be displayed in a consistent manner. The next step is to add the links to the navigation bar.

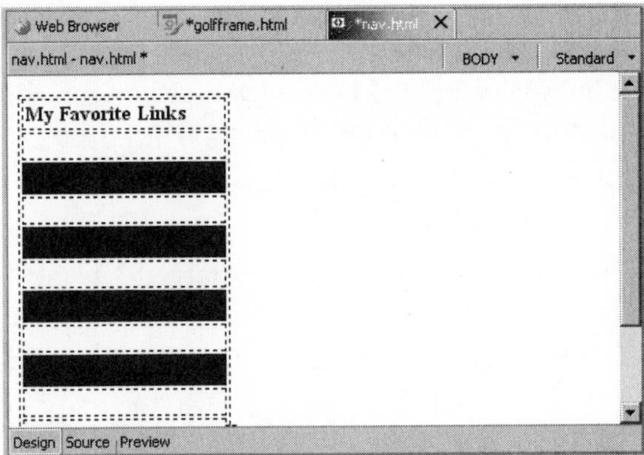

Figure 14.12 Initial navigation bar.

Adding Links

You will add four links to the navigation bar. The first link calls the handicap calculator page. The other three links are from the index.html file, and they go to outside Web pages. Add the links to the navigation bar with the following steps:

1. Select the third row of the navigation bar.
2. Select the menu items Insert > Link..., and the Insert Link window appears, as shown in Figure 14.13.
3. Make sure that the type is File. You can use this to put in a relative URL.
4. Enter **Calc Handicap** for the Link text.
5. Select **main** for the target.
6. Click the OK button to create the link.

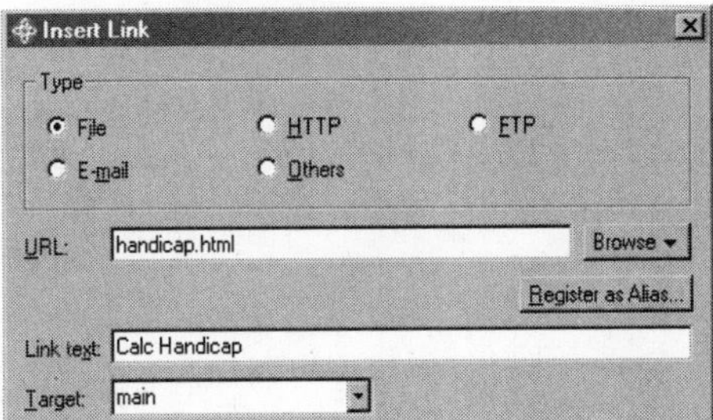

Figure 14.13 Insert Calc Handicap link.

You can use an Attribute Editor to change any of these values, or you can edit them in the HTML source code. The navigation bar needs three more links that were on the index.html file. You can create these links by using the Link wizard or you can add them to the HTML code. Add the other three links with the following steps:

1. Give row five the link <A href="http://www.usga.org/index.html" target="_blank">USGA</A>
2. Give row seven the link <A href="http://www.weather.com" target="_blank">The Weather</A>
3. Give row nine the link <A href="http://www.mapquest.com" target="_blank">Travel Maps</A>
4. Save the code.

Each of the links has the parameter target="_blank". This parameter causes the response to be displayed in a new browser window. The code for nav.html should look as follows:

```
<!DOCTYPE HTML PUBLIC "-//W3C//DTD HTML 4.01 Transitional//EN">
<HTML>
<HEAD>
<META http-equiv="Content-Type"
    content="text/html; charset=WINDOWS-1252">
<META name="GENERATOR" content="IBM WebSphere Studio">
<META http-equiv="Content-Style-Type" content="text/css">
<TITLE>nav.html</TITLE>
</HEAD>
<BODY>
<TABLE border="0">
    <TBODY>
        <TR>
            <TD nowrap align="left"><B>My Favorite Links</B></TD>
        </TR>
        <TR>
            <TD nowrap align="left"></TD>
        </TR>
        <TR bgcolor="#0000ff">
            <TD nowrap align="left"><A href="handicap.html" target= ⮐
"main">Calc
            Handicap</A></TD>
        </TR>
        <TR>
            <TD nowrap align="left"></TD>
        </TR>
        <TR bgcolor="#0000ff">
            <TD nowrap align="left"><A href="http://www.usga.org/ ⮐
index.html" target="_blank">USGA</A></TD>
```

```
        </TR>
        <TR>
            <TD nowrap align="left"></TD>
        </TR>
        <TR bgcolor="#0000ff">
            <TD nowrap align="left"><A href="http://www.weather.com" ⮐
target="_blank">The Weather</A></TD>
        </TR>
        <TR>
            <TD nowrap align="left"></TD>
        </TR>
        <TR bgcolor="#0000ff">
            <TD nowrap align="left"><A href="http://www.mapquest.com" ⮐
target="_blank">Travel Maps</A></TD>
        </TR>
        <TR>
            <TD nowrap align="left"></TD>
        </TR>
    </TBODY>
</TABLE>
</BODY>
</HTML>
```

If you look at the Design or Preview tabs, you can see that the link text does not show. The default color for a link is blue, and the navigation bar is blue. The navigation bar needs to be fixed so that the links appear with a different color. You will change the font and make other style changes using a style sheet.

Tuning the Fonts

The link fonts in the nav.html file are default fonts that can be changed easily. You could hard-code the anchor fonts in the body tag, but it is better to make these changes in a Cascading Style Sheet. You will add two new entries in the css file; one entry sets the font for the anchor tag and the other entry sets the color of the anchor tags when a mouse cursor is placed over the link. Create a new style sheet based on the Master.css file with the following steps:

1. Copy the Master.css file in the theme folder and make a new file in the theme folder called navstyle.css.
2. Double-click on the navstyle.css file in the theme folder, and the CSS Designer appears, as shown in Figure 14.14. You can use this editor to modify Cascading Style Sheets.
3. In the Source view of the style sheet, from the pop-up menu, select Add..., and the Set Selector of New Style window appears, as shown in Figure 14.15. This window allows you to pick the HTML tag that will have customized attributes.
4. Select the *A* tag name for the anchor tag, and click the OK button.

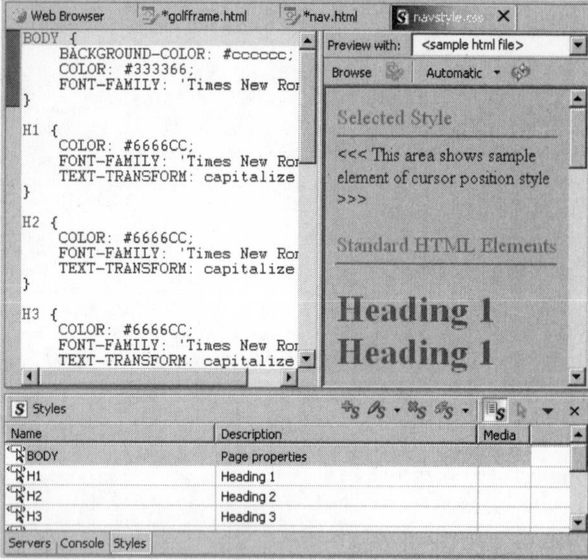

Figure 14.14 CSS Designer.

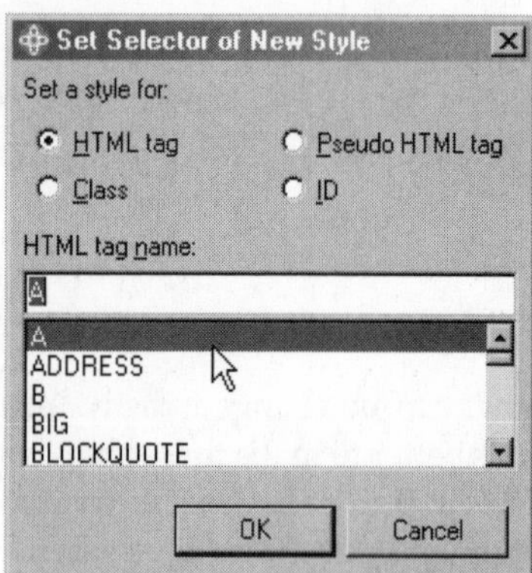

Figure 14.15 Set Tag Selector window.

The Add Style window appears; it has functions that help you customize a tag's font, layout, position, and list characteristics. You will set the font and the font style for the anchor tag. You will add the desired fonts for the style and set the font styles. The font will be bold white with no underlining. Make these changes with the following steps:

1. Select the Fonts item in tree view on the left, as shown in Figure 14.16.
2. Add the **Verdana** and **Arial** fonts using the Add button.
3. Choose **White** for the font color.
4. Select the Font styles item in the tree view on the left, and the Styles Properties window appears, as shown in Figure 14.17.

5. Select Styles as **Normal**.
6. Select Weight as **Bold**.
7. Set the Variant to **Normal**.
8. Set the Decoration to **None**. This removes the underlining that comes with the default link font.
9. Click the OK button to generate the style tag.

Editing Styles

You can also directly edit the style sheet code. You will make a simple change to the anchor tag font and the BODY tag. The `A:hover` tag controls the anchor tag when the mouse hovers over the link. You can use this tag to change the text color for links. This effect can also be accomplished with special JavaScript code for each link, but this technique is must faster and requires no JavaScript code. Add the following code to the style sheet source to make the font red:

```
A:hover {
    color: #ff0000;
}
```

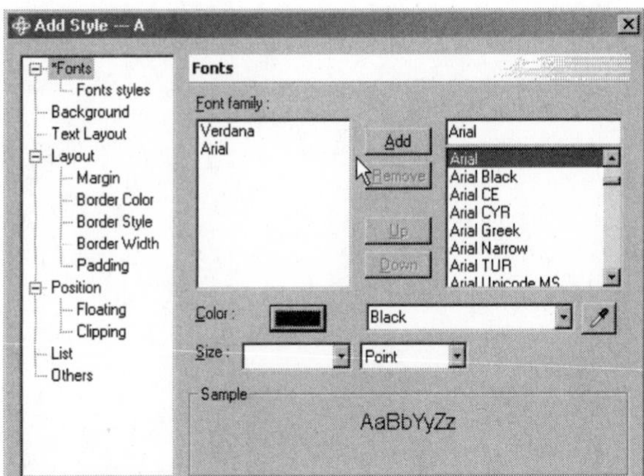

Figure 14.16 Add Style fonts.

Figure 14.17 Add Style font styles.

Change the BODY tag attribute so that the background is light gray. The code should be as follows:

```
BODY {
    BACKGROUND-COLOR: #cccccc;
    COLOR: #333366;
    FONT-FAMILY: 'Times New Roman'
}
```

Save the navstyles.css file. The source code for the completed Cascading Style Sheet should look as follows:

```
BODY {
  BACKGROUND-COLOR: #cccccc;
  COLOR: #333366;
  FONT-FAMILY: 'Times New Roman'
}
H1 {
  COLOR: #6666CC;
  FONT-FAMILY: 'Times New Roman';
  TEXT-TRANSFORM: capitalize
}
H2 {
  COLOR: #6666CC;
  FONT-FAMILY: 'Times New Roman';
  TEXT-TRANSFORM: capitalize
}
H3 {
  COLOR: #6666CC;
  FONT-FAMILY: 'Times New Roman';
  TEXT-TRANSFORM: capitalize
}
H4 {
  COLOR: #6666CC;
  FONT-FAMILY: 'Times New Roman';
  TEXT-TRANSFORM: capitalize
}
H5 {
  COLOR: #6666CC;
  FONT-FAMILY: 'Times New Roman';
  TEXT-TRANSFORM: capitalize
}
H6 {
  COLOR: #6666CC;
  FONT-FAMILY: 'Times New Roman';
  TEXT-TRANSFORM: capitalize
```

```
}
TH {
  color: #6060cc
}
A {
  color: white;
  font-family: Verdana, Arial;
  font-weight: bold;
  font-style: normal;
  font-variant: normal;
  text-decoration: none
}
A:hover {
  color: #ff0000;
}
```

You are ready to apply these styles to the navigation bar. When the navstyles.css file is added to the navigation bar, the font issues will be fixed. Drag the navstyles.css file and drop it on the nav.html file. The nav.html file should look like Figure 14.18 in the Design view.

The navigation bar has all the links in a convenient location. It is easy to maintain and enhance. The HTML code for the nav.html file should look as follows:

```
<!DOCTYPE HTML PUBLIC "-//W3C//DTD HTML 4.01 Transitional//EN">
<HTML>
<HEAD>
<META http-equiv="Content-Type"
    content="text/html; charset=WINDOWS-1252">
<META name="GENERATOR" content="IBM WebSphere Studio">
<META http-equiv="Content-Style-Type" content="text/css">
<TITLE>nav.html</TITLE>
<LINK rel="stylesheet" href="../theme/navstyle.css" type="text/css">
</HEAD>
<BODY bgcolor="#cccccc">
<TABLE border="0">
    <TBODY>
        <TR>
            <TD nowrap align="left"><B>My Favorite Links</B></TD>
        </TR>
        <TR>
            <TD nowrap align="left"></TD>
        </TR>
        <TR bgcolor="#0000ff">
            <TD nowrap align="left"><A href="handicap.html"
target="main">Calc
            Handicap</A></TD>
```

```
        </TR>
        <TR>
            <TD nowrap align="left"></TD>
        </TR>
        <TR bgcolor="#0000ff">
            <TD nowrap align="left"><A
href="http://www.usga.org/index.html" target="_blank">USGA</A></TD>
        </TR>
        <TR>
            <TD nowrap align="left"></TD>
        </TR>
        <TR bgcolor="#0000ff">
            <TD nowrap align="left"><A href="http://www.weather.com"
target="_blank">The Weather</A></TD>
        </TR>
        <TR>
            <TD nowrap align="left"></TD>
        </TR>
        <TR bgcolor="#0000ff">
            <TD nowrap align="left"><A href="http://www.mapquest.com"
target="_blank">Travel Maps</A></TD>
        </TR>
        <TR>
            <TD nowrap align="left"></TD>
        </TR>
    </TBODY>
</TABLE>
</BODY>
</HTML>
```

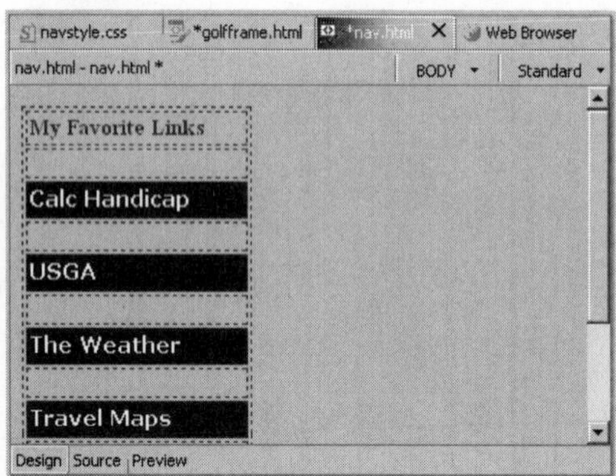

Figure 14.18 Updated navigation bar.

Incorporating Sound

It is not very common to encounter sounds on a Web page, but used in special cases they can be helpful. You can use sound to indicate that an error occurred or as a greeting on the initial page. You just need a sound file and a little JavaScript to make a Web page have sound.

Sounds are saved in special file formats such as .au, .wav, and .mid files. You can record your own sounds, and there are many sources for sound files on the Web such as the following:

- www.a1freesoundeffects.com
- www.soundamerica.com
- www.boogiejack.com

A short .wav file that makes the sound of applause is provided on the Web site for this book. You will add this .wav file to the Web page. The sound plays every time the Web page is displayed.

Adding Sound

It's easy to add sound to a Web page. All it takes is a sound file and a little bit of JavaScript code. Add sound to the golfframe.html file with the following steps:

1. Create a new folder under the Web Content folder named sounds.
2. Import the applause.wav file from the Web site for this book, and place it in the sounds folder.
3. Add the following JavaScript to the nav.html file within the <head> tags.

```
<SCRIPT language="JavaScript">
if (navigator.appName == "Netscape") {
  document.write('<EMBED SRC="../sounds/applause.wav" AUTOSTART=true
hidden=true LOOP=FALSE></EMBED>')
} else {
    if (navigator.appName == "Microsoft Internet Explorer")
    document.write('<BGSOUND SRC="../sounds/applause.wav">')
}
</SCRIPT>
```

The JavaScript code has an `if` statement that handles sound for Netscape Navigator and Internet Explorer. You can test the operation of the sound file. Change to the Preview tab, and when the golfframe appears you should hear applause.

Showing the Weather

It is a nice feature to add dynamic elements to your Web page. It is very easy to add a function to a Web page to dynamically display the weather. There are a few services that provide weather for Web pages:

- **www.wunderground.com** — This service provides some nice small display options for showing the weather.
- **www.weather.com** — This service is very popular and it provides display options for showing the weather with a lot of detail.

You can show the weather for a specific location, or you can pass a user's location to the weather service and dynamically display the weather for a specific user. The code that you get from these services has a link to the service provider for more information. Add a weather indicator to the bottom of the golf navigation bar with the following code:

```
<TR>
<TD valign="top"><FONT color="#000000"><B>Myrtle Beach
Weather</B></FONT><BR>
  <A href="http://www.wundergound.com"><IMG
src="http://banners.wunderground.com/banner/gizmotimetemp/US/SC/Myrtle_B
each.gif" alt="Local Forecast" height="41" width="127"></A></TD>
</TR>
```

If you want to add the weather to your own Web pages, you need to go to one of these weather providers and register. You will be provided with the desired code to display the weather on your HTML pages. The completed code for golfframe.html should look as follows:

```
<!DOCTYPE HTML PUBLIC "-//W3C//DTD HTML 4.01 Frameset//EN">
<HTML>
<HEAD>
<META http-equiv="Content-Type"
    content="text/html; charset=WINDOWS-1252">
<META name="GENERATOR" content="IBM WebSphere Studio">
<META http-equiv="Content-Style-Type" content="text/css">
<LINK href="../theme/Master.css" rel="stylesheet" type="text/css">
<TITLE>My Golf Page</TITLE>
<SCRIPT language="JavaScript">
if (navigator.appName == "Netscape") {
  document.write('<EMBED SRC="sounds/applause.wav" AUTOSTART=true
hidden=true LOOP=FALSE></EMBED>')
} else {
    if (navigator.appName == "Microsoft Internet Explorer")
    document.write('<BGSOUND SRC="../sounds/applause.wav">')
}
```

```
</SCRIPT>
</HEAD>
<FRAMESET cols="150,*" border="0" frameborder="0">
    <FRAME src="nav.html" name="nav" scrolling="NO" noresize="true">
    <FRAME src="main.html" name="main">
    <NOFRAMES>
    <BODY>
    <p>You must have a Browser that supports frames to view this
page.</p>
    </BODY>
    </NOFRAMES>
</FRAMESET>
</HTML>
```

The next step is to test all these changes to the Web Page. The Preview page provides a good view of how the page should look at runtime, but the real test needs to be done with the test server.

Testing the Updated Web Page

The Golf Web page is a lot more polished than the original index.html file. Test the page by running golfframe.html on the WSAD test server. When the Web page is displayed, it should look like Figure 14.19. The link to the handicap calculator loads an input page in the main frame. After entering some scores, the request goes to the GolfAVG servlet and the response, golfscores.jsp, is returned in the main frame, too. The external links work as they did in the original Web Page.

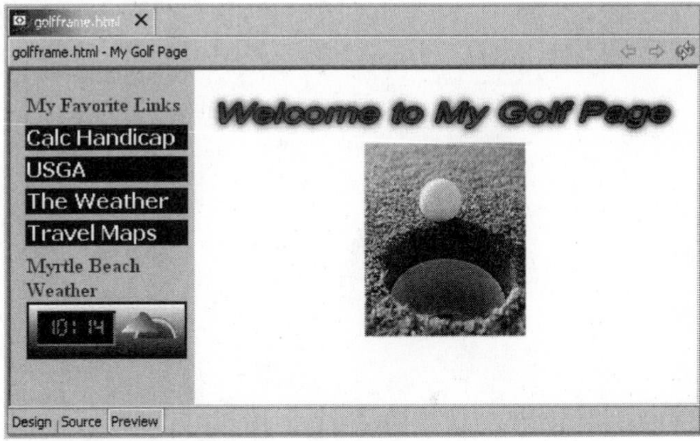

Figure 14.19 Polished Web page.

Summary

In this chapter, you learned many ways to improve the look of the Golf Web page. These techniques can be used to refine an existing Web page, or you can use them in the initial implementation. The key concepts covered include:

- Using framesets and frames in the Web page
- Adding pictures using the <IMG> tag
- Creating a logo using the WebArt Designer in WSAD
- Making a navigation bar and using it in a frame
- Incorporating sound into a Web page
- Showing the weather dynamically

There are still many other ways to make Web pages slick. You can develop animated messages and place them on a page using the image tag. You can also use flash files that have advanced multimedia effects. Most Web sites incorporate visual improvements to make them easier to use and to improve their overall appeal. In the next chapter, you will learn about Java Applets, a technique for running small Java applications on a Web page.

Building Applets

What's in Chapter 15?

When Java appeared, Sun's *HotJava* browser was able to download and run graphic user interface Java classes called *applets*. Some people saw this as the wave of the future. Browser vendors scrambled to incorporate applet technology. Today, the most-demanded Java technologies deal with server-side Java, but applets are still useful. In this chapter, we discuss:

- Java applet background
- How applets should be used in Web applications
- Java plug-in deployment and use
- Creation of a bar chart applet
- Applet testing
- An overview of how to integrate an applet into a Web site

Java applet technology has been deemphasized somewhat since its initial appearance. This technology seems to have followed the familiar technology adoption stages of hype, growth, disillusionment, and shrinkage, followed by stability. Part of the basis for this assertion lies in the tools. IBM's VisualAge for Java had explicit applet support. Its successor, WSAD, does not mention the word in its help screens. Granted, anybody may produce a plug-in for Java applet support, but there would have to be demand first. Java applets today have a role in J2EE programming that is limited, but useful when selectively applied.

Java Applets

An applet is a small application that runs inside another application or container. A Java applet is an instance of a subclass of either `java.awt.Applet` or `javax.swing.JApplet` that is embedded in an HTML page. We shall use the word "applet" to mean "Java Applet Technology" in this chapter.

A Web browser, or the *Java Applet Viewer* delivered in the JSDK, provides a window frame embedded in a rendered HTML page. Its size is supplied by HTML attributes. The applet is located and loaded based upon HTML elements. The Applet or JApplet class defines a standard interface that we selectively implement to define a useful applet. The applet takes its parameters from HTML tags. If the applet is well designed, a Web interface designer may modify its behavior extensively through HTML markup elements.

An applet extends the base AWT class `java.awt.Applet` or the Swing base class `javax.swing.JApplet`. A programming procedural difference between a Swing applet and an AWT applet is that child components are added to Swing's JApplet ContentPane instead of being added to the applet itself. Class `JApplet` directly extends class `Applet`, so the programmer is presented with a single set of base callback methods. Neither class is abstract, so the callback methods have default implementations. The set of commonly used callbacks are shown in Table 15.1. Related pairs of callbacks are grouped together. See the JavaDoc API documentation of the JSDK for reference.

Table 15.1 Common Applet Callback Methods

PUBLIC CALLBACK	DESCRIPTION
void Init()	Inform applet that it has been loaded into the system.
void destroy()	Inform applet that it is being reclaimed and that it should destroy any resources that it has allocated.
void start()	Inform applet that it should start its execution.
void stop()	Inform applet that it should stop its execution.
void paint(Graphics g)	Paints the container.
void update(Graphics g)	Updates the container. Usually calls `paint()`.
String getAppletInfo()	Returns information about this applet.
String[][]getParameterInfo()	Returns information about the parameters that are understood by this applet.

An applet uses the same visual components and event structure as a Java application. It may carry out networking on its own, subject to security restrictions. Trusted applets are allowed greater security leeway than anonymous applets. Trusted applets are established through a set of security procedures that involve the client. We do not address trusted applets here because applications should usually try to restrict applet use to presentation rendering effects.

Applet Advantages

Applet and Java seemed almost synonymous in the days of Java 1.0. The Web was new. It was often used only to present hierarchies of brochures. Two-tier client/server technology was entering the disillusionment side of the hype curve. The client was a problem. It was too hard to distribute and maintain. Differing levels of client platform software exacerbated maintenance dependency problems. Like client/server technology, applets provided an apparent benefit of offloading the business logic execution cycle to the client. The Web would be the maintenance distribution medium. Each new browser instance loads an entire new set of client bits when opened on the page containing the applet. Everything needed by the client, except the base Java libraries, was loaded with the applet. Client platform dependencies were eliminated because Java was a single unified platform.

Applet Disadvantages

Serious applications implemented as applets shared a problem with the traditional client/server model: intermediate result database rows flowed over the wire except where stored procedures were used. Worse, the DBMS server had to reside on the same host as the Web server that sent the applet, to meet security sandbox restrictions.

The *three-tier*, or *n-tier*, application server model emerged in the late 1990s to address the problems of two-tier client/server technology. In three-tier technology, the DBMS client application executes in a server. In effect, the client/server model's client moves into server such that it is shared across many thin clients that provide only presentation services. This focused application maintenance and deployment on the application server. Three-tier application design stressed separation of function such that back-end business domain logic could be shared across several applications without interference. The user interface was Web-based. Nothing had to be downloaded to the client except HTML, images, or specialized content.

Applets could participate in a thicker client three-tier application, but this could impose a dependency that could break across carefully crafted functional layers. This dependency could be a potential point of failure if the client browser could not handle the Java version of the applet.

Java Plug-In

Those interested in promoting Java applets wanted to prevent another debacle like the Java 1.0 to Java 1.1 transition where browsers were too slow to be updated. They reasoned that this problem would disappear if a browser could be dynamically modified to accept an arbitrary Java VM. They encountered difficulties because the two major browser vendors had extended HTML in different, incompatible ways. Remember that JavaScript programmers must sometimes take extraordinary measures to accommodate different browsers. A similar problem applies to anyone wanting to plug an arbitrary VM into a browser over the Web.

Netscape's browser was extensible through a standard downloadable plug-in framework. Microsoft's Internet Explorer browser was extensible through dynamically downloaded ActiveX controls. A solution addressed both browsers. It was named the "Java Plug-in." There were upsides and downsides to the solution.

Alas, the solution required that the HTML be modified. Worse, it required a different modification for each browser. Allowing both sets of HTML incantations to coexist in one HTML page mitigated this restriction. The normal applet tags used to specify an applet are simple. The HTML needed to use the plug-in was obtuse. A great feature of the design, however, provided for the proper JRE to be dynamically downloaded if it were not present on the client machine. The downside was that it was often a huge download. This was a lesser problem in speedy corporate LAN environments. SUN provides a utility with the JDK and JSDK to modify a standard HTML page to use the plug-in and to download it if it is not found. Invoke HtmlConverter from the bin directory of a JSDK to run the converter. The design provides the ability to specify a particular JRE level or minimum JRE level.

The plug-in situation is improved with J2EE, and you can download the plug-in from SUN. The download process offers to upgrade Internet Explorer 5 or greater, and any Netscape 6 found on the target system. These browsers do not require specialized applet HTML incantations. The ubiquitous Netscape 4.7x still requires specialized HTML to run a Java 2 JRE. The good news is that the old Netscape actually does operate under the plug-in, enabling Java 2 applets to operate on a browser that predates Java 2. See http://java.sun.com/products/plugin/versions.html for a treatise on how different versions of the Java Plug-in, running with different Web browsers and Web browser versions, behave when <object>, <embed>, and <applet> tags appear on an HTML page.

In addition, the plug-in caches applet classes. An administration application enables the end user to view and control this cache. You need to keep the cache in mind as you develop applets and test with a browser. If you make program changes that seem to be unheeded, you are probably executing an older version from the cache. The Java Applet Viewer doesn't use the Java Plug-in or a cache, so you may be better off testing with it initially.

You can download the plug-in from http://java.sun.com/products/plugin/. It carries out a simple installation procedure. Please obtain the latest plug-in to test the applet that you shall develop in the following sections of this chapter.

After a Windows installation, the plug-in installs an administration icon in the Windows Control Panel. The executing Plug-in Control Panel is shown in Figure 15.1. The plug-in application enables us to control settings for:

- Showing or hiding a Java console when an applet loads
- Specifying a particular JRE level

- Targeting a subset of browsers on a system
- IP proxies
- Cache settings and cache manipulation
- Certificates and security

When to Use Applets

We assert five praxes to consider when considering the use of applets in a Web application.

- Praxis 1: Today's Web applications should use applets only to apply special effects or to render data in ways that HTML or server-provided images cannot.
- Praxis 2: An application should function even when its component applet cannot.
- Praxis 3: Make the applet configurable through parameters.
- Praxis 4: Make the applet self-describing through overrides of `getAppletInfo()` and `getParameterInfo()`.
- Praxis 5: Events should modify applet operation, not server-side operations.

The first two praxes sound familiar after reading Chapter 12, "JavaScript." If the product is data rendered a special way in an applet, then praxis 2 is a moot point. Praxis 5 states that it is permissible to have sliders and buttons, but that these should modify local applet behavior or appearance, not provide input to the middle-tier application.

These rules seem restrictive enough to make applets seem irrelevant. Applets have lost stature if you compare the applet features of WSAD against its predecessor, IBM VisualAge for Java.

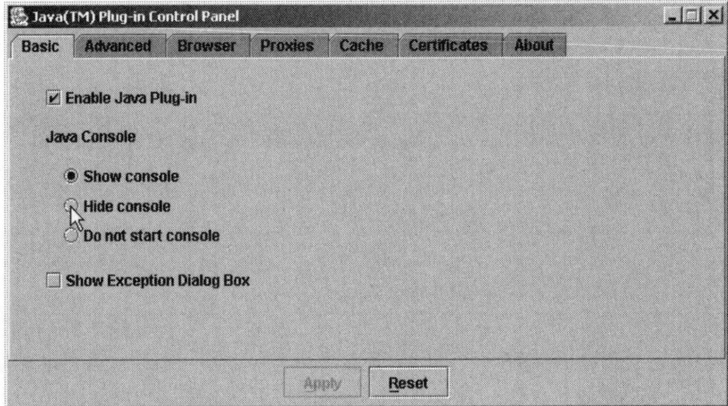

Figure 15.1 Java Plug-in Control Panel.

BarChart Applet

Bar charts, plots, and pie charts are one useful kind of rendering suited to applets. Sometimes it's easier for a human being to assimilate a picture than a table of numbers. Without an applet, a Java Web application would have to generate an image of a chart in the server, and then project it to the client. Here, an applet is usually more efficient. A huge amount of collateral classes is not needed. No outside communication is used. Only controls and events would possibly modify the presentation of a chart. A parameterized chart applet (praxis 4) enables reuse of the applet across a vast number of presentation jobs.

The remainder of this chapter steps through the creation of a bar chart applet that automatically scales its bar heights according to the input data values, number of values, and applet rectangle dimensions. The source code is on the book's Web site.

The colors of consecutive chart bars rotate through a default palette, or the HTML author may choose to impose colors on the some or all of the bars. Similarly, the labels of the bars have default values, or the HTML author may explicitly label them. The font default can be overridden. The background, font, and border colors may be specified or remain at default values. All of the parameters are described in the result of a `getParameterInfo()` call. The Java Applet Viewer can display the result.

How would the applet participate in a Web application? Consider a demographic application where an analyst wants to know the number of products sold by zip code. She could specify a product ID, and a set of zip codes in an HTML form. A servlet would obtain the data in a JavaBean from back-end domain logic. The servlet would forward the JavaBean to a JSP that builds applet tags from the data. The browser would download the JSP, which would render a custom date in a pleasing, graphical, understandable manner.

Let us create the bar chart applet. This applet will collect parameters, calculate operational characteristics such as bar height and spacing, and then render a vertical bar chart using the parameters and calculated characteristics. In addition, the applet will display information about itself if queried. Thus, you must implement the top-level public methods shown in Table 15.2.

Table 15.2 Public Bar Chart Applet Methods

METHOD	ACTION
void init()	Get parameters, calculate scaling factor, margins, gutters
void paint(Graphics gc)	Render the data based upon parameters and defaults
String getAppletInfo()	Return "about" information
String[][] getParameterInfo()	Return name, type, and description of each possible parameter

Parameters

Let us establish the parameters that this applet will accept. Applet parameter names and values are strings since they originate in HTML, but they may represent numeric values. A parameter is a name-value pair. A parameter originates in an HTML <param> element such as the following example:

```
<param name="B1" value="16" />
```

The applet will render vertical bars for an open-ended number of data values. Each value is a positive floating point number expressed in a string. Any negative value will be treated as zero. A non-numeric string value will also be treated as zero. The applet will determine the number of bars by the number of data values that it finds in the parameters. You could have a parameter that states the number of data value parameters. Instead, you shall simply let the init() method query for parameters until it finds no more of them. You shall use a naming convention for the bar data values that consists of a base name having a bar number suffix. The base name is "b" for "bar." Keep the name simple because someone may have to enter many of these. Therefore, a three-bar chart would have parameters named "b1","b2", and "b3."

Each bar has a label. If none is supplied, the label defaults to the bar number. Thus, bar three would have a default label of "3." An explicit label parameter follows the same scheme as the bar data parameter, except that the base name is "l" for "label." It is okay to supply labels for a subset of the bars.

Each bar is colored by its position in a color collection unless a color parameter is supplied. The color parameter name follows the same scheme as the bar parameter except that the prefix is "c" for "color." The value is taken from the set of standard Java color names.

These parameters and the remaining parameters are described in Table 15.3.

Table 15.3 Bar Chart Parameters

NAME	VALUE
bgColor	Java color name of chart background (optional)
fgColor	Java color name used to render fonts, borders (optional)
fontName	Font face name (optional)
pointSize	Font point size (optional)
gutterFraction	Inter-bar spacing–float fraction of bar width (optional)
title	Applet title (optional)
b1 ... bn	Positive floating point; e.g. 10.2, or 10.E1 (required)
l1 ... ln	Bar label (optional)
c1 ... ln	Java color name (optional)

A typical HTML test page for this applet follows:

```
<html><head><title>BarChart</title></head>
<body>
<applet CODE="com.xyz.applet.chart.BarChart"
  CODEBASE="applet" ARCHIVE="barchart.jar" ALT="BarChart Applet"
  ALIGN=""MIDDLE"" HEIGHT="300" WIDTH="400" NAME="BarChart" >
  <param name="bgColor" value="lightGray" />
  <param name="fgColor" value="black" />
  <param name="fontName" value="SanSerif" />
  <param name="pointSize" value="12" />
  <param name="gutterFraction" value="0.4" />
  <param name="title" value="Thousands of Factory Orders - Seasonally
Adjusted " />
  <param name="B1" value="16" />
  <param name="B2" value="14" />
  <param name="B3" value="17" />
  <param name="B4" value="18" />
  <param name="B5" value="21" />
  <param name="B6" value="20" />
  <param name="B7" value="21" />
  <param name="B8" value="22" />
  <param name="B9" value="6" />
  <param name="B10" value="23" />
  <param name="B11" value="8" />
  <param name="B12" value="12" />
  <param name="L1" value="Jan" />
  <param name="L2" value="Feb" />
  <param name="L3" value="Mar" />
  <param name="L4" value="Apr" />
  <param name="L5" value="May" />
  <param name="L6" value="Jun" />
  <param name="L7" value="Jul" />
  <param name="L8" value="Aug" />
  <param name="L9" value="Sep" />
  <param name="L10" value="Oct" />
  <param name="L11" value="Nov" />
  <param name="L12" value="Dec" />
  <param name="C3" value="white" />
  </applet>
</body>
</html>
```

Let us begin to code the applet by adding support for the parameters. First, you shall create an interface that defines the parameter names as follows:

1. Create a project in the WSAD Java perspective named "bar-chart."
2. Create a package in the project. Name it `com.xyz.applet.chart`.
3. Within that package, create an interface named `BarChartAppletParams`.
4. Define the body of the interface as follows:

```
package com.xyz.applet.chart;
/**
 * Defines manifest constants used as name attributes for
*/
public interface BarChartAppletParams {
    public static final String BAR_PARAM_PREFIX = "B";
    public static final String LAB_PARAM_PREFIX = "L";
    public static final String CLR_PARAM_PREFIX = "C";
    public static final String BGCOLOR = "bgColor";
    public static final String FGCOLOR = "fgColor";
    public static final String FONTNAME = "fontName";
    public static final String POINTSIZE = "pointSize";
    public static final String TITLE = "title";
    public static final String GUTTERFRACTION = "gutterFraction";
}
```

This interface supplies manifest constants representing the parameters. These enforce an agreement of names that is important because the applet is still happy if it can't find a parameter, but the applet's client author may not be.

The next step is to define the actual applet class. Let us continue:

5. Create a class within the `com.xyz.applet.chart` package. Name it `BarChart`. Extend `java.awt.Applet`, and implement `BarChartAppletParams`.
6. Define Java fields (instance variables) as follows:

```
private ArrayList data;
private int barWidth;
private int gutter;
private int margin;
private Font font;
private String title;
private double gutterFraction;
private int vmargin;
private Color bgColor;
private Color fgColor;
private static final HashMap colorMap;
```

7. A HashMap is used to map color names to Color values. Add a static initializer as follows:

```
static {
    // Build color map
    colorMap = new HashMap();
    colorMap.put("black", Color.black);
    colorMap.put("blue", Color.blue);
    colorMap.put("cyan", Color.cyan);
    colorMap.put("darkGray", Color.darkGray);
    colorMap.put("gray", Color.gray);
    colorMap.put("green", Color.green);
```

```
        colorMap.put("lightGray", Color.lightGray);
        colorMap.put("magenta", Color.magenta);
        colorMap.put("orange", Color.orange);
        colorMap.put("pink", Color.pink);
        colorMap.put("red", Color.red);
        colorMap.put("white", Color.white);
        colorMap.put("yellow", Color.yellow);
    };
```

The next set of steps adds code to initialize the fields. You shall override the `public void Applet.init()` method. About half of the applet's processing is carried out in this method. Let us continue:

8. Create a `public void init()` method in class `BarChart`.
9. Provide the method implementation seen following. Read the comments for each step of the initialization:

```
/**
 * Called once by Applet framework after this Applet is
 * loaded, but before start() is called.
 */
public void init() {
    // 1. Collect the data values
    // Number of elements is bar count
    initData();
    // 2. Set font .
    // Governs margins and and scaling
    String fontName = getParameter(FONTNAME);
    if (fontName == null)
        fontName = "SansSerif";
    String pointSize = getParameter(POINTSIZE);
    if (pointSize == null)
        pointSize = "10";
    font = new Font(fontName, Font.BOLD,
Integer.parseInt(pointSize));
    // 3. Compute vertical margin
    Graphics gc = this.getGraphics();
    gc.setFont(font);
    vmargin = gc.getFontMetrics().getHeight() * 2;
    // 4. Compute the scale factor
    double scaleFactor = getScaleFactor(data);
    // 5. Scale the data -- translate into graphic units
    // that fit the height of the applet rectangle
    applyScaleFactor(data, scaleFactor);
    // 6. Get the gutter fraction. Used to calculate space between
bars
    String param = getParameter(GUTTERFRACTION);
```

```
        if (param == null)
            param = "0.333";
        gutterFraction = Double.parseDouble(param);
        // 7. Compute bar width, gutter, and horiz margin
        // as a function of gutter fraction, data and frame rect
        double oneBar = (double) getWidth() / data.size();
        gutter = (int) Math.round(gutterFraction * oneBar);
        barWidth = (int) Math.round(oneBar - gutter);
        margin = gutter / 2;
        // 8. Miscellaneous
        // Set background color
        param = getParameter(BGCOLOR);
        if (param == null)
            param = "lightGray";
        bgColor = (Color) colorMap.get(param);
        // Set foreground color
        param = getParameter(FGCOLOR);
        if (param == null)
            param = "black";
        fgColor = (Color) colorMap.get(param);
        // Set title
        param = getParameter(TITLE);
        if (param == null)
           param = "Bar Chart";
        title = param;
    }
```

If you were to build the project now, you would receive "missing method" errors. Let us supply the missing private helper methods used during initialization:

10. Create a protected void `initData()` method.
11. This method gets the data values along with optional colors and labels. Implement it as follows:

```
    /**
     * Initialize the data from applet parameters.
     * Each bar is captured in an instance of BarChartBean.
     * Rotate the bar colors across bars not having "cn" parameters.
     * Each label defaults to ordinal number if no "Ln" found. Capture
    raw
     * data both as a string and a double.
     */
    protected void initData() {
        // Color rotation
        final Color[] barColors =
            {Color.blue, Color.cyan, Color.green, Color.magenta,
             Color.orange, Color.pink, Color.red, Color.yellow };
        data = new ArrayList(5);
```

```
        for (int di = 1;; di++) {
            String rawValue = getParameter(BAR_PARAM_PREFIX + di);
            // If no param, no more data
            if (rawValue == null)
                break;
            double value;
            try {
                value = Double.parseDouble(rawValue);
            } catch (NumberFormatException ex) {
                value = 0.0;
            }
            String label = getParameter(LAB_PARAM_PREFIX + di);
            if (label == null)
                label = Integer.toString(di);
            Color color = barColors[di % barColors.length];
            String param = getParameter(CLR_PARAM_PREFIX + di);
            if (param != null)
                color = (Color) colorMap.get(param);
            data.add(new BarChartBean(rawValue, value, label, color));
        }
    }
```

Notice that a NumberFormatException forces a bad input parameter to 0.0. Further, notice that the number of "b" values dictates the number of bars. Any missing or excessive "l" and "c" parameters are ignored. Missing "l" and "c" parameters receive default values. Let us continue by creating the method that calculates the scale factor.

12. Create method:

    ```
    protected double getScaleFactor(Collection data)
    ```

13. Implement the method as shown following while reading the comments:

    ```
    /**
     * Returns the computed scale factor of the given
     * collection assumed to contain BarChartBeans.
     * Uses the height of the Applet frame and the
     * values in the collection to determine a scale
     * factor such that the tallest bar, in pixels,
     * fits in the applet rectangle.
     * @param data java.util.Collection BarChartBeans
     * @return double, a scale factor
     */
     protected double getScaleFactor(Collection data) {
         // Find max data value
         double maxValue = Double.MIN_VALUE;
         Iterator it = data.iterator();
         while (it.hasNext()) {
             BarChartBean bcb = (BarChartBean) it.next();
    ```

```
            double curValue = bcb.getValue();
            if (curValue > maxValue) {
                maxValue = curValue;
                bcb.setValue(curValue);
            }
        }
        // Compute scale factor
        double maxbar = getHeight() - 2.5 * vmargin;
        return maxbar / maxValue;
    }
```

You have a scale factor that the `init()` method needs to apply to the data. Notice that the data resides in a collection of JavaBeans. You will create that JavaBean after you finish the remaining helper methods for `init()`.

14. The next method will apply the scale factor to the collection of JavaBeans that contains the data points creation method. Implement the method as follows:

```
    /**
     * Applies the given scale factor to the specified
     * collection BarChartBeans
     * @param data java.util.Collection, BarChartBeans
     * @param scaleFactor double
     */
    protected void applyScaleFactor(
            Collection data,
            double scaleFactor) {
        Iterator it = data.iterator();
        while (it.hasNext()) {
            BarChartBean bcb = (BarChartBean) it.next();
            bcb.setValue(bcb.getValue() * scaleFactor);
        }
    }
```

That completes coding for applet parameter extraction and initialization, except for the missing JavaBean that holds a data point.

Data

You need to create a simple JavaBean that holds one data point. Each data point has a raw data value, a scaled data value, a label, and a color. Let us create this simple class so that you may move on to the fun part of the project. Use the following steps:

1. Create a class named BarChartBean in package com.xyz.applet.chart. Implement java.lang.Serializable. Provide a default (no-argument) constructor.
2. Implement the constructor body by providing non-null values for the class types. You may set the strings to a value of "". Set the Color to `Color.white`.
3. Create private fields as shown in Table 15.4.

Table 15.4 BarChartBean Private Fields

TYPE	NAME
double	value
java.lang.String	label
java.lang.String	rawValue
Java.awt.Color	color

4. Display the Outline view of the Java Perspective.
5. Right-click each field, and then select Generate Getter and Setter.
6. Create a convenience constructor having the following signature:

```
public BarChartBean(String aRawValue, double aValue,
            String aLabel, Color aColor)
```

7. Implement the constructor body by setting the fields to the corresponding parameter values.

That completes the JavaBean used to hold a data point.

Rendering

The bar chart applet does not contain any Swing or AWT components in its content pane. The applet simply initializes itself and then renders graphics in its rectangle. There are no events because there are no event-emitting components involved. You override `Applet.paint()` to carry out the rendering in response to a call from `Applet.update()`. The paint method calls three helper methods. Once you implement those methods, you'll have an operational bar chart applet except for supplying parameter and applet information implementations. Let us begin by creating the `paint()` override method.

1. Create the method in class BarChart as follows:

```
/**
 * Render the frame of this Applet.
 * Called by the applet framework.
 * @param aGraphics java.awt.Graphics
 */
public void paint(Graphics gc) {
    super.paint(gc);
    // Use specified font
    gc.setFont(font);
    FontMetrics fm = gc.getFontMetrics();
    // Set background
    setBackground(bgColor);
    // Draw Title
```

```
        drawTitle(gc, font, fgColor, title);
        // Draw border
        gc.setColor(fgColor);
        gc.drawRect(0, 0, getWidth() - 1, getHeight() - 1);
        // Draw footer line
        int y = getHeight() - vmargin;
        gc.setColor(fgColor);
        gc.drawLine(0, y, getWidth() - 1, y);
        // Draw bars on chart
        int barNum = 0;
        Iterator it = data.iterator();
        while (it.hasNext()) {
            // Determine height and x cooridnate of  bar
            BarChartBean bcb = (BarChartBean) it.next();
            int value = (int) bcb.getValue();
            int x = barNum * (barWidth + gutter) + margin;
            // Draw  bar
            drawBar(gc, bcb.getColor(), x, value);
            // Display numeric value atop bar
            String txt = bcb.getRawValue();
            Rectangle2D rect = fm.getStringBounds(txt, gc);
            int xd = (int) ((barWidth - rect.getWidth()) * 0.5);
            y = getHeight() - (int) (value + vmargin + 2);
            drawText(gc, font, fgColor, txt, x + xd, y);
            // Label the bar
            rect = fm.getStringBounds(bcb.getLabel(), gc);
            xd = (int) ((barWidth - rect.getWidth()) * 0.5);
            y = getHeight() - vmargin + (int) rect.getHeight();
            drawText(gc, font, fgColor, bcb.getLabel(), x + xd, y);
            barNum++;
        }
}
```

This straightforward method draws the background, borders, and title using the fields initialized by `init()`. Next, it iterates over the collection of BarChartBean JavaBeans created by `init()`. The loop body delegates the rendering of each bar, labeling it, and decorating it with a text value. Next, you shall implement the three delegate methods.

2. Create the following `drawbar()` method in the `Barchart` class as follows. Notice that the AWT method `drawRect()` does most of the work:

```
/**
 * Draw one colored bar at the indicated (x,y) location,
 * using the passed color, width and height
 * @param gc java.awt.Graphics
 * @param color java.awt.Color
 * @param x int, distance from Applet left border in pixels
```

```
 * @param cy int, height of bar in pixels
 */
protected void drawBar(Graphics gc, Color color, int x, int cy) {
    int y = getHeight() - cy - vmargin;
    gc.setColor(color);
    gc.fillRect(x, y, barWidth, cy);
    gc.setColor(fgColor);
    gc.drawRect(x, y, barWidth, cy);
}
```

The following helper delegate draws text at a given point in a specified color.

3. Create and implement the following method:

```
/**
 * Draw text at the given point using the specified font
 * in the given color.
 * @param gc java.awt.Graphics
 * @param aFont java.awt.Font
 * @param color java.awt.Color
 * @param txt java.langString
 * @param x int
 * @param y int
 */
protected void drawText(Graphics gc, Font aFont, Color color,
    String txt, int x, int y) {
    if (txt != null && txt.length() > 0) {
        gc.setFont(aFont);
        gc.setColor(color);
        gc.drawString(txt, x, y);
    }
}
```

The final helper delegate simply draws the centered title of the bar chart in a specified color using a given font.

4. Create and implement the following method:

```
/**
 * Draws the title in the top margin
 * @param gc java.awt.Graphics
 */
protected void drawTitle(Graphics gc, Font aFont, Color color, String
aTitle) {
    gc.setFont(aFont);
    Rectangle2D rect = gc.getFontMetrics().getStringBounds(aTitle,
gc);
    int x = (int) ((getWidth() - rect.getWidth()) * 0.5);
    int y = (int) rect.getHeight();
```

```
        gc.setColor(color);
        gc.drawString(aTitle, x, y);
    }
```

That completes the initialization and rendering parts of the applet. You do not have any resources to dispose, so don't implement `destroy()`. You don't need to be notified when the applet is started or stopped, so don't implement `start()` and `stop()`.

Information Callbacks

To ease the job of using this applet in a Web-authoring environment, you should provide overrides of the two informational methods.

1. In the BarChart class create and implement the following method, substituting meaningful contact information:

```
/**
 * Returns information about this applet.
 * @return a string of information about this applet
 */
public String getAppletInfo() {
    StringBuffer sb = new StringBuffer();
    sb.append("BarChart\nDisplays a bar chart\n");
    sb.append("Author Louis E. Mauget\n");
    sb.append("Date: 06/29/2006\n");
    return sb.toString();
}
```

2. In the BarChart class create and implement the `getParameterInfo()` method. Each row is a string triplet consisting of a parameter name, a type, and a description. Note that the type indicates the kind of string data desired. Use the body that follows as a guide:

```
/**
 * Returns parameters defined by this applet.
 * @return an array of descriptions of the receiver's parameters
 */
public java.lang.String[][] getParameterInfo() {
    String[][] info = {
    {"fgColor", "Color", "Text and border color" },
    {"bgColor", "Color", "Background color" },
    {"fontName", "String",
         "Name of font face used to render the text" },
    {"pointSize", "Integer", "Point size of the font" },
    {"title", "String", "The title of this chart" },
    {"gutterFraction", "Float",
         "Bar separator as fraction of bar width" },
    {"bx", "Float", "Data value. One bar per bx where x = 1..n" },
```

```
        {"lx", "String", "Label of bar x (optional)" },
        {"cx", "Color", "Color of bar x (optional)" },
        };
        return info;
    }
```

That completes the applet. Build it and check it for any errors in the Task view. Repair any errors found. Then, it is time to exercise the BarChart applet.

Testing

One approach to testing and debugging an applet is to give it an optional frame and `main()` method to allow it to be also executed as an application. You could export a JAR file to a directory referenced by a test HTML page. Then, you use either the Java Applet Viewer or a Web browser to test the applet. If you need the WSAD debugger, then you may run the applet directly in WSAD. In our experience, a well-written applet should be highly parameterized. It should have a nontrivial `init()` method to configure itself from parametric input.

Let us test the applet by exporting it as a JAR file to a code base directory referenced by a test HTML page. Create a directory structure that looks like that seen in Figure 15.2

Export the applet to a JAR file in the applet test directory as follows:

1. Ensure that all classes of the applet are saved with no errors. Select package `com.xyz.applet.barchart` in the Packages view of the Java Perspective.
2. Select the menu item File / Export, choose Jar File from the Export dialog, and then press Next.
3. Use the Browse button to navigate to the test applet folder, and then press Finish.
4. Reply Yes to any confirmation dialog.

The applet JAR file is created by the export operation. WSAD will remember where you last exported the JAR file, if you need to repeat the cycle later. Next, create an HTML page that exercises the applet. Try the HTML page shown previously near Table 15.3. Place the HTML file into the docroot directory. Open that directory from the Windows or Linux desktop. Open the file using the default file association (e.g. double-click it). If you obtained the Java Plug-in and have a browser that does not need HTML conversion to be carried out on the HTML page, you should see a result resembling Figure 15.3.

Figure 15.2 Applet test directory.

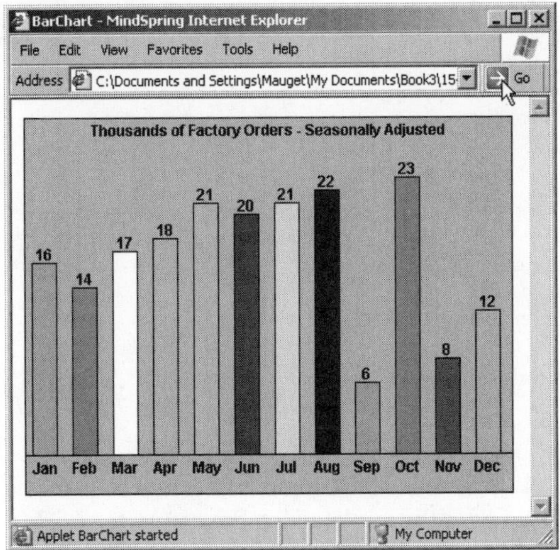

Figure 15.3 BarChart using IE with Java Plug-in.

If you enabled the Java Console in the plug-in administration application, you will see a window that resembles that shown in Figure 15.4.

The Java Console may be helpful during debugging, but keep in mind that the applet should be small and not complex.

If the default browser is Netscape 4.7x or some other browser that doesn't accept the plug-in without special HTML tags, you will see an error on the status line. The applet rectangle will not show a bar chart. You must convert the HTML file using the HTML converter that is part of the Java 2 SDK. Simply execute the converter, navigate to the HTML file, and then press the Convert button. Any browser that does not have the plug-in will present the dialog shown in Figure 15.5, offering to download it.

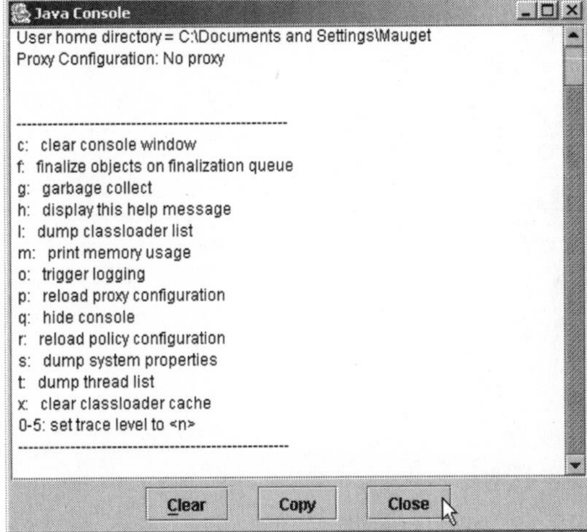

Figure 15.4 Java Plug-in console.

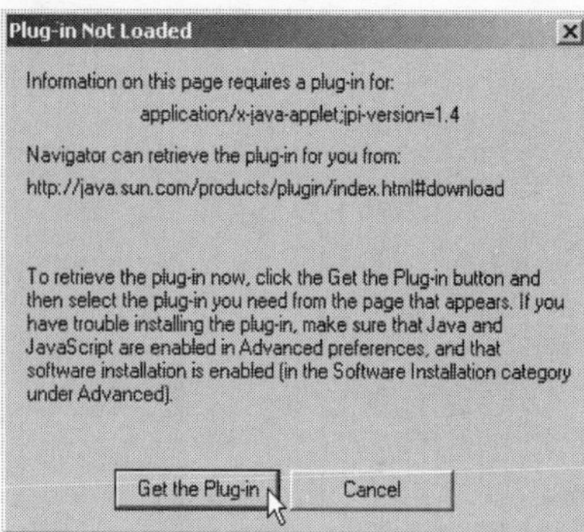

Figure 15.5 Plug-in automatic download.

After installing the plug-in, you can click the browser screen and cause it to load the applet. This version of Netscape can only render the applet using the converted HTML page. Netscape 6 and Internet Explorer 5 or greater are each capable of running the applet without converted HTML, provided that each has the plug-in loaded. Figure 15.6 shows Netscape 6 using the unconverted HTML.

The browsers are not the best vehicles for initial testing. The plug-in caches classes to prevent needless downloads of the applet bits. The Java Applet Viewer may be a better applet testing choice. It also displays the parameter information and applet information provided by an applet. In addition, it is possible to start the Java Applet Viewer in the Java debugger. The Java Applet Viewer also allows us to reload, start, stop, and clone the applet.

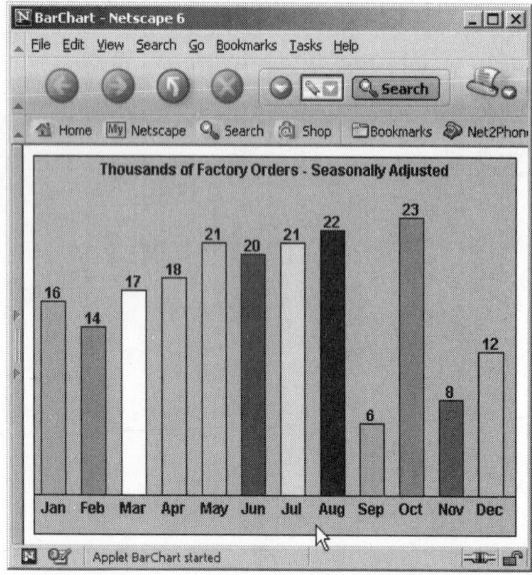

Figure 15.6 Netscape 6 using unconverted HTML.

Extending the Chart Applet

The operation of the BarChart applet involves gathering parameters, supplying default values for parameters not specified, calculating internal parameters, and finally drawing bars decorated with text. In the end, the fundamental API used is java.awt.Graphics .fillRect(). Let us enumerate some possible enhancements to the chart that could be controlled by parameters:

- Parameter-driven alternative to use: `java.awt.Graphics.drawPolygon()` or `java.awt.Graphics.fillPolygon()` to plot the values as points on a curve or filled curve.
- An option to present a horizontal bar chart.
- A base parameter value subtracted from all data values to accentuate small variations in data points (for example 1005, 1004, 1003, 1002 would be plotted as 5, 4, 3, 2 if the base were 1000).
- An option to allow signed data points. The vertical bar chart would extend each side of the baseline.
- An option to Add Swing components that allow the user to cause events that alter the display. Some of the previous enhancement candidates could be wired to these components.

Applets in Web Applications

Applets are used with Web applications in combination with other J2EE technologies. For instance, a parameterized applet used for specialized output can be a friend in developing a sophisticated Web application. Picture a retail demographic application that tracks numbers of customers by zip code. Humans often cognize data better graphically than textually. The BarChart applet could provide a graphic representation of customers by zip code. An analyst would request customer counts for, say, five zip codes. A JSP would generate dynamic applet <param ..> tags from a collection of JavaBeans returned by business logic invoked from a servlet. If the JSP needs the HTML conversion treatment, the scriptlet used to generate the parameters is not harmed. You will incorporate the BarChart applet into a Web client for an application involving Enterprise JavaBeans in Chapter 23, "Entity EJBs."

Summary

Java Applets have a narrow, important role in rendering data visually for Web applications. The applet should limit its participation to special effects and rendering, without being part of the application logic. A JSP may generate applet HTML elements based upon dynamic data. This can provide a customized graphical rendering of complex data, aiding understanding. The Java Plug-in reduces a time-related disconnect between browser versions and JRE versions. Some older browsers may need modified HTML to use the plug-in. This chapter covered:

- Java applet background
- How applets should be used in Web applications
- Java plug-in deployment and use
- Creation of a bar chart applet
- Applet testing
- An overview of how to integrate an applet into a Web site

We will cover deployment of Web applications in the next chapter.

CHAPTER

16

J2EE Application Deployment

What's in Chapter 16?

WSAD enables a developer to develop, deploy, and debug a J2EE application. In this chapter, we discuss deployment issues and touch on debugging a deployed Web application. We will cover:

- Deployable J2EE archive forms
- WSAD Web and enterprise projects
- Importing WAR files into WSAD
- Web application debugging
- Exporting Web applications from WSAD
- WSAD Web application and J2EE packaging
- Testing on local and remote servers
- Exporting an EAR file from WSAD
- Defining an enterprise application in WAS
- Importing an application into WAS
- Running applications outside the WSAD IDE

Web applications are composed of disparate static Web pages, servlets, JSPs, a deployment descriptor, and other Web resources. Each part must be addressable by the application. The Web application executes within an application server, but how are its parts given to the server? How is one application distinguished from another? How does the application find its component parts? What is an enterprise application? How does a Web application relate to an enterprise application? What are J2EE modules? The next section covers these issues of Web application deployment.

Deployable Archives

The J2EE standard defines a standard format for packaging a Web application described by an XML deployment descriptor. The files are structured into a directory tree that is packaged with a deployment descriptor into a Web Application Archive, or WAR file, as defined by the *Sun Microsystems Java Servlet 2.2 Specification*. A WAR is a structured JAR file that contains a Web module. A Web module contains one or more Web components that provide a service in response to a remote request. Static HTML, image files, JSPs, Java servlets, style sheets, and tag libraries are typical components. Thus, a WAR file is a packaged Web application that may be used to import the application into a Web server. A WAR file contains an XML document that describes deployment information such as servlet configurations, MIME types, and a document context root. WSAD provides the wizards for importing and exporting WAR files.

In addition, the J2EE standard defines an EAR file that is a structured JAR file containing a J2EE application as a deployable unit of J2EE functionality. The functionality could include one or more Web applications, EJB JAR files, resource archive (RAR) files, or J2EE connector modules. A J2EE application may be deployed across multiple computational tiers.

EAR files and WAR files are J2EE deployable units within the J2EE standard. They are deployable to any container or server that is compliant with the J2EE standard. IBM's Websphere Application Server 5 product is compliant. WSAD can create Web projects and enterprise application projects that may export WAR files and EAR files, respectively. In addition, WSAD will deploy Web projects and enterprise application projects directly to a local or remote application server.

WAR File

A WAR file has a specific directory structure, as shown in Figure 16.1. The top-level directory is the document root of the Web application. The JSPs, and static files such as HTML and GIFs are stored here, or in subdirectories under the document root. Every WAR contains `WEB-INF` subdirectory of the document root. This directory contains the `web.xml` deployment descriptor, any tag library xml descriptors used, a `classes` directory that holds server-side classes of the application, and a `lib` directory that holds JAR files used by the application. The WAR file does not need a JAR manifest entry, although it is permitted to be present.

You could create a WAR file from a Web application directory by executing the following command from the document root directory:

```
jar cvf ../webappname.war .
```

There is a better approach for the WSAD user. WSAD maintains a WAR directory structure within each Web application project. You can easily export the WSAD Web application directly to a WAR file.

EAR File

A J2EE application is packaged as an EAR file, which is a structured JAR file that has the .ear file extension and contains well-defined contents. This is a format that is portable across compliant J2EE platforms. A J2EE application consists of independently deployable units called *modules*. This allows parties to provide independent modules without needing to implement a full-scale application. These modules may be one or more Enterprise JavaBean (EJB), Web, or application client modules. We have discussed Web application packaging in WAR files. EJBs and application client modules are packaged in JAR files, which contain an XML-based deployment descriptor, along with other needed resources. All J2EE modules are independently deployable units.

Let us discuss the modules that compose an EAR file. Each module is composed of components. For example, a Web module may contain a deployment descriptor and any or all of the following: servlets, tag libraries, static HTML files, filters, JSPs, CSS files, necessary dependent JAR files, and other resources. It may contain JNDI references to resources in the environment or the EAR file.

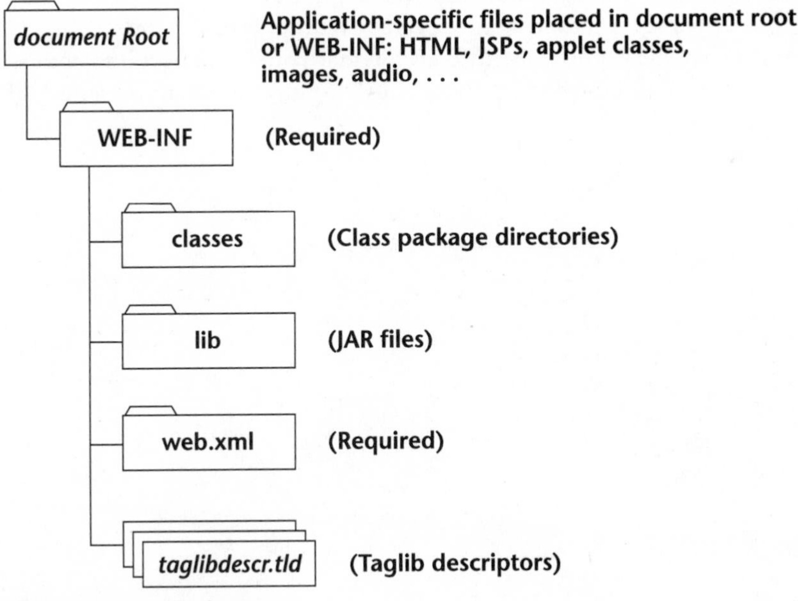

Figure 16.1 WAR format.

An EJB module contains a deployment descriptor, EJBs, RMI stubs, deployment classes, dependent JAR files, and JNDI references. The deployment descriptor is created by a J2EE-compliant *Application Assembler*. Its job is to link dependencies within and between deployment descriptors of the module archives. For example, a servlet in a Web application may be a client of a session EJB deployed in an EJB JAR within the J2EE application. The result is an EAR file that contains J2EE modules and a deployment descriptor, shown conceptually in Figure 16.2.

After the application assembler completes, a J2EE-compliant verification process should be executed to ensure that the application is consistent with the J2EE specification. WSAD encompasses each of these J2EE processes. You can create an enterprise project in WSAD that has dependencies on Web projects. Indeed, Web projects destined to run in the Websphere test environment are normally associated with an enterprise project. A DefaultEAR project is provided in case you have no enterprise application project. You will create an explicit enterprise application project in the section in this chapter entitled "Packaging for J2EE."

Web and Enterprise Projects

WSAD supports a local test environment consisting of the Apache Tomcat Web application server. User-supplied releases 3.2, 4.0, and 4.1 are supported. Tomcat is suitable for testing Web application projects, but it has no J2EE enterprise application support. For more information on obtaining Tomcat, go to jakarta.apache.org/tomcat. For full J2EE 1.3 support, WSAD supplies a WebSphere version 5.0 test server environment. WSAD also supplies a WebSphere version 4.0 test server that supports J2EE 1.2. You can create a Web application project in WSAD that will deploy to Tomcat, WAS, or any external application server that supports J2EE Web applications.

An enterprise application may contain several Web application projects as one deployable unit. It may be exported to an EAR file that you can import into another WSAD instance as a project, or deploy from WSAD to any compliant remote J2EE implementation.

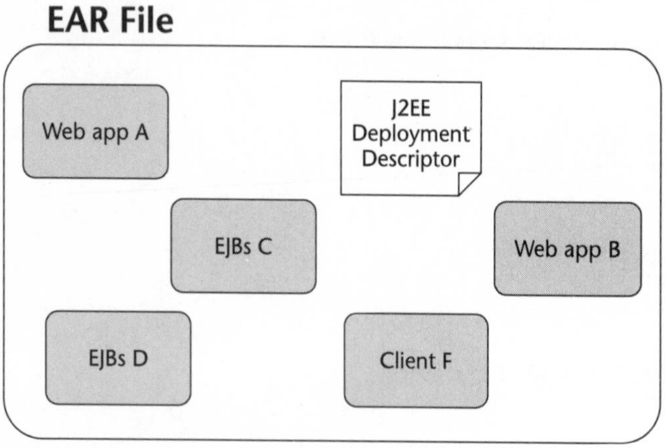

Figure 16.2 Conceptual EAR file.

Importing a WAR File into WSAD

A WAR file embodies a Web application. WSAD can import a WAR file. You can create a Web project in the WSAD workbench when you need to create and update resources for a Web application. Now, you will create a Web application and then import a WAR file into it.

1. Choose main menu items File > Open > Web Perspective to open the Web perspective. You may need to choose File > Open > Other first, if the Web Perspective has not been opened recently.
2. Select main menu items File > New > Web Project. The Create a Web Project wizard opens.
3. Enter **CalcWeb** in the Project name field. Let the other options keep their default values. The wizard should resemble Figure 16.3. Press Next.
4. Let the Enterprise application project name default to DefaultEAR. Remember, an EAR file contains a J2EE application. See Figure 16.4. You shall create an explicit EAR file in the section,"Packaging for J2EE."
5. Accept the remaining default settings by pressing Finish.

This creates an empty project container having the correct folder structure with a web.xml deployment descriptor. You could have created a default CSS file and entered dependent JAR file dependencies. The DefaultEAR project will contain the Web application along with other Web applications that compose the default enterprise application. The two projects are shown in the J2EE Navigator in Figure 16.5. Later, you will create your own enterprise application.

Now, you will continue by importing a WAR file to populate your CalcWeb Web project.

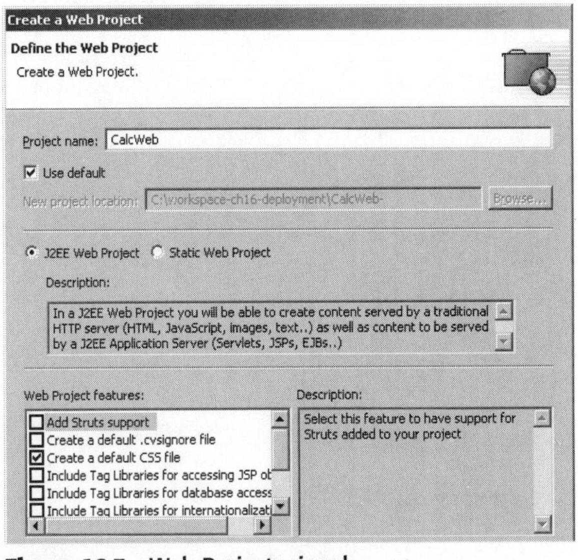

Figure 16.3 Web Project wizard.

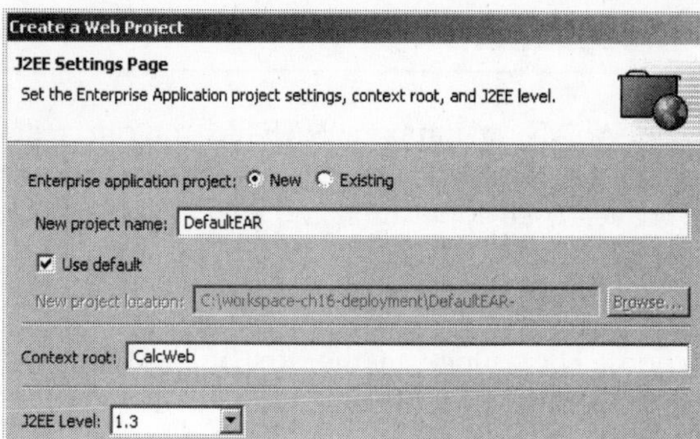

Figure 16.4 J2EE settings of a Web project.

6. Select the CalcWeb project in the Navigator. Choose the menu item File > Import. The Import dialog appears.
7. Choose WAR file, and then press Next.
8. Browse the CalcWeb.war file downloaded from the book Web site, as shown in Figure 16.6. Notice that you could have specified a new Web project here instead of importing into an existing Web project.
9. Press Finish. The project is populated with the application from the WAR file.
10. Display the web.xml file seen under Web Content/WEB-INF.

Inspect the Servlets tab and then the Source tab. Observe that the project now contains a servlet. You imported the Web application into a Web project. Now, you will inspect and modify its properties.

11. Right-click the CalcWeb project. Choose Properties.
12. Select Server Preference. Choose Websphere v5.0 Test Environment. This enables you to run and debug the application on the version 5.0 single-server test WAS bundled within WSAD.

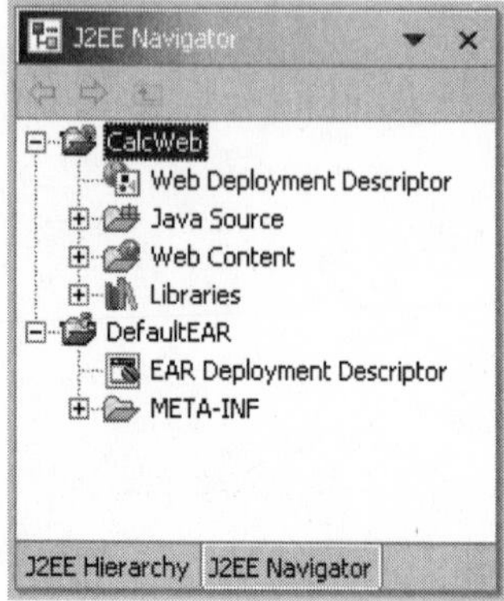

Figure 16.5 Web project with default enterprise project.

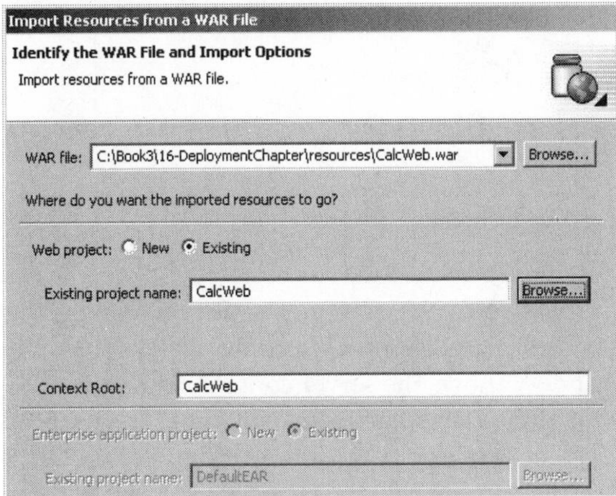

Figure 16.6 Import WAR file.

13. Ensure that the option Prompt for server before running is set.
14. Select Web. Ensure that CalcWeb is the context root. Notice the support for Apache Jakarta Struts and various kinds of tag libraries. You won't use any of these in the calculator, but you could change your mind in the future. This is where the support would be added.
15. Close the Properties dialog by pressing OK.

The properties are set such that the application is ready to deploy and execute. This requires just two clicks of the mouse in WSAD.

16. Right-click project CalcWeb, and then select Run on Server. You can do this from any Internet Explorer or Navigator view. The Server Preference dialog appears since you set the property earlier saying that you wanted to be prompted for server preference before running the application.
17. Use the existing server WebSphere v5.0 Test Environment. Press Finish.

The project is automatically published to the server. The server starts if it is not running. Notice the views that appear, which are listed in Table 16.1.

Table 16.1 Server Debugging Views

VIEW	DESCRIPTION
Console	Displays transcript of server messages
Processes	A tree of server processes
Debug	Thread tree; debug controls: suspend, resume, terminate, start, stop, step over, step into, return, show qualified names
Servers	A list of defined server instances, their run states, and synchronized states
Variables	The variables at a particular scope during debugging

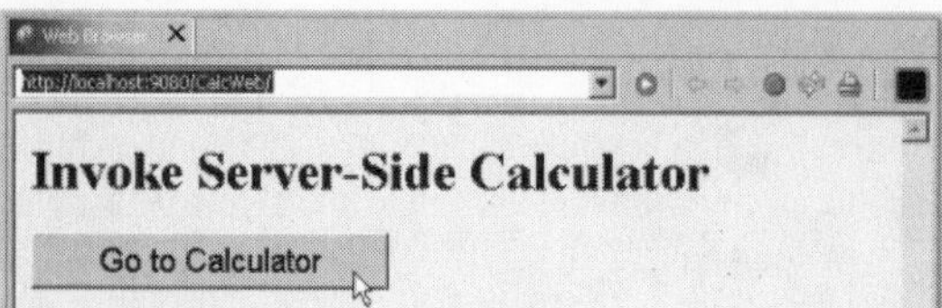

Figure 16.7 Executing an imported Web application.

The application is deployed or published to the server. The Server Perspective opens. An integrated browser pane opens the application's welcome page, as shown in Figure 16.7. Notice that the console window shows the server console messages.

This imported application is based upon the calculator application previously used in this book. That application was designed around a mediator design pattern. This enabled its Swing UI to be replaced with a servlet controller and a JSP view with no modification to the application model and domain layers. This is not the most practical use of servlet technology because it requires round trips to the server for every keystroke. It does make a good server-side debugging example. That a Swing application could be mutated into a Web application, without changing the application model, shows the power of isolating the application module using a mediator design pattern. The calculator is shown in Figure 16.8 in the WSAD Web Browser view.

If you were to alter the code, rebuild the project, and then choose Run on Server again, the application would automatically republish and open to the welcome page once more.

Any HTML updates to the JSP would be incorporated automatically because the server would detect the timestamp difference between its compiled servlet rendition of the JSP and the timestamp of the updated JSP source. It would page-compile the JSP into a new servlet and then run its `init` method. The associated *init* message would appear on the Console view for the server. An HTML change to the static HTML file would be incorporated immediately.

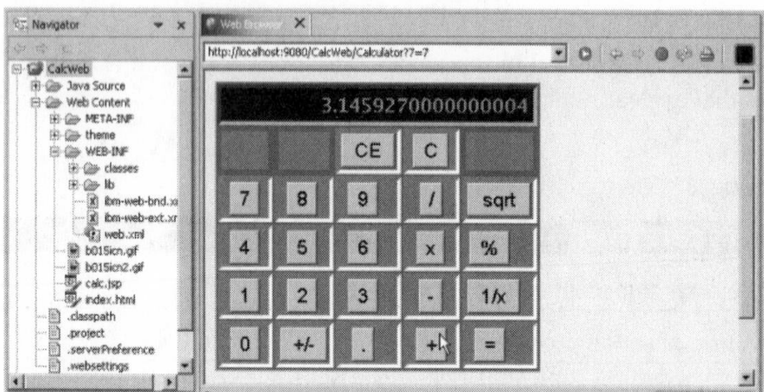

Figure 16.8 Calculator Web application running In WSAD.

Exporting a WAR File from WSAD

Where did the CalcWeb.war file originate? You created a Web project around the mediator and domain layers that were taken from the Swing-based calculator application. Then, you exported the project as a WAR file, remembering the option to attach the Java source code.

Carry out the following steps to export a WAR file:

1. Perform a WAR export operation by right-clicking the CalcWeb Web application project.
2. Select Export, and then choose WAR file from the resulting Export dialog. Press Next >. The WAR Export wizard panel appears.
3. Select Export source files if backing up the project.
4. Use the Browse button to select the name and target location for the WAR file. Choose c:\temp\CalcWeb.war. Press OK to close the Browse navigation dialog.
5. Click Finish to export the WAR file.

Remember that a WAR is a structured JAR file, and that a JAR file is stored in zip format. If you open the WAR file with a program such as WinZip, you can examine the contents. They would appear as seen in Figure 16.9.

The deployment descriptor follows:

```
<?xml version="1.0" encoding="UTF-8"?>
<!DOCTYPE web-app PUBLIC "-//Sun Microsystems, Inc.//DTD Web Application
2.3//EN" "http://java.sun.com/dtd/web-app_2_3.dtd">
<web-app id="WebApp">
    <display-name>CalcWeb</display-name>
    <servlet>
        <servlet-name>Calculator</servlet-name>
        <display-name>Calculator</display-name>
        <description>Conroller</description>
        <servlet-class>bellmeade.calculator.servlet.Calculator</servlet-
class>
    </servlet>
    <servlet-mapping>
        <servlet-name>Calculator</servlet-name>
        <url-pattern>/Calculator</url-pattern>
    </servlet-mapping>
    <welcome-file-list>
        <welcome-file>index.html</welcome-file>
        <welcome-file>index.htm</welcome-file>
        <welcome-file>index.jsp</welcome-file>
        <welcome-file>default.html</welcome-file>
        <welcome-file>default.htm</welcome-file>
        <welcome-file>default.jsp</welcome-file>
    </welcome-file-list>
</web-app>
```

WinZip (Evaluation Version) - CalcWeb.war

File Actions Options Help

New Open Favorites Add Extract View CheckOut Wizard

Name	Type	Size	Ratio	Packed	Path
b015icn.gif	PSP7.Image	966	12%	849	
b015icn2.gif	PSP7.Image	829	9%	755	
calc.jsp	JSP File	5,140	79%	1,092	
index.html	HTML Document	468	34%	307	
Manifest.mf	MF File	39	0%	41	meta-inf\
Master.css	Cascading Styl...	1,225	66%	411	theme\
ibm-web-bnd.xmi	XMI File	276	38%	170	web-inf\
ibm-web-ext.xmi	XMI File	481	45%	263	web-inf\
web.xml	XML Document	873	61%	344	web-inf\
Calculator.class	CLASS File	2,204	54%	1,015	WEB-INF\classes\bellmeade\calculator\servlet\
calculator-lib.jar	Executable Jar...	5,007	16%	4,191	WEB-INF\lib\
Calculator.java	JAVA File	2,236	60%	898	WEB-INF\source\bellmeade\calculator\servlet\

Selected 0 files, 0 bytes   Total 12 files, 20KB

Figure 16.9 CalcWeb.war contents.

WSAD Web Application Packaging

WSAD Web applications are created in the Web Perspective. They are usually manipulated in the Web Perspective, in the Server Perspective, in the Java Perspective, and perhaps, in the Resource Perspective. A WSAD Web project enforces the packaging standard of a WAR file. The Server Perspective may be used to deploy and test the application from the WSAD Workbench. The project structure for the CalcWeb project is shown in Figure 16.10.

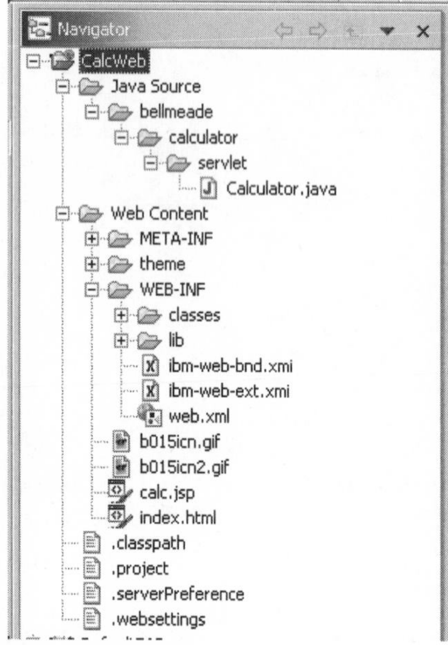

Figure 16.10 CalcWeb application structure.

Look at the location of the Java source file package, inside of Web Content folder. This folder mirrors the structure of a WAR file. The WEB-INF folder always exists in a WAR file. It must contain a deployment descriptor named web.xml. Directory-based Java packages located in the classes folder are placed on the Web application's class loader class path during deployment. Any JAR files placed in the lib folder are also placed on the application's class loader class path during deployment. Web content files and directories are placed directly under the Web Content folder. Their path is relative to the content root defined in the web.xml deployment descriptor. WSAD provides a form-based editor for these files as well as a syntax-colored text-based source edit view of it. Figure 16.11 shows the deployment information for the Calculator servlet.

Bottom tabs provide entry into various elements of the web.xml deployment descriptor. A Source tab lets you view the syntax-highlighted source text of the file.

Packaging for J2EE

We touched on J2EE application packaging previously. WSAD defines this packaging in an enterprise application project. Let us look at one of these. Open the WSAD J2EE Perspective. The J2EE view shows a tree of modules, server configurations, server instances, and databases. Remember that WSAD supplies a DefaultEAR project that you used to hold the CalcWeb Web module. It is a better practice to supply an explicit enterprise application for related Web modules instead of directing unrelated Web projects into DefaultEAR. This way, unrelated Web applications such as the IBM Universal Test Client don't coexist, and the problem of namespace collisions is reduced. The argument resembles that against using Java's default package for class files.

Expand the Enterprise Applications node of the J2EE view. The DefaultEAR project shows every Web module that it holds. You should see the CalcWeb.war archive there.

The CalcWeb Web application should also appear under the Web Modules node, where you can expand it to inspect its deployment elements. Notice that you can run a J2EE validation against it from its context menu.

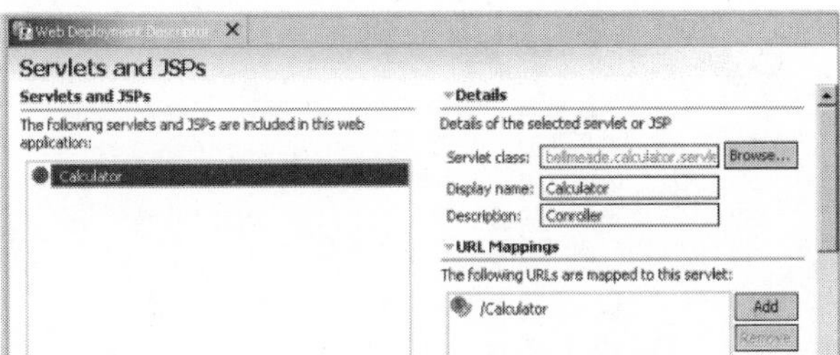

Figure 16.11 Servlet deployment descriptor.

Because it is good practice to isolate related Web applications in their own EAR file, let us create a new enterprise application project to hold the CalcWeb module.

1. Open the J2EE Perspective.
2. Select the menu items File > New > Enterprise Application Project. The Enterprise Application Creation wizard opens.
3. Specify Create J2EE 1.3 Enterprise Application project, as shown in Figure 16.12. This application will run on any J2EE 1.3-compliant server such as WebSphere Application Server v5.0. Press Next >.
4. Enter CalcApp for the enterprise application project name. Notice that you receive default J2EE module names for the application client project, an EJB project, and a Web project. You can disable any or all of these for an enterprise project so that you can import and attach one or more later.
5. For this exercise, you do not want to create default modules. Uncheck all three modules. Leave Use default set for the location of the project directory tree. See Figure 16.13.
6. Press Finish.

The CalcApp node appears in the J2EE Navigator view. It has no J2EE modules. It is currently a null enterprise application. Let us add the CalcWeb Web application to it.

7. Expand CalcApp / META-INF in the J2EE Navigator view.
8. Select Open from the EAR Deployment Descriptor context menu. The Application Deployment Descriptor view opens. Select the Module tab at the bottom.
9. Press Add.
10. Navigate to and select the project CalcWeb. Press Finish. The module CalcWeb.war appears in the Module list.
11. Select the CalcWeb.war module in the list. Observe the correct URI, Context root, and Project information appearing at the right side of the view.
12. Save and close the Application Deployment Descriptor file.

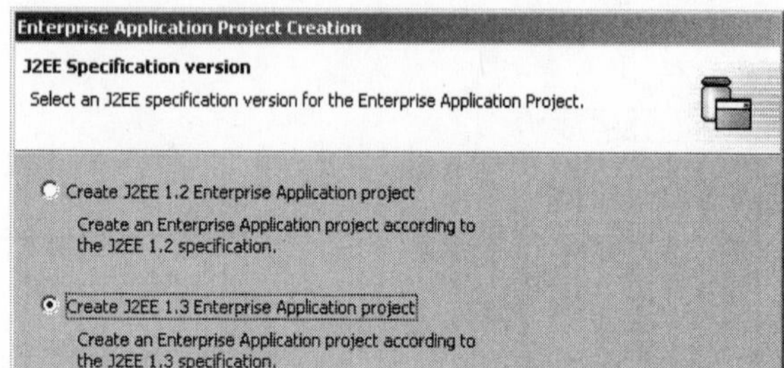

Figure 16.12 Specify J2EE 1.3 project.

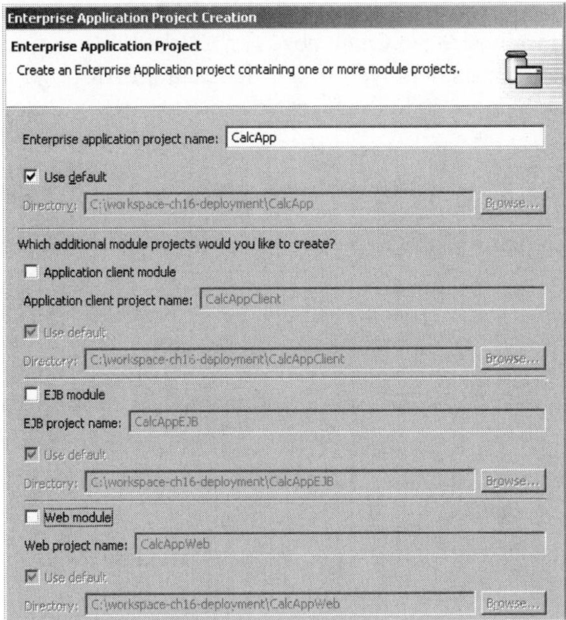

Figure 16.13 Create an enterprise application project.

Web module CalcWeb appears in two J2EE applications now. If you wish, you can open the Application Deployment Descriptor view of the DefaultEAR project and remove it from its Modules list.

Configure Local Server

The new CalcApp is not yet configured to run on a J2EE server. You will remove DefaultEAR from the WebSphere v5.0 Test Environment and add CalcApp.

1. Open the Server Perspective.
2. Ensure that no server is running. Use the Stop context menu item if necessary.
3. Expand and right-click Servers / WebSphere v5.0 Test Environment / DefaultEAR.
4. Choose Remove from the DefaultEAR context menu. The server configuration now has no configured enterprise applications.
5. Right-click Servers / WebSphere v5.0 Test Environment.
6. Choose Add > CalcApp from the context menu. CalcApp now appears as a configured application for WebSphere v5.0 Test Environment.
7. Display project CalcApp in the Navigator view.
8. Select Run on Server from the CalcApp project context menu.

After Websphere is initialized, choose Run on Server on the CalcWeb context menu or open a browser on URL http://localhost:9080/CalcWeb/. The CalcWeb Web application should operate as it did when it was deployed under the DefaultEAR project. Stop the server when you are ready to move on to the following section.

Configure Remote Server

That was easy. Now, you will try configuring and deploying CalcApp to a remote IBM WebSphere v5.0 Application Server (WAS). You will begin by configuring the remote server instance. You need a copy of WAS to carry out these steps, otherwise simply read them to understand the process. The WAS is on a separate machine from WSAD. You deploy it from WSAD to the remote server, using a Windows file share. You could use FTP instead if the host had an operational FTP service or daemon. See the documentation about this. You will use the file share method in the following steps:

1. At the WAS host, share the WAS installation root directory so that the WSAD installation can access it as a drive letter.
2. Open the WAS Administration Console. Ensure that WAS is started on the WAS host.
3. Return to the WSAD machine. Map the share created in Step 1 to a drive letter such as "Z."
4. Open the WSAD Server Perspective.
5. Use the context menu of the Server Configuration view to invoke New > Server and Server Configuration. The Create a New Server and Server Configuration dialog opens.
6. Enter a unique recognizable instance name such as **WAS Remote**.
7. Choose Websphere v5.0 > Remote Server for the Server type. Notice the live description of the server type.

In future development work you could specify a Remote Attach server type here. This would enable you to use WSAD as a debug client to a remote WAS host running in debug mode. The Debug Perspective would operate as discussed previously in the "Web Application Debugging" section.

8. Press Next>. The WebSphere Remote Server settings appear.
9. Enter the remote host name or IP address. See Figure 16.14. Press Next >.
10. Set the installed root location of the remote WAS. Additionally, set its deployment directory. These paths are local to the remote host. See Figure 16.15. Press Next>.

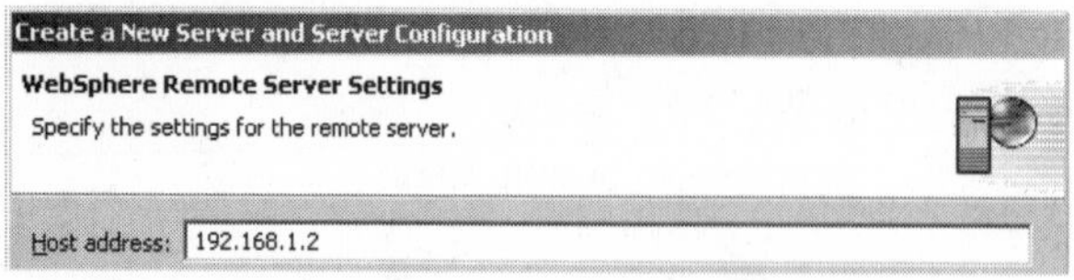

Create a New Server and Server Configuration
WebSphere Remote Server Settings
Specify the settings for the remote server.
Host address: 192.168.1.2

Figure 16.14 Specify remote host address.

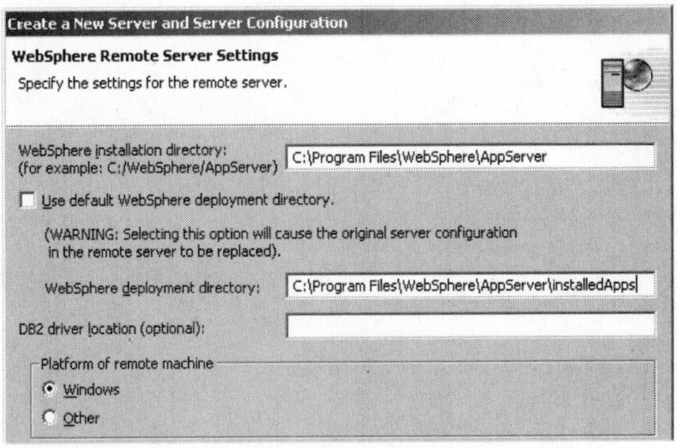

Figure 16.15 Specify remote Installation directory.

Now, you must choose to use the remote file share or FTP. You will use the remote file share in this example. If you were using Unix or Linux for either machine, this would require SAMBA on that machine.

11. Create a new remote file transfer instance using the copy file transfer mechanism, as shown in Figure 16.16. Press Next>.
12. Enter the mapped drive path (such as z:/) in the Remote target directory field, as shown in Figure 16.17. Press Finish.

WSAD creates the server instance. Now, you must associate a server configuration with it with the following steps:

13. In the Server Configuration view, open the context menu on Servers > WAS Remote. Choose Add > CalcApp.

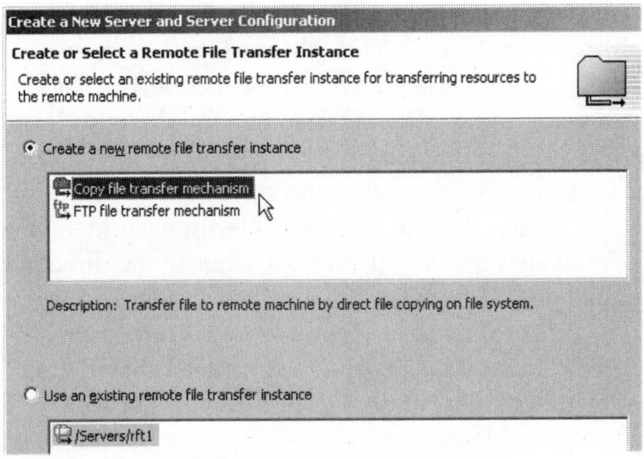

Figure 16.16 Remote file transfer instance.

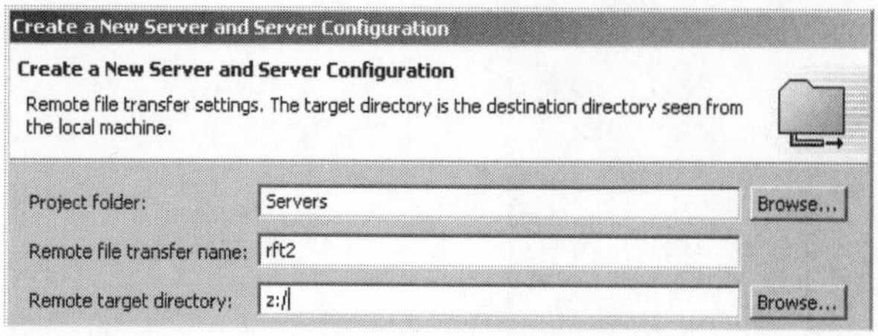

Figure 16.17 Remote file transfer settings.

Carry out the following set of steps to deploy CalcApp to the remote server from its context menu:

14. Select the Servers tab of the Servers view.
15. Right-click the WAS Remote server instance. Select Publish. The application deploys to the remote WAS instance.

Ensure that the remote instance is running, and then open a browser on the CalcWeb context of the remote server URL. For example, your URL was http://mauget1:9080/calculator-webapp/. You should be able to run the calculator as usual.

If you ever needed to view or modify a setting, you would open Server / WAS Remote from the Server Configuration view. Similarly, you can open the remote transfer instance from the Navigator Servers node.

Use the Services Control Panel applet on Windows to control the IBM Agent Controller. Use the normal daemon control scripts on Unix or Linux to control it on those platforms.

Control the Remote Server from WSAD

It is possible to publish to a remote server from WSAD, but it would be still better to operate it remotely from the Server Perspective as you did with the test environment. WSAD ships the IBM Agent Controller with WSAD. This feature runs as a service. It controls small programs called agents. WAS has an agent within it that will control WAS as if it were a proxy for remote operations. WSAD uses the agent controller to control WAS, or to carry out remote profiling and debugging. You want to use it to control a remote WAS instance as if it were the bundled test environment.

Look for the IBM Agent Controller in the install medium under the IBM_Agent_Controller directory. There are eight subdirectories. Choose the directory that matches the WAS platform name, and then install the installation file. For example, on Windows run windows/setup.exe. When asked if you want secure, encrypted communications, say no, assuming that you develop and test on an isolated LAN. Otherwise, you must consult the documentation to configure a Secure Socket Layer (SSL) connection. See Figure 16.18. You will have an opportunity to restrict the hosts that can access the agent controller, but remember that all communications are in the clear unless you use SSL.

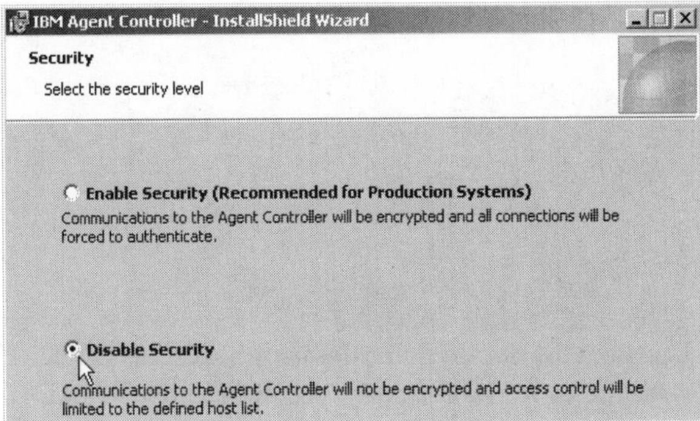

Figure 16.18 IBM Agent Controller security settings.

Once the agent controller is installed, it will start automatically as a service or daemon. At that point, you can use the WSAD server configuration you created in the previous section, "Configure Remote Server," to control the server. On WSAD, try invoking Run on Server against CalcWeb while WAS Remote is stopped. The remote WAS server should start after a time, and then the WSAD integrated browser will render the calculator application.

Export an EAR from WSAD

You have a new CalcApp enterprise application. Now, you will deploy it as an EAR file that is suitable for deployment to any J2EE application server. If you attach the Java source code to the EAR, the file may be imported as a project into another copy of WSAD, or used for offline project archival.

1. Invoke the context menu of CalcApp.
2. Select Export. The Export wizard opens.
3. Choose **EAR file** and then press **Next** >.
4. Use the Browse button to navigate to a destination. For example, use c:\temp\CalcApp.ear.
5. Select the option Export source files because you want to use this EAR as a project source backup in addition to deploying it to an application server.
6. Press Finish.

That is all there is to creating an EAR file in WSAD. Keep this file. You will import it into WAS locally. The contents, as seen using WinZip, appear in Figure 16.19. Notice the WSAD .project file that describes the CalcApp project.

Name	Type	Size	Ratio	Packed	Path
.project	PROJECT File	424	50%	211	
.serverPreference	SERVERPREFE...	202	25%	152	
CalcWeb.war	WAR File	13,...	9%	11,903	
.modulemaps	MODULEMAPS...	445	45%	244	meta-inf\
application.xml	XML Document	412	36%	264	meta-inf\
ibm-application-e...	XMI File	347	50%	175	meta-inf\
Manifest.mf	MF File	25	0%	27	meta-inf\

Figure 16.19 CalcApp.ear contents.

The enterprise application application.xml deployment descriptor defines the J2EE modules of the application along with its settings. Normally, you would use WSAD to view and edit the deployment descriptor in a structured manner by opening it from the Navigator, but it is instructive to look at the XML Source view also. Each module is contained in a module XML element. A J2EE module has its own deployment descriptor within its own archive. CalcWeb.war is the only Web module in CalcApp. See the source listing of application.xml that follows:

```
<?xml version="1.0" encoding="UTF-8"?>
<!DOCTYPE application PUBLIC "-//Sun Microsystems, Inc.//DTD J2EE
Application 1.3//EN" "http://java.sun.com/dtd/application_1_3.dtd">
<application id="Application_ID">
    <display-name>CalcApp</display-name>
    <module id="WebModule_1038866962554">
        <web>
            <web-uri>CalcWeb.war</web-uri>
            <context-root>CalcWeb</context-root>
        </web>
    </module>
</application>
```

Defining Enterprise Applications in WAS

You have defined a J2EE project in WSAD, then incorporated a Web module into it, and finally published (deployed or installed) it to WAS through WSAD. Instead, you could have defined the enterprise application directly in WAS and then incorporated the Web module at that point. The WAS Application Assembly Tool has wizards used to create the following:

- J2EE applications
- EJB modules
- Web modules
- J2EE application client modules

The application assembly tool can create a new application or J2EE module or import exiting modules. These can be combined into a new application. You will use the tool to create a new enterprise application named CalcApp2 that will contain the CalcWeb.war Web module with the following steps:

1. Open the Application Assembly Tool from the operating system menu, or from the WAS Administration Console main menu item Tools > Application Assembly Tool. The welcome panel shown in Figure 16.20 appears.
2. Select Application, and then press OK. The tool opens with a tree view of an EAR file structure in the left-hand pane. A right-hand tabbed pane displays a detail view.
3. Enter a Display Name of **CalcApp2.ear**. Enter a description. See Figure 16.21. Press Apply.
4. Click the Bindings tab. Enter CalcApp2 as the Enterprise application name. Press Apply.
5. Select Web Modules from the tree view. Invoke the context menu Import item, then navigate to and select CalcWeb.war. The Confirm Values dialog appears after you choose the file.
6. Enter CalcWeb as the context root. Press OK.

The new EAR file is defined at this point, but not saved in a file. You can display its characteristics in the tool, as shown in Figure 16.22.

7. Press Apply, and then use main menu item File > Save As to save the EAR as CalcApp2.ear in a location of your choice, such as c:\temp\CalcApp2.ear, or /tmp/CalcApp2.ear.
8. Use main menu item File > Verify to verify the work. Notice that you can view the deployment descriptor from the View Descriptor option on the File menu.
9. Exit the Application Assembly Tool.

You created an EAR but it is not yet deployed to WAS. You must remember its name and location for the deployment steps in the following section.

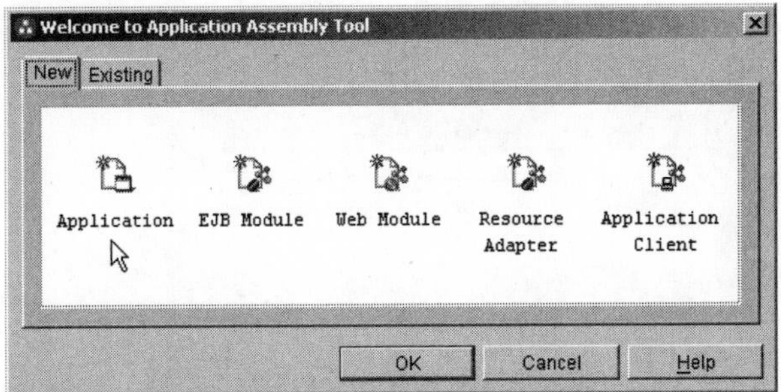

Figure 16.20 Assembly tool welcome panel.

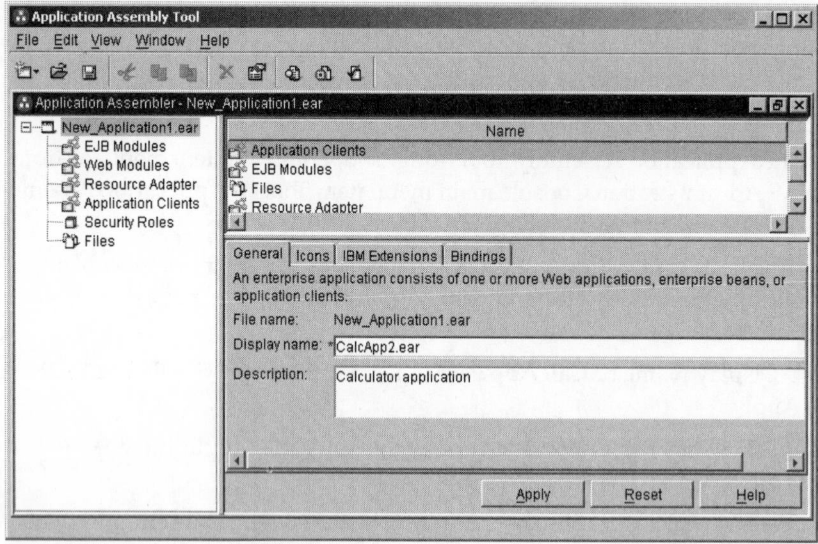

Figure 16.21 New application.

Importing to WAS

You created an enterprise application CalcApp2.ear by using the deployment tool. Now, you will deploy it to WAS by installing it from the Administrative Console.

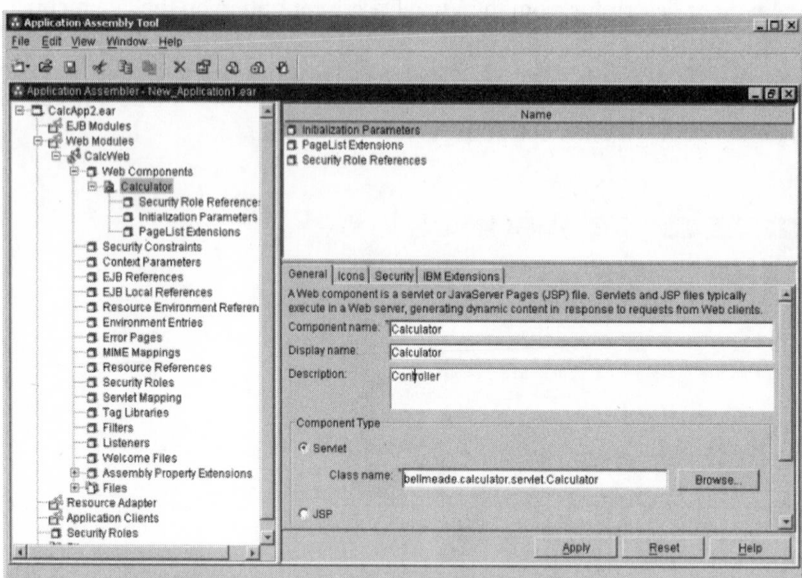

Figure 16.22 CalcApp2.ear in Application Assembly Tool.

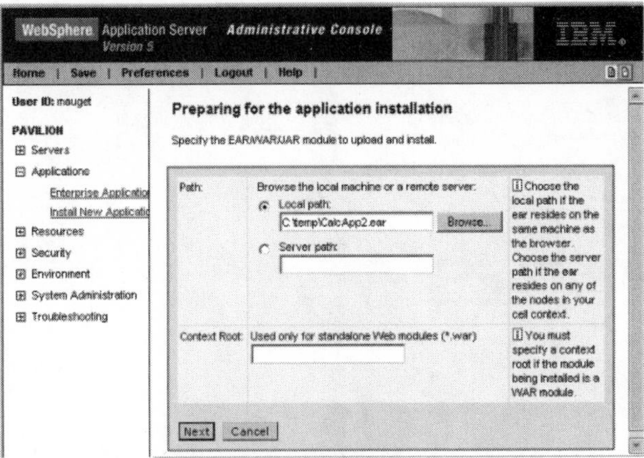

Figure 16.23 Choose Import EAR file.

1. Open the WAS Administrative Console.
2. Choose (*Server Name*) / Applications / Install New Application from the Tree view pane. The right-hand pane details the means to navigate to a local or remote archive file.
3. Browse to the CalcApp2.ear file you created in the previous section. The console should resemble Figure 16.23. Press Next three times.
4. The wizard invites you to select a module. Select CalcWeb. The console should resemble Figure 16.24. Press Next.
5. The next panel should resemble Figure 16.25, except for cell and node specifics. Select your module, and then press Next.

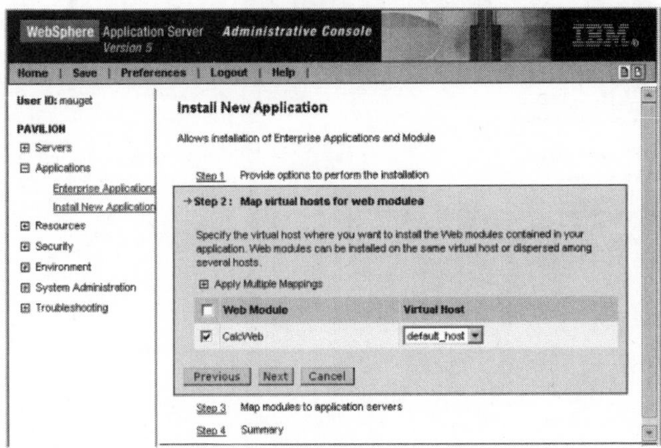

Figure 16.24 Select Web module.

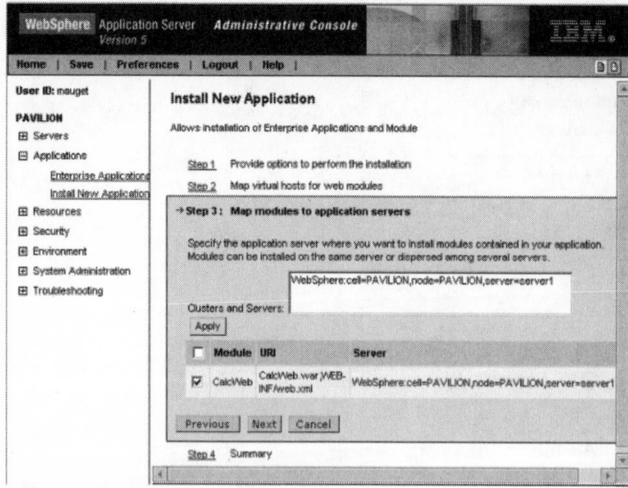

Figure 16.25 Map module to server.

6. Observe the final summary panel as shown in Figure 16.26.
7. Press Finish to carry out the deployment.
8. Although you pressed Finish, you actually are not finished. Click the link the reads Save to Master Configuration, and then press Save to update the master repository with your changes.
9. Click the Enterprise Applications link in the left-hand pane. Note that CalcApp2 appears in the list of applications shown in the right-hand pane, but that it is stopped. See Figure 16.27.

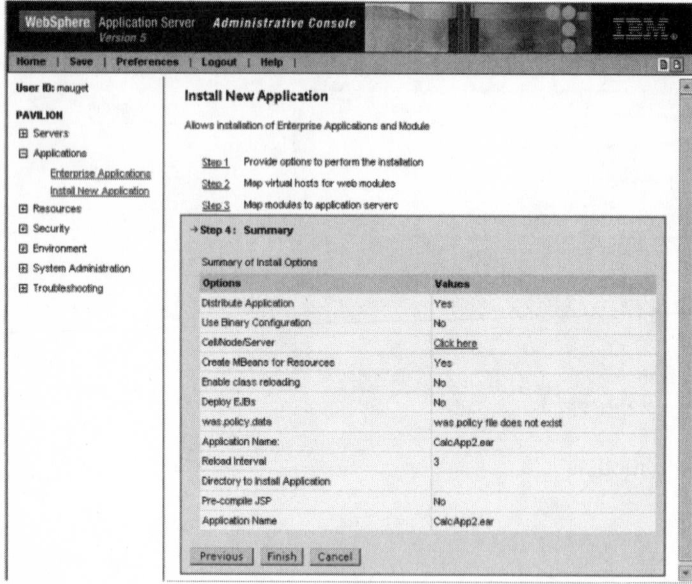

Figure 16.26 New application summary.

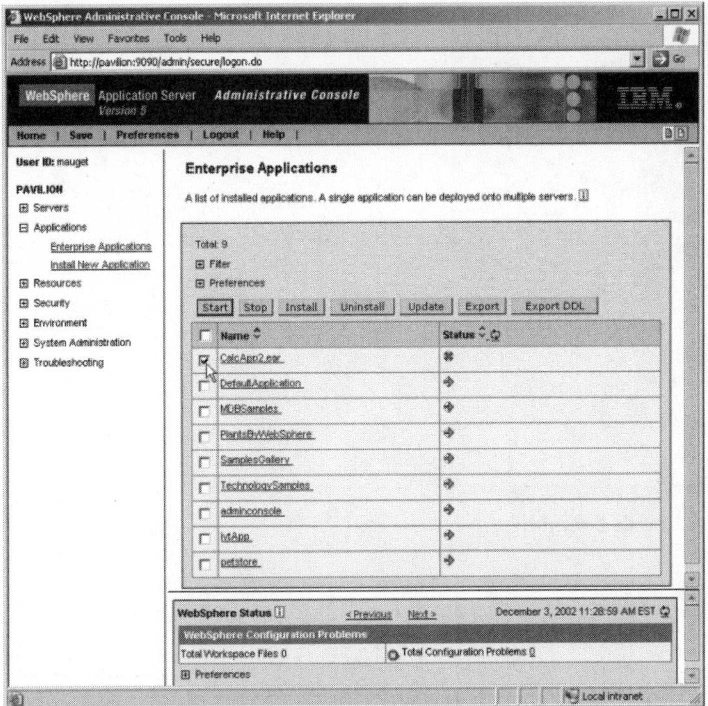

Figure 16.27 Deployed applications.

10. Select CalcApp2.ear, then press Start.

The red CalcApp2 application status will change to a green "running" indication. This means that you have successfully defined and deployed the application using WAS tools. It is ready for access.

Running Applications outside the IDE

You assembled the CalcApp2 enterprise application using the Application Assembly Tool, and then deployed it. To run the application, use a URL that addresses the WAS default host using the port number that you defined for that host. Append the context root /CalcWeb to complete the URL. For example, the URL on host netvista was http:netvista:9080/CalcWeb/ and you used a browser on another machine to run the application from that URL, as seen in Figure 16.28.

The application shown is served directly from the WAS node. Remember that the application also has a static HTML start page. It would be better to serve this page from a Web server. You use IBM Http Server. A plug-in decides what requests to forward to WAS. Choose Environment > Update Web Server Plugin from the WAS Administration Console Tree view to update the plug-in from the master configuration registry. Afterward a port 80 URL of the following form could access the application: http://pavilion/CalcWeb/.

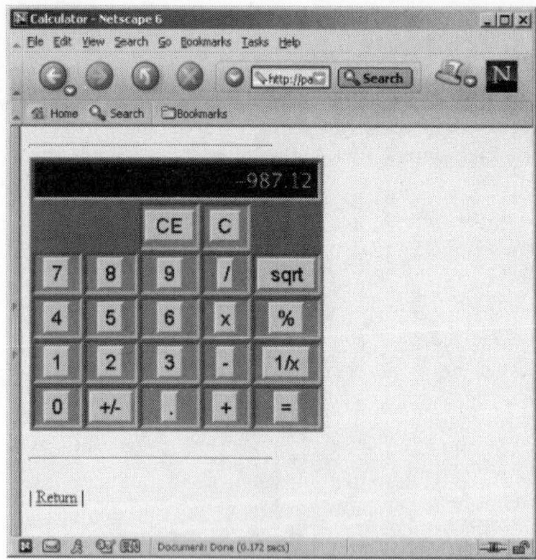

Figure 16.28 CalcApp2 hosted remotely.

Summary

J2EE defines three kinds of modules that may be separately deployed to an application server. In addition, modules may be composed into an enterprise application. WSAD provides the tools to create and test J2EE modules within its IDE. The full capabilities of the WSAD debugger are available for modules running in the test environment. In addition, WSAD can deploy modules to a remote application server or simply export and import them as archives. WAS contains an Application Assembly Tool to enable you to define modules and applications that are created by importing archives created by WSAD or other J2EE-compliant tools. This chapter covered the following items:

- Deployable archive forms
- WSAD Web and enterprise projects
- Importing WAR files into WSAD
- Web application debugging
- Exporting Web applications from WSAD
- WSAD Web application and J2EE packaging
- Testing on local and remote servers
- Exporting an EAR file from WSAD
- Defining an enterprise application in WAS
- Importing an application into WAS
- Running applications outside the WSAD IDE

We did not discuss EJB modules or enterprise client modules because we have not covered EJBs. These two kinds of modules are deployed in JAR files that may be incorporated into an EAR file. Chapter 22,"Enterprise JavaBeans," and Chapter 23, "Entity EJBs," will cover Enterprise JavaBeans, building upon concepts presented in this chapter. Meanwhile, let us move onto a discussion of layered architecture in Chapter 17, "Struts."

Struts

What's in Chapter 17?

This chapter shows you how to use the Struts framework in WSAD. It also has an overview of the Struts framework and its components. This chapter covers the following topics:

- Struts concepts
- Building a Struts application
- Testing a Struts application

This chapter takes you through the many steps to create a Struts application. You will use a number of wizards in WSAD to generate the base code for a Struts application. You will modify the generated code with the desired behavior for the application.

There are many advanced concepts associated with Struts. This chapter is an introduction to Struts, and you will make a basic Struts application. You can build on this knowledge and create more robust Struts applications.

What Is Struts?

Struts is a Java framework from the Apache group designed to make Web application programming easier. Struts combines servlet and JSPs with some special conventions that use the J2EE model two discussed in Chapter 11, "JavaServer Pages." Struts uses good model-view-controller design with tag libraries in JSP 1.1. The Struts framework provides some good conventions for implementing J2EE Web applications.

Model-View-Controller

Struts has specific components that fulfill the roles of model, view, and controller, as seen in Figure 17.1. Struts utilizes JSP files for the input and response pages. The Input page calls the Action servlet, which in turn calls the `perform()` method in the Action class, passing the ActionForm. The Action class then forwards the response to a JSP, completing the cycle.

Tag Libraries

The Struts framework relies on special tags provided in tag libraries. The libraries can be included JSP files, and they are used to reference Struts components and perform common display functions. Taglibs are referenced using a JSP page directive tag that identifies the .tld file with the desired tags. The following taglibs are part of Struts:

- struts-bean has tags for referencing JavaBeans.
- struts-html has tags for the basic HTML elements.
- struts-logic has tags for boolean operators, redirect, and forwarding.
- struts-form has tags for HTML form attributes.
- struts-template has the Put, Insert, and get tags.

The taglibs are XML files that specify the valid tags and their attributes. The taglib specifies tags and their name, tagclass, and attributes. Each attribute has a name and specifies if it is required. Following is the definition for HTML hidden tag from the struts-html taglib:

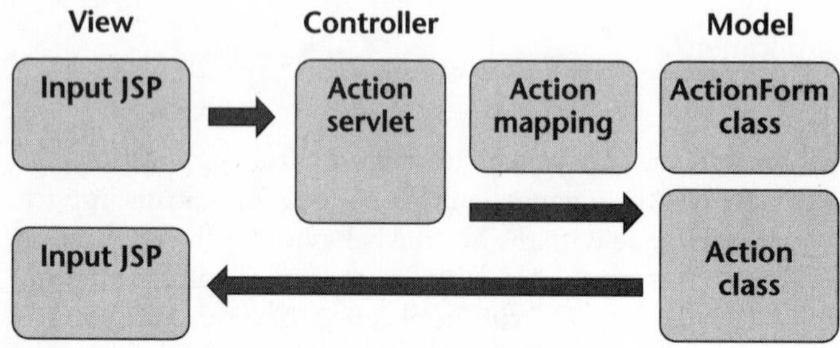

Figure 17.1 Struts model-view-controller.

```
<tag>
<name>hidden</name>
<tagclass>org.apache.struts.taglib.html.HiddenTag</tagclass>
<attribute>
<name>name</name>
<required>false</required>
<rtexprvalue>true</rtexprvalue>
</attribute>
<attribute>
<name>property</name>
<required>true</required>
<rtexprvalue>true</rtexprvalue>
</attribute>
<attribute>
<name>value</name>
<required>false</required>
<rtexprvalue>true</rtexprvalue>
</attribute>
</tag>
```

Taglibs provide English-type tags for JSPs that replace some of the awkward Java code that can be used in JSP scriptlets and expressions. You will use taglibs to build a Struts application in this chapter.

Struts Components

The Struts framework is open and extensible, and these are key reasons that it has become so popular. There are a number of components in the framework, but you need to focus on the core components to start. Struts has the following core components:

- The Action servlet acts as the controller and calls the appropriate Action class for processing requests.
- The Action class has a `perform()` method that handles requests. When processing is complete, a response is forwarded to the client.
- ActionForm holds the data for processing and is usually a JavaBean.
- Action mapping is an XML file that ties the Action class and ActionForm to the Action servlet.
- Error classes are additional utility functions that provide an easy and consistent mechanism for handling detectable errors.

There are many classes in the Struts framework. You will create a Struts project that has the struts.jar file with the framework files. Figure 17.2 shows the packages that come in the struts.jar file.

```
Web Content/WEB-INF/lib/struts.jar
    org.apache.struts.action
    org.apache.struts.actions
    org.apache.struts.digester
    org.apache.struts.taglib
    org.apache.struts.taglib.bean
    org.apache.struts.taglib.html
    org.apache.struts.taglib.logic
    org.apache.struts.taglib.template
    org.apache.struts.taglib.template.util
    org.apache.struts.upload
    org.apache.struts.util
```

Figure 17.2 Struts packages.

You are ready to start building a Struts application now that you know the basic background of the Struts framework. The next sections guide you though the many steps needed to create the five basic elements needed for a Struts application.

Building a Struts Application

WSAD has special wizards that help you develop Struts components. You will use these wizards to create a Struts application. Even though the wizards generate an application, you still need a design for the Struts application. You will build the five key components for a basic Struts application in this chapter.

The new Struts application is a simple data entry application to capture contact information for an address book. There is an input JSP, an ActionForm, an Action class, a configuration file, and a response JSP. The application will take a name, phone number, and a category for each contact. The input JSP information is passed to the Action class with the ActionForm. The response is a confirmation page, but the application code to actually save the data has been omitted. Data access topics are covered in Chapter 18, "Data Access." First, you will set up a Web project for the Struts application.

Making a Struts Project

WSAD has a wizard that makes a blank Struts project with the required libraries for the application. Make a new WSAD project with the following steps:

1. Select the menu items File > New > Project, and the New Project window appears, as shown in Figure 17.3.
2. On the New Project Window, select Examples > Web > Struts > Struts 1.02.
3. Select the Struts 1.0.2 Blank option.
4. Click the Next button, and the Web Project definition page appears, as shown in Figure 17.4.

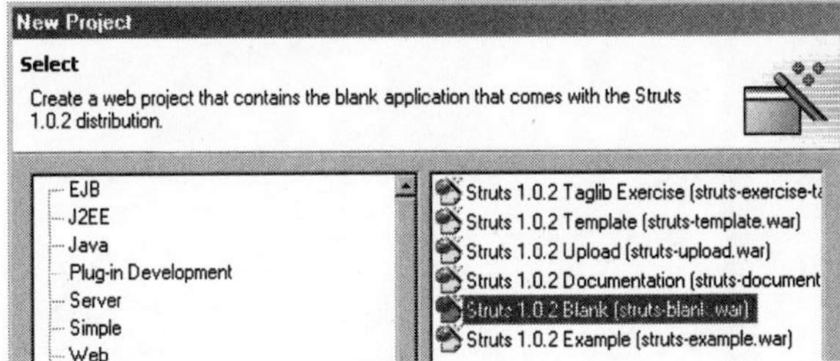

Figure 17.3 Struts project.

5. Enter **StrutsProject** for the project name.
6. Enter **StrutsProjectEAR** for the Enterprise Application project name.
7. Enter **StrutsProject** for the Context root.
8. Click the Finish button to create the Struts project.

WSAD generates the files for a blank Struts application, as shown in Figure 17.5. You may not use all of these Struts taglibs, but they are available in the project. The Libraries folder contains the struts.jar file with the Struts framework code. The struts.jar file is required to run a Struts application.

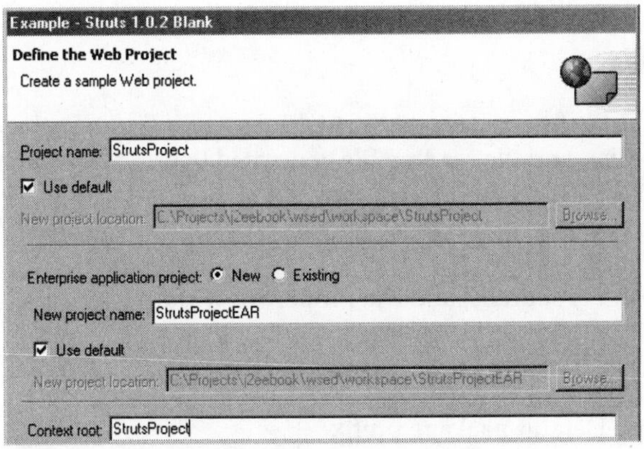

Figure 17.4 J2EE Struts project settings.

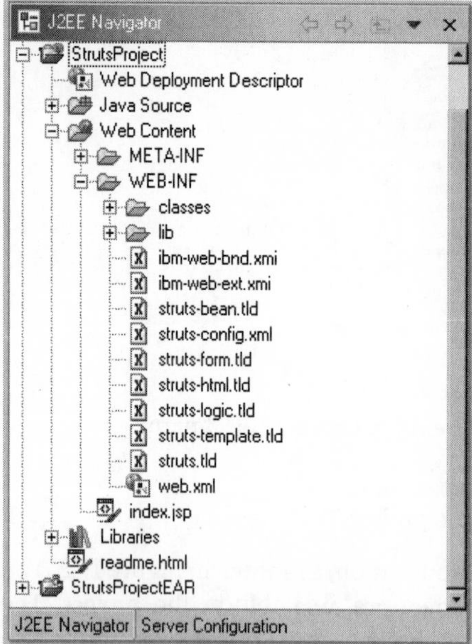

Figure 17.5 Struts files.

Struts Project Settings

There are a few items that should be changed in the StrutsProject. The StrutsProject should have a default package setting, and the readme file generated by WSAD should be deleted. Update the Struts project settings with the following steps:

1. Select the StrutsProject.
2. From the pop-up menu, select Properties, and the Properties window appears, as shown in Figure 17.6.
3. On the left panel, select Struts.
4. Enter **j2eebook.struts** for the Default package prefix.
5. Click the OK button to make this change.

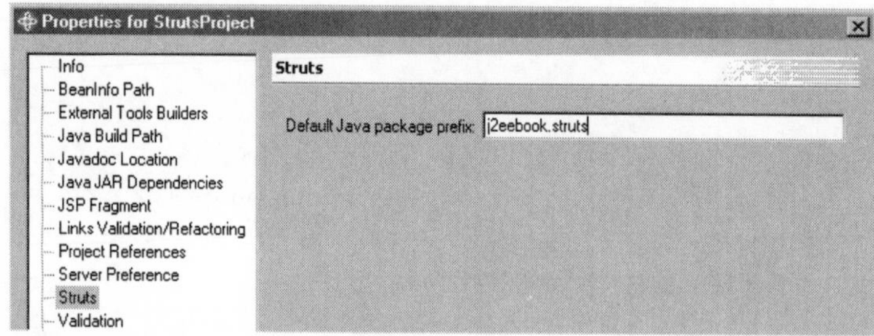

Figure 17.6 Struts package prefix.

WSAD created a readme file when it generated the new Struts application. The readme file displays after the code is generated showing Disclamer – Non-IBM Code. The readme file is not needed, so you should delete it from the Web Content folder.

Making a Configuration File

The first Struts component you will build is the Struts configuration file. WSAD copied a sample configuration file, but it will be easier to start with a new one. Make a new Struts configuration file with the following steps:

1. Delete the struts-config.xml file under the Web-INF folder.
2. Select the menu items File > New > Other.
3. Select Web > Struts > Struts Configuration File. Click the Next button to proceed.
4. The Configuration File Location window appears, as seen in Figure 17.7. Select the WEB-INF folder under the StrutsProject.
5. Click the Finish button to generate a new Struts configuration file.

The configuration file is an XML file that specifies that data sources, form beans, forwards, and action mappings for the Struts application. You can view the configuration by double-clicking the struts-config.xml file. The source code for the configuration file should look as follows:

```
<?xml version="1.0" encoding="UTF-8"?>
<!DOCTYPE struts-config PUBLIC "-//Apache Software Foundation//DTD
Struts Configuration 1.0//EN"
"http://jakarta.apache.org/struts/dtds/struts-config_1_0.dtd">
<struts-config>
    <!-- Data Sources -->
    <data-sources>
    </data-sources>
    <!-- Form Beans -->
    <form-beans>
    </form-beans>
    <!-- Global Forwards -->
    <global-forwards>
    </global-forwards>
    <!-- Action Mappings -->
    <action-mappings>
    </action-mappings>
</struts-config>
```

The next step is to make the Form bean and the Action class. Theses classes are registered in the configuration file. The WSAD wizard adds the mapping information to the Struts configuration file. You will need to save the configuration file after the wizards make these changes. Now, let's make a Struts form.

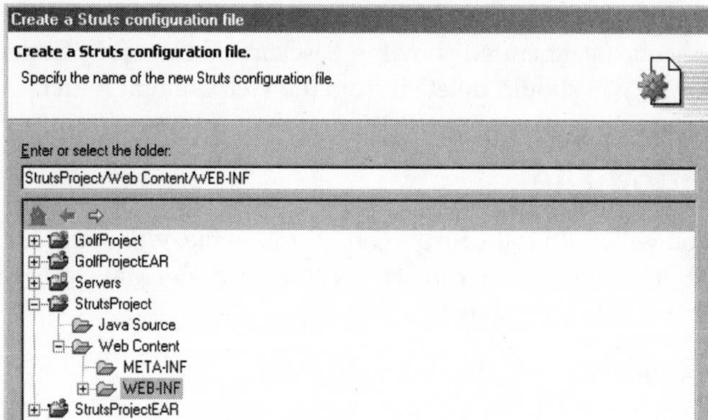

Figure 17.7 Configuration file information.

Making a Form Bean

The next Struts component you will build is Form bean. The Form bean subclasses the Struts ActionForm class and should follow the JavaBean conventions covered in Chapter 7, "Making JavaBeans." The form class is named ContactForm, and it will have three properties. Start making a Form bean with the following steps:

1. Select the Java Source folder in StrutsProject.
2. Select the menu items File > New > Other > Web > Struts, as shown in Figure 17.8.
3. Select the ActionForm Class.
4. Select the Next button to proceed.

The second page of the wizard appears, as shown in Figure 17.9. Complete the following steps:

5. Make sure that the Folder is /StrutsProject/Java Source.
6. Make sure that the package is j2eebook.struts.forms.
7. Enter **ContactForm** for the ActionForm class name.

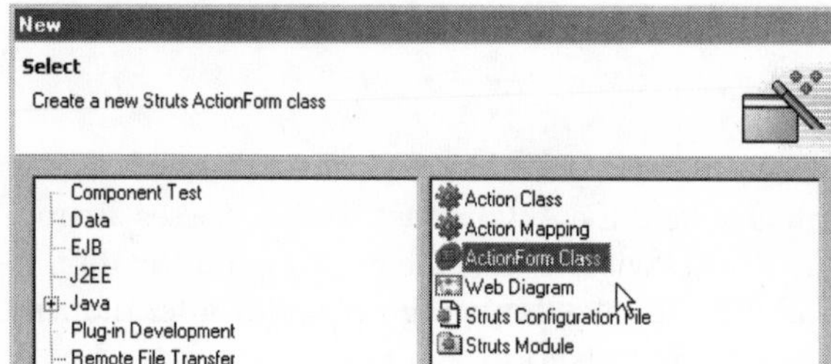

Figure 17.8 New Struts ActionForm.

8. Make sure the superclass is the ActionForm. If WSAD does not allow the ActionForm class. Then, there is a problem with the project's classpath.
9. Select constructors from superclass.
10. Click the Next button to proceed.
11. Skip the third page titled *Choose new accessors for your ActionForm class*, and click the Next button.

The new accessors page appears, as shown in Figure 17.10. This page helps you create the JavaBean Properties for the ActionForm. You will add three properties, named fullname, phone, and category, to the ActionForm. Add the three bean properties with the following steps:

12. Click the Add button, enter **fullname** for the Name, and click Add to save the property.
13. Click the Add button, enter **phone** for the Name, and click Add to save the property.
14. Click the Add button, enter **category** for the Name, and click Add to save the property.
15. Click the Next button to proceed.

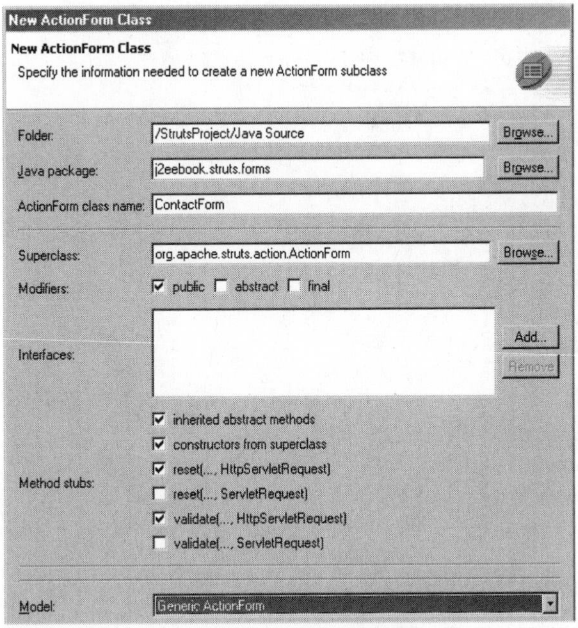

Figure 17.9 New Struts ActionForm location.

New ActionForm Class

Create new accessors for your ActionForm class

A field, getter, and setter will be created for each item you define

Name	Type
fullname	String
phone	String
category	String

Figure 17.10 Struts accessors.

The mapping page appears, as shown in Figure 17.11. This information is added to the Struts configuration file. Enter the following mapping information:

16. Select the struts-config.xml file from the drop-down list.
17. Enter **ContactForm** for the Mapping Name.
18. Click the Finish button to generate the ActionForm.

WSAD generates the ContactForm and adds its mapping to the configuration. The ContactForm has all the properties needed for the application. The wizard also creates two useful methods, namely `reset()` and `validate()`. You can add more properties and utility methods as needed. The code for the ContactForm should look as follows:

```
package j2eebook.struts.forms;
import javax.servlet.http.HttpServletRequest;
import org.apache.struts.action.ActionError;
import org.apache.struts.action.ActionErrors;
import org.apache.struts.action.ActionForm;
import org.apache.struts.action.ActionMapping;
/**
 * Form bean for a Struts application.
 * Users may access three fields on this form:
 * <ul>
 * <li>name - [your comment here]
 * <li>phone - [your comment here]
 * <li>category - [your comment here]
 * </ul>
*/
public class ContactForm extends ActionForm {
    private String name = null;
    private String phone = null;
```

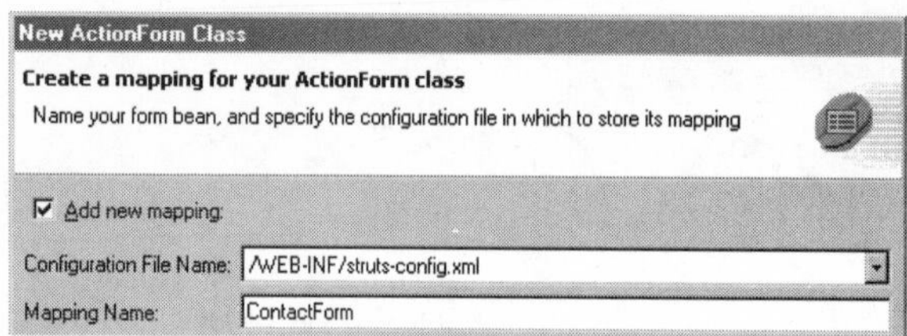

Figure 17.11 Struts mappings.

```
private String category = null;
/**
 * Get name
 * @return String
 */
public String getName() {
    return name;
}
/**
 * Set name
 * @param <code>String</code>
 */
public void setName(String n) {
    name = n;
}
/**
 * Get phone
 * @return String
 */
public String getPhone() {
    return phone;
}
/**
 * Set phone
 * @param <code>String</code>
 */
public void setPhone(String p) {
    phone = p;
}
/**
 * Get category
 * @return String
 */
public String getCategory() {
    return category;
}
/**
 * Set category
 * @param <code>String</code>
 */
public void setCategory(String c) {
    category = c;
}
/**
* Constructor
*/
public ContactForm() {
    super();
}
public void reset(ActionMapping mapping, HttpServletRequest request)
```

```
{
        // Reset values are provided as samples only.
        // Change as appropriate.
        name = null;
        phone = null;
        category = null;
    }
    public ActionErrors validate(
        ActionMapping mapping,
        HttpServletRequest request) {
        ActionErrors errors = new ActionErrors();
        // Validate the fields in your form, adding
        // adding each error to this.errors as found, e.g.
        // if ((field == null) || (field.length() == 0)) {
        //   errors.add("field", new
        // ActionError("error.field.required"));
        // }
        return errors;
    }
}
```

Making an Action Class

The next class needed for the application is an Action class that handles specific requests from the Action servlet. The wizard can help you create the Action class, then you must update the Action class with the specific Java code to handle the request.

Generating an Action Class

WSAD has a special wizard for creating an Action class. You will make an Action class called ContactAction, and then edit the class with code to store the ContactForm JavaBean in the session. Make a new Action class with the following steps:

1. Select the Java Source folder in the StrutsProject.
2. Select the menu items File > New > Other, and the Select windows appears.
3. Select Web > Struts > Action Class, and click the Next button to proceed.

The New Action Class window appears, as shown in Figure 17.12. Make the settings for the Action class as follows:

1. Make sure the Folder is /StrutsProject/Java Source.
2. Make sure the Java package is j2eebook.struts.action.

3. Enter ContactAction as the Action class name.
4. Make sure the Superclass is org.apache.struts.action.Action.
5. Make sure the default method stubs perform(..., HttpServletRequest, HttpServletResponse) and inherited abstract methods are selected.
6. Make sure the Model is Generic Action Class.
7. Click the Next button to proceed.

The mapping window appears, as shown in Figure 17.13. This page lets you specify the configuration information for the Action class. The mapping information goes in the Struts mapping file, struts-config.xml. You will add the response JSP file for the ContactAction class on this page with the following steps:

1. Click the Add button.
2. Enter **confirm** for the Name.
3. Enter **/pages/confirm.jsp** for the Path.
4. Click the Finish button to generate the Action class.

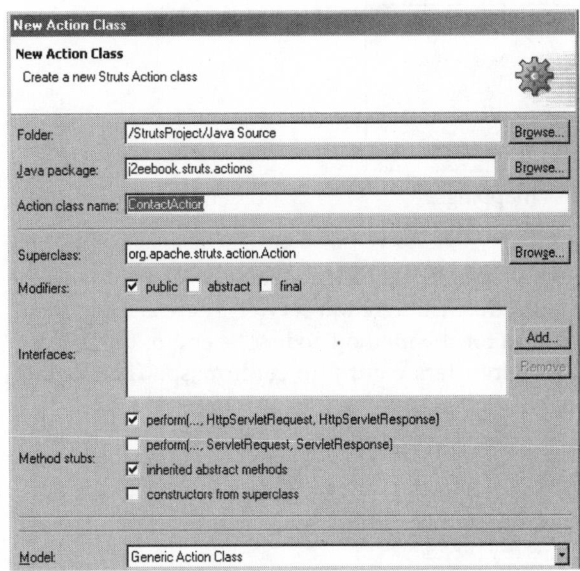

Figure 17.12 New Struts action class details.

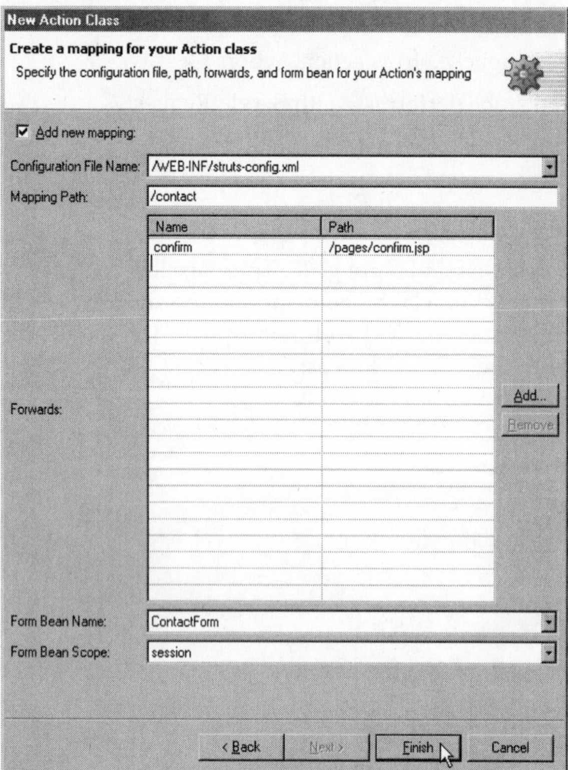

Figure 17.13 New Struts action class mappings.

WSAD generates the ContactAction class. It includes a default constructor and the `perform()` method that is called from the Struts Action servlet. There is a comment, *do something here*, indicating the location for the method code. The end of the perform method has a forward statement that transfers control to confirm.jsp. The ContactAction class should look as follows:

```
package j2eebook.struts.actions;
import java.io.IOException;
import javax.servlet.ServletException;
import javax.servlet.http.HttpServletRequest;
import javax.servlet.http.HttpServletResponse;
import org.apache.struts.action.Action;
import org.apache.struts.action.ActionError;
import org.apache.struts.action.ActionErrors;
import org.apache.struts.action.ActionForm;
import org.apache.struts.action.ActionForward;
import org.apache.struts.action.ActionMapping;
public class ContactAction extends Action {
    /**
```

```
    * Constructor
    */
    public ContactAction() {
        super();
    }
    public ActionForward perform(
        ActionMapping mapping,
        ActionForm form,
        HttpServletRequest request,
        HttpServletResponse response)
        throws IOException, ServletException {
        ActionErrors errors = new ActionErrors();
        ActionForward forward = new ActionForward();
        // return value
        try {
            // do something here
        } catch (Exception e) {
            // Report the error using the appropriate name and ID.
            errors.add("name", new ActionError("id"));
        }
        // If a message is required, save the specified key(s)
        // into the request for use by the <struts:errors> tag.
        if (!errors.empty()) {
            saveErrors(request, errors);
        }
        // Write logic determining how the user should be forwarded.
        forward = mapping.findForward("confirm");
        // Finish with
        return (forward);
    }
}
```

Adding Logic to the Action Class

The ContactAction needs to store the ContactForm in the Session. It can be helpful to put a message in the console showing that the ContactAction has executed. This can be done in a couple of lines of Java code. Add the following code to the ContactAction class in the try/catch block replacing the comment do something here:

```
HttpSession session = request.getSession(true);
session.setAttribute("contactform", form);
System.out.println("ContactAction processed");
```

Save this change to the ContactAction class. You would add code to save the entries to a database in this section. This sample does not include the code to save the contacts, rather it is intended to introduce the Struts framework and how to use Struts in WebSphere. The next step is to verify the settings in the Struts configuration file.

Verifying the Struts Configuration

The Struts configuration file is key to linking the Struts components together. Review the updated struts-config.xml file, and save the code. This is a very important step. Some of the WSAD tools cannot see the ContactForm or the ContactAction if you do not save the updated configuration file. You can edit the file to fix errors or use the editors to register ActionForms or Action classes that you code by hand. The Struts configuration file should look as follows:

```
<?xml version="1.0" encoding="UTF-8"?>
<!DOCTYPE struts-config PUBLIC "-//Apache Software Foundation//DTD
Struts Configuration 1.0//EN"
"http://jakarta.apache.org/struts/dtds/struts-config_1_0.dtd">
<struts-config>
    <!-- Data Sources -->
    <data-sources></data-sources>
    <!-- Form Beans -->
        <form-beans>
        <form-bean name="ContactForm"
         type="j2eebook.struts.forms.ContactForm"></form-bean>
    </form-beans>
<!-- Global Forwards -->
    <global-forwards></global-forwards>
    <!-- Action Mappings -->
    <action-mappings>
        <action path="/ContactAction"
         type="j2eebook.struts.actions.ContactAction" name="ContactForm"
         scope="session">
           <forward name="confirm" path="/pages/confirm.jsp"></forward>
        </action>
    </action-mappings>
</struts-config>
```

Making an Input Page

There are two more components to build for the application, namely the input and response JSP pages. WSAD has a special wizard that helps you create the input JSP file for a Struts application. You will create an input JSP page that has textfields for the ContactForm attributes on an HTML form. A Submit button calls the Struts Action servlet and passes the values to the server. Create the input form with the following steps:

1. First create a folder named **pages** under the Web Content folder. This folder holds the JSPs pages in a common location.
2. Select the **pages** folder that you just created.
3. Select the menu items File > New > JSP file, and the new JSP window appears, as seen in Figure 17.14.

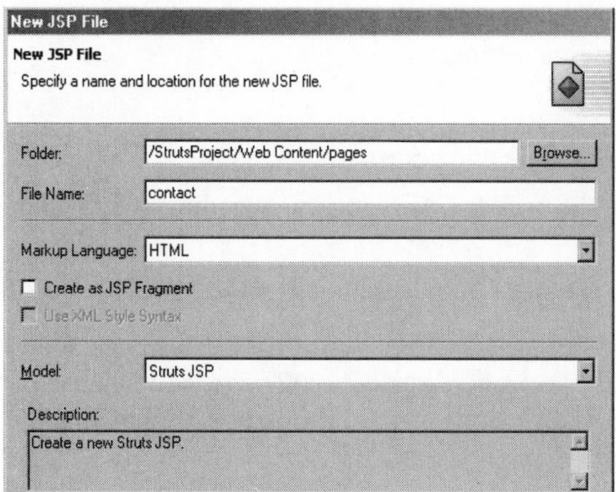

Figure 17.14 New Input JSP.

4. Make sure that the Folder is /StrutsProject/Web Content/pages.
5. Enter **contact** for the File Name.
6. The Markup Language should be **HTML**.
7. Select **Struts JSP** for the Model. This option provides the additional wizard pages for a Struts JSP.
8. Click the Next button to proceed.

The Struts tag library page appears, as shown in Figure 17.15. The JSP will use the struts-html library, but it does not need the struts-bean tag library for this page. Remove it with the following steps:

1. Select the struts-bean.tld tag library.
2. Click the Remove button, and the tag library is removed from the list.
3. Click Next to proceed.

New JSP File
New JSP File
Select any Tag Libraries you want to be included in the generated page.
Choose any additional Tag Libraries you want to import

Prefix	URI
html	/WEB-INF/struts-html.tld
bean	/WEB-INF/struts-bean.tld

Add Tag Library...
Remove

Figure 17.15 Tag libraries.

The page directive information page appears, as shown in Figure 17.16. There is no error page for this JSP. Make the following settings:

1. Deselect the Error Page checkbox.
2. Click the Next button on the page directive information page.
3. Click the Next button and skip the page for changing the encoding and content type.
4. Click the Next button and skip the page for generating method stubs.

The Form Field Selection page appears, as shown in Figure 17.17. This page allows you to select an ActionForm and select the properties for the JSP page. You will use the ContactForm and select the fullname, phone, and category properties for the JSP page. Set the fields with the following steps:

1. Select the **ContactForm** for the Form bean entry.
2. Enter **ContactForm** for the Bean name.
3. Enter **/ContractAction** for the Action.
4. Highlight the three properties **category**, **fullname**, and **phone**. These properties must be highlighted for them to be used in the JSP.
5. Click the Next button to proceed.

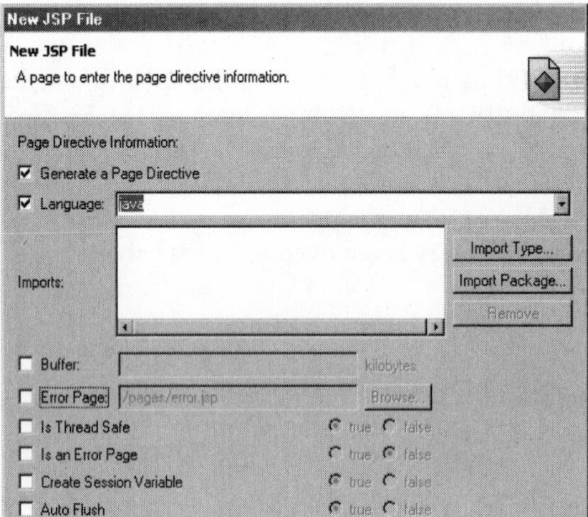

Figure 17.16 Page directive settings.

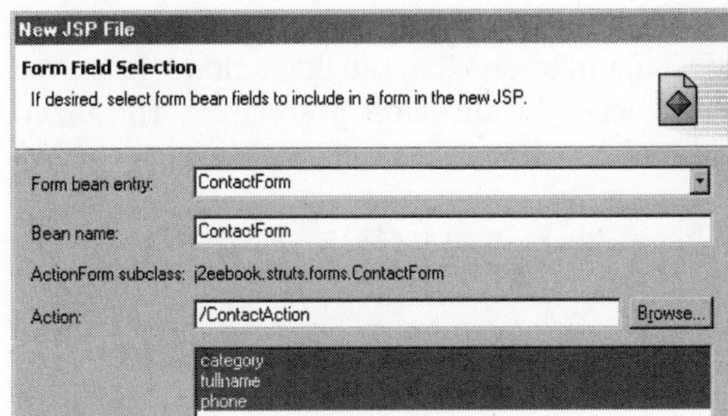

Figure 17.17 Form field selection.

The Design the Form page appears, as shown in Figure 17.18. This page lets you modify the attributes for the textfields that will be generated for the JSP. You will change the order of the properties and modify the labels for each of the properties. Make the following settings:

1. Change the order of the properties to be fullname, phone, and category.
2. Edit the Label for fullname so that it is **Full Name**:.
3. Edit the Label for phone so that it is **Phone**:.
4. Edit the Label for category so that it is **Category**.
5. Click the Finish button to generate the input JSP file.

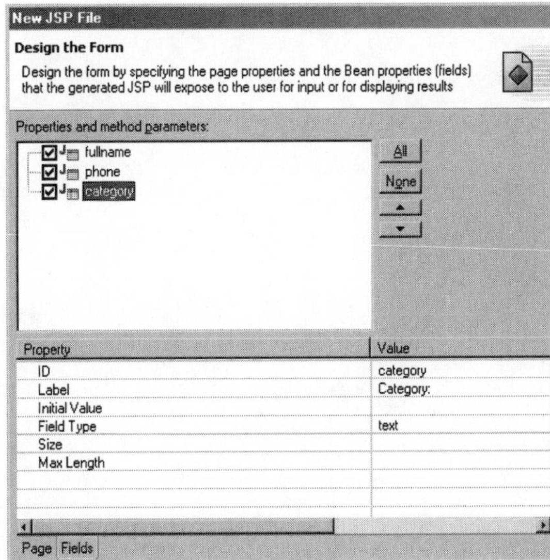

Figure 17.18 Attribute settings.

WSAD generated the initial code for the input page. The page includes textfields for each of the ActionForm properties and a Submit button that call the Action servlet. You will need to make a few changes to the generated code before proceeding. The generated code for the contact.jsp file should look as follows:

```
<!DOCTYPE HTML PUBLIC "-//W3C//DTD HTML 4.01 Transitional//EN">
<%@ taglib uri="/WEB-INF/struts-html.tld" prefix="html" %>
<html:html>
<HEAD>
<%@ page language="java"
contentType="text/html; charset=ISO-8859-1" %>
<META http-equiv="Content-Type" content="text/html; charset=ISO-8859-1">
<META name="GENERATOR" content="IBM WebSphere Studio">
<TITLE>contact.jsp</TITLE>
</HEAD>
<BODY>
<html:form action="/ContactAction">
    <TABLE border="0">
        <TBODY>
            <TR>
                <TH>Full Name:</TH>
                <TD><html:text property='fullname' value='' /></TD>
            </TR>
            <TR>
                <TH>Phone Number:</TH>
                <TD><html:text property='phone' value='' /></TD>
            </TR>
            <TR>
                <TH>Category:</TH>
                <TD><html:text property='category' value='' /></TD>
            </TR>
            <TR>
                <TD><html:submit property="submit"
                     value="Submit" /></TD>
                <TD><html:reset /></TD>
            </TR>
        </TBODY>
    </TABLE>
</html:form>
</BODY>
</html:html>
```

Updating the input Page

The input page has the basic elements that you need, but the code needs to be updated. You will change the JSP so that it looks like Figure 17.19. The page needs a title, the labels need to be left-aligned, and the category input should use a drop-down listbox. Make these changes with the following steps:

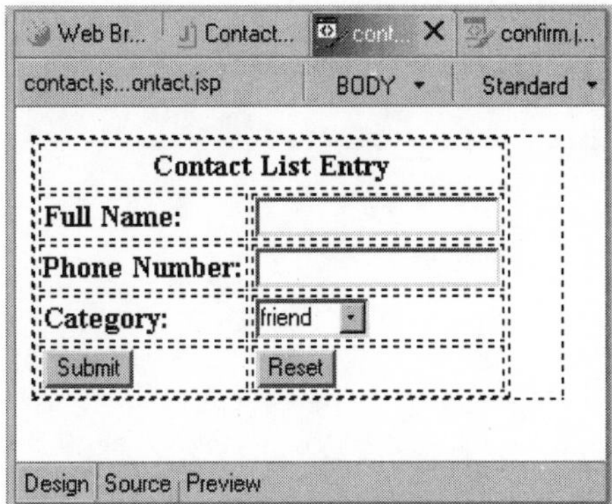

Figure 17.19 Struts input page.

1. Add the alignment tag align="left" to the three <td> columns.
2. Add new row to the top of the table.
3. Add a table heading <th> with text Contact List Entry.
4. Change the category textfield to a select list with the options friend, family, and business. Save the changes.

Theses changes don't change how the JSP works, they improve how it looks. The completed contact.jsp should look as follows:

```
<BODY>
<html:form action="/ContactAction">
  <TABLE border="0">
    <TBODY>
      <TR>
        <TH colspan="2">Contact List Entry</TH>
      </TR>
      <TR>
        <TH align="left">Full Name:</TH>
        <TD><html:text property='fullname' value='' /></TD>
      </TR>
      <TR>
        <TH align="left">Phone Number:</TH>
        <TD><html:text property='phone' value='' /></TD>
      </TR>
       <TR>
         <TH align="left">Category:</TH>
         <TD><html:select property='category' value=''>
             <html:option value='friend'>friend
             </html:option>
             <html:option value='family'>family
             </html:option>
             <html:option value='business'>business
             </html:option>
```

```
                </html:select></TD>
          </TR>
        <TR>
          <TD><html:submit property="submit" value="Submit" /></TD>
          <TD><html:reset /></TD>
        </TR>
      </TBODY>
    </TABLE>
  </html:form>
  </BODY>
  </html:html>
```

Making a Response Page

The last piece of the puzzle is the response page. The response page is named confirm.jsp, as entered in the Action class. The response page will display a simple confirmation message that includes the contact name that was entered on the input page. The response page could be much more intricate, but this chapter is focused on demonstrating how Struts works. Make a response JSP with the following steps:

1. Select the **pages** folder.
2. Select the menu items File > New > JSP File, and the new JSP File window appears, as shown in Figure 17.20.
3. Make sure the Folder is /StrutsProject/Web Content/pages.
4. Enter **confirm** for the File Name.
5. Make sure the Markup Language is HTML.
6. Make sure the Model is **None**.
7. Click the Next button to proceed.
8. The tag library page appears. This response page does not need any special tags. Remove the two libraries, as shown in Figure 17.21.
9. Click the Finish button to generate the JSP.

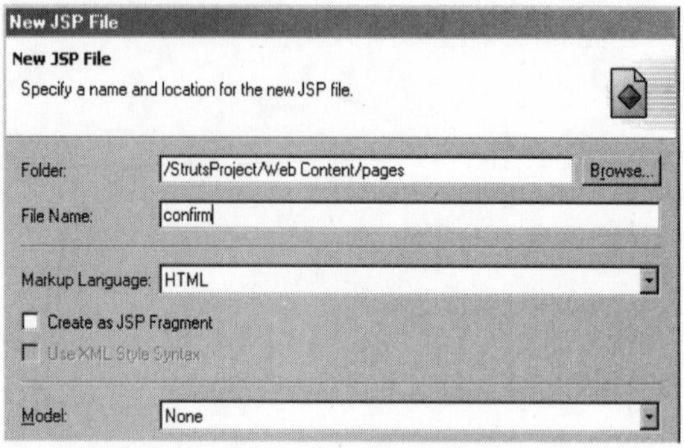

Figure 17.20 JSP response settings.

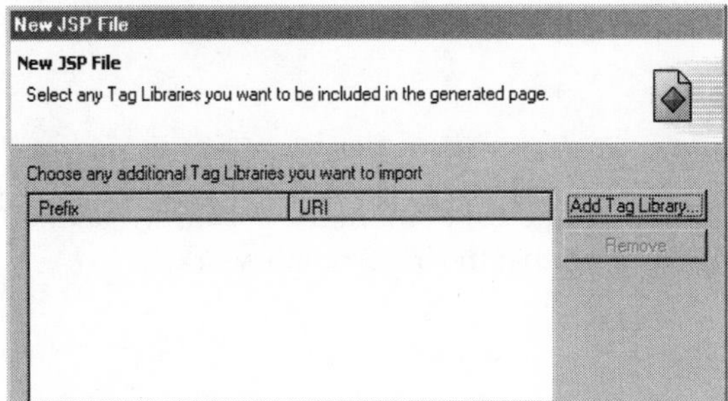

Figure 17.21 Response tag libraries.

The generated JSP file has some placeholder text and needs a few items. You will add the ContactForm bean to the page and a confirmation message that displays the contact name that was entered on the input page. Make these changes with the following steps:

1. On the Design tab, drag and drop a ContactForm bean to the confirm.jsp.
2. Edit the HTML source and add the attribute `id="contactform"` to the useBean tag.
3. Add the attribute `scope="session"` to the useBean tab.
4. Add a link back to the contact.jsp to the bottom of the JSP with the following code:

```
<A href="/StrutsProject/pages/contact.jsp">Add another contact</A>
```

5. Replace the placeholder text with the following line that displays a confirmation message and the fullname attribute from the ContactForm bean:

```
<P>Contact <jsp:getProperty name="contactform" property="fullname" />
added to list</P>
```

Save these changes to the confirm.jsp, and it should look as follows:

```
<!DOCTYPE HTML PUBLIC "-//W3C//DTD HTML 4.01 Transitional//EN">
<HTML>
<HEAD>
<%@ page language="java" contentType="text/html;
charset=ISO-8859-1" %>
<META http-equiv="Content-Type" content="text/html; charset=ISO-8859-1">
<META name="GENERATOR" content="IBM WebSphere Studio">
<TITLE>confirm.jsp</TITLE>
</HEAD>
  <BODY>
  <jsp:useBean id="contactform"
class="j2eebook.struts.forms.ContactForm" scope="session"></jsp:useBean>
  <P>Contact <jsp:getProperty name="contactform" property="fullname" />
  added to list</P>
  <P><BR>
  <A href="/StrutsProject/pages/contact.jsp">Add another contact</A>
```

```
    </P>
    </BODY>
  </HTML>
```

The next step is testing that all these Struts components work together. If you have problems, try debugging the Action class with a breakpoint in the perform() method. Remember to start the server in debug mode so that the breakpoints work.

Testing Struts

You can test the Struts application now that all the components are complete. All the Struts runtime files are already in the project, so there are no modifications needed to run the test. You will run the input page on the test server, enter data, and submit the form for processing. Test the Struts application with the following steps:

1. Select the contact.jsp file.
2. Select Run on Server...
3. The server Selection appears, as shown in Figure 17.22. Select the Test Server by clicking the OK button.

The contact.jsp file appears, as shown in Figure 17.23. Test the Struts application with the following steps:

1. Enter a name.
2. Enter a phone number.
3. Select a category.
4. Click the Submit button.

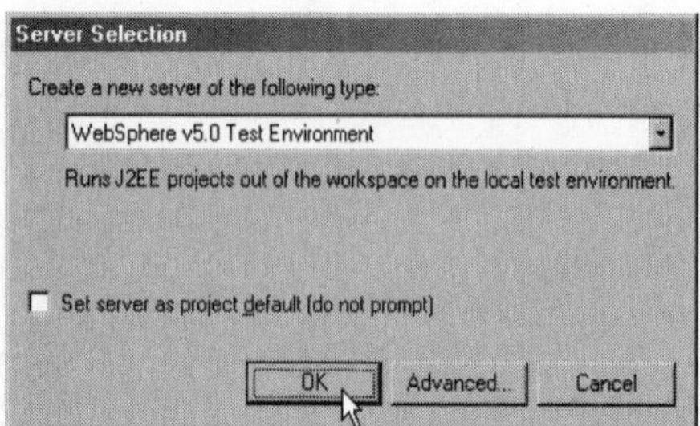

Figure 17.22 Server selection message.

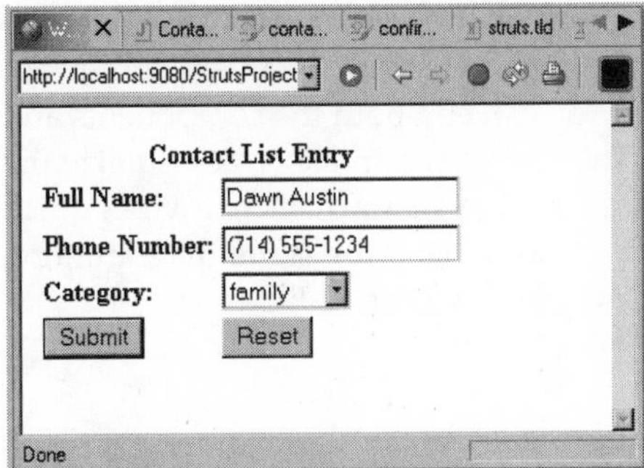

Figure 17.23 Contact.jsp input.

The Action class is called and the ActionForm is added to the session. The response is forwarded to the confirmation page that appears, as seen in Figure 17.24. It is a simple application, but it has the basic elements for a Struts application. You can select the link on the confirmation page and the initial contact entry page appears. This completes the basic Struts application. There are a lot of enhancements that can be made to this application such as error handling, persistence, and user interface improvements.

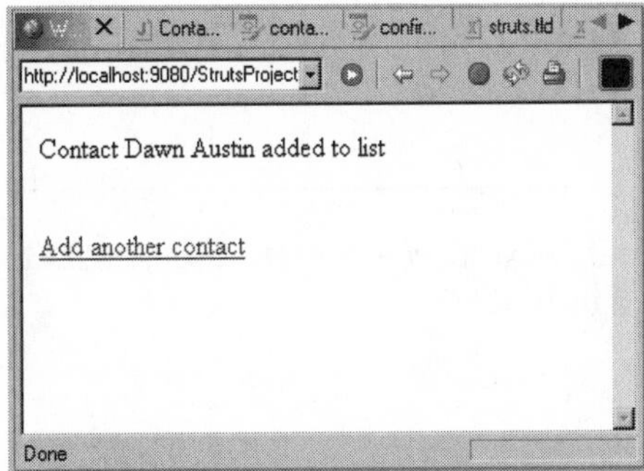

Figure 17.24 Confirm.jsp response.

The Web Diagram Tool

WSAD has another tool that helps you develop Struts applications with a Web diagram. The tool that makes Web diagrams is a lot like the VisualAge for Java Visual Composition Editor. The tool is a graphical editor that provides a free-form surface on which to place Struts components, as shown in Figure 17.25. Components can be Web pages, Action classes, ActionForms, JavaBeans, or Web applications. Components placed on the free-form surface that are not implemented appear gray and blurry. When the components are implemented their icon becomes colorful and clear. You can make visual connections that represent relationships between the components.

It is easy to make a Web diagram. You can create a new Web diagram file in the project with the Struts application. You can add Struts components to the free-form surface and draw connections using the pop-up menu. You can edit both the components and the connections using the Web diagram tool. The Web diagram lets you visualize the different components in a Struts application and how they relate. It also provides quick access for editing the components. It would be nice to have the same diagramming function for other J2EE Web applications that include servlets and EJBs.

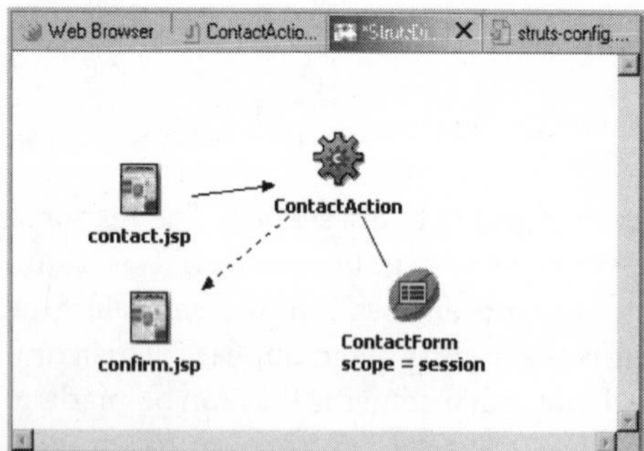

Figure 17.25 Web diagram.

Summary

This chapter described the Struts concepts and showed you how to use WSAD to develop Struts applications. The topics covered include:

- Struts concepts
- Building a Struts application by creating:
  - A configuration file
  - An ActionForm
  - An Action class
  - An input JSP
  - A response JSP
- Testing a Struts application

The wizards in WSAD make it easy to create new Struts applications. The Action class and ActionForm are automatically registered in the Struts configuration file. You can test and debug a Struts application just like any other J2EE application. There is more information on Struts at http://jakarta.apache.org/struts/index.html.

Data Access

What's in Chapter 18?

Most business applications rely heavily on persistent structured data. The relational data model has a huge installed base. There are several ways to access this kind of data using Java. JDBC is the most popular, but applications usually use higher-level layers to access JDBC. In this chapter, we discuss how to:

- Use raw JDBC
- Work with a database in WSAD
- Use the SQL Builder or the SQL wizard to create SQL statements
- Export a data definition to a database
- Execute SQL statements in the Data Perspective
- Generate a JavaBean from an SQL statement
- Create an application that uses an SQL JavaBean

The relational data model has existed since 1970, before the wide emergence of object-oriented programming. This model forms data relationships by joining tables at common columns. On the other hand, object models form relationships through inheritance and aggregation. Much of today's data manipulation occurs in object-oriented applications such as Java-based implementations, yet the persistent form of this data often resides in a relational database management system (RDBMS) or in hierarchical DBMS such as IBM's IMS.

WSAD enables you to write classes that use JDBC directly, or it can generate wrappers for SQL statements. The Data Perspective presents an SQL Builder to help build and test schemata and complex SQL statements, and then generate access classes from them. An SQL wizard enables us to build SQL statements for any kind of project. WSAD can import or export database definitions to or from an operational database. We will discuss JDBC at a high level in this chapter, and then build a data project that will lead into the next chapter about using data at the presentation layer.

JDBC Overview

The J2SE SDK supplies JDBC in package java.sql. JDBC resembles a Java rendition of *Object Database Connectivity* (ODBC), first promoted by Microsoft in the 1990s. JDBC is a thin Java wrapper for SQL. It uses a driver class for each RDMS. It even has drivers for ODBC, extending the range of implementations available. JDBC does not hide SQL from its API. The current level is JDBC 2.0 as part of J2EE. It extends the API to hide more of SQL, but JDBC remains squarely an API pinned to RDBMS technology. It isn't abstract enough to easily adapt to manipulating data stores that don't use SQL, such as messaging models.

We discuss JDBC basics here. A JDBC client follows these general steps to access a database:

1. Load a JDBC driver class for the target RDBMS.
2. Obtain an active Connection object to the database.
3. Create one or more Statement objects or PreparedStatement objects from the Connection. Optionally set parameter values in a PreparedStatement.
4. Issue `executeUpdate()` or `executeQuery()` on a Statement object or PreparedStatment.
5. If desired, use `executeQuery()` to process rows from the returned ResultSet object.
6. Close all statements and the Connection object when finished.

JDBC 2 adds SQL 3 data types such as pooled connection support, batch updates, scrollable result sets, disconnected row sets, and programmatically updatable record sets. These optional extensions offer choices in the way you process data, but the general flow remains. The following sections offer brief code examples of the major steps. JDBC classes reside in the J2SE package named java.sql. The package named javax.sql contains standard JDBC extensions, including connection pooling and distributed transaction classes.

JDBC Driver

The top-level object in a JDBC application is an instance of the proper driver class for the given RDBMS. The following statement loads the Cloudscape driver bundled with WebSphere Application Server V5.0:

```
Class.forName("com.ibm.db2j.jdbc.DB2jDriver";
```

The following statement loads an ODBC driver:

```
Class.forName("sun.jdbc.odbc.JdbcOdbcDriver");
```

Naturally, the performance and portability of the application depend on the JDBC driver implementation. There are four classifications of driver, as shown in Table 18.1.

In the previous example snippets, the Cloudscape driver is a type four driver. The ODBC driver is a type one driver.

Connection

JDBC operations require a Connection object obtained from the JCBC driver manager. The driver manager requires a vendor-dependent JDBC URL that describes the location of the database. It carries out optional authentication with optionally specified user account and password parameters. The following is a typical example:

```
Connection con = DriverManager.getConnection(url, "id", "pw");
```

If the RDBMS installation accepts anonymous connections the overloaded call is:

```
Connection con = DriverManager.getConnection(url);
```

Table 18.1 JDBC Driver Types

TYPE	DESCRIPTION
One	A bridge to an ODBC driver. ODBC native binary must be present at client. DBMS native binary must usually be loaded on client.
Two	Driver uses hybrid Java and native code. Some native binary code must be loaded on client.
Three	Java-based driver uses DBMS-independent network protocol to access DBMS network API. The most flexible kind of driver since most vendors provide network connection.
Four	Java-based driver uses DBMS protocol directly. High performance, but dependent upon vendor supplying driver for proprietary native protocol.

The vendor-specfic URL format is:

```
jdbc:<dbms name>:<db locator>
```

For example, a Cloudscape database named EmployeeDB would be located by the URL that follows:

```
jdbc:db2j:EmployeeDB;create=true
```

Notice that this vendor accepts extra parameters following the database name. Here, the Cloudscape database is created in the current directory if it does not exist.

Statement

It is necessary to use a Statement object or a PreparedStatement object to access the database. Create a statement from an open Connection object as follows:

```
Statement stm = con.createStatement();
```

Then, you may issue any of the method calls shown in Table 18.2 on the statement.

An RDBMS has a notion for a reusable precompiled statement. JDBC models this as a PreparedStatement object. If you need to execute a statement many times, perhaps using different column values, a PreparedStatement is appropriate to improve performance. For instance, a mass data insert operation could be implemented using a PreparedStatement created from an open Connection object.

```
String sql = "INSERT INTO EMPLOYEE (EMPID, NAME, DEPT, EMAIL)
             VALUES(?, ?, ?, ?)";
PreparedStatement pstm = con.prepareStatement(sql);
```

Table 18.2 Statement Execute Methods

METHOD	RETURN	DESCRIPTION
execute(String sql)	boolean	Executes an SQL statement that may return multiple results. Returns true if the next result is a ResultSet object, or false if it is an update count or there are no more results.
executeBatch()	int[ ]	Submits a batch of commands to the database for execution. Returns an array of update counts. Available since Java 1.3.
executeQuery(String sql)	ResultSet	Executes an SQL statement that returns a single ResultSet object that contains the data produced by the given query. Never returns null.

Table 18.2 *(continued)*

METHOD	RETURN	DESCRIPTION
executeUpdate(String sql)	int	Executes an SQL INSERT, UPDATE, or DELETE statement or an SQL statement that returns nothing. Returns either the affected row count for INSERT, UPDATE, or DELETE statements, or 0 for SQL statements that return nothing.

The SQL statement used to create the object can use "?" parameter markers in place of values. Then you would use PreparedStatement `setXxxx()` methods to set values before executing the PreparedStatement. These methods take an index of the value position and a typed value as parameters. The index base is one, not zero. There is a method for each data type accepted by JDBC.

All of the execute methods used by the Statement are accepted by class PreparedStatement. There are also no-argument overloads for the `execute()`, `executeUpdate()`, and `executeQuery()` methods, because the PreparedStatement often already contains the prepared SQL statement.

Result Set

JDBC 2.0 enhanced the options available for a ResultSet returned by an `executeQuery()` method, but the core function represents a group of rows returned by an SQL query. JDBC uses an SQL cursor to scroll forward through the ResultSet, producing each row for processing in turn. It is helpful to think of the ResultSet as containing all of the results, but each row could actually be fetched just in time as its turn arrives. The snippet that follows displays the name of each employee from an EMPLOYEE table.

```
ResultSet rs = stm.executeQuery("SELECT * FROM EMPLOYEE");
while (rs.next()) {
    System.out.println("Name: " + rs.getString(2));
}
```

The ResultSet class has many `getXxxx` methods other than `getString()`, but `getString()` always returns a string from any column type. These accessors take a column number as a parameter. The origin is one. If you don't like retrieving values by index, the `getXxxx()` methods are overloaded to accept the column name string instead, but this takes somewhat more processing.

Metadata

JDBC provides a metadata API that provides data about a database or query results. This promotes late bound, flexible applications at the expense of some extra processing. JDBC metadata is like a Java reflection API for a database. The class DatabaseMetaData provides information about the database.

The ResultSetMetaData class provides information about a given ResultSet object such as column count. You could use the `getColumnCount()` method in conjunction with `getString()` to display all of the data values in a row without knowing the column names or types. If the column type is important, the `getColumntType()` method will supply it. The `getColumntTypeName()` returns the RDBMS name for the type. If you need to display column heading names, `getColumntName()` returns a column name, given a column index. See the JDBC API documentation for information about ResultSetMetaData methods.

Exceptions and Warnings

Many JDBC methods throw java.sql.SQLException. It has three descendents, making four exceptions defined in JDBC. See Table 18.3.

SQL warnings are attached to the offending method's object when the SQLWarning exception is thrown. You can use the object's `getSQLWarning()` method to obtain any associated SQLWarning exception object. This object has `getMessage()`, `getSQLState()`, and `getErrorCode()` methods that each return a string having the indicated kind of information. See the J2SE API for more information about these values. Multiple SQLWarning objects could be linked. Each has a getNextWarning() method.

Transactions

A DBMS handles transactions automatically, but most DBMS can be set to allow explicit control by the client. This may be useful when you need to update two databases in one transaction, and you are not using a distributed transaction monitor. Use a `setAutoCommit(false)` method call on the Connection object to take control of transaction management. When you wish to give control back to the DBMS, you issue `setAutoCommit(true)` against the Connection object. Use the Connection object methods `commit()` or `rollback()` to complete or abort the transaction.

Table 18.3 JDBC java.sql Exceptions

EXCEPTION	DESCRIPTION
SQLException	Provides information on a database access error or other errors. Extends java.lang.Exception.
SQLWarning	Provides information on database access warnings. Extends SQLException.
BatchUpdateException	An error occurred during a batch update operation. Extends SQLException. Since JDBC 2.0.
DataTruncation	JDBC unexpectedly truncated a data value. Extends SQLWarning.

Stored Procedures

Most DBMS support precompiled procedures stored within the database itself for better performance. Rows do not flow across the network or IPC mechanism used by the DBMS API. The disadvantage is that vendor implementations vary.

To publish a stored procedure using JDBC, you usually may create a procedure in a string, and then issue `executeUpdate()` against a Statement object, passing the string that contains the procedure text.

You call a stored procedure from JDBC using a third kind of statement object class named CallableStatement. The following snippet shows the general idea. The parameter format used is vendor dependent.

JDBC 2.0

The JDBC 2.0 API adds the following functions:

- Scroll forward and backward in a result set or position to a given row.
- Update tables using Java methods instead of SQL commands.
- Send multiple SQL statements to a database in a batch.
- Give columns SQL3 data types.

In particular, a scrollable result set enables an application to browse to any row under user control. Another use is to position to a row to update it.

Standard Extension

The `javax.sql` package implements a standard extension to the Java programming language. It provides the features in Table 18.4.

Table 18.4 JDBC Standard Extension

FEATURE	DESCRIPTION
Rowsets	A JavaBean that encapsulates rows from a result set. It may be disconnected from the DBMS.
JNDI Names for Databases	Connect to a database using a published logical name from a JNDI service. Eliminates hard-coding deployable enterprise components.
Connection Pooling	A cache of reusable open database connections. Mitigates the considerable overhead in creating and destroying connections.
Distributed Transaction Support	Supports Java Transaction API two-phase commit. Enables Enterprise JavaBeans to use JDBC.

JDBC Example

Let us create an example of JDBC. Use the following steps:

1. Create a project in WSAD named JdbcDemo having a package named `com.xyz.demo`.
2. Place db2j.jar on the Java Build Path in the JdbcDemo project properties.
3. Click the Libraries tab, press Add Variable, select WAS_50_PLUGINDIR, press Extend, pick lib / db2j.jar, and finally press OK.
4. Within the package, place the following monolithic class that connects to a Cloudscape database, creating it if not found:

```
package com.xyz.demo;
import java.sql.Connection;
import java.sql.DriverManager;
import java.sql.PreparedStatement;
import java.sql.ResultSet;
import java.sql.SQLException;
import java.sql.Statement;
/**
 * Create database and table. Insert data. Display data.
*/
public class JdbcDemo {
    private final static String DRIVER = "com.ibm.db2j.
jdbc.DB2jDriver";
    private final static String URL =
        "jdbc:db2j:c:/db2j/databases/EmployeeDB;create=true";
    private final static String TABLE = "EMPLOYEE";
    /**
     * Entry point. Instantiate, the class, execute.
     * @param args[], java.lang.String
     */
    public static void main(String[] args) {
        new JdbcDemo().execute();
    }
    // Executes the demo
    public void execute() {
        try {
            // Load driver and connect
            Class.forName(DRIVER);
            // Connect, createing DB if not found
            Connection con = DriverManager.getConnection(URL);
            // Create statement
            Statement stm = con.createStatement();
            // Drop table
            dropTable(stm, TABLE);
            // Create table
```

```
            createEmployeeTable(stm);
            // Insert rows
            insertEmployees(con);
            // Update a row
            updateDepartment(con, 1003, "999");
            // Retrieve rows
            displayAll(stm, TABLE);
            // Close
            stm.close();
            con.close();
        } catch (ClassNotFoundException ex) {
            System.out.println(ex);
        } catch (SQLException ex) {
            System.out.println(ex);
        }
    }
    /**
     * Drops given table name using passed statement
     * @param stm java.sql.Statement
     * @param table java.lang.String, table name
     */
    protected void dropTable(Statement stm, String table) {
        try {
            StringBuffer buf = new StringBuffer();
            buf.append("DROP TABLE ");
            buf.append(table);
            stm.executeUpdate(buf.toString());
            System.out.print(table);
            System.out.println(" table dropped");
        } catch (SQLException ex) {
            System.out.println(" table doesn't exist");
        }
    }
    /**
     * Creates employee table
     * @param stm java.sql.Statement
     */
    protected void createEmployeeTable(Statement stm) {
        final String sql1 =
            "CREATE TABLE EMPLOYEE (EMPID BIGINT, NAME
                 VARCHAR(40), DEPT CHAR(3), EMAIL VARCHAR(40))";
        final String sql2 =
            "ALTER TABLE EMPLOYEE ADD CONSTRAINT EMPID "
                +" PRIMARY KEY (EMPID)";
        try {
            stm.executeUpdate(sql1);
            stm.executeUpdate(sql2);
```

```
            System.out.println("EMPLOYEE table created");
        } catch (SQLException ex) {
            System.out.println("EMPLOYEE table not created" +ex);
        }
    }
    /**
     * Inserts canned set of employee rows
     * @param con java.sql.Connection
     */
    protected void insertEmployees(Connection con) {
        final String[][] rows =
            { { "Bolliver Schagnasty", "C01", "schag@acme.com" }, {
                "Ellwood Suggins", "C01", "sugg@acme.com" }, {
                "Carl Wigbottom", "D11", "wig@acme.com" }, {
                "Constance Wutherby", "D11", "connie@acme.com" }, {
                "Lamar McCraken", "E02", "lamar@acme.com" }, {
                "Audry Schwartz", "C01", "audry@acme.com" }, };
        final String sql = "INSERT INTO EMPLOYEE (EMPID, NAME, DEPT, "
            +" EMAIL) VALUES(?, ?, ?, ?)";
        long idStream = 1000;
        try {
            PreparedStatement pstm = con.prepareStatement(sql);
            for (int i = 0; i < rows.length; ++i) {
                String row[] = rows[i];
                int colIndex = 1;
                pstm.setLong(colIndex++, ++idStream);
                for (int fldIndex = 0; fldIndex < row.length;
                    ++fldIndex)
                    pstm.setString(colIndex++, row[fldIndex]);
                int count = pstm.executeUpdate();
                if (count < 1)
                    throw (new SQLException("Insertion trouble!"));
            }
            System.out.println("Employees inserted");
        } catch (SQLException ex) {
            System.out.println("EMPLOYEE table not created" + ex);
        }
    }
    /**
     * Displays all employees on System.out
     * @param stm java.sql.Statement
     * @param table java.lang.String, table to access
     */
    protected void displayAll(Statement stm, String table) {
        final int LAST = 4; // Last column number
        StringBuffer buf = new StringBuffer();
        buf.append("SELECT * FROM ");
        buf.append(table);
```

```
        System.out.println("All Employees:");
        System.out.println(
            "EMPID \t\t\tNAME \t\t\tDEPT \t\t\tEMAIL");
        try {
            ResultSet rs = stm.executeQuery(buf.toString());
            // For each row: gather cols from row, display row
            while (rs.next()) {
                buf = new StringBuffer();
                for (int col = 1; col < LAST; ++col) {
                    buf.append(rs.getString(col));
                    buf.append(", ");
                }
                buf.append(rs.getString(LAST));
                System.out.println(buf);
            }
        } catch (SQLException ex) {
            System.out.println("Employees not found");
        }
    }
    /**
     * Updates the department for a specified employee
     * @param con java.sql.Connection
     * @param empid long
     * @param dept java.lang.String
     */
    protected void updateDepartment(Connection con, long empid,
            String dept) {
        final String sql = "UPDATE EMPLOYEE SET DEPT = ? "
            +"WHERE EMPID = ?";
        try {
            PreparedStatement pstm = con.prepareStatement(sql);
            pstm.setString(1, dept);
            pstm.setLong(2, empid);
            int count = pstm.executeUpdate();
            if (count < 1)
                throw (new SQLException("Update trouble!"));
        } catch (SQLException ex) {
            System.out.println(ex);
        }
    }
}
```

The code drops the EMPLOYEE table, recreates it, loads a batch of employees, updates one employee, displays all employees, closes the connection, and exits. The program is not layered. It mixes presentation with data access in the interest showing a suite of end-to-end JDBC-1 calls in a minimum space. The program exhibits basic create, read, update, and delete (CRUD) JDBC operations.

Notice that the URL references an absolute path to the database. This is because you used an embedded Cloudscape database. The JDBC driver references the database directly instead of interposing a server. An advantage of this embedded approach is that this full-featured Java-based DBMS is bundled with WSAD in the WebSphere V5.0 test environment. Another advantage is that this simple demonstration doesn't need instructions for dealing with a server. A disadvantage is that only one client may connect to the database simultaneously.

The output follows. Notice that employee 1003 was successfully updated to be a member of department 999.

```
EMPLOYEE table dropped
EMPLOYEE table created
EMPLOYEE inserted
All Employees:
EMPID NAME              DEPT        EMAIL
1001, Bolliver Schagnasty, C01, schag@acme.com
1002, Ellwood Suggins, C01, sugg@acme.com
1003, Carl Wigbottom, 999, wig@acme.com
1004, Constance Wutherby, D11, connie@acme.com
1005, Lamar McCraken, E02, lamar@acme.com
1006, Audry Schwartz, C01, audry@acme.com
```

WSAD Database Tools

Now, you will leverage the capability of WSAD to create and work with a database without directly dropping down to the JDBC programming level. You will still create and use SQL statements, but WSAD enables you to create Java wrapper classes for them. These classes use JDBC, but you will not need to code directly in JDBC unless you need to do something extraordinary.

Create a Data Connection

WSAD and its associated application servers use a data connection to abstract the details of accessing a database. You will use WSAD to create a database, a schema, tables, and suite of SQL query statements. Later, you will generate Java classes to access the database.

If you use a DBMS other than Cloudscape, you would adjust the JDBC driver information and URL in the following instructions. In this case, you would need to first create the database from the DBMS vendor tools unless the vendor supplies a means to create the database from a URL specification.

You will use the Cloudscape URL suffix create=true to create the database when you create the data connection. Create a directory location for the database folder if you use the Cloudscape DBMS (also called DB2j) bundled with WebSphere Application Server V5.0. Create the directory tree C:\db2j\databases if you use a Windows system. If the platform is Linux or Unix, then /tmp/db2j/databases is a workable choice. Create a data connection as follows:

1. Create a new Java project named DataAccess.
2. Open the Data Perspective for project DataAccess.
3. Right-click the DB Servers view client area. Invoke New Connection from the context menu. The New Connection wizard appears.
4. Set Database to DemoDB.
5. Select the Database vendor type drop-down value Cloudscape, v5.0.
6. Select the JDBC driver pull-down value Other Cloudscape Driver.
7. Use the JDBC driver drop-down list to select Cloudscape Embedded JDBC Driver.
8. Set the Database Location to c:/db2j/databases/DemoDB;create=true. This creates the database if it does not exist, provided that you create directories c:\db2j\database.
9. Set the Class location to that of the db2j.jar file by using the associated Browse button to navigate to <WSAD>\runtimes\base_v5\lib\db2j.jar.

See Figure 18.1. Notice the absolute location of the database name field of the URL. You will use forward slashes in the path on Windows because they work in Java, and because you will eventually generate Java classes that contain this URL in a String constant. A reverse slash would look like an escape sequence. If you use reverse slashes, you can repair the problem in the generated source when you come to that part of the chapter.

10. Press Finish.

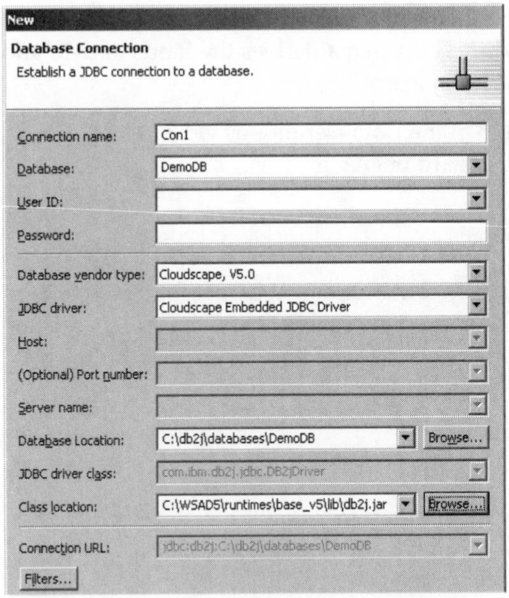

Figure 18.1 Database Connection wizard.

If you make a mistake entering a field, you should receive an immediate error. If so, close the message. The wizard remains open to let you fix the problem. When the wizard accepts the input there is a processing delay after you press Finish while WSAD loads the driver and accesses the DBMS. The new connection appears in the DB Servers view, as seen in Figure 18.2.

Define a Database to a Project

You have a connection to an empty DemoDB. The project needs a database definition that references that database so that you can define a schema and SQL queries for the database. Later, you will generate Java access classes from those queries. Follow these steps to define the database in the new DataAccess project.

1. Open the Data perspective Data Definition view.
2. Use the DataAccess project context menu to invoke New > Database definition. The New wizard opens.
3. Ensure that the Folder is set to /DataAccess. Set Database name to DemoDB. Set Database vendor type to Cloudscape, v5.0.
4. Enter a comment. The wizard should resemble Figure 18.3. Press Finish.

The definition appears under the DataAccess project folder. You will use this definition to manipulate the database structure and to make queries with WSAD tools.

Create a Schema

You created a connection to a database defined in the DataAccess Java project. The next step is to create a schema for the database. The schema defines the kinds of data and relationships that may be inserted into the database.

1. Right-click DataAccess > DEMODB in the Data Definitions view. Select New > New schema definition. The New wizard opens.
2. Enter APP as the Schema name.
3. Press Finish.

The schema appears in the DEMODB tree view. Notice that empty folders for tables, views, aliases, indexes, triggers, and structured types are contained in the schema shown in Figure 18.4. Each folder has its respective context menu, enabling us to create and edit its kind of database entity.

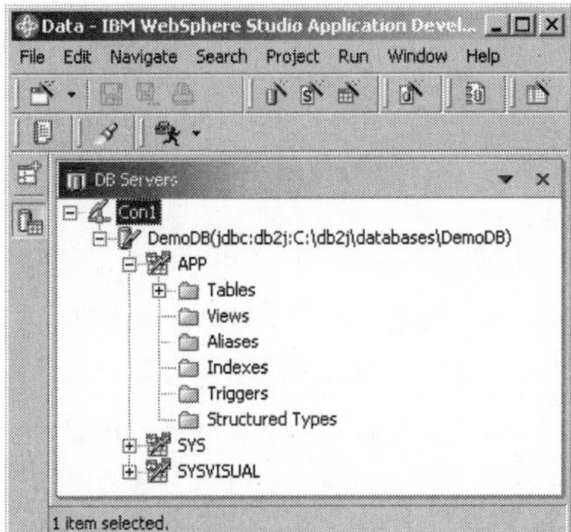

Figure 18.2 Completed connection.

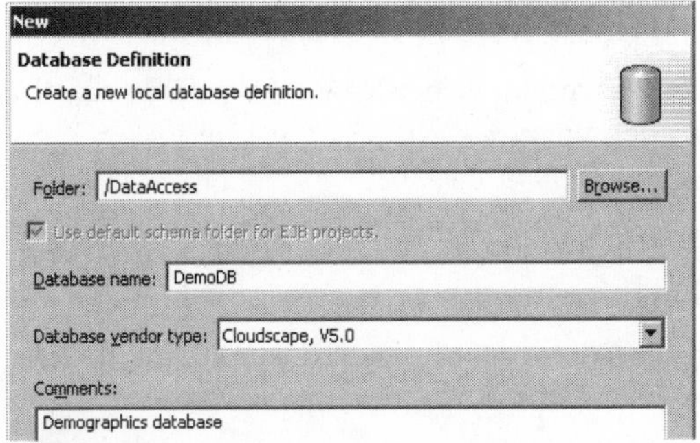

Figure 18.3 New database definition.

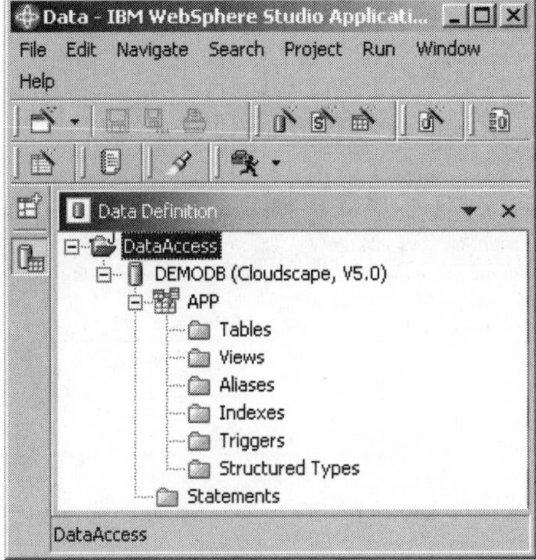

Figure 18.4 Schema.

Create Tables

You have a DEMODB APP schema. Let us create a LOCATION table in that schema. This table defines a United States city and state keyed by a postal Zip Code. Follow these steps:

1. Display the pop-up menu of DataAccess > DEMODB > APP > Tables.
2. Choose New > New table definition to invoke the New Table Definition wizard.
3. Set Table name to Location. Press Next >. The Table Columns panel appears.
4. Use the Add another button to add columns as shown in Table 18.5. Each entry is live. You do not need to press a button to keep the column value. Use Add another for each subsequent column. Check the work by highlighting each column name, and then checking its values in the right-hand pane. Press Next > when satisfied that the values are correct. The Primary Key panel appears.
5. Ensure the primary key name is ZipCode. The ZipCode column should be the only column name in the right-hand pane. Press Finish to generate the table.
6. Again, choose invoke the Tables context menu. Select New > New table definition to invoke the New Table Definition wizard.
7. Name this table Responder, and then press Next.
8. Add columns using the previously described process. Refer to Table 18.6. Press Next > when satisfied that the columns are properly defined.
9. Set the Primary key name to ID in the Primary Key panel. Ensure that only ID appears in the right-hand column. Press Next >. The Foreign Keys panel appears.
10. Choose APP.LOCATION from the Target Table pull-down list. Use the > button to send LOCATIONFK to the right-hand column under Source Columns.
11. Set Foreign key name to LocationFK. The panel should appear as shown in Figure 18.5. Press Finish.

Table 18.5 Location Columns

COLUMN NAME	COLUMN TYPE	NULLABLE	KEY	STRING LENGTH
City	VARCHAR			40
State	CHAR			2
ZipCode	CHAR		Yes	5
AreaCode	CHAR	Yes		3

Table 18.6 Responder Columns

COLUMN NAME	COLUMN TYPE	NULLABLE	KEY	STRING LENGTH
Id	BIGINT		Yes	
Sex	CHAR			1
AgeRange	VARCHAR			10
LocationFK	VARCHAR		Yes	5

Expand the new APP.LOCATION and APP.RESPONDER tables under DataAccess / DEMODB / APP. The new column definitions and the key columns appear. Notice the icons for primary keys and for the foreign key. See Figure 18.6. The tables are ready to accept inserted rows.

You can display and edit the database definition, the schema, or any entity within the schema. Use the APP.LOCATION context menu Open command to display or edit its definition. See Figure 18.7.

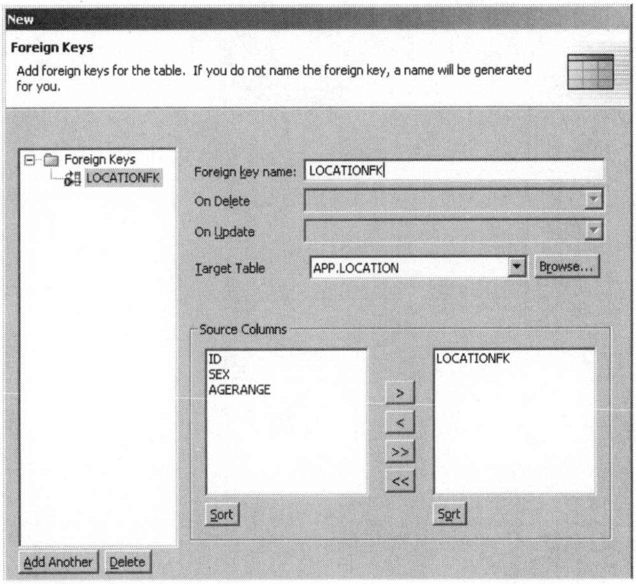

Figure 18.5 Foreign key.

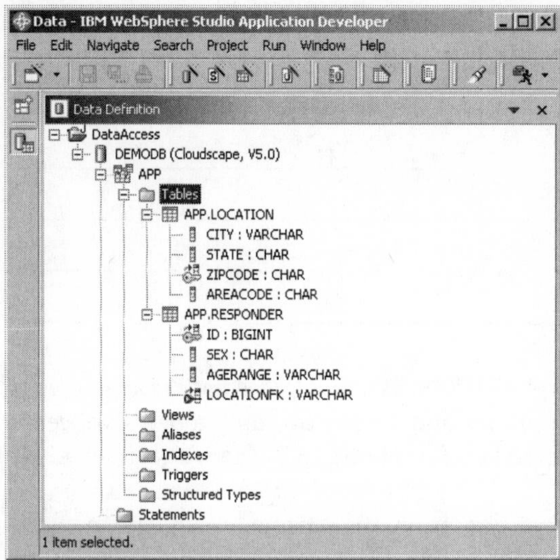

Figure 18.6 New tables.

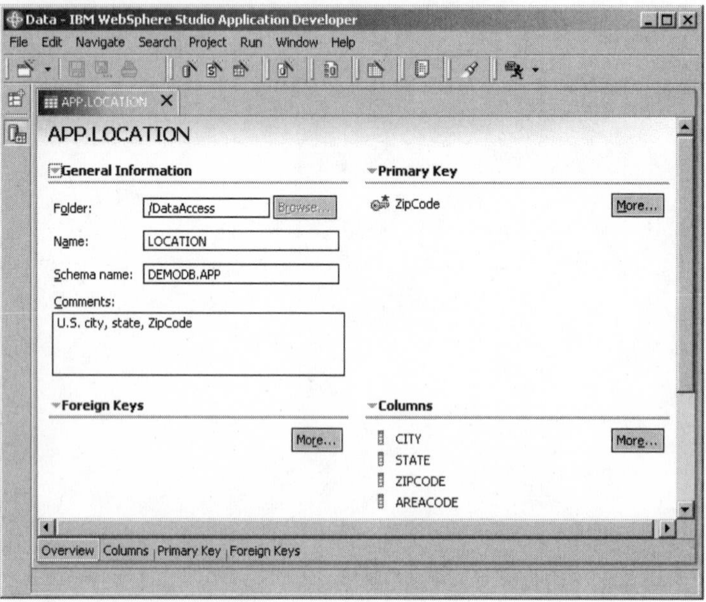

Figure 18.7 Table Editor.

Notice that the tabs at the bottom of the editor correspond to the forms that the Table Creation wizard showed. You can use this editor to alter and repair a table. If you created another entity such as an index, you can invoke its editor from its pop-up menu.

Generating DDL

You used interactive features of WSAD to create an operable database in the previous sections. If you deleted the database, you would need to duplicate these steps, correct? No, not if you captured the database definition in SQL data definition language (DDL). The DBMS executes the DDL to define the schema and its contained entities, such as tables containing column definitions and key declarations.

You can use WSAD to generate the DDL from the pop-up menu of the DEMODB database definition in the Data Definitions view. The Generate DLL menu item invokes the Generate SQL DLL wizard shown in Figure 18.8. Select any extra options, and then press Finish to create the DemoDB.sql file in the project folder.

You can open the Location.sql file in the editor to view or modify it. Following is the DDL generated using the fully qualified names option. Notice that comments entered in the Table Creation wizard or using the Table Editor are SQL comments.

```
-- Generated by Relational Schema Center
-- Demographics database
CREATE SCHEMA APP;
-- City, state, ZipCode, area code. PK is ZipCode,
CREATE TABLE APP.LOCATION
  (CITY VARCHAR(40) NOT NULL,
   STATE CHAR(2) NOT NULL,
   ZIPCODE CHAR(5) NOT NULL,
   AREACODE VARCHAR(3));
ALTER TABLE APP.LOCATION
  ADD CONSTRAINT ZIPCODE PRIMARY KEY (ZIPCODE);
-- Holds demographic data for one responder.
-- Foreign key to LOCATION table
CREATE TABLE APP.RESPONDER
  (ID BIGINT NOT NULL, SEX CHAR(1) NOT NULL,
   AGERANGE VARCHAR(10) NOT NULL, LOCATIONFK VARCHAR(5) NOT NULL);
ALTER TABLE APP.RESPONDER
  ADD CONSTRAINT ID PRIMARY KEY (ID);
ALTER TABLE APP.RESPONDER
  ADD CONSTRAINT LOCATIONFK FOREIGN KEY (LOCATIONFK)
  REFERENCES APP.LOCATION(ZIPCODE);
```

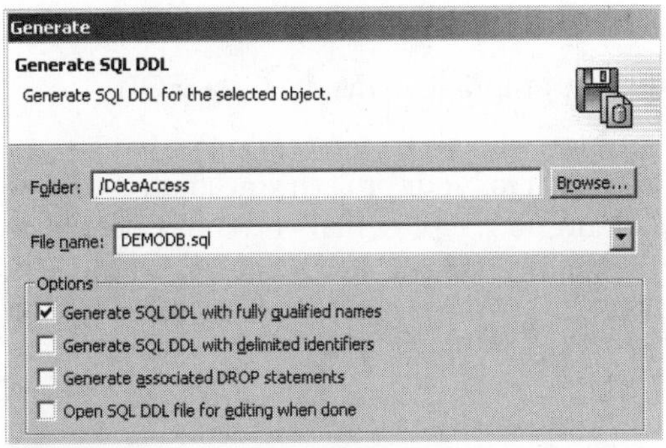

Figure 18.8 Generate SQL DDL.

This DDL creates the schema, then the tables, altering each table to add primary and foreign keys.

Using DDL

If you have a DDL file how do you use it? The vendor's DBMS tools could accept it to define the data. You don't have to use the vendor's tools since you have WSAD available. The DLL file context menu in the WSAD Data Definition view contains a suite of menu items used to edit the file, delete it, or apply it to a database definition in the Data Definition view or a database server in the DB Servers view. The Set Vendor Type menu item is used to associate a particular vendor with the DDL file, to adjust for vendor-specific characteristics.

You won't need to run the DEMODB.sql DDL at this point, since you still have the database definition that you used to generate the DDL. It is a good idea to generate and save DLL so that the database definition can be reconstituted later.

Create SQL Statements

You created a database schema that defines what kinds of data can be inserted into the database. The DDL phase is behind you. Now, you need data manipulation language statements (DML) to carry out data insertion, query, update, and deletion. You will refer to these statements as SQL, as WSAD does, although DDL and DML are each classifications of SQL statements. There are two ways to create an SQL statement in WSAD. The first is by using the SQL Wizard. The other method is called the SQL Builder. You will use the SQL builder to create your SQL, but first let us look at the SQL wizard.

SQL Wizard

You will not use the SQL wizard for the demographics project, but you will see the general usage here. Invoke the SQL wizard to create an SQL statement in any project. Follow these general steps:

1. Create or select a project.
2. Right-click the project folder. Choose File > New > Other > Data > SQL Statement.
3. Press Next to start the wizard.
4. Complete the wizard using the values appropriate to the database, SQL statement type, and project.

If you needed to create an SQL insert statement for your project, you could complete the first panel of the wizard as shown in Figure 18.9. Notice that you could elect to be guided through the statement creation, manually enter the statement, or call the SQL Builder that you will use in the next section.

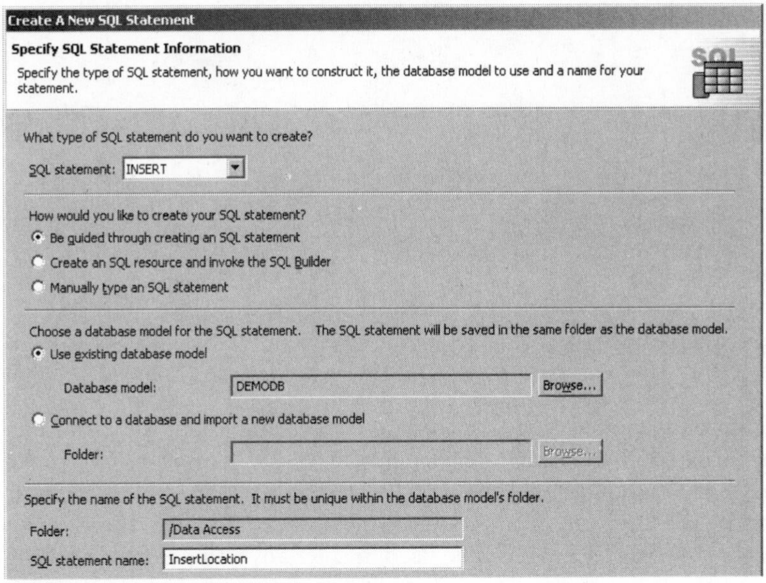

Figure 18.9 SQL wizard Start panel.

Recall that you created a database definition in your project. Since you already had the database defined in the server, you could have used this panel to import the model to the project. This is another area where WSAD offers flexibility through alternatives.

The next panel of the guided creation option varies with the statement type chosen. You chose INSERT, so the next panel shown has an Insert tab in addition to a Table tab as seen in Figure 18.10. You would choose a table by using the > button and then selecting the Insert tab. If you had chosen some other kind of SQL statement, you would open its tab now.

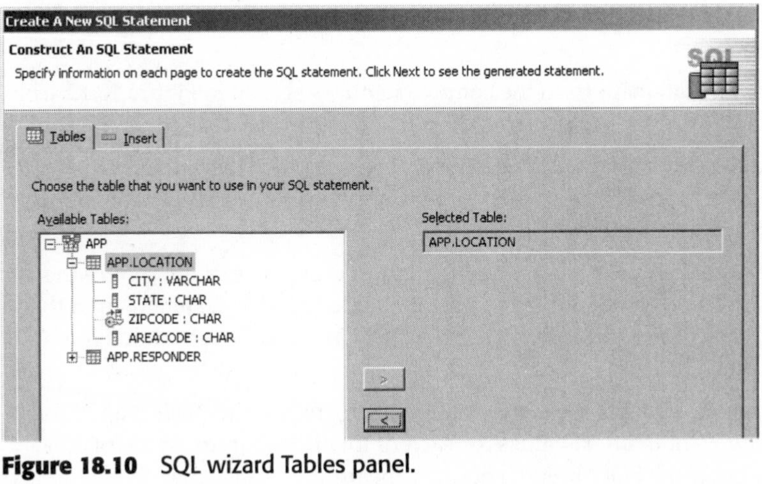

Figure 18.10 SQL wizard Tables panel.

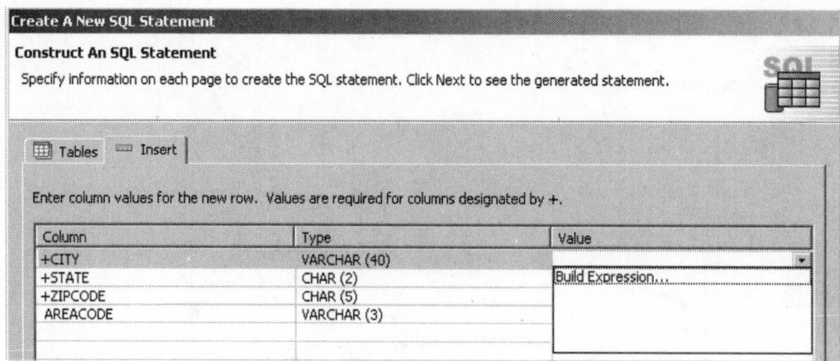

Figure 18.11 SQL wizard Insert panel.

The panel in Figure 18.11 invites you to enter values for each column. You could simply type a value into the Value column or click on its right side to invoke a pull-down as shown in the figure. The pull-down contains a link to an Expression Builder wizard. You would normally use the Expression Builder to create host variables. These generalize your INSERT statement so that it can be used to enter any value instead of being hard-coded to one value. Once you create an expression value, the pull-down contents change to let you edit the value if you desire. You won't put details into the Expression Builder here because this will be covered in the following section.

SQL Builder

Now, you will create the necessary SQL statements for the project by using the SQL Builder approach. After you create the statements, you can test them against DemoDB in WSAD. Later, you will have WSAD create Java wrapper classes for the statements so that a Java or Web application may access the database in an object-oriented fashion. You will step through creating an insert statement at a high level, and then apply those steps in creating several other statements.

1. Open the **Data Definition** view. Select the DataAccess project. Right-click the Statements folder.
2. Choose Insert Statement from the context menu, as shown in Figure 18.12. This launches a prompt for a statement name.
3. Enter LocationInsert for the statement name. Press OK. This launches the SQL Builder that consists of a specialized editor and the Outline view showing the statement you just named.
4. Right-click the `LocationInsert` statement in the Outline view. Notice the menu items. Choose Add Table to append a table to the SQL statement in the Raw Text pane of the editor. Select LOCATION in the table selection dialog, and then press OK.
5. The columns of the table appear in middle pane of the editor. Select all of them because you want to insert values for each of them. See Figure 18.13 for an example of how the SQL Builder should appear now. Notice that generated text accumulated as you made selections. So far you have not had to type anything, but you will need to enter values in the next step.

6. Look at the Value column of the bottom pane of the SQL Builder. Click the right side of the CITY value column to see the pull-down list. Choose Build Expression. The Expression Builder appears.
7. Choose Constant – numeric, string, or host variable. See Figure 18.14. You need host variables so that the statement can be used to insert variable data. Press Next, and the Constant Options Page appears.

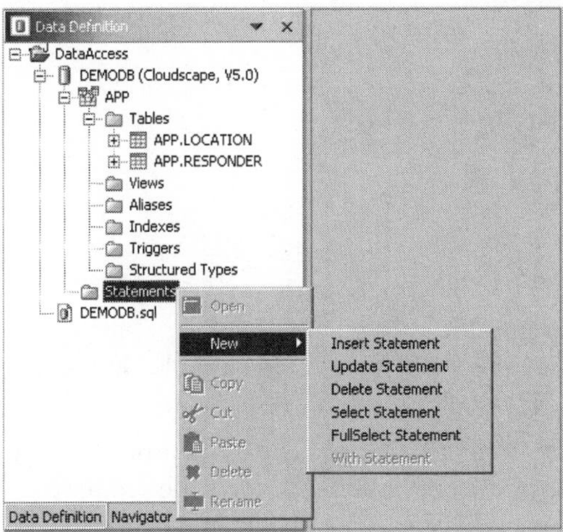

Figure 18.12 New SQL statement menu.

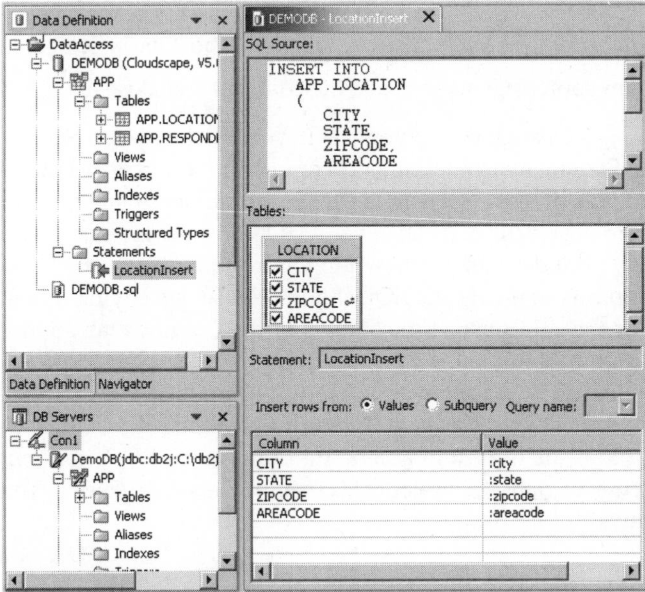

Figure 18.13 SQL Builder.

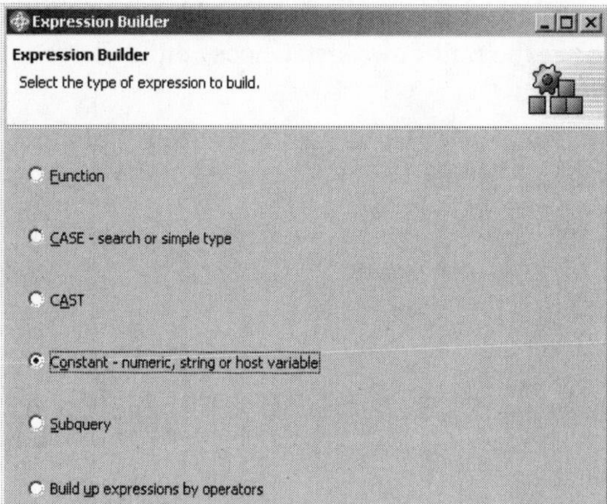

Figure 18.14 Expression type.

8. Choose String constant: character or graphic string, hexadecimal, or host variable names. See Figure 18.15. You will use the phrase "host variable" in making the choice. Press Next >. The String Constant Builder Page appears.
9. Select Host variable name. Enter city in the entry field. This is the first time you have had to type anything. Notice that the preview field shows the proper prefix for a host variable name, as shown in Figure 18.16.
10. Press Finish. The SQL Builder shows the host variable name in the Value column.
11. Now that you see what belongs in the Value column, you can simply enter the host variables directly. Enter **:state**, **:zipcode**, and **:areacode** in the respective rows. Do not forget the leading colon (:), which signifies a host variable name.
12. Review the SQL Builder source pane, then save the contents and close it.

The SQL INSERT statement is created. Before you test it, you need a way to retrieve a LOCATION row. Use the Statements context menu command New > Select statement to invoke the SQL Builder process to create a `Select` statement named LocationOfZipCode. It should retrieve all columns of a LOCATION row, given a Zip Code value. The corresponding SQL Builder view is shown in Figure 18.17. Notice that you used the Conditions tab columns to create the SQL `WHERE` clause, specifying a host variable value of zipcode for the ZIPCODE. The contents of the Columns tab are not shown, but they specify that all columns should be output.

Use similar steps to produce an SQL statement named LocationListState that produces a list of rows that equal a host variable :state. The output columns are CITY, ZIPCODE, and AREACODE. Order the output in ascending order of the CITY column. Save the statement and execute it against a two-letter state abbreviation to check it. The desired SQL statement follows:

```
SELECT APP.LOCATION.CITY, APP.LOCATION.ZIPCODE, APP.LOCATION.AREACODE
FROM APP.LOCATION
WHERE APP.LOCATION.STATE = :state
ORDER BY CITY ASC
```

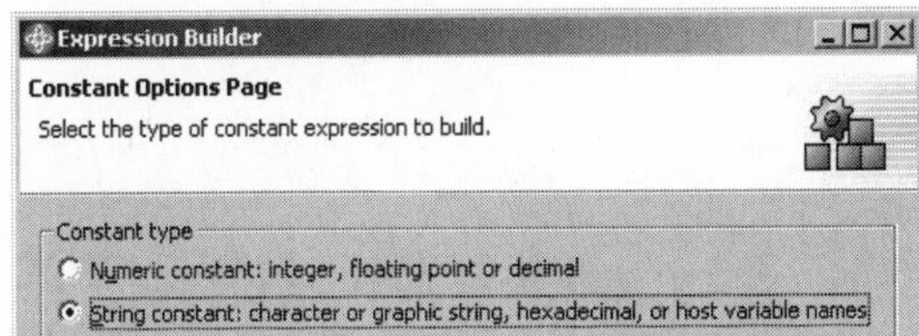

Figure 18.15 Host variable names option.

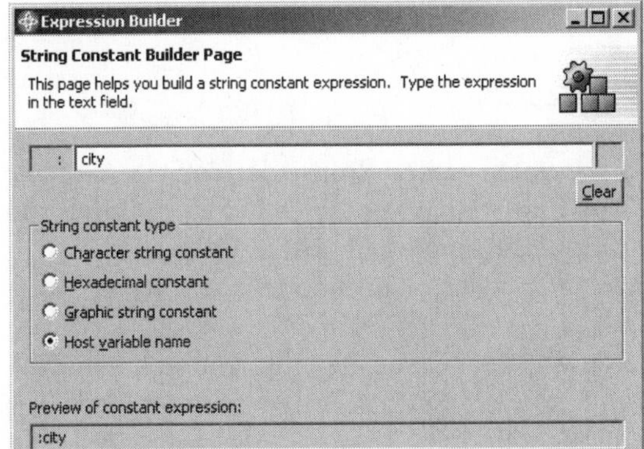

Figure 18.16 Define a host variable.

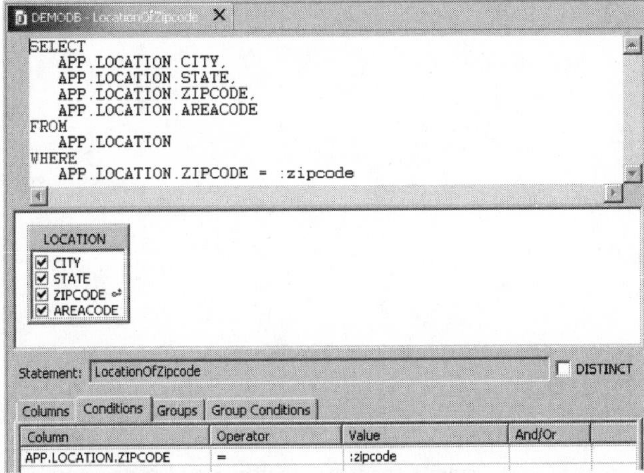

Figure 18.17 Select location of a Zip Code.

You will need to list all of the unique states in the LOCATION table in Chapter 19, "Displaying Data." An SQL GROUP BY clause will ensure that the rows are unique. Create an SQL statement named LocationListAllStates. Select only column STATE listed in ascending order. Eliminate duplicate rows by using the Groups tab to choose APP.LOCATION.STATE. Save the statement, and then execute it to verify that all states are listed once in ascending alphabetical order. The desired SQL statement follows:

```
SELECT APP.LOCATION.STATE
FROM APP.LOCATION
GROUP BY APP.LOCATION.STATE
ORDER BY STATE ASC
```

Let us turn our attention to the RESPONDER table. Create an insert statement named ResponderInsert that uses host variables for all column values. Use :zipcode for the host variable of column LOCATIONFK as a reminder of the kind of data values used for the key. The SQL text should read:

```
INSERT INTO APP.RESPONDER
   (ID, SEX, AGERANGE, LOCATIONFK)
   VALUES ( :id, :sex, :agerange, :zipcode)
```

Use the SQL Builder to create a Select statement named ResponderListState to query all responders in a given U.S. state. This time, add both tables before building the query. The query uses an inner join, using the Responder.LocationFK foreign key to reference the Location.ZipCode primary key when a Location.State column value matches a host variable value.

The SQL Builder view is shown in Figure 18.18. Notice the inner join in the middle panel. Depress the left pointer button on RESPONDER.LOCATIONFK, and then drag and release on LOCATION.ZIPCODE to create the join. Right-click to view or alter the join. Choose the default inner join type. Use the Columns tab to cause output of the result in ascending order on the Location.City, Location.ZipCode, Responder.Sex, and Responder.AgeRange column values. The generated SQL follows:

```
SELECT
   APP.RESPONDER.ID,
   APP.RESPONDER.SEX,
   APP.RESPONDER.AGERANGE,
   APP.LOCATION.CITY,
   APP.LOCATION.STATE,
   APP.LOCATION.ZIPCODE,
   APP.LOCATION.AREACODE
FROM APP.RESPONDER, APP.LOCATION
WHERE
   APP.RESPONDER.LOCATIONFK = APP.LOCATION.ZIPCODE
   AND APP.LOCATION.STATE = :state
ORDER BY CITY ASC, ZIPCODE ASC, SEX ASC, AGERANGE ASC
```

Your suite of new SQL statements is sufficient for now. If you need more you can create them in the future, while feeling free to experiment with temporary creations meanwhile. You can always delete them later if you do not need them.

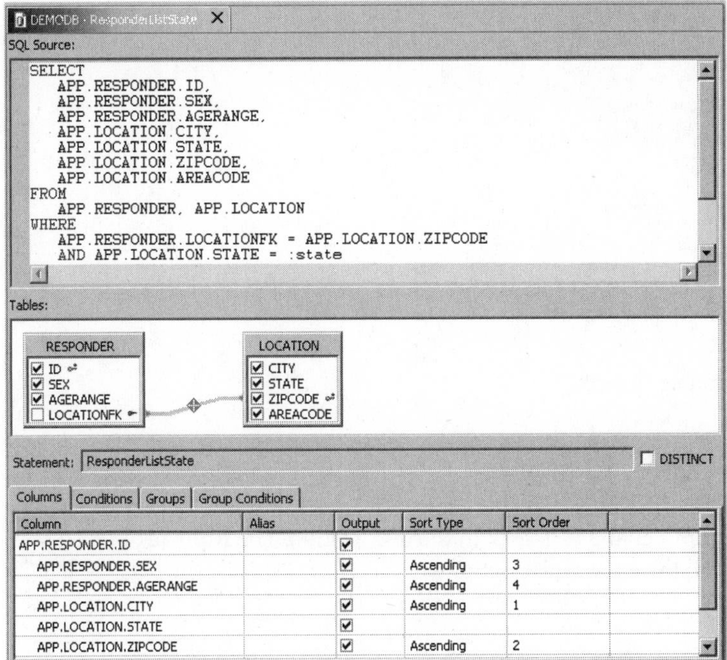

Figure 18.18 Inner join.

Export the Data Definition

The schema and tables that you created only exist in the database definition stored in DataAccess project. You must export these database objects to the actual DBMS.

1. Open the Data Definition view.
2. Right-click the DEMODB node. Invoke Export to server. The Data Export wizard opens. See Figure 18.19.
3. Select the data to export. Ensure that the LocationInsert, LocationOfZipcode, ResponderInsert, and ResponderListState statements are selected. Press Next >.
4. Keep the default settings of Commit changes only upon success and Generate fully qualified names selected. Press Next >.
5. The next panel invites you to create a DBMS connection. You created one previously, so check Use existing connection, and then specify that connection, Con1. If you wanted to export the same definition to another database, you could create a connection for it and carry out the export here. If you had deleted your connection you could have recreated it here.

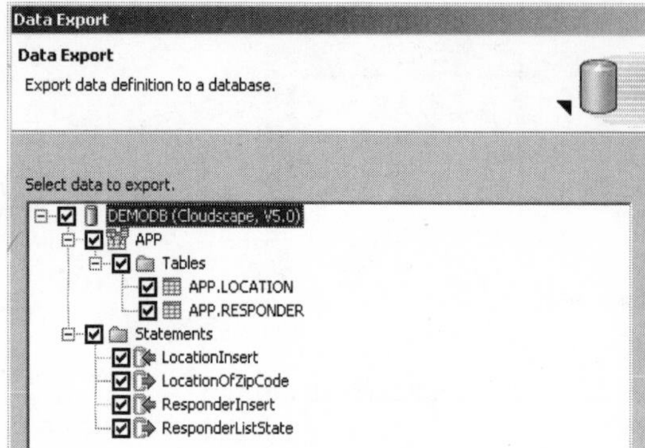

Figure 18.19 Export data objects.

6. Press Finish to carry out the export.
7. The Confirm export results panel appears. It shows the status of each export task. Press Commit changes to lock in the task results. The Rollback button would nullify all the export task actions.

Execute SQL

The DemoDB database now contains the schema and tables you defined. Now, you can test your SQL statements. The database contains no data, so you will execute the LocationInsert SQL statement to insert a row into the LOCATION table with the following steps:

1. Ensure that the Data Definition view is open.
2. Right-click DataAccess > DemoDB > LocationInsert. Choose Execute. The Execute SQL dialog appears, showing the SQL text in the SQL statement field.
3. Press the Execute button. Since the SQL statement uses host variables, the Specify Variable Values dialog appears. Enter a valid U.S. location, as shown in Figure 18.20. All of the values are strings, so they need to be nested in single quotes.
4. Press Finish. The Execute SQL Statement dialog shows success. Press Close.

Specify Variable Values

Host Variable Values

Specify the variable values to use

Name	Type	Value
:city	VARCHAR	'Raleigh'
:state	CHAR	'NC'
:zipcode	CHAR	'27613'
:areacode	VARCHAR	'919'

Figure 18.20 Specify host variable values.

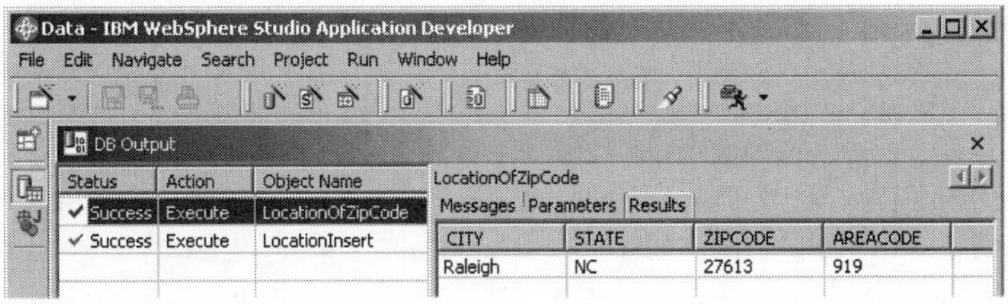

Figure 18.21 Query result.

If the ZipCode key already existed a Failure status line in DB Output would appear and the Message tab would contain a complaint about the duplicate key insertion attempt. Either way, the Results tab should show nothing because an Insert does not return data.

After inserting the row, retrieve it using the LocationOfZipcode SQL statement by using the previous directions as your guide. The result is shown in Figure 18.21.

Create a JavaBean from SQL

The manual SQL execution you carried out is impressive, but how does this relate to an application? You previously executed JDBC queries directly against an employee database without assistance from WSAD. Afterward, you used structured tools of the Data Perspective to create a demographic database, a schema, tables, and SQL statements. You need to use those statements in a Java application or their value will be diminished. The approach is to use the Data Definition view to generate a JavaBean for each SQL statement. These wrapper classes would be used in applications that need to use the database.

You need to insert rows into the Location table because it consists of static data joined to Responder rows. Then, you can present and manipulate the data in the next chapter. The first step is to generate a JavaBean for each SQL statement. Use the Java Perspective to create a package named com.xyx.data in the DataAccess project. Then, switch to the Data Perspective. Expand node DEMODB / Statements in the Data Definition view. Carry out the following steps for each DEMODB SQL statement.

1. Right-click the desired SQL statement. Execute Generate Java Bean. The Create a JavaBean that executes an SQL statement wizard appears.
2. Use the Source Folder browse button to set the folder to the DataAccess project folder.
3. Use the Package browse button to set the package to com.xyx.data.
4. Enter the name of the SQL statement as the class name.
5. Press Next >.
6. Review the information. It should contain connection information for DemoDB. Use the default settings. Press Next >.
7. Review the method specifications. Press Finish to generate the JavaBean.

When finished, the Java Perspective should show a JavaBean in package com.xyz.data for each SQL statement. Each may have an invalid escape sequence error if reverse slashes appeared the database connection URL. Double each reverse slash or substitute forward slashes to repair the error.

You will write a utility that uses the InsertLocation JavaBean to populate the LOCATION table. The source data resides in a resource file named ZIPa.csv loaded from a stream created by the class loader.

Use the Java perspective to create a package named com.xyz.utility under the DataAccess project. Drag external file ZIPa.csv to the folder DataAccess/com/xyz/utility in WSAD. Each line of the file is a comma-delimited row of city, state, Zip Code, area code values as in the follow example:

```
"Spokane","WA","99207","509"
```

If you wish, you can create your own ZIPa.csv file, but it must be in the indicated format that is expected by the LocationVO value object class to follow. An instance of the class holds one location having city, state, ZipCode, and area code attributes. The constructor is given a java.io.BufferedReader object positioned to a line of the ZIPa.csv file. Thus, attributes of the object may be set into an InsertLocation object to be sent to code to carry out insertion into the DemoDB.

Create a package named com.xyz.utility in project DataAccess. Within the package, create a LocationVO value object class. Implement it with the Java source code that follows:

```
package com.xyz.utility;
import java.io.BufferedReader;
import java.io.EOFException;
import java.io.IOException;
import java.util.StringTokenizer;
/**
 * This is a value object used for Location
 * insertions. It is constructed from the current
 * comma-separated record in a java.io.BufferedReader.
*/
public class LocationVO {
    private String city;
    private String state;
    private String zip;
    private String area;
    static private final String delim = "\",\n\r";
    /**
     * Creates new LocationVO object given an open Buffered reader on a
     * CSV stream consisting of records that look like this: <br />
     * "Buncombe","IL","62912","618"
     * @throws java.io.IOException, forwarded BufferedReader
     * @throws java.io.EOFException
     */
    public LocationVO(BufferedReader ins)
        throws EOFException, IOException {
        String buffer = ins.readLine();
```

```
        if (buffer == null)
            throw (new EOFException("ZIP data"));
        StringTokenizer st = new StringTokenizer(
            buffer, delim, false);
        if (st.hasMoreTokens())
            city = st.nextToken();
        if (st.hasMoreTokens())
            state = st.nextToken();
        if (st.hasMoreTokens())
            zip = st.nextToken();
        if (st.hasMoreTokens())
            area = st.nextToken();
    }
    /**
     * Overrides Object.toString() to return readable Location
     * @return java.lang.String, a location
     */
    public java.lang.String toString() {
        StringBuffer buf = new StringBuffer();
        buf.append(city);
        buf.append(", ");
        buf.append(state);
        buf.append(", ");
        buf.append(zip);
        buf.append(", ");
        buf.append(area);
        return buf.toString();
    }
    /**
     * Gets the city
     * @return Returns a String
     */
    public String getCity() {
        return city;
    }
    /**
     * Gets the state
     * @return Returns a String
     */
    public String getState() {
        return state;
    }
    /**
     * Gets the zip
     * @return Returns a String
     */
    public String getZip() {
        return zip;
    }
    /**
     * Gets the area
     * @return Returns a String
```

```
     */
    public String getArea() {
        return area;
    }
}
```

The Java application class LoadLocation uses the LocationVO and InsertLocation classes to insert the data from the ZIPa.csv file into the DemoDB. Create the `LoadLocation` class in the com.xyz.utility package. Implement LoadLocations with the following Java source code:

```
package com.xyz.utility;
import java.io.BufferedReader;
import java.io.FileReader;
import java.io.InputStream;
import java.io.InputStreamReader;
import com.xyz.data.LocationInsert;
public class LoadLocations {
/**
 * @param args java.lang.String[], file URL override
 */
    public static void main(String[] args) {
        new LoadLocations().execute();
    }
// Carry out database insertion on the Location table
    public void execute() {
        insert();
    }
    /**
     * Insert Location data
     */
    protected boolean insert() {
        try {
            InputStream ins =
                ClassLoader.getSystemResourceAsStream(
                    "com/xyz/utility/ZIPa.csv");
            BufferedReader br = new BufferedReader(
                new InputStreamReader(ins));
            LocationInsert location = new LocationInsert();
            while (true) {
                LocationVO vo = new LocationVO(br);
                location.execute("", "", vo.getCity(),
                    vo.getState(), vo.getZip(), vo.getArea());
                System.out.println(vo);
            }
```

```
        } catch (java.io.EOFException ex) {
            System.out.println(ex);
        } catch (java.io.IOException ex) {
            System.out.println(ex);
        } catch (java.sql.SQLException ex) {
            System.out.println(ex);
        }
        return true;
    }
}
```

The heart of the application is the `insert()` method, which creates a reader on the input file. For each input line, it creates a value object, transfers the value object contents to the generated InsertLocation JavaBean, calls its `execute()` method, and finally displays the value object.

Execute LoadLocations as a Java application. It may take up to a half-hour to parse and carry out the insertions because there are 45,000 records. What happens if you execute it twice? Duplicate key exceptions will cause the inserts to fail, leaving the original data intact.

Use the Data Perspective to execute the LocationOfZipcode SQL statement. It should be able to resolve any U.S. Zip Code that existed when the file was created.

Next, execute ResponderInsert. Supply the host variable values. Do not forget to enclose string values in single quotes. Use unique values for the ID primary key. Create several records with this query using two U.S. states, for example, WA and NC.

Finally, execute the ResponderListState query supplying one of the states. Figure 18.22 shows a typical query result.

The query used an inner join on the LOCATION and RESPONDER tables. You mapped this query to a JavaBean for use in a Web application to be discussed in the next chapter. There, you will add more SQL statements and generate JavaBeans.

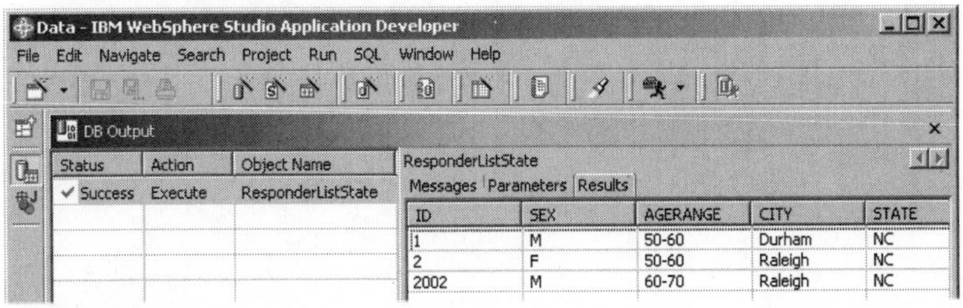

Figure 18.22 List query.

Summary

We discussed WSAD data tools and features in this chapter. We covered how to:

- Use raw JDBC
- Work with a database in WSAD
- Use the SQL Builder or SQL wizard to create SQL statements
- Export a data definition to a database
- Execute SQL statements in the Data Perspective
- Generate a JavaBean from an SQL statement
- Create an application that uses an SQL JavaBean

This chapter was an enabling chapter. It presented the foundation for using JDBC and WSAD tools to access persistent relational data. The next chapter builds on this foundation by demonstrating how to display and manipulate the data from a Web application. In Chapter 22, "Enterprise JavaBeans," and Chapter 23, "Entity EJBs," we will show how to use a J2EE Enterprise JavaBean container as an alternative to access persistent data.

Displaying Data

What's in Chapter 19?

In this chapter, we cover ways to access data, and how a human can view and interact with the data, especially in a J2EE application environment. The topics we cover include:

- Data client application model types
- JSP model one design
- Data rendering through a custom tag library
- JSP model two design
- The mediator design pattern
- The front controller design pattern
- The command design pattern
- Value objects
- Handling no data situations
- Pros and cons of the design models
- A survey of data rendering enhancements

You have seen how to create an SQL statement, test its execution in WSAD, and then generate a JavaBean from that SQL statement. Any Java client that subsequently needs to manipulate that SQL query would execute methods on that JavaBean to access or manipulate the corresponding data through the DBMS. The JavaBean is an object-oriented façade for a non-objected-oriented SQL relational query.

We will discuss high-level approaches to Web-based data client design, since Web applications are used to project data to multitudes of interactive users, many of whom are interested only in the data, not in overcoming the idiosyncrasies of the application carrying the data. The Web application paradigm is multitiered, potentially yielding high parallelism, but is sometimes perplexing to programmers because of its distributed nature and its stateless tendency.

Data Clients

The data access JavaBeans you generated through WSAD in Chapter 18, "Data Access," seem to be a boon for the Java programmer, but you could create a spaghetti-like coding mess if you do not segregate the responsibilities of client components into defined layers. A model-view-controller (MVC) layered design decomposes an application into an application logic layer and a presentation layer. An intervening controller layer translates presentation events into application actions and modifies the presentation based upon application results. Many multitier applications need a still more structured design approach to enhance reuse while reducing maintenance costs.

Figure 19.1 shows the three-layer MVC design as compared to the EitaSoft Corporation's Strata five-layer philosophy, where the presentation layer corresponds to the MVC view, but the controller is split into a controller and mediator pair.

The mediator is independent of the presentation so that the application could conceivably be moved from a Web application to a Java-based fat client application without rewriting the mediator or any layer to its right, as seen at the bottom of figure 19.1. The mediator represents the MVC model in a sense, because it contains the top-level logic of the application.

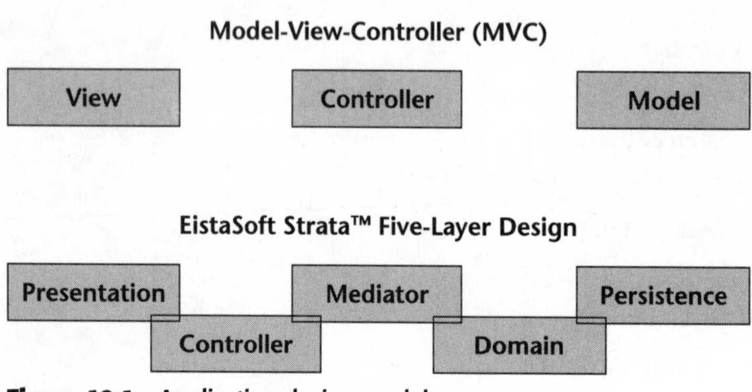

Figure 19.1 Application design models.

By comparison, the domain layer that contains reusable business logic that is independent of the application. The domain represents the family jewels of an organization's component library. Java-based domain logic is sometimes implemented as Enterprise JavaBeans (EJB) because they are configurable and deployable in multiple situations without the need for source code access. For example an EJB could be configured for fine-grained security roles per method, and then deployed into a load-balanced and fail-over application server cluster without modifying the EJB source code.

The persistence layer deals with long-lived data that could reside in a DBMS, a messaging system or any form of external storage. The persistence layer may contain an object-to-relational mapping scheme. The JavaBeans that you generated to encapsulate an SQL statement are a form of O-R mapping. Entity EJBs are another form of O-R mapping that could bridge the persistence layer to the domain layer.

Try to organize designs into well-defined layers, minimizing connections and dependencies between layers. Each layer should have no knowledge of layers beyond its contiguous neighbor. For instance, a mediator should know nothing of presentation details. Recall the calculator you built in a previous chapter. It was based upon a mediator that would operate in a Java Swing application or in a Web application. Strive for that kind of independence, especially when you need to interact with or render data.

The design that we present in a following section, "JSP Model Two," is a reasonable pattern for creating and maintaining five-layer data manipulation applications. These would have clear separation of responsibilities to enhance extensibility, maintainability, reuse, and the division of human skills.

Design Options

In this chapter, we show three approaches to rendering data in a Web application. Let us investigate Web-based design options that use a JSP to render query results. The J2EE literature refers to two major JSP design approaches: JSP model one and JSP model two.

To help you understand the difference between the two models, you will create a simple application that will query the user for a U.S. state, responding with a list of all of the cities and the U.S. Postal Service Zip Codes in that state. You will write this Web application three times: once for each design, and you will create a variation of the model one Web application that uses a tag library. The tag library will supplant a JSP model one scriptlet in iterating through the result rows. After you create and run the tree applications we discuss the advantages and disadvantages of each design approach.

JSP Model One

Recall that a JSP is only a servlet that was produced from a different source form. After it is compiled it is a servlet composed of println statements to emit any contained HTML, and it has Java code to implement scriptlets. Thus, you could construct your entire application in JSPs if you desired. This is the JSP model one philosophy shown in Figure 19.2.

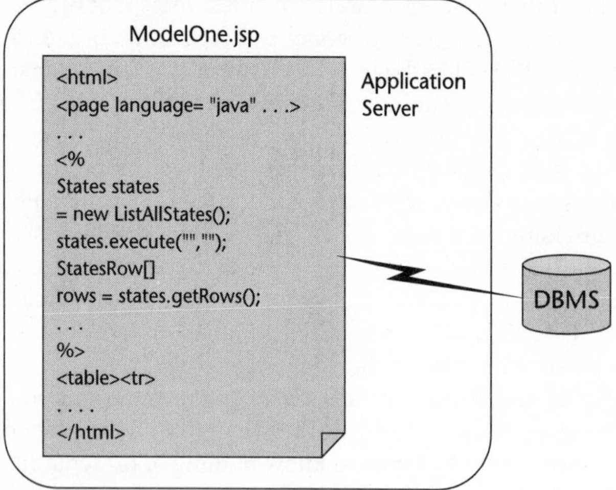

Figure 19.2 JSP model one.

You could segregate JSPs into view and model JSPs. A view JSP would obtain user input and render responses. It could forward user input to a model JSP that may query a database for a collection of rows. The model JSP could forward the collection to a view JSP that would render the results.

You will create a simple Web application named JspModelOne that uses a pick list to prompt the user for a U.S. state and returns a table of the cities and Zip Codes for the chosen state. This exercise uses the com.xyz.data.LocationListAllStates and com.xyz.data.LocationListAllStatesRow data access JavaBeans that you generated from an SQL statement in the last chapter.

Create the Model One Web Project

Begin by creating the Web project for the application. Afterward you will populate it with JSPs and deploy and run them. Create the Web project with the following steps:

1. Open the Web Perspective.
2. Use the main menu item File > New Web Project to create a J2EE Web project named JspModelOne. Check only the Web project features shown in Table 19.1. The wizard should match Figure 19.3. Not all of these features are needed for this project, but, for simplicity, you will create subsequent projects using these directions.
3. Press Next >. Elect to create DataDisplayApp as the associated J2EE application. Use the default context root of JspModelOne. The J2EE level should be set to 1.3. See Figure 19.4.

Table 19.1 Web Project Features

NUMBER	FEATURE
1.	Create a default CSS file
2.	Include Tag Libraries for accessing JSP objects
3.	Include Tag Libraries for database access
4.	Include the standard JSP library
5.	Include utility Tag Libraries

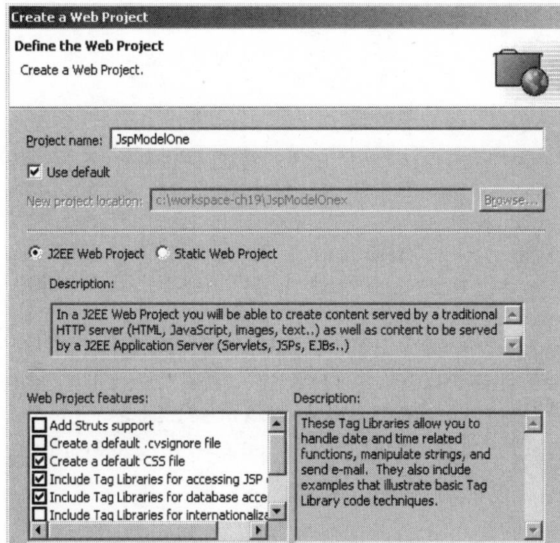

Figure 19.3 Create Web project.

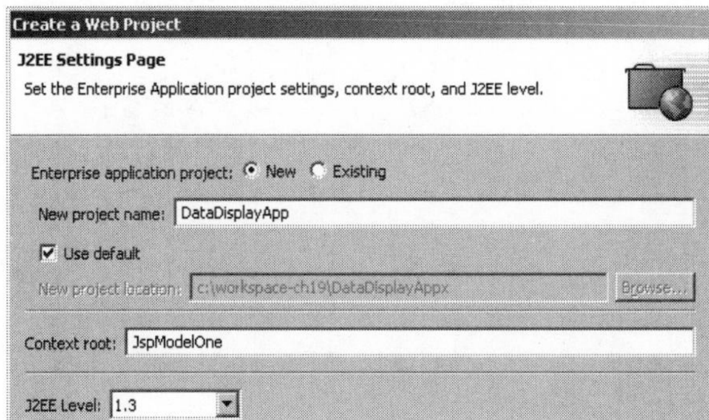

Figure 19.4 Model one Web project J2EE settings.

4. Press Finish to create the JspModelOne project and associate it with the DataDisplayApp J2EE project.
5. Open the Web Deployment Descriptor by using the Open item on the JspModelOne context menu.
6. Locate the Web Library Projects group on the Overview page. Use the Add button to include the DataAccess project as a dependent jar named DataAccess.jar.

This is the project you created to contain the data JavaBeans you generated from SQL statements in Chapter 18. The Web Library Projects group should resemble Figure 19.5. The dependent data project classes are deployed in a JAR file automatically by WSAD.

That completes the Web project's creation. Next, you will populate it with JSPs.

Create Application JSPs

This application uses two JSPs. The first is a default start page named index.jsp. It presents a pick list of U.S. states and possessions. All of the Java code needed to access the data JavaBeans to populate the pick list is contained within scriptlets on the page. The user picks an item and then submits the page.

The other JSP, named state.jsp, handles the request. It uses a data JavaBean to obtain an ordered list of city/Zip Code rows, and then generates an HTML table containing the rows. That's the entire application.

First you will create index.jsp. Consult the Design view shown in Figure 19.6.

The JSP declaration tag content contained within the HTML <HEAD> element follows. Notice the import tags that reference the data JavaBeans. Those classes will load from the dependent JAR named DataAccess.jar that you specified previously in the deployment descriptor.

```
<%@ page language="java" contentType="text/html; charset=WINDOWS-1252"
pageEncoding="WINDOWS-1252"
import="com.xyz.data.LocationListAllStates"
import="com.xyz.data.LocationListAllStatesRow"%>
```

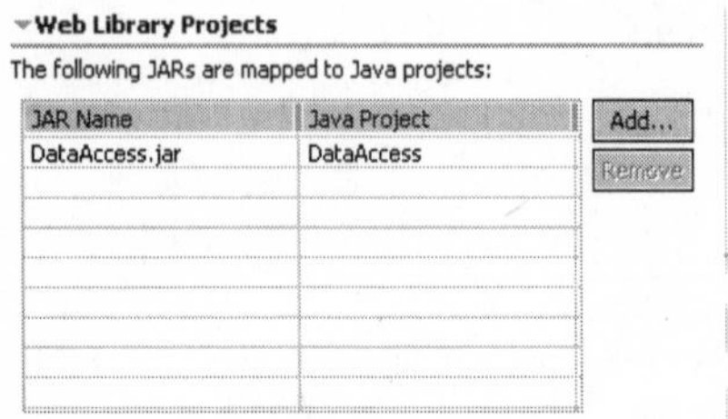

Figure 19.5 Deployment descriptor library JAR.

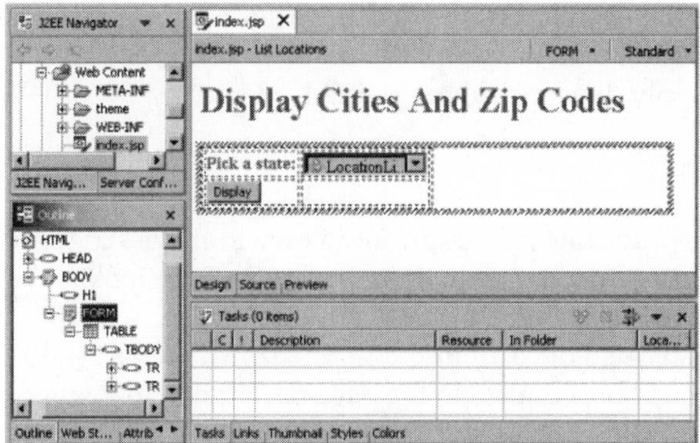

Figure 19.6 Design view of index.jsp.

You will use a borderless table to control the rendering layout. An encompassing <FORM> tag targets state.jsp as its handler. The Display button submits the form. A <SELECT> form drop-down menu contains the pick list of all the U.S. states and possessions. A list generator scriptlet uses Java classes `LocationListAllStates` and `LocationListAllStatesRow` to execute out the LocationListAllStates SQL query that you created in Chapter 18. Refer to the entire <BODY> element following to create the JSP:

```
<BODY><H1>Display Cities and Zip Codes</H1>
<FORM method="get" action="/JspModelOne/state.jsp"><TABLE border="0">
    <TBODY>
        <TR>
            <TH>Pick a state:</TH>
            <TD><SELECT name="state">
<% LocationListAllStates los = new LocationListAllStates();
    los.execute("","");
    LocationListAllStatesRow[] rows = los.getRows();
    for (int i= 0; i < rows.length; ++i) {
        LocationListAllStatesRow thisRow = rows[i];
        out.print("<option name=\"");
        out.print(thisRow.getLOCATION_STATE());
        out.print("\">");
        out.print(thisRow.getLOCATION_STATE());
        out.println("</option>");
    } %>
            </SELECT></TD>
        </TR>
        <TR>
            <TD><INPUT type="submit" name="display"
value="Display"></TD>
            <TD></TD>
        </TR>
    </TBODY>
</TABLE>
</FORM>
</BODY>
```

Notice that you have supplied one contiguous scriptlet that used `out.print()` to emit HTML tags. An alternative is to break the scriptlet into parts using JSP expressions, such as the following, to supply dynamic values to HTML elements.

```
<%= thisRow.getLOCATION_STATE() %>
```

You have enough information to duplicate index.jsp. Now, you will create states.jsp, which will render the requested results according to the user's pick. First, look at the Design view, shown in Figure 19.7.

This JSP uses two data JavaBeans generated from the `LocationListState` SQL statement in Chapter 18. Notice the import clauses in the page declaration following:

```
<%@ page language="java" contentType="text/html; charset=WINDOWS-1252"
pageEncoding="WINDOWS-1252" import="com.xyz.data.LocationListState"
import="com.xyz.data.LocationListStateRow"%>
```

A table controls the layout, but this time it contains rendered result rows. This JSP appears more complex until you analyze the contents of the HTML <BODY> element. First, it renders the name of the chosen state, as passed in the request object. Then it passes the state's name string to LocationListState that returns an array of Location-ListStateRow. Finally, it renders each element as an HTML table row.

If no results were returned, an empty HTML table body would result. Alternately, you could handle a no data situation by testing for a zero sized `LocationList StateRow` array and emitting a message instead of the table. This situation shouldn't happen in this situation since your pick list came from the same static database table that is queried here.

It is straightforward to duplicate this JSP once you see the HTML body element contained source tags. It is probably best to create the body visually, and then insert the scriptlets seen within the following page tags:

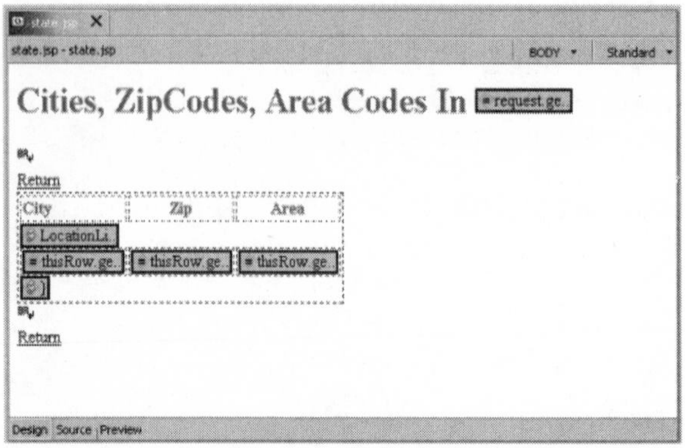

Figure 19.7 Design view of state.jsp.

```
<H1>Cities, ZipCodes, Area Codes in <%= request.getParameter("state") ⮐
%></H1>
<BR /><A href="/JspModelOne/index.jsp">Return</A>
<TABLE border="0">
    <TBODY>
        <TR>
            <TH align="left">City</TH>
            <TH>Zip</TH>
            <TH>Area</TH>
        </TR>
<%  LocationListState lls = new LocationListState();
    lls.execute("","", 7000, request.getParameter("state"));
    LocationListStateRow[] rows = lls.getRows();
    for (int i= 0; i < rows.length; ++i) {
        LocationListStateRow thisRow = rows[i];%>
        <TR>
            <TD><%= thisRow.getLOCATION_CITY() %></TD>
            <TD><%= thisRow.getLOCATION_ZIPCODE() %></TD>
            <TD><%= thisRow.getLOCATION_AREACODE() %></TD>
        </TR>
<% } %>
    </TBODY>
</TABLE>
<BR /><A href="/JspModelOne/index.jsp">Return</A>
</BODY>
```

Save the work. That completes the JSP model one application.

Publish and Test the Model One Application

JSP model one designs have a low fixed overhead, making them easy to create for small applications that aren't expected to grow. Now, you will publish the application and then test it. WSAD uses the term "publish" for the deployment process. An easy approach is to choose Run on Server from the JspModelOne context menu. If no test server is configured, WSAD will lead you through the steps to configure and start WebSphere v5.0 Test. Otherwise, you will be offered the chance to deploy and run on an existing configuration.

Refer to Figure 19.8 to see the application after Run on Server has triggered a publish operation followed by starting the WebSpere v5.0 test server. A request to run the Web application JspModelOne causes the encompassing J2EE application to execute, resulting in its contained J2EE modules starting. JspModelOne is among these.

If the Web request returns a "no class definition found" error for a class such as LocationListState, ensure that DataAccess.jar is in Web Library Projects on the Overview page of the JspModelOne deployment descriptor.

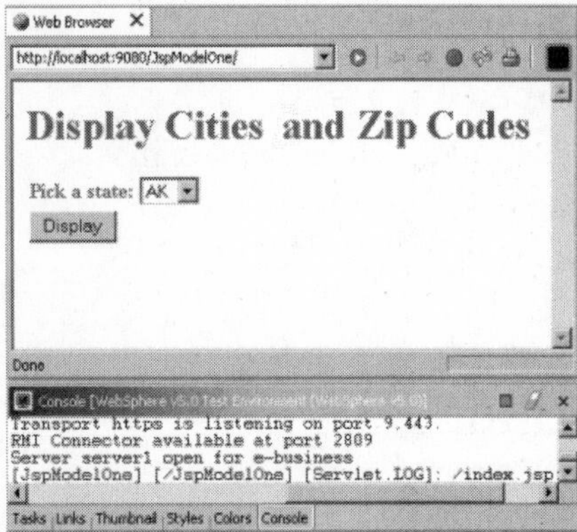

Figure 19.8 Model one start page.

Figure 19.9 shows the rendered state.jsp after it generated and rendered results for "NC." Try using the Web Browser view context menu to display the source tags. Notice that the scriptlets are stripped from the output, leaving only generated and static HTML. Recall that the page has been translated into an HTTP servlet that emits HTML strings to the output stream from print statements.

Critique of JspModelOne

WSAD helped make the application easy to create, since you had the DB access JavaBeans handy from Chapter 18. Before you congratulate yourself, you should realize that while the amount of Java scriptlet code wasn't excessive, this application involves only a couple of simple queries against a single static table in a relational database. Imagine a complex application that tends to have release cycles to enhance it or to simply maintain it. Further consider that it would likely use a larger SQL repertoire against joined tables to create, read, update, and delete (CRUD) rows or maybe entire tables.

http://localhost:9080/JspModelOne/state.jsp?state=NC&display=Display

Cities, ZipCodes, Area Codes in NC

Return

City	Zip	Area
Aberdeen	28315	919
Ahoskie	27910	919
Alamance	27201	919
Albemarle	28002	704
Albemarle	28001	704
Albertson	28508	919
Alexander	28701	704
Alexis	28006	704

Figure 19.9 Model one result page.

It is possible to imagine an out-of-control tangle of HTML, Java, and even SQL that would bring even the most brilliant designer to his or her knees. Imposing good organization processes can mitigate these issues, but the upcoming JSP model two design is better, albeit at the expense of more fixed overhead. A model one JSP design is good for small applications that are not expected to grow, because of its low fixed overhead. Model one is unwieldy where growth, reuse, separation of development skills, and lower maintenance costs are concerns. The JSP model two design in a following section is superior when these issues are important.

JSP Model One Using DB Tags

Before you do a JSP model two version of the project, let us segue into a cleaner model one approach. This project will use a tag library provided by WSAD in place of raw Java scriptlets. You will still implement the entire Web application in JSPs, but there will be just one small scriptlet used to display the state abbreviation. A data access tag library provided by WSAD will carry out the rest of the logic. One scriptlet expression will feed the chosen state abbreviation to a parameter tag. Figure 19.10 depicts the tags used to populate the body of the rendered table.

This tag library approach can promote increased model view separation because little Java code is exposed to the UI designer. A downside is that the SQL statement is exposed to the UI designer as a tag parameter instead of using our DB access Java Beans. Let us revise the previous JSP model one application to see the difference in the JSP implementations.

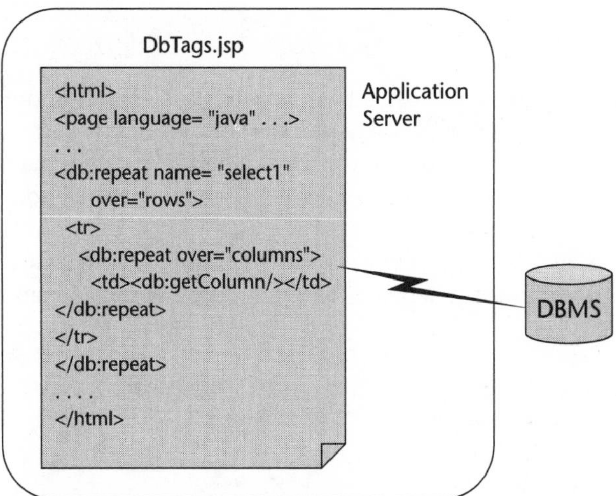

Figure 19.10 Model one JSP using DB tag library.

Create the DB Tags Project

Create a new Web project as you did for the JSP model one example. Name it JspDbTags. Keep the document root default value of JspDbTags as well. Be sure to specify the tag libraries as listed in Table 19.1. Use the same options as you did for JspModelOne, being sure to add DataAccess as a Web library project.

Create the DB Tags Web Application

You will implement the application entirely within new versions of index.jsp and state.jsp. Start by creating two JSPs in the new project with the following steps:

1. Ensure that the J2EE Navigator view is open.
2. Create a new blank JSP named index.jsp in the JspDbTags project. Press Next.
3. Press Add Tag Library. Choose jspsql. Supply a prefix value db.
4. Press Finish to create the page.

Repeat Steps one through four using the page name state.jsp. These JSPs do not need import attributes in the page descriptor in the <HEAD> element. The descriptor in each JSP should resemble the following:

```
<%@ page language="java" contentType="text/html; charset=WINDOWS-1252"
pageEncoding="WINDOWS-1252" %>
```

Each JSP should contain a directive used to load the jspsql tag library. Verify that the following directive appears just after the <HEAD> element in the source view:

```
<%@ taglib uri="jspsql" prefix="db" %>
```

The URI attribute refers to the bits that compose the tag library classes. The db prefix is an arbitrary namespace prefix used to reference tags of the jspsql tag library in the JSP. The DB tag library is used to create code tags to connect to the JDBC driver manager, along with another tag that specifies a parameterized SQL statement embedded in a tag.

Open the index.jsp page. The final Design view is superficially identical to that of the model one JSP. Use the Source view to insert the following two DB tag elements prior to the </HEAD> HTML tag:

```
<db:driverManagerSpec id="conn1" driver="com.ibm.db2j.jdbc.DB2jDriver"
    url="jdbc:db2j:c:/db2j/databases/DemoDB"
    userid="" password="" />
<db:select id="select1" scope="page" connectionSpec="conn1"
        readOnly="true">
    <db:sql>
        SELECT DISTINCT APP.LOCATION.STATE
        FROM APP.LOCATION
        ORDER BY STATE ASC
    </db:sql>
</db:select>
```

The first tag creates a connection to the database. Modify the URL attribute if the database resides at a different location. The second tag defines a `select` statement to query the database. You will use a reference to this tag in the body of the JSP to populate the state pick list. Replace the body of the JSP with the following:

```
<BODY>
<H1>Display Cities and Zip Codes</H1>
<FORM method="get" action="/JspDbTags/state.jsp"><TABLE border="0">
    <TBODY>
        <TR>
            <TH>Pick a state:</TH>
            <TD><SELECT name="state">
                <db:repeat name="select1" over="rows">
                    <OPTION name=
                        '<db:getColumn index="1" />'>
                        <db:getColumn index="1" />
                    </OPTION>
                </db:repeat>
            </SELECT></TD>
        </TR>
        <TR>
            <TD><INPUT type="submit" name="display"
                       value="Display"></TD>
            <TD></TD>
        </TR>
    </TBODY>
</TABLE>
</FORM>
</BODY>
```

Notice how the db prefix is used to qualify jspsql tags. The state.jsp page is your action handler. Notice that the <db:repeat> tag populates the HTML table through a named reference to the <db:select> tag.

Save the work. You are halfway finished with this version of the Web application. Open the Source view of state.jsp. Insert the following tags just before the </head> tag:

```
<db:driverManagerSpec id="conn1" driver="com.ibm.db2j.jdbc.DB2jDriver"
    url="jdbc:db2j:c:/db2j/databases/DemoDB" userid="" password="" />
<db:select id="select1" scope="page" connectionSpec="conn1"
        readOnly="true">
    <db:sql>
        SELECT
               APP.LOCATION.CITY,
               APP.LOCATION.ZIPCODE,
               APP.LOCATION.AREACODE
        FROM APP.LOCATION
        WHERE APP.LOCATION.STATE = :state
        ORDER BY CITY ASC, ZIPCODE ASC
    </db:sql>
    <db:parameter
        parmName="state"
```

```
            type="CHAR"
            value='<%= request.getParameter("state") %>'/>
</db:select>
```

This should look familiar by now. Here, you have passed the state parameter by extracting its attribute from the request object using a small scriptlet expression. The parameter tag is used to set the :state host variable in the select statement. The SQL is a duplicate of the source input you used for the corresponding SQL input to generate the data access JavaBean model one in the last chapter. The body of this state.jsp page is not complex, although it renders a large result. Replace the body of state.jsp with the following:

```
<BODY>
<H1>Cities, ZipCodes, Area Codes in <%= request.getParameter("state")
%></H1>
<BR /><A href="/JspDbTags/index.jsp">Return</A>
<TABLE border="0">
    <TBODY>
        <TR>
            <TH align="left">City</TH>
            <TH>Zip</TH>
            <TH>Area</TH>
        </TR>
        <db:repeat name="select1" over="rows">
            <TR>
                <db:repeat over="columns">
                    <TD><db:getColumn /></TD>
                </db:repeat>
            </TR>
        </db:repeat>
    </TBODY>
</TABLE>
<BR /><A href="/JspDbTags/index.jsp">Return</A>
</BODY>
```

Again, most of the rendering here is carried out by the <db:repeat> tag using the defined select1 query as an attribute. Save the work. This completes the implementation.

Publish and Test the DbTagsJsp Application

Now, you can publish and test the application. Select Run on Server from the DbTagsJsp project context menu in the J2EE Explorer. The application should look and feel the same as the previous model one JSP application. The implementation of this application is more interesting than seeing it run. Try viewing the source by using the context menu on the browser page. Notice that the server consumed the DB tags, leaving only the generated HTML tags.

Critique of DBTagsJsp

What did you accomplish? You polished the two JSPs by using higher-level tag elements instead of lower-level raw Java scriptlets. You used two small scriptlet expressions, but now the overall application logic is more declarative than procedural. One problem with using this tag library is that SQL is exposed in the presentation markup although it is not exposed to the end user. This may be a problem when you wish to not expose logic to Web authoring personnel.

It would be better to have the SQL and all application logic relegated to a back-end layer that the presentation cannot see or discern. This approach could promote separation of skills so that a presentation designer could change the look and feel of the application without breaking it. Conversely, the SQL programmer or Java programmer could change his or her code without necessarily disturbing the look and feel of the presentation layer.

JSP Model Two

In this section, you will create the same simple application you did in the previous two projects, except that you will need more work to create the higher fixed overhead of JSP model two. See Figure 19.11.

You will handle all HTTP requests with a single servlet written in the Front Controller J2EE pattern. This controller servlet will translate an input dispatch parameter to a command that is part of the Command pattern, and then instantiate and execute the object for that command. The command object will carry out any necessary application work by making a method call on a Mediator design pattern instance kept in the HTTP session. Thus, all state is maintained in the mediator. The goal is to keep the number of instance variables in the mediator low and keep each small. You do not want to use too much session resource or the number of possible simultaneous requests will be reduced. You may eventually evolve an application to handling tens or hundreds of simultaneous requests.

When the mediator method returns to the command object, the command object returns a string containing the target URL for forwarding the request. The front controller servlet forwards the request to the specified target. This is normally the JSP that will render the results of the request.

Remember that the model two JSP design restricts the JSP role to that of rendering dynamic data passed as a request attribute. This attribute usually references a Java Bean. The JavaBean implements the J2EE Value Object design pattern. How is the value object populated with data for rendering? A method in the mediator returns it to its calling command object. That object may set the reference to the value object in the request object for retrieval by the target JSP.

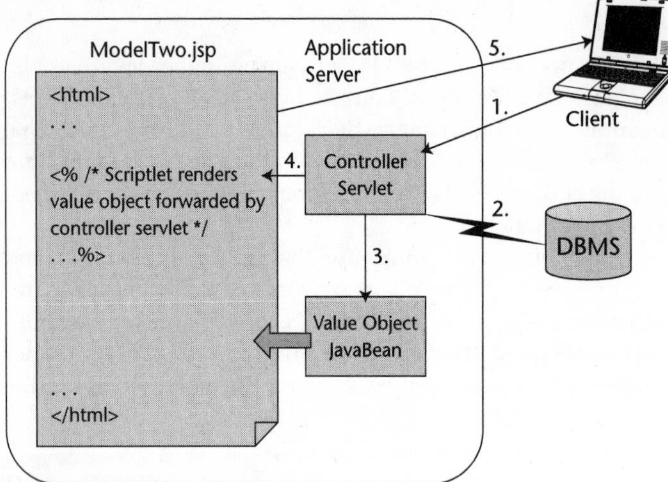

Figure 19.11 JSP model two.

Create the Model Two JSP Project

Create a new Web project as you did for each of the previous examples. Name it Jsp-ModelTwo. Again, let the document root default to the project name. Specify the options you used in the JSP model one project, remembering to associate the project with the DisplayApp J2EE project.

Add the DataAccess.jar composed in the DataAccess project to the project Web Library Projects group as you did for the previous two projects. Now, you can move on to creating the application.

Create the Model Two JSPs

Create blank index.jsp and state.jsp pages as you did previously. These JSPs will have scriptlets that deal only with rendering data passed in a value object JavaBean. Forms in the JSPs use the front controller servlet that you will create in a following section. Additionally, create a JSP named error.jsp to use as a target for possible application error states.

Creating error.jsp is trivial. It displays a static error message along with a hyperlink to the start page. Later, you may wish to display dynamic error information. For this exercise, implement its <BODY> tag as follows:

```
<BODY>
<H1>Error</H1>
<P>Sorry! The Demographic application suffered an error.</P>
<br />
<a href="/JspModelTwo/index.html">| Return |</a>
</BODY>
```

The Preview appears as seen in Figure 19.12.

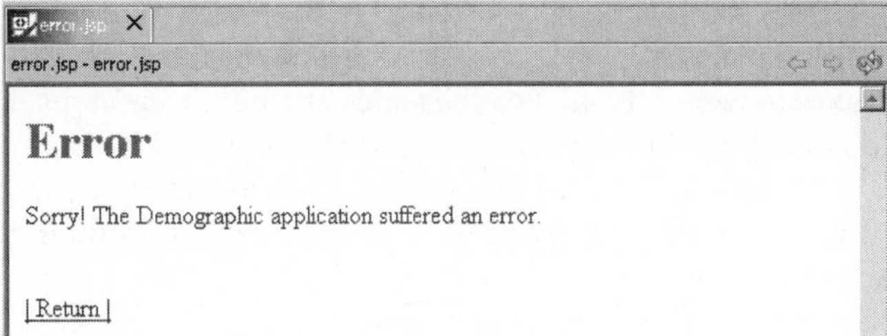

Figure 19.12 Preview of error.jsp.

The index.jsp displays the state pick list. This version has no application model logic. It only displays rows passed in a JavaBean. A scriplet renders the row data, but it cannot see nor influence any model logic. Add an import attributes to the page declaration for a DB access JavaBean as follows:

```
<%@ page language="java" contentType="text/html; charset=WINDOWS-1252"
pageEncoding="WINDOWS-1252"
import="com.xyz.data.LocationListAllStatesRow" %>
```

Substitute the following for the boilerplate body:

```
<BODY>
<H1>Display Cities and Zip Codes</H1>
<FORM method="get" action="/JspModelTwo/Controller">
<INPUT type="hidden" name="dispatch" value="CmdCities">
<TABLE border="0">
    <TBODY>
        <TR>
            <TH>Pick a state:</TH>
            <TD><SELECT name="state">
<% LocationListAllStatesRow[] states =
        (LocationListAllStatesRow[])request.getAttribute("states");
    if (states != null)
        for (int i=0; i < states.length; ++i) {
            LocationListAllStatesRow thisRow = states[i]; %>
            <option name="<%= thisRow.getLOCATION_STATE() %>">
            <%= thisRow.getLOCATION_STATE() %>
            </option>
<% } %>
            </SELECT></TD>
        </TR>
        <TR>
            <TD><INPUT type="submit" name="display"
                       value="Display"></TD>
            <TD></TD>
        </TR>
    </TBODY>
</TABLE>
</FORM>
</BODY>
```

Notice how the scriptlet obtains the JavaBean instance from the states attribute of the request object. A `for` loop emits HTML table rows that are populated with data from the JavaBean array. If no data were returned or the states attribute were not set, the drop-down menu would be empty, but the page would still be rendered normally. A better approach may be to conditionally forward processing to a dynamic error page. The error page is static, but it could easily be changed to display error information placed in a request attribute by the forwarder.

Add a JavaBean import statement to the state.jsp as follows:

```
<%@ page language="java" contentType="text/html; charset=WINDOWS-1252"
pageEncoding="WINDOWS-1252" import="com.xyz.data.LocationListStateRow"%>
```

Now, substitute the following for the dummy HTML body element of state.jsp:

```
<BODY>
<H1>Cities, ZipCodes, Area Codes in <%= request.getParameter("state")
%></H1>
<BR /><A href="/JspModelTwo/Controller?dispatch=CmdHome">Return</A>
<TABLE border="0">
    <TBODY>
        <TR>
            <TH align="left">City</TH>
            <TH>Zip</TH>
            <TH>Area</TH>
        </TR>
<% LocationListStateRow[] rows =
(LocationListStateRow[])request.getAttribute("cities");
    if (rows != null)
        for (int i= 0; i < rows.length; ++i) {
            LocationListStateRow thisRow = rows[i];
%>
            <TR>
                <TD><%= thisRow.getLOCATION_CITY() %></TD>
                <TD><%= thisRow.getLOCATION_ZIPCODE() %></TD>
                <TD><%= thisRow.getLOCATION_AREACODE() %></TD>
            </TR>
<% } %>
    </TBODY>
</TABLE>
<BR /><A href="/JspModelTwo/Controller?dispatch=CmdHome">Return</A>
</BODY>
```

The state.jsp renders its LocationListStateRow array into an HTML table by using a simple scriptlet. Again, there is no direct coupling to the application model. A `for` loop emits HTML table rows that are populated with data from the LocationListStateRow array. If no data were returned or the cities attribute were not set, the HTML table would display no rows, but the page would still render normally. A better tactic may be to conditionally display text such as "No data found."

Create a Static HTML Start Page

Create a blank index.html page. This page is used to enter the application through the controller servlet when no session is established. By default, this page takes precedence over index.jsp when no page is specified in the request URL. Replace the **<BODY>** element of the page with the following:

```
<BODY>
<h1>Demographics Application</h1>
<P><A href="/JspModelTwo/Controller?dispatch=CmdHome">Enter Demographics
Application</A></P>
</BODY>
```

The front controller always expects the dispatch parameter to name a valid command.

Create a Mediator

The mediator forms the top-level application model layer. Refer to Figure 19.13. It is called by commands that are dispatched by the front controller. The mediator must have no knowledge of the presentation layer. This promotes low coupling and reusability. Now, you will create the mediator.

1. Select the JspModelTwo / Java Source folder in the Package Explorer of the Java Perspective.
2. Use the context menu item New > Package to create package com.xyz.mediator.
3. Create the Mediator class in the com.xyz.mediator package.
4. Add the following field and two methods to the Mediator class. These implement the top-level logic called by command objects. The field keeps the application state (no pun intended—really), since the mediator instance will reside in the HTTP session object.

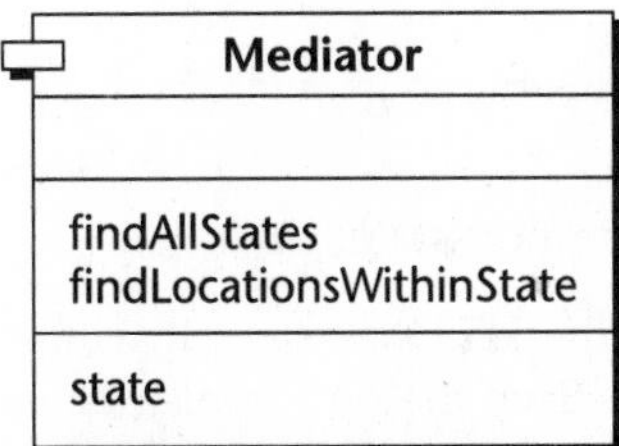

Figure 19.13 Mediator.

```
private String state;
/**
 * @return com.xyz.data.LocationListAllStatesRow[]
 * sorted distinct states
 */
public LocationListAllStatesRow[] findAllStates() {
    LocationListAllStatesRow[] result = null;
    try {
        LocationListAllStates data = new LocationListAllStates();
        data.execute("", "");
        result = data.getRows();
    } catch (SQLException ex) {
        ex.printStackTrace();
    }
    return result;
}
/**
 * @return com.xyz.data.LocationListStateRow[]
 * sorted distinct states
 */
public LocationListStateRow[]
                findLocationsWithinState(String state) {
    LocationListStateRow[] result = null;
    try {
        LocationListState data = new LocationListState();
        data.execute("", "", 5000, state);
        result = data.getRows();
    } catch (SQLException ex) {
       ex.printStackTrace();
    }
    return result;
}
```

5. Select the field state : String in the Outline view.
6. Invoke its context menu. Select Generate Getter and Setter to generate both a getter and setter accessor for the field.
7. Use import assistance to generate all the necessary import statements.

That completes the mediator. Its object will reside in the HTTP session. It will be retrieved and its methods invoked by command objects. Each method implemented thus far returns an array of DB access JavaBeans. It is up to the invoking command to handle these results.

Create Commands

The front controller servlet invokes commands. A command may use the mediator to carry out logical application activities. Our command package will contain a set of command classes that extend a `Command` base class, and additionally implement an `ICommand` interface. The base class provides common fields and a method to access the mediator for all commands. The interface is used by the front controller to access the common command `execute()` method. See Figure 19.14.

Create the com.xyz.command package in JspModelTwo / Java Source. The classes and interface that follow will reside in this package.

Create class `Command` in the com.xyz.command package. Implement the class as shown in the following code. It is easier to supply the fields and method first, and then let WSAD assist in creating the import statements. Note that the `getMediator()` method manages the mediator instance in the HTTP session.

```
package com.xyz.command;
import javax.jms.Session;
import javax.servlet.http.HttpServletRequest;
import javax.servlet.http.HttpSession;
import com.xyz.mediator.Mediator;
/**
 * Base class providing methods for command pattern
 */
public class Command {
    private static final String mediatorName = "MEDIATOR";
    /**
     * @return com.xyz.mediator.Mediator
     */
    public Mediator getMediator(HttpServletRequest req) {
        Object mediator = null;
        HttpSession session = req.getSession();
        mediator = session.getAttribute(mediatorName);
        if (mediator == null) {
            mediator = new Mediator();
            session.setAttribute(mediatorName, mediator);
        }
        return (Mediator) mediator;
    }
}
```

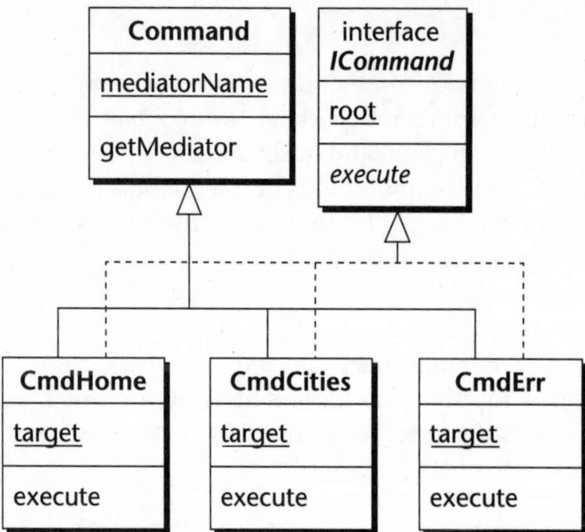

Figure 19.14 Commands.

Create the `ICommand` interface in the com.xyz.command package. The front controller uses it to execute commands that implement it. Define this interface as follows:

```
package com.xyz.command;
import javax.servlet.http.HttpServletRequest;
import javax.servlet.http.HttpServletResponse;
/**
 * Declares a commnand plugin point used by a front controller.
 */
public interface ICommand {
    public static String root = "/JspModelTwo";
    /**
     * Possibly causes side-effects.Returns a relative URL string.
     * @param req javax.servlet.http.HttpServletRequest
     * @param res javax.servlet.http.HttpServletResponse
     */
    public String execute(HttpServletRequest req, HttpServletResponse ⮐
res);
}
```

Now, you have the required classes needed to create the three command classes. For each, remember to extend the `com.xyz.command.Command` class and implement the `com.xyz.command.ICommand`. interface. Begin by creating com.xyx.command.CmdErr. It should resemble the following:

```
package com.xyz.command;
import javax.servlet.http.HttpServletRequest;
import javax.servlet.http.HttpServletResponse;
/**
 * Dispatch an error presentation JSP
 */
```

```
public class CmdErr extends Command implements ICommand {
    private static String target = "error.jsp";
    /**
     * @see com.xyz.command.ICommand#execute(HttpServletRequest,
     *   HttpServletResponse)
     */
    public String execute(HttpServletRequest req,
                          HttpServletResponse res) {
        return target;
    }
}
```

Create the `com.xyz.command.CmdHome` class, and implement it as follows:

```
package com.xyz.command;
import javax.servlet.http.HttpServletRequest;
import javax.servlet.http.HttpServletResponse;
import com.xyz.data.LocationListAllStatesRow;
import com.xyz.mediator.Mediator;
/**
 * Targets start page as next page, passing it a bean[]
 * containing all istinct US states and possessions.
 */
public class CmdHome extends Command implements ICommand {
    private final static String target = "index.jsp";
    /**
     * @see com.xyz.command.ICommand#execute(
     *          HttpServletRequest, HttpServletResponse)
     */
    public String execute(HttpServletRequest req,
                          HttpServletResponse res) {
        Mediator mediator = getMediator(req);
        LocationListAllStatesRow[] bean = mediator.findAllStates();
        req.setAttribute("states", bean);
        return target;
    }
}
```

Finally, create com.xyz.command.CmdCities, the most complex of the commands, as shown following:

```
package com.xyz.command;
import javax.servlet.http.HttpServletRequest;
import javax.servlet.http.HttpServletResponse;
import com.xyz.data.LocationListStateRow;
import com.xyz.mediator.Mediator;
/**
 * Return all cities for the current state
 */
public class CmdCities extends Command implements ICommand {
```

```
    private final static String target = "state.jsp";
    /**
     * @see com.xyz.command.ICommand#execute(HttpServletRequest,
     *                                      HttpServletResponse)
     */
    public String execute(HttpServletRequest req,
                          HttpServletResponse res) {
        String result = target;
        Mediator mediator = getMediator(req);

        // If new current state given, set it into mediator
        String state = req.getParameter("state");
        if (state != null)
            mediator.setState(state);
        // Have mediator return all locations in current state
        state = mediator.getState();
        if (state == null) {
            result = "error.jsp";
        } else {
            LocationListStateRow[] cities =
                mediator.findLocationsWithinState(state);
            req.setAttribute("cities", cities);
        }
        return result;
    }
}
```

Create a Front Controller Servlet

The front controller servlet implements the application controller layer that manages client requests by using the previous commands to interact through the mediator. Refer to the class diagram shown in Figure 19.15 to understand how the front controller relates to the command and to the mediator. Create the servlet as follows:

1. Open the JspModelTwo project in the Web Perspective.
2. Use the context menu item JspModelTwo / Java Source in the J2EE Navigator to invoke New > Package.
3. Name the package com.xyz.controller, and then press Finish.
4. Invoke the context menu on the JspModelTwo / Java Source / com.xyz.controller package and select New > Servlet.
5. Name the servlet Controller. When the wizard resembles Figure 19.16, press Finish.

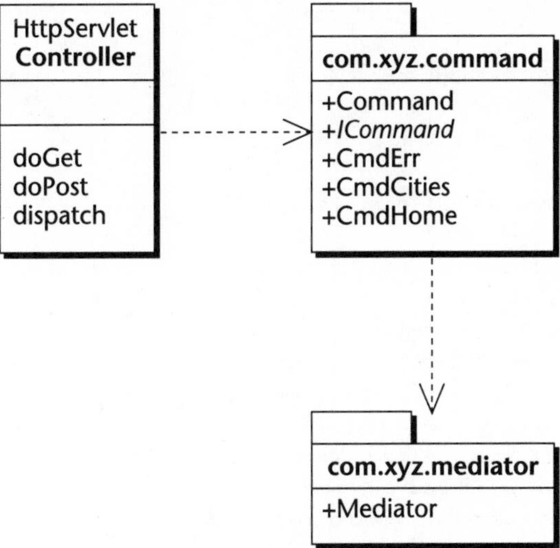

Figure 19.15 Front controller dependencies.

New Servlet

New Servlet
Create a new Servlet.

Folder: /JspModelTwo/Java Source Browse...
Java package: com.xyz.controller Browse...
Class Name: Controller
Superclass: javax.servlet.http.HttpServlet Browse...
Modifiers: Public Abstract Final
Options: Use Single Thread Model
Interfaces: Add... Remove
Code Generation Model: None

Figure 19.16 Create controller servlet.

6. Edit Controller.java. Insert the following method:

```
/**
 * Execute a command object according to the value of the
 * "dispatch" parameter. Forward control to the result of
 * the command. Dispatch CmdErr if no match
 * @param req javax.servlet.http.HttpServletRequest
 * @param res javax.servlet.http.HttpServletResponse
 */
```

```
protected void dispatch(HttpServletRequest req,
        HttpServletResponse resp)
    throws ServletException, IOException {
    String target = "error.jsp";
    // Decode and execute command given by "dispatch"
    // parameter value
    String cmdStr = req.getParameter("dispatch");
    if (cmdStr == null)
        target = new CmdErr().execute(req, resp);
    else if (cmdStr.equals("CmdHome"))
        target = new CmdHome().execute(req, resp);
    else if (cmdStr.equals("CmdCities"))
        target = new CmdCities().execute(req, resp);
    else
        target = new CmdErr().execute(req, resp);
    // Forward control to JSP selected by command
    req.getRequestDispatcher(target).forward(req, resp);
}
```

7. Replace the bodies of the `doGet()` and `doPut()` methods with the following statement:

   ```
   dispatch(req, resp);
   ```

8. Supply missing import statements by using content assistance at the lines flagged by the light bulb icon.
9. Save your work.

Ensure that the project builds correctly. This completes the initial application development.

Publish JspModelTwo and Test

Use the context menu to invoke Run on Server against project JspModelTwo in the J2EE Navigator. The project will be published automatically. The default test server will start if it is not running. The Static HTML start page will appear in the Web Browser view. This apparent difference from the other two renditions of the application ensures that the front controller servlet is called instead of the index.jsp because the servlet handles all requests. Aside from the start page, the application's appearance and behavior matches that of the previous two renditions. Figures 19.17 and 19.18 show external browser panels that rendered location data about Washington State.

Critique of JspModelTwo

That seemed like a great deal of work compared to the model one rendition. Recall that one advantage of a small model one application is low fixed overhead. You threw several design patterns at the model two design. These impose structure on the application but entail fixed overhead.

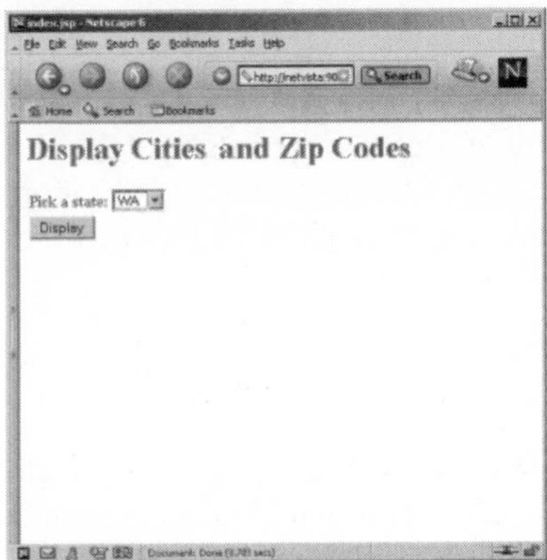

Figure 19.17 Model two pick list from index.jsp.

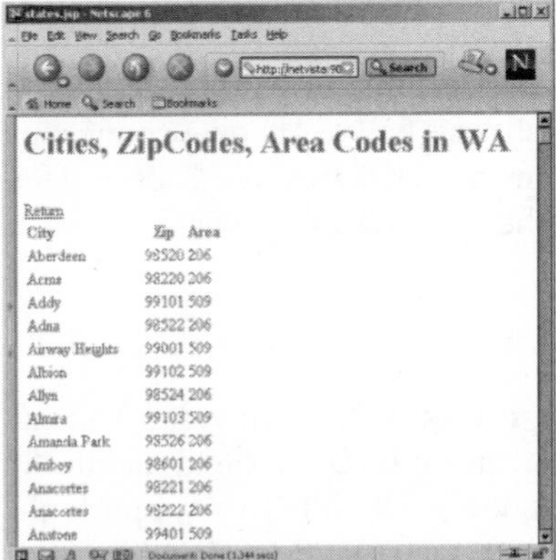

Figure 19.18 Example of model two states.jsp.

Assume that this small query application could be the beginning of a larger demographics program. Imagine how you would add to it to capture survey responder demographics, leveraging data access JavaBeans from more SQL statements such as those you developed in Chapter 18. Think of the application as having a view portion and a model portion that are as loosely coupled as possible. Develop a new model feature and only then develop the presentation view. Perhaps you want to set a current location for a session, and then add survey responder information for that location. You could add a radio button or Submit button beside each row displayed by states.jsp. The form submission would send the chosen location to the mediator, which would save it in an instance variable. The mediator instance is kept in the session, so the default location persists for the session duration.

Enhancements

This application is merely a demonstration of techniques used out of sight of the end user at this point. It is only one piece of a potential survey demographics application. Following are some techniques and features that could be applied to this or other applications that deal with persistent data.

DBMS Server

We chose a JDBC driver that used an embedded database. This is bad for real-world applications if only because an embedded database cannot be shared across multiple applications. We used this approach because DB2j Cloudscape is bundled with WSAD, so that we were able to avoid stating the steps to obtain, configure, and start a server-based DBMS. Additionally, a Cloudscape URL can specify that its database be created if it doesn't exist. This is good for creating a sample application.

If you have an available DBMS such as IBM DB2, Oracle, MySql, or Postgresql, you can use it by all means. These data stores mainly require a different driver and JDBC URL, and require manually creating an empty database. The WSAD data connection wizard will supply default values for many mainstream databases. If a chosen database is not listed you can elect to access it through the JDBC ODBC driver.

JNDI

J2EE mandates that compliant application servers include a JNDI provider. You can define named resource locations or services such that any application can dynamically bind to any published resource or service by using the JNDI API. This supports the J2EE philosophy of using an external level of indirection to avoid hard-coding locations in the code. This enhances deployment flexibility and tuning capability by avoiding the need to rebuild code every time the execution environment changes.

A database connection is one kind of resource that lends itself to being published under a JDNI name. When you generated JavaBeans from SQL statements in Chapter 18, you should have specified a published data source name instead of a hard-coded URL, except that you would have needed to configure the server and have it running to do the exercise. In Chapter 23, "Entity EJBs," you will use a published data source to access data. The subject of data sources leads into the discussion of connection pooling in the following section.

Connection Pooling

Connection pooling is an easy improvement that may vastly increase data performance. A DBMS suffers a glut of processing cycles in order to provide an application with a database connection, especially if the DBMS is remote. A Web application that displays or manipulates data may need at least one database connection per request. This connection has identical characteristics to connections needed for all requests in all sessions for all users. Why close the connection and dispose of it? Consider the concept of recycling.

It would be better to have a pool of reusable database connections. Each request handler would obtain a connection from a pool of identical preestablished requests, carry out SQL operations, return the connection to its initial state, and finally return it to the pool. A connection pool manager could heuristically grow or shrink the pool according to demand tracking.

JDBC 2 specifies connection pooling. A compliant DBMS implements a JDBC 2 provider that pools connections based upon a data source defined in the server. For example, you will define a pooled data source for our DemoDb database.

1. Open the WebSphere v5.0 Test Environment using its context menu in the Server Configuration view.
2. Click the Data source tab. Expand the Server Settings group. Notice that there is already a provider named com.ibm.db2j.jdbc.DB2jConnectionPoolData-Source defined. Select it.
3. Click the Add button to the right of the box labeled Data source.
4. Choose Version 5.0 data source in the wizard. Press Next >.
5. Complete the Modify Data Source panel as shown in Figure 19.19. Press Next >.
6. Set the DemoDb path as shown in Figure 19.20. Press Finish, and then save and close the configuration.

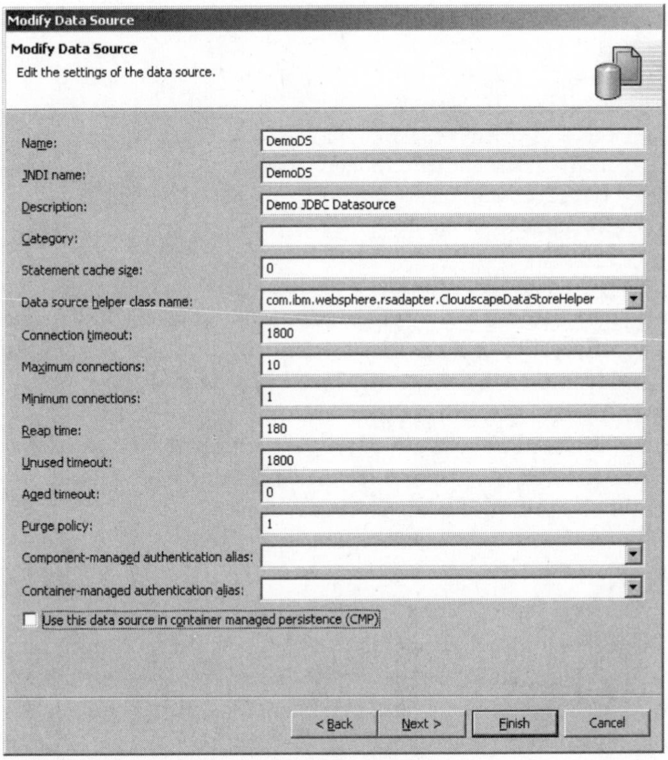

Modify Data Source

Modify Data Source

Edit the settings of the data source.

Name:	DemoDS
JNDI name:	DemoDS
Description:	Demo JDBC Datasource
Category:	
Statement cache size:	0
Data source helper class name:	com.ibm.websphere.rsadapter.CloudscapeDataStoreHelper
Connection timeout:	1800
Maximum connections:	10
Minimum connections:	1
Reap time:	180
Unused timeout:	1800
Aged timeout:	0
Purge policy:	1
Component-managed authentication alias:	
Container-managed authentication alias:	

☐ Use this data source in container managed persistence (CMP)

< Back | Next > | Finish | Cancel

Figure 19.19 Data source used in pool.

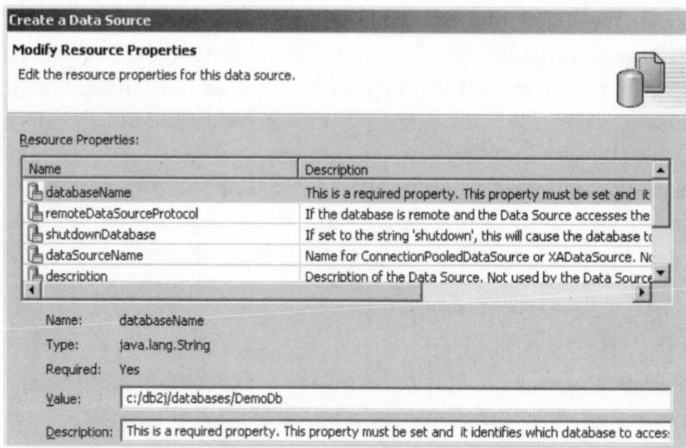

Figure 19.20 Pooled data source database name.

That completes the pooled data source definition. The Data sources group of the server configuration should resemble Figure 19.21.

How do you use this pooled data source? First, obtain a context from the JNDI provider, then make a lookup method call on it to find the data source, and finally get the connection from the data source, as shown in the following code snippet:

```
import java.sql.Connection;
import javax.naming.InitialContext;
import javax.sql.DataSource;
// Class definition removed for clarity
InitialContext jndiContext = new InitialContext();
DataSource ds = (DataSource) jndiContext.lookup("DemoDS");
Connection connection = ds.getConnection();
// Carry out JDBC calls using the connection
```

Not shown is the requirement to handle or declare a throws clause for the exceptions java.sql.SQLException and javax.naming.NamingException. The constructor for the InitialContext may need a location URL and security credentials, depending upon the application server vendor, its location, and the security lockdown imposed on the database. Our DB2j examples will work with a no-argument `InitialContext()` constructor. When the connection is closed or goes out of scope it is returned to the pool.

Using a pooled data source enables an application to scale better. The JNDI indirection also increases its flexibility by promoting late configuration.

Enterprise JavaBeans

Entity Enterprise JavaBeans (EJBs) normally use a pooled connection found through a JNDI lookup for container-managed entity beans. Entity beans represent persistent data. EJBs are worth considering for the domain and persistence layers of a J2EE application. We shall discuss EJBs in detail in Chapter 22, "Enterprise JavaBeans," and Chapter 23, "Entity EJBs."

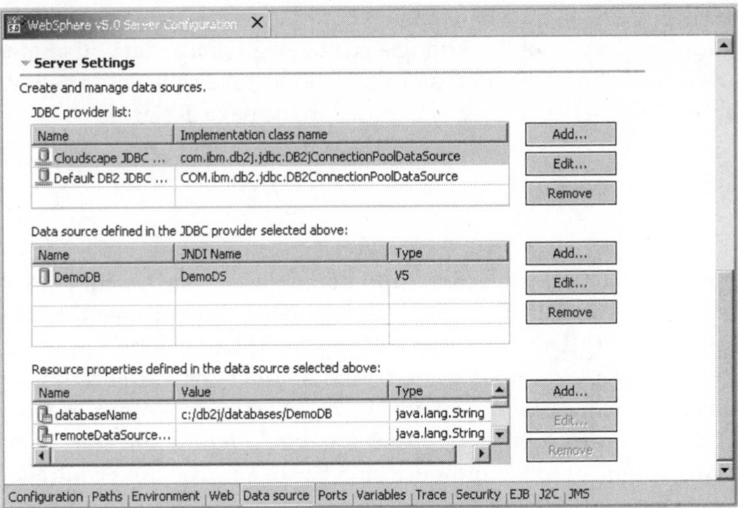

Figure 19.21 Completed pooled data source.

Complete the Application

We presented part of a potential demographic survey application. You created a RESPONDER database table and several SQL statements for it in Chapter 18. A `ResponderInsert` statement creates rows of survey response data. The Responder ListState query uses a join on the RESPONDER table and LOCATION table to list data about survey responders from a given U.S. Postal Service Zip Code. The data access JavaBeans for these statements can enhance the application.

We recommend the model two JSP approach. The necessary pattern-based infrastructure is already in place. Recall that the front controller dispatches the correct command based upon the dispatch parameter value. Add new model capability by coding a new method in the mediator along with a command object to call it. That's often all there is to adding capability to the model side.

The command returns the URL string for the JSP to render the result after setting a value object reference into the request object. The front controller then forwards control to the JSP specified. This would probably be a new JSP if it renders new functionality. It would find the value object by looking up its name in the request object. Then, it would render the data in the value object using scriptlets or a custom tag library.

Custom Tag Library

J2EE tag libraries are a way to isolate Java code from JSPs. You used a tag library supplied by WSAD to implement JSP model one dynamic actions in the JspDbTags rendition of the sample application. This mitigated the issue of exposing the presentation layer to mixed HTML tags and Java code.

For the same reason, it is a good idea to use a tag library to render value objects in a JSP model two application. This involves writing a custom tag library that will render value objects or Java collection classes used as value objects. Java code still provides the dynamic rendering; it is just never directly exposed to the page designer.

XML

Many DBMS, such as IBM DB2 with XML Extender, can accept or return data as an XML document. The WSAD Data Perspective supports the use of XML with a database. When a query result is returned as an XML document, the document can be transformed to any desired HTML rendition by applying an XSL transform document to it. Thus, you could dispense with a JSP that uses scriptlets or tag libraries for dynamic presentation in favor of emitting a custom HTML document. A command that produces HTML would not return a JSP URL. Instead, it would return null after sending a generated HTML document to the response object's stream. The front controller would not carry out a request forwarding operation in this case. The base Command class of JSP model two would contain the `transform` method used to produce the HTML document. We will show how XML can be transformed into HTML in Chapter 20, "XML in WebSphere Studio Application Developer," where you will create an online trivia examination Web application.

Frames

After the application is enhanced, it will have more presentation function points. There will be additional kinds of requests and updates that the user can request. It may be good to provide a more hierarchical view of the application's functionality. One easy approach is to use a simple two-pane HTML frameset. The left-hand pane would be a navigation page having textual or graphical hyperlinks to major application functions. The right-hand pane would contain the detailed view of the current function. The user could easily abandon a sequence of functional panels by clicking on a new major function in the left-hand pane. The parent attribute of a left-hand navigation pane hyperlink would direct the new page to the right-hand detail pane.

Interface Synchronizer Token

Our pages expect to be called with value objects in the request object. What happens if you directly execute one of them by manually entering its URL? Try it. This is a good way to test the "no data" scenario. The user should not be given an avenue to cause the application to show its ugly side. The problem is to keep a JSP from being rendered unless it was called correctly. One approach is to use an interface synchronizer token.

The Command base class could contain a method that generates a unique one-time use ID string that it saves in the session under a well-known name. Additionally, each JSP would have scriptlet logic or a custom tag that delegates to the `Command` class to insert the same ID value into a hidden text field. When the page is submitted from the client, the front controller delegates to the `Command` class to compare the hidden field ID value with that in the session. If there is a mismatch, control is forwarded to the error page. Thus, the user cannot use bookmarks or the Back button to cause state mismatches. The application is more bulletproof and makes a better impression on the user.

Summary

This chapter discussed ways to render data in J2EE Web applications. We covered:

- Data client application model types
- JSP model one design
- Data rendering through a custom tag library
- JSP model two design
- The mediator design pattern
- The front controller design pattern
- The command design pattern
- Value objects
- Handling no data situations
- Pros and cons of the design models
- A survey of data rendering enhancements

Although the JSP model two design has an initial higher fixed coding overhead due to the several design patterns you incorporated, once this infrastructure is present, understanding, maintaining, and extending the model can be fairly routine. We recommend this design for serious data-related applications.

The next chapter examines the use of WSAD in creating XML-enabled applications.

XML in WebSphere Studio Application Developer

What's in Chapter 20?

XML has emerged as a document meta-language standard that has wide use in data representation and manipulation. XML is often used as the underpinnings of higher-level technologies such as J2EE. This chapter covers:

- An overview of WSAD XML tools
- Using the XML Editor to create an XML document
- Creating a DTD from XML
- Generating JavaBeans for a DTD or XML schema
- Writing an XLT transform
- Tracing an XSL transform
- Integrating XML into a Web application
- Deploying XML content and transforms in a Web application
- Running an XML Web application in WSAD

We assume that you have some knowledge of XML, XSL, DTD, and XML schema. The chapter focus is on using WSAD with these technologies. It starts with an overview of the XML tools provided by WSAD. This suite of tools holds its own with development products that target XML only. WSAD adds the ability to integrate XML into projects that use its other tools such as Web application authoring, deployment, and integrated testing and debugging.

The second part of the chapter steps through a project that delivers a trivia quiz to a Web community. WSAD tools are used throughout. Our exposure to raw XML angle brackets is minimized except for the coding of transformation templates to render an HTML form. The chapter ends by listing possible enhancements to the project.

WSAD XML Tools

WSAD incorporates an extensive set of visual XML development tools. These include features for building DTDs, XML schemas, XML, XSL transforms, and mappings between XML and various backend data storage systems. These tools compare well with competing tools that only address XML. Let us survey the bundled WSAD XML tools.

XML Editor

WSAD contains an XML editor used for creating and viewing XML files. We may use it to create a new XML file by entering elements and attributes directly, or create its skeleton from an existing DTD, or similarly create boilerplate from an existing XML schema. In addition, we may use the XML editor to edit an existing XML file, and then associate it with a DTD or schema, and finally validate it against the DTD or schema.

DTD Editor

The DTD editor is a tool that creates, views, and modifies a DTD. It operates similarly to the XML editor. You can use the DTD editor to generate a default HTML form based on a DTD. Additionally, the DTD editor can create a new DTD, generate a corresponding XML schema file, or generate JavaBeans that will create and manipulate instances of an XML schema. The JavaBean representation of a DTD is powerful. It enables us to create, process, save, or load an XML stream that is an instance of the schema for the JavaBeans.

XML Schema Editor

The XML schema editor is the schema analog of the DTD editor. It is used to edit an XML schema instead of a DTD. Like the DTD editor, it can generate JavaBeans that handle instances of that schema. In addition, we may use the XML schema editor to generate relational table definitions from the schema.

XSL Debugger

The XSL Debugger works with an XSL transformation against an XML file. It enables us to set breakpoints in the XSL script, or to visually step through the XSL script, watching the transformation rules fire. The debugger displays the current XSL element, the XSL template call stack, and the list of set breakpoints. In addition, the user may view the XML source and the corresponding text, XML, or HTML result. We shall use this capability to develop an XSL script that renders XML in an HTML page.

XML to XML Mapping Editor

The XML to XML mapping editor maps one or more source XML files to one result XML file. We may add Java methods, XPath groups, and expressions to a mapping. We may generate an XSLT script from the mapping. That script may be used to map XML files for the source DTDs into a result XML file.

XML and SQL Query Wizard

The XML and SQL query wizard to create an XML file from an SQL query result table. The wizard gives us the option to create an XML schema or DTD that describes the XML instance. The wizard can create a DADX file the represents our SQL query for use with the Web services tools.

RDB to XML Mapping Editor

The RDB to XML mapping editor defines a mapping between relational tables and an XML file. We may produce a document access definition (DAD) script for use by IBM DB2 with XML Extender support. The DAD script enables the composition of XML files from DB2 data, or the reverse decomposition of XML files into DB2 relational data.

XML-Based Web Project

An online knowledge testing system is a good candidate for an XML Web project. We shall design a small system that features a trivia test that is defined as an XML DTD. An XML instance of that DTD is transformed by a servlet into an HTML form by use of an XSL transform. The user selects answers to question prompts by selecting radio buttons that appear next to answer choices. We shall use WSAD XML tools and WSAD Web tools to create our trivia examination system.

High-Level Design

The XML document contains question elements. Each question element contains several choice elements. A correct choice element is marked by an attribute. This attribute is never transformed to HTML, so the user cannot discern correct answers by viewing HTML source. When the user presses the submit button, the user's answers are sent to a scoring servlet. That servlet loads the XML document into the JavaBeans for the trivia schema. The user's answers are matched to the correct answers and the scoring servlet emits a score as HTML created by another XSL transformation.

Create a Trivia DTD

We do not necessarily need to use an XML schema for this project. The XML schema provides fine-grained control over allowable XML document characteristics, and it supports XML name spaces. If we use a DTD, we may create many other kinds of entities from it in WSAD, including an XML schema, should we later decide to use one. For simplicity, we choose to define our trivia document syntax using a DTD.

We could create the DTD from scratch, or let WSAD create it from an XML file. Start by using WSAD to create an example XML document having the desired structure, next use WSAD and create a DTD from that document, and then perhaps to modify the DTD a bit. WSAD makes this easy. Let us begin by creating a trivia XML document with the following.

1. Open the **XML Perspective** in WSAD. Observe the toolbar icons and the XML-specific menus. Notice that we may create XML examples. We may wish to explore these examples before continuing.
2. Create a project named **exam-system** to contain our XML-related files, and JavaBeans that we will generate from a DTD.
3. Invoke the pop-up menu on the **exam-system** project in the Navigator view. Choose New > XML. Notice the other XML-related menu items available like DTD, Schema, and XSL.
4. The **Create XML File** wizard appears. Select **Create XML File from Scratch**. Press Next **>**.
5. Name the file **quiz.xml**. Press Finish. The skeleton file appears in the XML editor.
6. Select the **Design** tab of the XML editor. Right-click the **??xml** processing instruction symbol. Chose item Add After > New Element as shown in Figure 20.1.
7. A dialog box appears. Name the element **quiz** in the dialog box, and then press **OK**. This is the quiz document root element.
8. Right-click the quiz element. Choose Add Attribute > New Attribute as shown in Figure 20.2.

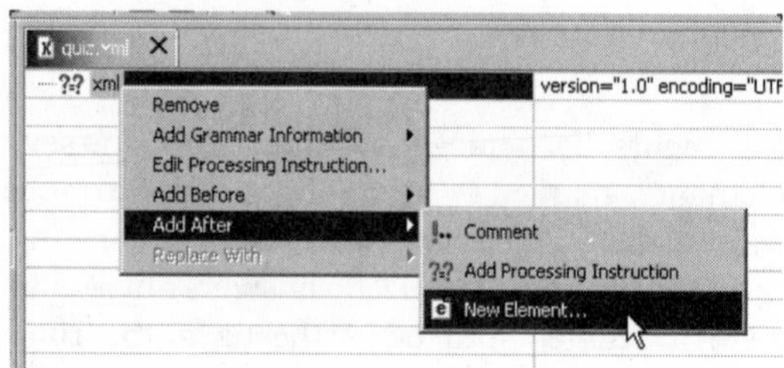

Figure 20.1 Add new XML element

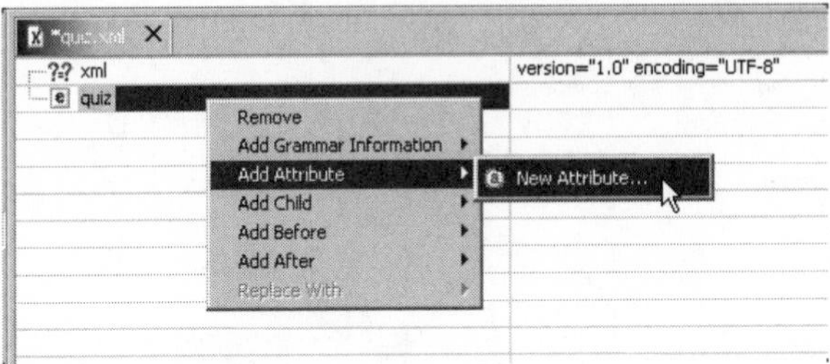

Figure 20.2 Add attribute.

9. A **New Attribute** dialog appears. Name the attribute **id**. Set its value to **e501**, a unique ID. This ID would be used to uniquely distinguish this quiz instance in a future enhancement. Press **OK** to set the name and value.
10. Right-click the **quiz** element. Choose Add Child > New Element to add a child element named **name**. Then type the character data value **Trivia** in the right-hand column of the new element's row.
11. Add a new element after element **name**. Call it **description**. Set its character data to **Trivia quiz.**
12. Add a new element after element **description**. Name it **question.**
13. Add a child element to **question** named **prompt**. Type **Prompt 1** for the value in the right-hand column of the new element.
14. Add a new element after **prompt**. Name it **choice**. Enter **Choice 1** for the value of the new element.
15. Add an attribute to **choice** named **id**. Set its value to **c01.**
16. Add another attribute to **choice**. Name it **correct**. Set its value to **1.**
17. Use **Add After > New Element** to add another **choice** element after the current **choice** element. Add an **id** attribute having value **c02**. Omit the **correct** attribute this time. Set the character data to **Choice 2.**
18. Duplicate the **question** element, adding the new **question** after it. This is best carried out using copy > past from the **Source** tab rendition.
19. Return to the **Design** tab. Change the **id** attributes on the choices to make them unique. Change the character data for the prompt element to **Prompt 2.**
20. Save the file.
21. Check the work by using main menu **XML > Validate the current state of the XML file.**

Choose main menu **XML > Expand all**. The Design tab contents of the XML editor should match the document shown in Figure 20.3. The next steps are to create a DTD from the dummy XML file and impose some settings. Then the DTD will be complete. We created two questions having two choices each only as a hint to the DTD generator that these elements occur multiple times. Generate the DTD by carrying out the following steps:

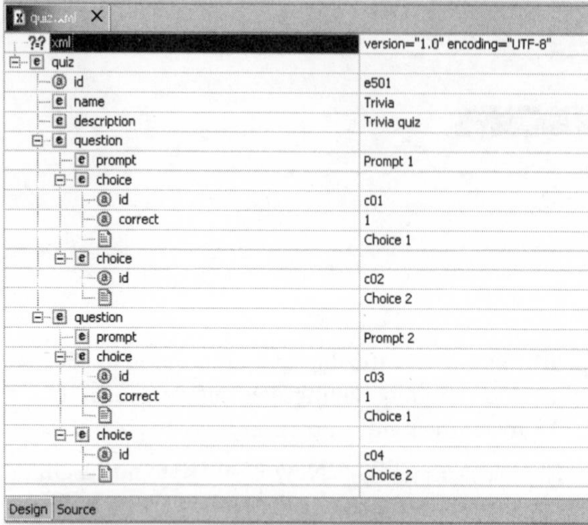

Figure 20.3 Dummy quiz document.

1. Select the "Create a New DTD File" icon from the toolbar as shown in Figure 20.4.
2. The **Create DTD** wizard appears. Choose the option **Create a DTD from an XML file**. Press **Next.**
3. Set field **Enter File name** to **quiz.dtd**. Press **Next >.**
4. Navigate to and select the **quiz.xml** document from project **exam-system**. Notice that multiple XML files could contribute to a DTD. We have just one. Move **quiz.xml** to the right-hand column by selecting it and pressing the right-arrow icon. Press **Finish.**
5. The DTD appears in the Navigator view. Open it in the DTD Editor by choosing Open from its pop-up menu.
6. Select the **Source** tab of the editor. Find and click on the **quiz id** attribute. Reselect the **Design** tab, and then select the **#required** radio button.
7. Repeat the sequence to set the remaining **choice id** attribute to **#required**. These settings force unique identification of the **quiz** and each **choice**.
8. Save the work. We need the **choice id** to enable us to check a user choice against the correct choice. We may need the **quiz id** if the test document were to be extracted from a DBMS.
9. Now edit the **quiz.xml** document. Select the **Design** tab.
10. Right-click the **?? xml** processing instruction at the beginning.
11. Choose **Add Grammar Information > Add DTD Information.**
12. Press OK on the resulting dialog, accepting the defaults.
13. Choose main menu **XML ‡ Validate the current state of the XML file**. The message should report a valid XML file.
14. Save the file.

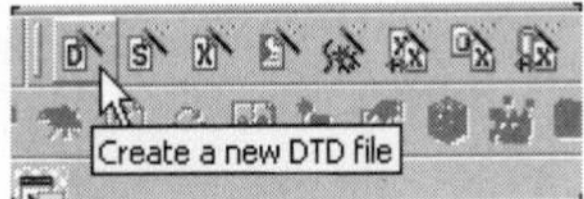

Figure 20.4 Create a new DTD file.

We have the desired DTD and a valid skeleton trivia examination instance now. A valid XML file obeys its XML schema or DTD. Observe that we did not need to look at source tag angle brackets very often in this process. We could have carried out the steps without looking at XML source, but we did use a copy / paste shortcut to duplicate the **question** element. Moreover, we could have created the DTD from scratch, but it is easier to create the initial trivia quiz that we desire, and then create a DTD from it. Thereafter the DTD will be the defining authority for document validity and for generating JavaBeans that manipulate XML documents according to its definition.

Create a Trivia Test XML Document

The next step is to edit the dummy quiz to create an actual trivia quiz suitable for testing our upcoming XSL transform, which is used to render an HTML quiz form. We may either copy file **quiz.xml** from the CDROM material, or enter source into the XML editor **Source** tab view, or we may enter elements, attributes, and character data in the XML editor structured **Design** tab view. The source is easy to present here. White space is not significant except within character data—a string bounded by an element. Our **quiz.xml** source file contents should resemble the XML source that follows:

```
<?xml version="1.0" encoding="UTF-8"?>
<!DOCTYPE quiz SYSTEM "quiz.dtd">
<quiz id="e501">
    <!--Exam definition -->
    <name>Triva</name>
    <description>Trivia quiz</description>
    <question>
        <prompt>Which country is the largest user of ketchup?</prompt>
        <choice id="c05">Australia</choice>
        <choice id="c06" correct="1">Sweden</choice>
        <choice id="c07">United States</choice>
        <choice id="c08">Germany</choice>
    </question>
    <question>
        <prompt>The most popular topic of public speakers is:</prompt>
        <choice id="c09">Leadership</choice>
        <choice id="c10">Sports</choice>
        <choice id="c11">Financial security</choice>
        <choice id="c12" correct="1">Motivation</choice>
    </question>
    <question>
        <prompt>Which country has the most bicycles?</prompt>
        <choice id="c13" correct="1">Netherlands</choice>
```

```
            <choice id="c14">Italy</choice>
            <choice id="c15">Vietnam</choice>
            <choice id="c16">Germany</choice>
        </question>
        <question>
            <prompt>ZIP code 12345 is assigned to:</prompt>
            <choice id="c17">Hicksville, New York</choice>
            <choice id="c18">Morristown, New Jersey</choice>
            <choice id="c19">Scranton, Pennsylvania</choice>
            <choice id="c20" correct="1">General Electric in Schenectady,
    New York</choice>
        </question>
        <question>
            <prompt>What is the most common place name in Britain?</prompt>
            <choice id="c01">Hursley</choice>
            <choice id="c02">Waterford</choice>
            <choice id="c03" correct="1">Newton</choice>
            <choice id="c04">Greenwich</choice>
        </question>
    </quiz>
```

Use main menu item **XML / Validate the current state of the XML file** to validate the file against the DTD. Repair any deviations. An XML file is either valid according to its DTD or XML schema or it isn't. We need this **quiz.xml** file to be valid because the JavaBeans representation of the DTD will be used to process the XML document.

Create an XML-to-HTML XSL Transform

The trivia examination system will convert an XML quiz document to an HTML form. Why not simply write the exam document in HTML in the first place? It is true that the exam is data that we want to present to a user. HTML can present data, but we need to process responses against that same document. Moreover we need to use the same system against any arbitrary examination document. Thus, we need the document to stand for the complete examination. This means that it must contain the correct response indicators. We don't want the end user to see the correct answers. In addition, we may want to change the look and feel of the presentation independently of the examination data. Clearly, we need to represent the data separately from its presentation. We choose to represent the data in an XML document, but present it as an HTML document. An XSL transformation is just the ticket for doing this. There are other ways to present data, such as JSPs and servlets. XSL is a also a good choice because it enforces model-view separation while reducing the need for raw Java coding.

WSAD will help us create and test the required XSL transform using the XSL Debugger. Carry out the following steps to create the transform script:

1. Open the **exam-system** project in the XML Perspective. Select the project in the Navigator.
2. Create a new XSL transform file using the toolbar icon shown in Figure 20.5 or choose New > XSL from the project's pop-up menu.

Figure 20.5 Create an XSL file.

3. Name the file "quiz2html.xsl." Press "Finish". Now we have an empty XSL transform appearing as shown following:

```
<?xml version="1.0" encoding="UTF-8"?>
<xsl:transform xmlns:xsl="http://www.w3.org/1999/XSL/Transform"
    version="1.0"
    xmlns:xalan="http://xml.apache.org/xslt">
</xsl:transform>
```

The desired XSL file consists of four templates that are children of the <xsl:transform> element. The root template emits the base HTML file. A template is said to *fire* by matching a path expression within the parsed XML document. Nested templates are to be fired within our XSL document to create our test form. One template iterates over the **question** elements. Another iterates across the **choice** elements within a question. We may enter each template from the text to follow, or import the **quiz2html.xsl** file into the project from the Chapter 20 resources on the CDROM. Insert each template as an XML element child of the <xsl:transform> element.

Insert the root template that follows. It fires first, applying the template that matches the **quiz** element.

```
<xsl:template match="/">
   <xsl:comment>Render an HTML document</xsl:comment>
   <HTML>
      <xsl:apply-templates select="quiz"/>
   </HTML>
</xsl:template>
```

Insert the following **quiz** template. It applies the **description** and **question** templates. There is no template for **description** so the XSLT processor simply the text of the element into the output stream.

```
<xsl:template match="quiz">
   <xsl:comment>Render HTML HEAD and BODY elements</xsl:comment>
      <HEAD>
         <TITLE>
            <xsl:apply-templates select="name"/>
         </TITLE>
       </HEAD>
       <BODY bgcolor="#dddddd">
          <xsl:processing-instruction name="body"/>
          <H1>
             <xsl:apply-templates select="description"/>
          </H1>
          <FORM method="post" action="Score">
```

```
                <xsl:processing-instruction name="form"/>
                <HR/>
                <TABLE>
                   <TR><TD>
                         <xsl:for-each select="question">
                            <xsl:apply-templates select="."/>
                         </xsl:for-each>
                       </TD>
                    </TR>
                    <TR><TD>
                          <INPUT type="submit" id="score" value="Score"/>
                       </TD>
                    </TR>
                </TABLE>
             </FORM>
          </BODY>
</xsl:template>
```

Next is the template for the **question** element. It iteratively applies the **choice** template. Insert the following **question** template:

```
<xsl:template match="question">
   <xsl:comment>Render one question with its choices</xsl:comment>
   <TABLE>
      <TR>
         <TH>
            <xsl:number format="1."/>
         </TH>
         <TH align="left" colspan="2">
            <xsl:apply-templates select="prompt"/>
         </TH>
      </TR>
         <xsl:for-each select="choice">
            <xsl:apply-templates select="."/>
         </xsl:for-each>
       <TR>
          <TD colspan="3">
             <HR/>
          </TD>
       </TR>
    </TABLE>
</xsl:template>
```

Only the **choice** template remains. Insert the following text to create it:

```
<xsl:template match="choice">
   <xsl:comment>Render one choice</xsl:comment>
      <xsl:variable name="cnum">
         <xsl:value-of select="."/>
      </xsl:variable>
      <TR>
```

```
        <TD width="5%">
            <INPUT type="radio">
                <xsl:attribute name="name">
                    <xsl:number level="multiple" count="question"/>
                </xsl:attribute>
                <xsl:attribute name="value">
                    <xsl:value-of select="@id"/>
                </xsl:attribute>
            </INPUT>
        </TD>
        <TD width="5%">
                <xsl:number format="a)"/>
        </TD>
        <TD align="left">
                <xsl:value-of select="."/>
        </TD>
    </TR>
</xsl:template>
```

Save the file. That completes the XSL file used to transform the XML **quiz.xml** document to an HTML stream.

XSL Debug

We have been hasty declaring that the XSL file is complete, because it hasn't been tested. Perhaps we made a mistake constructing it. The WSAD **XML Debugger** eliminates our needing to code a test program for our transform. Execute it from the XML Perspective by selecting both the XSL file and the input XML file in the Navigator view. Hold the Ctrl key down while selecting **quiz.xml** and **quiz2html.xsl**. Right-click the selection. Choose Apply **XSL > As HTML**. An XML debugging session appears. Press F5 on the keyboard to step to the first XSL element. The debugger should resemble Figure 20.6. Notice that the transform, and the output appear in separate panes. Observe the wealth of information available in the **Current XSL Element** pane. Continue pressing the F5 key to observe the details of the transformation. Look at the Template Call Stack tab when the current template is nested within an outer match.

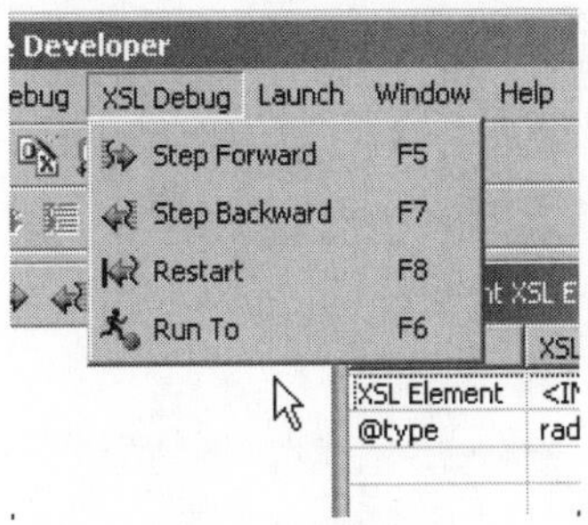

Figure 20.6 XSL debug.

We chose HTML output, therefore the result renders as "Result HTML" in its own pane. Had we chosen XML output, the result pane would show the source of the result XML document. If we misspelled a match argument, the output from the matching template would be missing. If an illegal character were detected, an error message box indicating the error location and description would appear during the transform.

Aside from pressing **F5** for Step Forward, there are alternative ways to control the trace like Step Back, Restart, and Run to. Additionally, the icons shown in the menu are duplicated in the title bar of the **Sessions** pane. If we have a problem in our XSL file, the use of these execution controls may help us pinpoint it. This facility also has breakpoints that we may set in the marker bar of the XSL file, just as we did with Java code in Chapter 4. Use **Run To** after setting breakpoints. If we lose our way, we can try **Restart**.

Position the pointer over the button just left of the close button on the Session pane. The text should read: **Open the browser on the transformation result**. Assuming that our XSL file and XML file are correct, click the button. The integrated Web browser will open in a pane of the XML Debugger. The contents should resemble those seen in Figure 20.7.

Reopen the XML Perspective. Notice that a new file appears under the **exam-system** project. It is named **quiz_qiz2html_transform.html** or something close to that name. This is the HTML file resulting from the transformation. We intend to generate our application's HTML dynamically, so this file isn't needed. We may delete it if we wish.

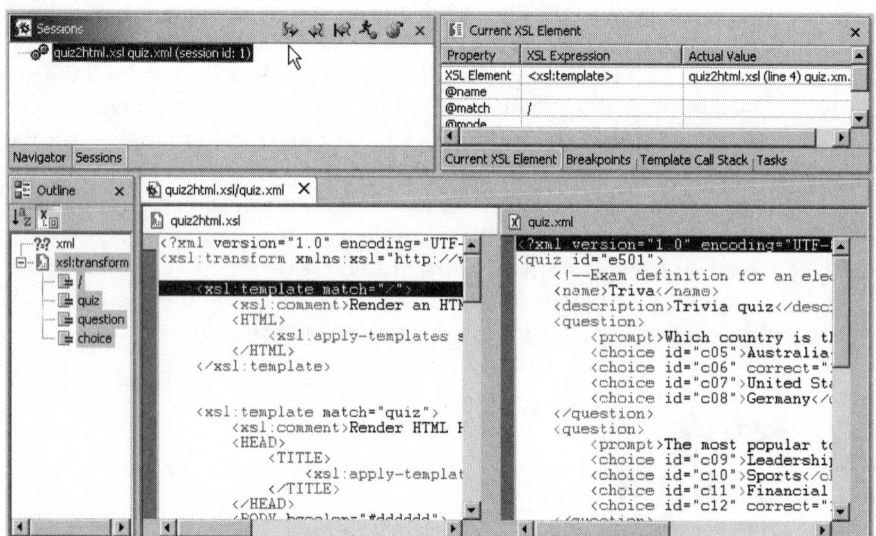

Figure 20.7 Viewing an XSL transform result.

Create a Score Result XSL Document

The **quiz.xml** document renders as HTML with the help of the **quiz2html.xsl** transformation document, but how will the application present the quiz results? Let us design a simple page that shows the number of possible questions and the number of questions answered correctly. Later, we will discus how these two values originate.

An XSL document may accept parameters from the transformation engine. Assume that we will pass the two score values into the transformation process once we write our application code. Our score page will be extremely simple. It will only need the two parameters, using no information from the input XML document. Any dummy XML document will do, even **quiz.xml**. It is wasteful, however, to parse an unused large document. Let us simply create a null XML document for use in the scoring transformation. The HTML will be derived from the two parameters and canned HTML contained within the scoring XSL script.

We know how to create an XML document now. Create one named **null.xml** in project exam-system. Give it one empty element named **nothing**. The source representation follows:

```
<?xml version="1.0" encoding="UTF-8"?>
<nothing></nothing>
```

The needed transform document is fairly trivial. Create it from the following information, naming it **score.xsl**:

```
<?xml version="1.0" encoding="UTF-8"?>
<xsl:stylesheet
  xmlns:xsl="http://www.w3.org/1999/XSL/Transform"
  version="1.0"
  xmlns:xalan="http://xml.apache.org/xslt">
    <xsl:param name="score" select="0"/>
    <xsl:param name="possible" select="0"/>
  <xsl:template match="/">
    <xsl:comment>Render an HTML document</xsl:comment>
    <html>
      <body bgcolor="#cccccc">
        <h1 align="center">Score</h1>
        <table align="center">
          <tr>
            <td align="center">You scored
              <strong>
                <xsl:value-of select="$score" />
              </strong>
              correct out of
              <strong>
                <xsl:value-of select="$possible" />
              </strong>
            </td>
          </tr>
```

```
            <tr>
              <td align="center">
                <form action="index.html" method="get">
                  <input type="submit" value="Home" />
                </form>
              </td>
            </tr>
          </table>
        </body>
      </html>
    </xsl:template>
  </xsl:stylesheet>
```

Notice the **xsl:param** declarations at the beginning of the document. The application would pass named parameter values into the output stream using **xsl:value-of** elements near the middle of the document. Try running **Apply XSL > As HTML** while **null.xml** and **score.xsl** are selected. Display the results in the browser. The results should resemble Figure 20.8. Notice that the default values of the parameters are rendered because no actual values were by the debugger. Erase the **null_score_transform.html** result file. We will not need it here.

Integrating XML Into a Web Application

We have a valid XML quiz document that may be transformed into HTML. The HTML presents a form used to send user examination responses to the scoring subsystem. We need to implement an end-to-end approach to sending the HTML to the trivia test user, accepting that user responses, scoring those responses, and finally rendering results for user viewing.

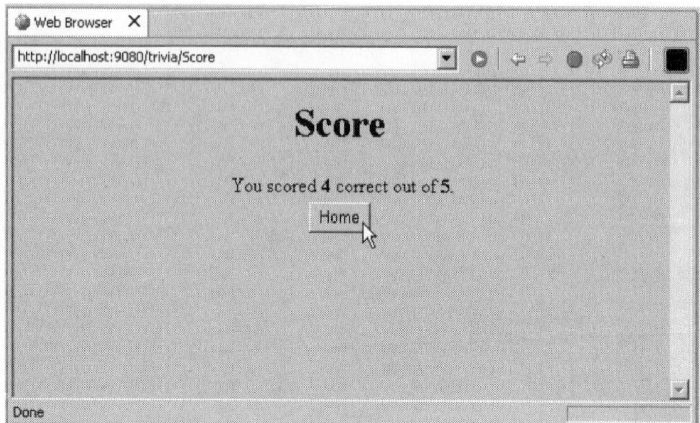

Figure 20.8 Quiz score transformation.

You shall use a **Quiz** servlet to do the transform that you tested in the XSL Debugger. The HTML form will target a **Score** servlet that carries out the scoring, and then sends the rendered score to the user. This application will use no JSPs nor will it emit HTML from servlets, aside for exception information. The XSL transform paradigm is the sole presentation technology-chosen for the examination system. The following sections step us through the integration of our previous XML work into a new Web application.

Generating JavaBeans for a DTD

We will implement scoring through JavaBeans that search the parsed XML DOM to enable the Score servlet to carry out correct choice matching. WSAD will generate the equivalent JavaBeans for **quiz.dtd** that will represent the DTD as Java classes. We need a package to contain those classes. Use the following steps to create the package:

1. Open the XML Perspective to the **exam-system** project.
2. Use the pop-up menu to invoke New > Package. The **New** wizard appears.
3. Enter **com.xyz.quiz.beans** in the Name field.
4. Press Finish to create the package.

Follow these steps to generate JavaBeans into the package:

5. Right-click the **quiz.dtd** file. Choose Generate > JavaBeans. Notice the other kinds of artifacts we may generate from a DTD or schema.
6. Take care to select **quiz** as the **Root Element**. When the Generate dialog matches that seen in Figure 20.9, press Finish.
7. Expand the **com.xyz.quiz.beans** package to verify that the JavaBeans were generated.

Thanks to WSAD, we avoided a span of boring, repetitious, error-prone programming. Notice that there are errors due to missing packages. Continue with the following steps to place the necessary classes on the class path.

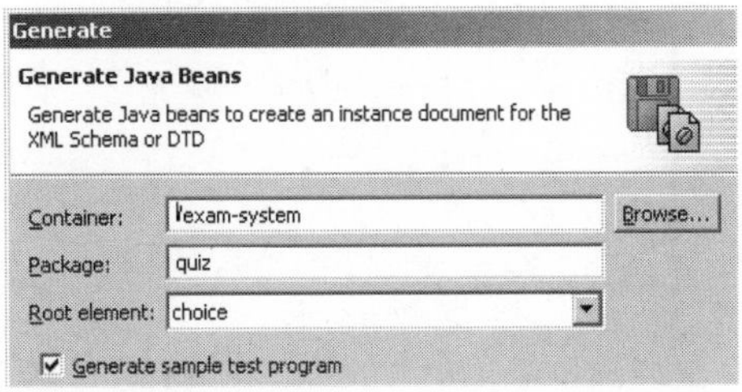

Figure 20.9 Generate JavaBeans for DTD.

8. Open the properties of the **exam-system** project, and then choose **Java Build Path.**
9. Select the **Libraries** tab. Use Add Variable to add the following path variables: **JRE_LIB, WAS_50_PLUGINDIR** (Use **Extend** button to pick **j2ee.jar** from **lib**), **WAS_V5_XALAN, WAS_V5_XERCES,** and **XSDBEANS.**
10. Close the properties by pressing OK.
11. Inspect the Task view for errors.

The names of the JavaBeans should be familiar. They are the element names from **quiz.dtd**. An accompanying sample test program gives us an idea of how to use the JavaBeans.

Web Application Design

The Web application will be composed of two servlets and no JSPs. The servlets request dynamic rendering through an XSL transformation to the servlet print writer stream. A static HTML page is the home page for the application. Figure 20.10 shows the overall class design of the Web application.

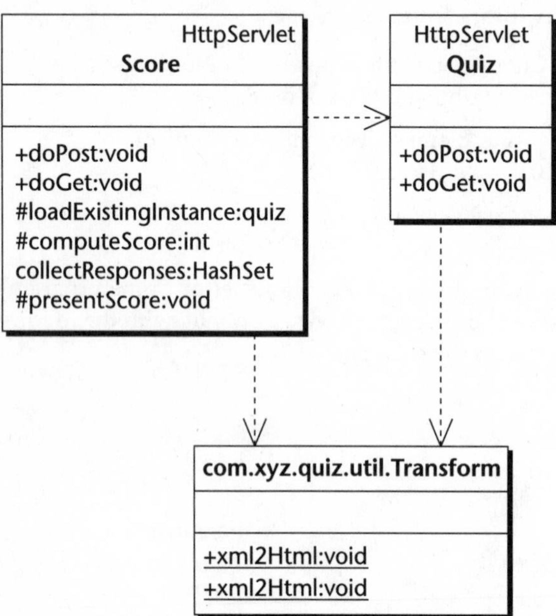

Figure 20.10 Web application class diagram.

Web Application

Next, we need to create a Web application to contain the executable code. Carry out the following steps to create the Web application having two servlets:

1. Open the Web Perspective. Create a project named **trivia**. The Web application document root will default to that name.
2. Select trivia > Java Source. Create a package named **com.xyz.quiz.servlet.**
3. Use the pop-up menu New > Servlet item to create servlet classes named **Quiz** and **Score** in the new com.xyz.quiz.servlet package.
4. Edit class **Quiz**. Insert the following implementation of `doPost()`, and then make `doGet()` delegate to this method.

```
public void doPost(javax.servlet.http.HttpServletRequest request,
    javax.servlet.http.HttpServletResponse response)
        throws javax.servlet.ServletException, java.io.IOException {
    response.setContentType("text/html; charset=UTF-8");
    response.setHeader("pragma", "no-cache");
    PrintWriter out = response.getWriter();
    try {
        Transform.xml2Html(out, "/xmlcontent/quiz.xml",
                "/xmlcontent/quiz2html.xsl");
    }
    // Display exceptions on the client browser.
    catch (Exception e) {
        out.write(e.toString());
    }
    // Close the PrintWriter.
    out.close();
}
```

Notice that we process the XML and XSL files through a call to **Transform.xml2 Html**. We will create this utility in the following section entitled *Transform Utility*. Further, observe that the parameters specify a relative path to the files. This allows them to be delivered in the same WAR file as the Web application while keeping them out of exposed Web documents. We will cover this in a following section named *Deploy XML Content*.

This little application has some issues. We have hard coded the transform and XML source names. In a production application, the names would originate from properties, or perhaps from a JNDI lookup. There is no error page. An error JSP or servlet should be provided in production.

The remaining servlet is named **Score**. Continue the following steps to provide its implementation logic:

5. Remain in the Java Perspective of project **trivia**. Implement the `doPost()` method of the **Score** servlet as shown following, and then make the `doGet()` method delegate to it:

```
public void doPost(javax.servlet.http.HttpServletRequest request,
    javax.servlet.http.HttpServletResponse response)
    throws javax.servlet.ServletException, java.io.IOException {
    response.setContentType("text/html; charset=UTF-8");
    response.setHeader("pragma", "no-cache");
    PrintWriter out = response.getWriter();
    // Load the XML input document
    java.net.URL xmlUrl =
    com.xyz.quiz.servlet.Score.class.getResource(
        "/xmlcontent/quiz.xml");
    quiz iQuiz = loadExistingInstance(xmlUrl.getFile());
    // Get answer, score and question count
    HashSet answers = collectResponses(request);
    int score = computeScore(iQuiz, answers);
    int possible = iQuiz.getquestionCount();
    // Give response
    presentScore(possible, score, out);
    // Close the PrintWriter
    out.close();
}
```

6. Add the helper method that follows to the **Score** servlet. It loads the generated **quizFactory** class. The non-standard capitalization was generated based upon DTD element name **quiz** being a lower case name. The **quizFactory** class produces instances of our generated JavaBeans by parsing the **quiz.xml** document. Thus, we need only work with JavaBeans, not XML parsing.

```
/**
 * Load an XML document using the generated quizFactory class
 *   @param filename An existing XML file name
 */
protected quiz loadExistingInstance(String filename) {
    quizFactory iQuizFactory = new quizFactory();
    iQuizFactory.setPackageName("com.xyz.quiz.beans");
    // Load the document
    quiz iQuiz = (quiz) iQuizFactory.loadDocument(filename);
    return iQuiz;
}
```

7. Continue implementing logic in servlet **Score** by adding the following method that implements a scoring algorithm:

```
/**
 * Return number of correct answers given a quiz.
 * @param iQuiz quiz
 * @param answerSet java.util.Hashset of HTML form values
* @return int, count of correct answers
```

```
 */
protected int computeScore(quiz iQuiz, HashSet answerSet) {
    // Count user responses that match correct choices
    int numCorrect = 0;
    final int possible = iQuiz.getquestionCount();
    // For each question:
    for (int qi = 0; qi < possible; ++qi) {
        question qn = iQuiz.getQuestion(qi);
        final int numC = qn.getchoiceCount();
        // For each possible choice for this question:
        for (int ci = 0; ci < numC; ++ci) {
            choice ch = qn.getChoice(ci);
            String ca = ch.getCorrect();
            // Is this one a correct choice?
            if (ca != null && ca.equals("1")) {
                String id = ch.getId();
                // Did user choose it? If so, count it correct
                if (answerSet.contains(id))
                    numCorrect++;
                }
        }
    }
    return numCorrect;
}
```

The scoring algorithm uses the WSAD-generated JavaBeans to access the **correct** and **id** attributes of **choice** elements. Notice that we obtain a count of questions from the quiz even though the XML document contains no explicit count. The magic is in letting the generated `quiz.getquestionCount()` method implementation enumerate all of the parsed **question** elements for us.

For each **question**, the algorithm searches for the correct **choice**. It uses the **id** attribute of this choice to match against attributes returned in the HTML form. If there is a match the user is credited with a correct choice. The HTML form choices are built with the choice attributes contained in the **quiz.xml** document because the HTML transform mapped each choice id attribute to a radio button attribute.

Continue creating the **Score** servlet by carrying out the following steps:

8. We use a `HashSet` for fast lookup of user choice **id** attributes. Insert the following method to build the `HashSet`:

```
/**
 * Collect user responses
 */
HashSet collectResponses(javax.servlet.http.HttpServletRequest
request) {
    // Collect user responses for fast retrieval
    HashSet answerSet = new HashSet();
    Enumeration enum = request.getParameterNames();
    while (enum.hasMoreElements()) {
```

```
            String name = (String) enum.nextElement();
            String value[] = request.getParameterValues(name);
            if (value != null && value.length > 0) {
                answerSet.add(value[0]);
            }
        }
        return answerSet;
    }
```

9. The **Score** servlet uses a transform to present the score. The central task is to pass the number of possible questions and the user score to the transformation method. Implement the **presentScore** method as follows:

```
protected void presentScore(int possible, int score, PrintWriter out)
{
    try {
        // Build XSL parameter map
        HashMap params = new HashMap();
        params.put("score", Integer.toString(score));
        params.put("possible", Integer.toString(possible));
        // Emit HTML
        Transform.xml2Html(out, "/xmlcontent/null.xml",
                "/xmlcontent/score.xsl", params);
    }
    // Display exceptions on the client's browser.
    catch (Exception e) {
        out.write(e.toString());
    }
}
```

10. Open the Web Perspective on project **trivia**. Create an **index.html** page that links to relative URL `Quiz`, our trivia test servlet name.

This completes the servlet programming. Now we need to supply a common XSL transform utility for servlet use.

Transform Utility

Each servlet uses an overloaded static **xml2Htlm** transform method located in utility class **com.xyz.quiz.util.Transform**. The first overload takes no XSL parameters. The second overload accepts a hash map containing name and value pairs to be passed to the XSL transform operation. Use the following steps to create the utility:

1. Open project **trivia** in the Java Perspective.
2. Create package **com.xyz.quiz.util.Transform** in the **trivia > Web Content** folder.
3. Create class **Transform** within the package. Accept the default values.
4. Edit class **Transform**. We may use **Ctrl+a** to select the entire boilerplate contents for replacement. Enter the following source code. We may want to omit the **import** statements, afterward, letting content assistance find and insert them.

```
package com.xyz.quiz.util;
import java.io.InputStream;
import java.io.PrintWriter;
import java.util.HashMap;
import java.util.Iterator;
import java.util.Set;
import javax.xml.transform.TransformerConfigurationException;
import javax.xml.transform.TransformerException;
/**
 * Carries out XML to HTML transformations
 */
public class Transform {
    // No XSL parameters used in this overload
    public static void xml2Html(PrintWriter out, String xml, String
xsl)
        throws TransformerConfigurationException,
TransformerException {
        xml2Html(out, xml, xsl, null);
    }
    // XSL parameters passed in HashMap
    public static void xml2Html(PrintWriter out, String xml,
        String xsl, HashMap map)
        throws TransformerConfigurationException,
TransformerException {
        javax.xml.transform.TransformerFactory tFactory =
            javax.xml.transform.TransformerFactory.newInstance();
        // Get the XML input document and the stylesheet
        InputStream xmlStream =
Transform.class.getResourceAsStream(xml);
        InputStream xslStream =
Transform.class.getResourceAsStream(xsl);
        // Set the transform sources
        javax.xml.transform.Source xmlSource =
            new javax.xml.transform.stream.StreamSource(xmlStream);
        javax.xml.transform.Source xslSource =
            new javax.xml.transform.stream.StreamSource(xslStream);
        // Create a transformer
        javax.xml.transform.Transformer transformer =
            tFactory.newTransformer(xslSource);
        // Set XSL parameters, if any
        if (map != null) {
            Set keys = map.keySet();
            Iterator it = keys.iterator();
            while (it.hasNext()) {
                String aKey = (String) it.next();
                String aVal = (String) map.get(aKey);
```

```
                    transformer.setParameter(aKey, aVal);
                }
            }
            // Transform XML to HTML; send to the response PrintWriter
            transformer.transform(
                xmlSource,
                new javax.xml.transform.stream.StreamResult(out));
        }
    }
```

5. Save the file.

That completes the transform utility class and the Java coding for the Web application. Now, we need to supply the XML content to the Web application.

Deploying XML Content

The **Transform** class **xml2Html** transform method reference the input XML and XSL documents through document relative path strings passed as parameters, but where do the actual files reside? Remember, this application will be deployed to an application server. It would be cumbersome and against standards to assign an absolute location for loading such resources. A full-blown examination application would probably keep the documents in a DBMS, obtaining the document through the services of a product such as IBM's *DB2 XML Extender*, directly supported by the WSAD XML Perspective. Since we are only presenting one examination, we will let the Java class loader load the files from the class path. The following statements show how to cause loading of an XSL file:

```
String relativePath = "/xmlcontent/score.xsl";
Transform.class.getResourceAsStream(String relativePath);
```

A corresponding incantation loads an XML file. The Java class loader used for class **Transform** does the job. We need only to place the files on the relative class path, and then specify that relative path in the parameters to the **xml2Html** method.

Carry out the following steps to insert the two XML and two XSL files as deployable Web application resources:

1. Open the Resource Perspective on project **trivia.**
2. Create a folder named **xmlcontent** under **trivia > Java Source.**
3. Navigate to file **quiz.xml**, **null.xml**, **score.xsl**, and **quiz2html.xsl** under project **exam-system**. Hold the Ctrl key depressed to multi-select the four files.
4. Drag the entire selection to the **xmlcontent** folder in the **trivia** project. Drop the files, and then press **OK.**

At this point, the XML content and transform, as well as the servlets and HTML page, are deployable in a WAR file. Notice the missing DTD file. We didn't install it because the transform engine does not have the information to find it relative to where we placed the other two files. Furthermore, we validated the static XML file when we created it, so let us not waste cycles in revalidating it. We shall remove the relative reference to the DTD from the `quiz.xml` file. Be sure to impose the DTD reference when authoring a new quiz.

5. Remain in the Resource Perspective. Open the **quiz.xml** file. Remove the DOCTYPE construct in the Source pane of XML Editor. Save the file.

Deploy and Test

We are ready to deploy and test the **trivia** Web application. Before testing, we need to give the application access to the generated JavaBeans in the **exam-system** project. Those JavaBeans need the **xsdbeans.jar** file on the application class path as well. If we place the file in the application **WEB-INF/lib** directory the application server will automatically place it on the Web module class path at deployment time. Follow these steps to ensure that runtime dependencies are satisfied:

1. Use the Navigator to select **trivia/Web Content/ WEB-INF/lib.**
2. Invoke the pop-up menu, and then select **Import**. The Import wizard appears.
3. Choose **Import File System,** and then press **Next >.**
4. Use the **Browse** button to navigate to **[install-dir] > wstools > eclipse > plugins > com.ibm.etools.xsd_1.0.0 > runtime.**
5. Select **xsdbeans.jar**. The wizard should resemble Figure 20.11. Press Finish.

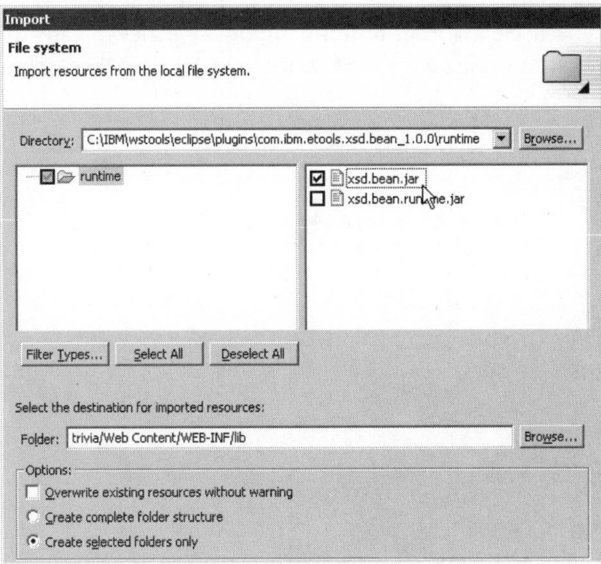

Figure 20.11 Import supporting JAR.

6. Open the Web Perspective.
7. Open the Web Deployment Descriptor for project trivia.
8. Use the Web Library Projects group's Add button to select project **exam-system** as a library jar named **exam-system.jar.**
9. Save the **Web Deployment Descriptor.**

That completes the dependent JAR information needed by the application on the application server. The two library JAR files will be deployed with the **trivia** Web application. Continue the following steps to deploy and execute the application:

10. Right click the project, and then choose "Run on Server." If we have previously defined a server, it will start. If no server is defined, we encounter a series of wizard screens. Follow the steps to configure a server. We ensure that we choose **WebSphere v5.0 Test Environment** as the test server unless we have another server available. We retain the remaining default values. The new server will initialize and start after we complete the wizard's steps.
11. After the server starts, we obtain the HTML start page. Click button labeled **Take a Trivia Test**. A quiz should appear in the Browser View as shown in Figure 20.12.

That concludes project development and deployment. Take the trivia quiz. When you submit choices, the **Score** servlet will render a page resembling that shown in the Browser in Figure 20.13. The servlet used the JavaBeans that WSAD generated from our DTD to access correct choices. It matched them against the user's actual choices returned in the HMTL form. It was not necessary to understand the JavaBeans' operation. We simply created JavaBean instances from the XML document, and then accessed their properties. This is a clean programming model. We never directly parsed XML. The JavaBeans XSD support used a class factory to instantiate them from the XML quiz document.

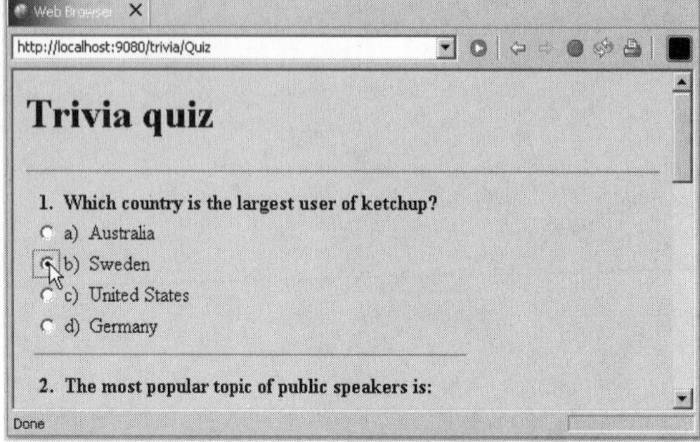

Figure 20.12 Trivia quiz in Browser view.

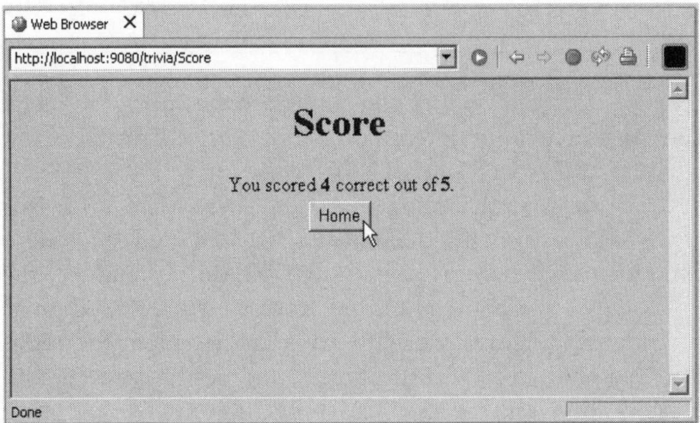

Figure 20.13 Live quiz score results.

Try accessing the application from an arbitrary browser – on another machine if possible. The transform and parsing executes rapidly after the servlet initializes at the first access, especially if the browser doesn't compete with the server for execution.

Enhancements

Our time and space are almost exhausted for this chapter. The trivia examination system is hard-coded to present one exam. It doesn't give much information on the score page. Possible enhancements are:

- Use the SQL mapping capabilities of WSAD to store XML documents in DB2 using **DB2 XML Extender**. The documents may be stored as relational tables that are retrieved as XML or they may be stored in an XML column in a relational table.
- Dynamically generate a quiz from a pool of question XML documents stored in a database.
- Write a Web-based authoring tool for quiz instances.
- Incorporate user authentication and authorization. Distinguish roles such as user, subject matter expert, author, and administrator. Use the system as a certification examination practice system.
- Make a finer-grained DTD or XML schema that groups questions into categories, scoring each category separately. This is another feature candidate for a certification practice examination system.
- Use just one servlet. Make it a front controller that implements a command design pattern or a business delegate pattern.

Summary

Why did you use XML in our quiz project? So that you could use the application data model—the quiz—as the central source for both rendering and scoring. This was easy, given XML's standardized nature and WSAD's set of XML tools.

What are the alternatives? The most attractive may be a DBMS-based design. Our quiz project would benefit by DBMS-resident test documents, but we would opt to store them in XML form or at least retrieve SQL rows as XML using DB2 XML Extender or the equivalent. The advantage of using XML technology as the processing target medium is that XML may easily be manipulated and transformed in ways unforeseen by the application designer. The standardized nature of XML, its parsers, and derivative technologies is the attraction for application and process designers. Revisit the previous "Enhancements" section while considering how we would apply those enhancements in a non-XML-based design. We covered the following areas in this chapter:

- An overview of WSAD XML tools
- Using the XML Editor to create an XML document
- Creating a DTD from XML
- Generating JavaBeans for a DTD or XML schema
- Writing XLT transforms
- Tracing an XSL transform
- Integrating XML documents into a Web application
- Deploying XML content and transforms in a Web application
- Test-running an XML Web application in a WebSphere v5.0 test environment

In Chapter 21 we will cover version management for a team environment.

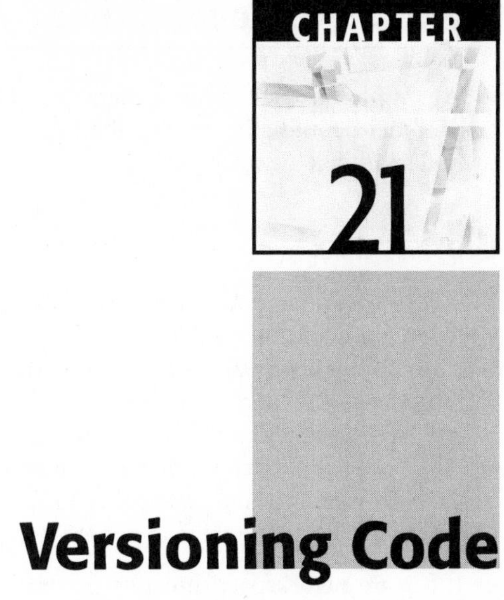

Versioning Code

What's in Chapter 21?

A useful development product must maintain code revisions for recovery or auditing. WSAD maintains recoverable local file history. Additionally, today's projects involve teams of coders, testers, and maintainers. This requires a tool to accommodate team development. WSAD is integrated with the Concurrent Version System (CVS). It also integrates with an open-ended set of alternative version control and management tools through its plug-in capability. This chapter discusses:

- Standalone development
- Versioning overview
- Versioning products
- The Concurrent Version System (CVS)
- CVS integration with WSAD
- Working with repositories

We move from a discussion of standalone development through working with the WSAD CVS integration details. For those who do not have a CVS repository, you will see ways to create one that can be used with WSAD.

Standalone Development

WSAD supports team development in addition to standalone development. Both development paradigms involve the WSAD workspace and a local history record of each file within it.

Workspace

WSAD project files reside in a workspace. Each time you save a file, its changes are stored in the workspace, replacing the previous data of that file. The default behavior is to prompt for a workspace location on the local file system when WSAD starts.

You may specify another workspace by using a command-line switch to WSAD or Eclipse. Add a –data <*workspacedirectory*> parameter to the command line used to start WSAD. The directory could be a file share on a distributed file system. A customized desktop shortcut is a convenient way to specify a workspace parameter on Windows. Carry out the following steps to use a remote share from a Windows-based WSAD:

1. Create a workspace directory on the remote system. This example remote is named Pavilion in this example.
2. Share the workspace directory on the network. You should ensure that the WSAD host user has create and write access. A sample share access name is \\Pavilion\eclipse-share.
3. Return to the local system. Map a drive letter to the share; this example uses Y.
4. Create a directory named Y:\workspace.
5. Create a shortcut to WSAD on the desktop.
6. Display the properties of the shortcut by right-clicking it and choosing Properties.
7. Append **–data Y:\workspace** to the Target field in the Shortcut tab. Be sure to supply a space between it and the command portion. The shortcut appears in Figure 21.1.
8. Rename the shortcut on the General tab to something appropriate, such as WSAD Workspace on Remote.
9. Press OK to finish modifying the shortcut.

Now, you can use the shortcut to launch a WSAD instance that uses the remote workspace. It does not prompt for a workspace if it sees a valid command-line data parameter. Try creating a Hello World application, and then verify that the project appears on the remote share.

Could you share your work with somebody else in this manner? Certainly, but you would need to agree that only one person may use the workspace at a time. WSAD writes to the workspace when you compile or save. Two users in the workspace could lead to file corruption because there is no locking imposed by WSAD in this mode of operation. WSAD does not know that another instance of itself is using the workspace. Some form of external locking could be imposed. This could be carried out by imposing a limit of one on the number of users allowed to use the share simultaneously.

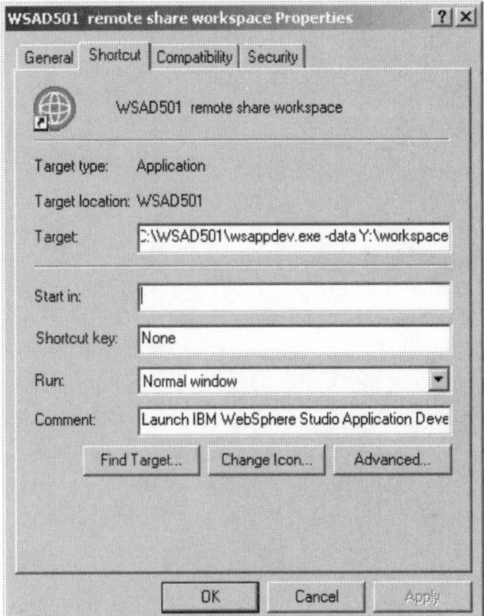

Figure 21.1 Remote shared workspace.

The memory overhead of WSAD is a function of the number of projects and files in the workspace. Project build paths may refer to other projects. It is convenient to configure different workspaces for separate development projects for performance reasons and for the encapsulation or separation of work products. Use the technique described previously to target a local directory as a workspace. Use an absolute file path instead of a share name for the workspace.

Local History

Happily, there is a way to recover from undesired file modifications. WSAD maintains a local history of each file that is updated when you create or modify the file. You can compare a file to a previous state and elect to replace it with a previous state with the following steps:

1. Select a file in a view such as Package Explorer or Navigator.
2. From the pop-up menu, choose Compare With > Local History to obtain a before-and-after differential view, as shown in Figure 21.2.

You can choose Replace With > Local History to invoke the same differential view with a Replace button. Highlight a version in the upper pane, and then press Replace to revert to that version. If you delete or rename a file only to regret it later, you may recover it by choosing Restore From Local History from the context menu. This is a great feature as long as you remember that it is available.

TIP **Local history is maintained for files, not folders or projects.**

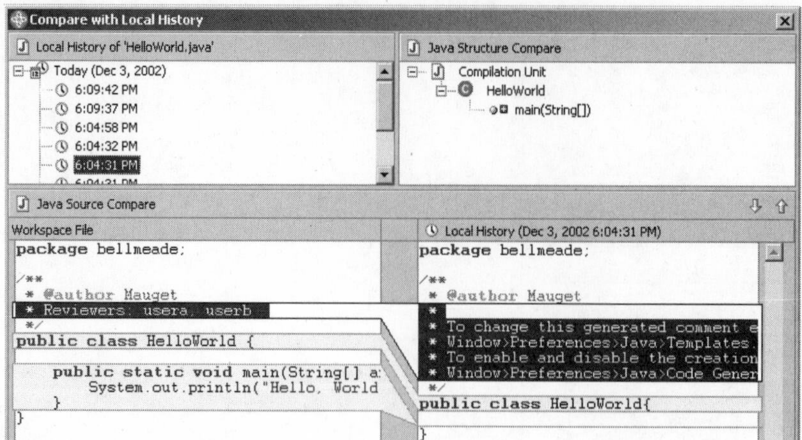

Figure 21.2 Local history.

Versioning Overview

The local history feature of WSAD enables us to roll back to a previous version of a file or recall a deleted file. It has limitations, however. It does not enable us to manage directories. A team develops most real coding products, but there is no default coordination between local histories of different WSAD workspaces.

It is clear that some kind of smart shared workspace is needed for team development. The simple shared workspace on the network won't work because there is no team modification control in that mode. Team development requires coordinated multiuser access to shared software projects and snapshots of that software. These artifacts would reside in a *shared repository*. There are numerous kinds of shared repositories available. WSAD can use a repository, but which one? WSAD enables the use of a pluggable repository.

A *software configuration management* system, or SCM, manages such a repository. A similar term used in the industry is version control system, or VCS. Such products exhibit these two features:

1. Coordination and integration of work through a stream model that ensures that only one copy of the current project exists at a given time.
2. A history of the work carried out by a team so that a current artifact may be reverted to a previous version if desired.

Version Control System Products

The default repository for WSAD is CVS, which is tightly integrated with the WSAD Workbench. IBM's Rational ClearCase is included as an installation option. This plug-in tightly integrates with WSAD. You will need a Rational ClearCase repository to use it. Additionally, you may choose another version control system if you obtain and install its corresponding WSAD plug-in. See the *Team Repository Providers* heading at www.eclipse.org/community/plugins.html. Each system has its unique terminology, but several fixed concepts map among them. Table 21.1 shows how some of the terms equate.

Concurrent Version System

The Concurrent Version System (CVS) is an open source version control system that saves multiple versions of files in one or more repositories. CVS enables more than one person to work with files from its repository. It uses a non-reserve paradigm where more than one person may check out a file simultaneously. Contrast this with other systems where one person locks a file when he or she checks it out of the repository.

The CVS Bible is named *Version Management with CVS*. It is included on the Web site for this book. Its short name is the *Cederqvist* manual, after its primary author, Per Cederqvist. The manual details CVS operation along with its commands. You need not know CVS commands to use CVS in WSAD or Eclipse, but additional knowledge is helpful. You will use a few CVS commands from a command window in setting up a repository in a following section.entitled CVS for NT.

Table 21.1 WSAD CVS ClearCase Terminology Comparison

WSAD	CVS	CLEARCASE
Workspace	File System	Work area
Repository	Repository	VOB
Stream	Branch (tag)	Stream and Project
Project	Folder	View
Resource	File	Element
Release	Revision	Check-in
Update	Update	Compare with
Version	Commit (tag)	Version

Team Perspective

The non-reserve characteristic of CVS is called the optimistic concurrency model. Multiple persons may check out a file, change it, and then check it back into the repository. Conflicts are resolved almost automatically on a time basis through a catch-up mechanism using the CVS update command. Figure 21.3 shows a typical sequence involving two developers. The stream is the series of changes to a single file. If two people modify the same piece of a file, the winner must be decided manually; otherwise conflict resolution is almost automatic. Thus, every developer edits a local copy of the file in his or her own workspace, and CVS merges the work when each finishes.

Does allowing two people to edit pieces of one file create an integrity problem? It could if two people change the same part of the file. CVS detects this condition, requiring a manual decision. Isn't this why other version control systems lock files that are checked out? Yes, but this doesn't guarantee integrity. The last person to change the file can easily undo the previous person's work. Version control is not a substitute for developer communication. No version control system can detect when changes to a single file, or across a set of files, will conflict.

The optimistic concurrency model of CVS works well in practice. Many commercial products are developed from build code extracted nightly from a CVS repository. For example, you can extract the nightly build of CVS from a public CVS repository. Eclipse resides in CVS. Use the WSAD CVS Repository Exploring Perspective to work with CVS. Use the CVS Repositories view context menu to access New > Repository Location to access a CVS repository.

Try this with host dev.eclipse.org. Specify a repository path of /home/eclipse and a user named anonymous, as shown in Figure 21.4. This enables the viewing of Eclipse source code or extracting it to a local project.

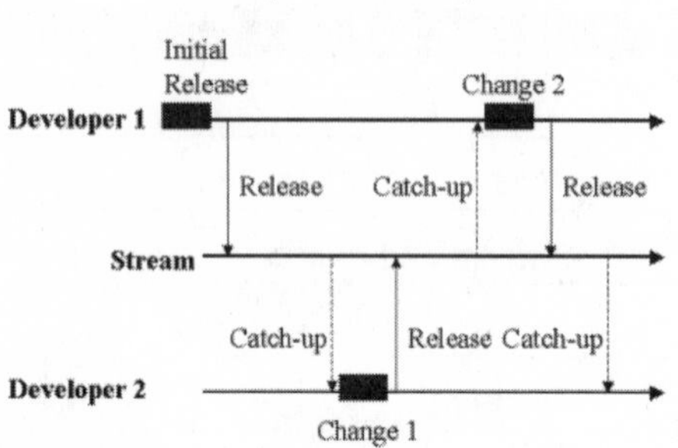

Figure 21.3 Optimistic concurrently model.

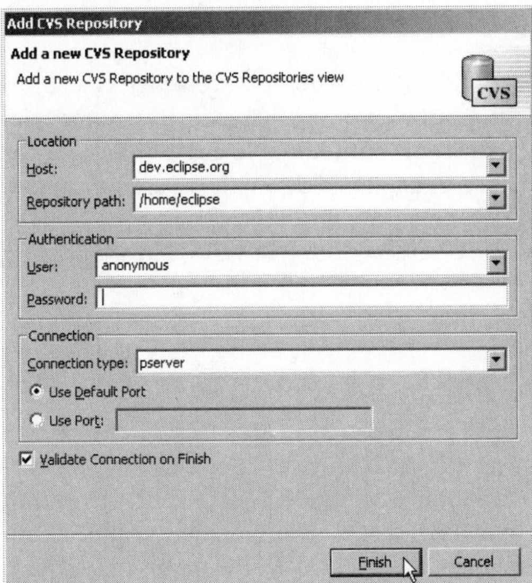

Figure 21.4 Add Eclipse repository.

Try expanding the HEAD stream to see the Eclipse packages, as shown in Figure 21.5. Notice that you browsed a Java source file directly from the CVS server. The anonymous login for this repository provides read-only access, so you cannot hurt anything. Another repository germane to this discussion is the CVS repository itself. Visit www.cvshome.org/ for instructions about this repository.

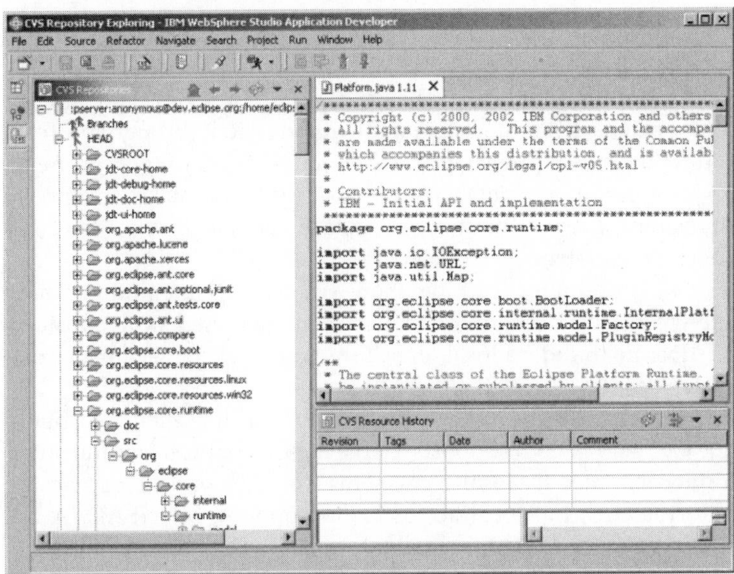

Figure 21.5 Access Eclipse public repository.

Versions

CVS deals with resources such as files and folders. A version of a resource is a saved snapshot of its state at a given time. You carry out versioning by tagging resource with a version label. Afterward, anyone may extract an unmodifiable copy of it from the repository. Resources are recursive, so you can version a folder with the assurance that its contents become versioned also.

You will see how to version a file using the CVS integration in WSAD in a following section. Let us discuss branches first.

Branches

Teams that share work through CVS integrate their work in branches. A branch is a shared work area that any team member may update. Each member may change resources in an individual workbench in isolation. The person must explicitly commit changes to the branch for the work to be available to other team members. This is considered an outgoing change. Each team member should ideally update his or her local workspace with changes others have made in the branch before committing work to it. This ensures that the latest state is available in the local workspace. As each member commits changes other team members will see these as incoming changes.

Every CVS repository has one branch called HEAD, as you saw in Figure 21.6. HEAD is usually used as a development stream. Other branches are often used for maintenance work.

WSAD CVS Integration

We will discuss CVS integration, and then create a repository for experimentation so that you can begin working with repositories. WSAD incorporates a visual CVS client in the CVS Repository Exploring Perspective. The Package Explorer view and Navigator view, visible in other perspectives, are integrated with the client through the Team context menu item. You can share a project with a CVS repository through this menu. You can synchronize all or part of a project with a repository. If you make a change to a local copy of a repository file, you may commit those changes to the repository through the Team context menu item.

A local CVS repository is useful for learning about WSAD CVS integration. Those coming from a Visual Age for Java background may seek an integrated local repository in WSAD, but WSAD does not bundle a local repository. You must connect to an existing repository or create one.

The open source CVS executable may be used as a command-line client. Additionally, it implements the CVS server. CVS supports a large number of protocols for client-server access. One protocol is used for local access. This would be perfect for learning about WSAD repository access, but local access isn't supported by WSAD. A full authenticating client-server protocol is mandated by the protocol choices available in

WSAD. WSAD encapsulates the connection URL notation, but you must supply the fields in a wizard. It's easier to understand the fields if you understand how they form a URL path to a remote repository. If you used a CVS command-line client the following URL format would specify the repository:

```
:protocol:[[user][:password]@]hostname[:[port]]/path/to/repository
```

Table 21.2 is an enumeration of several protocols. There are many supported protocols, but WSAD supports just the three remote protocols and the local protocol shown. WSAD refers to a CVS protocol as a connection type. Notice that there may be security issues with some connection types. The following sections cover using a CVS repository and learning the WSAD team concepts.

CVS for NT

If you use a single Windows NT, Windows 2000, or a Windows XP machine, and you simply want to learn about CVS under WSAD, then CVS for NT (CVSNT) is a good choice. Read about CVSNT and download it at www.cvsnt.org. CVSNT listens on port 2401 for a password server (pserver) protocol connection. It additionally supports Kerberos authentication or Windows NT domain authentication in both client and server modes.

WSAD narrows the options for using CVSNT. Let us look at using CVSNT in pserver mode because WSAS supports this protocol. Download the installation file for Windows. The version is named cvsnt_1.11.1.3.exe. Execute the file directly or double-click its name to start the Installation wizard. Skip the first page of the wizard. You can choose a default installation or a custom installation. The options do not use much space so install everything. Press Next > to complete the installation. Use the Browse button to choose a simple installation root. The wizard wants to install CVS for NT in the Program Files directory. This is inconvenient because it causes a wordy path with embedded blanks. Use the Browse button to choose C:\CVSNT. This eases the next step because the wizard may complain that it could not set the system path.

Table 21.2 Common CVS Protocol

PROTOCOL	WSAD	DESCRIPTION
:local:	No	Direct access on the local machine.
:pserver:	Yes	Password Server. Remote CVS invoked by inetd. Password authentication by CVS in clear text. Well-known listen port is 2401.
:ext:	Yes	Passes commands and responses using rsh. All data passed in clear text. Uses rhost authentication.
:extssh:	Yes	Passes commands and responses using SSH. Authentication and data are encrypted.

After the installation is complete, you need to update the system environment variable path. Use the Windows control panel to execute the System control panel applet. Click the Advanced tab. Press the Environment Variables button. Use the Edit button of the System variables section to add a path entry. You specified the installation root of C:\CVSNT. Be sure to place it ahead of any other path that may have a cvs.exe file in it, because CVSNT supplies its own version of cvs.exe with Windows-specific functionality.

The installation creates a CVSNT service. A control panel applet provides a way to start and stop this service. The service starts automatically each time the system boots, unless it is set to start manually by using the Windows Services management console.

Before you can use the CVS server with WSAD, you must define at least one repository and add some users. First, click the Advanced tab of the CVSNT applet to set some options. For simplicity, turn on Use local users instead of domain, especially if the machine is not a member of a Windows NT or Windows 2000 domain. See Figure 21.6 for an example.

Next, create a repository by clicking the Repositories tab. Use the Add button to specify C:\cvsroot. The applet offers to create the directory. The result is shown in Figure 21.7.

Note that you may create and serve multiple repositories. WSAD allows you to move a project from repository to repository on a given server. Stop and restart CVSNT from the Service Status tab each time you add or delete repositories so that it will use the current repository environment.

Adding users is the final step in readying CVSNT for serving requests. CVS pserver protocol uses a file named <cvsroot>/CVSROOT/passwd to manage authentication. The file contains a list of user records. Each record has the following format:

```
<CVS user>:<encrypted password>:<mapped system user>
```

This is the only file that you should edit directly. Any other file would be checked out, modified, and checked in. If the CVS username does not match a local Windows user account name, then supply a mapped user ID of a Windows user. Add one or more users using a text editor such as Notepad. Omit the password at this point. A sample initial passwd file follows. Users mauget and db2admin are real Windows accounts. Names usera, userb, and userc are CVS users that will map to these real accounts, because authentication against real user IDs is a requirement.

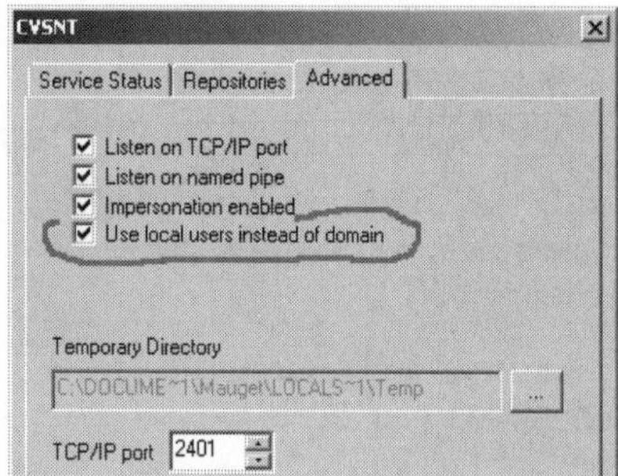

Figure 21.6 Use local Windows authentication.

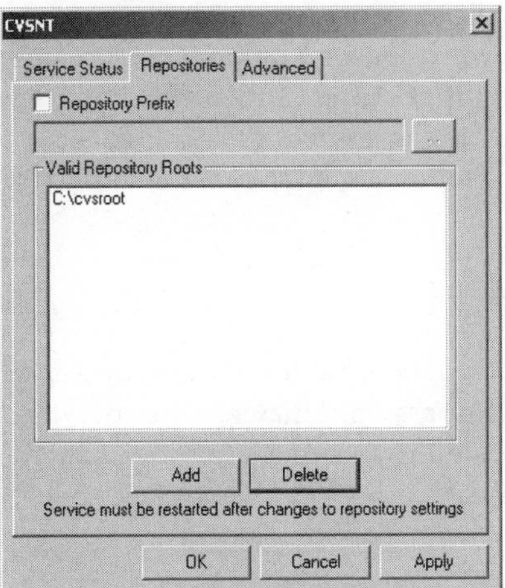

Figure 21.7 Added repository.

```
mauget:
usera::mauget
userb::db2admin
userc::db2admin
```

User mauget is a real Windows user. Therefore, he authenticates by passing his Windows password. The other users must connect to CVS by issuing the Windows password for the mapped user. This is a security exposure. CVS uses clear text passwords that may be compromised. The CVS user's Windows password is passed in the clear. The passwd file user record has its own optional password field. This password should be different than the Windows account password or there would be no use using the CVS password field. This password may be compromised but the user's Window password is not exposed. You could impose a secure protocol atop pserver to prevent this exposure. Security is not an issue since you will run the server on your local machine.

The CVS password is stored in Unix crypt form. How can you produce this form on Windows? CVSNT adds a passwd command to set the password for a user. How can you set the password if you do not want to expose it in the clear? Do not log on, but instead use the local protocol. This is the default if you do not specify a protocol. Open a command window. Issue the CVS passwd command, supplying the repository –d parameter as follows:

```
cvs -d c:\cvsroot passwd usera
```

The CVS client will prompt for the password twice. Issue this form of CVS command for each desired user. A sample passwd file appears as follows:

```
mauget:pDY1uUPd8L5t6
usera:jB9h7fc5xKJB6:mauget
userb:0CRhkgsamzKoM:db2admin
userc:7CwTpG7Yo19zU:db2admin
```

Notice that every password field is different. This is interesting because you set the same password for all four users. The crypt algorithm imposes a random perturbation that enables 4096 possible representations of one input string. This makes the password more difficult to crack if someone should obtain the passwd file.

The CVSNT repository is ready for use. Issue the following form of command to log into CVS in password server mode:

```
cvs -d :pserver:usera@localhost:C:\cvsroot login
```

The CVS client asks for the authentication password, which it forwards to the server in relatively clear text. The server grants access if the password matches the encrypted password stored in the passwd file. List the CVS modules in a repository by using the ls command as follows:

```
cvs -d :pserver:usera@localhost:C:\cvsroot ls
```

You see only the CVSROOT module if nothing has been placed into the repository. Log the user out of CVS using the following form of command:

```
cvs -d :pserver:usera@localhost:C:\cvsroot logout
```

If you have access to CVS installed on another machine on the network, you may issue the previous commands by using the CVSNT machine's DNS name or its IP address in the repository URL.

The point of this section is to give the isolated Windows user a repository for learning version control under WSAD. Now, you will connect to the new CVSNT repository using WSAD. Invoke WSAD. Show the CVS Repository Exploring Perspective. Right-click anywhere in the CVS Repositories view to invoke the context menu. Choose New > Repository Location, as shown in Figure 21.8.

The Add CVS Repository wizard appears. Specify field values as shown in Table 21.3.

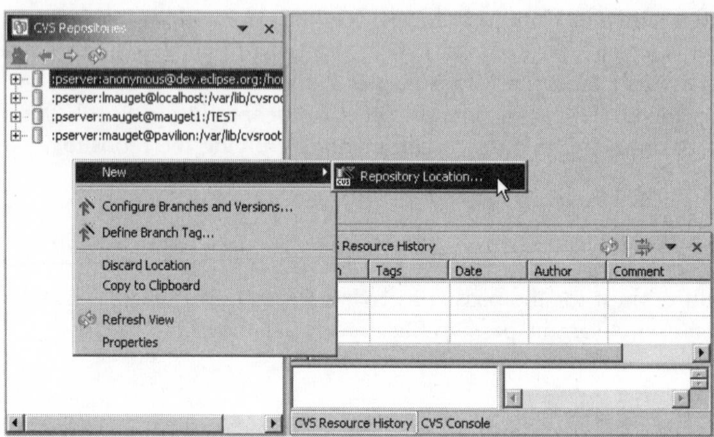

Figure 21.8 New repository.

Table 21.3 Sample Values for Adding a CVSNT Repository

LABEL	VALUE
Host:	localhost
Repository path:	c:\cvsroot
User:	usera
Password:	(the password you installed)
Connection type:	pserver

Use the default port 2401 by not specifying a port in the Host field. Set the connection validation option. The wizard should appear as shown in Figure 21.9. Press Finish.

The new repository should then appear in the CVS Repositories view. It will contain only a CVSROOT module. Expand the HEAD branch, and then expand its CVSROOT module. It should resemble the CVSROOT module seen in Figure 21.10. Display the context menu of config file and select the Show in Resource History context menu item. The history of that file in CVS appears in the CVS Resource History view. If the procedure is successful, WSAD is connected to a repository, and you can version code in the CVS repository.

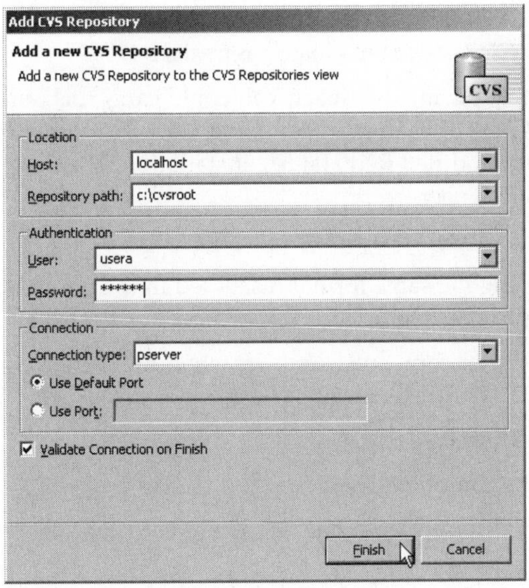

Figure 21.9 Add CVS repository.

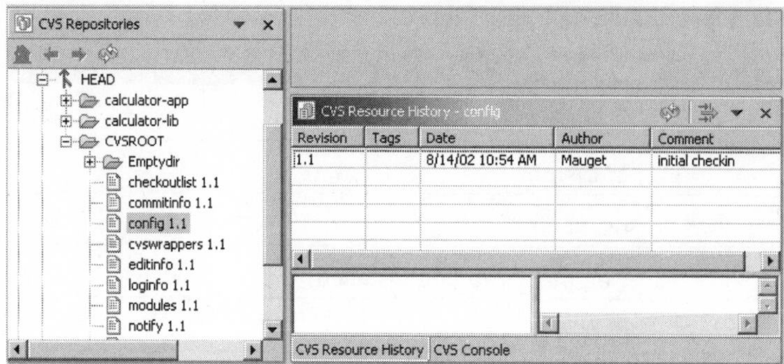

Figure 21.10 CVS resource history.

Linux CVS Server

You can use Linux as a CVS server without reservation. If you have a Linux machine, chances are that it has CVS installed. A small, older machine is sufficient for learning about CVS on WSAD. You will step through the process of turning it into a CVS server that listens for pserver connections. These instructions are based on a Red Hat Linux 8.0 system configuration. The instructions follow:

1. Log into Linux as root. Open a shell window unless at a command prompt now.
2. Issue the command cvs –init /var/lib/cvsroot to create a repository.
3. Create username of cvsuser in a group named cvsuser. You could carry this out from the Red Hat User Manager GUI application by invoking Start > Programs > System > User Manager on an unmodified Red Hat 8.0. installation. The user cvsuser will become the mapped CVS user.
4. Use the command shell to switch to directory `/var/lib/CVSROOT`.
5. Create a user in the passwd file using the same format discussed in the previous CVSNT section. Map the user to cvsuser.
6. Either create an encrypted password or copy one from /etc/shadow. Place it between the colons, as seen in the following example:

   ```
   mauget:$1$/PD/ÛiRc$wmPskgD0geEjfYUhxrzqW1:cvsuser
   ```
7. Change to directory /var/lib in the command shell.
8. Issue command shown –R cvsuser:cvsuser. This gives ownership of the repository to the mapped CVS user.
9. Navigate to directory /etc/xinetd.d.

10. Create a file named cvspserver. Use an editor to set its contents to execute cvs when a request arrives on TCP port 2401: The contents follow:

```
service cvspserver { port = 2401 socket_type = stream
    protocol = tcp wait = no user = root
    passenv = PATH server = /usr/bin/cvs
    server_args = -f --allow-root=/var/lib/cvsroot pserver
}
```

11. Issue the command /sbin/chkconfig cvspserver on. This enables the boot-time automatic starting of the cvspserver service you just created.
12. Start the cvspserver service by issuing command /etc/init.d/cvspserver start.
13. Log out of root. Log in as a normal user on the local system.
14. Start a cvs client, as shown in the following example, except specify the user name in place of *mauget*:

```
cvs -d :pserver:mauget@localhost/var/lib/cvsroot
```

Now, you have a working CVS server. Use WSAD to try to connect to the new repository by following the procedure shown previously for CVSNT. If you already created the CVSNT repository or connected to the Eclipse repository, you may keep those connections. It is instructive to have multiple repositories while learning CVS. Connect as shown in Figure 21.11, but use the locally defined Linux host, user, and password.

If you create each repository reference discussed so far, the WSAD window will resemble Figure 21.12. The Linux machine is named pavilion in the figure. This Linux repository is useful for production, but a production CVS machine may be restricted to repository service. You should never edit a production CVS repository.

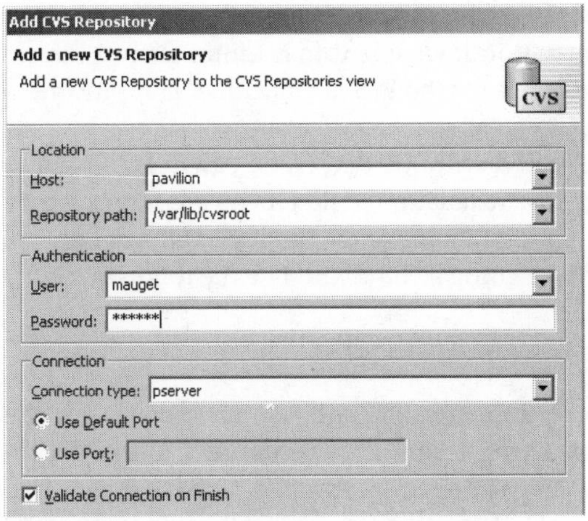

Figure 21.11 Linux pserver connection.

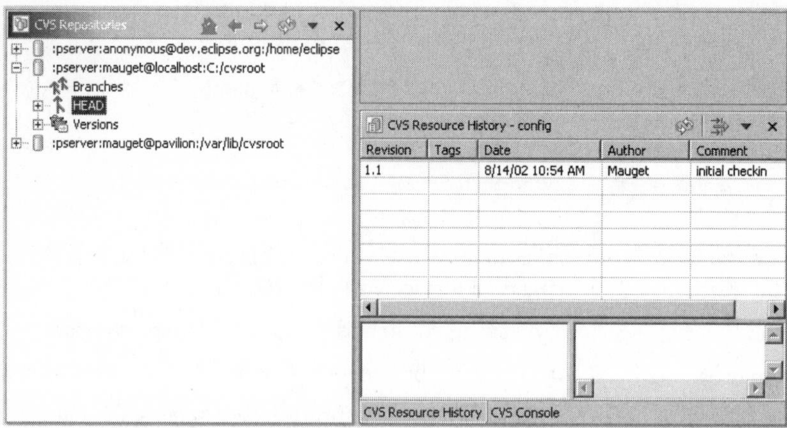

Figure 21.12 CVSNT and Linux CVS repositories.

SSH Tunneling

Recall that the pserver protocol is insecure. You can address this problem by using a network link where all authentication and data traffic is encrypted. Consider using Secure Shell (SSH) if the server is on Linux or Unix. SSH is built into Red Hat Linux and most other distributions. SSH enables a tunneling mode whereby a client connects to a port on its local machine that is forwarded over an encrypted connection to the server. Here, a WSAD repository connection to port 2401 on the local machine would surface on port 2401 on the remote CVS server machine. The client acts as if it were talking to the localhost. The remote pserver CVS cannot distinguish that the connection is special. SSH handles tunneling the traffic between the two machines.

You can institute this procedure from a Windows client to a Linux client with no additional investment. You need an SSH client for the WSAD machine. Happily, there are at least two free options.

You could use the OpenSSH client delivered with the Red Hat Cygwin POSIX environment for Windows. Cygwin has a network installation option if you are connected by broadband. OpenSSH doesn't install by default. You must choose it from the net group. You would establish a tunnel connection by issuing a command like the following:

```
ssh -L2401:localhost:2401 -l <user> <remote_host>
```

Substitute an actual remote host for <remote_host> and use an account on the remote machine in place of <user>. This account must also be defined in the remote CVS passwd file. A command shell window will open on the CVS host. Leave it open while carrying out CVS operations in WSAD. Remember to use localhost for the repository location because the connection is directed to localhost:2401 at the client end. The first time you connect, SSH will say that it cannot verify the authenticity of the remote host. It will display an RSA key fingerprint and ask if you want to proceed. Reply yes. Thereafter, the connection will be carried out without fanfare. The remote host will prompt you for a password as if it were a simple Telnet connection.

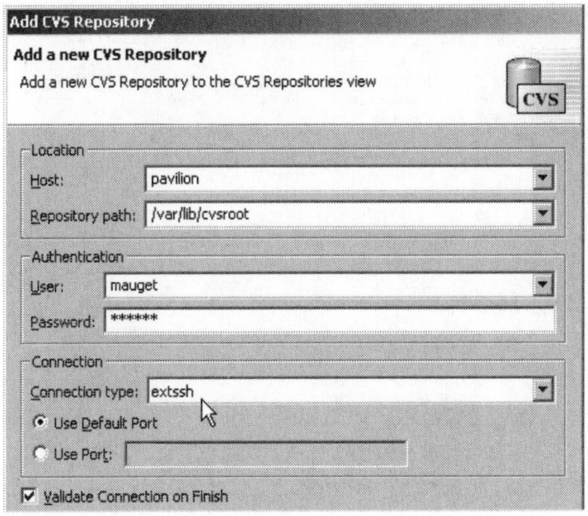

Figure 21.13 Connection type extssh.

WSAD :extssh:

It is a bother to log into an SSH session to secure a pserver connection. WSAD provides its own SSH session if you specify the *extssh* connection type. Here, you connect to the remote machine as you would using a pserver connection type, except that you specify a connection type of extssh, as shown in Figure 21.13.

Working with Repositories

The information in the previous sections enables you to work with a repository as a learning exercise. Now, you will use a repository to work with projects in a version-controlled team situation. Use the CVS Repositories Perspective to work with repositories directly. Use the CVS Repositories view to manipulate a repository. It has a drop-down menu that toggles the view between showing CVS folders and showing CVS modules in a tree view. You can use the Package Explorer view or Navigator view in other perspectives to work with resources under CVS control. If you have set up a repository as discussed previously, try some of the actions discussed in the following sections.

CVS Label Decorations

It is helpful to see the state of each CVS resource displayed in the workbench. The CVS icon and label decorations indicate the state of each resource. To enble CVS label decorations, open the preferences dialog by clicking main menu item Window > Preferences. Select Workbench > Label Decorations, and then set and apply the CVS option, as shown in Figure 21.14.

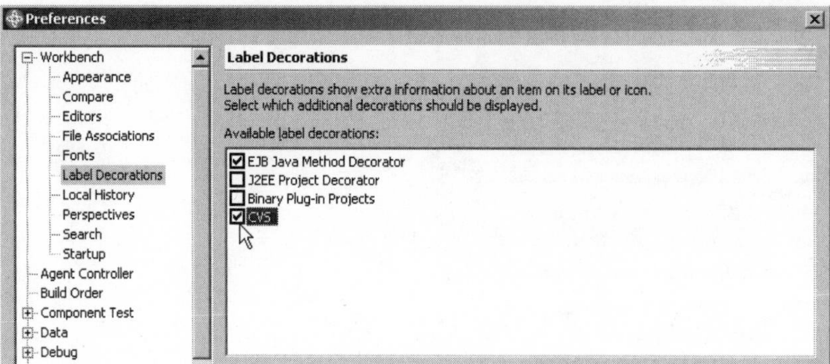

Figure 21.14 CVS resource decorations.

Figure 21.15 shows an example of the resulting decorated resources. Each project location is shown in square brackets. The kind of resource is noted within parentheses. A tiny icon resembling the flowchart symbol for a file is attached to the lower-right corner of any resource that resides in the repository.

Once CVS label decorations are enabled, you can reconfigure the decorations themselves. Open the preferences dialog again by clicking main menu item Window > Preferences. This time select Team > CVS > Label Decorations in the Preferences dialog. You should select the checkbox option **Indicate is outgoing** in the Icons group, as shown in Figure 21.16. This flags an item that is altered since it was checked out.

Project to Repository

How would you initially place a WSAD project into a CVS repository? Carry out the following steps:

1. Create or select a reference to the repository in the CVS Repositories view, as carried out previously.
2. Display the desired project in the Navigator view.
3. Invoke Team > Share Project from the project's context menu. The Share Project with CVS Repository wizard appears, resembling Figure 21.17.
4. Choose a repository location or create a new repository reference. Press Finish to check in the project using the project name as the CVS module name.

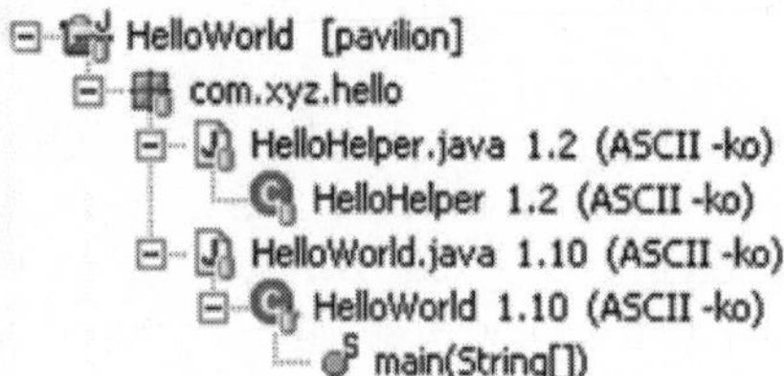

Figure 21.15 Examples of CVS resource decorations.

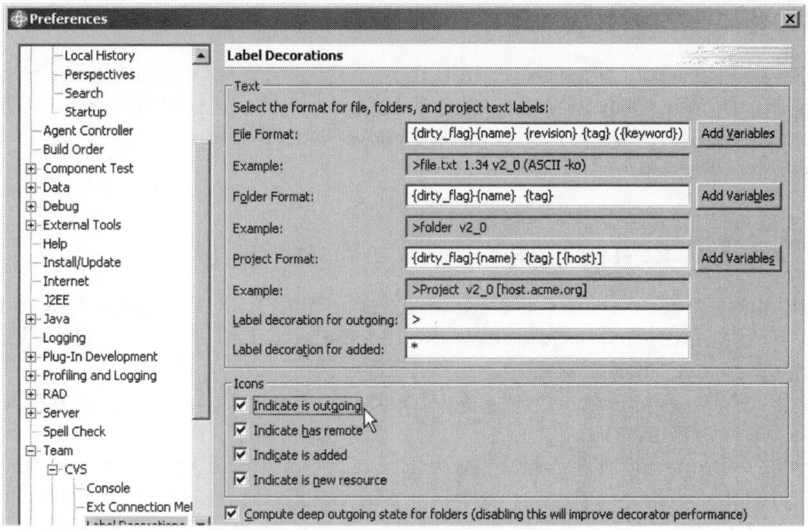

Figure 21.16 Configure CVS label decorations.

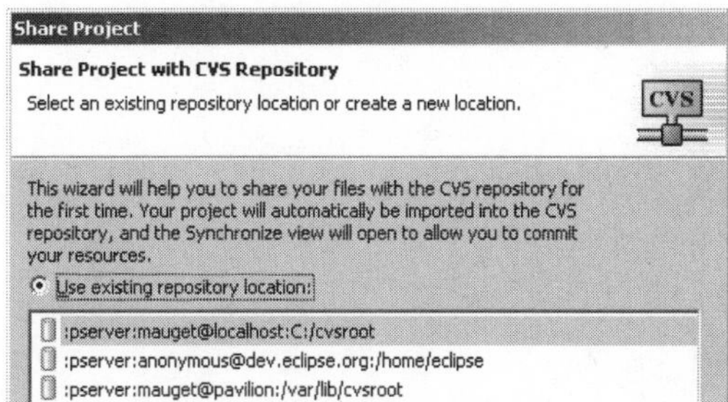

Figure 21.17 Share project with repository.

The project is placed under version control in the CVS repository HEAD stream. Others can see it, and they may create local projects from it. We explain the HEAD stream when we discuss branches and streams in a following section titled Branches.

Repository to Project

Team members can now see the project if they have a reference to the repository, but how can they create a local project from your new repository resource? They would carry out the following two steps:

1. Select the resource in the repository.
2. Choose Check Out as Project from the resource pop-up menu.

Check Out As is a more flexible approach. This menu item will invoke the New Project dialog, enabling the workbench user to make a project of a given kind to receive the resource. You would use this method to create a Java project from the resource so that it would appear in the Package Explorer.

Add to Version Control

If you place a project under version control, thus making it available to others in a team. When you subsequently create another Java class or file as part of the project, you must add that resource to version control. Choose Team > Add to Version Control from the resource's pop-up.

Committing Outgoing Work

You have a resource under version control, and then you modify that resource. How do you update the repository so that the team can use the modified resource? The CVS commit command carries out this operation. WSAD encapsulates the command in the Team > Commit context menu item. WSAD will ask for a commit comment during the operation, as seen in Figure 21.18.

After the commit operation the outgoing tag, if it is enabled, disappears from the resource name in the Package Explorer view. The comment becomes part of the history of the resource. Use the Team > Show in resource history context menu item for the resource to check the comments for all of its committed revisions. An asterisk marks the most recent revision as shown in Figure 21.19. Notice the Tags column. You will learn about tags when we discuss branches and versions.

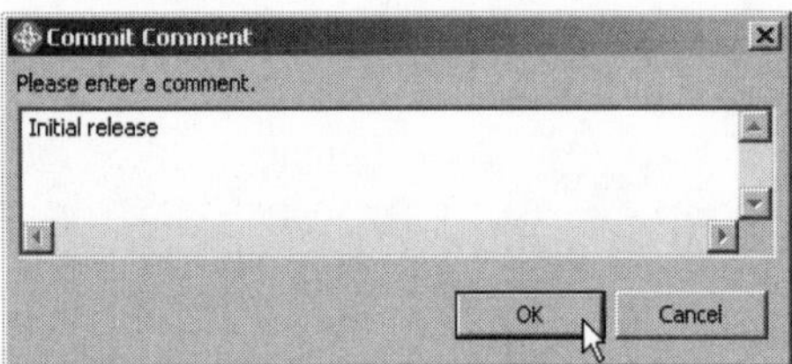

Figure 21.18 Commit comment.

CVS Resource History - HelloWorld.java

Revision	Tags	Date	Author	Comment
*1.11		12/4/02 10:58 AM	mauget	Test outgoing changes
1.10		8/17/02 3:22 PM	mauget	Update some stuff
1.9.2.1		8/17/02 3:06 PM	mauget	Branch alpha-1
1.9	Alpha-1, Root_Alpha-1, version-1_2, version-1_1	8/17/02 12:30 PM	mauget	Adding a reviewer : usera
1.8		8/17/02 12:20 PM	mauget	Reviewer comment
1.7		8/17/02 12:17 PM	mauget	Reviewer comment
1.6		8/17/02 12:01 PM	mauget	Adding a reviewer : usera
1.5		8/17/02 11:21 AM	mauget	Reviewer comment
1.4		8/17/02 11:09 AM	mauget	Fix displayed text
1.3		8/16/02 8:44 PM	mauget	Misc changes
1.2	Maintenance	8/16/02 5:28 PM	mauget	Fix comments
1.1	Book, Root_Book, HelloWorld, Root_HelloWorld	8/15/02 8:57 PM	mauget	Initial release

Figure 21.19 Resource history.

Update

Version control technology is supposed to enable a team to work on one project. Let us postulate that you and Carey each have a copy of the repository resource HelloWorld.java in your workspaces. Each of you modifies the source code in your local workspaces. Each change is against a different part of the file, but you changed independent copies of the file. The label decoration for the file is prefixed with a ">," meaning that the location copy has been modified.

Carey commits her copy to the repository. Her ">" label prefix on the resource disappears, signifying that her local copy is clean. Later, as you try to commit your change, WSAD, through CVS, will detect the conflict. You will receive a message box resembling that seen in Figure 21.20.

How do you proceed? You can use the context menu item Team > Update to tell WSAD to carry out a CVS update command that merges Carey's changes into your local HelloWorld.java resource. Since each of you modified different parts of the file, no manual winner decision is necessary. Your resource still shows the ">," which means that the resource is not committed, but now it has Carey's change merged. Now, you can retry the commit operation. If nobody modified HelloWorld.java while you were updating your local copy, then the commit will be completed.

Synchronize with Repository

It is good practice to carry out an update before synchronizing. This minimizes exposure to the ugly conflict message seen previously. WSAD, as a façade for CVS, bundles these steps in a user-friendly manner where you can check the difference between the repository resource and your local copy of the resource. The context menu item Team > Synchronize with Repository compares the local copy of a resource with the repository copy. It distinguishes between incoming and outgoing changes.

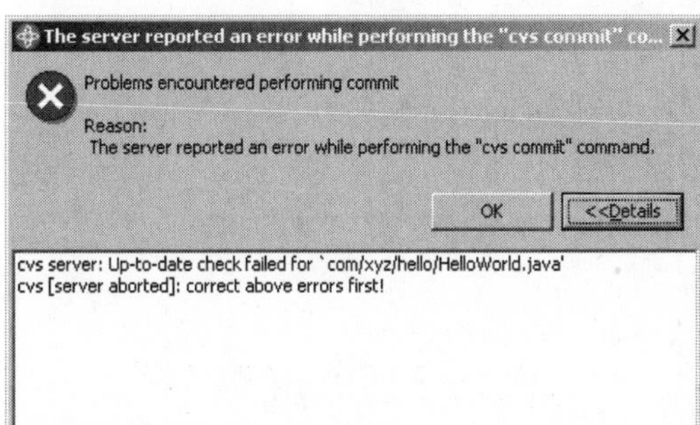

Figure 21.20 Commit conflict.

For instance, if Carey modifies HelloWorld.java after you commit a change to it, her local copy matches the repository while yours does not. You may not know of the change, but you can invoke Team > Synchronize with Repository at any time to ensure that your copy matches the repository. In this case, the Synchronize view would appear in incoming mode, meaning that a potential update is inbound to your workspace. A Structure Compare pane shows the resource in its hierarchy. It has a blue left-arrow icon suffix, showing the direction of synchronization. If you double-click the resource, a pair of differential comparison view panes shows highlighted textual differences. This is the kind of comparison view you saw previously when we discussed local resource history. The context menu item Override and Update item will carry out an update of the local copy of HelloWorld.java. See Figure 21.21. WSAD will ask you to choose if you want to only update resources that can automatically be merged, or if you want to update all changes, overwriting local changes with remote contents. Since the source comparison in Figure 21.21 shows that no change affects the same source lines, you will let the contents be merged automatically.

Now, the local copy matches the latest revision in the repository until somebody changes the resource after you.

If you now make a new modification that you want to commit, you use the context menu item Synchronize Outgoing Changes. Here, the Synchronize view appears in outgoing mode. The decoration arrow on the resource points to the right. You can open the resource to Comparison view, as shown in Figure 21.22. You would choose Commit to post the update to the repository. The decoration arrow would disappear from the Navigator.

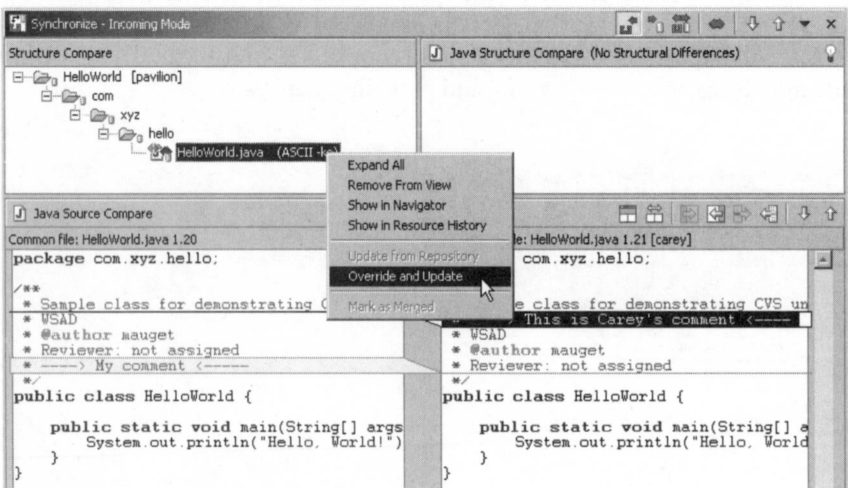

Figure 21.21 Synchronize incoming mode.

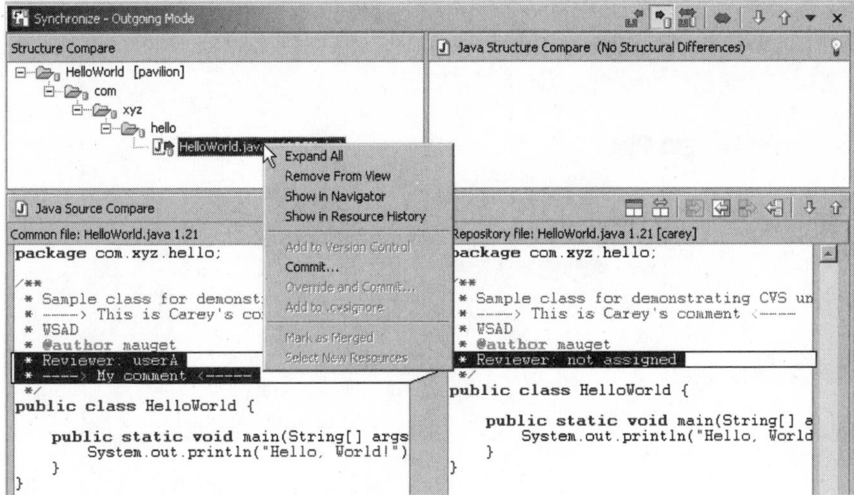

Figure 21.22 Synchronize outgoing mode.

How do you know when to use Synchronize Outgoing Changes as opposed to Synchronize with Repository? You could have used Synchronize with Repository to obtain the same outgoing mode Synchronize view. The Synchronize Outgoing Changes operation declares the desired direction of synchronization, but the CVS will not miss conflicts if you use either operation. You can use Synchronize with Repository when you have outgoing changes. The CVS will detect any conflicts. WSAD will present the comparison panes for you to check when you double-click a node decorated with a blue comparison arrow.

We skirted the issue of what happens when you and Carey each change the same area of a given resource. Let us say that Carey adds a reviewer name to a comment line and commits the change to the repository. Now, you add another reviewer name to the same comment line and try to commit the change. The Synchronize view shows a red status line that reads: 1 conflicts, no incoming changes, no outgoing changes, no new resources. See Figure 21.23 for an example.

The context menu offers to let us Override and Update. If you do this, the local copy will be updated from the repository copy, but you will lose the change on the conflicting source line. If you switch the Synchronize view to Incoming / Outgoing mode by clicking the third icon from the left in the top-right of the title bar, the context menu will change. You will be allowed to choose Override and Commit. You can change the conflicting text to reflect your change and hers, and then choose Override and Commit. WSAD will offer to save the file. Let us say that you change the conflict line to read: Reviewers: usera, userb, userc, and then commit, letting WSAD first save the file. WSAD replies with an information dialog box with text: You have changes that conflict with the server. Release those changes? When you release those changes, Carey will receive them the next time she synchronizes or updates. If you made the modification correctly, her changes will be merged with yours.

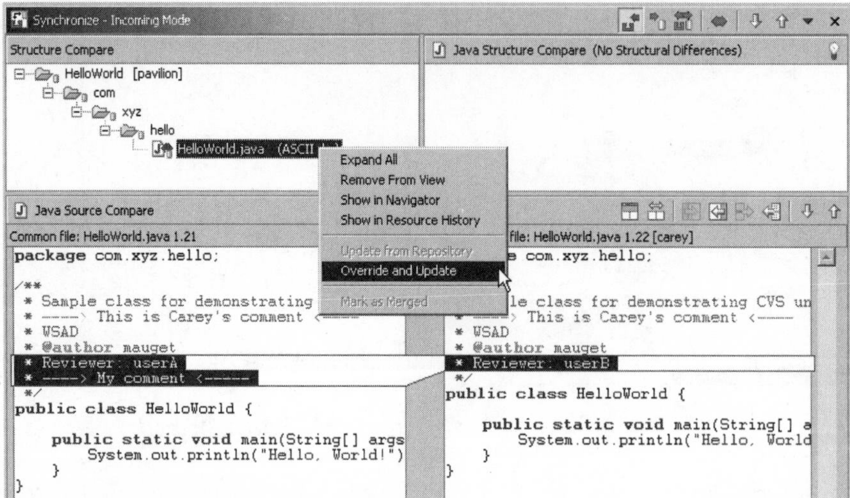

Figure 21.23 Synchronization conflict.

This seems onerous, but these kinds of conflicts shouldn't happen often in a team where members communicate. The alternative paradigm, where an entire resource is locked, presents a set of problems that some consider more difficult.

CVS Ignore

Some resources are regenerated locally, are not part of the state of a project, or are pinned to a location. For instance, binary Java class files are regenerated during a build. Perhaps you only want the source files under version control. CVS maintains a list of file name patterns that it ignores. WSAD exposes an interface to this list through the Team pop-up menu.

Branches

A CVS repository has one or more streams of resources under control. It always has a HEAD stream. This is often used as the development stream.

Recall that CVS allows you to tag resources. You use those tags to assign resources to distinct streams. For instance a team may need to fix a problem in their released product while they are working on the next release. They cannot release the development stream as a fix since its target product is in an incomplete state. Instead, they could create a branch in the revision stream below where they started work on the new release. Maintenance personnel could check out, repair, and commit the failing resource to the branch. Thus, maintenance personnel create a new revision of the failing resource on a separate branch from the new product stream of revisions in the development HEAD stream. Later, the two branches may be merged so that the development stream picks up the repair.

You should synchronize with the repository first. Then, invoke the Team > Branch context menu on the desired resource—usually a project. The Create a New CVS Branch dialog appears. Create a name for the branch. The dialog will enforce CVS character set rules as you type. See Figure 21.24 for an example. A suggested version name is automatically composed from the branch name as you type. You can modify the version name if your organization dictates a naming convention. The Details >> button displays information about existing branches and versions. The Start working in the branch option means that your local resource will be assigned to the new branch. Press OK to create the branch.

At this point, the CVS Repository view shows the new Beta-1 branch, as shown in Figure 21.25.

If you commit a change, will other developers get it when they synchronize? Not unless their workspaces are working in the new branch. Will team member Jeremy's CVS Repositories view show the new branch? Yes, he can use the context menu Configure Branches and Versions command to discover branches that exist in the repository, and then add Beta-1 to the Repositories view so that he can browse it or import it into a project. Additionally, the Show in Resource History pop-up menu of an individual resource will display the resource history of all revisions and tags for that resource.

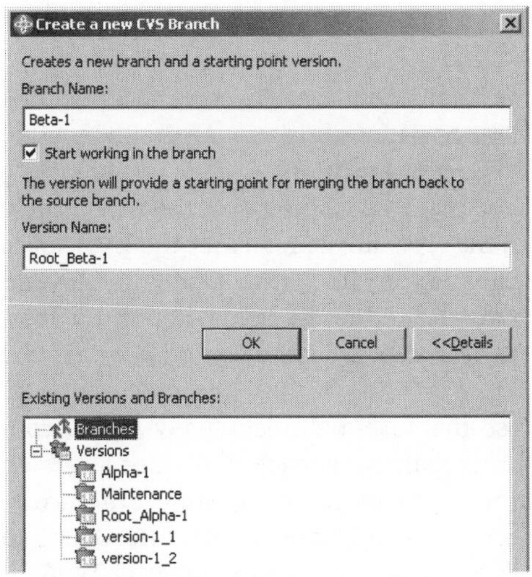

Figure 21.24 Create CVS branch.

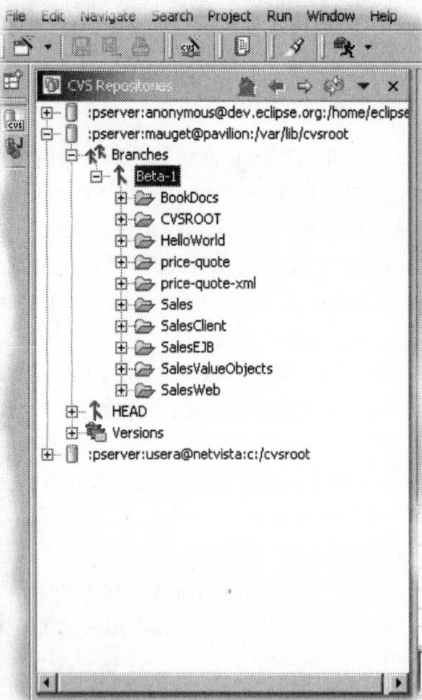

Figure 21.25 Beta-1 branch.

Versions

A version is an immutable snapshot of a stream in the *versions* section of the repository, but the HEAD stream and branches are still the basis for revisions. A version is often used as input to build a product release. Let us create a version.

When you create a version of a resource, you use it as it appears in the workbench. Therefore, it is important to synchronize with the repository first. After the workspace state is satisfactory, use the context menu command Replace With > Revision followed by the Get Contents command to work with the desired resource revision in the local workspace. Then, choose the Team > Tag as Version context menu command to tag the resource as a version.

Often you will do this on a project node so that CVS will recursively tag all contained resources as a version. The Tag Resources dialog invites you to enter a version tag. This is a name for the version. Some characters are illegal in the name, but the dialog live validity checking will not let you enter an invalid name. Expand the dialog to show existing versions by pressing the Details >> button, as shown in Figure 21.26.

Use the Configure Tags button to display and choose any existing tags in your resources for the new version, as shown in Figure 21.27. Chosen tags are added to the resource and all of its children when you press the OK button. Afterward, press the OK button on the Tag Resources dialog to create the new version.

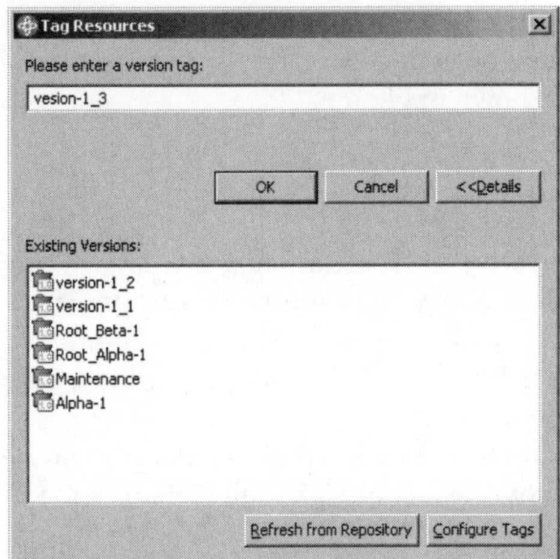

Figure 21.26 Tag resources.

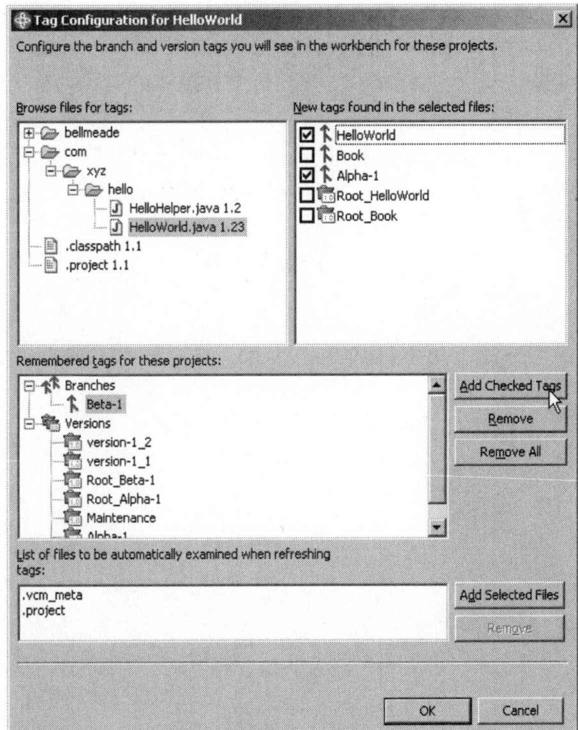

Figure 21.27 Tag configuration.

To see the new version in the repository, select the CVS Repositories view, expand Versions, and then expand the project. You tagged your example project with version-1_2. There is a version-1_2 in your node list, shown in Figure 21.28.

Replacing

You may decide that your latest revision is incorrect. You can replace your working copy of a resource with an earlier version from the repository. This is similar to replacing the copy from local history, except that the revision comes from the shared repository. Use the context menu item Replace With > Branch or Version to choose the desired revision to overwrite your local resource copy.

You can always restore code to the latest revision in the repository. Simply choose context menu item Replace With > Latest From Repository. The full suite of replacement options is shown in Figure 21.29.

Merge

Recall the previous scenario where a maintenance branch would eventually merge with a development branch. Use the context menu item Team > Merge command to invoke a Merge wizard to carry out the merger of two branches. The first panel appears as shown in Figure 21.30.

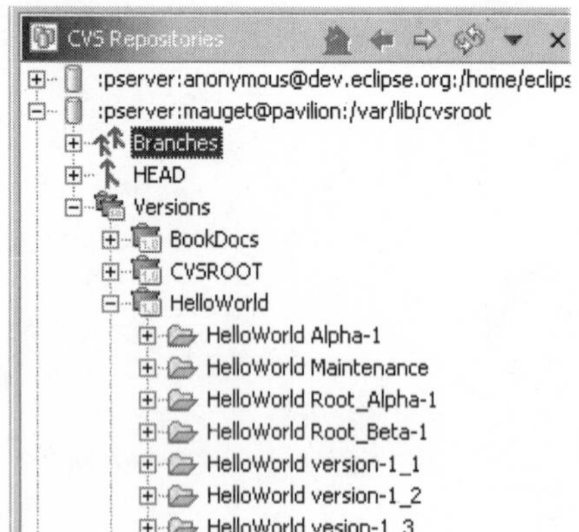

Figure 21.28 Versions.

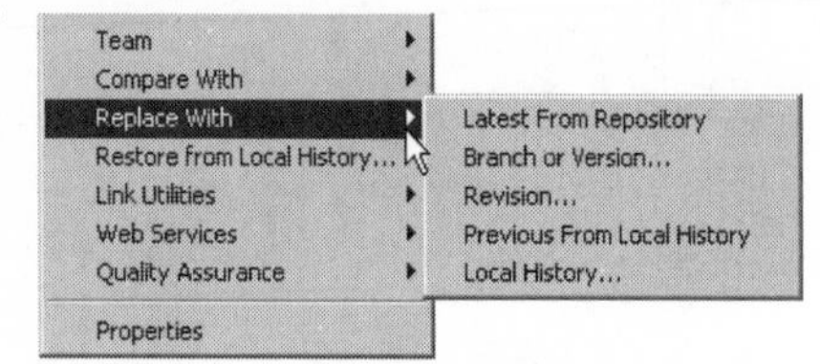

Figure 21.29 Replacement choices.

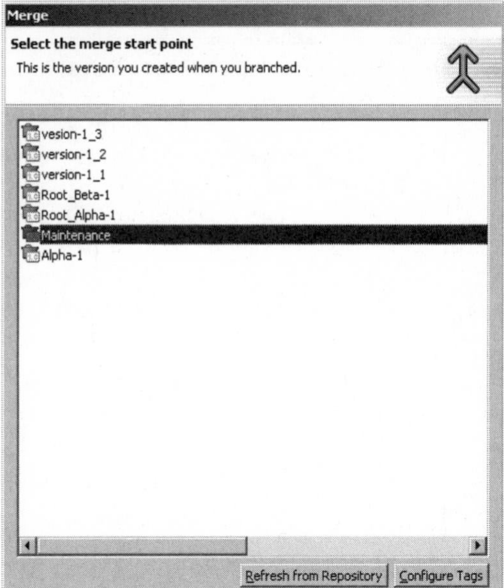

Figure 21.30 Merger target.

Select the target version from the list, and then press Next >. The next panel invites you to select the source branch or version to be merged into the target, as shown in Figure 21.31. Select a branch or version, and then press Finish. Changes are merged into the target.

Create Patch

WSAD enables you to create a patch file based upon the delta between a workspace file and a repository revision. Try this by changing and saving a file that is under version control. Don't synchronize it. Instead, use the context menu item Team > Create Patch to create a diff file or Clipboard entry by pressing Finish. For example, if you added "Patch this" to a comment in a HelloWorld.java resource, deleted a line, and saved the file without synchronizing it, then you created a patch on the clipboard with the following contents:

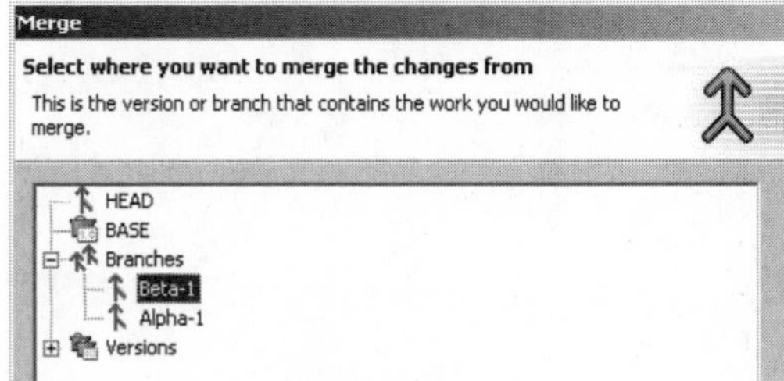

Figure 21.31 Merger source.

```
Index: HelloWorld.java
===================================================================
RCS file: /var/lib/cvsroot/HelloWorld/com/xyz/hello/HelloWorld.java,v
retrieving revision 1.23
diff -u -r1.23 HelloWorld.java
--- HelloWorld.java                                9 Dec 2002 21:43:03 -0000
1.23
+++ HelloWorld.java                               10 Dec 2002 02:20:05 -0000
@@ -2,10 +2,10 @@

 /**
   * Sample class for demonstrating CVS under
- * ----> This is Carey's comment <----
   * WSAD
   * @author mauget
   * Reviewer: userA, userB, userC
+ * Patch this
   */
 public class HelloWorld {
```

Notice that the addition is prefixed by a plus. The deleted line prefix is a minus. The next situation simulates a patch situation by using Replace With > Latest From Repository to replace the local copy from the latest revision in the repository. This undid the changes to the file. Then, you use the context menu item Compare With > Patch. This results in a dialog where you chose the HelloWorld.java file from a hierarchy and elected to compare it to the patch on the Clipboard. The next panel appears, as seen in Figure 21.32. Pressing Finish returned the local copy of HelloWorld.java to the local modification state. The repository was unchanged because this was a local patch.

This patch capability could be used to apply maintenance to source code that isn't under CVS control. For instance, some open source programs are distributed in source form. The end user builds the application based upon custom input. Maintenance may be distributed in the form of patch files. This is common in the Linux kernel community.

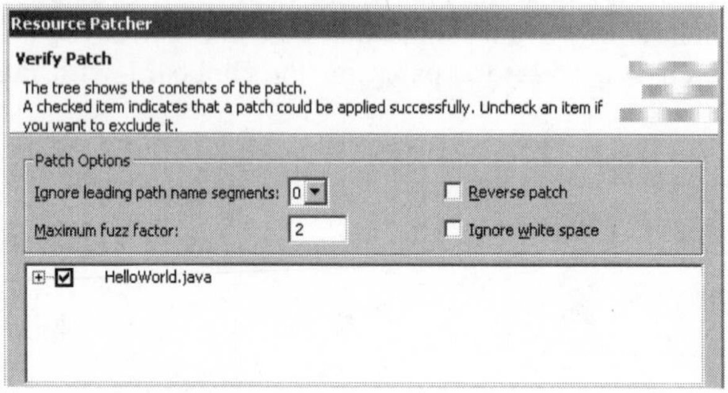

Figure 21.32 Verify patch.

Comparison

You saw the Compare With context menu previously. It presents the *diff* comparison between the selected file and a choice of sources.

- Latest from Repository
- Branch or Version
- Patch (seen previously)
- Each Other (a multiple file selection)
- Revision
- Local History (seen previously)

WSAD uses common diff window panes among these comparisons. They clearly show the differences.

CVS Console

WSAD imposes a graphical user interface façade over a set of CVS commands. This hides the actual CVS commands that are issued. This is normally good, but it may be helpful to trace the actual CVS commands that WSAD issues. The CVS Console view provides a transcript of WSAD CVS activity. Activate the console by choosing the main menu item Window > Show View > CVS Console. If you have not recently displayed this view, you can pick it from the tree of possible views shown by invoking Window > Show View > Other. The following console transcript shows the action of a CVS Repositories context menu Check Out As Project operation on module calculator-app. Notice that this CVS operation is simply a CVS checkout (co) command.

```
***
cvs co -d "calculator-app" -P -A "calculator-app"
  cvs server: Updating calculator-app
  U calculator-app/.classpath
  U calculator-app/.cvsignore
  U calculator-app/.project
  cvs server: Updating calculator-app/bellmeade
  cvs server: Updating calculator-app/bellmeade/calculator
  U calculator-app/bellmeade/calculator/Calculator.java
ok (took 0:00.781)
***
```

Disconnect

When you share a project or create a project from a repository, it is logically connected to that repository through CVS meta information contained in a local file. WSAD enables you to disconnect the project or a contained resource from the repository by using the context menu item Team > Disconnect. The confirmation asks you to choose whether you want to eliminate the meta information. If you do not delete the CVS meta information, you will not be allowed to place the project into another repository. After a disconnect operation, the CVS label decorations will disappear from the project.

Summary

WSAD acts as a façade for CVS access while providing integration with the development environment. It does not enable local CVS access. Thus, we covered how to create a remote repository for learning purposes, if only on the local machine. We discussed major version control operations on the CVS so that you could try the operations on your own repository. We covered:

- Standalone development
- Versioning overview
- Versioning products
- The Concurrent Version System
- CVS integration with WSAD
- Working with repositories

In Chapter 22, "Enterprise JavaBeans," we begin a discussion of using WSAD to develop and test Enterprise JavaBeans.

Enterprise JavaBeans

What's in Chapter 22?

The Enterprise JavaBeans (EJB) specification details standard component architecture for building distributed object-oriented business applications using Java. WSAD provides a comprehensive development, test, and deployment environment for EJBs. This chapter covers:

- Enterprise JavaBeans overview
- Creation of an enterprise application project
- Creating a stateless session bean
- Promoting methods to interfaces
- Generating deployment classes and RMI stubs
- Deployment to a test environment
- The IBM Universal Test Client
- Bottom-up creation of entity beans from a DBMS schema
- The RDB-EJB mapper
- Specifying a container-managed relationship (CMR)

- Creating a data source and registering its JDNI reference
- Bean debugging
- Exporting an EAR file
- Client API

A J2EE 1.3 specification application server hosts Java enterprise applications. WSAD bundles a test version of the WebSphere v5.0 application server. An enterprise application consists of one or more of the following kinds of modules:

- Enterprise JavaBeans (EJB) module
- Web application module
- Connector module
- Client module

These module types are exportable to an enterprise archive file (EAR), structured JAR file that contains a JAR file for each module, and any supporting classes. The EJB module resides in a structured EJB JAR file of its own within the EAR file.

This chapter discusses how to build an EJB module. You will exercise the module through the IBM Universal Test Client embedded in WSAD. We wrap up the chapter with a simple command-line Java application client that performs a query on one of the EJBs. The next chapter enhances the EJB module and adds a Web module used as an EJB client. The EJB module and the Web module together form a sales tracking application.

EJB Overview

Enterprise JavaBeans are nonvisual transactional components of transaction-oriented distributed enterprise applications. They can be developed once, and then reused in multiple applications. An EJB is deployed to a conceptual container in the server. Application requests are directed to the container, which operates on the beans on the client's behalf. WSAD and WebSphere v5.0 support the EJB 2.0 specification, which is part of J2EE 1.3. The Enterprise Javabeans Specification, Version 2.0 specifies the following kinds of beans:

- Entity beans, which represent persistent data
- Session beans, which house application flow and domain logic
- Message-driven beans, which receive messages from Java Messaging Service (JMS) queues or topics

The developer may implement the persistence mechanism of an entity bean. This is called bean-managed persistence (BMP). The alternative is container-managed persistence (CMP). Here, the container handles the details of communication with the back-end data store. EJB 2.0 enhanced CMP capabilities. The developer may specify queries to find bean instances in the EJB QL variant of SQL specified by J2EE 1.3. EJB 2.0 adds container-managed relationships (CMR) where relationships between EJBs are automatically handled by the container.

Session beans may be deployed as stateful or stateless beans. A stateful bean instance resembles part of the client residing in the application server. It belongs to one client and maintains state across requests. A stateless session bean instance does not maintain any state between requests. It resembles a taxicab that is sequentially shared across clients. An article left behind in a taxicab cannot be expected to appear in the next taxi. A stateless session bean resembles a taxi this way and in the way that it is a member of a reusable pool. Stateless session beans are usually used to manage application workflow to entity beans. In fact, production clients almost never directly reference entity beans.

All client requests of beans are carried out through interfaces. Each EJB has a home interface that operates as a class factory for creating and finding bean instances. A bean instance is represented by a remote interface. The bean client locates home interfaces through a JNDI repository supplied by the J2EE server. Other needed resources involved, such as the back-end data source, are located in this manner. Communications with the interfaces is carried out using RMI over IIOP. Some beans, such as session beans, are clients to other beans in the same container. EJB 2.0 added optional local interfaces that are only reachable within the local VM, but do not use the network. They are useful for entity beans that are only referenced by session beans in the same container.

EJBs are configurable. This means that many of a bean's operational characteristics are not contained within the bean. Instead, the characteristics are specified administratively in an XML document called a deployment descriptor. Here, transactional specifics, security aspects, CMR relationships, JNDI references, and other characteristics are specified without the need for a developer to open the Java code.

EJBs are reusable across J2EE-compliant application servers. They are reusable across J2EE applications. They may be configured into load-balanced and fail-over clusters. Therefore, EJB technology is worth considering for reusable domain logic within an enterprise.

WSAD is a superb tool for creating, testing, and deploying EJBs and J2EE applications. The rest of this chapter steps through the creation and testing of an EJB module.

Sales Project

In this chapter and the next, you will create a J2EE 1.3 application that tracks sales by postal code. This chapter addresses the EBJ module that comprises the business domain and back-end data model for the project.

A sales purchase is a moment in time. Each purchase is created when an order is placed. A purchase consists of a timestamp, an item, and a location. An order process creates each purchase. The location is specified by a U.S. Zip Code. A table relates the Zip Code to a U.S. city and state. A query of an item's purchases by Zip Code shows a geographical distribution of demand. A future enhancement could relate Zip Code to income bracket or other demographic data. The UML class model of the business domain is shown in Figure 22.1.

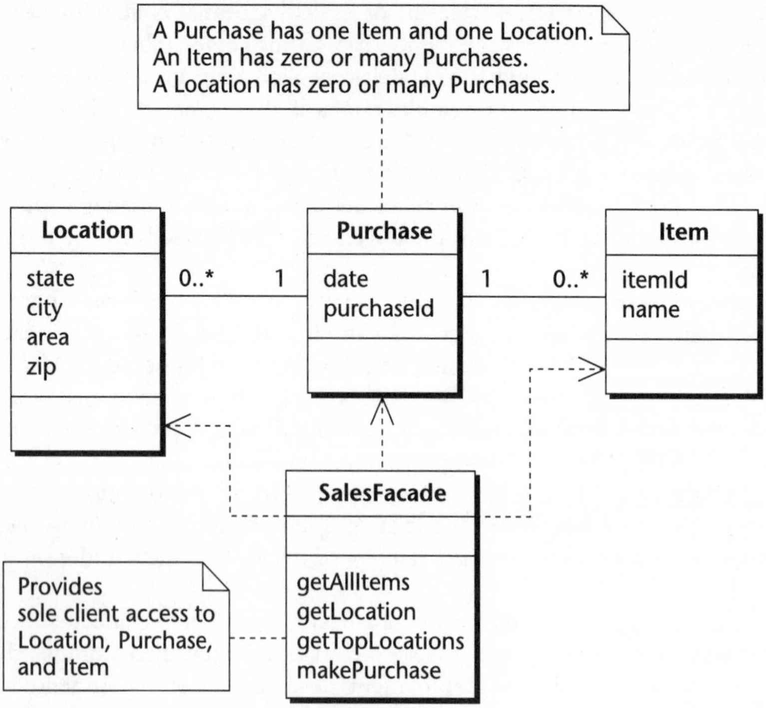

A Purchase has one Item and one Location.
An Item has zero or many Purchases.
A Location has zero or many Purchases.

Location
state
city
area
zip

0..* 1

Purchase
date
purchaseId

1 0..*

Item
itemId
name

SalesFacade
getAllItems
getLocation
getTopLocations
makePurchase

Provides
sole client access to
Location, Purchase,
and Item

Figure 22.1 Sales application diagram.

These classes represent persistent data instances. You'll implement the classes and their relationships as EJB 2.0 specification CMP entity EJBs. WSAD version 5 and WebSphere version 5 are the development and test environments. You will use Cloudscape, also known as DB2 for Java (DB2J), bundled in WSAD within the WebSphere v5.0 Test Environment to manage your persistent data.

Create an Enterprise Application

The Sales J2EE project will contain all three possible kinds of J2EE modules: client application, EJB application, and Web application. You will work on the client application and the Web application in the following chapter. Begin with the following steps:

1. Create a new WSAD workspace directory. The name and location are your choice, but WSAD must be able to write to it. The following is an example:

   ```
   C:\workspace-Sales22-GM
   ```

2. Make a shortcut or script that references the empty workspace. Append the `-data` switch to the WSAD start command. For example, the following works if the WSAD installation root is C:\WSAD5:

   ```
   C:\WSAD5\wsappdev.exe -data c:/workspace-Sales22-GM
   ```

3. Start WSAD. It will display a message saying that it is completing its installation. This is because it is initializing the new workspace metadata.
4. Select File > New > Project, J2EE, Enterprise Application Project.
5. Press Next >, and then choose Create J2EE 1.3 Enterprise Application Project. Be careful to choose J2EE 1.3. Press Next >.
6. Press Next >, and then name the project Sales. Take the default values as shown in Figure 22.2. Notice that the three module project names are generated. You can change their names, but accept the default names for this project. Press Finish.
7. The J2EE Perspective should resemble that shown in Figure 22.3. Notice the four new projects derived from your input.

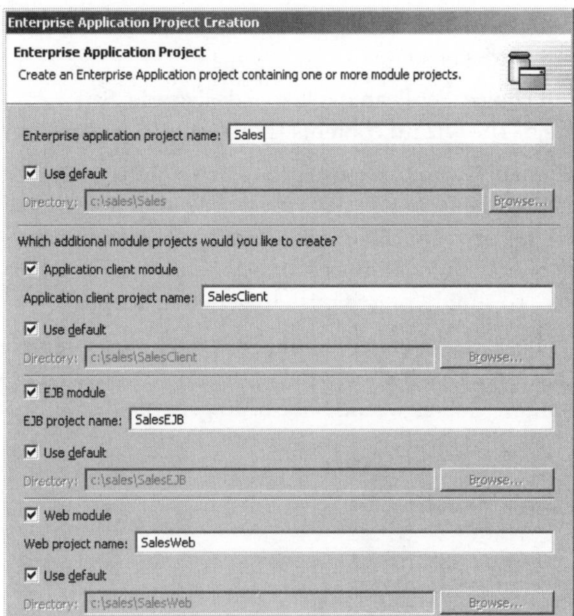

Figure 22.2 Sales enterprise application project.

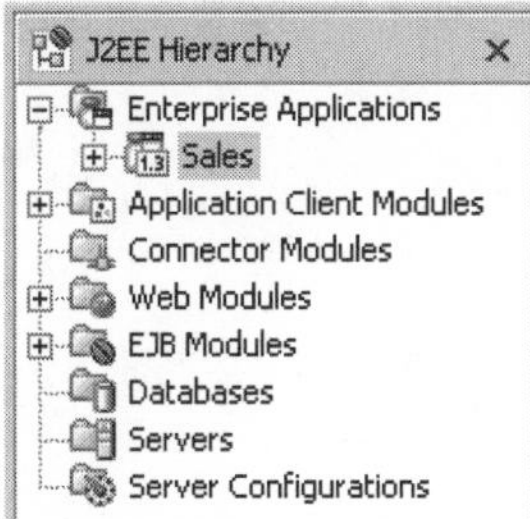

Figure 22.3 Sales application.

The workbench is now ready for some enterprise-level application coding. You do not need to be alarmed because WSAD will supply much of the initial code.

Create a Stateless Session Bean

The EJB application will use a stateless session bean façade layer to orchestrate client requests to the entity beans. This chapter largely addresses creating and testing the entity beans. You will create the stateless session bean first, because this is an easy path to exercise an EJB in the new project. The bean will have only an echo(String) method in this chapter. You will add business methods that use the back-end entity beans in the next chapter. Create the stateless session EJB with the following steps:

1. Select EJB Modules > SalesEJB in the J2EE Hierarchy view.
2. Choose New > Enterprise Bean from the SalesEJB context menu. The Enterprise Bean Creation wizard appears. Press Next >.
3. Keep the Session bean default choice. Set Bean name to SalesFacade. Set Default package to com.xyz.ejb. The wizard contents should match Figure 22.4.
4. Press Next >. The next panel enables you to choose between a stateful or stateless session type, dictate whether the bean will have remote or local interfaces (or both), and if it will use container-managed or bean-managed transactions. See Figure 22.5. You will use only remote interfaces for this bean. The default values are correct for the bean, so simply press Finish to generate the bean.

WSAD generates three classes: a bean class, a remote home interface, and a remote bean interface, as seen in the J2EE Hierarchy view shown in Figure 22.6. If you had chosen additional local interfaces, two more classes would have been generated.

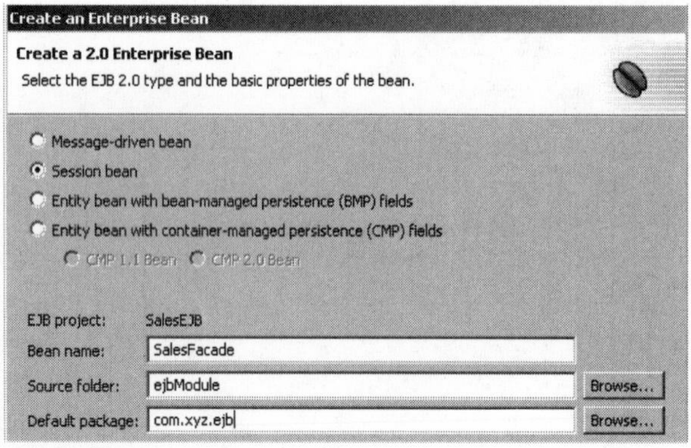

Figure 22.4 Create session bean.

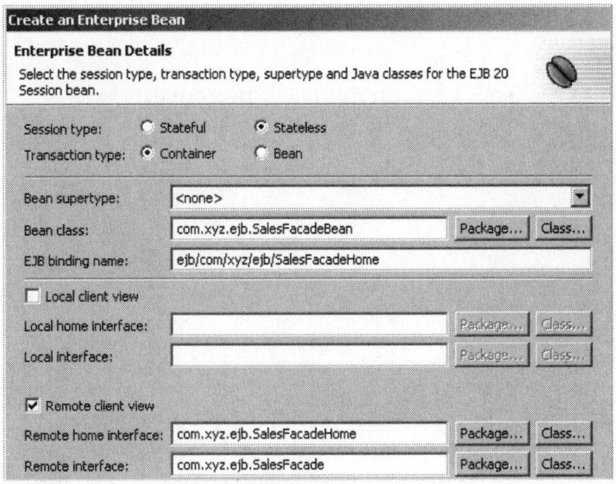

Figure 22.5 Set bean details.

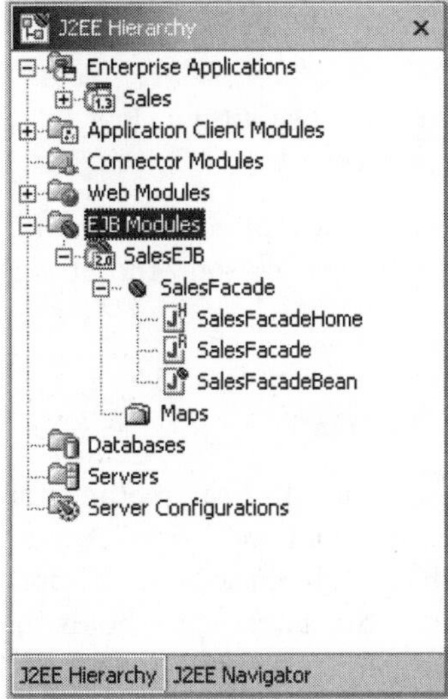

Figure 22.6 SalesFacade bean sources.

Add a Business Method

EJB specification 2.0 beans have four possible kinds of methods: finder methods that find a persistent instance, creation methods that construct an instance, business methods that carry out operations on the bean, and data selector methods used locally by beans. A stateless session bean has no persistent instances. WSAD generates a no-argument creation method for it. Thus, you need at least one business method for this bean to be of any use. You will create an echo(String) method that you can exercise in the WSAD Test Client.

1. Double-click the SalesFacadeBean source in the J2EE Hierarchy view to open the bean in the J2EE Editor.
2. Add the following method to the class beneath method ejbremove():

```
/**
 * echo a string
 * @param aString java.lang.String
 * @return java.lang.String
 */
public String echo(String aString) {
    return "SalesFacade: " + aString;
}
```

3. Save the class. The method appears in the Outline view of the SalesFacade-Bean. Notice that the other methods of the bean have small icon decorations. The new method has none. The echo(String) method is an orphan that is not exposed in the bean's remote interface. You must promote it to the remote interface.
4. Open the context menu of the echo(String) method in the Outline view by right-clicking the method signature.
5. Choose Enterprise Bean > Promote to Remote Interface. The Outline view shows an"R" icon decoration on the echo(String) method.

The SalesFacadeBean is almost ready for testing. Open the remote interface file named SalesFacade. Notice that WSAD inserted the prototype for the echo(String) method when the promotion was carried out.

Generate Deployment Code and RMI Stubs

An EJB cannot be used directly. It runs in a J2EE container that calls bean methods on behalf of client requests. WebSphere version 5 is the J2EE test container supplied with WSAD version 5. WSAD will deploy the bean, along with its encompassing J2EE application, to the WebSphere test environment. An XML deployment descriptor holds the configuration of the bean and its application. Java deployment classes and compiled remote method invocation (RMI) stubs are deployed with the application. Some J2EE servers generate this deployment code during deployment. WSAD generates it ahead of time. This way it doesn't necessarily need to be generated to deploy a change. Let us generate the deployment classes and RMI stubs for the new enterprise application.

1. Invoke the context menu of the EJB Modules > SalesEJB EJB module in the J2EE Hierarchy view.
2. Choose Generate > Deploy and RMIC Code.
3. A dialog appears, as shown in Figure 22.7. Set the SalesFacade option if it isn't already set. WSAD doesn't always correctly decide when the code needs regeneration. It is always okay to generate the code if you are not certain. Press Finish.
4. Check the Tasks view for errors. There should be none.

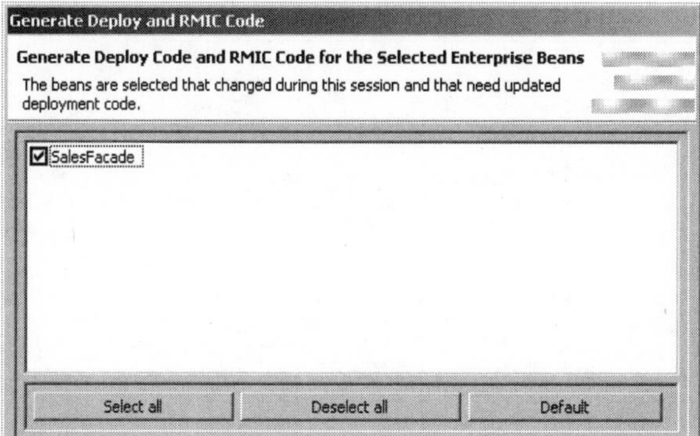

Figure 22.7 Generate deployment code and stubs.

Notice that the J2EE Navigator view shows that many classes were generated to deploy the application. These are the support classes and remote method invocation (RMI) stubs needed to deploy and operate the bean in an application server. You will deploy and operate the bean in the WebSphere v5.0 Test Environment bundled with WSAD.

Deploy

Once the RMI stubs and deployment classes are built, the EJB is ready for deployment. It is part of the SalesEJB module that resides in the Sales J2EE application. WSAD has a Server perspective where you can create a server project with a particular configuration. Then, you can start the server within WSAD, and then deploy the application to it. WSAD provides a Run on Server context menu item that will cause its target to be deployed, starting an associated server if it is not running. If you select Run on Server on the SalesEJB or on its encompassing Sales enterprise application, the WebSphere v5.0 Test Environment is configured and started, and then the application is deployed (published) to the server. Thereafter, a Run on Server will reuse the same server configuration unless you create and choose an alternate server and configuration.

Try it now, using the following steps:

1. Right-click the SalesEJB in the J2EE Hierarchy and select Run on Server. A prompt will appear that asks if the bean should be used on the WebSphere v5.0 Test Environment, attach to a remote WebSphere v5.0 application server, or use some other J2EE application server.

2. Accept the default by pressing OK. This will choose the bundled test environment. The server configuration starts, the console view displays the server starting messages, the Sales application deployment, and, finally, a server opens for eBusiness message.

After the server starts, the IBM Universal Test Client view appears. This automatically deployed Web application is rendered in the integrated Web browser, as shown in Figure 22.8. Additionally, you could open an external browser on URL http:localhost9080/UTC/initialize?port=2809.

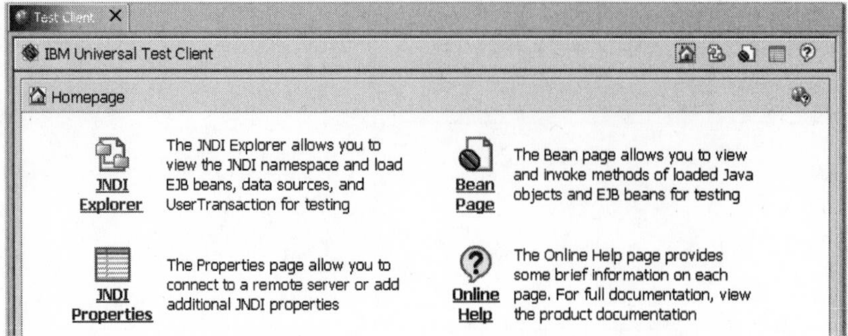

Figure 22.8 IBM Universal Test Client.

Test the SalesFacade Bean

A client locates the home interface for a desired bean by interrogating the JNDI service of the server. An explicit URL references the JNDI service unless it resides on localhost. Since the test client executes in the same server as the JNDI service, the client finds the service by default. Use the following steps to test the bean:

1. Click the JNDI Explorer link in the test client. The explorer opens, displaying a tree view of the names registered in the JNDI service.
2. Expand the node ejb > com > xyx > ejb. This is the fully qualified package name that WSAD registered for the SalesBean. The remote home interface stub of the bean appears as a hyperlink. See Figure 22.9.

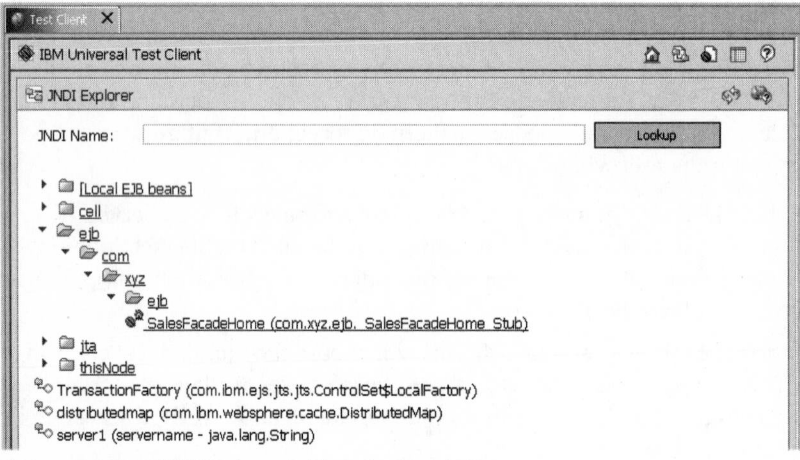

Figure 22.9 JNDI Explorer with SalesFacadeHome.

The next step is to obtain a reference to the remote home interface. This interface acts as a factory that is used to create (or obtain from a pool) an instance of the bean.

3. Click the SalesFacadeHome hyperlink. This invokes the test client's Bean Page, which shows references and parameters.
4. Expand the node EJB References > SalesFacade > SalesFacadeHome. The bean's create() method becomes visible.
5. Expose the creation method parameters by clicking SalesFacade create().

The Parameters pane shows the method above an Invoke button. The client should appear as shown in Figure 22.10.

Learn this user interface. This is how to invoke bean methods in the test client. If a method requires parameters, the Parameters pane will provide a list of constructors for them, allowing the instances to be passed to the method at hand. Continue with the following steps:

6. Create an instance of the SalesFacade remote interface by clicking the Invoke button. The resulting SalesFacade remote interface instance appears beneath the Invoke button followed by a Work with Object button.
7. Press Work with Object to insert the instance into the References pane. The SalesFacade reference appears under the remote home interface in the References pane.
8. Expand the SalesFacade reference node to see its defined methods, as shown in Figure 22.11. The single method String echo(String) that you created appears in the tree. Notice the scissors icon to its right. This icon is used to release a reference when you are finished with it. Continue with the following steps:

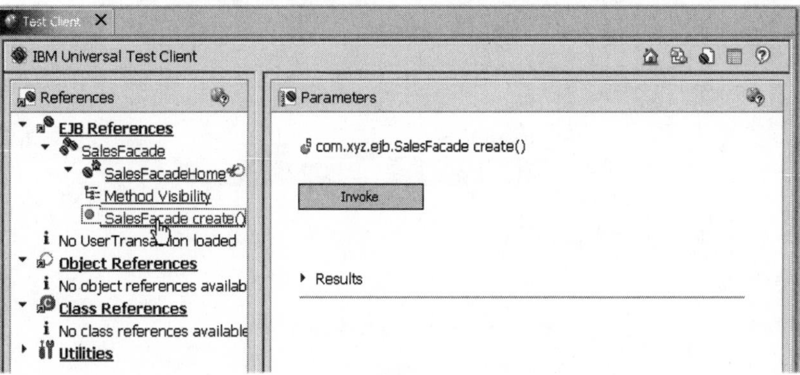

Figure 22.10 Invoke the create method.

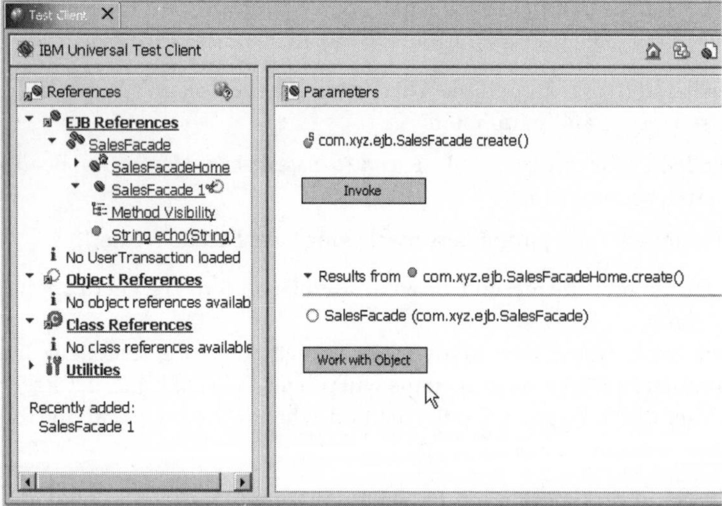

Figure 22.11 SalesFacade remote Interface reference.

9. Invoke the `echo(String)` method by clicking its hyperlink in the References node tree. The Parameters pane renders a set of choices for creating the method parameter.
10. Enter **Hello World** into the parameter String value field, and then press Invoke. The echo text appears in the Results portion of the Parameters pane, as seen in Figure 22.12.

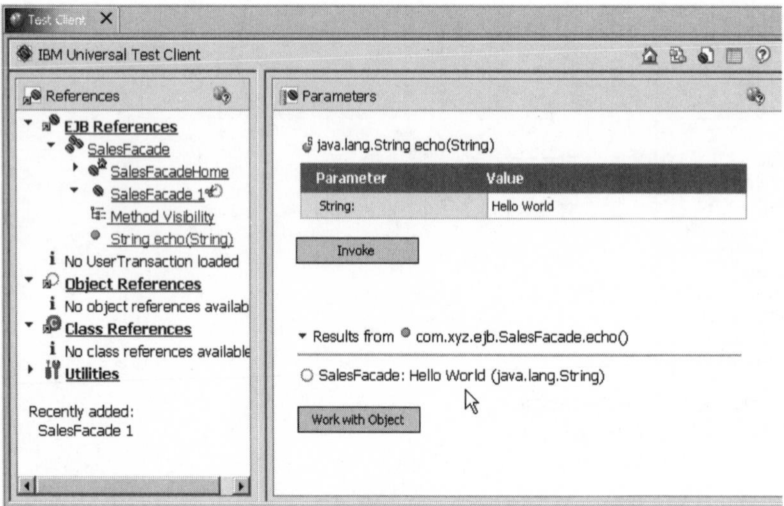

Figure 22.12 Result of method Invocation.

That concludes the demonstration of the stateless session bean. If you wish to work with a result object, you can press the Work with Object button at the bottom of the Parameters pane (scrolled off the screen in the figure). This inserts the instance into the Object References node tree in the References pane. You could operate on the object using operations found under the Utilities node. You click the scissors icon to release an object when you are done using it. When you are finished with the SalesFacade remote reference, click its scissors icon to release its reference.

You will leave the SalesFacadeBean for now. Later, you will add business methods that control the flow of client requests to the set of entity beans that you are about to create.

CMP Entity Beans with CMR Relationships

You will use CMP beans because there are no requirements that must be handled by BMP. EJB 2.0 container management is more full-featured than EJB 1.1, reducing the need for BMP. You wish to leverage the power of the J2EE container and tools. Had you chosen BMP, you would need to implement callback code that carried out the necessary JDBC calls to handle the persistent aspect of the bean. Instead, let us try to minimize or eliminate manually writing Java code in the entity beans.

WSAD presents three choices in designing entity beans. If you have an existing database that you wish to map to entity beans, you choose the bottom-up approach. If you design the beans first, and then implement a database schema from them, this is top-down design. If you need to marry existing beans to an existing database schema, this is called meet-in-the-middle design.

Assume that you have an existing Cloudscape database that contains ITEM, LOCATION, and PURCHASE tables. You want to map those tables to corresponding entity beans, and then access those beans through the stateless session façade bean that you created previously.

Copy the db2j folder from this book's Web site to the C:\ drive on Windows, or to the temp directory on Linux. We use Windows path notation in this chapter. The database location is C:/db2j/databases/SalesDB. Its db2j JDBC URL follows:

```
jdbc:db2j:C:/db2j/databases/SalesDB
```

Tables 22.1, 22.2, and 22.3 show the schemata of the SalesDB tables. If you do not use the database from the book Web site, you can create the database and the schema using Java-based Cview utility archived in the <WSAD>\eclipse\base_v5\lib directory. The db2jcview.jar, db2j.jar, and jh.jar files must appear on the classpath. Execute class com.ibm.db2j.tools.cview in a VM. The supplied C:\db2j\cview.bat file is an example of how to invoke Cview. You can use the utility to enter data rows, or import the c:\LOCATION.DAT, c:\ITEM.DAT, and c:\PURCHASE.DAT files to their respective tables.

Table 22.1 Location Bean Table

NAME	TYPE	PK	FK	NULLABLE
CITY	VARCHAR(40)			
STATE	CHAR(2)			
ZIPCODE	CHAR(5)	X		
AREACODE	CHAR(3)			X

Table 22.2 Item Bean Table

NAME	TYPE	PK	FK	NULLABLE
ITEMID	BIGINT	X		
NAME	VARCHAR(40)			

Table 22.3 Purchase Bean Table

NAME	TYPE	PK	FK	NULLABLE
PURCHASEID	BIGINT	X		
TIMESTMP	VARCHAR(40)			
ITEMID	BIGINT		X	X
LOCATIONID	CHAR(5)		X	X

Before proceeding, ensure that you have the database created or copied from the Web site for this book. You will continue by creating three entity EJBs that model the UML class diagram shown in Figure 22.3. Carry out the following steps:

1. Open the J2EE Perspective, display the J2EE Hierarchy view, expand the EJB Modules folder, and then select project SalesEJB.
2. Select the SalesEJB context menu item Generate > EJB to RDB Mapping. The EJB to RDB Mapping wizard offers to create a new folder to contain the generated mapping file, as shown in Figure 22.13. Press Next.
3. The next wizard panel offers to carry out bottom-up mapping to create the beans from a database schema, as shown in Figure 22.14. Press Next.

The database connection needs some care in specifying a JDBC driver class, its location on the system, and a connection URL.

4. Enter the values shown in Figure 22.15. Note that DB2 for Java uses a Cloudscape driver. The database portion of the URL specifies the absolute path of the database on the system.
5. Press Next.

6. If a panel like that shown in Figure 22.16 does not appear, press < Back to check the work.
7. After success in getting to the next panel, select the APP.ITEM, APP.LOCATION, and APP.PURCHASE tables, as shown in Figure 22.16. Press Next.
8. The next panel allows us to specify EJB 2.0 beans, a prefix, and a package name. Select Generate 2.0 enterprise beans. Leave the prefix blank.
9. Important: set the package name to com.xyz.ejb so that all of the beans occupy the same package. When the screen matches that shown in Figure 22.17, press Finish.

The Map map.xmi view appears. You generated three entity beans in a bottom-up fashion from tables in a relational DBMS. Notice the three new generated beans on the left. The corresponding tables appear at the right.

10. Expand the Purchase EJB and the PURCHASE table. The field-to-column mappings should appear as seen in Figure 22.18.

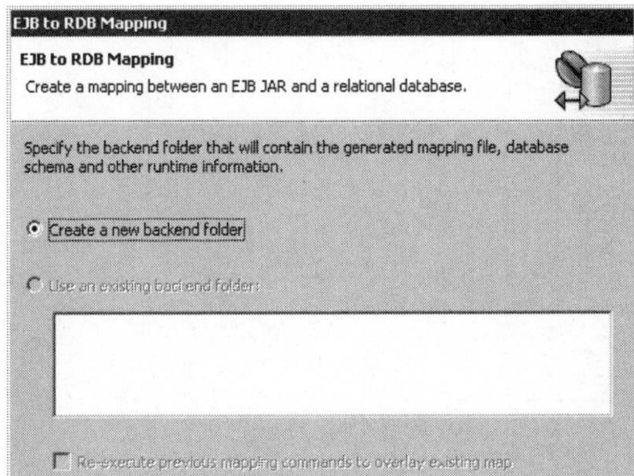

Figure 22.13 Create back-end mapping folder.

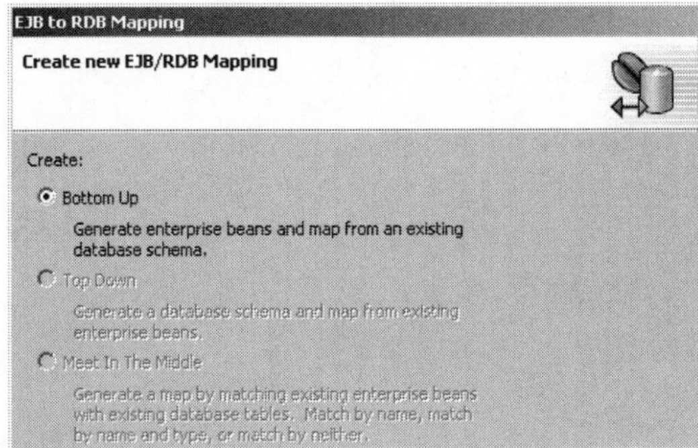

Figure 22.14 Bottom-up mapping.

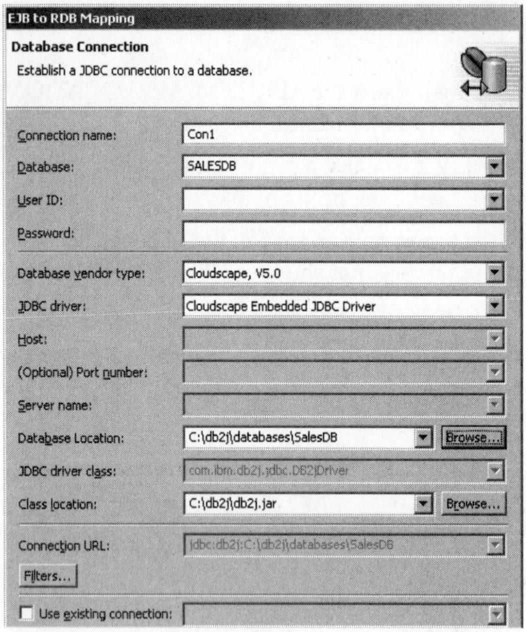

Figure 22.15 Data connection for mapping.

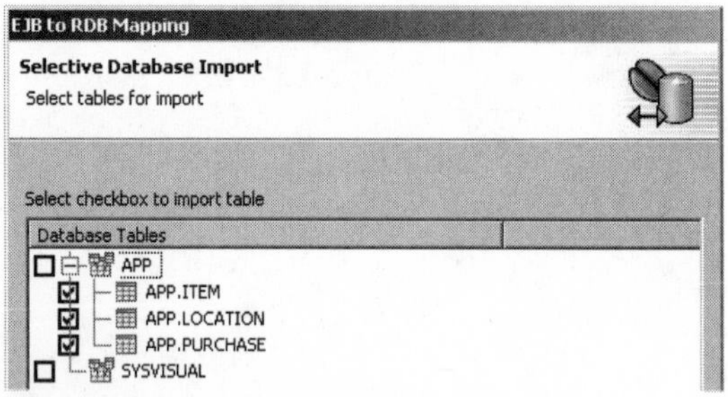

Figure 22.16 Select tables for mapping.

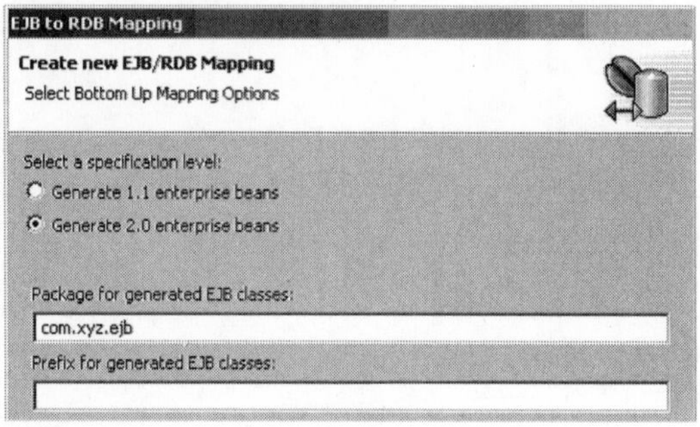

Figure 22.17 Set EJB package name.

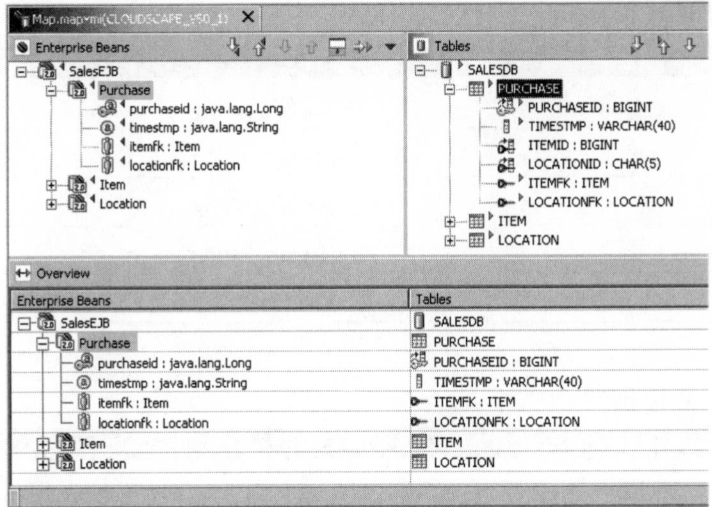

Figure 22.18 Beans mapped to tables.

Expand the beans in the J2EE Hierarchy. Notice that only local interfaces were generated. This means that the beans can only be accessed locally within the virtual machine. You will use the stateless session bean as a remote façade to provide coarse-grained access to the entity beans. This eliminates many resource-holding stubs in the server when concurrent sessions are accessing the beans. It also reduces network traffic since one course-grained method call on the session façade bean results may result in many fine-grained requests of the entity beans. In addition, local interfaces are required for beans that participate in CMR.

The Java Perspective Package Explorer view of the project shows generated source code for each bean, named <bean name>Bean. There is a key class named <bean name>Key, and a source file for each kind of interface for each bean. An XML deployment descriptor and an XMI file is generated in the required META-INF folder of a J2EE EJB module JAR file directory structure. You could code the JavaBeans and other structures manually, but the work is exacting and boring. This is a recipe for human error and frustration, but it is the kind of work at which computers excel.

You did not explicitly add CMP attributes to any of the beans. The mapping procedure derived them from table columns. Tables 22.4, 22.5, and 22.6 show the generated CMP attributes.

Notice the generated CMR attributes. Each CMR attribute represents a relationship with another bean. You created attributed beans, but the mapper cannot read your mind regarding the specific characteristics of the associations shown on the UML diagram.

Table 22.4 Location Bean Attributes

ATTRIBUTE	KEY	CMR	TYPE
city			java.lang.string
state			java.lang.string
zipcode	X		java.lang.string
areacode			java.lang.string
purchase		X	Purchase

Table 22.5 Purchase Bean Attributes

ATTRIBUTE	KEY	CMR	TYPE
purchaseId	X		long
timestmp			java.lang.String
locationfk		X	Location
itemfk		X	Item

Table 22.6 Item Bean Attributes

ATTRIBUTE	KEY	CMR	TYPE
itemId	X		long
name			java.lang.string
purchase		X	Purchase

CMR Relationships

CMR attributes are described in the XML deployment descriptor that is part of the SalesEJB jar file. You will use the Deployment Descriptor Editor to update or create relationships that implement associations. You will adjust the multiplicity and navigation attributes of the two CMR relationships generated by the mapper using the following steps:

1. Use the SalesEJB context menu to invoke Open with > Deployment Descriptor Editor. This editor is divided into tabbed pages. Each page has two columns of expandable categories. The right-most Source tab opens the raw deployment descriptor. Browse the XML source for a moment to get a notion of the information contained within.

2. Select the Overview tab and then expand the Relationships 2.0 category found in the left-hand column toward the bottom. The two relationships created by the mapper appear there. Look for the following:

   - Purchase_To_Item
   - Purchase_To_Location

3. You can expand them to see their endpoint names. Select Purchase_To_Location, and then press the Edit button.
4. The Edit Relationship wizard appears. Enter a description on the first panel. Press Next > to display the roles. Carefully set the roles as shown in Figure 22.19. Specifically, deselect the Navigable option for Location because you don't want to have references to purchases in your relatively static Location table. Press Finish when the roles are set.
5. Similarly, edit role Purchase To Item, as shown in Figure 22.20, turning off the Navigable option for Item, and then press Finish.
6. Save the EJB Deployment Descriptor. The Tasks view should show no errors for any resource in the workspace. Leave the deployment descriptor open.

Now, there are three CMP entity beans with relationships handled by the container. Open the Java Perspective to inspect the generated Java files. Notice the additional two pairs of link files composed of the role names that you specified. There are many custom files, but you didn't write even one line of Java code for the entity beans.

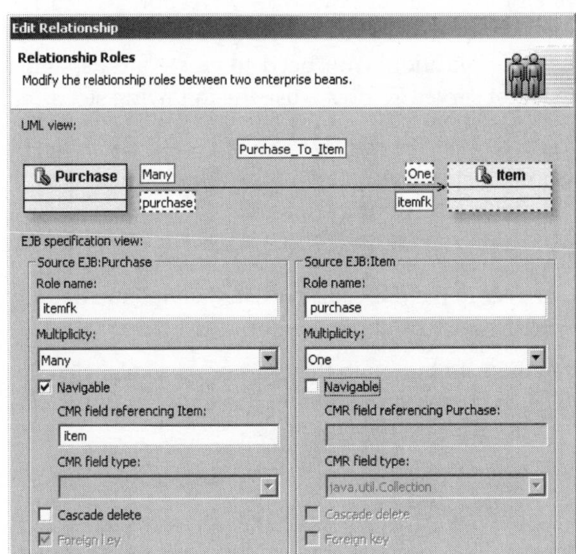

Figure 22.19 Purchase-to-Location role.

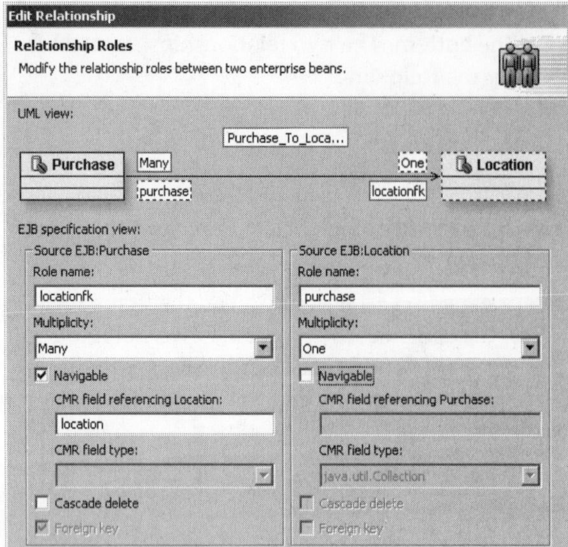

Figure 22.20 Purchase-to-Item role.

Create a Data Source JNDI Reference

Let us take inventory. You have a session bean and three related CMP entity beans. The entity beans map to a DB2 for Java DBMS. You chose the WSAD WebSphere v5.0 Test Environment for the J2EE application server when you created the session bean. What is missing before you can deploy the application? You need to create a data source JNDI reference for the beans in the target server. To do so, use the following steps:

1. Open the Server Perspective. Select WebSphere v5.0 Test Environment in the Servers node of the Server Configuration view. Open it by double-clicking or picking Open from its context menu. The Configuration Editor opens.
2. Click the Data source tab. View the Server Settings category.
3. Select the CloudScape JDBC Driver in the JDBC driver list. Its implementation class should read: com.ibm.db2j.jdbc.Db2jConnectionPoolDataSource.
4. With the driver selected, push the Add button to the right of the list labeled Data source defined in the JDBC driver selected above. The Create a Data Source wizard appears.
5. The type of JDBC provider appears as Cloudscape JDBC Provider 5.0. Keep the default Version 5.0 data source choice, and press Next >.
6. Set the Add a Data Source form values to access the SALES database, as shown in Figure 22.21. Remember the JNDI name setting. You will need it for the EJB deployment descriptor.

Modify Data Source

Modify Data Source

Edit the settings of the data source.

Name:	Sales data source
JNDI name:	jdbc/sales
Description:	Sales JDBC Datasource
Category:	Sales
Statement cache size:	0
Data source helper class name:	com.ibm.websphere.rsadapter.CloudscapeDataStoreHelper
Connection timeout:	1800
Maximum connections:	10
Minimum connections:	1
Reap time:	180
Unused timeout:	1800
Aged timeout:	0
Purge policy:	1
Component-managed authentication alias:	
Container-managed authentication alias:	

☑ Use this data source in container managed persistence (CMP)

Figure 22.21 Sales data source.

TIP **Set Use this data source in container managed persistence (CMP) or the CMP entity beans will not operate with this data source.**

7. Press Next >. This wizard panel invites you to set data source properties. The important property here is the database name. The wizard suggests c:/db2j/databases/sample. Set it to c:/db2j/databases/salesDB, as shown in Figure 22.22. Let the other default values remain. Press Finish.

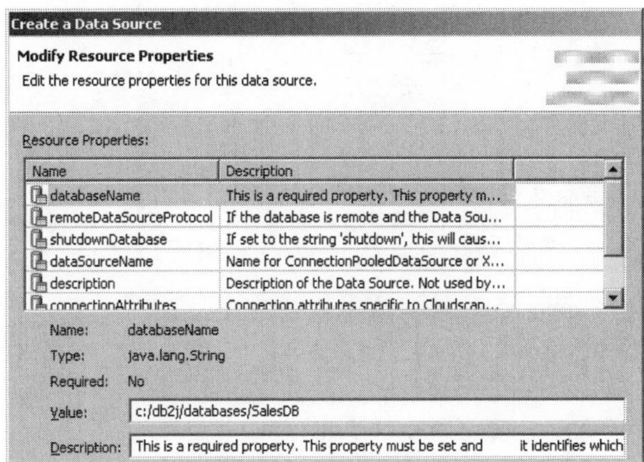

Figure 22.22 Set database name in the data source.

8. Save the test environment configuration using File > Save WebSphere v5.0 Test Environment. The data source appears as shown in Figure 22.23.
9. Now, set the data source JNDI name reference in the EJB deployment descriptor. Display the J2EE Hierarchy. Open the Deployment Descriptor Editor from the SalesEJB context menu. Select the Overview tab.
10. Expand the WebSphere Bindings category (bottommost). Enter **jdbc/sales** in the JNDI name field near the bottom right. This is the value you configured in the JDNI server previously.
11. Set Container authorization type to Per_connection_factory.
12. Pull down the Backend-ID on bottom left pull-down list. Select CLOUDSCAPE_V50_1.
13. Save and close the EJB Deployment Descriptor Editor.

The EJB module now references a JNDI name that is registered in the application server. The application server contains a data source keyed by that name. Any client may obtain the data source via a JDNI lookup on the server.

TIP **You used Cloudscape as an embedded DBMS. That means only one application may open each database simultaneously. You must close other applications, including the bundled CloudView utility, when WSAD needs to open the SalesDB database.**

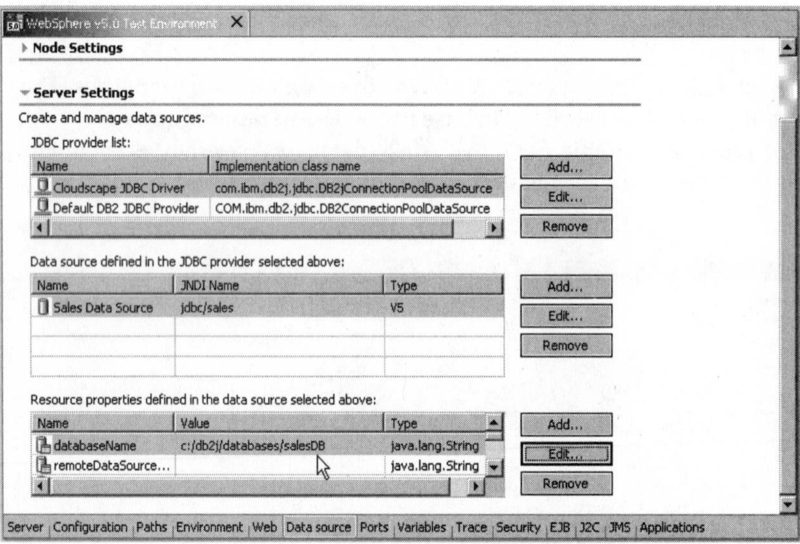

Figure 22.23 Sales data Source In server settings.

Deploy the EJB Module

You are nearly ready to deploy the EJB module again. You have to generate deployment files and RMI stubs for the new beans. Do so with the following steps:

1. Select Generate > Deploy and RMIC Code from the SalesEJB context menu. The Generate Deploy and RMIC Code dialog appears.
2. Select all EJBs. Press Finish.
3. Wait for processing to be completed.

Afterward, the Java view shows an increase in the Java file population. You now have the resources needed to deploy and test the application. Deploy the module using the following last step:

4. Click Run on Server from the context menu of the SalesEJB project. Ensure that the WebSphere v5.0 Test Environment is chosen. Press Finish.

The project is published (deployed) to the associated server. You can see the JNDI binding of the jdbc/db2/sales data source in the Console view, along with the SalesEJB module starting indication.

When the server is ready, the console will display Server server1 open for eBusiness. The IBM Universal Test Client will automatically start as it did for the previous session bean exercise.

Exercise the Beans

Observe the IBM Universal Test Client embedded browser page. Click the JNDI Explorer link to open the tree view of the references registered in JNDI. Expand the tree to see the Local EJB Beans, EJB, and JDBC JNDI references for the application, as shown in Figure 22.24. Notice that all of the entity beans are local beans, meaning that they must be accessed locally within the virtual machine, not over a network.

You will work with the Item bean as follows:

1. Click on ejb > com > xyz > ejb > LocalItemHome. This opens the references page to the Item bean in the Bean Page. You will use this page to carry out the same steps that a client must to use a bean.
2. Expand the ItemLocal > ItemLocalHome node. Click the method ItemLocal findByPrimaryKey(ItemKey).
3. Now, you must create an ItemKey. Select ItemKey(Long) from the Constructors drop-down list in the Parameters pane.
4. Expand the parameter ItemKey: > Constructor:ItemKey: > Long:.
5. Enter a value of 1005, and then press Invoke. This creates a new parameter instance with a value of 1005 used to find and return an ItemLocal bean interface object with the key 1005—provided that you have previously created this bean from the preloaded database.

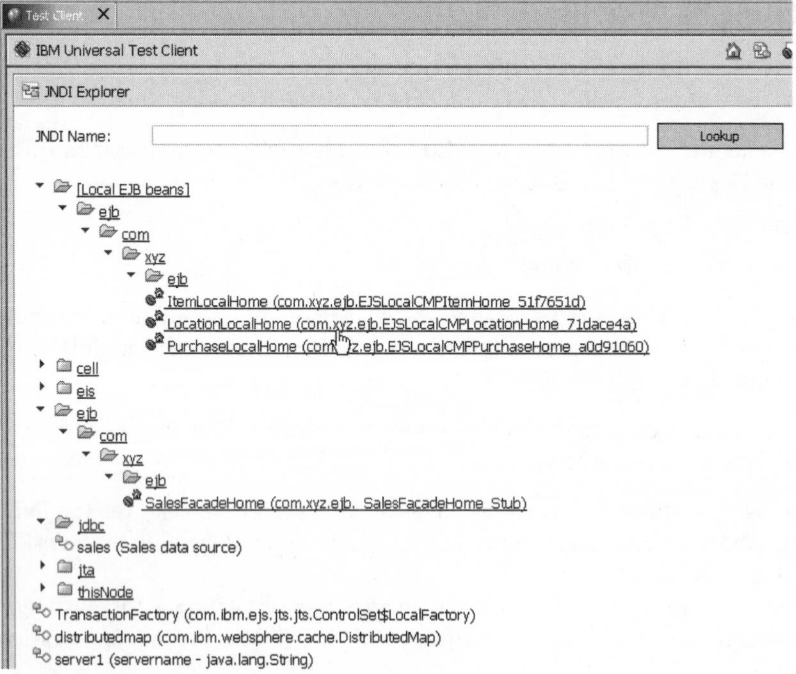

Figure 22.24 EJBS and JDBC data sources.

6. Press Work with Object. The ItemLocal interface reference should appear in the References pane. The ItemKey object used to find the reference should show under Item References. Each has a scissors icon used for releasing the reference.
7. Expand the ItemLocal reference. Click String getName(). The method appears in the Parameters pane above an Invoke button.
8. Press the Invoke button. The result should read Promised LAN Switch, as seen near the bottom right of Figure 22.25.
9. Release the references by pressing the scissors icon in the References pane.

That was a sanity check on the Item bean. Try the analogous operation with the Location bean. Here, you would pass a U.S. Zip Code as a String key. Try a value of 12345. Find the bean with that Zip Code. Then invoke its String getCity() method. The result would be Schenectady. You will create Purchase instances related to Item and Location instances in the next chapter when you use the SalesEJB module with a client.

Debugging a Bean

You can debug a bean locally or remotely on a WebSphere Application Server. The infrastructure behind this server-side debugging technique was mentioned previously in remote debugging. The project instance should be associated with a server configuration and instance configured to start in debug mode when Run on Server is chosen.

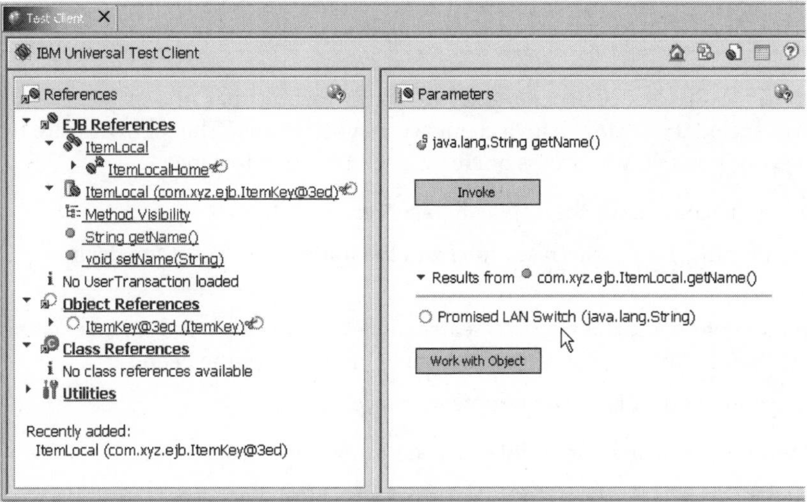

Figure 22.25 Invocation of Item.getName().

Simply set a breakpoint in the bean, and then choose Run on Server from the context menu of its EJB project or the encompassing Enterprise Applications project. The IBM Universal Test Client will execute after the server finishes initializing. Create or find the bean using the test client as discussed previously. Exercise a method that will attempt to execute through a breakpoint. When the container thread suspends, you can inspect variables, step code, set other breakpoints, and resume, as you would when carrying out local debugging. Of course, you would limit such a debugging session to a test server.

Export an EAR File

You have not written many lines of Java code, but you have invested a considerable number of mouse clicks and entered a few text values. Now, you will back up your enterprise application to an EAR file. This file may be imported into a WSAD project or deployed to a server. To back up your application, use the following steps:

1. Access the J2EE Perspective.
2. Select Export EAR File from the Enterprise Applications Sales project context menu. Attach the source, since you will use the EAR as backup. Name the EAR Sales.jar. Choose a location in a backup directory.
3. Press Finish to carry out the export.

Client Applications

You used the IBM EJB Test Client to get that warm feeling that one of your beans responds as expected. How does a Java client access your beans? The following are the high-level steps for one way to access or create a remote bean instance:

1. Get an initial context for the application server.
2. Obtain a remote home interface stub from the initial context for the desired bean.
3. Use the remote home interface to create a new bean instance or find an existing bean instance. This process returns a remote interface for the bean.
4. Carry out method calls on the remote interface.

The analogous steps using a local interface are as follows:

1. Find the local home interface through a JNDI lookup on the ENC.
2. Obtain a local home interface.
3. Create a new bean instance or find an existing bean instance through the local home interface.
4. Carry out method calls on the local interface.

Remember that local interfaces are only available within a single VM. They are not distributed on the network. The client of a bean is often in the same VM. If the bean has no remote interfaces, it cannot be available to remote clients. If it has no local interfaces it cannot participate in CMR. It is okay to present both kinds of interfaces. The WSAD RDB to EJB Mapper generated each kind of interface for your entity beans. You generated only remote interfaces for your SalesFacade session bean. This bean will become the client intermediary for the entity beans. It will leverage their local interfaces to take advantage of the reduced overhead offered.

Summary

In this chapter, you created and exercised a J2EE EJB module. The chapter covered:

- EJB overview
- Creation of an enterprise application project
- Creating a stateless session bean
- Promoting methods to interfaces
- Generating deployment classes and RMI stubs
- Deployment to a test environment
- The IBM Universal Test Client
- Bottom-up creation of entity beans from a DBMS schema

- The RDB-EJB mapper
- Specifying a CMR relationship
- Creating a data source and registering its JDNI reference
- Bean debugging
- Exporting an EAR file
- Client API

In the next chapter, you will use the Deployment Descriptor Editor to set transaction characteristics and additional details for the beans. You will learn how to use access beans generated by WSAD to make accessing an EJB resemble accessing a JavaBean. Then, you'll add and promote four business methods to the SalesFacade session bean, and then introduce a Web module as the client for the Sales application.

Entity EJBs

What's in Chapter 23?

This chapter continues the Sales EJB project that you started in Chapter 22, "Enterprise JavaBeans." This chapter covers the following:

- How to configure EJB transactions
- Creating a custom `find` method
- The session façade business tier J2EE pattern
- How to use value objects as a pattern
- The front controller presentation pattern
- How to implement a Web module in a J2EE application
- A brief introduction to message-driven beans, access beans, and security

A J2EE application may consist of one or more of three kinds of modules: EJB, Web, and client. You started the SalesApp J2EE application in the last chapter. Now, you will add more functionality to the entity beans and create a stateless session façade bean for client access. Then, you will implement the SalesWeb module as a SalesApp client. Finally, you will survey some miscellaneous WSAD and EJB 2.0 features.

Transactions

The EJB container encapsulates a transaction monitor. Transactions are about error management—bulletproof error management. A *transaction* is a set of tasks that are executed together as a unit of work. It is atomic; that is, all of its encompassed tasks must complete successfully for the transaction to succeed. If one of the embodied tasks fails, the effect of each of the tasks is reset to its initial state.

When you use an ATM to transfer money from one account to another, a deposit follows a withdrawal. A transaction encompasses the two tasks so that you do not lose the transfer amount if the deposit fails. The transaction is rolled back after a failure so that the withdrawal amount still resides in the first account. If the data for both accounts resides in a transaction-aware DBMS, the operation was protected by a *local transaction*. What about a wire transfer between two banks? Each bank's DBMS must participate in a *distributed transaction*. A distributed transaction monitor, such as CICS, could protect a wire transfer by orchestrating the operation of each DBMS local transaction monitor.

Transactions must be *atomic*, *consistent*, *isolated*, and *durable* (ACID). These terms are defined in Table 23.1.

Conversational transaction monitor (CTM) programming can be complex. Enterprise JavaBeans are a server-side component model for CTMs. The EJB declarative model extends robust transaction support to each bean type: session, entity, and message-driven. An administrator controls a bean's transaction characteristics through a *declarative transaction management* paradigm.

Transaction Scope

The application server manages all the EJBs deployed in its container. The container resembles the Golf proxy design pattern. It executes methods on behalf of distributed client requests. The programmer does not interact directly with an EJB. Thus, the container can manage all aspects of EJB life cycle and transaction scope. What is transaction scope? It is the set of EJBs that participates in a unit of work.

The thread of execution encompasses all of the EJBs that could possibly be included in the transaction scope. If all of the method calls within the transaction scope complete successfully, the associated transaction is *rolled forward*—it succeeds. A system exception causes a rollback resembling an undo operation. A system exception extends java.lang.RunTimeException or java.rmi.RemoteException. An application exception does not extend either class, so it does not cause rollback.

Table 23.1 Transaction Characteristics

Atomic	The transaction must execute completely or not at all.
Consistent	Data must remain in harmony with its model. The previous example's first account debit amount must match the second account.
Isolated	One transaction cannot interfere with another.
Durable	All data changes must be written to physical storage before transaction completion.

Transaction Demarcation

The execution thread does not guarantee that an EJB is a member of the transaction scope. The declarative transaction management capability of the EJB container means that the programmer does not have to deal with explicit transaction demarcation. You may use explicit demarcation through the Java Transaction Service (JTS), or the OMG Object Transaction Service (OTS), but this leads to inflexible distributed objects, murky code, and it has a significant learning curve.

It is better to control EJB transactional behavior through its deployment descriptor. This way its business logic does not have to be modified to fit a given application's transactional behavior. This promotes reusability for the bean by future applications.

Transaction Attributes

Recall that a bean in a thread of execution *could* be included in the transaction scope. This depends upon the transaction attributes set in the deployment descriptor for the bean as part of its declarative transaction management. The bean's transaction attribute would be one of those shown in Table 23.2.

Table 23.2 Transaction Attributes

Not Supported	This EJB method or any EBJ that it calls is not a member of the current transaction scope. The success or failure of this method does not affect the current transaction.
Supports	This EJB method will be included in a transaction scope only if the caller is a member of a transaction scope. The success or failure of this method does not affect the current transaction unless the caller is a member of a transaction scope.
Required	This EJB method will be included in the current transaction scope. If there is no transaction, the EJB starts a new one that ends when the current method exits. The success or failure of this method always affects a transaction.
Requires New	A transaction is always started regardless of whether the caller is part of a transaction scope. Any caller transaction is suspended until the method ends. The new transaction covers the current method and any EJBs it accesses. The success or failure of this method always affects its own transaction, not that of the caller.
Mandatory	The EJB method must be included in the caller's transaction scope. If the caller is not part of the transaction, the invocation fails, throwing *javax.transaction.TransactionRequriedException*. The success or failure of this method always affects the caller's transaction unless the caller has no transaction.
Never	The EJB method must never be invoked within a transaction scope. The EJB will execute normally without a transaction in this case. It will throw an exception if is invoked in a transaction scope. The success or failure of this method never affects the caller's transaction because the caller cannot be part of a transaction.

Notice that the descriptions in Table 23.2 refer to an EJB method. An administrator may assign a transaction attribute either at the EJB level or at the method level.

Setting Transaction Attributes

You assigned no transaction attributes to EJBs in the EmployeeEJB module developed in the previous chapter. All EJB methods have a transaction attribute inherited from the encompassing EJB. The EJB default transaction attribute is NotSupported, so that is the attribute assigned to all methods of the three CMR EJBs. The term "CMR" should be a red flag when you consider transaction attributes, because the state of one instance may depend upon the state of a related instance. The EJB 2.0 specification recommends that such CMP 2.0 entity beans use only the Required, RequiresNew, and Mandatory transaction attributes. This ensures that database access happens in a transaction scope, ensuring consistent persistent state. Usually, Required will satisfy the requirements of most applications.

Your three SalesEJB entity beans will never be called directly by an application client, except during testing by the IBM Universal Test client. Instead, you will use the single stateless session bean in a façade design pattern to mediate application logic flow to the entity beans. If you set a transaction attribute of Required on all four beans, then each client request will be wrapped in a transaction that succeeds or fails based upon the success of all nested method calls used to fulfill a request. Your nontest clients will only call methods on the session bean. If a client doesn't use explicit transaction management, then the session bean will start a new transaction when one of its methods is called. If a client does institute its own transaction (client-side transaction demarcation), then the session bean will become part of that transaction scope. Thus, the Required attribute is normally the first choice during transaction attribute assignment. Certain methods could be assigned overriding attributes.

The session bean will have a method to create Purchase instances, each related to an Item instance and a Location instance. You need to assign a transaction attribute of Required to each of the four beans. Use the following steps:

1. In the J2EE Hierarchy view, choose Open with > Deployment Descriptor Editor from the context menu of SalesEJB.
2. Click the Assembly Descriptor tab at the bottom.
3. Find and expand Container Transactions in the right-hand column.
4. Press Add to invoke the Add Container Transaction wizard. The four beans should be listed.
5. Press Select All. The wizard should appear as seen in Figure 23.1.
6. Press Next >. The next panel invites you to select the transaction type and the beans or individual method to which the transaction type will be applied.

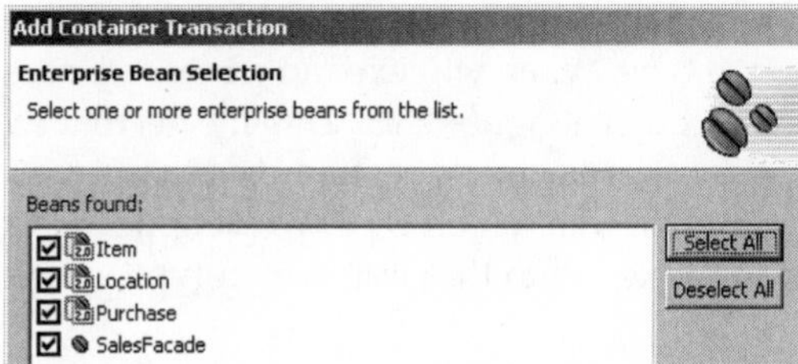

Figure 23.1 Beans for container transaction.

7. Open Container transaction type, and then select Required.

   You will set all methods of all beans to transaction type Required. Press Select All. The list expands to show all methods, as shown in Figure 23.2. Notice that you could use the wizard to change the attribute for a single method. Each method inherits a transaction type from its encompassing EJB if nothing is checked beside it.

Press Finish. Save the editor to carry out the transaction type assignment.

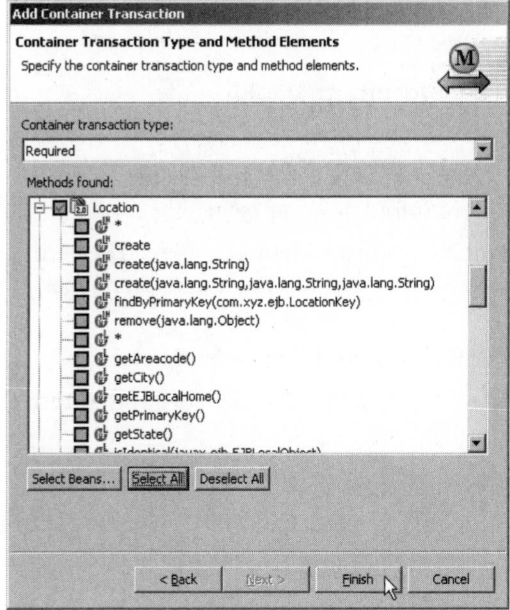

Figure 23.2 Transaction type assignment.

Notice that the Container Transactions section of the Deployment Descriptor Editor shows a tree view of the beans by transaction type. When you expand a bean, you see a blue method icon with an asterisk to its right. See Figure 23.3. This means that all methods of that bean receive the encompassing transaction type. If you were to assign a different transaction type to some methods, that transaction type would appear as a new top-level tree node. Bean with methods assigned to that transaction type would appear under it.

Now, all methods of the beans in the SalesEJB module will always run in a transaction scope, imparting the ACID protection services of the EJB container's transaction monitor. This is all that is necessary. You didn't need to program any API calls or alter the EJB Java code. The SalesFacade session bean has no useful methods. Later, you will add methods. These will inherit the Required transaction attribute from the SalesFacade bean unless you specify otherwise.

Custom Find Method

The clients need a list of all items represented by the Item entity bean. You construct a custom find method to return all Item objects by using the Deployment Descriptor Editor. You used CMP for all of the entity beans, so you can do all of the work in the XML deployment descriptor, with the following steps:

1. Open the Deployment Descriptor Editor for project SalesEJB.
2. Choose the Beans tab, and then select the Item bean.
3. Locate the section in the right-hand column called Queries. Press the Add button seen there. The Add Finder Descriptor wizard appears.
4. Leave the Method Type set to find method, and set Method to New. The panel will reconstitute itself, and a red message that the "Method name cannot be 'find'" will appear near the title.
5. Specify a new find method name of `findAll` that takes no parameters.
6. Use the Return type drop-down list to choose java.util.Collection. The correct settings are shown in Figure 23.4.
7. Press Next >. A subsequent wizard panel invites you to specify the EJB QL query.

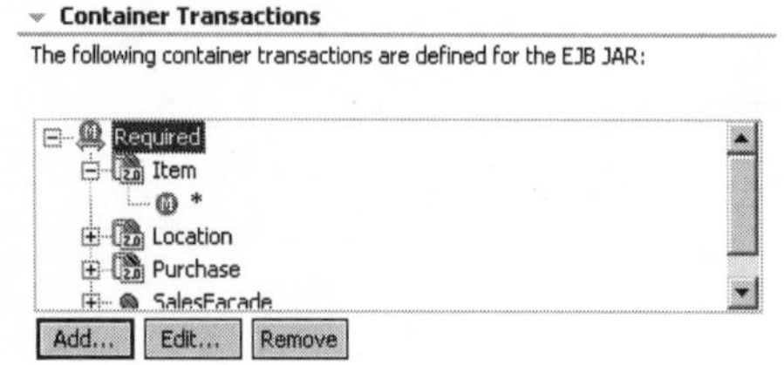

Figure 23.3 Defined container transactions.

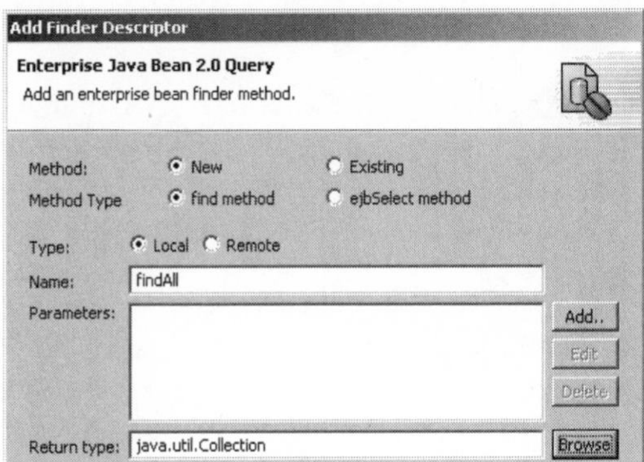

Figure 23.4 Add a finder descriptor.

How does the container know the selection criteria for the objects you want returned? You convey the information through an EJB QL query against the Item abstract schema name. You decide to order the results by item name for comprehension by the client user. EJB QL resembles SQL but it omits some SQL constructs. EJB QL contains no ORDER BY clause, but a WebSphere extension supports this clause. You will use the extension, although this pins the deployment to WebSphere. If you desire more generality, you could write a business method that calls to data access object that implements direct JDBC calls.

8. Use the Select a sample query drop-down to choose Find All Query to prime the Query statement text area with a boilerplate query.
9. Add a description like Return a collection of all Item references sorted by name.
10. Alter the boilerplate query to the following by appending order by o.name:

    ```
    SELECT OBJECT(itm) from Item AS item ORDER BY itm.name
    ```

11. Ensure that the field contents resemble Figure 23.5, press Finish, and save the deployment descriptor to commit the changes. The Tasks view will show one error because one of the generated deployment classes is obsolete.
12. Invoke the context menu of EJB Modules > SalesEJB. Choose Generate Deploy and RMIC Code for all beans for completeness. The Tasks view should be error free afterward.

If you make a mistake in the query or want to experiment with it later, use the Edit button in the Queries group of the deployment descriptor to alter it.

EJB QL allows a SELECT clause to return any CMP or single CMR field. It will not return multiple fields. Notice the identifier variable is named **o**. You could not use item because EJB QL identifiers are case insensitive, which means they cannot be the same as existing abstract schema names—Item in this case.

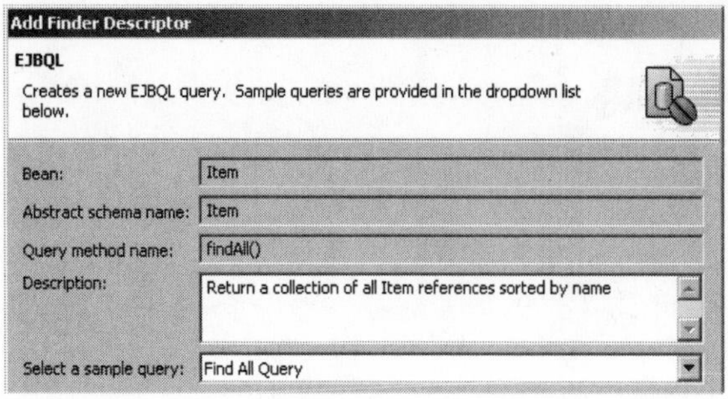

Figure 23.5 Finder EJB QL.

At this point, you can use a Run on Server context menu command. Exercise the new finder method in the IBM Universal Test Client by using the steps you learned in Chapter 22, "Enterprise JavaBeans." The `findAll()` method will appear in the ItemLocalHome reference. Invoke it to receive a collection of ItemLocal references. Press Work with Contained Objects to store the references in the References tree. Then, you may invoke the getName() method of any ItemLocal reference.

Notice that the order of successive references is determined by the sort order of their contained names. The container did this because the EJB QL had an **order by** clause. This clause is a WebSphere extension not guaranteed to work with other J2EE-compliant application servers.

Business Tier J2EE Patterns

The SalesApp enterprise application is specifically a J2EE application. Here, the goals of performance, maintainability, reuse, and extensibility are not always governed by the same practices that you learned when designing monolithic applications or even client/server applications. For instance, it may be better to retrieve or regenerate data anew rather than stash it in the session. You must keep in mind that 1,000 lines of code could be expected to handle tens or hundreds of simultaneous requests while yielding one-second response times.

A J2EE application sits astride a network. EJB method calls flow over the network easily. It is tempting to say that the network is transparent, and then simply program as if it were not there. This is a mistake. It is better to send a larger amount of data across a network relatively infrequently than it is to make frequent calls involving smaller amounts of data.

Architects using J2EE technology have found workable approaches and some that do not work. They distilled workable approaches into J2EE design patterns. You will use a few of them in the Sales business tier that the SalesEJB module implements.

Value Object

Data must flow between your Sales EJBs and a client. Your Location bean has city, state, zipCode, and areaCode attributes. A client could obtain a Location reference and then call `getCity()`, `getState()`, and `getAreaCode()` to obtain a record for a Zip Code. This is a chatty solution, involving multiple network calls, each having a measure of fixed overhead. It would be better to package the attributes into a single object and then send it over the network. This is analogous to buffering bytes of data from a block device, and then reading them in a chunk instead of individually.

The Value Object business tier pattern encapsulates all of the business data of a session bean, an entity bean, or some kind of data access object. The value object is sent in a single method call. Normally, a value object is immutable; that is, it has no set access methods. Its constructor establishes its value. Obtain its attributes from its get access methods. The immutability makes it unlikely that a client programmer will believe he is modifying an attribute of the EJB by setting it in the value object.

You foresee a need to access the Item bean and Location bean attributes. Accordingly, you will create them using the following steps:

1. Open the Java Perspective. Create a Java project named SalesValueObjects.
2. Create the package com.xyz.data in the new project.
3. Display the properties of the SalesEJB project. Add project SalesValueObjects to the Java Build Path using the Project tab selection so that future build dependencies will be resolved.

Note that this does not place the JAR file on the SalesEJB class path in the application server. You resolve that issue in a following section, "Jar Dependencies."

4. Create class named `ItemVO` in the `com.xyz.data` package. Implement the `java.io.Serializable` interface. Clear all check boxes in the New wizard. Press Finish.
5. Create private Java fields in the ItemVO class as in the following:

```
private long itemId;
private String name;
```

6. Use the pop-up menu item Generate Getter and Setter of the ItemVO outline view to generate getters (no setters), as shown in Figure 23.6.

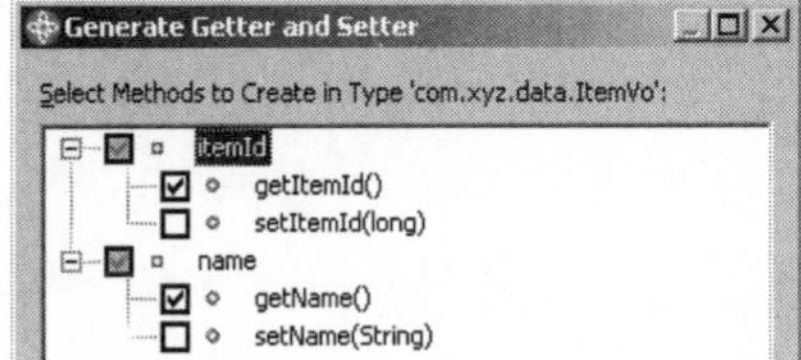

Figure 23.6 Generate ItemVO getters.

7. Add the following constructor:

```
/**
 * Create an ItemVO given an ID and a name
 * @param anItemID long
 * @param aName java.lang.String
 */
public ItemVO(long anItemId, String aName) {
    itemId = anItemId;
    name = aName;
}
```

8. Save ItemVO error free.

Follow the same procedure to create serializable class `LocationVO`. Use the previous package com.xyz.data under project SalesValueObjects. This time insert the private field attributes shown in the following and create getters for them.

```
private String city;
private String state
private String zipCode
private String areaCode
private int salesCount;
```

LocationVO has three constructors because it will be used several ways. Add the following three constructors to LocationVO:

```
public LocationVO(String aCity, String aState, String aZipCode,
    String anAreaCode) {
    city = aCity;
    state = aState;
    zipCode = aZipCode;
    areaCode = anAreaCode;
}
public LocationVO(String aCity, String aState, String aZipCode,
    String anAreaCode, int aSalesCount) {
    city = aCity;
    state = aState;
    zipCode = aZipCode;
    areaCode = anAreaCode;
    salesCount = aSalesCount;
}
public LocationVO(LocationVO locationVO, int aSalesCount) {
    city = locationVO.city;
    state = locationVO.state;
    zipCode = locationVO.zipCode;
    areaCode = locationVO.areaCode;
    salesCount = aSalesCount;
}
```

Session Facade

The client may obtain a reference to the EJB home interface, and then find or create a bean or collection of references using the home interface. What is a reference? It's an instance of a stub that handles the marshaling of parameters and results across the network. Each stub represents a resource drain on the server and network overhead during data transfers. Fine-grained access to entity bean attributes could result in many stubs being open simultaneously. This resource drain, along with the attendant network may be detrimental to performance. It is helpful to multiply each resource instance by the number of simultaneous client accesses expected. This helps us stay grounded the design goal of accommodating many simultaneous clients. The Session Façade business tier pattern addresses the following issues:

- Reduces tight coupling between clients and business objects
- Reduces the number of business method invocations between client and server
- Protects business objects from misuse by imposing a uniform access strategy for clients

You will use the Session Façade business tier pattern to encapsulate the complexity of interactions between business objects participating in the application workflow. This means that no client, except the IBM Universal Test Client, will directly access the three entity beans. The SalesFacade bean will provide a course-grained access point for clients. It will access the entity beans through their local interfaces, thus reducing potential network access to local VM calls. The client will receive a value object or a collection of them in response to a coarse-grained request. Thus, network traffic will be far less frequent and far fewer stubs will be needed per client. In addition, if the client resides in the same VM as the SalesFacade, then the WebSphere Application Server will optimize the network call to a local call.

At this point, the SalesFacade bean has only an echo method that you used to illustrate how to access an EJB. Now, you will add the business methods that you will need to implement the SalesApp workflow. The methods use value objects; so first add project SalesValueObject to the SalesEJB build path through its properties dialog.

Add Local References

The session bean will access the entity beans through their local interfaces. It will find the interfaces through environmental naming convention (ENC) EJB references that you will register in the server now, with the following steps:

1. Use the J2EE Hierarchy view to open the Deployment Descriptor Editor. Choose the References tab.
2. Select SalesFacade under References.
3. Use the Add button to invoke the Add Reference wizard to add three EJB local references. Use the information shown in Table 23.3.
4. Save the deployment descriptor to commit the additions.

Table 23.3 SalesFacade EJB References

REF NAME	LINK
ejb/Item	Item
ejb/Location	Location
ejb/Purchase	Purchase

Get a Location

This first façade business method returns a LocationVO, given a ZipCode string. It encapsulates a call to the Location entity bean using its local interface. It uses the ejb/Location reference that you created previously to find the local reference in the JNDI environmental naming context (ENC). The ENC naming tree root is java:comp/env/.

Use the Navigator view to open SalesFacadeBean.java in the Java Editor. Insert the following method, using code assist to insert needed import statements, save the code to build it, and repair any errors.

```
/**
 * Return a LocationVO, given a ZipCode
 * @return com.xyz.data.LocationVO, a location
 */
public LocationVO getLocation(String zipCode) {
    final String loRef = "java:comp/env/ejb/Location";
    LocationVO locationDO = null;
    try {
        Context jndiContext = new InitialContext();
        LocationLocalHome localHome = (LocationLocalHome)
            jndiContext.lookup(loRef);
        LocationLocal locationLocal =
            localHome.findByPrimaryKey(new LocationKey(zipCode));
        locationDO = new LocationVO(locationLocal.getCity(),
            locationLocal.getState(), zipCode,
            locationLocal.getAreacode());
    } catch (javax.naming.NamingException ex) {
            throw new EJBException(ex);
    } catch (javax.ejb.FinderException ex) {
            locationDO = new LocationVO("", "", "", "");
    }
    return locationDO;
}
```

Use the content assistant to supply missing import statements by clicking on the yellow light bulb icons in the left margin. Build the project successfully. Finally, promote the method to the remote interface as you did with the **echo()** method in the previous chapter. Use the following steps:

1. Ensure that SalesFacadeBean.java is still displayed in the J2EE Editor.
2. Make sure that the Outline view is displayed.
3. Right-click `getLocation(String)` in the Outline view to open its context menu.
4. Choose Enterprise Bean > Promote to Remote Interface.

Afterward, the method should have an **R** icon prefix in the Outline view, as shown in Figure 23.7. Errors will appear at this point because the deployment classes need to be regenerated. Regenerate them from the J2EE Hierarchy view context menu of EJB Modules / SalesEJB, by choosing Generate > Deploy and RMIC Code as you did previously. All errors should disappear from the Task view.

Get All Items

Clients need to list all items in the business tier. The Items finder returns a collection of local EJB references to Item objects. You don't want the client to have these references. Each stub uses server resources. Additionally, the client would need to make method calls on each stub to collect the desired attributes. This increases the network load. Remember that the number of concurrent clients multiplies these two effects. Instead, you choose to have the session façade return an array of lightweight value objects. Returning a collection of value objects is a common alternative, but the array is more type-safe, and it eliminates the added overhead of the collection object. Insert the following method into SalesFacadeBean.java:

```
/**
* Return array of Item data objects
* @return com.xyz.data.LocationVO[], an array of all locations
*/
public ItemVO[] getAllItems() {
    final String loRef = "java:comp/env/ejb/Item";
    ItemVO[] data = null;
    try {
        Context jndiContext = new InitialContext();
```

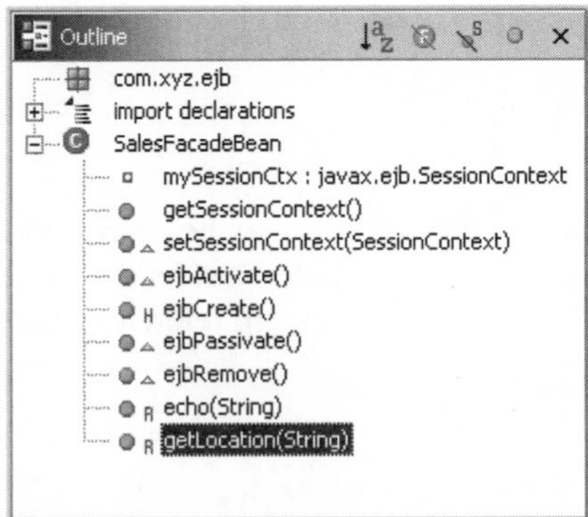

Figure 23.7 Promote to remote Interface.

```
            ItemLocalHome itemLocalHome =
                (ItemLocalHome)jndiContext.lookup(loRef);
            Collection items = itemLocalHome.findAll();
            data = new ItemVO[items.size()];
            int i = 0;
            Iterator it = items.iterator();
            while (it.hasNext()) {
                ItemLocal item = (ItemLocal) it.next();
                long key = (ItemKey)
                    item.getPrimaryKey()).getItemid().longValue();
                data[i++] = new ItemVO(key, item.getName());
            }
        } catch (javax.naming.NamingException ex) {
            throw new EJBException(ex);
        } catch (javax.ejb.FinderException ex) {
            data = new ItemVO[0];
        }
        return data;
    }
```

Use content assist to supply the missing import statements and then save. Switch to the Java Perspective, use the Outline view to promote `getAllItems()` to the `SalesFacade` remote interface, and regenerate the deployment code as you did previously. There should be no errors after completion.

This method delegates to the `findAll()` Item finder that you declared using EJB QL previously. You create the returned array of value objects by extracting attributes from each Item reference enumerated from the collection returned by the multiple find. Notice that if no items are found, it returns a zero-length array of value objects. A NamingException is converted to an EJBException. This will cause the required encompassing transaction to roll back.

Make a Purchase

So far, the session bean knows how to retrieve relatively static items and locations. Now, you will insert a creational method to build a PurchaseLocal instance that has an Item and a Location. You need only store an ItemLocal instance and a LocationLocal instance in their respective CMR fields using the following generated method signatures:

```
PurchaseLocal.setLocationfk(LocationLocal)
PurchaseLocal.setItemfk(ItemLocal)
```

The container handles the mechanics of the relationship according to the description you defined previously. Insert the following method into the SalesFacadeBean, and then promote it to the remote interface. Notice that it uses all three EJB references that you defined for the JNDI ENC.

```
/**
 * Create Purchase objects from list of items for a given Zip Code
 * @return boolean, true if and only if successful
```

```
 */
public boolean makePurchase(String zipCode, Long[] items) {
    final String pcRef = "java:comp/env/ejb/Purchase";
    final String loRef = "java:comp/env/ejb/Location";
    final String itRef = "java:comp/env/ejb/Item";
    long key = System.currentTimeMillis();
    try {
        Context jndiContext = new InitialContext();
        // Find local homes
        PurchaseLocalHome purchaseLocalHome =
            (PurchaseLocalHome) jndiContext.lookup(pcRef);
        LocationLocalHome locationLocalHome =
            (LocationLocalHome)jndiContext.lookup(loRef);
        ItemLocalHome itemLocalHome =
            (ItemLocalHome)jndiContext.lookup(itRef);
        // Get loop-invariant timestamp and location
        String timeStamp = new java.util.Date().toString();
        LocationLocal locationLocal =
            locationLocalHome.findByPrimaryKey(
                new LocationKey(zipCode));
        // Create Purchases
        for (int i = 0; i < items.length; i++) {
           ItemLocal itemLocal =
               itemLocalHome.findByPrimaryKey(new ItemKey(items[i]));
            // Create new purchase
            PurchaseLocal purchaseLocal =
                purchaseLocalHome.create(new Long(++key), timeStamp);
            // Set location
            purchaseLocal.setLocation(locationLocal);
            // Set item
            purchaseLocal.setItem(itemLocal);
        }
    } catch (javax.naming.NamingException ex) {
        throw new EJBException(ex);
    } catch (javax.ejb.FinderException ex) {
        return false;
    } catch (javax.ejb.CreateException ex) {
        throw new EJBException(ex);
    }
    return true;
}
```

Return Top Sales Locations

An ordered list of top sales locations is one of the major features of the sales application. You need business logic to count purchases by location, and then return a list of the top sales locations sorted by units purchased. A Location find method returns locations, but a Location has no knowledge of purchases and items in the CMR scheme.

Additionally, how would you craft an EJB QL query to return locations sorted by purchase volume? A home method in the Purchase bean could call upon an `ejbSelect` method to do a query against the abstract schema. An SQL `COUNT()` function with a `GROUP BY` clause can do the task, but EJB QL cannot support multivalued `SELECT` clauses. In addition EJB QL does not support the SQL `GROUP BY` clause or `COUNT()` function needed to return a count and a location. If you used bean-managed persistence (BMP), you could write a find method that uses this JDBC SQL statement to produce an ordered list of key/count pairs:

```
SELECT locationid, count(*) FROM purchase
    group by locationid ORDER BY 2 DESC
```

You want to leverage CMP, not BMP, but CMP seems to be inadequate here. You could consider writing a data access object (DAO) that you would invoke from the session façade, but this J2EE pattern could be a book chapter by itself. Instead, you will place a JDBC call using the previous SQL statement within a `SalesFacade` method, noting that this trade-off removes a measure of generality from the bean. You will locate the data source using a JNDI reference, so that the bean isn't hard-coded to its persistent storage. Enter the following two methods into the SalesFacadeBean:

```
/**
 * Returns an array of LocationVO ordered by number of purchase
.* transactions. Each location contains purchase unit count.
 * @return com.xyz.data.LocationVO[], an array of locations
 */
public LocationVO[] getTopLocations() {
    final String dsRef = "jdbc/sales";
    final String sql = "SELECT locationid, count(*) FROM purchase "
            + " group by locationid ORDER BY 2 DESC ";
    final int LIMIT = 10;
    LocationVO[] locationDO = new LocationVO[0];
    PreparedStatement ps = null;
    ResultSet result = null;
    try {
        InitialContext jndiContext = new InitialContext();
        DataSource ds = (DataSource) jndiContext.lookup(dsRef);
        Connection con = ds.getConnection();
        ps = con.prepareStatement(sql);
        result = ps.executeQuery();
        ArrayList col = new ArrayList(LIMIT);
        int line = 0;
        while (result.next()) {
            String zipCode = result.getString(1);
            int count = result.getInt(2);
            LocationLocal location = findLocation(
                jndiContext, zipCode);
            LocationVO thisLoc =
                new LocationVO(location.getCity(), location.getState(),
                    zipCode, location.getAreacode(), count);
```

```
                col.add(thisLoc);
                if (++line >= LIMIT)
                    break;
            }
            locationDO = (LocationVO[])col.toArray(
                new LocationVO[col.size()]);
        } catch (java.sql.SQLException ex) {
            locationDO = new LocationVO[0];
        } catch (javax.naming.NamingException ex) {
            throw new EJBException(ex);
        } catch (javax.ejb.FinderException ex) {
            locationDO = new LocationVO[0];
        }
        return locationDO;
    }
    /**
     * Returns a Location, given a JndiContext and a Zip Code String
     * @param jndiContext javax.naming.Context
     * @param zipCode java.lang.String
     * @returns com.xyz.ejb.LocationLocal
     */
    private LocationLocal findLocation(
        javax.naming.Context jndiContext,
        String zipCode) throws
            javax.ejb.FinderException, javax.naming.NamingException {
        final String loRef = "java:comp/env/ejb/Location";
        LocationLocalHome localHome =
                (LocationLocalHome) jndiContext.lookup(loRef);
        return (LocationLocal) localHome.findByPrimaryKey(
                new LocationKey(zipCode));
    }
```

Generate the import statements. Be careful to select JDBC packages—some names occur in more than one package. Promote method `getTopLocations()` to the remote interface and generate SalesFacade bean deployment classes. The Tasks view should show no errors.

The new session bean method uses JDBC to obtain an ordered list of LOCATION table ID/item count pairs. It constructs the usual LocationVO array result be retrieving the specified Location instances. This time, you set the count field of each LocationVO instance. Notice the hard-coded limit of 10. This is not a best practice. It would be better to register an environment value in the deployment descriptor for this limit, and then query it using JNDI. This would make the code somewhat larger, so you elected brevity over generality.

JAR Dependencies

A deployed application often JAR files aside from those provided by the J2EE environment. These are deployed in the EAR file that embodies the application. The J2EE modules within the application may reference such dependent jar files. For example, the SalesEJB module used the value objects that you use to convey data between the EJBs and the client. The Sales enterprise application would contain a SalesValueObjects.jar file that would be referenced by the SalesEJB module. Use the following steps to configure the dependent JAR:

1. Expand the Enterprise Applications mode in the J2EE Hierarchy view.
2. Open the Sales context menu. Choose Open with > Deployment Descriptor Editor.
3. Choose the Module tab. Expand the Project Utility JARs section.
4. Press the Add button. Choose project SalesValueObjects, as seen in Figure 23.8.
5. Press Finish. Save and close the Application Deployment Descriptor.

Notice that SalesValueObjects.jar now sits under the Utility JARs node of the application. At this point the Sales application could be deployed with the SalesValueObjects.jar on its class path. The JAR file contains the two value objects needed by clients and the SalesEJB module, but the EJB module doesn't yet know about the JAR file. You use the Jar Dependency Editor to set a reference to it in the EJB module. Continue with the following steps:

1. Expand the EJB Modules node in the J2EE Hierarchy view.
2. Use the SalesEJB context menu to invoke Open with > JAR Dependency Editor.
3. This editor lists the entire set of JAR files contained in the application **EAR** file. Only SalesValueObjects.jar exists in the Sales application. Check its box.
4. Save and exit the JAR Dependency Editor.

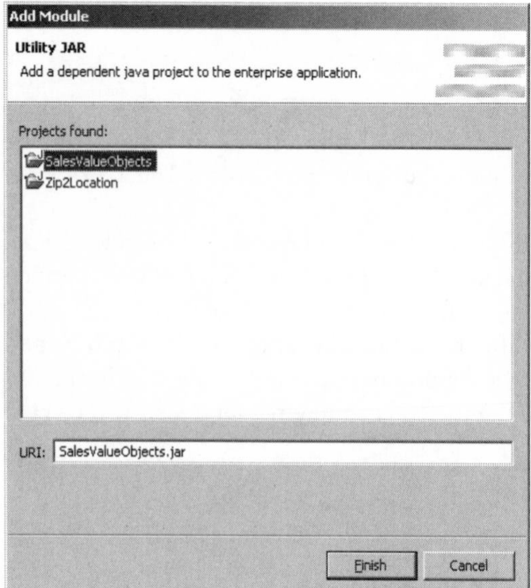

Figure 23.8 Add dependent project.

Now, the class loader for the EJB module will find the value objects on the Sales application class path in the application server.

Generate, Deploy, and Test

Build the project error-free. Generate deployment classes and RMI stubs once more and check them for errors. Publish the application to the server test environment. Test the new SalesFacade bean methods by carrying out Run on Server against SalesEJB, and then using the IBM Universal Test Client with the procedures shown previously.

TIP The Utilities / Object / List node on the EJB page will allow you to work with the value objects returned by methods that return multivalued results.

This concludes the business tier J2EE patterns that you will implement. The SalesEJB module is complete. There are more patterns that you could have used, but these patterns will operate well in this small application.

Web Client

Many J2EE applications use a Web module for a client. The HTTP protocol is allowed through most firewalls, while the EJB IIOP protocol does not because it uses arbitrary port ranges. The Web module may run in the same VM as the EJB module, which presents an opportunity to use a direct path to the EJB container. In addition, the Web module and the EJB module may be packaged as a J2EE application in a single deployable EAR file as you did with the Sales application.

You will access the remote interface methods that you added to the SalesFacade bean from the SalesWeb module. The application will resolve a U.S. postal Zip Code to a city, state, and area code. Please don't rely on this information, especially the area code. You are only using the information as part of this exercise. Your application will enable a user to record a purchase of an item at a given Zip Code. Finally, it will display the top sales locations by number of units purchased.

Figure 23.9 shows a state diagram of the Web client pages. Command objects dispatched by a front controller servlet carry out state transitions. Each page has implied transitions to the error page, start page, or out of the application that are omitted to avoid diagram clutter.

Front Controller

A Web module is defined by the J2EE specification. You will use the SalesWeb module for the presentation services of the Sales enterprise application. There are J2EE design patterns for the presentation layer. You will use the Front Controller pattern to construct the one and only servlet used in the application.

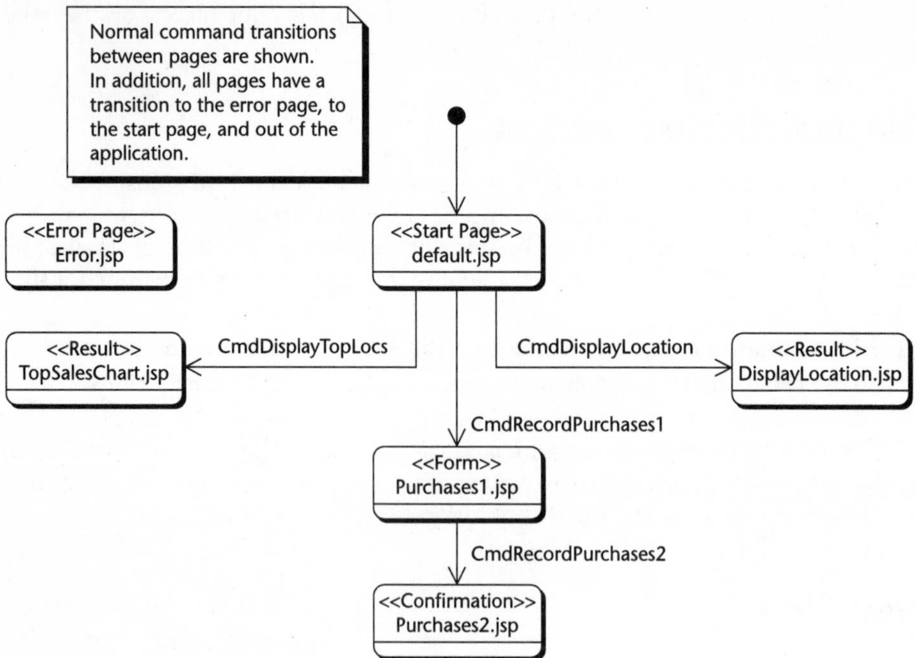

Figure 23.9 JSP state diagram.

Here, JSPs are used for dynamic presentation only. Each request from a JSP is handled by a single controller servlet that uses a Gof command pattern to delegate the request to a command handler. Each decoded command resolves to a simple, unique class that implements a common command interface. Each command class may delegate work to the business tier—EJBs in this case. Each command always stipulates a JSP that will be dispatched afterward. Any value object returned from the business tier would be rendered by the receiving JSP.

Figure 23.10 depicts the front controller arrangement that you will use. Each command implements `ICommand.execute()`, which returns a JSP name, given HTTP request and response objects. Each request contains an action parameter that designates which command object should be instantiated and dispatched. The servlet maps the value from a set of well-known action parameter to a command, calls the command's execute method, and finally dispatches the JSP name returned by the command. Some commands, such as CmdDisplayLocation, may execute a method of the session façade bean, placing the returned value object reference in the HTTP request attribute for retrieval during JSP rendering of the result. Some commands manage a cookie that holds the current Zip Code used to prime form fields for user convenience. This Web application does not use the HTTP session object because no state is maintained beyond remembering that ZipCode value.

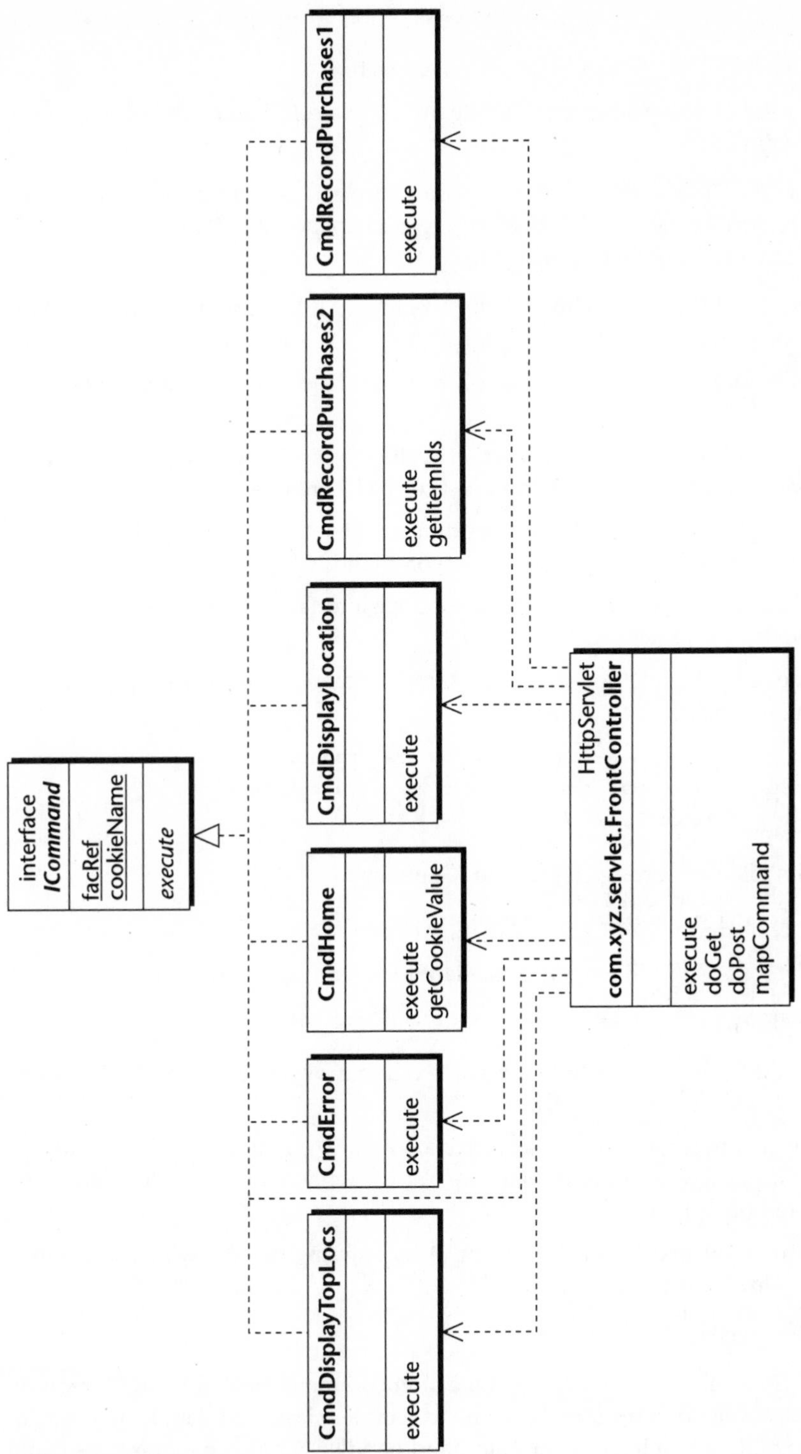

Figure 23.10 SalesWeb front Controller.

Now, you will create the front controller servlet first, using the following steps:

1. Open the SalesWeb project in the Web Perspective.
2. Display the project properties. Include projects SalesEJB and SalesValueObjects in the build path.

This enables the client to refer to classes in those projects at build time. You also need to state that you need project SalesValueObjects as a dependent JAR in the deployment descriptor. Continue with the following steps:

3. Use the J2EE Hierarchy to invoke Open With > JAR Dependency Editor on Web Modules > SalesWeb.
4. In the Dependencies group, set SalesEJB.jar and SalesValueObject.jar to be dependent JAR files.
5. Save the deployment descriptor. A SalesValueObjects.jar will be placed on the deployed SalesWeb class path in the server Web container.
6. Invoke the Java Source folder's context menu. Use New > Package to create packages com.xyz.servlet and com.xyz.command.
7. In package com.xyz.command create a public interface named ICommand. Use the default values.
8. Add the following method declaration to ICommand, and then supply the missing imports:

```
public String execute(HttpServletRequest request,
  HttpServletResponse response) throws ServletException,
  java.io.IOException;
```

9. Add the following string constant to ICommand:

```
final String cookieName = "zipcode";
```

10. Add the following EJB reference constant to ICommand, and then save it:

```
final static String facRef = "java:comp/env/ejb/SalesFacade";
```

11. Invoke the SalesWeb > Java Source context menu, and then use New > Servlet to invoke the New Servlet wizard.
12. Specify Java package com.xyz.servlet, class name `FrontController`, and then add the new `ICommand` interface. Use the default values for the other settings, and press Finish.
13. Force `doGet()` to delegate to `doPost()` by entering the following statement as the entire `doGet()` body:

```
doPost(request, response);
```

The Front Controller pattern decodes an action command passed by a JSP request, delegates the command to the target command handler class, and then forwards control to the next JSP determined by the command handler. A given handler class could invoke methods from the business tier, setting a value object in the request object for the target JSP to render. You will continue your implementation work by providing a decode method for the request.

14. Insert the following command decoder into the servlet. You will have unresolved references for the command handlers. Implement them as follows:

```
/**
* Returns an ICommand object corresponding to the passed
* command string in the set. Returns an error
* ICommand object if the string is null or unidentifiable
* @param set java.util.HashSet
*/
protected ICommand mapCommand(HashSet set) {
    ICommand result = null;
    if (set == null)
        result = new CmdError();
    else if (set.contains("CmdHome"))
        result = new CmdHome();
    else if (set.contains("CmdRecordPurchases1"))
        result = new CmdRecordPurchases1();
    else if (set.contains("CmdRecordPurchases2"))
        result = new CmdRecordPurchases2();
    else if (set.contains("CmdDisplayLocation "))
        result = new CmdDisplayLocation();
    else if (set.contains("CmdDisplayTopLocs"))
        result = new CmdDisplayTopLocs ();
    else
        result = new CmdError();
    return result;
}
```

15. Supply the following implementation of the `doPost()` method. This is the heart of the Front Controller pattern. It extracts parameters from the requesting JSP, maps the request to a target command handler, executes, the command, and then forwards the request to a JSP designated by the command handler.

```
public void doPost(HttpServletRequest req, HttpServletResponse resp)
        throws ServletException, IOException {
    Enumeration enum = req.getParameterNames();
    HashSet set = new HashSet();
    while (enum.hasMoreElements())
        set.add(enum.nextElement());
    ICommand cmd = mapCommand(set);
    String target = cmd.execute(req, resp);
    req.getRequestDispatcher(target).forward(req, resp);
}
```

That completes the servlet portion of the pattern. This is the only servlet in the entire Web module. It still has errors because you have not implemented the command handlers referenced by the servlet. You will add the command handlers in the following sections. Each command class name matches the parameter name used to request it from a JSP. Each returns the name of the next JSP to be displayed. The graph of command paths resembles a finite state machine that has JSP nodes and command edges. Some of those edges have side effects caused by calling EJB business logic through the session façade bean.

CmdHome

In package com.xyz.command, create class `CmdHome`, implementing the interface `ICommand` in package com.xyz.command. Have the wizard build stubs for inherited methods. Implement the `execute()` method as follows:

```
public String execute(HttpServletRequest request,
    HttpServletResponse response) throws ServletException, IOException {
    String zipCode = getCookieValue(request, cookieName, "27703");
    request.setAttribute(cookieName, zipCode);
    return "default.jsp";
}
```

This command uses a private helper method to get a cookie that contains the last Zip Code specified by the user providing. This provides a value for the user's convenience. Add the following to the class:

```
/**
 * Returns cookie value if found, or default value if not found.
*/
private String getCookieValue(HttpServletRequest request,
    String cookieName, String defaultValue) {
    String value = defaultValue;
    Cookie[] cookies = request.getCookies();
    for (int index = 0; index < cookies.length; ++index) {
        Cookie cookie = cookies[index];
        if (cookieName.equals(cookie.getName()))
            value = cookie.getValue();
    }
    return value;
}
```

CmdError

In package com.xyz.command, create class `CmdError`, implementing interface `ICommand` in package com.xyz.command. Have the wizard build stubs for inherited methods. Implement the `execute()` method as follows:

```
public String execute(HttpServletRequest request,
    HttpServletResponse response) throws ServletException, IOException {
    return "error.jsp";
}
```

CmdDisplayLocation

In package com.xyz.command, create class `CmdDisplayLocation`, implementing interface `ICommand` in package com.xyz.command. Have the wizard build stubs for inherited methods. Implement the `execute()` method as follows:

```
public String execute(HttpServletRequest request,
    HttpServletResponse response) throws ServletException, IOException {
    try {
        Context jndiContext = new InitialContext();
        Object ref = jndiContext.lookup(facRef);
        SalesFacadeHome home =
            (SalesFacadeHome) PortableRemoteObject.narrow(
                ref, SalesFacadeHome.class);
        SalesFacade facade = home.create();
        String zipCode = request.getParameter("zipcode");
        if (zipCode != null) {
            LocationVO locationDO = facade.getLocation(zipCode);
            request.setAttribute("location", locationDO);
            response.addCookie(new Cookie(cookieName, zipCode));
        }
    } catch (javax.naming.NamingException ex) {
    throw new EJBException();
    } catch (java.rmi.RemoteException ex) {
    throw new EJBException();
    } catch (javax.ejb.CreateException ex) {
    throw new EJBException();
    }
    return "DisplayLocation.jsp";
}
```

This command method calls business logic before returning. It uses the facRef constant defined in ICommand to find the SalesFacade bean. Supply the missing import statements using import assistance. You convert exceptions to EJBException, signifying that you want the current transaction rolled back if you get into trouble.

CmdRecordPurchases1

In package com.xyz.command, create class CmdRecordPurchases1, implementing interface `ICommand` in package com.xyz.command. Have the wizard build stubs for inherited methods. Implement the `execute()` method as follows:

```
public String execute(HttpServletRequest request,
    HttpServletResponse response) throws ServletException, IOException {
    try {
        Context jndiContext = new InitialContext();
        Object ref = jndiContext.lookup(facRef);
        SalesFacadeHome home =
            (SalesFacadeHome) PortableRemoteObject.narrow(
                ref, SalesFacadeHome.class);
        SalesFacade facade = home.create();
        ItemVO[] data = facade.getAllItems();
        request.setAttribute("item", data);
    } catch (javax.naming.NamingException ex) {
            throw new EJBException();
    } catch (java.rmi.RemoteException ex) {
            throw new EJBException();
    } catch (javax.ejb.CreateException ex) {
            throw new EJBException();
    }
    return "Purchases1.jsp";
}
```

Use WSAD content assistance to supply missing imports by selecting the light bulb icons. The CmdHome command `execute()` method returns a list of all items that it forwards to a JSP for rendering. The user would select items from that list to be recorded as sales by the next command.

CmdRecordPurchases2

In package com.xyz.command, create class CmdRecordPurchases2, implementing interface `ICommand` in package com.xyz.command. Have the wizard build stubs for inherited methods. Implement the execute() method as follows:

```
public String execute(HttpServletRequest request,
    HttpServletResponse response) throws ServletException, IOException {
    String targetPage = "ErrorPage.jsp";
    Long[] itemIds = getItemIds(request);
    try {
        Context jndiContext = new InitialContext();
        Object ref = jndiContext.lookup(facRef);
        SalesFacadeHome home =
            (SalesFacadeHome) PortableRemoteObject.narrow(
                ref, SalesFacadeHome.class);
        SalesFacade facade = home.create();
        String zipcode = request.getParameter("purchasezip");
        if (zipcode != null && facade.makePurchase(zipcode, itemIds))
            targetPage = "Purchases2.jsp";
    } catch (javax.naming.NamingException ex) {
        throw new EJBException();
    } catch (java.rmi.RemoteException ex) {
```

```
            throw new EJBException();
        } catch (javax.ejb.CreateException ex) {
            throw new EJBException();
        }
        return targetPage;
    }
```

This command uses a private helper method to extract the user's item choices. Add the following to the class:

```
    /**
     * Helper method returns an array of Long Item IDs
    */
    private Long[] getItemIds(HttpServletRequest request) {
        ArrayList list = new ArrayList(20);
        Enumeration enum = request.getParameterNames();
        while (enum.hasMoreElements()) {
            String idStr = (String) enum.nextElement();
            if (idStr.startsWith("buy")) {
                String key = request.getParameter(idStr);
                Long id = new Long(Long.parseLong(key));
                list.add(id);
            }
        }
        return (Long[]) list.toArray(new Long[list.size()]);
    }
```

CmdDisplayTopLocs

In package com.xyz.command, create class `CmdDisplayTopLocs`, implementing interface `ICommand` in package com.xyz.command. Have the wizard build stubs for inherited methods. Implement the `execute()` method as follows:

```
    public String execute(HttpServletRequest request,
        HttpServletResponse response) throws ServletException, IOException {
        try {
            Context jndiContext = new InitialContext();
            Object ref = jndiContext.lookup(facRef);
            SalesFacadeHome home = (SalesFacadeHome)
                   PortableRemoteObject.narrow(ref, SalesFacadeHome.class);
            SalesFacade location = home.create();
            LocationVO[] topLocs = location.getTopLocations();
            request.setAttribute("toplocs", topLocs);
        } catch (javax.naming.NamingException ex) {
            throw new EJBException();
        } catch (java.rmi.RemoteException ex) {
            throw new EJBException();
        } catch (javax.ejb.CreateException ex) {
```

```
            throw new EJBException();
        }
        return "TopLocations.jsp";
    }
```

Add Imports

Edit the `FrontController` class. Use import assistance to supply the imports for the command classes. This completes the front controller command implementation for the SalesWeb module.

EJB Reference

Many of the front controller command handler classes reference the SalesFacade bean because they are clients of its business logic with the reference string in ICommand. You need to define the reference in the SalesWeb deployment descriptor to locate the EJB. Do so with the following steps:

1. Open the Deployment Descriptor Editor. Select the References tab.
2. Press the EJB tab at the top so you can target a remote interface. Press the Add button. A prototype reference appears.
3. Use the Link Browse button to choose the SalesFacade bean. The other fields are automatically shown.
4. Important: Overtype the new object reference name with **ejb/SalesFacadeHome**.
5. Save the editor's contents.

Before you leave the Deployment Descriptor Editor, you may want to browse its contents to view the kind of information contained in a Web deployment descriptor. Notice the definition for your front controller servlet when you press the Servlets tab.

Java Server Pages

The servlet, along with its dependent logic, is complete. The entire SalesWeb client is approaching completion. It needs the view layer consisting of JSPs to make requests of the front controller and render the results. You will create the pages in the next sections.

Web Content Folders

You need to create folders to place house auxiliary Web artifacts such as a style sheet, an image, and an applet. The JSPs will reside in the content root. You will create a series of folders by repeating the following steps for targets named applet, image, and theme:

1. Invoke the context menu on project SalesWeb, folder Web Content.
2. Choose New Folder. This invokes the New Folder wizard.
3. Supply the given folder name, and then press Finish.

Cascading Style Sheet

Each JSP will use a single CSS for style conformance and centralized look and feel. Carry out the following steps to create it:

1. In the J2EE Naviagator, invoke New > CSS on the theme folder's context menu.
2. Name the theme Master.css, and then press Finish.
3. The CSS editor opens. Enter the following code, and then save it:

```
BODY {color: black;
    font-family: "Comic Sans MS", Arial;
    background-color: white;
    font-size: 10pt
}
H1 {color: black;
    font-family: Arial;
    font-size: 20pt
}
H2 {color: black;
    font-family: Arial;
    font-size: 18pt
}
H3 {color: black;
    font-family: Arial;
    font-size: 16pt
}
.button {color: white;
    font-family: sans-serif;
    background-color: green;
    font-size: 10pt;
    font-weight: 600
}
```

Image

The user interface of even a learning exercise should be esthetically pleasing. You will use one thematic image on your pages.

1. In the Web perspective, invoke New Image File from the SalesWeb / image folder context menu. The New Image File wizard appears.
2. Choose a GIF file type. Name the image sales.gif. Press Finish.
3. Open the image with the Web Art designer.
4. Use the tool to create a logo from text, or pick a graphic from the gallery.
5. Save the file as sales.gif, and close it.

Applet

Locate the JAR file named barchart.jar that you created in Chapter 15. It contains the applet named com.xyz.applet.chart.Barchart. Copy the barchart.jar file into the Web Content / applet folder. Use main menu item File > Refresh to cause the file to appear in the applet folder in the J2EE Navigator. You will reference this applet in a JSP that renders the top sales locations returned from the façade.

JSP Source

This application needs the JSPs so the user can make requests of EJB business logic and to render the results. HTML source is too verbose for including the JSP source tags here. You may copy the JSP source from the book's Web site or create pages of your liking using the parameters and scriptlets detailed in the following material. Place each page in the Web Content folder in the SalesWeb project. Create each using the JSP editor in the Web Perspective. On each page, you may display the .gif image that you installed previously to give the user a sense that the pages belong to a single application. Turn off caching on all pages by specifying the following HTML elements:

```
<meta HTTP-EQUIV="Expires" CONTENT="0">
<meta HTTP-EQUIV="Pragma" CONTENT="no-cache">
<meta HTTP-EQUIV="Cache-Control" CONTENT="no-cache">
```

Default Page

The default.jsp start page or home page of the Web application will be rendered when a browser references URL http://localhost:9080/SalesWeb/ because its name is on the welcome list in the deployment descriptor. The content root defaults to the project name unless otherwise specified in the deployment descriptor. Insert the following scriptlet used as a value to prime the single input field:

```
<% String zipCode = (String)request.getAttribute("zipcode");
   if (zipCode == null) zipCode = "12345"; %>
```

The default page is a form with an action attribute of FrontController, since you use this single servlet to handle all requests. Use a method attribute of get so you can see the parameters in the URL. Include form input elements shown in Table 23.4.

Table 23.4 default.jsp Form Elements

TYPE=	NAME=	VALUE=	CLASS=
"text"	"zipcode"	"<%= zipCode %>"	
"submit"	"CmdDisplayLocation"	"Display Location"	"button"
"submit"	"CmdRecordPurchases1"	"Record Purchases"	"button"
"submit"	"CmdDisplayTopLocs"	"Query Top Locations"	"button"

The submit buttons request the three activities that this application can carry out. The text element is not used by CmdDisplayTopLocs. You may choose to group the other three input elements separately. An HTML table helps to control layout. The page included on the book Web site is rendered as shown in Figure 23.11.

Error Page

When a command detects trouble, it calls the error page named Error.jsp. Use this simple page to display an indication of an error. The page uses a JSP directive and a scriptlet. Its source code follows:

```
<%@ page isErrorPage="true" %>
<pre>
<% exception.printStackTrace(new java.io.PrintWriter(out)); %>
</pre>
```

Display Location

The page named DisplayLocation.jsp renders the city, state, Zip Code, and area code attributes of a returned LocationVO value object returned by the session bean. Insert the following JSP directive to get a reference to it set by the CmdDisplayLocation command object.

```
<jsp:useBean id="location" class="com.xyz.data.LocationVO"
scope="request"/>
```

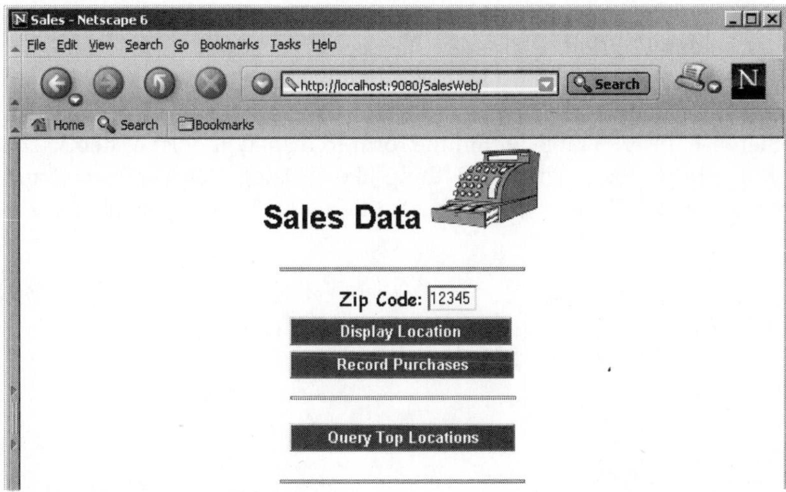

Figure 23.11 Start page.

The scriptlet renders the contents of the value object as shown in the following table snippet:

```
<TR>
  <TD><jsp:getProperty name="location" property="city"/></TD>
  <TD><jsp:getProperty name="location" property="state"/></TD>
  <TD><jsp:getProperty name="location" property="zipCode"/></TD>
  <TD><jsp:getProperty name="location" property="areaCode"/></TD>
</TR>
```

The page included on the Web site for this book is rendered as shown in Figure 23.12.

Record Purchases

When a user wishes to record purchases using Purchases1.jsp, the CmdRecordPurchase1 command issues the `getAllItems()` method call on the session bean. The bean returns the result as an array of LocationVO. The command sets the reference into a request attribute named item. The default.jsp caller passes a parameter named zipcode that contains the Zip Code for which purchases are to be recorded. This value is displayed on the page, and it is propagated to the next command through a hidden input field named zipcode. Insert the following source to implement the display and propagation of the Zip Code value:

```
<% String zip = (String)request.getParameter("zipcode"); %>
<P>Purchaser Zip Code <%= zip %></P>
<INPUT size="20" type="hidden" name="zipcode" value="<%= zip %>" >
```

The page displays a table of all items for sale. The user checks the items to record, and then presses a submit button. The session façade bean uses the CMR fields that you defined in the Purchase bean to record the purchases. The form should have an action attribute of FrontController. The method should be `post` since a too-long URL could result otherwise. Insert a table within the form to display the list of items. The column headers should contain values something like, Catalog Number, Name, and Purchase. Render the detail rows using a scriptlet and HTML resembling the following:

```
<% com.xyz.data.ItemVO[] item =
    (com.xyz.data.ItemVO[]) request.getAttribute("item");
for (int i=0; i < item.length; i++) {
  String buy = "buy" + i; %>
  <TR>
    <TD><%= item[i].getItemId() %></TD>
    <TD><%= item[i].getName() %></TD>
    <TD valign="middle" align="center">
      <INPUT type="checkbox" name="<%= buy %>"
            value="<%= item[i].getItemId() %>"></TD>
  </TR>
<% } %>
```

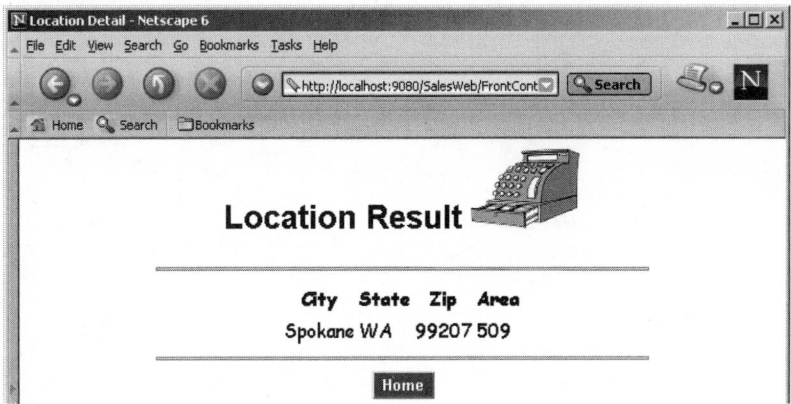

Figure 23.12 DisplayLocation.jsp.

The selection targets the CmdRecordPurchases2 command through the normal Submit button. Create Submit, Reset, and Cancel buttons using the following elements:

```
<TD><INPUT type="submit" name="CmdRecordPurchases2" value="Submit"
    class="button"></TD>
<TD><INPUT type="reset" name="reset" value="Reset"
    class="button"></TD>
<TD><INPUT type="submit" name="CmdHome" value="Cancel"
    class="button"></TD>
```

The page included on the Web site for this book is rendered as shown in Figure 23.13.

Confirm Purchase Recording

The CmdRecordPurchases2 command targets Purchases2.jsp to render the results of the successful conclusion of recording purchases. This JSP is a simple confirmation page that routes control to CmdHome through its single submit button. Include the following snippet in a table embodied within a form that has an action parameter of FrontController:

```
<TR><TD>Purchases Recorded for Zip Code
  <%= (String)request.getParameter("zipcode")%></TD>
</TR>
<TR><TD>
  <INPUT type="submit" name="CmdHome" value="Home" class="button">
  </TD>
</TR>
```

The page included on the Web site WAR file is rendered as shown in Figure 23.14.

Record Purchases

Purchaser Zip Code 99207

Catalog Number	Name	Purchase?
1002	BelchFire RAID	☐
1004	Extreme Computer	☐
1009	Holstein Ultralite Notebook	☐
1011	Juke Joint DVD array	☑
1003	Kozmo eSurfer	☑
1005	Promised LAN Switch	☐
1010	Route THIS router	☐
1012	Roving Eye Webcam	☑
1007	Site Control Gateway	☐
1001	Summit K280, 3.0 GHZ	☐
1006	The HUB	☐
1008	Total Computing Palmtop	☐

Submit Reset Cancel

Figure 23.13 RecordPurchases.jsp.

Display Top Locations

The TopSalesChart.jsp is your *piece de résistance*. It uses the fruits of all the business methods in the session façade bean, rendering tabular results and graphical results. The command CmdDisplayTopLocs carries out a **getTopLocations()** method call on the session bean. The result is a reference to an array of LocationVO containing an array of the top few sales locations ordered by volume. The EJBs did all the work. The JSP simply renders the array of LocationVO twice, in different ways.

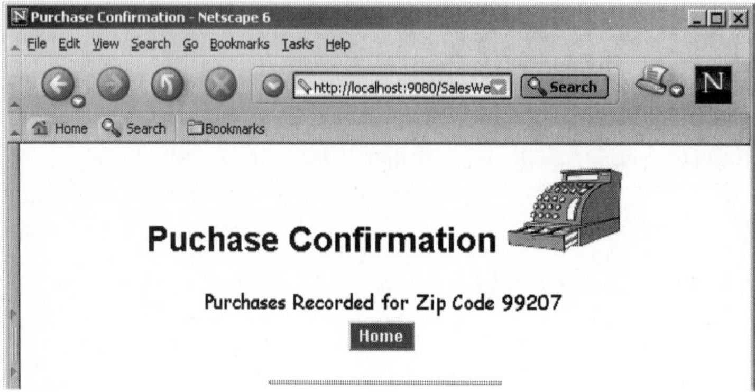

Figure 23.14 RecordPurchases2.jsp.

The CmdDisplayTopLocs command sets the result reference into the request object under name toplocs. Use the following scriptlet to retrieve the reference in the TopSalesChart.jsp:

```
<% com.xyz.data.LocationVO[] location =
    (com.xyz.data.LocationVO[])request.getAttribute("toplocs"); %>
```

The visual gratification of this client stems from an applet. You render the results using the BarChart applet you developed previously:

```
<APPLET code="com.xyz.applet.chart.BarChart" codebase="applet" alt="Bar
Chart Applet: Sales Ranking" width="500" height="280"
archive="barchart.jar" hspace="50">
  <param name="bgColor" value="white" />
  <param name="fgColor" value="black" />
  <param name="fontName" value="SanSerif" />
  <param name="pointSize" value="16" />
  <param name="gutterFraction" value="0.4" />
  <param name="title" value="Ranked Sales Locations by ZipCode" />
<% for (int i=0; i < location.length; i++) {
  com.xyz.data.LocationVO ldo = location[i];
  int col = i + 1;
  String bar = "B" + col;
  String lab = "L" + col;
%>
  <param name="<%= bar %>" value="<%= ldo.getSalesCount()%>" />
  <param name="<%= lab %>" value="<%= ldo.getZipCode()%>" />
<% } %>
</APPLET>
```

The applet assigns Zip Code labels to the bars. Add the following snippet to a table to render the ordered results for use as a legend:

```
<TABLE>
    <COL span="6" align="center">
    <TBODY>
        <TR>
            <TH>Rank</TH>
            <TH>Units</TH>
            <TH>City</TH>
            <TH>State</TH>
            <TH>Zip</TH>
            <TH>Area</TH>
        </TR>
<% for (int i=0; i < location.length; i++) {  %>
        <TR>
            <TD><%= Integer.toString(i+1) %></TD>
            <TD><%= location[i].getSalesCount() %></TD>
            <TD><%= location[i].getCity() %></TD>
            <TD><%= location[i].getState() %></TD>
```

```
                <TD><%= location[i].getZipCode() %></TD>
                <TD><%= location[i].getAreaCode() %></TD>
            </TR>
<% } %>
        </TBODY>
</TABLE>
```

After you enter some purchases, the page resembles that shown in Figure 23.15.

Deploy and Test

Invoke Project > Rebuild All from the main menu to ensure that the application is up to date. After you check for errors, you start the test server by choosing Run on Server from the Sales application context menu. WSAD publishes and deploys any module that needs a refreshed deployment, specifically SalesWeb. You can point a browser at URL http://localhost:9080/SalesWeb/, because you used the default WebSphere v5.0 Test Environment with a document root of SalesWeb. You are able to navigate the application, querying locations of any U.S. Zip Code, recording purchases for a given Zip Code, and displaying the resulting ranked top sales locations. The WSAD embedded browser works for all but the TopLocations.jsp. The integrated browser will not load the applet.

Advanced Topics

That wraps up the EJB project. There are other EJB technologies that you didn't exploit for lack of space. We will touch upon them briefly now.

Message-Driven Beans

The EJB 2.0 specification added message-driven beans (MDB). These resemble stateless session beans, except that they can receive and process JMS messages. This makes the MDB the only asynchronous bean in the EJB 2.0 specification. It is important to know that an MDB can receive and process messages concurrently. In addition, you should know that an MDB does not have component interfaces because no client can invoke an MDB through the Java RMI API, as is the case with the other kinds of beans. The MDB's container takes care of transactions, resources, concurrency, and message acknowledgement. The developer need only implement the bean's `public onMessage (javax.jms.Message)` method, much like any callback method.

You create an MDB in WSAD by invoking New > EJB from an EJB project context menu, as you did with the other kinds of beans. Then, you select Message-driven bean in the Create an Enterprise Bean wizard. After creation you flesh out the `onMessage()` method to suit. You need to create a reference to JMS queue or topic connection factory and a reference to a JMS queue or topic in the Deployment Descriptor Editor. These entities would need to exist in the application server. For example, you would use the WebSphere Application Server administration facilities to configure a topic or a queue reference as you did for a data source reference.

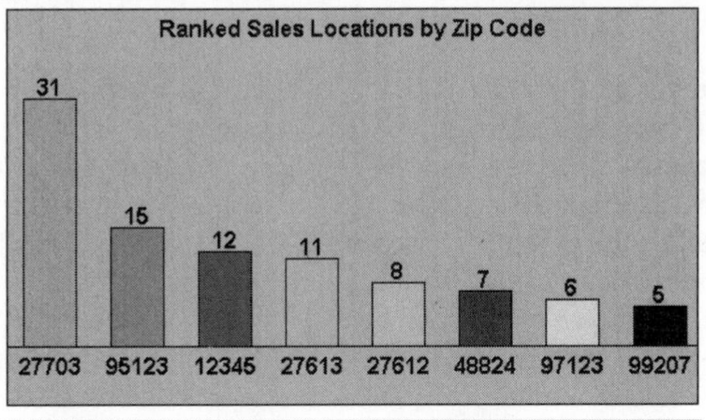

Rank	Units	City	State	Zip Code	Area Code
1	31	Durham	NC	27703	919
2	15	San Jose	CA	95123	408
3	12	Schenectady	NY	12345	518
4	11	Raleigh	NC	27613	919
5	8	Raleigh	NC	27612	919
6	7	East Lansing	MI	48824	517
7	6	Hillsboro	OR	97123	503
8	5	Spokane	WA	99207	509

Home

Figure 23.15 TopLocations.jsp.

Access Beans

WSAD provides several variations of JavaBean wrappers used to encapsulate EJB access. You may create these by invoking New > Access Bean from an EBJ Project's context menu. Here, you have a choice of three kinds of access bean. Each has an explanatory paragraph beside its choice. Read this carefully, because there are trade-offs. For example, two kinds of access bean do not support local interfaces. Informed use of these beans may help with performance issues. For example, a copy helper access bean may present a local copy of a remote bean attributes for a single entity bean instance. You can set these attributes locally without needing multiple server round trips.

You addressed the same issue by using a stateless session façade that references the EJB local interfaces. You didn't use access beans in your project because we wanted to show you how to use a couple of J2EE patterns directly. In addition, the access beans need a runtime JAR file. It is not clear that this works on all J2EE-compliant servers.

When you edit EJBs and have access beans, you may need to edit or regenerate the access beans. Use the EJB context menu on the EJB project in the J2EE Perspective to invoke Access Beans > Generate Access Beans or Access Beans > Edit Access Beans.

Security

The EJB 2.0 specification specifies access control security. It is up to the J2EE server to handle authentication and secure communications. Access control is also called authorization. Jeff is known to the server but can he invoke `getAllItems()` on the Session Façade bean?

If Websphere Application Server or any other J2EE compliant application server is configured to use one of several choices of security, the client is represented as either a user or a role. The server tracks each client as a security principle. In EJB, the security identity is encapsulated in a javax.security.Principal object. The principal becomes the client representative to the EJB access control mechanism. You can use the EJB Deployement Descriptor Editor to assign logical roles to principals. See the Assembly Descriptor tab to open the Security Roles group. Use the Add button to add security roles to the EJB JAR. Just below it is the Method Permissions group, where you can assign roles to methods. The Access tab enables you to add a user or role-based security identity at the bean level.

Summary

In this chapter we covered many EJB topics including:

- How to configure EJB transactions
- Creating a custom `find` method
- The session façade business tier J2EE pattern
- How to use value objects as a pattern
- The front controller presentation pattern
- How to implement a Web module in a J2EE application
- A brief introduction to message-driven beans, access beans, and security

You have finished the SalesApp J2EE project started in Chapter 22, "Enterprise JavaBeans." You used CMR relationships to facilitate recording purchases by location and by item. The Web client used the BarChart applet developed in Chapter 15, "Building Applets," to render the comparative sales results by U.S. postal Zip Code location. You used several J2EE patterns in this project. Read more about J2EE patterns in *Core J2EE Patterns Best Practices and Design Strategies,* Alue et al, Prentice Hall, 2001. The service locator and the business delegate would fit into the SalesApp project.

We will move on to coverage of Web services in the next chapter.

Web Services

What's in Chapter 24?

A Web service is a unit of functionality available over the Internet that uses a standardized platform-independent XML message transport that is not tied to a particular computer language. WSAD enables you to create and test Web services that use the Simple Object Access Protocol (SOAP) transport. In this chapter, you learn about:

- Web services concepts, including applications of XML named SOAP, WSDL, UDDI, and WSIL
- Developing Web services using WSAD
- Publishing a Java class or other entities as a Web service
- Using the WSAD-generated Web service test client
- Using the generated Web service proxy class
- The SOAP administration client
- Developing a custom Web client for a Web service
- How to develop a Java application client for a Web service
- Exporting a WSDL file
- How to use WSAD to generate a Web service proxy from a WSDL file

- The use of the WSAD Web Services Explorer
- Using UDDI with the IBM UDDI Test Registry
- Publishing a service to UDDI
- Installing the WSAD local test UDDI registry

Much literature that covers Web services gives a great deal of information about SOAP architecture. Here, you will treat SOAP as an alternative to RMI, whose internals are almost never discussed. In this chapter, you will concentrate on using WSAD to produce, publish, and consume SOAP-based Web services.

Concepts

A Web service is a service available over the Internet that uses a standardized XML message transport, which is platform independent and is not tied to a particular computer language. WSAD enables us to create and test a Web service that uses SOAP over an HTTP transport. The implementation language of the service wrapper is Java, but the service would be able to communicate with any kind of client, anywhere in the world, provided that the client has a working SOAP binding.

SOAP

Almost any software that accepts machine-readable inputs and produces machine-readable outputs may be published as a SOAP-based Web service. A method call on a service uses pass-by-value parameters. A called method is described by an XML element. Its parameter values are packed into self-describing XML structures, sent over the wire, and reconstituted at the service side for input into the published service. Results get the same treatment going in the return direction. SOAP provides an API to carry out the details of connecting to the service, packaging parameters, making the call, and extracting the result. The client normally calls a stub that uses the proxy design pattern to mask the details of the SOAP API.

The SOAP transport, at a high level, resembles a world parallel to that of EJBs. Parameters are passed by value. The client binds to a service, and then calls a stub or proxy to invoke methods on that service. Where do Web services fit with respect to EJBs? One answer is that the EJB architecture is designed for tighter binding and security suitable to an enterprise intranet. A SOAP Web service is designed to penetrate firewalls to reach the Internet, usually by using HTTP port 80. A given Web service could be made available to the entire World. An EJB uses RMI/IIOP, which uses a wide range of ports, making it firewall unfriendly, but it may be published as a Web service to make it available on the Internet. A non-Java client of an EJB would need to consider using JMS (to an MDB) or CORBA to access it, but those access methods may not be available to an arbitrary Web application located on the Internet. SOAP is a great leveler. It binds program components without regard to platform or language. This is possible only because of its acceptance as an emerging standard by an assortment of competing vendors and software producers.

There is more to a Web service than a SOAP transport that can bind a local component to a remote component. A Web service may also be self-describing so that it may be published, discovered, and consumed. Cooperation within the industry is producing more emerging standards toward this end.

Web Services Description Language

Web Services Description Language (WSDL) is an XML grammar for describing network services as a set of endpoints. It is independent of network protocols and message formats, but it is commonly used with SOAP, MIME, and HTTP GET/POST endpoint bindings. WSDL 1.1 is a W3C note described at www.w3.org/TR/wsdl.

The specification depicts eight major parts, shown in Table 24.1.

The WSDL format is boring for humans, but it lends itself to computer generation from easily specified or obtained information. Happily, the existence of WSAD means that you will almost never need to manually compose a WSDL document.

How is a WSDL document useful? It contains sufficient information to enable WSAD to generate a static client proxy for a Web service from a WSDL document. Conversely, WSAD can create a WSDL file from a Web service. In addition, an invocation tool such as IBM Web Services Invocation Framework (WSIF) can dynamically invoke a Web service, given a WSDL document. Thus, if a client must choose among providers of a given kind of service, it could select a WSDL document from a collection of documents that represent that kind of service of a kind of business based on some factor such as cost or distance.

Table 24.1 Major WSDL Parts

definitions	The XML root element. It contains the Web service name, name space declarations, and the remaining services elements that follow.
types	Defines the data types recognized by the endpoints.
message	Names the request and response messages. It may contain optional part elements that describe parameters or return values.
portType	Composes multiple message elements, such as a request and a response message, into a single operation.
binding	Describes the wire implementation of the service. SOAP-specific information resides here.
service	Contains the address of the described service. A URL is used to define a SOAP address here.
documentation	Encapsulates human-readable documentation. It may be nested within any other WSDL element.
import	Used to embed other WSDL documents or XML schemas into the current document for increased modularity and reuse.

Universal Description, Discovery and Integration

Where would the client find a collection WSDL documents that represent a kind of business or kind of service? How would it access the documents? How would the documents be placed in the collection?

Universal Description, Discovery and Integration (UDDI) is a specification for describing, discovering, and publishing Web services. It is described at www.uddi.org/. UDDI is a technical specification for building a distributed XML-based repository of businesses and Web services. In addition, UDDI is a set of well-known operational business registries operated by IBM, Microsoft, SAP, and XMethods. These operator sites form UDDI *cloud services*, operating together as a loosely coupled multimaster registry. That means that an update to or deletion from one registry will eventually propagate to the others.

Some of the registry operators operate a test registry where you can register a test business that has test services. You need only obtain a free user ID and password. See www.uddi.org/register.html for the current list of public UDDI registries and test registries. WSAD supplies a local test registry that you can use on your local machine. WSAD has a *Web Services Explorer*, which you may use to access the local test registry or any of the well-known registries on the Internet. You can use it to publish a business entity and its Web services.

A repository data is divided into three major categories, shown in Table 24.2.

A well-known registry, such as UDDI, facilitates just-in-time application integration by enabling the dynamic querying of service providers for a given industry or service type. The application could choose different providers each time it executes a request. For example, picture an order fulfillment application that selects a shipper based upon price and geographic factors.

UDDI has three major aspects: publishing, querying, and cloud services. The specification includes an XML schema that describes four kinds of data, shown in Table 24.3.

Table 24.2 Repository Data Categories

White pages	Contain general information about a given company, such as name, description, address, phone numbers, and other contact information.
Yellow pages	Classification data for a service or business. This may include standardized product, industry, or geographical codes.
Green pages	Technical description of a Web service, such as the external service type specification and address for invocation. The service type could be HTTP, SMTP, CORBA, or RMI, or, usually, SOAP.

Table 24.3 XML Schema Data Classifications

businessEntity	Information about the actual business
businessService	Information about a single Web service or group
bindingTemplate	Information about how to access a specific Web service
tModel	Descriptions or pointers to external technical specifications or taxonomies

WSAD, along with the public registries, registries, implements UDDI version 2 at the time of this writing. Recently UDDI specification version 3 was announced. It is described at http://uddi.org/pubs/uddi_v3_features.htm.

Web Services Inspection Language

Some applications may need the full power of a registry of businesses or services. Such an application may know the host that provides a service, or even be bound to a certain host. It only needs the WSDL document for that service. WSIL enables the client to directly reference the service provider to ask for the services it provides. WSIL is sometimes discussed as a bridge to UDDI, but it can also be used as an adjunct to UDDI. WSAD supports querying WSIL documents through the Web Services Explorer.

Developing Web Services

An HTTP transport Web service in WSAD uses the SOAP messaging model. It is created within a Web project. Remember that a Web project creates a J2EE module (WAR file) that is deployed in an enterprise project (EAR). The facilitator of an RPC-based SOAP endpoint is a servlet named rpcrouter. If only accepts HTTP POST operations that contain SOAP messages. It parses each SOAP request, extracting a target class, method, and any necessary parameters. It instantiates the target class if necessary, calls the method, packages the result into a SOAP response, and sends it to the client in an HTTP response.

Almost any Java class may be exposed as a Web service, provided that it isn't a user interface class. This means that anything that a Java class encapsulates and exposes in public methods can be exposed as a Web service by using the exposed class in an adapter pattern. WSAD wizards can expose the following kinds of entities as Web services in the ways shown in Table 24.4.

Table 24.4 Web Service Targets

JavaBean	Almost any Java class with a no-argument constructor
EJB	A class in the service acts as an EJB proxy
URL	Exposes an application referenced by a URL
ISD	Web service description document
DADX	Data description used with IBM DB2 XML Extender

Currency Conversion Java Class

Now, you will create a simple JavaBean class that carries out currency conversion. Afterward, you will expose it as a Web service with the assistance of a WSAD wizard. It will have a simple main method that exercises one of the conversions, but this method will not be exposed as part of the service.

Create a Java project named ConvertCurrency. Within it, make a package named com.xyz.conversion. Insert the following class Conversion into the package:

```
package com.xyz.conversion;
/**
 * Currency conversion class
 */
public class Conversion {
    public double dollar2Euro(double dollars) {
        return dollars * 1.01981d;
    }
    public double euro2Dollar(double euros) {
        return euros * 0.980653d;
    }
    public double dollar2Yen(double dollars) {
        return dollars * 120.126d;
    }
    public double yen2Dollar(double yen) {
        return yen * 0.00832494d;
    }
    public double dollar2MexPeso(double dollars) {
        return dollars * 9.97010d;
    }
    public double mexPeso2Dollar(double pesos) {
        return pesos * 0.100305d;
    }
    /**
     * Test script for dollar2Euro
     * @param arg String[], arg[0] contains dollars
     */
```

```
    public static void main(String[] arg) {
        String bucks = "1.00";
        if (arg.length > 0)
            bucks = arg[0];
        StringBuffer buf = new StringBuffer();
        buf.append("$");
        buf.append(bucks);
        buf.append(" is ");
        buf.append(new Conversion().dollar2Euro(
            Double.parseDouble(bucks)));
        buf.append(" Euros");
        System.out.println(buf);
    }
}
```

When you run this class as a Java application, the result is the following:

```
$1.00 is 1.01981 Euros
```

Expose a Class as a Web Service

The previous exercise was a simple command-based Java application. Now, you will expose the `com.xyz.conversion.Conversion` class as a Web service. You will create a proxy and a Web-based test client. The Web Service wizard makes this task easy. The following instructions assume that a WebSphere v5 Test Environment or equivalent server configuration has been created.

1. Create a Web project by invoking New > Project Web > Web Project. Press Next >.
2. Set Project name to WebService. Press Next >.
3. Set Enterprise Application Project to New.
4. Set the New project name to WebServiceApp. Press Finish to generate the projects WebService and WebServiceApp.
5. Invoke the Properties context menu command of project WebService. Select the Projects tab, and then set ConvertCurrency to be on the build path. Press OK. This sets the build path. Now, you must set the execution path.
6. Open the WebServiceApp deployment descriptor. Select the Module tab. Locate the Project Utility JARs group. Use the Add button to place ConvertCurrency.jar into the application. Save and close the deployment descriptor.
7. Invoke the context menu of project WebService, choose Open with > JAR Dependency Editor, and then select option ConvertCurrency under Dependencies. Save and close the JAR Dependency Editor. Now, the ConvertCurrency class will be on the Web service class path.
8. Use the Package Explorer view to select the Conversion.java file of Convert Currency project within the com/xyz/conversion folder.

9. Choose New > Other from the context menu. Choose Web Services wizard in the left-hand pane. Select Web Service in the right-hand pane. Press Next >.
10. Set Web service type drop-down to Java bean Web Service in the Web Service wizard. Set the options listed in Table 24.5. When panel appears as seen in Figure 24.1, press Next >.
11. Choose Use Defaults on the Web Service Deployment Settings panel. Select the project, as shown in Figure 24.2. Press Next >.
12. Verify that the com.xyz.conversion.Conversion bean is the target. Press Next >.
13. Set the Scope to Request. Review the various documents to be generated as shown in Figure 24.3. You would change the DNS name in the Web service URI to an actual DNS name in a production Web service. The tempuri.org name is used only for testing and demonstrations such as those you carry out here. Press Next >.

Table 24.5 Conversion Web Service Options

Start Web service in Web project
Generate a proxy
Test the generated proxy
Overwrite files without warning
Create folders when necessary

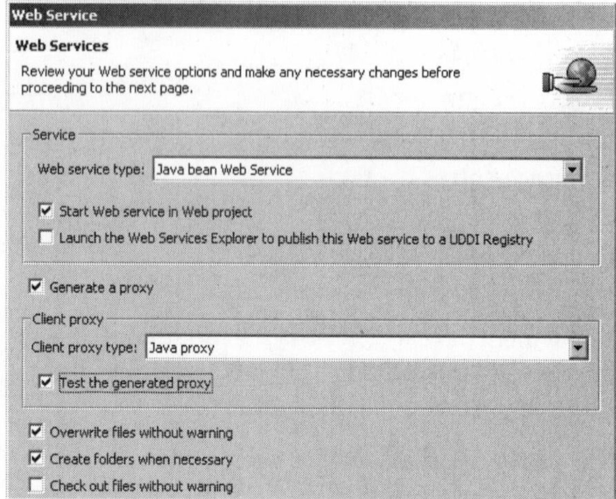

Figure 24.1 Generate Web service.

Web Service
Web Service Deployment Settings
Choose from the list of supported run-time protocols and deployment servers, or use the default settings.
Web service deployment environment selection:
Use Defaults
Choose run-time protocol first
Choose server first
Explore options
Run-time Protocol Selection:
IBM SOAP run-time
Server Selection:
WebSphere v5.0 Test Environment
Web project:
WebService
< Back
Next >
Finish
Cancel

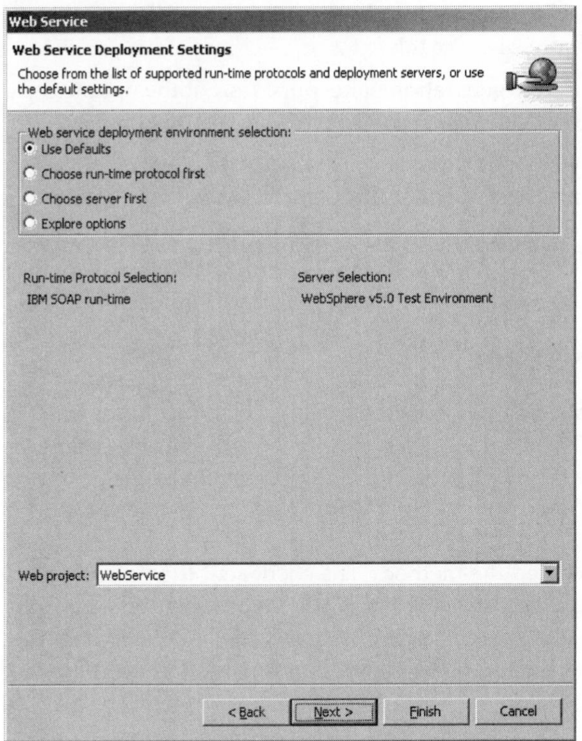

Figure 24.2 Web service deployment settings.

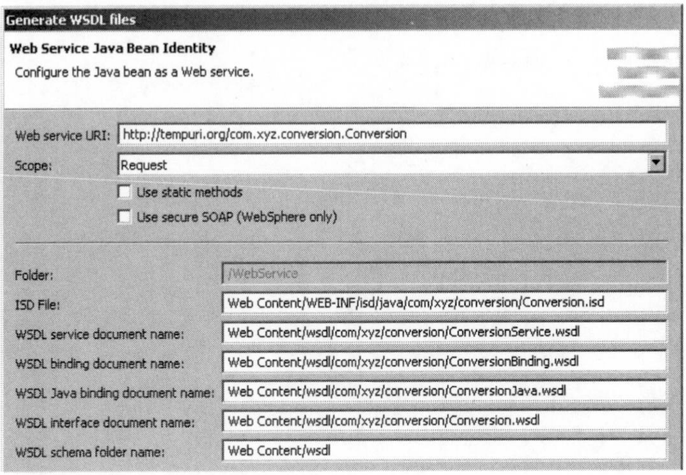

Generate WSDL files
Web Service Java Bean Identity
Configure the Java bean as a Web service.
Web service URI:
http://tempuri.org/com.xyz.conversion.Conversion
Scope:
Request
Use static methods
Use secure SOAP (WebSphere only)
Folder:
/WebService
ISD File:
Web Content/WEB-INF/isd/java/com/xyz/conversion/Conversion.isd
WSDL service document name:
Web Content/wsdl/com/xyz/conversion/ConversionService.wsdl
WSDL binding document name:
Web Content/wsdl/com/xyz/conversion/ConversionBinding.wsdl
WSDL Java binding document name:
Web Content/wsdl/com/xyz/conversion/ConversionJava.wsdl
WSDL interface document name:
Web Content/wsdl/com/xyz/conversion/Conversion.wsdl
WSDL schema folder name:
Web Content/wsdl

Figure 24.3 JavaBean identity.

14. Deselect the `main()` method since it is not to be exposed in the Web service. The panel should match Figure 24.4. Press Next >.
15. After a processing delay, a proxy generation panel appears. Set the option Generate proxy methods with the "synchronized" keyword. Press Next >.
16. Another processing delay yields to a proxy test panel that displays all of the exposed methods. Press Finish to begin to publish and test the Web service.

After more processing, the TestClient.jsp will appear in the WSAD Web browser. You use the client in the following section.

Use the Generated Test Client

Select the `dollar2MexPeso(double)` method in the Methods frame. Enter 10.00 in the Inputs frame. Press Invoke. The result, 99.70, will appear in the Results frame, as shown in Figure 24.5. To invoke the test client in the future, simply choose Run on Server from the context menu of WebServiceClient / Sample Conversion in the J2EE Navigator.

What happened when you executed the method? The client sent the parameters to the method of the generated proxy. The proxy sent a SOAP invocation message to the Web service, receiving a response message from it. It forwarded the response that resulted in the result page. You will examine the proxy in more depth in the following section.

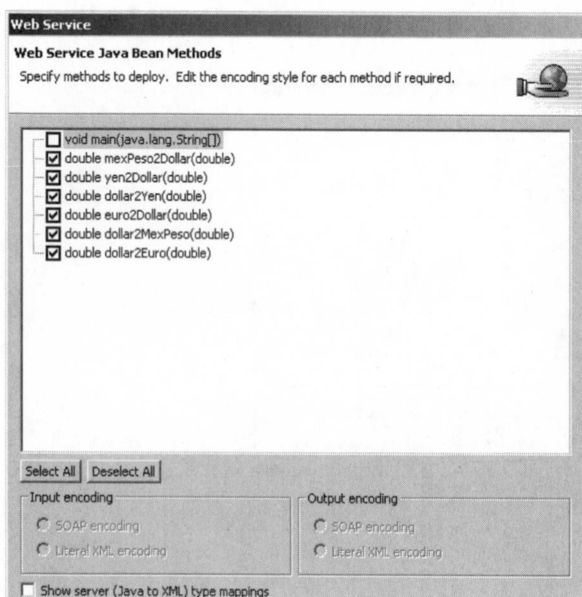

Figure 24.4 Method exposure.

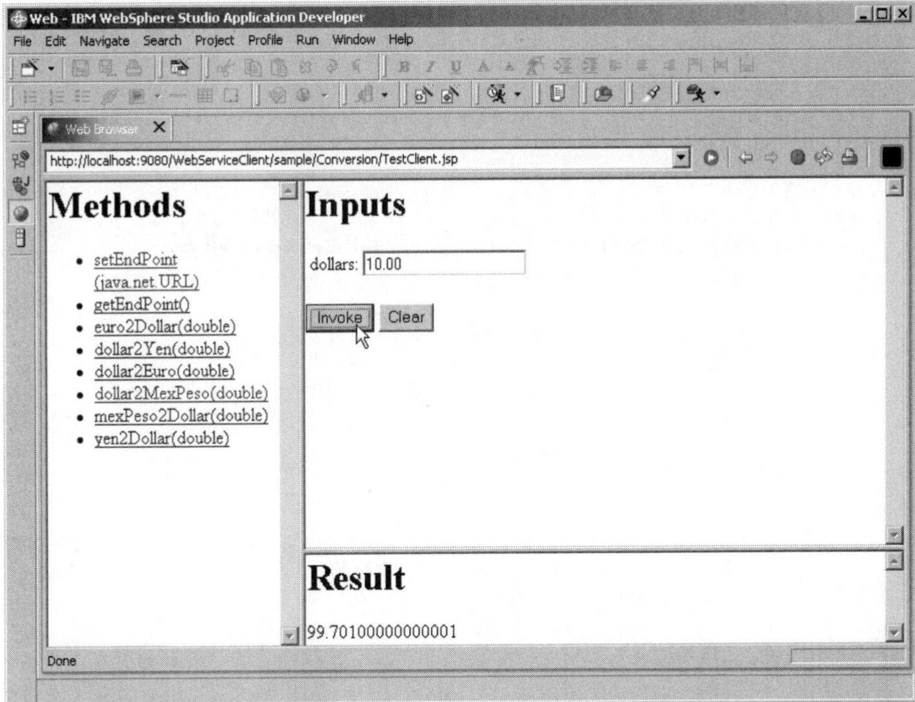

Figure 24.5 Input form.

Notice that the output format did not resemble a currency format. This is the case because the test client has no notion of currency. It only knows that it must render some returned double values. You will create your own client that knows how to format these results in the following section.named Client Servlet.

Generated Proxy

The test client uses the generated `proxy.soap.ConvertCurrencyProxy` class that you specified during service generation. Any servlet, applet, or application class may use this proxy, provided that it has the dependent JAR files on its class path.

Part of the generated proxy follows. If you plan to access its service remotely, you must modify its stringURL value to reference the actual host's external DNS name or IP address.

```
package proxy.soap;
import java.net.*;
import java.util.*;
import org.w3c.dom.*;
import org.apache.soap.*;
import org.apache.soap.encoding.*;
import org.apache.soap.encoding.soapenc.*;
```

```
import org.apache.soap.rpc.*;
import org.apache.soap.util.xml.*;
import org.apache.soap.messaging.*;

public class ConvertCurrencyProxy {
    private Call call = createCall();
    private URL url = null;
    private String stringURL =
        "http://localhost:9080/WebService/servlet/rpcrouter";
    public ConvertCurrencyProxy() {
    }
    public synchronized void setEndPoint(URL url) {
        this.url = url;
    }
    public synchronized URL getEndPoint()
            throws MalformedURLException {
        return getURL();
    }
    private URL getURL() throws MalformedURLException {
        if (url == null && stringURL != null &&
                stringURL.length() > 0) {
            url = new URL(stringURL);
        }
        return url;
    }
    public synchronized double dollar2Euro(double dollars)
            throws Exception {
        String targetObjectURI =
            "http://tempuri.org/com.xyz.conversion.Conversion";
        String SOAPActionURI = "";
        if (getURL() == null) {
            throw new SOAPException(
                Constants.FAULT_CODE_CLIENT,
                "A URL must be specified via
                 ConvertCurrencyProxy.setEndPoint(URL).");
        }
        call.setMethodName("dollar2Euro");
        call.setEncodingStyleURI(Constants.NS_URI_SOAP_ENC);
        call.setTargetObjectURI(targetObjectURI);
        Vector params = new Vector();
        Parameter dollarsParam =
            new Parameter(
                "dollars",
                double.class,
                new Double(dollars),
                Constants.NS_URI_SOAP_ENC);
        params.addElement(dollarsParam);
        call.setParams(params);
        Response resp = call.invoke(getURL(), SOAPActionURI);
        //Check the response.
```

```
            if (resp.generatedFault()) {
                Fault fault = resp.getFault();
                call.setFullTargetObjectURI(targetObjectURI);
                throw new SOAPException(
                    fault.getFaultCode(),
                    fault.getFaultString());
            } else {
                Parameter refValue = resp.getReturnValue();
                return ((java.lang.Double)
                    refValue.getValue()).doubleValue();
            }
        }
         <<< Similar method stubs removed for clarity >>>
    }
```

The proxy creates a SOAP `Call` object, it sets a remote method name into the `Call` object, and then it builds a parameter collection for the method, setting it into the call object. Next, it invokes the method on the call object, passing the URL of the remote SOAP RPC router. This action passes an XML SOAP document to the router via an HTTP POST operation. The router decodes the document, including the service, the method, and any parameters values. It issues the method call on behalf of the client, packaging the response into a new XML SOAP document, and returning it within an HTTP response. The client `Call.invoke()` returns a new `Response` object that encapsulates the decoded SOAP response. If the response document doesn't contain a fault, the client issues a `Response.getReturnValue()` to obtain the Java primitive or object value of the response.

The GoF proxy pattern encapsulates these simple details of the SOAP API, freeing the actual client to simply access the method as if it were local, aside from network latency issues and the passing of parameters by value instead of by reference.

In addition, you can directly invoke the proxy from the IBM Universal Test Client using the following browser URL:

```
http://localhost:9080/UTC/preload?object=proxy.soap.ConversionProxy
```

The proxy will appear as a reference that you can use to invoke the service methods as you did with EJB methods in Chapter 22, "Enterprise JavaBeans, and Chapter 23, "Entity EJBs." See Figure 24.6.

SOAP Administration

You published a SOAP-based Web service that answers client requests, but can you list the Web services that you published, or can you start and stop a Web service? Yes you can do this because the SOAP access point in WAS v5.0 is based upon Apache SOAP. It includes a rendition of the Apache SOAP administrative console. You can access it from URL `http://localhost:9080/WebService/admin/` to start and stop services or to inspect the service description. Figure 24.7 shows the Detail view of the currency conversion service that you published previously.

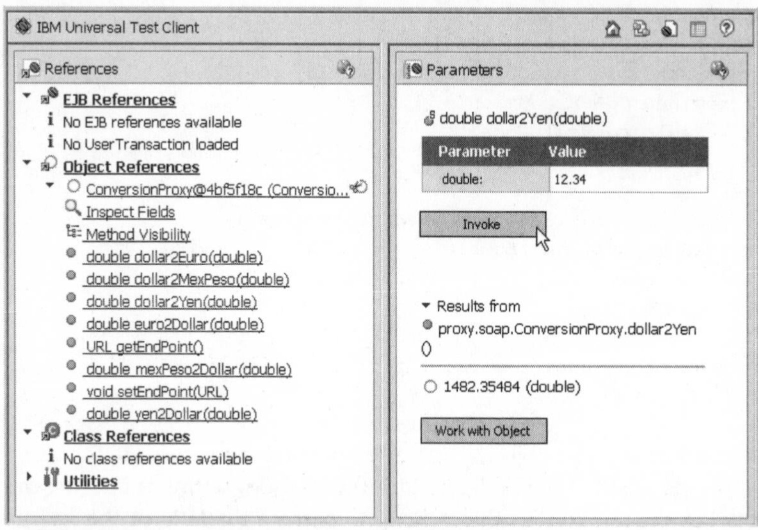

Figure 24.6 Proxy with IBM Universal Test Client.

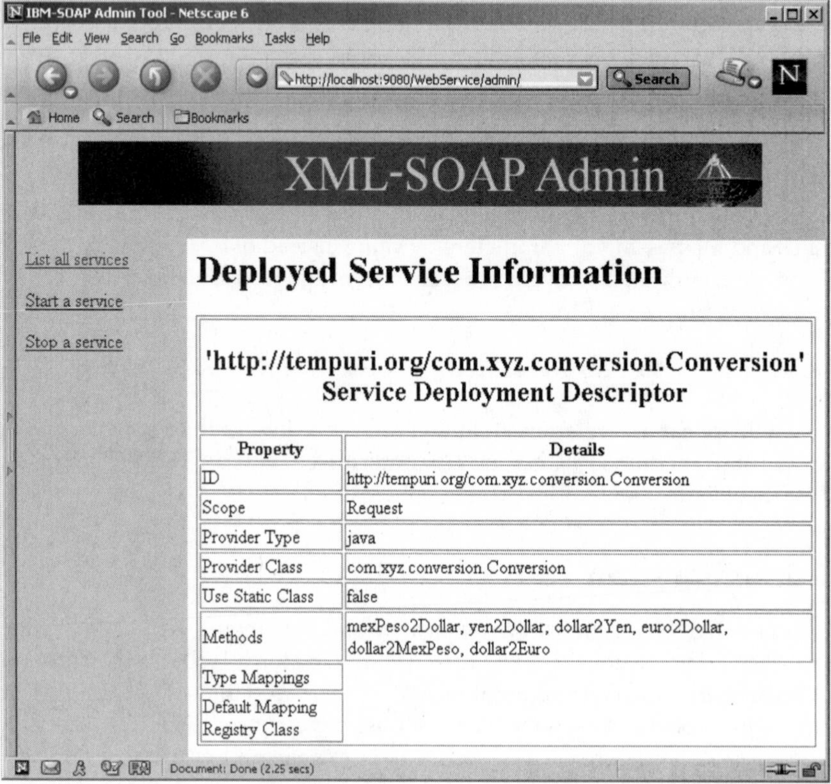

Property	Details
ID	http://tempuri.org/com.xyz.conversion.Conversion
Scope	Request
Provider Type	java
Provider Class	com.xyz.conversion.Conversion
Use Static Class	false
Methods	mexPeso2Dollar, yen2Dollar, dollar2Yen, euro2Dollar, dollar2MexPeso, dollar2Euro
Type Mappings	
Default Mapping Registry Class	

Figure 24.7 SOAP administration Client.

A Custom Web Client

A custom Web client for the Web service operates much like a client for an EJB or some other kind of back-end service. You use a servlet to accept a parameterized request from the browser. The servlet calls the service proxy as if it were a local class, except that the parameters are copies, not references. This is like calling an EJB interface, except that the proxy intrinsically knows the service address. The proxy resembles a WebSphere EJB access bean in this respect. The servlet sets the results returned by the proxy as attributes of the request object. Finally, it forwards the request to the JSP, which renders the attributes. The JSP is ready to accept a new dollar amount from the user to begin a new conversion cycle.

To distinguish the client from the Web service server, create an enterprise project named ConvertCurrencyApp. Do not let the wizard create any J2EE modules.

Client Servlet

The servlet uses a `formatMoney(double):String` private helper method to format the double results returned by the proxy into a string that contains two decimal positions. This alleviates the strange-looking money values seen in the generated test client results. Carry out the following steps to create the servlet:

1. Create a Web project named ConvertCurrencyClient. Associate it with enterprise application ConvertCurrencyApp. This will contain your client of the Web service.
2. Create a package in the Web Content folder of the project named com.xyz.servlet.
3. Create a Java project called ConversionProxy, and then create a package in it named com.xyz.proxy.soap.
4. Invoke the properties of the ConversionProxy project, and then add the path variables SOAPJAR and XERCESJAR on the Libraries tab.
5. Hold the control key depressed while dragging the file ConversionProxy.java from the soap.proxy package in the WebServiceClient project to your new package, com.xyz.proxy.soap, in the ConvertCurrencyClient project.
6. Use content assist to repair import statements in the ConversionProxy.java.
7. Open the ConvertCurrencyApp deployment descriptor. Add the project ConversionProxy as a utility JAR on the Module tab. Save the descriptor and close it.
8. Use the context menu of the ConvertCurrencyClient project to open the JAR Dependency Editor. Select ConversionProxy.jar, and then save and close the editor. The proxy is now available to the Web client that you are constructing.
9. In the Servers view select Add > ConvertCurrencyApp from the WebSphere v5.0 Test Environment context menu. This adds the new enterprise application to the server configuration.

10. In the ConvertCurrencyClient project, create a servlet named Conversion in the com.xyz.servlet.

11. Implement the servlet with the following source code. Notice the `formatMoney()` helper method used to format results.

```
package com.xyz.servlet;
import java.io.IOException;
import java.io.PrintWriter;
import java.math.BigDecimal;
import java.text.NumberFormat;
import java.util.Locale;
import javax.servlet.ServletException;
import javax.servlet.http.HttpServlet;
import javax.servlet.http.HttpServletRequest;
import javax.servlet.http.HttpServletResponse;
import proxy.soap.ConversionProxy;
/**
 * Currency conversion controller
 */
public class Conversion extends HttpServlet {
    public void doGet(HttpServletRequest req, HttpServletResponse resp)
        throws ServletException, IOException {
        doPost(req, resp);
    }
    public void doPost(HttpServletRequest req, HttpServletResponse resp)
        throws ServletException, IOException {
        ConversionProxy proxy = new ConversionProxy();
        String dollarsStr = req.getParameter("dollars");
        double dollarsNumeric = Double.parseDouble(dollarsStr);
        dollarsStr = formatMoney(dollarsNumeric);
        req.getSession().setAttribute("dollars", dollarsStr);
        try {
            double euros = proxy.dollar2Euro(dollarsNumeric);
            req.setAttribute("euros", formatMoney(euros));
            double mexpesos = proxy.dollar2MexPeso(dollarsNumeric);
            req.setAttribute("mexpesos", formatMoney(mexpesos));
            double yen = proxy.dollar2Yen(dollarsNumeric);
            req.setAttribute("yen", formatMoney(yen));
            req.getRequestDispatcher("default.jsp").
                forward(req, resp);
        } catch (Exception ex) {
            resp.setContentType("text/html");
            PrintWriter writer = resp.getWriter();
            writer.println(ex);
            writer.println(
                "<br /><a href=\"/WebServiceClient/default.jsp\">
                 Home</a>");
        }
    }
```

```
    /**
     * Return arg as string format nnn.nn
     * @param arg double, money value
     */
    protected String formatMoney(double arg) {
        BigDecimal payment = new BigDecimal(arg);
        NumberFormat formatter = NumberFormat.getCurrencyInstance();
        double doublePayment = payment.doubleValue();
        return formatter.format(doublePayment).substring(1);
    }
}
```

Client JSP

A JSP provides dynamic presentation services. The input dollar amount is preserved from screen-to-screen to prime the input field for user convenience. The dollars value is held in the session object although you could have used a cookie instead. The value defaults to 1.00 when the session is established. The JSP renders the converted values passed in the request object by the servlet. See the `request.getAttribute(String)` scriptlets in the listing of the JSP. Carry out the following steps to create the JSP:

1. Create a JSP named default.jsp in the Web Content folder of project Convert-CurrencyClient.
2. Implement the page such that its source conforms to the following listing and its preview format is something like that seen in Figure 24.7.

```
<!DOCTYPE HTML PUBLIC "-//W3C//DTD HTML 4.01 Transitional//EN">
<HTML>
<HEAD>
<%@ page language="java" contentType="text/html; charset=WINDOWS-1252"
pageEncoding="WINDOWS-1252" %>
<META http-equiv="Content-Type"
    content="text/html; charset=WINDOWS-1252">
<META name="GENERATOR" content="IBM WebSphere Studio">
<META HTTP-EQUIV="Expires" CONTENT="0">
<META HTTP-EQUIV="Pragma" CONTENT="no-cache">
<META HTTP-EQUIV="Cache-Control" CONTENT="no-cache"
<TITLE>Currency Conversion</TITLE>
</HEAD>
<BODY>
<% String dollars =  (String)session.getAttribute( "dollars");
if (dollars == null)
  dollars = "1.00";
%>
<h1 align="center">Convert Dollars</h1>
<FORM methnod="get" action="Conversion">
```

```
<CENTER>
<TABLE border="0">
    <TBODY>
        <TR>
            <TH align="right">Dollars:</TH>
            <TD align="right"><INPUT type="text" name="dollars"
size="8"
                value="<%= dollars %>" maxlength="10"></TD>
        </TR>
        <TR>
            <TD COLSPAN="2" align="center"><INPUT type="submit"
                name="convert" value="Convert to:"></TD>
        </TR>
        <TR>
            <TH align="right">Euros:</TH>
            <TD align="right"><%=request.getAttribute("euros")%></TD>
        </TR>
        <TR>
            <TH align="right">Mex Pesos:</TH>
            <TD
align="right"><%=request.getAttribute("mexpesos")%></TD>
        </TR>
        <TR>
            <TH align="right">Yen:</TH>
            <TD align="right"><%=request.getAttribute("yen")%></TD>
        </TR>
    </TBODY>
</TABLE>
</CENTER>
</FORM>
</BODY>
</HTML>
```

3. Publish the WebService client, restart the server, and choose Run on Server from the project context menu.
4. Use Run on Server to test the client.

Additionally, try the client from an external browser. The URL to invoke the application from an external browser follows:

```
http://localhost:9080/ConvertCurrencyClient/
```

See Figure 24.8 for an example.

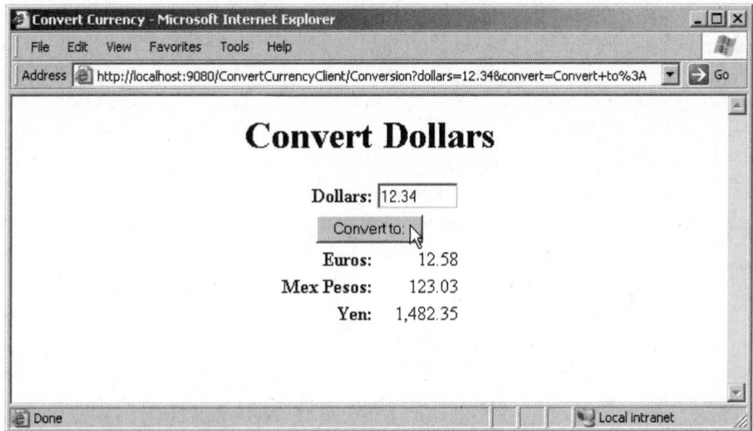

Figure 24.8 Custom Web client.

Java Application Client

A Web client of a Web service is useful because it has the qualities of reach and platform independence. The Web service itself has those same qualities, but it is not tied to Web clients. Any code on any platform, implemented in any language that can access an HTTP transport and use the SOAP protocol can use a SOAP-based Web service.

Now, you will create a simple static Java client for the currency conversion service. Its operation will resemble the servlet you wrote for the Web client except that its dollars input is a command-line argument value, and its presentation is carried out by `System.out.println()`. Carry out the following steps:

1. Create a Java project named ConversionClient.
2. Add project ConversionProxy to the build path.
3. Create a package named com.xyz.conversion.client.
4. Make a class named Conversion in that package. Create it with a `main()` method.
5. Instantiate ConvertCurrencyProxy.
6. Check for command-line argument for dollars. Provide a default value if none is supplied.
7. Convert the dollars to a string, and then pass it to the conversion methods of the proxy.
8. Display each result.

A rendition of the application follows. You use two overloads of `formatMoney()` to format money values either from a `double` or from a `String`.

```
package com.xyz.conversion.client;
import java.text.NumberFormat;
import proxy.soap.ConvertCurrencyProxy;
import com.ibm.math.BigDecimal;
public class ConversionClient {
    private final static String bucks = "10.00";
    public static void main(String[] args) {
        ConvertCurrencyProxy proxy = new ConvertCurrencyProxy();
        StringBuffer buf = new StringBuffer();
        String dollarStr = bucks;
        if (args.length > 0)
            dollarStr = args[0];
        dollarStr = formatMoney(dollarStr);
        double dollars = Double.parseDouble(dollarStr);
        try {
            buf.append("$");
            buf.append(dollars);
            buf.append(" is:\n\t");
            buf.append(formatMoney(proxy.dollar2Euro(dollars)));
            buf.append(" Euros\n\t");
            buf.append(formatMoney(proxy.dollar2MexPeso(dollars)));
            buf.append(" Mexican Pesos\n\t");
            buf.append(formatMoney(proxy.dollar2Yen(dollars)));
            buf.append(" Yen\n");
            System.out.println(buf);
        } catch (Exception ex) {
            ex.printStackTrace();
        }
    }
    /**
     * Return arg as string format nnn.nn
     * @param arg String, money string (no symbols allowed)
     */
    protected static String formatMoney(String arg) {
        BigDecimal payment = new BigDecimal(arg);
        NumberFormat formatter = NumberFormat.
                getCurrencyInstance();
        double doublePayment = payment.doubleValue();
        return formatter.format(doublePayment).substring(1);
    }
    /**
     * Return arg as string format nnn.nn
     * @param arg String, money string (no symbols allowed)
     */
    protected static String formatMoney(double arg) {
        return formatMoney(Double.toString(arg));
    }
}
```

This application will execute as-is in the WSAD environment, provided that you set the path to the WSAD library variable names shown in Table 24.6. If you want to export the application, it needs the JAR files referenced by those variable names on its class path. It also requires the `proxy.soap.ConvertCurrencyProxy` class to be on its path. If you run the application on a remote machine, you must modify the URL in the proxy to reference the Web service host by its remote host name instead of localhost.

The Web service must be running in the server before you execute ConversionClient as a Java application. Sample output follows:

```
$10.0 is:
    10.20 Euros
    99.70 Mexican Pesos
    1,201.26 Yen
```

Export a WSDL File

Invoke the context menu of the `Conversion.java` class, that you exposed as a Web service, and select Web Services > Generate WSDL Files item to generate a WSDL file that is logically equivalent to a proxy. Don't forget to set the Web project field to Web-Service because that module contains the deployed service. Set the Scope to Request, and deselect the `main()` as you did previously. Refer to the wizard panels that you saw when you generated and deployed the Web service for the class previously.

A client implemented in an arbitrary language on a foreign platform could use the generated WSDL information to generate its own proxy binding. WSAD uses the import statement to compose a WSDL file from separate documents. The first document is the WSDL service document. It defines the service having a collection of related ports. A port represents a network endpoint, consisting of a network address and a binding. This is shown in the service document for the ConversionService service, which follows. Notice that it imports a conversion binding document.

Table 24.6 Required JAR Files

WSAD LIB VARIABLE NAME	JAR FILE NAME
ACTIVATIONJAR	activation.jar
JRE_LIB	rt.jar
SOAPJAR	soap.jar
MAILJAR	mail.jar
XERCES	xercesImpl.jar

```
<?xml version="1.0" encoding="UTF-8"?>
<definitions name="ConversionService"
    targetNamespace="http://conversion.xyz.com/"
    xmlns:tns="http://conversion.xyz.com/"
    xmlns:soap="http://schemas.xmlsoap.org/wsdl/soap/"
    xmlns="http://schemas.xmlsoap.org/wsdl/">
  <import namespace="http://conversion.xyz.com/" location=
"http://localhost:9080/WebService/wsdl/com/xyz/conversion/ ⮐
ConversionBinding.wsdl"/>
  <service name="ConversionService">
    <port name="ConversionPort" binding="tns:ConversionBinding">
      <soap:address location=
          "http://localhost:9080/WebService/servlet/rpcrouter"/>
    </port>
  </service>
</definitions>
```

The next imported WSDL file is a service binding document. It defines the defined operations and messages for a particular port. The binding information contains the protocol name, the invocation style, a service ID, and the encoding for each operation. Following is a fragment that shows the `euro2DollarRequest` method depicted as an operation. Notice the input and output definitions. This document is imported by the binding document. In turn, it imports the Java binding document.

```
<?xml version="1.0" encoding="UTF-8"?>
<definitions name="ConversionBinding"
    targetNamespace="http://conversion.xyz.com/"
    xmlns="http://schemas.xmlsoap.org/wsdl/"
    xmlns:soap="http://schemas.xmlsoap.org/wsdl/soap/"
    xmlns:tns="http://conversion.xyz.com/">
  <import location="Conversion.wsdl"
      namespace="http://conversion.xyz.com/"/>
    <binding name="ConversionBinding" type="tns:Conversion">
      <soap:binding style="rpc" transport=
            "http://schemas.xmlsoap.org/soap/http"/>
      <operation name="euro2Dollar">
        <soap:operation soapAction="" style="rpc"/>
          <input name="euro2DollarRequest">
            <soap:body
              encodingStyle=
                  "http://schemas.xmlsoap.org/soap/encoding/"
              namespace=
                 "http://tempuri.org/com.xyz.conversion.Conversion"
              parts="euros" use="encoded"/>
            </input>
            <output name="euro2DollarResponse">
              <soap:body
                  encodingStyle=
                    "http://schemas.xmlsoap.org/soap/encoding/"
                namespace=
                  "http://tempuri.org/com.xyz.conversion.Conversion"
```

```
                use="encoded"/>
            </output>
        </operation>
        <!-- Remaining operation elements removed for clarity -->
    </binding>
</definitions>
```

Following is an example of the WSDL Java binding document for the Web service. It contains the Java binding information that is used by WSAD.

```
<?xml version="1.0" encoding="UTF-8"?>
<definitions name="Conversion"
      targetNamespace="http://conversion.xyz.com/"
      xmlns="http://schemas.xmlsoap.org/wsdl/"
      xmlns:tns=
      "http://conversion.xyz.com/"
      xmlns:xsd="http://www.w3.org/2001/XMLSchema">
  <message name="euro2DollarRequest">
    <part name="euros" type="xsd:double"/>
  </message>
  <!-- Remaining message elements removed for clarity -->
  <portType name="Conversion">
    <operation name="euro2Dollar" parameterOrder="euros">
      <input message="tns:euro2DollarRequest"
          name="euro2DollarRequest"/>
      <output message="tns:euro2DollarResponse"
          name="euro2DollarResponse"/>
    </operation>
    <!-- Remaining operation elements removed for clarity -->
  </portType>
</definitions>
```

Had you published an EJB as a Web service, you would see an EJB binding document. These aggregate documents form a logical WSDL file sufficient for a tool such as WSAD to produce a proxy that will access a Web service.

Generate a Proxy from WSDL

WSAD can generate a proxy for a Web service from its WSDL document. This is sufficient when it is the only information supplied about a service by a query to a service registry. The sequence of wizard panels resembles those you saw when you generated the Web service itself.

1. Expand the WebService project in the Navigator view of the Resources Perspective.
2. Select Web Content > wsdl > com > xyz > conversion > ConversionService.wsdl.
3. Choose the New > Other wizard from the context menu. Choose Web Services from the left-hand pane. Select Web Service Client from the right-hand pane. Press Next >.

4. Choose Java Proxy and Create folders when necessary. Press Next >.
5. Verify that the WSDL file name or URL setting is the path to Conversion-Service.wsdl. Press Next >.
6. Set the fully qualified proxy class name to `com.xyz.proxy.soap.ConversionProxy2`, and then press Next >.
7. Set the option to test the generated proxy, and then press Finish to generate the proxy.
8. Press Finish to generate the proxy.
9. When the test client appears in the browser view, test its methods as you did previously for the earlier ConversionProxy class.

At this point, the fully qualified proxy class is available for use by clients. Notice that you could have specified a URL for the input WSDL file. This means that WSAD can generate a proxy for an arbitrary public service as long as it has a published WSDL file available. You only need a means to find and query published services.

Web Services Explorer

There is a currency conversion Web service that you can access from a proxy. You've seen how to generate the proxy from the WSDL description of the Web service. Presumably, a client could choose among several WSDL documents that supply currency conversion calculations, but how would the client find them? We previously discussed the role of UDDI as a repository of information that enables a client to discover a service provided for a particular kind of business. Cloud services handle propagating the publication to the other UDDI sites. Thus, you could publish a business description in a UDDI site, and then link your service description to that business. A client could discover your business and its service, download the description in the form of WSDL document, generate a proxy, and invoke your service through that proxy. This assumes that similar kinds of services implement a common interface so that the method signatures of the generated proxy are identical across the set of possible services.

WSAD provides the Web Services Explorer utility to access any UDDI registry. Invoke it from the main menu item Window > Launch the Web Services Explorer. This launches the default browser, rendering this start page of this Web-based tool. It consists of three panes. The Navigator occupies the left pane. The Actions pane is at the top right. The Status pane sits at the bottom right. A set of icon buttons sits at the top right, above the Actions pane. These, along with other controls that appear in the panes as needed, control the utility.

Using UDDI

The Web Services Explorer will create, find, view, update, or delete UDDI entries in any UDDI registry. A Favorites button enables you to access a list of them in the Navigator pane. The Navigator contains only the UDDI Main node when you first invoke the utility. Click it to use the Actions pane to open a registry. It is prefilled with the information to access the IBM UDDI Test Registry, as seen in Figure 24.9.

Now, you will try it, pressing the Go button to proceed. If you don't have a user ID and password for the registry, you should first use the hyperlink Click here to obtain a user ID and password for this registry to access to the site with the default browser for registration. At this point, you may use the Find button (third from right in Actions pane) to carry out queries of businesses and services. Use the Publish button (third from right in Actions pane) to create a business or a service within a business. The utility supplies both simple and advanced forms for these two operations. It is better to use the Simple option at first, and then explore the fine-grained inputs available under the Advanced option.

For example, you may try publishing a business to the IBM Test Registry using the simple option. Supply the business name and description along with a valid user ID and password for the registry on the form. Press Go. The business is published. Use the Find button to retrieve the information using the Simple version of the query. Notice that % is used as a wildcard character. See Figure 24.10 for an example of a find result on a sample business named ACE that carries out currency conversion. It appears in a pick list along with other businesses having the ACE prefix.

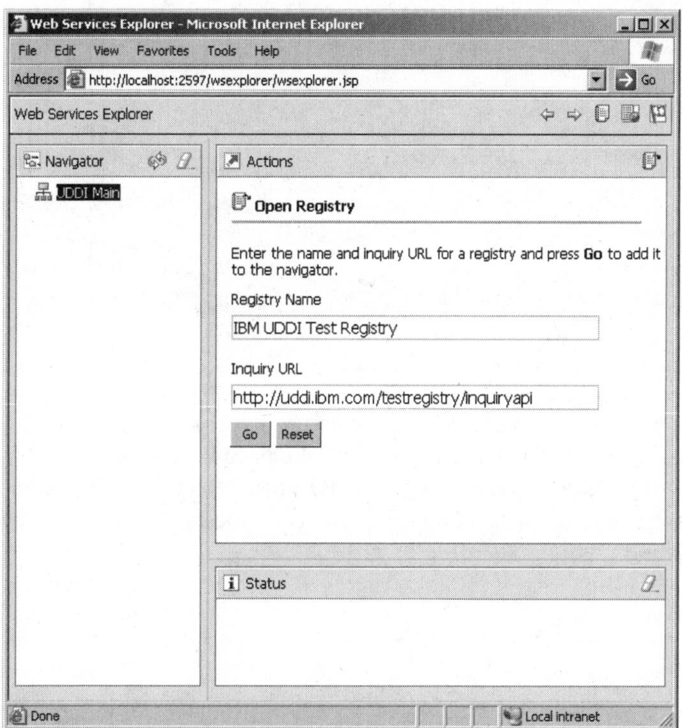

Figure 24.9 Open a UDDI registry.

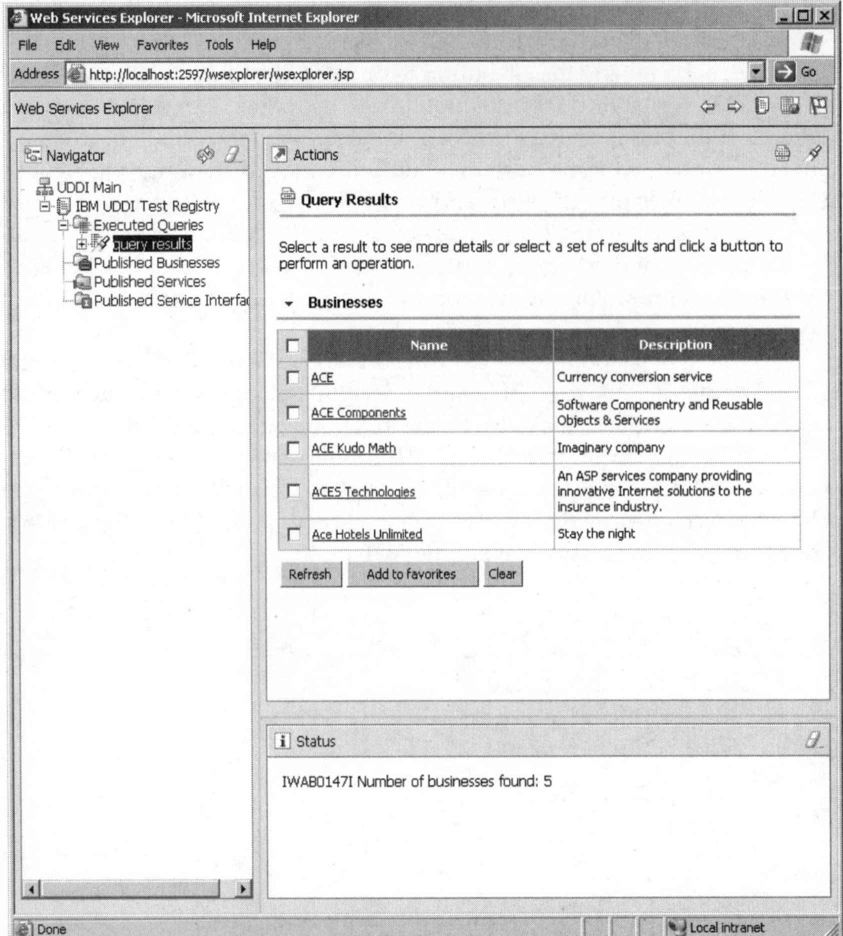

Figure 24.10 Find a business In UDDI.

If you select the check box beside your ACE business and press Add to favorites, that business will appear in the favorites list you can invoke from the Favorites button at the top right of the Actions pane. If you press the ACE hyperlink, you see the details of that business, as shown in Figure 24.11. Notice that you can modify the details if you have the correct user ID and password.

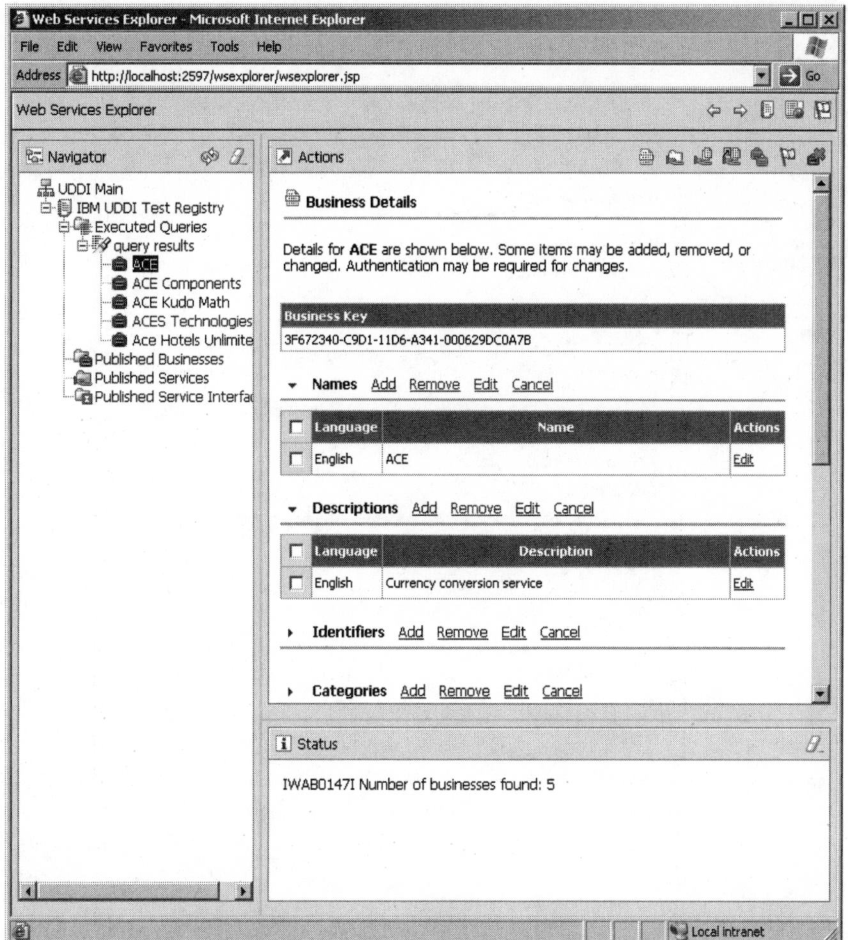

Figure 24.11 Business detail.

Observe the larger set of buttons at the top of the Actions pane. As always, you may determine what each means by hovering the pointer over it.

The fifth icon from the right enables you to publish a service for this business. This requires that a WSDL document for the service be accessible on the Web by the UDDI service. As an exercise, you copied the four WSDL document fragments that compose the WSDL description of the Conversion service to a Web server on the Internet. They were situated in the `WebService\Web Content\wsdl\com\xyz\conversion` directory of the WebService project. Then, you pressed the Publish button of the ACE business Actions pane. You supplied the Web URL of the root WSDL document to the Simple publish service form. The input form is shown in Figure 24.12. The WSDL URL is that of the public Web server that contains the WSDL documents describing the service.

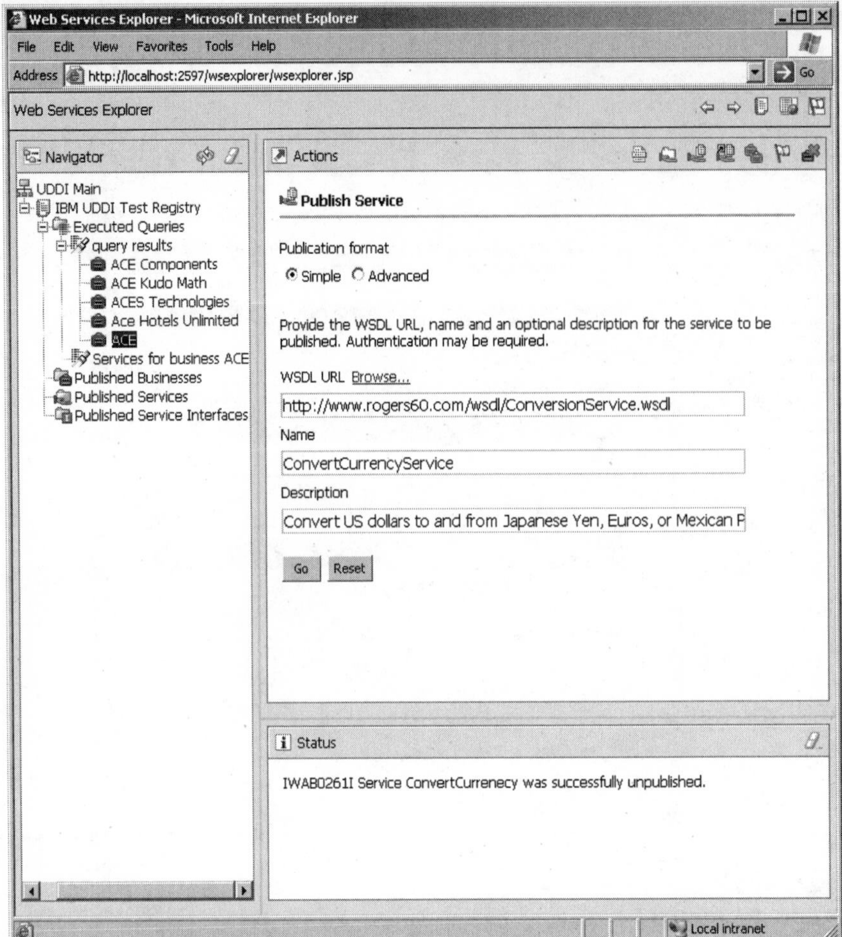

Figure 24.12 Publish a service.

Figure 24.13 shows the result after pressing the Go button.

You may use the Find icon to locate this service at any time in the future. How is this useful? Here is where the fun starts. If you find the service, then the Actions pane icons allow you to query the service interfaces or to import the WSDL document into the WSAD Workbench or into the file system. You've seen that a proxy may be generated from a WSDL document so that you may access the corresponding service. Now, you will import the WSDL document back into your system by querying the services for the ACE business and setting the resulting form to import into the Convert.wsdl file in a simple project named Imports, as shown in Figure 24.14.

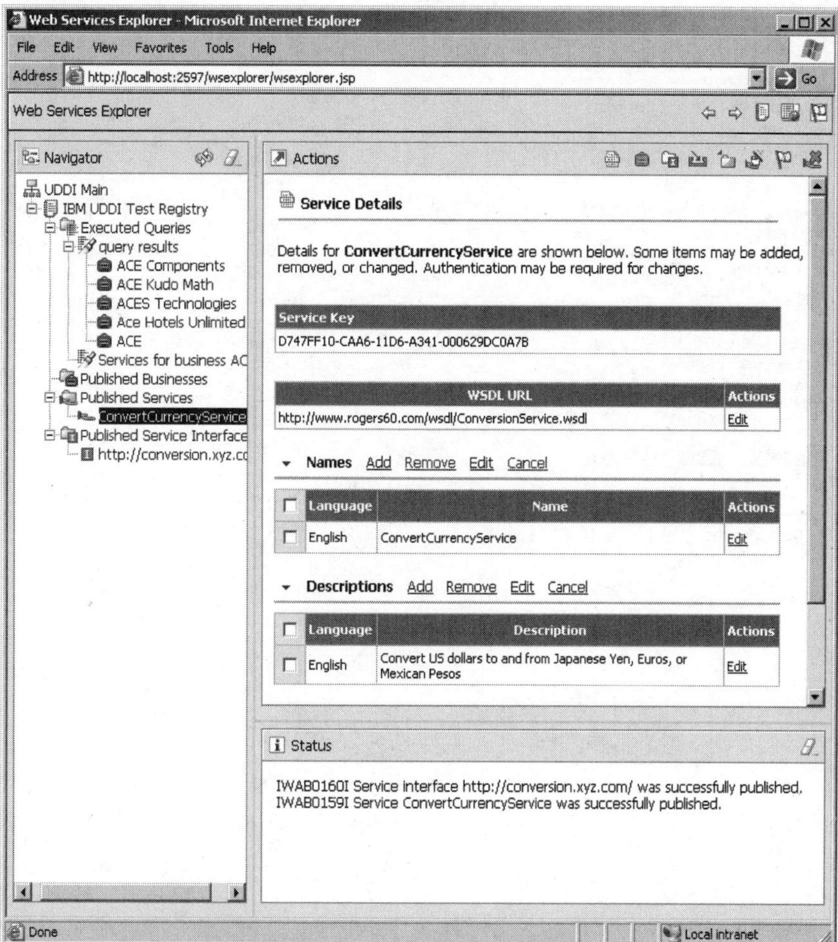

Figure 24.13 Published service.

The result is a copy of the root WSDL file that you published previously. Notice that all of your successful queries are recorded in the Navigation pane.

Please realize that you do not have to import your own service description. You may import anything you find. Further realize that the service does not have to be implemented in Java. You can create a proxy and access any service that speaks SOAP.

Local UDDI Test Registry

If you do not have access to a Web server on the Internet, you can use a local UDDI registry supplied by WSAD to interoperate with services published in the test server. WSAD contains a configurable UDDI registry that you can use to publish test local Web services through the Web Services Explorer. You can place it in the favorites list alongside the public registries.

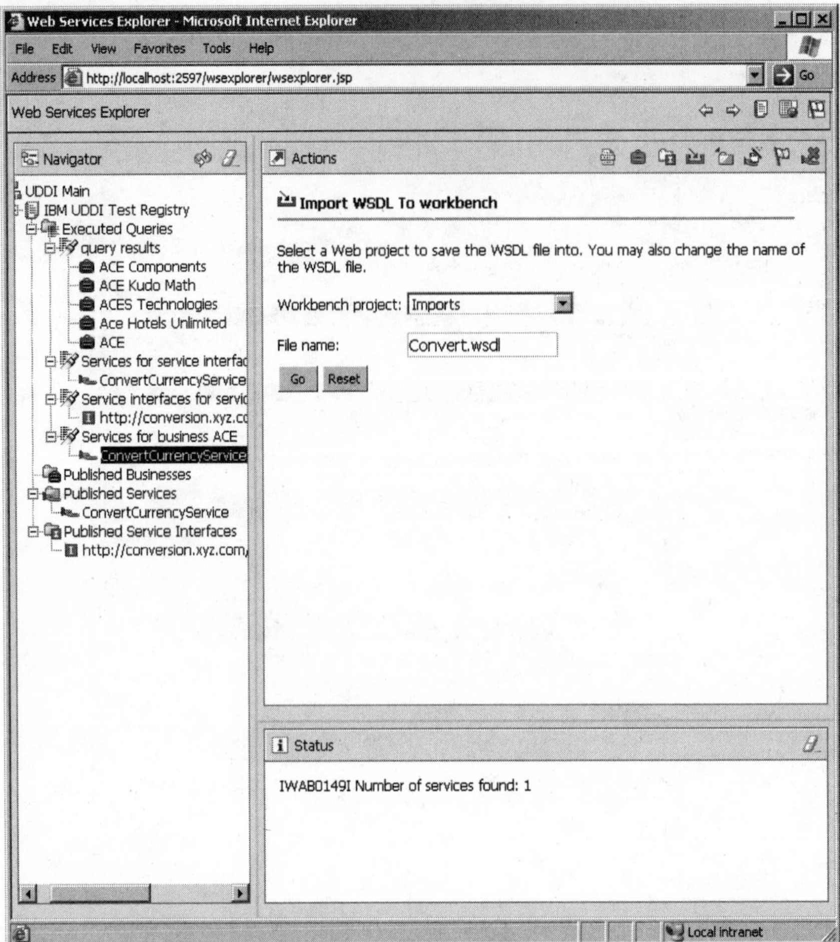

Figure 24.14 Import a service.

The local registry is implemented as an enterprise application deployed to the WSAD WebSphere v5.0 Test Server. It uses a DBMS to hold its content. You can configure it to use the supplied IBM Cloudscape DBMS or a separately available IBM DB2 DBMS. Carry out the following steps to configure the WSDAD unit test UDDI registry:

1. Invoke the New wizard by selecting File > New > Other.
2. Display the list of Web services wizards by selecting Web Services in the left-hand pane.
3. Choose Unit Test UDDI in the right-hand list of wizards. Press Next >.
4. Choose Deploy the Unit Test UDDI Registry and Private UDDI Registry For WAS v5 with Cloudscape. See Figure 24.15. Press Next >.

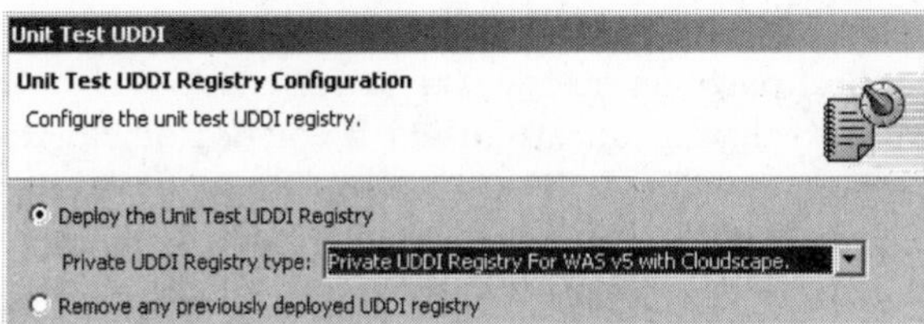

Figure 24.15 Deploy Test UDDI Registry.

5. You already have a configured server so choose Use an existing server. Ensure that it is selected in the Server name drop-down list, as shown in Figure 24.16.
6. Select Launch the Web Services Explorer. Press Finish to create the test UDDI registry.

The Web Services Explorer is automatically launched, as specified. You would normally choose the main menu item Window > Launch Web Services Explorer to invoke it on demand.

Three projects are created, as described in Table 24.7. The registry is also an example of a secure J2EE application. It is instructive to use the Deployment Descriptor Editor to see how the security roles are specified.

Table 24.7 WSAD Test Registry UDDI Projects

PROJECT NAME	J2EE MODULE TYPE	ARCHIVE	CONTENTS
UDDI-EAR	J2EE 1.2 Application	UDDI-EAR.ear	ejb.jar, soap.war, security decl
UDDI-EJB	EJB 1.1	ejb.jar	Inquiry and Publish stateless session beans; security roles
UDDI-SOAP	Web Application	soap.war	SOAP interface to UDDI; uddi, uddiPublish, uddiGet servlets; security roles

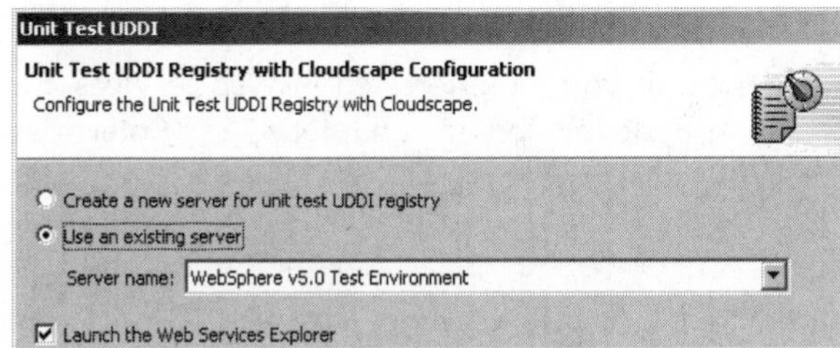

Figure 24.16 Cloudscape UDDI DBMS.

At this point, you may treat the local UDDI registry as if it were the IBM Test Registry on the Internet, except that no third-party services will be present.

Publish operation roles are mapped to all authenticated users. If you do not want to deal with authentication on a test server, open the UDDI-EAR deployment descriptor on the Security tab. Change all the roles that have "publish" in their names to map to Everyone in the WebSphere Bindings. Save the changes and restart the server.

Summary

Web services are useful for bridging any impendence mismatch between distributed components on different platforms and implemented in arbitrary languages. They are useful for applications that require late binding to business services, such as lowest bid service scenarios. The multimaster registry concept supplied by UDDI cloud services enables discovery of services such that a different service could fulfill the same need from day to day.

The rapidly emerging technology of Web services merits an entire book. In this chapter, we discussed the following items with respect to WSAD:

- Concepts, including applications of XML named SOAP, WSDL, UDDI, and WSIL
- Developing Web services using WSAD
- Publishing a Java class or other entities as a Web service
- Using the WSAD-generated Web service test client
- Use of the generated Web service proxy class
- The SOAP administration client
- Developing a custom Web client for a Web service
- How to develop a Java application client for a Web service
- Exporting a WSDL file
- How to use WSAD to generate a Web service proxy from a WSDL file
- The use of the WSAD Web Services Explorer
- Using UDDI with the IBM UDDI Test Registry
- Publishing a service to UDDI
- Installing the WSAD local test UDDI registry

This concludes the chapters in this book. If you are interested in Web services, try exposing the stateless session façade EJB developed in Chapters 22, "Enterprise JavaBeans," and Chapter 23, "Entity EJBs," as a Web service.

Index

Symbols and Numerics

A

D

U

W